Software Change Impact Analysis

Software Change Impact Analysis

Shawn A. Bohner
Robert S. Arnold

IEEE Computer Society Press
Los Alamitos, California

Washington • Brussels • Tokyo

Library of Congress Cataloging-in-Publication Data

Bohner, Shawn.
    Software change impact analysis / Shawn Bohner, Robert S. Arnold.
        p.   cm.
    Includes bibliographical references. (p.).
    ISBN 0-8186-7384-2
    1. Computer software—Evaluation.   I. Arnold, Robert S.   II. Title.
QA76.76.E93B65   1996
005.1 ' 6—dc20
                                          95-52098
                                              CIP

IEEE Computer Society Press
10662 Los Vaqueros Circle
P.O. Box 3014
Los Alamitos, CA 90720-1314

IEEE Computer Society Press Order Number BP07384
Library of Congress Number 95-52098
ISBN 0-8186-7384-2

Additional copies can be ordered from

IEEE Computer Society Press Customer Service Center 10662 Los Vaqueros Circle P.O. Box 3014 Los Alamitos, CA 90720-1314 Tel: (714) 821-8380 Fax: (714) 821-4641 Email: cs.books@computer.org	IEEE Service Center 445 Hoes Lane P.O. Box 1331 Piscataway, NJ 08855-1331 Tel: (908) 981-1393 Fax: (908) 981-9667 mis.custserv@computer.org	IEEE Computer Society 13, avenue de l'Aquilon B-1200 Brussels BELGIUM Tel: +32-2-770-2198 Fax: +32-2-770-8505 euro.ofc@computer.org	IEEE Computer Society Ooshima Building 2-19-1 Minami-Aoyama Minato-ku, Tokyo 107 JAPAN Tel: +81-3-3408-3118 Fax: +81-3-3408-3553 tokyo.ofc@computer.org

Assistant Publisher: Matt Loeb
Technical Editor: Jon Butler
Acquisitions Assistant: Cheryl Smith
Advertising/Promotions: Tom Fink
Production Editor: Lisa O'Conner
Cover Design: Joe Daigle

The Institute of Electrical and Electronics Engineers, Inc.

Contents

Preface

What is Software Change Impact Analysis?

Software change impact analysis, or *impact analysis* for short, estimates what will be affected in software and related documentation if a proposed software change is made. Impact-analysis information can be used for planning changes, making changes, accommodating certain types of software changes, and tracing through the effects of changes. Impact analysis provides visibility into the potential effects of changes before the changes are implemented. This can make it easier to perform changes more accurately.

Why This Book?

This book is a collection of tutorial papers, trade articles, and software-research literature that capture current impact-analysis techniques and technical results. Much has been written on impact analysis, but it is scattered across magazines and books and is time-consuming to collect, review, and evaluate. This book grew from our perception that, with the great interest in software change, people need a handy, one-volume source of useful information. We have collected scattered technical information on the science and art of determining what software parts affect one another. We have sifted through many papers, articles, and technical reports. We have distilled the themes, trends, and techniques of impact analysis so that our book can frame the field, focus attention, and temper expectations.

There is little general understanding of the technical aspects of this fundamental, yet somewhat invisible, technology. Few programmers relish tracking down the possible effects of change in hard-to-understand software. Yet there are techniques and tools that can render this task more systematic and accurate. The software community needs to know what impact analysis is about.

Why This Book Now?

Understanding the impacts of software change has been a challenge since software systems were first developed. With the increasing size and complexity of systems, this ability has become more difficult. New problems requiring substantial impact analysis have reached popular consciousness. For example, with the new century fewer than five years away, many legacy software systems will need inspection and change to ensure they handle date information correctly. Available technology must be brought to bear on these problems.

Scope

This book provides a battery of ideas for doing impact analysis better. You should gain a healthy respect for the strengths and limitations of impact-analysis technology — a solid background that will prove valuable for years to come.

But this book is not a "how-to" book on impact analysis. We have instead identified key impact-analysis themes and then reprinted papers that illustrate those themes effectively. In selecting papers, we considered their readability, technical content, currency, how well they illustrate the themes we wanted to show, and how well they would equip readers with a solid understanding for tackling impact-analysis problems.

We believe the papers reprinted here meet these criteria. Other papers you should be aware of are in the annotated bibliography at the end of the book.

There is much more information on impact analysis than we had space for here. The omission of any work does not imply that the work is any less significant than the work reprinted, annotated, or mentioned in this book. You should not immediately discount the impact-analysis work we have neither reprinted nor mentioned. Its omission reflects more on how much time and space could be devoted to preparing this volume, than on its relative importance to the work discussed. We hope that our book encourages you to explore the large body of work in impact analysis.

Intended Readership

This book is intended for software practitioners and researchers. For practitioners, such as software maintainers and other programmers, the book presents the technical ideas behind many kinds of automated impact-analysis techniques. This collection of papers is a sound basis for understanding software impact-analysis technology in many CASE tools.

For researchers, this book collects a substantial body of literature on impact analysis. Although it does not contain all known work on impact analysis, it does contain or mention many seminal works. This will save you days otherwise spent tracking these sources down. We have also organized the field into themes, which makes comparing impact-analysis work easier.

Content Summary

We selected papers that provide fundamental information, of enduring value, on impact analysis. We include work from source-code dependency analysis and traceability analysis. We show how results from both areas can more effectively support impact analysis in software-engineering repositories. We describe why techniques for impact representation and determination are at the heart of both source-code dependency analysis and traceability analysis.

The book's **Introduction, "An Introduction to Software Change Impact Analysis,"** defines impact-analysis terms, describes frequently occurring technical ideas, and presents an overview of the technology. It also describes dependency analysis and requirements traceability.

Chapter 1, "Nature of Impact Analysis," introduces impact analysis in the software-change process, establishes a framework for comparing various types of impact analysis, and illustrates impact analysis in a real-world situation — the upcoming "date change" problems for the 21st century. These papers will help you understand impact-analysis ideas, capabilities, and limitations.

Although impact analysis is an important area in software development and maintenance, it persists in being hard to do in practice. **Chapter 2, "State of the Practice,"** describes available technology that influences the effectiveness of impact analysis in practice: traceability-analysis techniques, impact-analysis techniques, and configuration management. Software traceability is important for modeling dependencies among software objects because it allows navigation to different objects to examine the extent of a change. These papers will introduce you to the fundamental ideas that permeate practical impact analysis.

Automated support is essential for effective impact analysis. There is considerable work in manually identifying change impacts in the plethora of software artifacts produced during development and maintenance. **Chapter 3, "Automated Support for Impact Analysis,"** describes sample prototype systems that support impact analysis. By giving examples of impact-analysis tools and environments, the chapter provides some background on automated support for different types of impact analysis and alerts you to some key technologies that can be applied to impact analysis. Impact analysis is not the primary topic of each paper, but it permeates several of the software-change processes described.

Chapter 4, "Dependency-Analysis Approaches," describes how to analyze source-code dependencies to create formal representations of data, control, and component dependencies. Impact analysis requires some model, explicit or implicit, of dependencies. Formal definitions of programming languages provide a reasonable structure to capture data definition and use information as well as control-flow information. With this information — often underlying impact-analysis tools — a programmer can make reasonable decisions on what statements, modules, and data elements might be affected if the software is changed. Many of the ideas here also pertain to the use of dependency information in impact analysis in general.

Advances in software-development environments and repository technology have enabled software engineers to trace the impacts of software changes using traceability relationships. **Chapter 5, "Traceability Approaches,"** describes traceability modeling among software artifacts of various types, such as requirements and design information. Much of this chapter is based on traceability in software-development environments and documentation systems. Traceability relationships are often represented in a graph structure, which is amenable to navigation with a hypertext system. The chapter also describes how to determine impacts from relationships among different types of software artifacts.

Impacts can be represented in many ways, from simple marks on program statements to sophisticated truth-maintenance rules. Effective analysis requires an understanding of software changes, the relationships among software life-cycle objects, a discipline to account for the changes, and automated support. **Chapter 6, "Impact Representation,"** describes more models of dependencies among software objects. Both formal and qualitative models are described. The papers are an important basis for capturing dependency knowledge. This chapter and Chapter 7 provide the most detailed technical information in the book. ⎮

Impact-determination techniques help programmers use formal models of dependencies to derive the impacts of a change. These techniques include transitive closure, heuristic search, and techniques based on logical inference, analogical reasoning, data-flow analysis, and program slicing. **Chapter 7, "Impact-Determination Techniques,"** describes algorithms and approaches for automatically determining what is affected when a change is proposed. These techniques are frequently encountered in impact-analysis tools today. Approaches such as transitive closure, program slicing, and inferential models are discussed.

Chapter 8, "Final Remarks," outlines material covered in the book and some important observations about impact analysis. The **Annotated Bibliography** provides references to and descriptions of other important impact-analysis papers in the literature. We encourage you to examine these interesting readings and obtain some for your library.

Reader's Guide

You may decide to read the papers out of sequence, but we encourage you to read the introduction and Chapter 1 to firmly establish concepts and ideas. This foundation will serve whatever reading path you choose. The table below summarizes a few suggested paths.

	Practical Understanding	In-Depth	Quick-Look
Introduction	1st	1st	1st
Chapter 1 - Nature of Impact Analysis	2nd	2nd	2nd
Chapter 2 - State of the Practice	3rd	3rd	Recommended
Chapter 3 - Automated Support	4th	4th	Optional
Chapter 4 - Dependency-Analysis Approaches	5th	5th	Optional
Chapter 5 - Traceability	6th	6th	Optional
Chapter 6 - Impact Representation	Optional	7th	Optional

Chapter 7 - Impact-Determination Techniques	Optional	8th	Optional
Chapter 8 - Final Remarks	9th	9th	Optional
Annotated Bibliography	Browse for further reading possibilities	Browse for further reading possibilities	For reference

The Practical Understanding path is for practitioners who want to know about the technology underlying impact analysis, without having to dive into formal impact analysis.

The In-Depth path includes quite detailed formal dependency-modeling and impact-analysis algorithms. It is recommended for researchers and those wanting to build impact-analysis tools.

The Quick-Look path is for those who want some idea of what impact analysis is about but have relatively little time to read.

Whatever path you choose, we hope you enjoy the many facets of software change impact analysis as much as we did in producing this book.

Shawn A Bohner and Robert S. Arnold

April 1996

Acknowledgments

It is a pleasure to acknowledge the help we received in preparing this book. We thank the authors of all the many fine papers on software change impact analysis that we reviewed. They represent the foundational work that makes a new field of study and ultimately a change in technology possible. We also thank the reviewers and IEEE Computer Society Press staff, who contributed many hours reading, constructively commenting, editing, and improving the manuscript for this work. We thank Jon Butler and Alan Davis, chief technical editors, Catherine Harris, editorial director of IEEE Computer Society Press during most of this book's production, Lisa O'Conner, production editor, and Nancy Talbert, for their efforts in seeing the book smoothly through production. Alan Davis counseled us about the book's size and paper selection. Jon Butler shepherded the book through technical review. Catherine Harris encouraged the book over the long haul and patiently awaited our manuscripts. Lisa O'Conner gently but diligently pushed the manuscript through to production. Nancy Talbert improved the book's readability by providing valuable editorial advice on the manuscript. The book manuscript referees — two sets of them — provided comments that improved the book's technical content.

This book is enhanced by research work from Shawn Bohner's Ph.D. dissertation. He is grateful to members of his dissertation committee — James D. Palmer, David Rine, Hassan Gomaa, and Jeff Offutt — for their technical guidance and contributions.

For their stimulating discussions and insight on software change impact analysis work, we thank Robert Charette, Keith Gallagher, Hausi Müller, Shari Lawrence Pfleeger, Vaclav Rajlich, and Norman Wilde.

We also thank our parents and friends for their support. Too often credit is given to parents after they have passed on, unable to see the tribute. But both sets of parents, John and Vera Rose Arnold, and Thomas and Phronia Bohner are fortunately very much with us. Special thanks go to them — and our friends — whose constant encouragement enabled us to see this work through.

Finally, we thank the Lord both for the opportunity to learn about impact analysis and write about it for others' benefit, and for all those who made it possible.

An Introduction to Software Change Impact Analysis

Shawn A. Bohner and Robert S. Arnold

1. Basic Concepts

Nearly all software undergoes some change in its lifetime. Changes can be large or small, simple or complex, important or trivial — all of which influence the effort needed to implement the changes. Experience over the last three decades shows that making software changes without visibility into their effects can lead to poor effort estimates, delays in release schedules, degraded software design, unreliable software products, and the premature retirement of the software system [Swanson 1989] [Lehman 1994]. The Year 2000 date-change problem is a good example of poor insight into the impacts of change.

With change comes a need to accurately estimate the scope (size and complexity) of the changes and plan for their implementation. Traditionally, determining the effects of software change has been something that software professionals do in their heads after some cursory examination of the code and documentation. This may be sufficient for small programs, but not for large systems. Large systems often require repositories to organize their software artifacts, which are becoming increasingly interdependent in subtle ways. Software change impact analysis, or *impact analysis* for short, offers considerable leverage in understanding and implementing change in these systems because it provides a detailed examination of the consequences of changes in software. Relationships among software artifacts — including requirements, design, source code, test material, operational guides, and associated management documents — are often implicit; impact analysis makes them more explicit.

A major goal of impact analysis is to identify the software work products affected by proposed changes. Conceptually, it takes a list of *software life-cycle objects* — from specifications to programs – analyzes these SLOs with respect to the software change, and produces a list of items that should be addressed during the change process. Software staff can use the information from such an analysis to evaluate the consequences of planned changes as well as the trade-offs among the approaches for implementing the change.

In this paper, we emphasize software maintenance, although impact analysis is certainly useful in software development. Typical examples of impact-analysis techniques include

- using cross-referenced listings to see what other parts of a program contain references to a given variable or procedure,
- using program slicing (described later) to determine the program subset that can affect the value of a given variable [Gallagher 1991], or
- browsing a program by opening and closing related files,
- using traceability relationships to identify software artifacts associated with a change,
- using configuration-management systems to track and find changes, and
- consulting designs and specifications to determine the scope of a change.

Figure 1 depicts the two major technology areas for impact analysis: dependency analysis and traceability analysis. These complementary areas approach impact analysis from quite different perspectives and have their respective advantages to enhancing the potential of identifying software impacts.

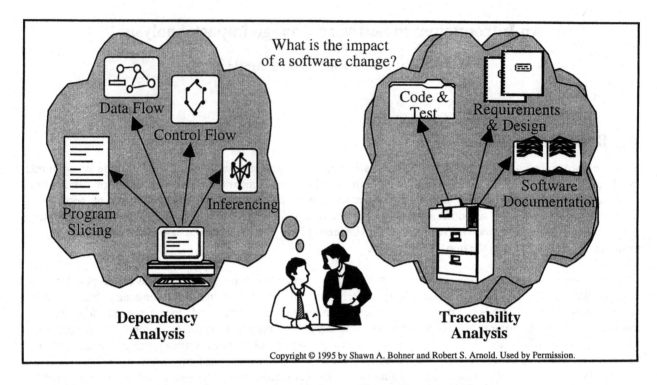

Figure 1. Major Areas of Software Change Impact Analysis

Dependency analysis involves examining detailed dependency relationships among program entities (variables, logic, modules, and the like). It provides a detailed evaluation of low-level dependencies in code but does little for SLOs at other levels. Hence, when we refer to dependency analysis, it is typically from the narrow perspective of source-code analysis.

Traceability analysis involves examining dependency relationships among all types of SLOs. As such, it addresses impact analysis from a broader perspective. For example, it can relate software artifacts (such as requirements) with associated design components. Although traceability covers many of the relationships among artifacts that a software project library or repository might store, these relationships typically are not very detailed.

1.1 Concepts and Terms

To understand the boundaries of impact-analysis technology and appreciate some of its risks, it is helpful to review some terms and definitions concerning the maintenance, improvement, or understanding of existing source code.

1.1.1 Impact analysis

Impact analysis has been practiced for years, yet there is no commonly accepted definition. For example, the term "impact analysis" does not appear in the *IEEE Glossary of Software Engineering Terminology* [IEEE 1993]. Several definitions come from developers of tools and techniques that support impact analysis. The developers of Alicia, a prototype impact-analysis tool at Rome Laboratories (formerly the Rome Air Development Center), define impact analysis as "an examination of an impact to determine its parts or elements" [RADC 1986]. They define an impact as the "effect or result of making a change to a system or its software." Shari Pfleeger [Pfleeger 1991] defines impact analysis as "the evaluation of the many risks associated with the change, including estimates of the effects on resources, effort, and schedule." Richard Turver and Malcolm Munro [Turver 1994] define impact analysis as "the assessment of a change, to the source code of a module, on the other modules of the system. It determines the scope of a change and provides a measure of its complexity." Still other definitions exist. [Arthur 1988], [Gallagher 1991], [Loyall 1993].

We define impact analysis as *identifying the potential consequences of a change, or estimating what needs to be modified to accomplish a change.* An impact (noun) is a part determined to be affected, and therefore worthy of inspection. Our definition of impact analysis is similar to the ones above except that it emphasizes the *estimation* of impacts, since what was actually changed is not fully known until after the software change is complete. The RADC definition of impact analysis comes closest to our definition because it concentrates on the identification of impacts. The Pfleeger definition extends this to the evaluation of impacts.

Impact analysis precedes, or is used in conjunction with, making a change. *Static* impact analysis analyzes static code structure without executing the code. *Dynamic* impact analysis executes the software as an aid to determining the impacts within it.

1.1.2 Traceability

Traceability refers to the ability to define and trace relationships among entities such as software work products and their components, the SLOs.

The term "traceability" appears in *Webster's New World Dictionary* with its root "trace." The most appropriate definition given for trace is "to follow the development, process or history of . . . to determine a (source, date, etc.) by this procedure." A definition for requirements traceability is found in *ANSI/IEEE Standard 830-1984* [IEEE 1993], which states, "A software requirements specification is traceable if (i) the origin of each of its requirements is clear and if (ii) it facilitates the referencing of each requirement in future development or enhancement documentation." Similarly, *DoD Standard 2168* [DOD 1985a] defines traceability as "the association of data generated in a particular life-cycle activity with other data generated in predecessor and successor activities; an attribute of software requirements, design, the software product, or documentation indicating that they derive from a higher source and can be allocated to a lower level, if required." Orlena Gotel and Anthony Finkelstein [Gotel 1994] define requirements traceability as "the ability to describe and follow the life of a requirement, in both a forward and backward direction."

We define traceability as *the ability to trace between software artifacts generated and modified during the software product life cycle.*

1.1.3 Side and ripple effects

Other terms are related to impact analysis. A *side effect* is an "error or other undesirable behavior that occurs as a result of a modification" [Freedman 1981].

A *ripple effect* is the "effect caused by making a small change to a system which affects many other parts of a system" [Stevens 1974]. *Stability* is ". . . the resistance to the potential ripple effect which a program would have when it is modified" [Yau 1980]. *Ripple-effect analysis* emphasizes the tracing of impacts in source code when the source code is changed. It may also trace impacts in available documentation.

Three primary types of ripple effects are coding, data, and documentation [Freedman 1981]. Other important types of ripple effects include ripple effects on the following [RADC 1986]:

- *Requirements.* Influences the operation of the system.
- *Interface.* Results in a change in specification of the hardware or software interface.
- *Environment.* Impacts development, maintenance, or test environments.
- *Management and logistics.* Includes cost, schedule, resource, contractual, and deployment and training impacts.

Sometimes ripple effect is also used to denote an *unwanted* side effect of a change.

3

1.2 Difficulty of Impact Analysis

Impact analysis has long been one of the most tedious and difficult parts of software change. Manual impact analysis is labor intensive and ad hoc. Systematic approaches to impact analysis are frequently not part of formal software-engineering training, so programmers or analysts tend to develop their own impact-analysis approaches.

Another reason that impact analysis has been difficult in practice is the all too common low level of automated support for impact analysis typical in software-maintenance workplaces. Frequently less sophisticated tools are used for impact analysis, such as text editors and file-system "change directory" commands. These tools, readily available in many software-engineering environments, can require substantial human interaction to accomplish impact analysis.

A third difficulty is that automated impact-analysis tools often provide a rather limited analysis. Automated impact analysis depends on the ability to

- create models of relationships among SLOs,
- capture these relationships in software and associated representations,
- translate a specific software change into the impacted objects and relationships,
- trace relationships and reasonably bound the search for impacts, and
- retranslate the estimated affected objects back into software objects [Arnold 1993].

In short, automated impact analysis is a significant technical challenge. Fortunately, the commercial world is focusing on impact-analysis technology, especially on how to resolve the "Year 2000 problem" – how to convert legacy-system processing from two-digit years (99) to four-digit years (1999). This new attention will likely improve the quality of impact-analysis technology.

2. The Nature of Software Change

Because impact analysis involves a study of changes and their effects, a necessary first step in understanding impact analysis is to understand the characteristics of change and their effect on the analysis process.

2.1 Characteristics of Change

Much has been written about software changes and their consequences [Lehman 1991], [Lehman 1980], [Boehm 1987], [Swanson 1989], [Collofello 1987]. This is not surprising. We have only to survey the software life cycle to see the many sources of potential software changes.

But although many have studied the problem and offered solutions, the software community persistently struggles with issues of software change and software maintenance. Why?

There are several reasons. First, software requirements are continually changing to accommodate user expectations, new operational environment needs, and the like. This represents a key management challenge during software development because changes to requirements have a high potential for producing impacts. Seemingly slight requirements can affect pervasive system assumptions, leading to massive software changes. Some of these changes can alter the software design, which can have far-reaching consequences.

Second, the development cycles of large software systems can be quite long [SAD 1980]. Few people stay with the project for the entire development cycle. Even fewer people remember the initial requirements or the rationale behind them. Some systems may evolve over 10 to 15 years without being operational.

4

Finally, the software-change cycle for large, complex systems can be slow. Without the requisite change-management mechanisms, software changes during maintenance can have unpredictable consequences that often delay their implementation. For example, suppose a programmer changes a data element on the basis of incorrect information. Initially, the change appears to operate correctly and even passes functional tests. In the next release, however, another programmer discovers that the changed data element is used by a program previously considered to be independent of the change. The result is that someone must correct — possibly with a patch — the newly introduced error in the current release and schedule the fix for the next release.

2.2 Kinds of Change

Changes may be classified and studied in several ways, such as by the type of change activity, the kinds of items being changed, or the motivation for the change.

An example of the first category is a study by David Weiss and Victor Basili [Weiss 1985] of software-development changes made in projects at the NASA Software Engineering Laboratory. Weiss and Basili reported that the most frequent type of software change is the unplanned design modification. They found that such modifications are usually made to optimize the program, to improve the services the program offers to its users, or to clarify and improve the maintainability of the software work products.

In another study, Basili, Louis Chmura, and Weiss analyzed changes made to the *A7-E Software Requirements Document* [Basili 1980], [Chmura 1982]. They reported that 247 requirements errors were corrected from 1978 to 1981. Figure 2 depicts the reported error types and their respective percentages. Of the 206 non-clerical errors, 73 percent required less than one hour to correct, 22 percent required more than one day but less than one week, and one percent required more than one month.

Changes may also be classified and studied by the types of SLOs to which they are applied, such as requirements, designs, and programs. For example, typical requirements changes include changes to accommodate customer needs or wants (demand for enhanced functionality), changes in operational environment, changes due to obsolete or clarified requirements, and changes due to lessons learned from software prototypes.

Finally, studying the motivation for the change can be revealing. Typical reasons for design changes include requirements changes; design trade-offs and elaboration; interface changes; scope and visibility issues; performance, timing, and sizing issues; and feedback from prototypes. Typical reasons for program changes include bug fixes, algorithm-coding adjustments, arithmetic-precision modifications, data-structure modifications, initialization modifications, control and sequence changes, and parameter changes. The causes of a program change can also be similar to those for a design change.

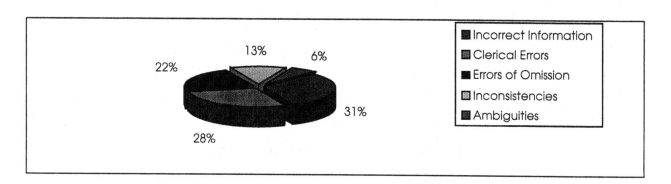

Figure 2. Types of Errors Corrected in Requirements for the NASA A7-E Software Requirements Document (based on data from [Basili 1980], [Chmura 1982])

3. Impact-Analysis Process

Programmers and analysts typically analyze the effects of software change informally as an iterative series of investigations and impact discoveries. Two ways to understand the impact-analysis process are (1) to observe the impact-analysis steps themselves and (2) to study impact analysis in the context of the software-change process. Figure 3 illustrates impact analysis with respect to software change and the continuous nature of the analysis during the change process.

As the figure shows, analysts first evaluate requirements for the software change from a change request with respect to the current system. During the software-change process, they discover additional ripple effects. They add these effects to the currently known impacts and extend the *change map*, a road map of SLOs related to the change. These currently known impacts provide valuable information for determining resource and schedule estimates. The change map provides a checklist of software work products that may require changes as a result of the change request as well as a road map to their location.

3.1 Process Steps

Figure 4 illustrates a typical impact-analysis cycle. The user, analyst, or programmer submits a change for approval, which a configuration-control board reviews and either approves, suspends, alters, returns for more information, or rejects. If the change is approved, it is passed to the programmer, who conducts an impact analysis to scope out the change and plan its implementation.

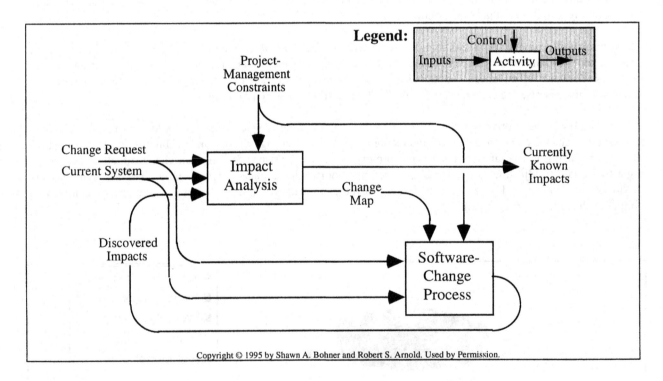

Figure 3. Impact Analysis as Part of Software Change

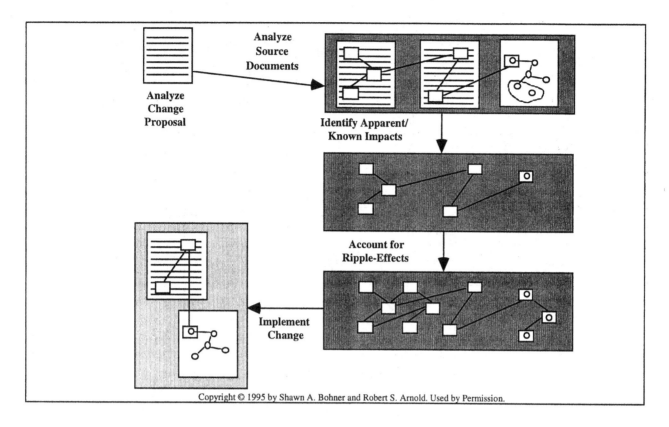

Figure 4. Key Steps in Impact-Analysis Process

To scope out the change, programmers determine the software items initially affected by the change. They may examine software requirements, design, source code, and test material to identify the apparent software artifacts involved in the change. This analysis of source documents leads to a clearer change specification and some mapping to the decomposition of associated SLOs.

Next, programmers identify the initial set of impacts from apparent or currently known impacts. From these impacts and their associated relationships to other SLOs, they can account for any potential ripple effects to obtain the impacts to be examined while making the software changes.

The analysis assumes there is a formal set of objects and relationships that characterize the impact structure of the software being changed. This is not critical to doing impact analysis, but can increase its speed and accuracy, especially if the analysis is automated. If objects and relationships are not available, programmers can use techniques similar to those used for quality assurance to define them, such as inspections, walkthroughs, desk-checking, and independent verification and validation.

3.2 Role in Software Change

Impact analysis occurs throughout the change process: as changes are made, more impacts are discovered, and the set of known impacts may grow. Consequently, as the change process progresses, more is known about the change, and the analysis becomes more concrete.

Figure 5 is a simplified view of the major software-change activities from the impact perspective. From this perspective, impact analysis is a supporting or an enabling technology.

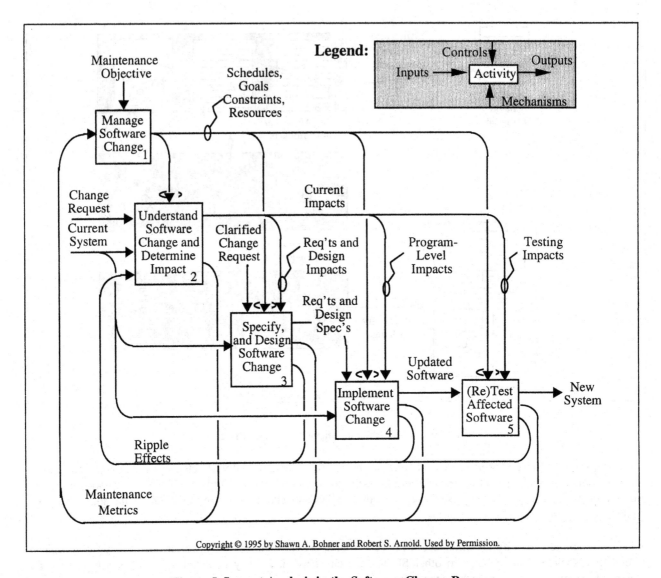

Legend:

Inputs → Activity → Outputs (with Controls above and Mechanisms below)

Figure 5. Impact Analysis in the Software-Change Process

Several important outputs from these activities drive the software-change process, including impact, traceability, stability, complexity, modularization, documentation, adaptability, self-descriptiveness, testability, verifiability, and completeness. These feedbacks, collectively labeled "maintenance metrics" (bottom left of Figure 5) indicate measurable attributes in the associated activities. The results are assessed by the software-change-management activity before the next activity is undertaken. Composite maintenance metrics act as a controlling mechanism in the iterative progression from the current system to the change requests for a new system.

The first step in Figure 5, *Manage Software Change,* controls the sequence of activities by analyzing the feedback from software-change activities in terms of the implications for change management and determining the appropriate actions with respect to goals, schedules, constraints, and resources. The second step, *Understand Software Change and Determine Impact,* evaluates the proposed change request, clarifies it, and determines the possible effects of the change. This activity produces current impacts such as requirements, design, program-level, and testing impacts to guide the other activities. Ripple effects discovered during these activities are recorded and used to refine the initial impact analysis.

The next step, *Specify and Design Software Change*, takes the clarified change request and generates requirements and design specifications. Using these specifications, the fourth step, *Implement Software Change*, generates the

8

proposed change to the software system and updates all the documentation associated with the software work product. In the last step, *(Re)Test Affected Software*, the modifications are tested to ensure that they meet new requirements, and the overall system is subjected to regression testing to verify that it meets existing requirements.

3.3 Products

Requirements, system descriptions, specifications, architectures, functional and detailed designs, source code (in its various forms), test specifications, test procedures, test reports, and verification plans are among the plethora of information that inundates the audit trail of the typical software effort. Impact analysis examines many of these work products using dependency information to produce sets of identified SLOs that should be examined when a change is implemented. Figure 6 summarizes the sets of impacts that can be determined from each activity in the change process.

The impact sets in the figure are taken from our impact-analysis framework [Arnold 1993]. The *starting impact set* is the set of objects thought to be initially affected by a change. The analyst or programmer determines the SIS while examining the change specification. The *estimated impact set* is the set of objects estimated to be affected. The analyst or programmer produces the EIS while conducting the impact analysis. The *actual impact set* is the set of objects actually modified as a result of the change. The AIS is normally not unique, since a change can be implemented in several ways.

3.4 Impact Representation

To identify the impact sets, a programmer must have information about the dependency relationships among the SLOs.

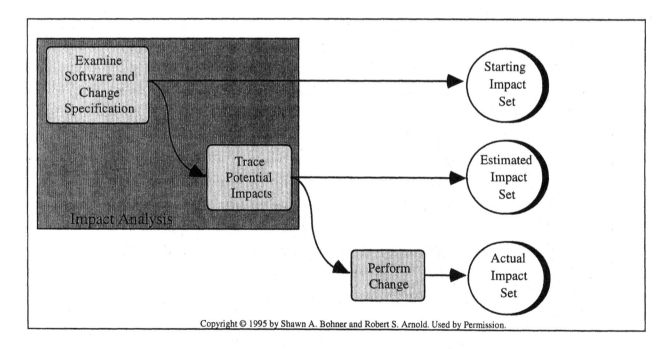

Figure 6. Key Sets of Software Life-Cycle Objects in Impact Analysis

Impacts among SLOs can be readily represented with graphs, such as that in Figure 7. The graph nodes represent the information in software work products. Each work product contains a node for each component, or SLO. In the figure, the design is represented as a collection of nodes, with one node for each design component; the requirements specification has one node for each requirement, the code has one node for each component, and so on. The arcs represent dependency relationships both among SLOs within a work product and among the work products themselves. The start node is the changed SLO (such as a changed requirement), the end node is the SLO affected (such as a design object), and the arc between them indicates that the end node depends on the start node. The nature of the relationship is captured as a label on the arc.

When one SLO depends on another, the change to the latter may affect the former. For example, when one source-code module calls another, the first is dependent on the second. That is, if the second module is changed, the result is likely to affect the first module, but a change to the first will not necessarily affect the second.

In a graph representation of dependencies, a direct impact occurs when the SLO affected is related by a dependency that directly connects a related SLO. This type of impact, also called a *first-order impact*, can be obtained from the connectivity graph. An indirect impact occurs when the object affected is related by the set of dependencies representing a path between the SLO and the affected object. This type of impact is also referred to as an *N-order impact*, where *N* is the number of intermediate relationships between the SLO and the affected object.

In Figure 7, "Design 1," "Req't 2," and "Test 1" are directly impacted when "Req't 1" is changed. The dashed lines that go from "Req't 2" through to "Test 3" denote an indirect impact. Using the ripple analogy, this indirect impact is a *third-order impact* because it ripples three times or has a path length of three.

Figure 8 illustrates a simple directed graph of 10 SLOs, 0 to 9. Each represents a software artifact (a requirement, design, code, or test fragment) connected to other SLOs by modeled relationships. As the figure shows, even with a fan-out, or *out-degree*, of three relationships per SLO, the network of nodes and edges can be quite complex.

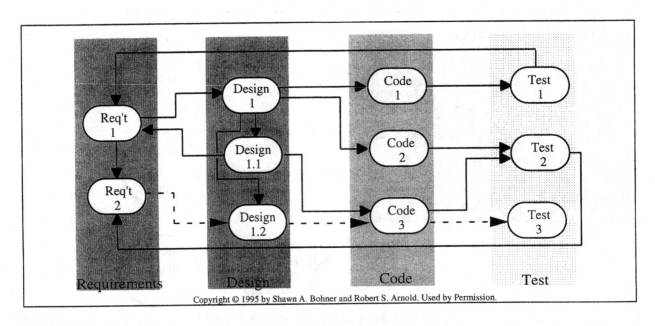

Figure 7. Examples of Direct and Indirect Impacts

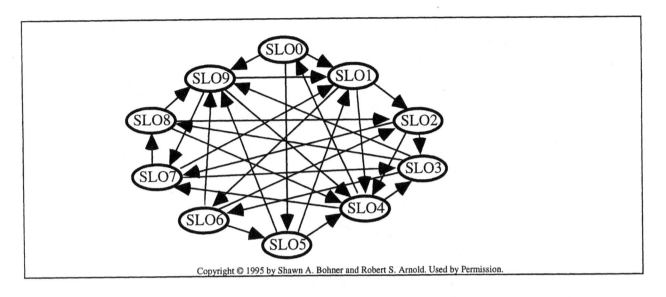

Figure 8. Simple Directed Graph of Software Life-Cycle Objects

The fan-in, or *in-degree,* of an SLO node indicates the number of known SLOs that depend on that particular SLO. In Figure 9a, four nodes depend on SLO1 (SLO0, SLO5, SLO7, and SLO9), so the in-degree of SLO1 is 4. This is a relatively high in-degree when compared with that of SLO2 (which is 2), but not as high as that of SLO4 (which is 5).

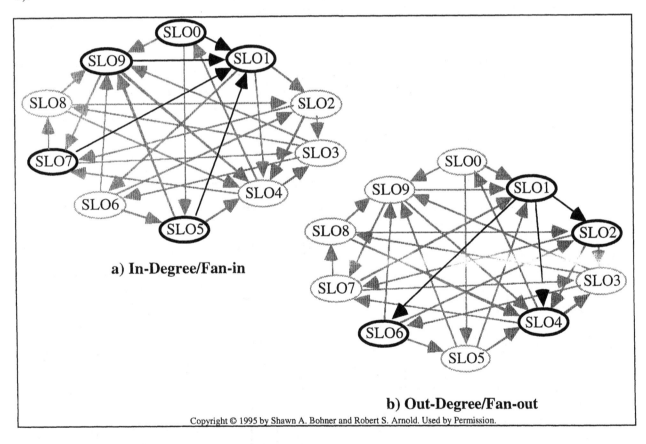

a) In-Degree/Fan-in

b) Out-Degree/Fan-out

Figure 9. In-degree and Out-degree of Traceability Relationships

Figure 9b depicts the out-degree of SLO1. SLO1 has an out-degree of 3 and is dependent on SLO2, SLO4, and SLO6. For this example, all SLOs have an out-degree of 3, which indicates a homogenous distribution of dependency. Although this is an unlikely situation under normal circumstances, we use it to show how even a small out-degree can have considerable potential effects.

Assuming that both in-degree and out-degree relationships have a bearing on a change to an SLO, a combination of these relationship for SLO1 is a useful indicator. In this case, the software engineer making the change might consider examining SLO0, SLO1, SLO2, SLO4, SLO5, SLO6, SLO7, and SLO9. In-degree and out-degree relationships also indicate what effort might be necessary to implement the change with respect to the existing software artifacts.

Graphs can be specified in ways other than the use of nodes and arcs. Software engineers might use connectivity matrices, for example, to describe first-order impacts. They could then transform the connectivity matrix into a reachability matrix with distance indicators, such as that in Table 1, which is based on the SLOs and associated relationships in Figure 8. A reachability matrix shows the objects that could be affected by a change to a particular SLO. Such a matrix also offers the distances (first, second, or third order) associated with each impact. (Entries with a blank indicate self-referenced items.) Engineers can transform a connectivity matrix to a reachability matrix by augmenting a transitive-closure algorithm [Warshall 1962] and using a dynamic programming technique to traverse memory about the nodes.

3.5 Identifying Impacts

In Table 1, SLO0 (first row of the matrix) has a 3 in the SLO8 column. This means that SLO8 represents a third-order impact for SLO1 and is not as important to track as SLO1, SLO5, or SLO9, which represent first-order impacts.

This distance information can also offer some insight into the relative ripple effect associated with each SLO. For example, SLO1 ($3 \cdot 1 + 5 \cdot 2 + 1 \cdot 3 = 16$) has a smaller overall ripple than SLO8 ($3 \cdot 1 + 3 \cdot 2 + 3 \cdot 3 = 18$) — possibly indicating that if given a choice, SLO1 would be preferable to change than SLO8. This very simplified example shows the power of accounting for and recording dependency information and analyzing it to make software-change decisions.

Table 1. Matrix of Traceability Relationships with Distance Indicators

	SLO0	SLO1	SLO2	SLO3	SLO4	SLO5	SLO6	SLO7	SLO8	SLO9
SLO0		1	2	3	2	1	2	2	3	1
SLO1	2		1	2	1	2	1	2	3	2
SLO2	2	2		1	1	3	2	1	2	2
SLO3	3	2	2		2	2	1	2	1	1
SLO4	1	2	3	1		2	2	1	2	2
SLO5	2	1	2	2	1		2	2	3	1
SLO6	3	2	1	2	2	1		2	3	1
SLO7	3	1	2	1	2	3	2		1	2
SLO8	3	2	1	2	1	3	3	2		1
SLO9	2	1	2	2	1	3	2	1	2	

3.6 Searching for Impacts

Impact-analysis methods use search algorithms to analyze relationships and identify the consequences of a change. There are several types of algorithms [Bohner 1995]:

- *Semantically guided.* Impact analysis is directed by predetermined semantics of objects and relationships derived from semantic network algorithms or a database view, for example.

- *Heuristically guided.* Impact identification is directed by predetermined rules or heuristics to suggest possible paths to examine or dubious ones to avoid. Such methods may use a rule base of system-change experience, for example.

- *Stochastically guided.* Impact determination is guided by probabilities derived for the situation, for example, probabilities based on characteristics of the SLOs, to determine the likelihood of the impact.

- *Hybrid guidance.* Impact identification uses a combination of the above methods, for example, transitive-closure algorithms coupled with probabilities of impact.

- *Unguided/exhaustive.* Impact identification is conducted in a brute-force manner using simple traceability relationships in the repository, through transitive-closure algorithms, for example.

Change impacts have been portrayed using other representation forms such as truth-maintenance rules in a rule-based system. Jon Doyle has examined this in detail [Doyle 1979] and presents a good perspective on the inferencing necessary to detect dependencies in a rule base. Although the paper concentrates on issues of artificial-intelligence belief systems, it provides good ideas that parallel application in impact analysis. Rather than focusing on a matrix or graph of dependencies, truth-maintenance systems use a set of rules for dependency-directed backtracking to change a set of assumptions. Truth-maintenance techniques show promise in reducing the search space of the impact analysis for large systems.

4. Methods and Tools

Both dependency analysis and traceability analysis have many supporting methods and tools. Those we describe here are primarily from the research community because we wanted to convey the capabilities of the technology. The techniques we describe are being used in source-code analysis, metrics, and CASE tools; documentation-management systems; traceability systems; software-project libraries; and software repositories.

4.1 Dependency Analysis

For dependency (or source-code) analysis, automated tools detect and capture dependency information, evaluating data, control, and component dependencies. A supporting method is *program slicing* a technique that takes advantage of data- and control-flow dependencies to capture "slices" of programs. Techniques for dependency analysis are used extensively in compilers and source-code analysis tools. Modeling data-, control-, and component-dependency relationships are fruitful ways to determine software-change impacts within the set of source-code artifacts. Although dependency analysis focuses narrowly on impact information captured from source code, it is the most mature impact-analysis technique available.

Impact-analysis techniques that support these sets of dependencies include data-flow analysis, control-flow analysis, program slicing, test-coverage analysis, cross referencing, and browsing. This list is by no means exhaustive, but it does give a reasonable sense of the technology that can be brought to bear on this important area.

Many commercially available software-analysis tools address source-code dependencies. These include program slicers, cross-referencers, data-flow and control-flow analyzers, source-code comparators, test-coverage analyzers, and interactive debuggers. Most of these tools answer questions about what and where data is defined or used, and what acts on the data. In terms of impact analysis, they provide automated assistance to software engineers in identifying the consequences of software changes. These techniques focus on data structures and the logical structure of programs to aid software engineers in understanding the source code.

4.1.1. Data Dependencies

Data dependencies are relationships among program statements that define or use data. A data dependence exists when a statement provides a value used directly or indirectly by another statement in a program [Ferrante 1987], [Loyall 1993]. Data definition and use graphs are typical representations of these dependencies.

Data-flow analysis produces dependency information on what data goes where in the software system [Taha 1988]. It identifies aggregates of data and the subelements they represent. Data-flow techniques analyze source code to determine paths and transformations that data can take through the system. These paths are typically represented as graphs or tables that assist software engineers in understanding key data flows.

The *Dependency Analysis Tool Set* is an example of what can be accomplished with data dependencies. This prototype system was developed by Norman Wilde at the University of West Florida [Wilde 1987] to assist in understanding the complex interrelationships found in large systems developed in C. Program-dependency classes include

- *data-flow dependencies* among data objects when the value held by an object may be used to calculate or set another value;
- *definition dependencies*, in which one program entity is used to define another;
- *calling dependencies* between two modules, in which one calls the other; and
- *functional dependencies* among program modules and global data objects that the module creates or updates.

Dependencies are stored in a *dependency graph,* in which each node represents a program entity and each arc represents a dependency between entities. A query mechanism lets the user select the types of dependencies to be analyzed from the dependency classes just listed. It assists in searching for indirect dependencies as well as filtering out unimportant dependencies.

Researchers have addressed dependency analysis from a program-viewing perspective using incremental data-flow techniques [Taha 1988]. Similar principles are applied in research on improving retesting strategies for modified systems using a combination of data-flow analysis and logic-coverage techniques [Harrold 1993], [Podgurski 1990].

4.1.2. Control Dependencies

Control dependencies are relationships among program statements that control program execution. There are several notions of control dependencies — strong and weak control [Loyall 1993], dominance [Podgurski 1990], [Ferrante 1987], and so on — but the primary idea is that the way statements relate can affect the program's execution. *Program-dependence graphs* are often used to account for control dependency [Ottenstein 1984], [Ferrante 1987].

Control-flow analysis provides information on the logical decision points in the software system and the complexity of their structure. Control-flow techniques identify procedure-calling dependencies, logical decisions (conditions such as IF-THEN-ELSE, LOOPS, CASE statements), and under what conditions these hold true. Software engineers can use these techniques to analyze the source code and determine the control paths through the system. These paths are typically represented as graphs or tables to aid in understanding the software's control flow.

An example of a tool that employs control-flow analysis techniques is the *McCabe Battlemap Analysis Tool* [McCabe 1992]. This tool decomposes source code into its control elements to create a view of the program that specifies the control flow for analysis. Although the semantics are limited to the decision logic and calling structures in the program, the information that can be gleaned provides considerable insight into the software's structure and complexity. In terms of impact analysis, the tool traces changes in control logic, alerting the software engineer and change originator to their potential consequences.

4.1.3. Component Dependencies

Here we present component dependencies as general relationships among source-code components such as modules, files, and test runs. Many techniques to detect component dependency are supported by software-engineering tools such as cross-referencers, test-coverage analyzers, and source-code comparators. The following paragraphs describe the purposes of these tools.

Inscape is an example of a software-engineering environment for large software systems [Perry 1989]. Software systems have become so large and complex that tracking the process of developing and enhancing the system requires automated support. Inscape provides a set of integrated tools that use formal module-interface specifications for examining component relationships and constructing the software. The specifications provide a formal semantic interconnection model that aids in relating software components for construction and change.

Cross-referencers help find impacts by indexing software information captured from source code. Because they bring together all object references (to a data field, disk file, flag, module, and so on), they help software engineers understand relationships among software artifacts. Cross-referencing tells where else in the program variables in the affected source-code statements appear. The software engineer can then go to those areas and continue checking for potential impacts. Cross-referencers used in conjunction with source-code browsers are effective for identifying component dependencies.

Test-coverage analyzers identify the parts of the system that were executed during testing and indicate where processing time was spent. Test-coverage analyzers can instrument programs being tested and collect runtime statistics on coverage during execution. Thus, they are highly effective in helping testers determine the areas covered by test cases — and even more important those not covered. This provides a basis for impact analysis.

Source-code comparators help in determining changes in the source code after the change has been made. For example, two people may have changed the program at the same time for different reasons. To determine where the changes may have overlapped, the software engineer can use a source-code comparator to identify the changed statements in both cases.

4.2 Traceability Analysis

Today's software-engineering projects are faced with producing and managing a large number and wide variety of software artifacts. They are able to store the SLOs in a repository and even get them out with relative efficiency. However, little attention has been paid to analyzing the SLOs while they are in the repository. Impact-analysis techniques are emerging to fill this void. Traceability techniques, which are generally manual, can be used to model dependencies among SLOs in the repository.

Traceability analysis identifies affected SLOs using their traceability relationships. SLOs represent documents of one kind or another containing varied levels of software information. In current traceability tools, the granularity of SLOs is typically somewhat coarse for accurate impact analysis. One type of traceability system is the *document-management system*. This system aids the software engineer in identifying SLOs, usually with a query mechanism, and makes it easy to browse documents. Another more passive approach is to record traceability data in traceability matrices and use them to identify the potential impacts of changes.

We discuss traceability analysis mostly from the perspective of software-engineering environments and documentation systems. Traceability relationships are often represented in a graph structure, which is amenable to navigation with a hypertext system. In the traceability methods and tools presented here, most systems do not support impact analysis directly but rather support navigation among SLOs.

4.2.1. Impact Analysis

An impact-analysis system lets software engineers identify, relate, navigate, and analyze SLOs to determine candidates for a software change. An impact-analysis technique supports specifying a software change, establishing the starting impact set, determining an estimated impact set, and performing the software change to identify the actual impact set.

Alicia (Automated Life Cycle Analysis System) is a prototype developed specifically for impact analysis [RADC 1986] by Software Productivity Solutions. Developed for the U.S. Air Force's Rome Laboratories, Alicia is the most comprehensive traceability-based impact-analysis system we identified. Its three chief traceability capabilities are

- It describes the change and lets the user select the traceability starting point.
- It marks the impacted objects in the project database.
- It lets the user visually traverse and browse the project database

Alicia represents one of the first attempts to address impact analysis with automated traceability mechanisms. Intended to support the entire software-development life cycle, Alicia provides a systematic method for analyzing a change in the context of development work products. Its six-step methodology lets the user postulate a change, designate an initial impact, evaluate the impact, decide if the change should be made, make the change, and verify the change. Alicia is not based on a document-oriented model. Rather, Alicia is based on the information context model of DoD-Std-2167 [DOD 1985b] software development. It supports the completeness and consistency checking of traceability relationships as well as navigation among SLOs in the project database.

4.2.2. Requirements

Requirements-traceability techniques assist software engineers and program managers in determining if the software requirements have been implemented in the system. In the past, manually created requirements-traceability matrices supported this function. As requirements-traceability techniques have matured, more of the work is becoming automated. Requirements traceability also involves identifying parts of the software that may change with changed requirements. Essentially, requirements traceability is an "accounting" function, accounting for relationships among SLOs.

READS (Requirements Entry Allocation Decomposition System) is an example of a requirements-traceability tool [Smith 1992]. This tool, developed by Paramax Systems Corp., is used in projects that produce large, textual requirements specifications. READS manages requirements represented as fragments of text. It accepts ASCII source documents as input and does basic requirements identification by recognizing any sentence containing the words "shall," "must," or "will." Remaining requirements must be identified manually. In addition to its text, a requirement is associated with a set of attributes, including a unique number and name; indicators of status, priority, and security; a document-section cross-reference; a version number; and the user ID and time of last update.

Once users have identified all the source requirements, they can develop additional parsed, interpreted, and derived requirements. Parsed requirements are multiple child requirements broken down from a parent requirement. An example is the parent "The system shall do A and B." broken into the children "The system shall do A." and "The system shall do B." READS maintains links between the child requirement and its parents. Users can also assign developed requirements to READS' *allocation division*, a hierarchical structure to which requirements are allocated. READS derives much of its power from this feature, because there can be many allocation divisions, and the association among requirements and nodes in an allocation division's hierarchical structure is many-to-many. This flexibility lets software engineers maintain almost any kind of information about requirements (such as mappings between a current version of a software object and the next revision and assignments to members of the development team). READS includes various online searching, querying, reporting, and browsing facilities. However, being limited to requirements traceability, it provides little support for other software artifacts.

The Software Productivity Consortium embarked on developing a requirements-traceability tool set for their member companies [Nejmeh 1988]. Although the project did not produce a deliverable product, the prototype developed for demonstration did show some significant enabling technologies to support traceability in a project library's database. The *SPC Traceability Tool Set* was designed to have five major subcomponents:

- *Decomposer.* This lets the user import documents from the document-processing system into a project database.

- *Schema Inferer.* This set of operations infers entity types, relationship types, attribute names, and attribute types from a project library's schema.

- *Constraint Analyzer.* This set of operations lets the project team define and verify completeness and consistency constraints among the entities in a project library.

- *Navigator.* These operations let the user browse SLOs in the project library, create/delete and traverse relationships among SLOs, and invoke tools on the SLOs.

- *Report Generator.* This mechanism produces traceability reports.

The SPC's demo prototype included the Decomposer, Navigator, and Report Generator. The prototype accepted DoD-Std-2167A [DOD 1987] SLOs from the documentation tool, decomposed them, and stored them in a project library. It generated lists of relationships among the captured SLOs and let the user navigate among the SLOs through windowing. A few reports were generated from the database to demonstrate the utility of collecting traceability information. Although this prototype did not address impact analysis or evaluation directly (as with READS), software engineers could manually implement impact analysis using the information provided by the SPC Traceability Tool Set.

4.2.3. Software Documentation

Software-documentation systems ordinarily offer little to support impact analysis. However, some systems provide services that support change and a documentation structure that assists in identifying the impacts of changes. Recognizing that software consists mostly of documents and that they change over the development cycle, several documentation-support facilities have started to support the relating of document objects for tracing changes.

Sodos (Software Document Support) is a prototype environment developed at the University of Southern California to support the development and maintenance of software documentation [Horowitz 1986]. Sodos supports system-requirements definition, functional requirements, preliminary design, detailed design, coding, integration and test, and maintenance. Additionally, its traceability support augments configuration management.

Sodos defines documents declaratively, using a structural hierarchy, the information content, and intra-/interdocument relationships. Developers and maintainers manually enter the document's content (text and graphics), as well as the requisite relationships among SLOs. Sodos then represents and stores documents and relationships in a database. Queries using predefined document relations (based on keywords and structure) provide Sodos users with a flexible set of tools for supporting SLO traceability.

Sodos supports traceability with both predefined and user-defined relationships among documents and components within documents. The underlying object model consists of objects, attributes of objects, relationships of objects, and a set of actions (called behavior) performed on the objects. It manages SLOs using an object-oriented model and a hypermedia graph of relationships. Sodos supports completeness and consistency checking of traceability relationships and navigation among SLOs. However, there is little direct support for impact analysis or change description.

SoftLib is a documentation-management system developed at the University of Strathclyde in Scotland [Sommerville 1986]. SoftLib provides assistance in managing software-development information, and its operation reflects the library metaphor, much like configuration-management systems. Through the central repository of documents, SoftLib can check out, modify, and return a document (or document set) requested by the user. For completeness checking of a document set, SoftLib ensures that software engineers make available all the documents required by a project according to the predetermined methodology. For consistency checking, SoftLib ensures that when a component is modified, all associated documents are modified in the same session.

The browsing features of SoftLib include searching for

- components in the central repository,
- documents for a particular component,
- components for a particular project,
- components for a particular version, and
- documents according to the operations performed on them.

Thus, users can identify components that change as a result of a modification to a particular component. Although this is a coarse-grained approach to traceability, it represents a useful application of document dependencies.

A more elaborate software-documentation system is *ISHYS* (Intelligent Software Hypertext System), developed as a documentation-integration facility of the USC Software Factory project [Garg 1989]. ISHYS helps software engineers develop and manage documentation throughout the development life cycle. Interesting features include

- facilities for browsing the hypertext of documents,
- interfaces to various software-development tools,
- task models of roles in software development and maintenance,
- reuse support through the creation of templates for software tasks and documents, and
- integration of documents within and across projects.

The Software Factory uses an automation-based life cycle that focuses on the roles played by development agents and the resulting products. Developer, manager, user, and maintainer roles are supported through agents in the development and maintenance of software documentation.

In ISHYS, basic templates are nodes of a hypertext that can have node-to-node and point-to-point links. The links represent various relationships among connected SLOs. ISHYS supports informal specifications, high-level specifications, formal development history, low-level specifications, decision and rationale notes, and source code. Although not the major intent of its design, ISHYS has the potential to provide traceability support for software artifacts represented in the basic templates. Traceability is enabled with the use of links and keyword-search mechanisms.

Links among the basic templates also provide useful navigation mechanisms for browsing related SLOs. ISHYS visualizes objects in the software system as a graph. Hierarchy charts display dependencies of related software objects. This aids in navigating through the body of software information and in identifying structural dependencies among SLOs.

4.2.4. Software-Project Database Systems

Database systems for software projects let the project team manage both project information and products. However, such systems do not directly support impact analysis. Instead, they provide database-query mechanisms that, when combined with a formally specified product structure, help software engineers determine the potential impacts of software changes.

An excellent example is *PMDB* (Project Master Database), developed at TRW [Penedo 1985] to provide an automated and integrated software-engineering environment database. The three principal components of PMDB are products, resources, and plans. *Products* are documents, executable software, and the like. *Resources* are consumable entities used to develop products, including staff-hours, computers, and money. *Plans* are the directing mechanisms for allocating, controlling, managing, and expending resources in the development of products. PMDB plans include schedules, budgets, technical plans, and management plans.

PMDB is based on the entity-relationship attribute model. It supports traceability, completeness, and consistency checking as well as navigation mechanisms for browsing the database. It does not support impact analysis directly, but its query capability provides data views of predetermined relationships and associated objects. Consequently, software engineers can use PMDB to identify potential high-level impacts.

RTTS (Requirements to Test Tracking System) was developed by Honeywell to track documents for software projects using Mil-Std-1679, the U.S. Navy's software-documentation standard [Rang 1985]. As the name indicates, RTTS concentrates on supporting testing activities, sometimes to the exclusion of other uses for traceability.

RTTS creates, analyzes, and maintains relationships among Mil-Std-1679-compliant program-performance specifications, program-design specifications, program-description document, code, informal procedure tests, interface-design specification, test plan, program-test specification, program-test procedures, and program-test reports. When the user enters these documents into the RTTS, it decomposes them into paragraphs and stores them in the database according to their paragraph numbers.

RTTS provides several capabilities for supporting requirements tracking:

- It creates, modifies, and deletes relations among documents and their contents.

- It identifies instances where no links exist for a particular document (for completeness checking).

- It detects the design, code, and test documentation associated with a particular system function or requirement.

- It finds the requirements that have been tested by a formal procedure.

- It lists the software procedures tested by a formal procedure.

- It identifies procedures that test a software procedure.

The user enters unnamed relationships among requirements, design, code, and test manually. These represent the primary traceability mechanism. RTTS also stores information about the date and time created/modified and the creator/modifier (such as initials). It supplies a set of predefined queries for performing the functions just listed.

4.3 Impact-Determination Techniques

Techniques to determine the impact of a change take the form of algorithms used to identify impacts in terms of the impact model. Software engineers apply these techniques to models of SLOs and their respective relationships to determine what other objects may be affected.

Impact-determination techniques underlie most automated impact-analysis approaches. Indeed, the effectiveness of impact analysis depends on the performance and accuracy of these techniques. These techniques, which are a subset of search techniques, include transitive-closure, inferencing, and program slicing. Regardless of the impact-determination technique employed, it is clear that the representation of software dependencies (whether graph, matrix, rules, or semantic networks) is important. We have attempted to present current thoughts on determining software-change impacts through representation methods.

4.3.1. Transitive Closure

Transitive closure is a fundamental impact-analysis technique. Transitive-closure algorithms take a graph of objects and relationships as input and determine all objects reachable from any object to any other object through paths of length 0 or more [Warshall 1962]. Transitive closure, as originally defined by Warshall, is in terms of a graph and does not use domain-dependent heuristics to perform the search.

Figure 10 illustrates transitive closure: Graph G defines a call graph among four modules. An arrow from module A to module B, for example, means that some function in A calls some function in B's interface. Graph G* shows the transitive closure for G, with arcs connecting any module that could directly or indirectly call another module. Graph G defines a direct-impact relationship set of ordered pairs {(A,B), (B,C), (C,D), (D,A)}. Each ordered pair of nodes represents a direct relationship between the nodes and is depicted as an arc between them. Graph G* gives the transitive closure, which is also a graph.

As G* shows, this is the worst case, in which every node in G could impact every other node in G. Because this gives little information about the impacts, the software engineer must further discriminate among relationships to determine a more suitable set of objects to examine.

Transitive closure is easy to explain and intuitively appealing for implementing impact analysis. Often it is a starting point for prototyping impact-analysis tools and for developing faster search techniques. Its advantage is the simplicity of its algorithm. Its disadvantage is that straightforward implementations are too slow for impact analysis on "non-toy" sets of objects.

The original transitive-closure algorithm [Warshall 1962] executes in $O(n^3)$ time, where n is the number of nodes in the input graph. $O(n^3)$ is a slow-running time for realistic sizes of n. Faster algorithms have since been developed [Purdom 1972], [Qadah 1991].

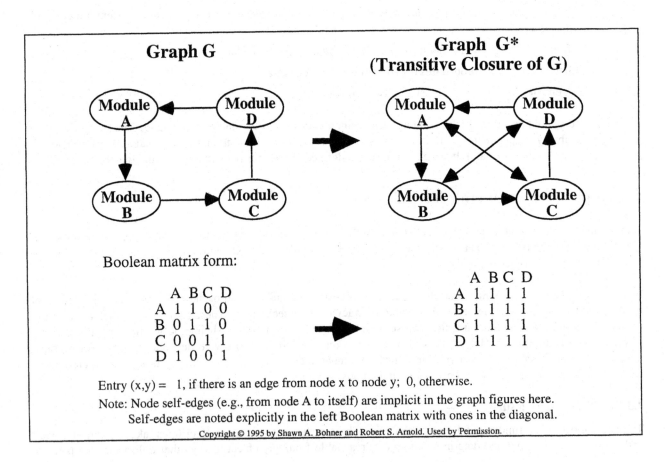

Boolean matrix form:

	A	B	C	D
A	1	1	0	0
B	0	1	1	0
C	0	0	1	1
D	1	0	0	1

	A	B	C	D
A	1	1	1	1
B	1	1	1	1
C	1	1	1	1
D	1	1	1	1

Entry (x,y) = 1, if there is an edge from node x to node y; 0, otherwise.
Note: Node self-edges (e.g., from node A to itself) are implicit in the graph figures here.
Self-edges are noted explicitly in the left Boolean matrix with ones in the diagonal.

Figure 10. Elements of Transitive Closure

Another appealing way to deal with transitive closure is to determine the distance of other potential impacts from the original impact. Through dynamic programming techniques [Sedgwick 1983], software engineers can determine the distance from the original node and narrow the evaluation of impacts to a given distance threshold.

4.3.2. Inferencing

Inferencing systems use rules to characterize relationships among objects. The rules define the search space or how it is explored, as well as the underlying relationships among entities or properties of entities. Inferencing systems usually consist of a database of facts, a way to infer new facts from previous ones, and some executive for managing the search. For example for graph G in Figure 10, the fact database might contain

$$Module(A), Module(B), Module(C), Module(D)$$

where Module(X) means that X is a module.

The database might also contain calling relationships from G:

$$Calls(A,B), Calls(B,C), Calls(C,D), Calls(D,A)$$

where calls(X,Y) means some function in module X calls some function at module Y's interface.

The simple transitive calling rule applies:

$$Calls(X,Y) \text{ and } Calls(Y,Z) \rightarrow Indirectly\_Calls(X,Z)$$

Given Calls(A,B) and Calls(B,C), software engineers can infer from this rule that Indirectly_Calls(A,C) is also a valid fact. From what "calling" normally implies, they might also conclude that a change to C could impact how A executes. Thus, inferencing helps determine a new fact, which in turn is used to assert a potential impact.

With inferencing, software engineers can compute the search space as needed, usually depending on how the search for impacts is going. Inferencing's power is in the reduction of the search space. In terms of impact analysis, it provides a flexible mechanism for determining impacts according to relationship rules. As a software system changes, engineers can update these relationship rules as well as object declarations.

Once the rules and objects are established, inferencing engines (production-rule systems and the like) provide the evaluation mechanisms to determine potential impacts. The strategy used to analyze impacts varies. Here we present two strategies: truth maintenance and semantic inferencing.

4.3.2.1. Truth Maintenance

Constraint systems use constraint rules to characterize relationships among objects. The relationships define and limit object properties, which is why the systems are called constraint systems. A truth-maintenance system [Doyle 1979] is a type of constraint system that maintains consistency in a model of assumptions. When the model is changed, the truth-maintenance system checks it for inconsistencies, identifies them, and brings them to the user's attention for resolution. Checking for boundary breaches or inconsistencies represents an impact-analysis technique because the objects identified with the breach or inconsistency represent an impact set.

Although truth maintenance is applied predominately in artificial-intelligence belief systems, it shows promise for impact analysis. With truth maintenance, the impact model is represented as facts and rules about objects, not as nodes and relationships.

Change dependencies can be represented with truth-maintenance rules. Doyle details the inferencing necessary to detect dependencies in a rule base [Doyle 1979]. A set of rules are used for dependency-directed backtracking to change a set of assumptions. Truth-maintenance techniques may help reduce the search space in impact analysis for large systems. In effect, the search space is computed as needed, rather than being precomputed, and it is made explicit.

4.3.2.2. *Semantic Inferencing*

Software engineers can also use semantic information to narrow the search space in impact analysis. Reasoning about the semantic effects of program changes can lead to a more focused and accurate determination of the impact of software changes.

Semantic networks have been applied successfully in a variety of contexts to represent knowledge. Figure 11 illustrates what semantic inferencing means in a software context. In Figure 11a, it is straightforward to infer that FRED has a TAIL since FRED is a DOG and a DOG has a TAIL. Similarly in Figure 11b, REQT 3.4.2 depends on X-WINDOW TEXT WIDGET, since REQT 3.4.2 is realized in PROGRAM (TEXT EDITOR), and PROGRAM (TEXT EDITOR) depends on X-WINDOW TEXT WIDGET. The depends-on relationship may be a synonym for "calls" or "uses" in this case. Representing software knowledge in this way provides a flexible medium for applying logic algorithms to determine the impacts of software changes.

Many researchers have addressed knowledge representation in the context of software changes. Mark Moriconi and Timothy Winkler describe a logic for determining impacts that is based on *information flow* [Moriconi 1990]. Information flow is defined simply as *A* affects *B* if a change in the value of *A* could affect the value of *B* when the program containing them is executed. This logic has some advantages because it lets software engineers

- derive a given impact from the logic's axioms (if it exists),
- handle impacts caused by new program constructs by adding new rules, and
- save proofs (how inferences are derived) and reuse them as artifacts in themselves to speed future impact analyses.

Remap is a system for capturing design knowledge and dependencies that supports impact determination using semantic inferences based on design dependencies [Dhar 1988]. Software engineers derive design knowledge by creating analogies based on the similarity of application among design components. Using these analogies, they can infer dependencies and see potential change effects. Remap also has a learning component, which it uses to derive dependency knowledge. The tool uses a breadth-first search to determine impacts.

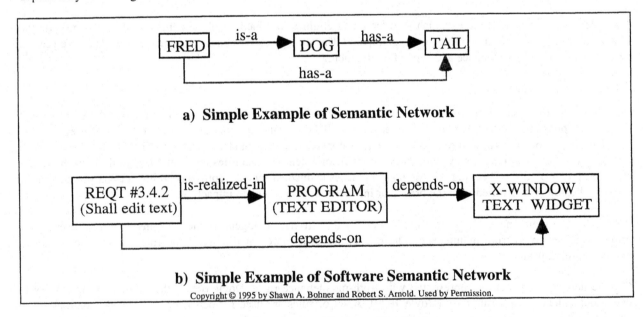

a) **Simple Example of Semantic Network**

b) **Simple Example of Software Semantic Network**

Figure 11. Examples of Semantic Inferencing

Knowledge about how software components interconnect is also important semantic information in the support of large-scale software modifications. Stephen Yau and Jeffrey Tsai represent such interconnection knowledge and show how to derive rules that characterize component dependencies [Yau 1987]. They use first-order logic to represent component-interconnection information and provide for integrity checking during development and maintenance activities. Automatic reasoning techniques in the first-order logic derive inferences that impact-analysis tools can use to detect change impacts.

4.3.3. Program Slicing

Another interesting impact-determination technique is program slicing. Program slicing provides a mechanism for constraining the view and behavior of a program to a specific area of interest [Weiser 1984], [Horwitz 1990], [Berzins 1995]. A *program slice* is an executable program that includes only the parts of the original program that are affected by the change. The slice is taken primarily from data- and control-flow information analyzed with respect to some slicing criteria. Basically, program slicers focus attention on a particular part of a program by eliminating parts that are not essential to execute the target area. This is particularly useful when debugging a complex program or testing a software change.

Surgeon's Assistant is an example of a prototype program slicer that lets users pull out parts of a program and analyze them in the context of data flow [Gallagher 1991]. It was developed at Loyola University to investigate decomposition slicing as a software-maintenance technique. Surgeon's Assistant provides semantic information and guidance to assist in formulating a maintenance strategy that is based on a slice of the software decomposed with respect to a change requirement. This view lets software testers test the slice with confidence that other parts of the program are not impacted, thus eliminating the need for regression testing. The decomposition is effectively an impact analysis of the change at the code level.

5. Conclusion

Software systems are subject to changes that often eat away at their maintainability and reliability. Costs to implement software changes are often disproportionately high because the tools and techniques to analyze their impacts are inadequate. More often than not, software-change impacts are investigated with little automated support. With the continued growth of today's software systems, however, this practice must change, or the longevity of these systems will be severely threatened.

The need for impact analysis is strong and pervasive. With business's current attention to the Year 2000 problem — in which impact analysis plays a prominent role — we can expect more commercial focus on both change processes and impact-analysis tools. This, in turn, will aid in evaluating a broad spectrum of software change as software continues to evolve.

Finally, software repositories are quickly becoming the vehicle for managing SLOs. Impact-analysis technology will become a valuable tool in conducting trade-offs of change strategies, in better estimating the costs of software changes, and ultimately in more efficiently executing those changes.

6. References

Items with an asterisk are papers that appear in this book.

*[Arnold 1993] R. S. Arnold and S. A. Bohner, "Impact Analysis — Towards A Framework for Comparison," *Proc. Conf. Software Maintenance*, IEEE CS Press, Los Alamitos, Calif., 1993, pp. 292–301.

[Arthur 1988] L. J. Arthur, *Software Evolution.*, John Wiley & Sons, New York, 1988.

[Basili 1980] V. Basili and D. Weiss, "Evaluation of a Software Requirements Document by Analysis of Change Data," *Proc. Int'l Conf. Software Eng.*, IEEE CS Press, Los Alamitos, Calif., 1981, pp. 314–323.

[Berzins 1995]   *Software Merging and Slicing*, V. Berzins, ed., IEEE CS Press, Los Alamitos, Calif., 1995.

[Boehm 1987] B. Boehm, "Improving Software Productivity," *Computer*, Sept. 1987, pp. 43–57.

[Bohner 1995] S. A. Bohner, "A Graph Traceability Approach to Software Change Impact Analysis," Ph.D. dissertation, George Mason University, Fairfax, Va., 1995.

[Chmura 1982]   L. Chmura and D. Weiss, "The A-7E Software Requirements Document: Three Years of Change Data," Naval Research Laboratory Memo, Report 4938, Naval Research Laboratory, Washington, DC, Nov. 1982.

[Collofello 1987] J. S. Collofello and J. J. Buck, "Software Quality Assurance for Maintenance" *IEEE Software*, Sept. 1987, pp. 46–51.

[Dhar 1988]   V. Dhar and M. Jarke, "Dependency Directed Reasoning and Learning in Systems Maintenance Support," *IEEE Trans. Software Eng.*, Feb. 1988, pp. 211–227.

[DOD 1985a] U.S. Department of Defense, "Military Standard for Software Quality Evaluation," DoD-Std-2168, Apr. 26, 1985.

[DOD 1985b] U.S. Department of Defense, "Defense System Software Development Standard, DoD-STD-2167, June 5, 1985.

[DOD 1987] U.S. Department of Defense, "Software Development Plan," DI-MCCR-80030A, DoD-STD-2167A, Defense System Software Development, Oct. 27, 1987.

[Doyle 1979] J. Doyle, "A Truth Maintenance System," *Artificial Intelligence*, Vol. 12, No. 3, 1979, pp. 231–272.

[Ferrante 1987]   J. Ferrante, K. J. Ottenstein, and J. D. Warren, "The Program Dependence Graph and Its Use in Optimization," *ACM Trans. Programming Languages and Systems*, July 1987, pp. 319–349.

[Freedman 1981] D. P. Freedman and G. M. Weinberg, "A Checklist for Potential Side Effects of a Maintenance Change," in *Techniques of Program and System Maintenance*, G. Parikh, ed., 1981, pp. 93–100.

*[Gallagher 1991]   K. B. Gallagher and J. R. Lyle, "Using Program Slicing in Software Maintenance," *IEEE Trans. Software Eng.*, Aug. 1991, pp. 751–761.

*[Garg 1989] P. Garg and W. Scacchi, "A Hypertext System to Manage Software Life Cycle Documents," *IEEE Software*, May 1990, pp. 90–98.

*[Gotel 1994] O. C. Gotel and A. C. Finkelstein, "An Analysis of the Requirements Traceability Problem," *Proc. First Conf. Requirements Eng.*, IEEE CS Press, Los Alamitos, Calif., 1994, pp. 94–101.

*[Harrold 1993] M. J. Harrold and B. Malloy, "A Unified Interprocedural Program Representation for a Maintenance Environment," *IEEE Trans. Software Eng.*, June 1993, pp. 584–593.

*[Horowitz 1986]   E. Horowitz and R. Williamson, "SODOS: A Software Document Support Environment — Its Definition," *IEEE Trans. Software Eng.*, Aug. 1986, pp. 849–859.

*[Horwitz 1990] S. Horwitz, T. Reps, and D. Binkley, "Interprocedural Slicing Using Dependence Graphs," *ACM Trans. Programming Languages and Systems*, Jan. 1990, pp. 26–60.

[IEEE 1993] "Glossary of Software Engineering Terminology," Std. 729-1993, in *IEEE Software Eng. Standards*, 5th ed., IEEE Press, New York, 1993.

[Lehman 1980] M. M. Lehman, "Programs, Life Cycles, and Laws of Software Evolution," *Proc. IEEE*, special issue on software eng., Sept. 1980, pp. 1060•01076.

[Lehman 1991] M. M. Lehman, "Software Engineering: the Software Processes and Their Support," *IEE Software Eng. Journal*, special issue on software environments and factories, Sept. 1991, pp. 243–258.

[Lehman 1994] M. M. Lehman, "Software Evolution," *Encyclopedia of Software Eng.*, 1994, pp. 1202–1208.

*[Loyall 1993] J. P. Loyall and S. A. Mathisen, "Using Dependence Analysis to Support Software Maintenance," *Proc. Conf. Software Maintenance*, IEEE CS Press, Los Alamitos, Calif., 1993, pp. 282–291.

[McCabe 1992] "Battlemap Analysis Tool Reference Manual," McCabe & Associates, Inc., Columbia, Md., Dec. 1992.

*[Moriconi 1990]M. Moriconi and T.C. Winkler, "Approximate Reasoning about the Semantic Effects of Program Changes," *IEEE Trans. Software Eng.*, Sept. 1990, pp. 980–992.

[Nejmeh 1988] B. A. Nejmeh and T. E. Dickey, "Traceability Technology at the Software Productivity Consortium," Tech. Report SPC-1.0-881130-40-00-N, Software Productivity Consortium, Herndon, Va., Nov. 1988.

[Ottenstein 1984] K. J. Ottenstein and L. M. Ottenstein, "The Program Dependence Graph in a Software Development Environment," *ACM SIGPLAN Notices*, May 1984, pp. 177–184.

[Penedo 1985] M. H. Penedo and E. D. Stuckle, "PMDB — A Project Master Database for Software Engineering Environments," *Proc.Int'l Conf. Software Eng.*, IEEE CS Press, Los Alamitos, Calif., 1985, pp. 150–157.

[Perry 1989] D. E. Perry, "The Inscape Environment," *Proc. Int'l Conf. Software Eng.*, IEEE CS Press, Los Alamitos, Calif., 1989, pp. 2–12.

[Pfleeger 1991] S. L. Pfleeger, *Software Engineering: The Production of Quality Software*, Macmillan, New York, 1991.

*[Podgurski 1990] A. Podgurski and L. A. Clarke, "A Formal Model of Program Dependencies and Its Implications for Software Testing, Debugging, and Maintenance," *IEEE Trans. Software Eng.*, Sept. 1990, pp. 965–979.

[Purdom 1972] P. Purdom, Jr., "A Transitive Closure Algorithm," *BIT*, Vol. 10, 1970, pp. 76–94.

*[Qadah 1991] G. Z. Qadah, L. J. Henschen, and J. J. Kim, "Efficient Algorithms for the Instantiated Transitive Closure Queries," *IEEE Trans. Software Eng.*, Mar. 1991, pp. 296–309.

[RADC 1986] "Automated Life Cycle Impact Analysis System," Tech. report RADC-TR-86-197, Rome Laboratories, Rome, N.Y., Dec. 1986.

[Rang 1985] E. R. Rang and K. H. Thelen, "A Requirements to Test Tracking System," *Proc. ACM Conf.*, ACM Press, New York, 1985, pp. 387–391.

[SAD 1980] "Final Report of the Software Acquisition and Development Group," Software Acquisition and Development Group, July 1980.

[Sedgwick 1983] R. Sedgwick, *Algorithms*, Addison-Wesley, Reading, Mass., 1983.

[Smith 1992] T. J. Smith, "System Development and Requirements Management," tech. report, Paramax Systems Corp. (now Loral Corp.), Reston, Va., Jan. 1992.

[Sommerville 1986] I. Sommerville et al., "SoftLib — A Documentation-Management System," *Software Practice and Experience*, Feb. 1986, pp. 131–143.

[Stevens 1974] W. Stevens, G. Meyers, and L. Constantine, "Structured Design," *IBM Systems J.*, Vol. 13, No. 2, 1974.

[Swanson 1989] E. R. Swanson and C. Beath, *Maintaining Information Systems Organizations*, John Wiley & Sons, New York, 1987.

[Taha 1988] A. Taha and S. Thebaut, "Program Change Analysis Using Incremental Data Flow Techniques," Tech. report SERC-TR-26-F, Software Eng. Research Center, Univ. of Florida, Gainesville, Fla., Jan. 1988.

*[Turver 1994] R. J. Turver and M. Munro, "An Early Impact Analysis Technique for Software Maintenance," *J. Software Maintenance: Research and Practice*, Vol. 6, No. 1, 1994, pp. 35–52.

[Warshall 1962] S. Warshall, "A Theorem on Boolean Matrices," *J. ACM*, Vol. 9, No. 1, 1962, pp. 11–12.

[Weiser 1984] M. Weiser, "Program Slicing," *IEEE Trans. Software Eng.*, July 1984, pp. 352–357.

[Weiss 1985] D. Weiss and V. Basili, "Evaluating Software Development by Analysis of Changes," *IEEE Trans. Software Eng.*, Feb. 1985, pp. 157–168.

[Wilde 1987] N. Wilde and B. A. Nejmeh, "Dependency Analysis: An Aid for Software Maintenance," Tech. report SERC-TR-23-F, Software Eng. Research Center, University of Florida, Gainesville, Fla., Jan. 1987.

[Yau 1980] S. S. Yau and J. Collofello, "Some Stability Measures for Software Maintenance," *IEEE Trans. Software Eng.*, Nov. 1980, pp. 545–552.

[Yau 1987] S. S. Yau and J. J. Tsai, "Knowledge Representation of Software Component Interconnection Information for Large-Scale Software Modifications," *IEEE Trans. Software Eng.*, Mar. 1987, pp. 545–552.

Chapter 1
Nature of Impact Analysis

Purpose

The papers in this chapter will help you understand software change and the importance of predicting the effects of changes to software before they are actually made. The papers also address where to apply impact analysis in the software-maintenance process. The chapter explains how you might determine if impact analysis is effective and presents a framework for comparing various types of impact analysis. The last paper describes a real-world problem that impact analysis could help solve.

The Papers

Software change is a fundamental ingredient of software maintenance. Impact analysis is key in analyzing change or potential change and in identifying the software objects the change might affect.

Even with the best-laid plans, software changes. Developers must understand *how* change occurs to effectively predict the impacts of that change.

One way to understand how change occurs is to understand how programs evolve. Over the last two decades, Manny Lehman and Laszlo Belady have proposed and refined "laws" of program evolution ([Belady 1976], [Lehman 1980] [Lehman 1985], [Lehman 1991], [Lehman 1994]). Although the statistical validity of these laws has been challenged [Yuen 1981], [Lawrence 1982], we believe they are helpful, if not absolute, comments on the nature of change.

Belady and Lehman studied several years of OS/360 development and change data. From this data, they proposed five laws that characterize the dynamics of program evolution:

1. *Change is continual.* "A program undergoes continuing change or becomes less useful. The change process continues until it becomes cost-effective to replace the program with a re-created version." That is, software systems change to meet the demands of users and environments until it is no longer cost-effective to change them.

2. *Complexity increases.* "As an evolving program is changed, its complexity, which reflects deteriorating structure, increases unless work is done to maintain or reduce the complexity." In other words, as the program is changed, the complexity of its structure is likely to increase unless proactively controlled.

3. *There is dynamic dependency.* This is what Belady and Lehman call the "fundamental" law of program evolution: "Program evolution is subject to a dynamic that makes the programming process, and hence measures of global project and system attributes, self-regulating with statistically determinable trends and invariances." In other words, program evolution is composed of several attributes that are dynamically related such that the change in one alters others (through feedback) and tends toward a goal.

4. *Organizational stability is preserved.* "The global activity rate in a project supporting an evolving program is statistically invariant." That is, the rate of work involved in changing an evolving program tends to remain constant despite resource changes.

5. *Familiarity is conserved.* "The release content (changes, additions, deletions) of the successive releases of an evolving program is statistically invariant." In other words, the content of successive software releases tends to remain the same in terms of changes.

The three papers in this chapter add to the understanding of these five laws. In the first, "A Process Model for Software Maintenance," Robert Moreton argues convincingly for an effective software-maintenance process in light of the increasing size and complexity of software systems. A key part of software maintenance is impact analysis, in which the effects of a change request are elaborated for estimates. Moreton clearly explains where and when impact analysis should be employed in the software-maintenance process.

Although impact-analysis technology is rapidly maturing, quantitatively assessing software-change impacts is (as of early 1995) more an art than a science. People who have considerable domain, system, and program experience or knowledge can give reasonable assessments of software-change impacts in relatively small scale situations. However, impact-analysis practices vary widely, even among experienced software professionals.

We need ways to measure the potential impacts of the change itself and the system to be changed. Software stability, traceability, complexity, and size are all measures that influence the impact assessment.

In the next paper, "Impact Analysis – Towards A Framework for Comparison," we introduce a definition of impact analysis that clearly delineates the basis for comparing impact-analysis capabilities. We present a framework model of impact analysis and put forth the ideas underlying impact analysis according to the definition. We also classify several impact-analysis approaches according to this definition. The framework is based on applications of impact analysis; parts are used to perform impact analysis and parts are used to measure the effectiveness of the impact-analysis techniques. We also model the effectiveness of impact analysis to illustrate the situations (both good and bad) that are likely to be found in impact sets.

Robert Arnold concludes the chapter with a paper that describes a real-world application for impact analysis. In "Millennium Now: Solutions for Century Data Change Impact," he describes the nature of the impact-analysis problem through the date-change problem that is likely to plague software organizations at the turn of the century. He suggests steps to take in planning for the transition as well as the tools and techniques necessary to accomplish the effort. Taking a software-assets approach, Arnold suggests

that early assessment is the key to addressing the impacts to an organization's software portfolio.

References

[Belady 1976]   L. A. Belady and M. M. Lehman, "A Model of Large Program Development," *IBM Systems J.,* Vol. 15, No. 3, 1976, pp. 225-252.

[Lawrence 1982] M. Lawrence, "An Examination of Evolution Dynamics," *Proc. Int'l Conf. Software Eng.,* IEEE CS Press, Los Alamitos, Calif., 1982, pp. 188-196.

[Lehman 1980]   M. M. Lehman, "Programs, Life Cycles, and Laws of Software Evolution," *Proc. IEEE*, special issue on software eng., IEEE Press, New York, Sept. 1980, pp. 1060-1076.

[Lehman 1985] M. M. Lehman and L. A. Belady, *Program Evolution: Processes of Software Change*, Academic Press, London, 1985.

[Lehman 1991] M. M. Lehman, "Software Engineering, the Software Process and Their Support," *IEE Software Eng. J.*, special issue on software environments and factories, Sept. 1991, pp. 243-258.

[Lehman 1994] M. M. Lehman, "Software Evolution," *Enc. Software Eng.*, 1994, pp. 1202-1208.

[Yuen 1981] C. K. S. Yuen, "A Phenomenology of Program Maintenance and Evolution," PhD dissertation, Dept. of Computing, Imperial College of Science and Technology, Univ. of London, London, 1981.

A process model for software maintenance

ROBERT MORETON

Director of Studies, Birmingham Polytechnic, UK

Abstract: This paper draws on work undertaken for the Butler Cox Productivity Enhancement Programme (PEP) to describe a process model which will provide a basis for overcoming the problems of cost and complexity associated with software maintenance. PEP is a continuous program that is open to organizations wishing to measure and improve systems development and productivity.

The paper argues that for maintenance work to be effective, it is vital to control the input to the process – the procedure by which change requests are notified and managed in the first place. The procedure of change management is followed by impact analysis, system release planning, change design, implementation, testing and system release/integration. These steps, which occur sequentially, are supported by a further activity that continues concurrently – progress monitoring.

The conclusion of the paper is that a coordinated program, effective across the whole maintenance process and designed to control changes to the system, will become more and more critical as the complexity of the system increases. Formal procedures are essential to ensure that software is not degraded and to provide an audit facility. At the same time there are several automated change and control packages now available that could help to reduce administrative overheads and increase control over system changes.

Introduction

Software maintenance is an expensive and complicated business. Research undertaken by Moreton (1988) for the Butler Cox Productivity Enhancement Programme (PEP), indicates that maintenance is generally undermanaged. As a result system changes are not always properly controlled and there is insufficient recognition of the benefits to be derived from the newer methods and tools. Recent articles by Glass (1988, 1989) highlight the need to formalize the maintenance process, to manage the software as a product and to link quality with maintenance processes. The purpose of this paper is to describe a process model for software maintenance which will provide a basis for rectifying the perceived deficiencies and exploiting the potential benefits.

For maintenance work to be effective, it is vital to control the input to the process – the procedure by which change requests are notified and managed in the first place. This procedure of change management is the first of several steps in the maintenance process. Change management is followed by impact analysis, system release planning, change design, implementation, testing and system release/integration. These steps, which occur sequentially, are supported by a further activity that continues concurrently – progress monitoring. The whole process is illustrated in Figure 1 (adapted from Arthur, 1988).

In a survey of 24 commercial organizations belonging to the Butler Cox PEP, respondents claimed to have a clearly defined procedure in place that corresponds to the first step, change management. Certainly, every respondent in the survey records all user requests and operational problems, but respondents admitted to some failings as well. Periodic formal audits, for instance, are in place in fewer than half of the survey respondents' businesses (see Figure 2). In order to achieve improvements in the maintainance environment, the steps in the process need to be carefully coordinated, not simply monitored individually.

Formalize the maintenance process

To appreciate the importance of formalizing the steps in the maintenance process, it helps to understand more precisely what they are.

Change management

Change management is the critical first step in the maintenance process. A formal procedure for change management is essential for two reasons: it provides a common communication channel between maintenance staff, users, project managers and operations staff, and it provides a directory of changes to the system, for status reporting, project management, auditing and quality control. The basic tool of the change-management procedure is a formal change-

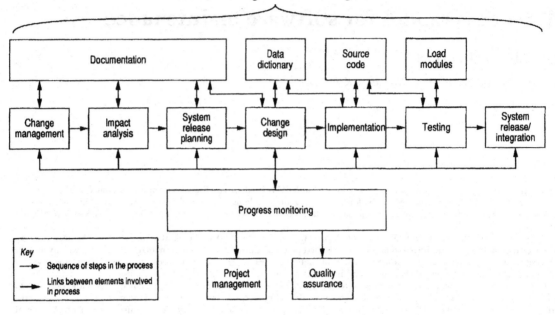

Figure 1. Define the steps in the maintenance process

Figure 2. Most organisations have control procedures in place

request document that forms the basis of a contract between the user and the maintainer.

An important element of change management is version control (or software configuration control). It means tracking different versions of programs, releases of software and generations of hardware, and it plays a major role in ensuring the quality of delivered systems. Version control also ensures that software is not degraded by uncontrolled or unapproved changes, and provides an essential audit facility.

Impact analysis

The purpose of impact analysis is to determine the scope of change requests as a basis for accurate resource planning and scheduling, and to confirm the cost/benefit justification. Impact analysis can be broken down into four stages. The first stage is determining the scope of the change request, by verifying the information contained within it, converting it into a systems requirement, and tracing the impact (via documented records) of the change on related systems and programs. In the second stage, resourcing estimates are developed, based on considerations such as size (in estimated lines of code) and software complexity. Code analysers that measure the quality of existing code can be helpful at this stage. The third stage is analysing the costs and benefits of the change request, in the same way as for a new application. In the fourth stage, the maintenance project manager advises the users of the implications of the change request, in business rather than in technical terms, for them to decide whether to authorize proceeding with the changes.

There are three benefits of impact analysis: improved accuracy of resourcing estimates and, hence, better scheduling; a reduction in the amount of corrective maintenance, because of fewer introduced errors; improved software quality.

System release planning

In this step, the system release schedule is planned. Although well established amongst software suppliers, system release planning is not widely practised by the data processing departments of the organizations surveyed, reflecting a difference in the extent to which formal maintenance contracting is established.

A system release batches together a succession of change requests into a smaller number of discrete revisions. System releases can take place according to a timetable that is planned in advance. The timetable planning gives users the chance to set priorities for their change requests, and makes testing activities easier to schedule. The problem with system releases comes, of course, when corrective maintenance is required urgently.

Software is available to help monitor system releases. The software records the changes incorporated in, and the date of, each release, and provides information for project control, auditing and management.

Change design and implementation

The common thread in the work in these two steps is that they are undertaken to satisfy an often short-term user requirement.

Corrective maintenance, in particular, will be undertaken in a limited time and will be concerned primarily with fault repair (with little regard for careful design and integration changes). Emergency repairs must subsequently be linked to the formal software-maintenance process and be treated as a new change request. This will ensure that the repairs are correctly implemented and that the design document-ation is updated.

Adaptive maintenance will functionally enhance an existing system. The design and implementation process is similar but more restricted than the design and implementation of new application systems. The major difference is that the design implications of enhancements must be taken into account in the subsequent program and module implementation. Failure to design the change at each level can result in an increasingly complex, unreliable and unmain-tainable system. This leads to higher maintenance costs and reduces the life of the system.

Perfective maintenance is concerned with improving the quality of existing systems. The effort is applied to software that is the most expensive to operate and maintain. The design tasks undertaken will range from complete redesign and rewrite to partial restructuring. The process combines the characteristics of the other two types of maintenance.

Testing

The purpose of maintenance testing is to ensure that the software complies with both the change request and the original requirement specification. It forms a major part of a successful quality-assurance plan. In principle, maintenance testing is much like develop-ment testing except that, because the scope of maint-enance testing is potentially narrower, fewer test cases have to be prepared, validated and filed in the test-case library.

The maintenance test cases should be created as a direct result of the first stage in the impact analysis. They should be sequenced according to the principle of incremental testing so that defects in the change-request specification and design can be identified early on. Walk-throughs and inspections should be imple-mented routinely as a formal element in the process.

The test-case library itself builds up over time. At first, it contains only the test cases prepared for and validated during original development. It grows as test cases for successive maintenance tests are added to it. A file of this sort is called a regression testing file. A few tools are available from suppliers (such as IBM and Digital) to help with regression testing. Although limited in what they can do (in terms of features such as automatic revalidation, for instance), they are able to provide administrative support.

System release/integration

This step consists of releasing the revised programs into live operation. The implications for maintenance staff are significant because it is their responsibility to ensure that any revised versions are completely inte-grated with other parts of the system, which may never have been revised or which may have been revised at different times.

Progress monitoring

Progress monitoring takes place concurrently with the other seven steps in the maintenance process. The sort of data that should be collected during progress monitoring includes the time taken per step, the effort involved and the scope of the change. Collecting and filing data of this sort so that performance can be monitored, both over time and between systems, is consistent with the disciplined formal approach to software development and maintenance implied by the terms software engineering. Improving software maintenance productivity is difficult if there is no record of where problems and successes have occurred in the past.

31

Coordinate the steps in the maintenance process

There is no panacea for solving the problems of maintenance. It is essential, however, to consider not only how each individual step in the process works, but also how the various steps fit together.

The software house, Peterborough Software (UK) Ltd, provides an example of how companies can successfully coordinate the steps in the software maintenance process. The problems that it faces are unusually demanding. The company maintains a range of payroll software packages. The packages run on a variety of computers, under the control of different operating systems, both within the UK and overseas. Altogether, Peterborough Software has around 400 customers. The software coding differs from country to country, to take account of local statutory regulations, such as taxation. Thus, several releases of the same package are current at a time, and all have to be supported in the field. The regulations change frequently and without warning, and maintenance changes therefore have to be implemented swiftly and accurately. The difficulties faced by Peterborough Software are further compounded when customers create nonstandard versions of the software by failing to apply maintenance modifications that are issued to them, or applying them in the wrong sequence.

How does Peterborough Software arrange its maintenance procedures against this background of complexity? The answer lies in disciplined adherence to procedural steps similar to the ones we have described here, and in the use of a computer-based program monitoring system known as the Problem Monitoring System (PMS).

The maintenance procedure is carried out by two divisions within Peterborough Software. One is the Customer Support Division, which effectively looks after management impact analysis and system release planning. The other is the Development Division, which is responsible for coding, testing and quality assurance.

Change requests received by the Customer Support Division come from three sources: customers, whose requests take the form of enhancements (called facility requests), queries and error reports; impending legislative changes; the market. To survive, Peterborough Software has to compete by offering products that are constantly being improved. Maintenance arising from customers is both adaptive and corrective in nature; from the other two sources, it is mostly adaptive and perfective.

Customers are the most important source of change requests – the Customer Support Division receives up to 400 telephone enquiries a day, for instance enquiries are routed to application-support groups organized by software product and by the kind of equipment it runs on. Within the application-support groups, consultants familiar with the way the software can be used, and with the way it works, form the first line of response. They are able to resolve most of the enquiries on the spot, but 20 per cent have to be passed to the Development Division for resolution. It is here that the PMS comes into its own. It logs problem reports at every stage of response and resolution, using customer references and event codes. When a coding change is made, for instance, the programmer records the details on the PMS. These are immediately available to others, so duplication is avoided. The PMS helps to coordinate adaptive and corrective maintenance work. It monitors maintenance progress and produces management statistics.

The Development Division is organized into groups that specialize in analysis, coding and quality assurance. Tested software is batched for release. Different forms of release reflect the level of support that Peterborough Software provides. For instance, versions for release which are necessitated by government legislation get full support. Any earlier versions still left in the field beyond a certain date no longer enjoy full support.

The Peterborough Software example is a model for the maintenance of any large application system, but particularly for multisite, multiversion implementation with large numbers of users. The principal lessons are as follows:

- Recognition of the cost and of the importance of the post-release phases of the system life cycle, and the consequent planning (for example, replacement, migration and technical design) for the maintenance effort
- The rigour applied to pre-release testing and post-release version identification and control
- The formal contractual basis that clearly specifies the responsibilities of supplier and customer
- Recognition of the relative importance of problems that occur in practice at the operational level (including those deriving from imperfect documentation or training), and at the code maintenance level and of the need to provide adequate support staff at both levels.

A coordinated programme, effective across the whole maintenance process, and designed to control changes to the system, will become more and more critical as the complexity of the systems increases. Formal procedures are essential to ensure that software is not degraded and to provide an audit facility. The experience of Peterborough Software may serve as a model. At the same time, there are several automated change-and-configuration-control packages currently being introduced to the market that could help to reduce administrative overheads and increase control over system changes.

References

Arthur, L.J. (1988) *Software Evolution,* Wiley, New York

Glass, R.L. (1988) Champions of the living software *Systems Development,* August.

Glass, R.L. (1989) Linking quality and maintenance *Systems Development,* July.

Moreton, R. (1988) Managing software maintenance *Butler Cox Productivity Enhancement Programme,* Paper 8.

Biographical notes

Robert Moreton is a principal lecturer at Birmingham Polytechnic. As Director of Studies within the Department of Computing, he is responsible for the academic quality of a range of professional and degree courses in computing and information technology. He is also an associate consultant with Butler-Cox, where he specializes in systems development methods and project management. In the past eight years, he has worked on both consultancy and research projects for the company. He has contributed to Butler-Cox reports on cost-effective systems development and maintenance, managing software maintenance and trends in information technology. He was also responsible for a study of the market for system-building tools in Europe. A common theme of his work has been tracking and evaluating developments in information technology and forecasting the potential impact of these developments.

He has a masters degree in computer science from Brunel University and is a member of the British Computer Society.

Address for correspondence: Department of Computing, Feeney Building, Birmingham Polytechnic, Perry Barr, Birmingham B42 2SU.

Impact Analysis - Towards A Framework for Comparison

Robert S. Arnold

Software Evolution Technology
12613 Rock Ridge Rd.
Herndon, VA 22070
703-450-6791
r.arnold@compmail.com

Shawn A. Bohner

MITRE Corporation
7525 Colshire Dr.
McLean, VA 22102
703-883-7354
bohner@mitre.org

ABSTRACT

The term "impact analysis" is used with many meanings. We define a three-part framework for characterizing and comparing diverse impact analysis approaches. The parts correspond to how an approach is used to accomplish impact analysis, how an approach does impact analysis internally, and the effectiveness of the impact analysis approach. To illustrate the framework's application, we classify five impact analysis approaches according to it.

1. Introduction

1.1. Purpose

Many activities are termed "impact analysis," yet it is difficult to relate them. Impact analysis (IA) approaches should be characterized so that IA approaches can be understood, compared, and assessed. This paper presents a framework for doing this.

The framework aids comparing IA approaches, assessing the strengths and weaknesses of individual IA approaches, and unifying the widely varying IA technology within a single conceptual framework. We present the framework, justify it, and use it to compare five IA approaches.[1]

1.2. How the Reader Can Use These Results

If the reader is interested in understanding, evaluating, or using IA technology, reading this paper will be helpful. By understanding the parts of the IA framework, the reader will see several features of IA that could be in a given IA approach, but may not be. This will help the reader assess the potential value of an IA approach. The reader can use the parts of the framework to critique claims of IA made by software tool vendors or by researchers.

Vendors and researchers may use the framework to redefine their work in terms comparable to other approaches and

---

[1] By "approach" we mean tools, semi-automatic procedures, and manual procedures.

tools. This will help them track IA technology improvements.

1.3. New Results

This paper has several new results. First, the framework for understanding and classifying IA approaches is new. We are unaware of any other such paper in the IA literature. The comparison of the five IA approaches systems using the framework is new. We have not seen different types of IA approaches compared according to a common framework.

1.4. Paper Structure

Section 2 discusses why an IA classification framework is needed and the issues such a framework should address. Section 3 presents the framework. Section 4 applies the framework to compare five IA approaches and tools. Section 5 relates our work to others'.

2. The Need for an Evaluation Framework

2.1. Definition

Impact analysis (IA) is the activity of identifying what to modify to accomplish a change, or of identifying the potential consequences of a change. Examples of IA are:

- using cross reference listings to see what other parts of a program contain references to a given variable or procedure,
- using program slicing to determine the program subset that can affect the value of a given variable [Gallagher1991],
- browsing a program by opening and closing related files,
- using traceability relationships to identify changing artifacts,
- using configuration management systems to track and find changes, and
- consulting designs and specifications to determine the scope of a change.

IA precedes, or is used in conjunction with, change. It

provides input to performing the change. Normally, nothing changes except our understanding of what may be involved with the change.[2]

2.2. No Consensus Definition

IA has been practiced in various forms for years, yet there is no consensus definition. For example, IA does not appear in the IEEE Glossary of Software Engineering Terminology [IEEE1983]. [RADC1986] defined IA as "an examination of an impact to determine its parts or elements." (They defined an impact as the "effect or result of making a change to a system or its software.") [Pfleeger91] defined IA as "the evaluation of the many risks associated with the change, including estimates of the effects on resources, effort, and the schedule." (p. 433)

2.3. Related Terms

There are other IA-related terms. An **impact** (noun) is a part determined to be affected, and therefore worthy of inspection. **Traceability** is the ability to determine what parts are related to what other parts according to specific relationships. A **side effect** is an "error or other undesirable behavior that occurs as a result of a modification " [Freedman1981]. **Stability** is "...the resistance to the potential ripple effect which a program would have when it is modified" ([Yau1980], p. 28). **Ripple effect** is the "effect caused by making a small change to a system which affects many other parts of a system." [Stevens1974]

2.4. Problems with Impact Analysis Divergence

The lack of a common view of IA, and the proliferation of related terms, has led to several problems:

- It is hard to decide what is meant by IA. People rarely give explicit definitions.
- There is a lack of dimensions for comparing one IA approach with another.
- It is hard to know if enough information is available for significant comparison.
- It is hard to discern when different work on IA is related.
- It is hard to discern what work contributes to IA and what does not, according to a basic framework for assessing the technology.

This paper presents a conceptual framework for resolving these problems.

---

[2]Some IA approaches, for specialized applications, have the option of actually performing a change once impacts are found. We consider this an added feature and not part of the basic impact analysis definition.

3. The Impact Analysis Framework

In this section we present the framework intuitively. First we summarize the major parts of the framework. Next we discuss each part in more detail. Then we summarize the collected features of the framework as a way to compare IA approaches.

3.1. Overview

Figure 3-1 outlines how to use the framework. The framework can be used to guide understanding of an IA approach, to compare or evaluate IA approaches, or to structure analyses of IA approaches. The framework provides several points for assessing an IA approach. This

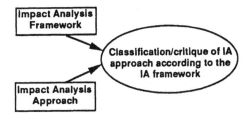

Figure 3-1. How to Use the Impact Analysis Framework

will result in a critique or assessment of the IA approach according to the framework.

Figure 3-2 summarizes the three parts of the IA framework: IA Application, IA Parts, and IA Effectiveness. IA Application examines how the IA approach is used to accomplish IA. It looks at the features offered by the IA approach interface. IA Parts examines the nature of the internal parts and methods used to actually perform the IA. IA Effectiveness examines properties of the resulting search for impacts, especially how well they accomplish the goals of IA.[3]

The following sections, describing each part of the framework, are structured as follows: First, the purpose of the framework part is given. Then a diagram is given to frame its context. The parts of the diagram are discussed. Finally, a table is given that summarizes the framework elements resulting from this part.

---

[3]It is common, in evaluations of tools and technology, to create evaluation criteria for technology-specific and technology-generic factors. The latter include reliability of the vendor, user-friendliness of the tool interface, level of customer service, etc. In discussing this framework, we just focus on the impact analysis-specific items. Non-functional criteria are not discussed in this paper, but often do form a part of a technology evaluation.

Figure 3-2. Parts of the Impact Analysis Framework

3.2. IA Application

IA Application examines how the approach is actually used to perform IA. To accomplish IA, we must have a proposed change, something to be changed, and a way to estimate what must be done to do the change.

Figure 3-3 pictures a generic IA process. A change is conceived in the real world, then reduced to a change specification.[4] The change specification uses objects and relationships familiar to the change specifier. These objects and relationships are drawn from the artifact object model. The change specification and knowledge of the item to be changed are used to specify what is initially impacted to the IA approach.

The IA approach then determines what else may be affected. These results are then translated, if necessary, back into real world terms. The results are then used to plan, to scope, or to accomplish the change.

The IA approach may also provide other features, such as

- explanations of why items are estimated to be impacted,
- measures of the IA itself,
- animation illustrating how the impacts ripple,
- access to change histories,
- suggested change strategies,
- actually performing the change,
- ways to test the change, and
- graphical views of impacts.

An example of IA is when a programmer is given an engineering change report and asked "what is involved" to do the change. The programmer should provide a difficulty assessment (how hard it will be for the programmer to do the change), a level of effort estimate (how long the

change should take) and perhaps a risk assessment (how complicated the change will be to perform). IA—here browsing program code and forming a strategy for a accomplishing the change—helps the programmer to answer all three points.

The key elements of IA application are given in Table 3-1.

3.3. IA Parts

This part of the framework concerns the functional parts of the IA approach—what the approach does, and how it does it, and the duties of the agents or tools involved.

Figure 3-4 illustrates the elements of IA Parts. To express a specific change, the IA approach has its own model of objects and relationships at its interface. The input, expressed in terms of the interface object model, is translated into the IA approach's internal object model.

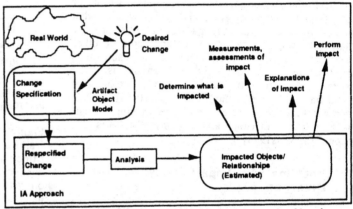

Figure 3-3. IA Application: Performing from the User's Viewpoint

The internal object model defines the objects and relationships (or dependencies) the approach uses to accomplish IA.

The internal object model is normally stored in a repository of some kind. The repository has its own features for loading, browsing, and modifying objects and relationships. The repository is loaded by decomposing the artifact into objects and relationships conforming to the internal object model.

The impact model defines the rules or embedded assumptions reflecting the semantics about what affects what. It defines the classes of objects and relationships used by the IA approach, and ways (rules, algorithms) for determining when a change to one object will affect another object. These may be embedded in the internal

---

[4] Often many intermediate steps are done before a change specification is reached. We focus here just on the key conceptual elements of the technical impact analysis process.

36

object model or the impact calculation algorithms. Sometimes they may appear as a separate rules base.

The tracing/impact approach implements the impact model. The tracing/impact approach defines how objects and dependencies are represented, how impact rules are captured (e.g., programmed), and the specific search algorithms used to find impacted objects and relationships.

Once the results of IA are obtained at the internal object model level, these must be translated back into the interface object model, then further interpreted to determine what parts of the original artifacts are impacted. For some artifacts (e.g., programs), often the directly impacted artifact objects are supplied by the impact analysis approach. For other artifact sets (e.g., requirements), significant manual work is needed to accomplish determine what is impacted.

Each of these parts has many variations that, for brevity, we do not discuss here. Table 3-2 summarizes the elements of "IA Parts."

An example illustrating IA Parts is incremental program recompilation.
The programmer makes a change to software and the compiler must determine the minimal parts that must be recompiled, and in what order. The change here is specified implicitly: the compiler detects which parts of the code have been modified. The change is then translated into the compiler's compilation graph, which captures compilation dependencies between compilable code units. The compilation graph was produced through earlier compilations of the code. The compiler than applies its impact algorithm to determine what program units must be recompiled and in what order. (Often this is not visible to the programmer, or is just taken for granted.) Though not part of IA, the compiler then often goes ahead and recompiles the affected program units. What the programmer sees is a program that has been recompiled.

3.4. IA Effectiveness

This part of the framework concerns how well the IA approach accomplishes IA. Once IA is done, how

Table 3-1. Framework Elements for IA Application

Element	Explanation	Rating Scale
Artifact Object Model (Domain)	What are the types of objects and relationships captured from the application domain?	Program objects and/or relationships; Predefined domain objects and/or relationships; User specifiable domain objects and/or relationships; None; Unknown
Decomposition	Can the item to be analyzed be automatically decomposed and stored within the IA approach/tool?	Yes, syntax with complete semantics; Yes, syntax with some semantics; Yes, syntax only; No; Unknown
Change specification	How is the change specified for the IA approach?	Yes, with detailed analysis; Yes, with some analysis; No, not applied; Unknown
Results specification	How are the results of IA expressed?	Report; Browsing; Database view; None; Unknown
Interpretation	How much effort by the user is needed to interpret the results (i.e., derive true impacts from IA)?	Significant; Some; None; Unknown
Other features	What other features are available to the user?	<The specific feature>. E.g.: explanations, metrics, impact animation, options to perform the change, access to change histories, suggested change strategies, ways to test the change; None; Unknown

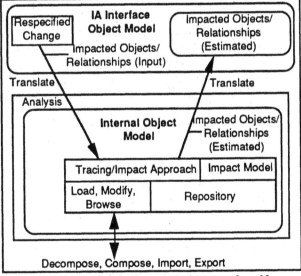

Figure 3-4. IA Parts: Functional parts of an IA approach.

accurate is it?

3.4.1. Definitions

To discuss effectiveness, we introduce the concepts pictured in Figure 3-5.

At the artifact object model level, IA is assumed to take place on a bounding set of objects, which we shall call the *System*. These objects are drawn from an encompassing model called the *Universe*.

At the interface object model level, the analogs of the System and the Universe are the *System#* and *Universe#*. (We append a "#" to sets that are at the interface object model level.) The *starting impact set* (SIS#) is the set of objects that are thought to be initially affected by a change. The *estimated impact set* (EIS#) is the set of objects estimated to be affected by the IA approach. The SIS# and EIS# are assumed to share the same object model, namely the interface object model. The *impact paths* are the search paths tying objects in the SIS# to objects in the EIS#.

The *actual impact set* (AIS) is the set of objects (in the artifact object model) actually modified as the result of performing the change. The AIS# is the image of the AIS in terms of objects and relationships in the interface object model.

The AIS is normally not unique, since a change can be implemented in several ways. (Nevertheless, in our discussion we will mention "the" AIS, meaning an AIS resulting from a particular impact analysis.) In our examples, we will also assume that the AIS reflects a correct implementation of a change.

It is also possible to characterize the SIS, EIS, and AIS in terms of the internal object model. For simplicity in discussing the framework, we shall discuss them at the level of the interface object model and above.

3.4.2. Effectiveness Concepts and Measures

We consider four areas that should be examined to determine the effectiveness of an IA approach.

3.4.2.1. SIS# and EIS#

This area looks at the relationship of the SIS# with EIS#. By definition, the EIS# always contains the SIS#. Yet the relative size of the EIS# influences the work to be

done later in checking the objects that the IA approach estimates to be affected.

Table 3-3 discusses the possibilities. For each case, a picture of the relationship, with defining conditions, is given. Then a metric with a measurement is given to detect when the case occurs. A point description (i.e., in looking at a single measurement) of the implications of the case is described. Finally, the "Desired Trends" indicates the desired, expected, and goal measurement tends that would be wanted over several applications of the IA

Table 3-2. Framework Elements for IA Parts		
Element	Explanation	Rating Scale
Interface Object Model	What objects and relationships can be expressed at the approach's interface?	Strings; Program objects; Predefined document objects; User specifiable document objects; Unknown
Internal Object Model	What objects and relationships does the approach use to accomplish IA?	Document oriented; Object based; Graph structure; None; Unknown
Impact Model	How are dependencies modeled? Where does the approach take these dependencies into account? How closely does the impact model mirror dependencies of the artifact's model of dependencies?	Data flow; Control flow; String matching; Object dependency; None; Unknown
Tracing/Impact Approach	How does the approach accomplish IA through tracing affected objects and relationships? What algorithms or procedures are used?	Decomposition; Pattern matching; Heuristic search; Stochastic search; Not explicit; None; Unknown
Decomposition	What objects and relationships are captured from the artifact and stored as objects and relationships within the repository?	Compiler; Database entity; Object filter; None; Unknown
Repository	What repository is used to store objects and relationships?	Relational Database Management System (RDBMS); File system; None; Unknown
Load, modify, browse	What features does the repository have for loading objects and relationships into it, modifying them, and browsing them?	Load; Modify; Browse; All three available; None; Unknown

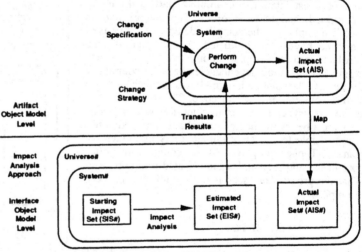

Figure 3-5. Key sets of objects in IA effectiveness.

approach. (The percentages in this column are suggested starting points. They may be tuned as desired.) The percentages in the "Expected" and "Goal" trends sum to 100% across the boxes, rather than within the boxes, because of mutually exclusive cases.

3.4.2.2. EIS# and System#

This area looks at the relationship of the EIS# with the System#. In general, we do not want the IA approach to estimate that everything is affected—that is, the EIS# is the same as the System#—unless that is indeed the case. The "distance" of the EIS# from the System# is a way to gauge the sharpness of the IA. Table 3-4 illustrates some

cases and interpretations.

3.4.2.3. EIS# and AIS#

The relationship between the EIS# and the AIS# is also meaningful. We want the AIS# to be contained regularly in the EIS#, and preferably very close or exactly the same. This would give us more confidence that IA approach results in estimated impacts that can be more carefully relied on to give the true scope of a change.

We do not want the AIS# greater than EIS#, since this means that the EIS# is less a reliable indicator of the true scope of a change. Table 3-5 illustrates some cases and

Case/Picture	Defining Conditions	Measurement When Present	Point Interpretation	Desired Trend
Table 3-3. SIS# and EIS# Possibilities				
1 System# SIS#, EIS#	EIS# = SIS#; EIS#, SIS# ⊆ System#	|SIS#| / |EIS#| = 1	Best. Estimated impact restricted to SIS#.	Desired: SIS# = EIS# always. Expected: SIS# = EIS# are equal in 5% of a random sample of impact analyses Goal: SIS# = EIS# in 20% of a random sample
2 System# SIS# EIS#	|EIS#| > |SIS#|; SIS# ⊂ EIS#; EIS#, SIS# ⊆ System#	K < |SIS#| / |EIS#| < 1, for some user-selected K such that 0 < K < 1	Expected. The estimated impacts are just a little more than the SIS#. "Little" is relative. We suggest K = .7 here.	Desired: 1 > |SIS#| / |EIS#| ≥ .70 never. Expected: 1 > |SIS#| / |EIS#| ≥ .70 in 40% of a random sample of impact analyses. Goal: 1 > |SIS#| / |EIS#| ≥ .70 in 60% of a random sample of impact analyses.
3 System# SIS# EIS#	|EIS#| >> |SIS#|, SIS# ⊂ EIS#; EIS#, SIS# ⊆ System#	|SIS#| / |EIS#| < K, where K is as in the preceding row	Not good. Big jump from SIS# to EIS# means a lot of things to check in the EIS#.	Desired: |SIS#| / |EIS#| < .70 never. Expected: |SIS#| / |EIS#| < .70 in 55% of a random sample of impact analyses. Goal: |SIS#| / |EIS#| < .70 in 10% of a random sample of impact analyses.

Case/Picture	Defining Condition	Measurement When Present	Point Interpretation	Desired Trend
Table 3-4. EIS# and System# Possibilities				
1 System#, EIS#	EIS# = System#	|EIS#| / |System#| = 1	Default, not so helpful for impact analysis. But may indicate a system with extreme ripple effect.	Desired: EIS# = System# should never occur. Expected: EIS# = System# in 30% of a random sample of impact analyses. Goal: EIS# = System# in 5% of a random sample of impact analyses.
2 System# EIS#	|System#| > |EIS#|; EIS# ⊂ System#	J < |EIS#| / |System#| < 1, for some user-selected J such that 0 < J < 1	Better. Change estimated not to affect entire system.	Desired: |EIS#| < |System#| always. Expected: |EIS#| < |System#| in 50% of a random sample of impact analyses Goal: |EIS#| < |System#| in 70% of a random sample of impact analyses.
3 System# EIS#	|System#| >> |EIS#|; EIS# ⊂ System#	|EIS#| / |System#| < J, where J is as in the preceding row	Even better. Change estimate is restricted to a relatively small subset of the system.	Desired: |EIS#| << |System#| always. Expected: |EIS#| << |System#| in 20% of a random sample of impact analyses. Goal: |EIS#| << |System#| in 25% of a random sample of impact analyses.

paragraphs, the *paragraph* containing the sentences is specified as the SIS# to the IA approach. The IA approach then does IA, resulting in an EIS# of five paragraphs (including the paragraph in the SIS#). Except for the SIS# paragraph, all four other paragraphs must be inspected, meaning 24 sentences must be inspected (6 sentences/paragraph in the figure). In contrast, if the granularity was at the level of sentences, then potentially only the two actually affected sentences (see figure) could have been found. Thus a finer granularity search would allow a potential search savings of 480% (= 24 predicted impacted sentences / 5 actually impacted sentences, including, in this example, the two sentences in the original SIS)).

Table 3-6 illustrates some possibilities with granularity. Similar comments and observations can be made between the relative granularities of the interface object model and the internal object model.

3.4.3. Summary Table

Table 3-7 summarizes the resulting framework elements from IA effectiveness.

4. Classify Systems According To Framework

To illustrate the use of, and provide some justification for, the IA framework, Table 4-1 uses the framework elements to compare five IA approaches. The first is a program slicer represented by the Surgeon's Assistant developed to investigate decomposition slicing as a software maintenance technique [Gallagher1991]. Decomposition here is effectively an impact analysis of the change at the code level. The second is a generic manual cross referencing that detect all references to a given software object (data field, disk file, flag, module, etc.) and assists in understanding relationships between software artifacts.

The third is a traceability system represented by the Automated Life Cycle IA System (ALICIA) [RADC1986]. ALICIA represents one of the first and most comprehensive attempts to address IA with automated traceability mechanisms. The

fourth is a Documenting System called Software Document Support (SODOS) environment [Horowitz1986]. It supports the development and maintenance of software documentation. Finally, a commercial tool called the Battlemap Analysis Tool™ (BAT) [McCabe1992] represents a control flow analyzer (among other capabilities). Control flow tools identify calling dependencies, logical decisions (conditions such as IF-THEN-ELSE, LOOPS, CASE statements, etc.), and other control information to examine control flow impacts.

We see two distinct approaches to IA here. The first type (represented by the program slicer, cross referencer, and control flow analyzer) is source code oriented and examines dependencies within the same artifact type. The second type (represented by ALICIA and SODOS) is life-cycle-document oriented and examines dependencies between differing artifact types. Generally speaking, the first type is more mature and provides a finer grained analysis of

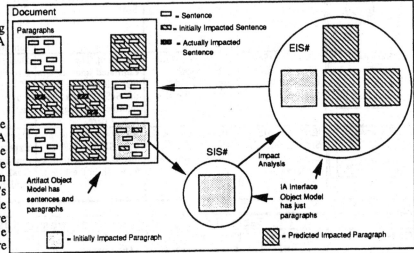

Figure 3-6. How granularity can influence the search for true impacts after impact analysis.

Table 3-6. Granularity Possibilities			
Case	Artifact Object Model	Interface Object Model	Comments
G1			Granularities are about equal. Potentially less work needed to translate impacts into the SIS#. Potentially less work needed to translate results from the EIS#.
G2			Artifact object model has finer granularity than the interface object model. Potentially more work in discovering true impacts (at artifact object model level) from those predicted in the EIS#.
G3			Artifact object model has coarser granularity than the interface object model. Potentially more work is needed to specify fine grained objects in the SIS#.

interpretations.

3.4.2.4. Granularity

In practice, the repeated translations from the artifact objects to interface and internal objects, and back, causes several kinds of problems. For example, there is the problem of predicting what artifact objects are actually affected from the EIS# (interface model objects). The translation from the artifact object model to the interface object model and back is usually manual.

Figure 3-6 illustrates this problem. If the artifact object model includes sentences and paragraphs as objects, but the interface object model includes only paragraphs as objects, then we must express a change to a sentence in the artifact model as an impacted paragraph in the interface object model. The resulting EIS# would then include impacted paragraphs. This means work is needed to look inside the impacted paragraphs to find the exact sentences that may be impacted. It also means many more spurious impacts would have to be looked at because the impact bandwidth of a paragraph is often bigger than that for a sentence.

In this example, the SIS has two sentences. Because the IA interface object model can only express impacts with

Case/Picture	Defining Conditions	Measurement When Present	Point Interpretation	Desired Trend
1 System# (AIS#, EIS#)	EIS# = AIS#; EIS# $\subseteq$ System#	|AIS#| / |EIS#| = 1	Best. Estimated impact set matches AIS#. If this happens regularly, usefulness of IA is substantially increased.	Desired: |AIS#| = |EIS#| always. Expected: |AIS#| = |EIS#| in 10% of a random sample of impact analyses Goal: |AIS#| = |EIS#| in 70% of a random sample of impact analyses
2 System# (AIS# EIS#)	|EIS#| > |AIS#|; AIS# $\subset$ EIS#; EIS# $\subseteq$ System#	H < |AIS#| / |EIS#| < 1, for some user-selected H such that 0 < H < 1	"Safe". The EIS# contains the AIS#, and the EIS# is not much bigger than the AIS#.	Desired: |AIS#| < |EIS#| never. Expected: |AIS#| < |EIS#| in 50% of a random sample of impact analyses Goal: |AIS#| < |EIS#| in 20% of a random sample of impact analyses
3 System# (AIS# EIS#)	|EIS#| >> |AIS#|; AIS# $\subset$ EIS#; EIS# $\subseteq$ System#	|AIS#| / |EIS#| < H, where H is as in the preceding row	Safe, but not so good. Big jump from AIS# to EIS# means a lot of things to check in EIS# before arriving at the AIS#.	Desired: |AIS#| << |EIS#| never. Expected: |AIS#| << |EIS#| in 40% of a random sample of impact analyses Goal: |AIS#| << |EIS#| in 10% of a random sample of impact analyses
4 System# (EIS# AIS#)	|AIS#| > |EIS#|; EIS# $\subset$ AIS#; EIS# $\subseteq$ System#	M < |EIS#| / |AIS#| < 1, for some user-selected M such that 0 < M < 1	Expected. IA approximates, and falls short of, what needs to be changed.	Desired: |EIS#| < |AIS#| never. Expected: |EIS#| < |AIS#| in 60% of a random sample of impact analyses Goal: |EIS#| < |AIS#|, in 20% of a random sample of impact analyses
5 System# (EIS# AIS#)	|AIS#| >> |EIS#|; EIS# $\subset$ AIS#; EIS#, SIS# $\subseteq$ System#	|EIS#| / |AIS#| < M, where M is as in the preceding row	Not so good. Big jump from EIS# to AIS# means extra work to discover AIS#.	Desired: |EIS#| << |AIS#| never. Expected: |EIS#| << |AIS#| in 30% of a random sample of impact analyses Goal: |EIS#| << |AIS#| in 10% of a random sample of impact analyses
6 System# (EIS# AIS#)	|AIS# $\cap$ EIS#| > 0, AIS# $\neq$ EIS#; EIS# $\subseteq$ System#	|EIS# $\cap$ AIS#| > 0	Not so good. Extra work to check EIS# objects that aren't in AIS#. Extra work to discover objects in AIS# not in EIS#	Desired: |EIS# $\cap$ AIS#| near 1 most of a random sample of impact analyses. Expected: .7 < |EIS# $\cap$ AIS#| < 1, in 60% of a random sample of impact analyses Goal: .9 < |EIS# $\cap$ AIS#| < 1, in 80% of a random sample of impact analyses
7 System# (EIS# AIS#)	|AIS# $\cap$ EIS#| = 0; EIS# $\subseteq$ System#	|EIS# $\cap$ AIS#| = 0	Not so good. A worse version of case 6.	Desired: |EIS# $\cap$ AIS#| = 0 never Expected: |EIS# $\cap$ AIS#| = 0 in 20% of a random sample of impact analyses Goal: |EIS# $\cap$ AIS#| = 0 in 5% of a random sample of impact analyses

Table 3-5. AIS# and EIS# Possibilities

impacts while the second type is less mature, but provides a broader analysis.

5. Relation to Other Work

This paper presents a variety of concepts relating IA technology. We are aware of other work for characterizing change, but have found no applicable evaluation criteria for IA technology.

In one characterization of change, Madhavji describes a broad perspective on change with respect to people, policies, laws, resources, processes, and results [Madhavji1991]. Madhavji distinguishes changes to described items from changes to the environment that houses these items. The Prism Dependency Structure facility supports describing items and their inter-dependencies as well as identifying possible effects of changes. The Prism Change Structure facility supports classifying, recording, and analyzing change-related data from a qualitative perspective.

Our work differs from Madhavji's in that his work focuses on the change process while ours focuses on IA

technology and a characterization of IA applications, parts, and effectiveness criteria.

6. Conclusions

IA has many meanings in industry today and the trend is to use the term for more and more situations. In this paper, we have attempted to bring some order and structure to the discussion of IA technology. We recognize the need for a framework to compare IA approaches. This paper presented a definition of IA and a framework that delineates clearly the basis for comparing IA capabilities. The framework

Table 3-7. Evaluation Parameters for Logical Performance Effectiveness

Element	Explanation	Desired IA Effectiveness Trends
SIS and EIS	What trend is observed in the relative size of the SIS and EIS when the approach is applied to typical problems? We would like the EIS to be as close as possible to the SIS.	$|SIS| / |EIS| = 1$, (i.e., SIS = EIS), or nearly 1
EIS and System#	What trend is observed in the relative size of the EIS and System# when the approach is applied to typical problems? We would like the EIS to be much smaller than the System#.	$|EIS| / |System\#| \leq N$, where N is some small tolerance level
EIS and AIS#	What trend is observed in the relative size of the EIS and AIS# when the approach is applied to typical problems? We would like the EIS to contain the AIS#, and the AIS# to equal to or smaller than the EIS.	$|EIS| / |AIS\#| = 1$, (i.e., EIS = AIS#), or nearly 1
Granularity	What is the relative granularity of the artifact object model vs. the interface object model? We would like the granularities to match, if possible.	G1, granularities match. (It is even better if granularities are fine enough too.)

Table 4-1. Comparison of Impact Analysis Systems with IA Framework
Table 4-1a. Framework Category: IA Application

IA Approach	Artifact Object Model	Decomposition	Change specification	Results specification	Interpretation of EIS# to Determine AIS	Other Features
Program Slicer – Surgeon's Assistant [Gallagher1991]	Programs & entities within them	Yes, with some semantics. Knows about programming language objects, control, & data flow relationships.	Yes, with some analysis. User must specify slice criteria & initially affected program, variables, etc	Browsing. Can browse the sliced pieces of the program.	Some effort. Slice approach may compute the slice for the programmer.	Testing, Browsing
Manual Cross Referencing, based on name id & cross reference listings.	Programs, predefined documents	No. Just passively identifies text strings according to match criteria.	No, not applied. User manually reviews cross reference listings	Report. Cross reference listing is the report	Significant. Much effort needed to locate secondary dependencies.	None.
Traceability System – Automated Life Cycle Impact Analysis System (ALICIA) [RADC1986]	DOD-STD-2167 documents & entities within them	Yes, with little semantics. software life cycle objects (SLOs) stored in a RDBMS with a schema that reflects the DOD-STD-2167 relationships.	Yes, with detailed analysis. Uses method. Requirements for a change are analyzed for tracing SLOs.	Report & Database View. ALICIA provides impact report & navigation through a view.	Significant. SLOs are not elaborated nor explained.	Methodology, Document-oriented database schema
Documenting System – Software Document Support (SODOS) environment [Horowitz1986]	Predefined document set & ASCII text.	Yes, with some semantics. Stores decomposed SLOs in a RDBMS based on an object model & predefined relationships.	Yes, with detailed analysis. Req'ts for change are incorporated in B-spec, then analyzed for tracing to SLOs.	Report, Browsing & Database View. Results of IA in hypermedia graph & view for browsing & report.	Significant. SODOS for document management. SLOs not elaborated nor explained thus the user must interpret results	Query – supports traceability with both predefined & user defined relationship Browsing – navigation/edit support.
Control Flow Analyzer – Battlemap Analysis Tool (BAT) [McCabe1992]	Source code programs	Yes, with little semantics. These are limited to decision logic & calling structures.	No, not applied. Control flow analyzers do not support change specification.	Report, Browsing, & Database View. Results stored as a graph & output in a report or editor.	Significant. Control flow impacts not explained by the tool. Interpretation is left to the user.	Call graphs Complexity Metrics Browsing/ editing Execution path slicer

Table 4-1b. Framework Category: IA Parts

IA Approach	Interface Object Model	Internal Object Model	Decomposition	Impact Model	Tracing/ Impact Approach	Repository	Load, Modify, Browse
Program Slicer – Surgeon's Assistant	Program objects such as variables, statements, etc	Data define-use graph & control flow graph	Similar to compiler	Slicing based on data & control flow dependencies	Decomposition slice, program slicing	File system	All three are available
Manual Cross Referencing	Character Strings, i.e., representing variables	None. Just matches characters	None	Matching between character strings	Pattern matching	File system	Not available
Traceability System – ALICIA	DOD-STD-2167 doc's (req'ts, design, code, test, etc.) & input templates	Meta-schema based on DOD-STD-2167 objects	Documents decomposed into relational database	Has user-defined & predefined relationships that have dependency info.	Based on traceability relationships. Heuristic & stochastic impact search algorithms	RDBMS	All three available
Documenting System – SODOS	Documents based on predefined object-based software life cycle	Manages SLOs using object-based model & hypermedia graph. Meta-schema based on predefined document & management objects.	Decomposes documents into object model using templates & filters	Object configuration management & navigation. User-defined & predefined relationships that have dependency information	Based on user-defined & predefined traceability relationships. This enables consistency checking of traceability relationships	RDBMS – Smalltalk-80 object-oriented front-end to RDBMS	All three available
Control Flow Analyzer – BAT	Program objects such as variables, statements, etc.	Control flow graph, calling hierarchies, module structure	Decomposes the code into its control flow elements	Based on control flow dependencies	Not explicit – identifies changes associated with control flow	File system	All three available

Table 4-1c. Framework Category: IA Effectiveness

IA Approach	SIS and EIS	EIS and System#	EIS and AIS#	Granularity
Program Slicer – Surgeon's Assistant	Could not determine from available sources.	Could not determine from available sources.	Could not determine from available sources.	Interface object model is finer-grained. Impacts between programs must be expressed in terms of subprogram entities.
Manual Cross Referencing	Could not determine from available sources.	Could not determine from available sources.	Could not determine from available sources.	Interface object model is finer grained. Impacts between documents must be re-expressed as items that are cross-referenced.
Traceability System – ALICIA	Could not determine from available sources.	Could not determine from available sources.	Could not determine from available sources.	Interface object model is more coarse grained. Impacts between documents must be re-expressed in impact model.
Documenting System – SODOS	Could not determine from available sources.	Could not determine from available sources.	Could not determine from available sources.	Interface object model is more coarse grained. Impacts between documents must be re-expressed in impact model.
Control Flow Analyzer – BAT	Could not determine from available sources.	Could not determine from available sources.	Could not determine from available sources.	Interface object model is finer grained. Impacts between programs must be expressed in terms of subprogram entities.

consists of three parts: IA Application, IA Parts, and IA Effectiveness. To demonstrate the use of this framework, we classified five existing IA technologies according to its criteria.

We believe this work will be helpful to those desiring to investigate the functionality of existing IA approaches. For those hoping to compare approaches, the framework should provide plenty of useful differentiators.

Bibliography

[Freedman1981] Freedman, D. P. and G. M. Weinberg, "A Checklist for Potential Side Effects of a Maintenance Change," In G. Parikh, Techniques of Program and System Maintenance, 1981, page(s) 93 - 100.

[Gallagher1991] Gallagher, K.B. and J.R. Lyle, "Using Program Slicing in Software Maintenance," IEEE Transactions on Software Engineering, Volume 17, Number 8, August 1991, page(s) 751 - 761.

[Horowitz1986] Horowitz, E. and R. Williamson, "SODOS: A Software Document Support Environment - Its Definition," IEEE Transactions on Software Engineering, Volume SE-12, Number 8, August 1986, page(s) 849 - 859.

[IEEE1983] IEEE, "Glossary of Software Engineering Terminology," Std. 729-1983, In IEEE, Software Engineering Standards, Third Edition, New York: IEEE, 1989., 1983.

[Madhavji1991] Madhavji, Nazim H., "The Prism Model of Changes," Proceedings of the International Conference on Software Engineering, IEEE Computer Society Press, 1991, page(s) 166 - 177.

[McCabe1992] McCabe & Associates, Inc., "Battlemap Analysis Tool Reference Manual," McCabe & Associates, Inc., Twin Knolls Professional Park, 5501 Twin Knolls Road, Columbia, MD, December 1992.

[Pfleeger1991] Pfleeger, Shari L., Software Engineering: The Production of Quality Software, New York, Macmillan Publishing Co., 1991.

[RADC1986] Rome Air Development Center, "Automated Life Cycle Impact Analysis System," RADC-TR-86-197, Rome Air Development Center, Air Force Systems Command, Griffiss Air Force Base, Rome, NY, December 1986.

[Stevens1974] Stevens, W., G. Meyers, and L. Constantine, "Structured Design," IBM Systems Journal, Volume 13, Number 2, 1974.

[Yau1978] Yau, S.S., J.S. Collofello, and T.M. MacGregor, "Ripple Effect Analysis of Software Maintenance," Proc. of COMPSAC, Washington, DC: IEEE Computer Society Press, 1978, page(s) 60 - 65.

[Yau1980] Yau, S.S. and J. Collofello, "Some Stability Measures for Software Maintenance," IEEE Transactions on Software Engineering, Volume SE-6, Number 6, November 1980, page(s) 545 - 552.

The Year 2000 Problem: Impact, Strategies, and Tools

Assessing and acting on your "Year 2000 Problems" in 1996 could save your organization costly embarrassments later on

Dr. Robert S. Arnold

February 12, 1996

Software Evolution Technology, Inc.
12613 Rock Ridge Rd.
Herndon, Virginia 22070
USA
703-450-6791
rarnold@sevtec.com

January 1, 2000 is less than four years away. When that happens, will your business stop working? It could if your systems handle dates with two-digit year fields. And if you don't have such systems, it could still happen to you. Especially if the systems or software packages, that you depend on, have the problem. Acting now could help you stay in business when year 2000 is upon you.[1]

THE PROBLEM

The Year 2000 Problem is the problem of assuming an insufficient number of digits in a year field in programs or data. For example, the year

---

[1] This paper is revised and updated from these papers by the same author: "Millennium Now: Solutions for Century Date Change Impact," *Application Development Trends*, Volume 2, Number 1, January 1995, pp. 60-62, 64-66; "Year 2000 Tools," *Year 2000 News*, Issue 1.1, August 4, 1995. Both papers are copyright © 1995 Software Evolution Technology, Inc. All rights reserved.

1995 is represented as "95." The year "1989" is represented "89." An so on.

Such a simple assumption. Why all the ruckus?

Say it's January 12, 2000 and your company sends out an invoice that day. Your accounts receivable legacy software represents years with two digits. So January 12, 2000 is represented as 01/12/00 (MMDDYY in your data). But your legacy code thinks this means January 12, *1900*. Yes, it should be year 2000, but your old, two-digit, code does not take this into account.

Now suppose your customer does not pay the bill by March 12, 2000. Your accounts aging software scans the data base to see what accounts receivable are due. It sees the January 12, (19)00 invoice. Since the invoice is over a 100 years old (!), the software could call this a really bad debt and cancel it!

The Year 2000 problem could be a problem well *before* the year 2000 arrives. Suppose it is July 1, 1999 and you decide to grant Sally a pay raise on January 1, 2000. The effective salary raise date, 1/1/00, is input to the code. The software may grant the pay raise *immediately* because 2/1/00 precedes the current date, 7/1/99, making the raise immediately effective! She might even receive back pay dating from 1900!

Similar problems can happen in other applications having dates of effect, such as bank interest rates, insurance policy premium rates, pension plan annuity checks, and shipping rates.

The Year 2000 Problem can affect any program that represents or assumes years are represented with only two digits, any data bases with two-digit year fields, and any query or screen that has two-digit year fields. It can also affect programs, systems, data bases, data base queries, etc. that depend on these programs and data.

In practice, COBOL and assembly code legacy systems are susceptible, though code in almost any language can have this problem. For example, a programmer could have built this assumption into C or C++ code.

Common sources for possible Year 2000 Problems are COBOL Procedure and Data divisions, CICS screens featuring date-oriented or time duration fields, copybooks, database queries, ISPF screens, and JCL procedures.

Are these risks worth it? Tom Oldenburger, Supervisor of Application Support with a health maintenance organization in California, feels that if the Year 2000 is not solved, all of his systems would be affected and business could stop. For him, the risks are not worth chancing.

WHY NOW?

"But January 1, 2000 is four years away. Why worry about this now?"

There are several reasons maintenance managers give for not acting now. Some reasons and responses are:

• "It will go away." The system will not be around on 01/01/2000. Why fix a problem that will not occur?

Systems tend to stay around longer than we expect. Some systems are rewrites of previous systems, perpetuating their errors. Someone may salvage this code in the future, not realizing it could have a Year 2000 bug in it. In the meantime, these systems may be outputting data with 2-digit years. When this is fixed there will be a cost for every 2-digit year you produce. Why perpetuate a reengineering problem?

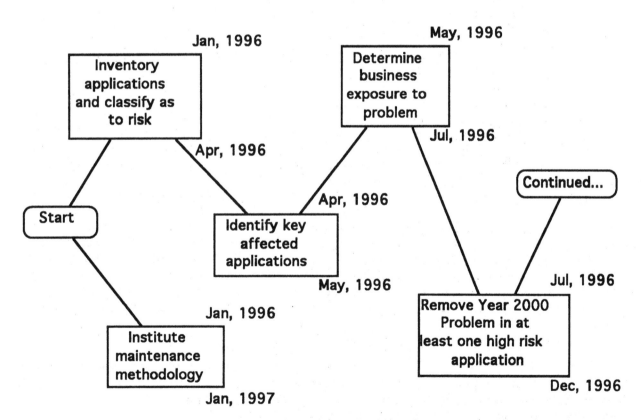

Figure 1. (1 of 2) High Level Steps In Year 2000 Problem Resolution. This is a conservative approach to assessing potential Year 2000 Problems in an application, and acting on them if necessary. Table 1 explains the steps. Time durations for the steps are illustrative only, and will need to be adjusted for each Year 2000 Problem resolution project.

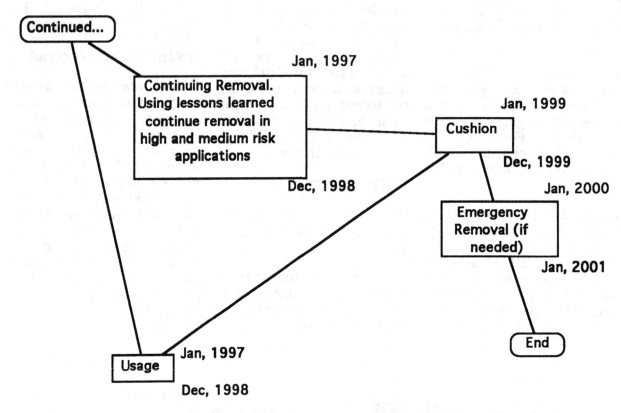

Figure 1. (2 of 2) High Level Steps In Year 2000 Problem Resolution.

• "Not on my watch." I probably won't be at this job on 1/1/2000. Why put my short term budget in jeopardy to solve this longer term problem?

The impact on your budget should be based on concrete analysis. It may not be as bad a problem as you expect. But you should determine your organizations exposure. A longer term view in this case could prevent panic fixing later on.

• "Too busy." We have our hands full with maintenance, why add to my backlog by putting the Year 2000 Problem on my plate?

Yes, it is a matter of priorities. But it is marvelous how a potential disaster can change this. You may be betting the farm without knowing it.

• "I really don't want to know." The problem could become a can of worms once we do some checking. If it is, management may question why I didn't look at this earlier.

Professional managers do not hide from reality, they deal with it. Superiors appreciate people that recognize a potentially serious problem and start to act on it. Unless they knew better, but didn't.

• "Just expand the year field. What's the big deal?" This is not as serious problem to solve as you're making it out to be.

A fair amount of reengineering may be involved to fix the problem. You may need to change data schemas, raw data, input screens, procedural logic, and so on. You will not know how much work is really involved until you actually roll up your sleeves and check for yourself.

But why act *now*, rather than six months or a year from now?

For some organizations, acting now is not mandatory. But it could save reengineering work later, particularly with data. For other organizations, delay could be deadly. The longer you delay, the harder (i.e., more costly) it can be to reengineer your code later. Just look at the new Denver airport baggage sorting system.

STRATEGIC PLANNING

Because the risks to your organization can be severe, and because Year 2000 Problems can occur long before 1/1/2000, you should at least determine your organization's exposure at this time.

To get concrete answers, you will need to understand the extent of the actual problem in your environment, what your solution options are (with cost-

Date	Activity	Explanation
1-4/1996	Inventory applications and classify as to risk	In your software portfolio, determine what applications are possibly affected by the Year 2000 Problem. Determine business or operations impact should these applications have serious Year 2000 Problems. Identify applications as high risk, medium risk, low risk.
4-5/1996	Identify key affected applications	Target high risk systems for Year 2000 Problem removal. Create plans for transitioning legacy code and data to use 4-digit years.
1/1996 - 1/1997	Institute maintenance methodology	If you have not already done so, institute procedures to avoid further propagating Year 2000 Problems. (This is a good idea even if you do not have Year 2000 Problems.)
5-7/1996	Determine business exposure	Determine your business exposure to the Year 2000 Problem. This means you have valid estimates of the real problem at your site. You then estimate what would happen to your business should serious problems actually occur. Will a problem bring your business to a halt? Require extra reengineering later on? Just be an occasional nuisance?
7-12/1996	Remove Year 2000 Problem in at least one high risk application.	Do this to get first hand data about how difficult the problem will be for you. This will help you gauge the difficulty in solving the problem for other systems. Delaying this could leave you with little time, before 2000, for removing the problem in all high risk applications.
1/1997 - 12/1998	Continuing removal	Eliminate Year 2000 in other high risk or medium risk applications. This may extend into 1999.
1/1997 - 12/1998	Usage	Some corrected applications should now be in production, especially those already encountering 21st century dates. Fix any Year 2000 Problems not caught by previous fixes. Feed this experience back into other Year 2000 removal efforts. Eliminate problem in low risk applications, as resources allow.
1/1999 - 12/1999	Cushion	This year is for slack in case you need more time to remove Year 2000 Problems in your applications.
1/2000 - 1/2001	Emergency removal (if necessary)	You should allow some time here in case you choose to delay and then do discover critical Year 2000 Problems in your software. Depending on Year 2000 outsourcing specialists to help you at this time could be problematic if outsourcers have their hands full with other customers needing help with Year 2000 Problems.

Table 1. Time Line for Resolving Year 2000 Problems in Your Applications. This table explains the steps in Figure 1.

benefit projections), and what your organizational exposure is in case you choose to do nothing now.

Figure 1 shows how checking your exposure now can be part of a more comprehensive schedule for resolving Year 2000 Problem difficulties.

This is a conservative plan. (Riskier plans will delay the steps.) It features determining true risk early on, removing Year 2000 Problems from one high risk application early on, and providing plenty of slack in 1997-1999 in case solving the problems are stickier than expected. Table 1 explains the steps in Figure 1 in more detail.

Tom Miele, Manager of Development Technologies at a data processing center supporting several health insurance providers in Pennsylvania, received a directive from top management to determine the extent of the Year 2000 Problem. This made eliminating the problem a matter of business importance, not just of software maintenance. He has completed a preliminary Year 2000 Problem impact study, with Viasoft's help. His goal is to be Year 2000 Problem "clean" in all affected applications by 1998. 1999 will be used to fix any remaining problems.

FINDING AND REMOVING YEAR 2000 PROBLEMS

Figure 2 presents a baseline process for finding and removing Year 2000 Problems from code and data. It just presents basic steps; many refinements are possible.

The process is to first place your system under control so that uncontrolled change does not introduce new problems while you are fixing Year 2000 Problems. Next comes an initial estimate of the cost of Year 2000 Problem removal. This will help temper your expectations as the work proceeds. Finding problem code looks at your code and data to discover date-oriented problems.

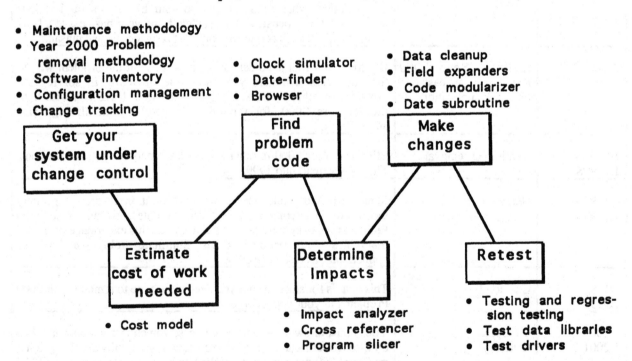

Figure 2. Process and Technology for Eliminating Year 2000 Problems.
Year 2000 Problems can be systematically reduced. This figure shows the process steps and supporting technology. Table 2 discusses the technology and gives examples of commercial technology.

Table 2. A Year 2000 Problem Removal Tool Kit

Classes of tools useful for solving Year 2000 Problems are listed here, along with sample commercially available technology. Technology specifically positioned for solving the Year 2000 Problem is emphasized. Most technology listed here works on COBOL legacy code and data. The technology is grouped by the Year 2000 Problem removal step, as shown in Figure 2, to which the technology applies. Some technology can be used with more than one step, even though it is not so listed. Because of this, the table should not be used for product comparison purposes. (Much more technology is available than shown here.)

1. GET YOUR SYSTEM UNDER CHANGE CONTROL

1.1 Maintenance Methodology

Having a sound approach to software maintenance will put order and discipline into software change. This will help in many areas, including instituting standards to lessen the insertion of Year 2000 Problems into your code. See [Hayes1994] for a recent discussion and list of available maintenance methodologies. Another maintenance methodology is the IEEE standard on software maintenance [IEEE1993].

1.2 Year 2000 Problem Removal Methodology

Several methodologies for approaching removal of Year 2000 Problems have recently appeared. These can save you time because they have already thought through how to systematically resolve Year 2000 Problems. *Year 2000 News*[2] also features articles on Year 2000 Problem methodology.

SEVTEC Reengineering Process Library	Software Evolution Technology (SEVTEC)
Viasoft's ENTERPRISE 2000	Viasoft
System Vision Year 2000	Adpac

1.3 Software Inventory

Inventorying your software will help you determine all the code, JCL, data bases, etc. that constitute your system. This is important for providing a complete system on which to for impact analysis. These tools can help you do this.

Century Source Conversion	Quintic Systems, Inc.
GILES	Global Software
VIA / Alliance	VIASOFT
Xpediter / Xchange	Compuware Corporation
System Vision Year 2000	Adpac

1.4 Configuration Management

Configuration management can turn your software into configurations. This is important as you modify and eliminate bugs in the code. You can then systematically record what software you have fixed and what needs fixing. Here are some sample configuration management tools.

Aide-de-Camp	Software Maintenance & Development Systems, Inc.
CCC	Softool Corporation
ChangeVision for SoftBench	Hewlett-Packard
Change Man	Optima Software, Inc.
ENDEVOR	LEGENT Corporation

---

[2]*Year 2000 News* is an Internet newsletter on the Year 2000 Problem. To subscribe, contact Robert Arnold at rarnold@sevtec.com or 703-450-6791.

PVCS   Intersolv, Inc.

1.5 Change Tracking

Change tracking will log requests for changes and track them to resolution. The change tracking database can be a useful place to look for changes regarding dates or bugs concerning dates. You can use an off-the-shelf tool, or create a change-tracking database application easily enough.

AWARE!	Integritech Systems, Inc.
CaseWare/PT	CaseWare
CCC/Pro	Softool Corporation
InfoTrak	Trident Software
IPM/MVS, IPM/PC	The Orcutt Group
Maestro II	Softlab

2. ESTIMATE COST OF WORK NEEDED

Cost Model

This tool, spreadsheet, or methodology predicts how much work will be needed to remove Year 2000 Problems. Check how the model you intend to use has been validated. That is, its predictions compared with actual human performance in removing the Year 2000 Problem. Because carefully measured empirical data on finding and removing Year 2000 Problems is currently hard to find, the cost model may not been separately calibrated with valid data collected from real Year 2000 Problem removal projects.

SEVTEC Reengineering Process Library	Software Evolution Technology, Inc.
IMPACT 2000	Viasoft
System Vision Year 2000	Adpac Corporation

3. FIND PROBLEM CODE

3.1 Clock simulator

These change your system clock, unknown to your programs. They are an easy way to quickly check if your code has Year 2000 Problems.

HourGlass 2000	MainWare, Inc.
TICTOC	Isogon Corporation
VIA / ValidDate	VIASOFT
Portal 2000	Prince Software Products
Xpediter / Xchange	Compuware Corporation

3.2 Date-finder

These tools or lists of names help you locate date-oriented data, variables, or information in the code.

Century Source Conversion	Quintic Systems, Inc.
General Purpose Systems Analyzer (GPSA/PC)	COBOL Maintenance Technologies
SE/ONE (D-Ray)	Software Eclectics, Inc.
System Vision Year 2000	Adpac Corporation

3.3 Browser

Browsing tools allow you to scan through code and inspect. Scanning can be speeded by looking at structure charts, selecting code, and immediately jumping to the code. They can save a lot of time over just using a text editor. Browsers can include some reverse engineering tools or maintenance workbenches.

COBOL / Softbench	Hewlett - Packard
General Purpose Systems Analyzer (GPSA/PC)	COBOL Maintenance Technologies
GILES	Global Software
InterCASE Reverse Engineering Workbench	Intersolv
Legacy Workbench	KnowledgeWare
McCabe Tools	McCabe & Associates
Micro Focus COBOL Workbench	Micro Focus
Refine / COBOL	Reasoning Systems
Revolve	Burl Software Laboratories / Micro Focus
SEEC/CARE Cobol Analyst	SEEC

4. DETERMINE IMPACTS

4.1 Impact Analyzer

These essential tools do the hard work of finding what is related to what. They can save you hours of grunge work. But they are subject to accuracy and "safety" limitations. Just because an impact analysis tool estimates that an item is affected, does not mean that the item will need to be changed to fix a specific Year 2000 Problem. Impact analysis tools will tend to overshoot their estimates of what is affected, to be on the safe side. The extent of the this overshoot, the difference between what actually needed to be changed and what was originally estimated to be changed, is not known.

McCabe Slice Tool	McCabe & Associates
Revolve	Burl Software Laboratories / Micro Focus
SEEC/CARE Cobol Analyst	SEEC
PM/SS, System Vision Year 2000	Adpac Corporation
Via / Alliance, VIA / Insight	Viasoft

4.2 Cross Referencer

These tools tell you where variables, procedures, or other items are in the code. They are helpful in speeding up browsing and providing a limited form of impact analysis.

Revolve	Burl Software Laboratories / Micro Focus
SEEC/CARE Cobol Analyst	SEEC
SE/ONE	Software Eclectics, Inc.
PM/SS, System Vision Year 2000	Adpac Corporation
Via / Insight, Via / Recap	Viasoft

4.3 Program Slicer

Code slicing tools--a powerful type of static impact analyzer--help you see all the code affecting a given variable or statement. Forward slicing starts with a name or statement, and tells you what it affects. Backward slicing also starts with a name or statement, but tells you all parts of the program that could affect it. Despite their power, the tools do not replace the need for regression testing.

INTERSOLV Maintenance Workbench	INTERSOLV
VIA / Renaissance	VIASOFT
REFINE / COBOL	Reasoning Systems

5. MAKE CHANGES

5.1 Data Cleanup

These tools help you improve the consistency and accuracy of your data. Sometimes this is done in the context of extracting and coverting data from a non-relational to a relational DBMS.

Bachman / Re-engineering Product Set	Bachman Information Systems

Extract Tool Suite	Evolutionary Technologies, Inc.
Legacy Data Mover	Legent
Pacreverse	CGI Systems
Warehouse Manager	Prism Solutions Warehouse Manager
Integrity	Vality Software
DATATEC	Compuware Corporation

5.2 Field Expanders

These tools help you automatically expand 2-digit year fields into 4-digit year fields. Some data cleanup tools (mentioned above) can also be used.

Century File Conversion	Quintic Systems, Inc.
Vantage YR2000	Great American Insurance Companies

5.3 Data Name Rationalization

These tools help you introduce standard or more uniform names to date-oriented fields.

DATATEC	Compuware Corporation
$NAME	Global Software
Revolve	Micro Focus
PM/SS	Adpac Corporation

5.4 Code Modularizer

These tools help you to identify chunks of code and may wrap an interface around them, making them into procedures or modules. Fall-throughs into this code are replaced by calls to it. This is helpful because certain changes in the module can be hidden without fear that other parts will be affected.

Via/Renaissance	Viasoft
REFINE / COBOL	Reasoning Systems

5.5 Date Subroutine

These subroutines are reusable code modules that have correctly implemented the handling of dates. If you're worried about the accuracy of your date handling, these tools could help.

COBOL Language Environment/370	IBM
TransCentury Calendar Routines	Transcentury Data Systems

6. RETEST

6.1 Testing and Regression Testing

Testing is essential for checking whether software changes introduced unwanted problems. Since automatic impact analyzers do not check impacts in all possible inter-code relationships (e.g., timing), testing is nearly always a necessary part of software change.

Automator QA	Direct Technology
CICS/Replay	Interactive Solutions, Inc.
CA-DATAMACS	Computer Associates International
QES/Architect	QES, Inc.
Playback	Compuware Corporation
SQA Manager	Software Quality Automation
SQA Robot	Software Quality Automation
STW/REG	Software Research, Inc.
CA-VERIFY	Computer Associates International

6.2 Test Data Libraries

These tools help you organize your test data for use and reuse. They often are part of test and retest tools, or you can create and manage your own.

6.3 Test Drivers

These tools take a lot of the drudgery out of running test cases and comparing actual with expected results. They are often part of test and retest tools.

[End of Table 2. A Year 2000 Problem Removal Tool Kit]

These initially discovered problems "prime the pump" for automatic impact analysis, which is the next step. Once you have an estimate of all affected code and data, you use this to plan and perform a systematic solution in your application. Finally you perform a retest since current impact analysis technology does not guarantee all possible date-oriented problems are revealed.

Table 2, "A Year 2000 Problem Removal Tool Kit," presents technology associated with each step in Figure 2.

IMPACT ANALYSIS METRICS AND THE YEAR 2000 PROBLEM

Articles have been published that estimate the cost to correct the Year 2000 Problem in the industry to be in the millions. For specific decision-making on the front lines of software maintenance, such numbers are not very helpful. Managers need to have specific, reliable estimates tailored for *their* environments. This information is important for deciding whether to act now or later.

One way to estimate how much of your code is affected by the Year 2000 Problem is to use an impact analysis tool. Figure 3 shows the steps, which are expanded in Table 3. The steps are based on the impact analysis capability comparison framework described in [Arnold1993].

To use an impact analysis tool to estimate the items you will need to change to solve a Year 2000 Problem, first you find date-oriented items in your code likely to be affected. This initial set of affected items is then input to the impact analysis tool. (For example tools, see Table 2.) The tool estimates other affected items that you should check. This estimate is used to gauge the size of your Year 2000 Problem.

Currently impact analysis tools have limitations that make their usefulness, *as estimators of the effort needed to solve a Year 2000 Problem*, unclear. You may be tempted to run an impact analysis tool, discover that the tool predicts most of your code is affected by a Year 2000 Problem, and conclude you have a serious problem on your hands. Maybe, but maybe not!

What we do not have yet are clear measurements of "safety" and "scope" of the analysis that impact analysis tools do. (The actual metrics are defined in [Arnold1993].) "Safety" checks whether the tool regularly includes, in its impact predictions, *all* the code that will *actually* be modified when the year 2000 is corrected. That factor will give you more confidence that the tool's impact analysis is reasonably complete for your purposes. "Scope" checks the extent to which the tool's impact predictions are excessive. This influences the amount of extra work you will need to do when checking affected code and data.

Impact analysis tools will tend to be conservative (overshoot) their estimates of what must actually be changed, to be on the safe side. The extent of the this overshoot, the difference between what actually needed to be changed and what was originally estimated to be changed, is not known.

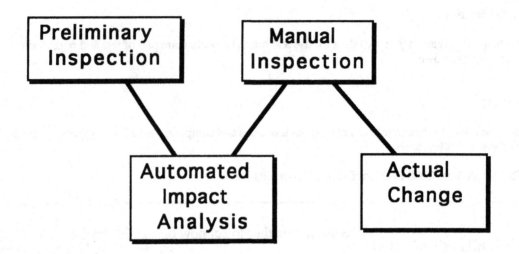

Figure 3. Basic Steps in Code-Level Impact Analysis. Impact analysis proceeds systematically from finding initially affected date-oriented items, to estimating other items that are affected, to planning and performing the change that reduces Year 2000 Problems. Table 3 expands on the steps listed here.

Unfortunately, most impact analysis tools today do not provide these impact analysis measurements. You will have to calculate them yourself. So be careful when using impact analysis tools to estimate the effort to resolve your Year 2000 Problems.

EARLY ASSESSMENT IS KEY

There is much technology and planning expertise available for resolving Year 2000 Problems in your applications. Whether you choose to act now or later can influence how your business will operate in several years. Certainly your business flexibility can be impacted, and embarrassing and costly problems could be coming your way. Assessing the problems at this time is key to covering yourself before disaster strikes.

REFERENCES

[Arnold1993] Arnold, Robert S. and Shawn Bohner, "Impact Analysis - Towards a Framework for Comparison," *Proceedings of the Conference on Software Maintenance*, Los Alamitos, CA: IEEE Computer Society Press, September 1993.

[Hayes1994] Hayes, Ian S., "Project Management: How It Can Improve the Maintenance Process," *Application Development Trends*, October 1994, page(s) 48 - 50, 52, 54 - 57, 60 - 61.

[IEEE1993] IEEE, "IEEE Standard for Software Maintenance," Standard 1219-1993, IEEE, 345 East 47th St., New York, NY 10017, June 2, 1993.

Step	Activity	Example
1. Preliminary Inspection	Done manually, with the help of browsing software or date-name finding software. The goal of this work is to "prime the pump" with entities (variables, statements) that are known to be date-oriented. This set of entities is called the "starting impact set."	Preliminary inspection finds 38 program variables that are date-like. These are contained in 5% of the system's lines of code. This example uses "percentage of non-commentary source lines of code" as the measure of impact.
2. Automated Impact Analysis	The starting impact set is input to the automated impact analysis tool. This may be done all at once, or piecemeal, depending on the tool. The tool then estimates the lines of code, or other entities, that are potentially affected. This collection of entities is called the "estimated impact set."	The tool predicts that 75% of the code is potentially affected by changes to the 38 variables. This 75% is what is most often used to estimate the size of your Year 2000 Problem. The estimate could vary from tool to tool.
3. Manual Inspection	This uses the impact estimate as a guide for checking the code manually. This is needed because impact analysis results do not imply that everything must be changed, just what is potentially affected. It is useful for creating a plan for systematically removing Year 2000 Problems in the code.	
4. Actual Change	The Year 2000 Problem is removed. The collection of entities actually modified is called the "actual impact set."	It is found that changes are needed in code lines comprising 25% of the lines of code. 8% was not in the estimated impact set.

Table 3. Basic Steps in Code-Level Impact Analysis. The steps are based on the impact analysis capability comparison framework described in [Arnold1993].

Chapter 2
State of the Practice

Purpose

The papers in this chapter describe the technology applied to managing software artifacts and their respective changes. For impact analysis, the technologies include tracing requirements to their associated life-cycle objects, supporting design evolution, and managing changes to the software artifacts (through configuration management, for example).

The Papers

As we mentioned in our introduction, software professionals often conduct impact analysis in an informal manner that is largely manual. They rarely use automated tools beyond automated browsers or cross referencers to determine software impacts.

After so many years of software technology progress, why is this still the case? One reason might be that, in the 1970s and 1980s, many software-technology investments concentrated on software development rather than maintenance. This left maintenance departments with sparse tools, methodologies, and labor resources, compared with those of developers. In short, although impact analysis was recognized as an important problem, little was done to help maintainers. Reengineering was at center stage.

Another reason impact analysis has been difficult is that performing industrial-strength impact analysis seems to require substantial computing resources. If attempted manually, it can be time-consuming, expensive, and exhausting.

With enabling technologies such as software repositories, faster central processors, and cheaper memory, the horsepower needed for powerful impact analysis is becoming more widely available. This technology, coupled with improved impact-analysis processes, is being used to bring previous impact-analysis-related ideas into prominence.

Requirements traceability is a property that lets developers determine where requirements have been implemented in software documents and source code. Traceability lets them tell whether or not requirements have been realized in a design or implementation. It is also useful in identifying software life-cycle objects that may need examination when requirements change. Traceability is commonly achieved with traceability links, a dependency relation connecting various SLOs.

The first paper, "An Analysis of the Requirements Traceability Problem" by Orlena Gotel and Anthony Finkelstein, introduces a formal definition of requirements traceability. It also presents a framework of issues for examining tool support. The authors investigate and discuss the requirements-traceability problem in considerable depth. They provide a detailed view of the traceability issues and approaches applied in today's environment. They divide the requirements traceability problem into dilemmas before requirements specification and after. Most traceability work is done after the requirements-specification stage. Impact analysis is done using these traceability relationships.

In the next paper, "Software Change Impact Analysis for Design Evolution," Shawn Bohner describes software impact analysis that incorporates both dependency analysis and traceability techniques to assist in evolving software-system designs. The paper combines horizontal traceability information (relationships among different types of SLOs) with vertical traceability information (relationships among the same types of SLOs) to analyze the effect of changes to the software design. Bohner discusses current impact-analysis technology issues and how the technologies need to evolve to use repositories more effectively.

Gene Forte concludes the chapter with "Configuration Management Survey," in which he reviews the capabilities and features available in configuration-management tools. If a configuration-management system is viewed as a repository for software artifacts, it is natural to think of the repository as the place where impact analysis can be accomplished. In some sense, impact analyses are conducted in current configuration-management systems through dependency tracking for objects in software construction as well as in release management and versioning. This dependency tracking is rapidly evolving to support traceability and impact analysis.

Forte relates the capabilities of configuration-management systems to the basic requirements for improved software development and maintenance. The paper gives good insight into the state of the practice in impact analysis through its discussion of commercial development and maintenance environments, presenting what they can do to support software change and what they are planning to do. Forte includes an insightful discussion that targets key configuration-management issues in software development and maintenance.

An Analysis of the Requirements Traceability Problem

Orlena C. Z. Gotel & Anthony C. W. Finkelstein

Imperial College of Science, Technology & Medicine
Department of Computing, 180 Queen's Gate
London SW7 2BZ   (oczg; acwf@doc.ic.ac.uk)

Abstract

In this paper[1], we investigate and discuss the underlying nature of the requirements traceability problem. Our work is based on empirical studies, involving over 100 practitioners, and an evaluation of current support. We introduce the distinction between pre-requirements specification (pre-RS) traceability and post-requirements specification (post-RS) traceability, to demonstrate why an all-encompassing solution to the problem is unlikely, and to provide a framework through which to understand its multifaceted nature. We report how the majority of the problems attributed to poor requirements traceability are due to inadequate pre-RS traceability and show the fundamental need for improvements here. In the remainder of the paper, we present an analysis of the main barriers confronting such improvements in practice, identify relevant areas in which advances have been (or can be) made, and make recommendations for research.

[Keywords: requirements traceability, pre-requirements specification traceability, post-requirements specification traceability, requirements engineering practice, requirements traceability tools.]

1:Introduction

Requirements traceability (RT) is recognised as a concern in an increasing number of standards and guidelines for requirements engineering (RE) [12]. This concern is reflected by the various systems that have been developed and a growing research interest in the area [25]. Despite many advances, RT remains a widely reported problem area by industry. We attribute this to inadequate problem analysis.

Definitions of "requirements traceability" are discussed in detail later, though we provide the following for orientation:

- **Requirements traceability** refers to the ability to describe and follow the life of a requirement, in both a forwards and backwards direction.
- **Pre-RS traceability** refers to those aspects of a requirement's life prior to inclusion in the RS.
- **Post-RS traceability** refers to those aspects of a requirement's life that result from inclusion in the RS.

In this paper, we analyse the RT problem in detail. We describe our empirical investigations in Section 2, review the current support in Section 3, examine the underlying causes of the problem in Section 4, and present a framework for addressing these in Section 5. Section 6 lists the main problems facing pre-RS traceability improvements, Section 7 identifies how some of these can be tackled, and Section 8 discusses that aspect of the composite problem which is the subject of our on-going research agenda at Imperial College.

2:Research method

Numerous data gathering techniques were used to define and analyse the RT problem. The empirical exercises took place over 1 year and involved more than 100 practitioners. Their work areas covered all aspects of development, maintenance and management; their experience ranged from 9 months to 30 years; and the projects they were involved with varied in number, type, and size. A detailed specification for RT support was produced in parallel. Here, introspection helped to identify requirements to support both this activity and its traceability.

2.1:Literature & tool reviews

The literature was surveyed, and over 100 commercial tools and research products were reviewed, to gather viewpoints regarding: what RT is; why it is needed; what problems it involves; and to locate relevant research and development.

2.2:Focus groups

5 semi-structured sessions were conducted. These involved 37 practitioners spread across 5 sites of a U.K. company. Each session lasted 1 hour, was audio taped, and transcribed. The data were used to: consolidate the above; discover how RT problems are overcome (if at all); get suggestions for improvements; and to inform questionnaire design.

2.3:Questionnaires & follow up interviews

A 2-stage questionnaire was used. Stage 1 was designed to rapidly gather data from a wide population of practitioners and to target those from whom more detail could be gathered. 80 were distributed and 69% returned. Stage 2 was tailored to the primary working areas and experiences of individual practitioners, using a reusable pool of questions. 39 were distributed and 85% returned. These provided a deeper understanding of the problems and preliminary requirements to address them. 2 informal interview sessions were subsequently conducted with the respondents. Each lasted 1.5 hours and were used to corroborate their answers, appraise their validity, extract additional information, and to check preliminary analysis.

2.4:Observation & participation

Data were also gathered following the observation of, and some participation in, a variety of RE exercises. For instance, Rapid Application Development workshops were observed,

---

[1] [23] is a longer version of this paper. The empirical work and surveys we refer to are fully documented as a BT/Oxford University research report.

where comprehensive notes were taken, and any informal documents produced were collected. Our analysis compared such artifacts with the workshop's end products.

3: Current support for requirements traceability

It has been noted that most tools do not cover RT [46], and that few support the RT requirements enforced by DOD STD-2167A [58]. Our survey further indicates that those which do, employ basically identical techniques. They differ mainly in cosmetics, and in the time, effort, and manual intervention they require to achieve RT. Both the type and extent of support provided depends on the underlying assumptions they embed about RT and the particular problems they focus on. However, they often suffer problems due to poor integration and inflexibility. These shortcomings are reflected by the preferred use of general-purpose tools in practice [38].

3.1: Basic techniques

Numerous techniques have been used for providing RT, including: cross referencing schemes [16]; keyphrase dependencies [28]; templates [27]; RT matrices [9]; matrix sequences [4]; hypertext [32]; integration documents [36]; assumption-based truth maintenance networks [53]; and constraint networks [2]. These differ in the quantity and diversity of information they can trace between, in the number of interconnections they can control between information, and in the extent to which they can maintain RT when faced with on-going changes to requirements.

Additionally, some form of RT can result from using certain languages, models, and methods for development. This is particularly exemplified by: the Requirements Statement Language [10]; process entity-relationship models [24]; the Planning and Design Methodology [42]; formal methods [8]; and Quality Function Deployment [59]. The quality of the resulting RT, however, depends on the rigid adherence to pre-specified procedures and notations for development.

3.2: Automated support

Many commercial tools and research products support RT, primarily because they embody manual or automated forms of the above techniques. We highlight some representative examples below and provide further details in Table 1.

General-purpose tools include: hypertext editors; word processors; spreadsheets; database systems; etc. They can be hand-configured to allow previously manual and paper-based RT tasks to be carried out on-line. This generally involves defining cross references and specifying their update criteria.

Special-purpose tools support dedicated activities related to RE and some achieve restricted RT. For example: the KJ-editor provides traceability between ideas and requirements [56]; and the T tool provides traceability between requirements and test cases [54]. Support is implicit in tool use, by automation of any mundane tasks needed to provide RT, and guidance is limited.

Workbenches contain a collection of the above to support coherent sets of activities. Less restricted RT can be achieved, but the quality depends on the focal workbench activity. Those in which RT and RT management are focal (such as the Automated Requirements Traceability System [21] and the Requirements Traceability and Management System [41]), are what we refer to as RT workbenches. They are typically centred around a database management system, and have tools to document, parse, organise, edit, interlink, change, and manage requirements. Other upper-CASE workbenches which assist RE activities frequently provide some support. This is either from explicit RT components (e.g., a Coupling Module in AGE [34]), or from having carried out other activities using its tools (e.g., the Requirements Apprentice [51]). Those workbenches which accept requirements documents, from which to drive the design and implementation, commonly provide coarse-grained RT between requirements and their realisation.

Environments, which integrate tools for all aspects of development, can enable RT throughout a project's life. The basis for integration defines how RT is established: a common language (e.g., Input/Output Requirements Language in Technology for the Automated Generation of Systems [54]); a common structure (e.g., relations of an Entity-Relation-Attribute Model in Genesis [48]); a common method (e.g., Information Engineering Method in the Information Engineering Facility [57]); or (where the tools are combined to support multiplicity) a specialised RT tool or repository structure (e.g., Teamwork/RqT [5]). Those which incorporate third-party tools use powerful repositories and database management systems to relate their products (e.g., the Digital CASE Environment [54]).

4: Why there is still a traceability problem

To date, techniques have been thrown at the RT problem without any thorough investigation of what this problem is. Despite a growth in specialised tools, and inflated claims of RT functionality from tool vendors, their use is not as widespread in practice as the importance of RT would suggest. RT problems even remain cited where they are used. Following investigations with practitioners, we have found that the RT problem is not perceived to be uniform, and attribute its persistence to diverse definitions and a number of fundamental conflicts.

4.1: Lack of common definition

Definitions of "requirements traceability", either by practitioners or in the literature, were found to be either:

- **Purpose-driven** (defined in terms of what it should do):
  "...the ability to adhere to the business position, project scope and key requirements that have been signed off" [Focus group practitioner].
- **Solution-driven** (defined in terms of how it should do it):
  "...the ability of tracing from one entity to another based on given semantic relations" [47].
- **Information-driven** (emphasising traceable information):
  "...the ability to link between functions, data, requirements and any text in the statement of requirements that refers to them" [Focus group practitioner].
- **Direction-driven** (emphasising traceability direction):
  "...the ability to follow a specific item at input of a phase of the software lifecycle to a specific item at the output of that phase" [15].

Each definition differs in emphasis and delimits scope. No single one covers all concerns. This has implications for the

RT	(A) General-purpose tools	(B) Special-purpose tools	(C) Workbenches	(D) Environments and beyond
(1) Priority given to RT	Any general-purpose tool can potentially be configured for RT purposes, though RT is not a concern of the basic tool.	Those that support RE activities (e.g., analysis techniques), often provide some form of RT as a by-product of use, but RT is not focal.	Priority depends on the focal set of activities. Where these are RT and management (in RT workbenches), RT is the main concern. Where other RE activities are focal, RT is a side concern.	Typically a side concern, though the extent of this depends on whether or not there are dedicated tools for RT contained in the composite environment.
(2) Support provided for RT	No explicit support is provided. RT must be hand-crafted and the resulting support provided depends on the initial effort expended in doing this. The focus can easily become configuring the tool to enable RT rather than ensuring RT itself.	Support is implicit in the framework provided for carrying out the main activity of the tool. Mundane and repetitive tasks, which are usually necessary to provide basic RT, are typically automated as a consequence of proper use of the tool.	In RT workbenches, support is explicit (else as B). No real analytical ability is provided, but they offer: (i) Guidance - through adherence to RE approach (typically top-down decomposition), types of information to collect, and link types to establish. (ii) Assistance - by parsing textual documents to tag requirements, establishing (syntactic) links between them, and through a repository which manages any bookkeeping and rudimentary checking.	Provided as a by-product of coordinated tool use and adherence to RE philosophy. Extent of support depends on the internal integration strategy and/or repository structure. More guidance and assistance if it has dedicated RT tools, or if it is a main concern. RT maintenance is supported if the repository can manage quantities of information and reconfigure after change.
(3) Requirements-related information that can be made traceable	Ability to trace any information which can be input to the tool (be this textual, graphical, etc.), so potentially able to trace all requirements-related information if sufficient effort and time, are exercised.	Predefines the amount and type of information that can be input and made traceable. This is typically restricted to that information necessary to carry out the activity the tool supports. Only a limited scope of requirements-related information can be traced.	Potential to trace a diversity of requirements-related information. RT workbenches often impose arbitrary limits on the amount and type of information. They trace how an RS was produced, but usually only its derivation from a textual baseline, not its exploratory development, refinement, and context of production. Additional information (e.g., informal notes) can often be recorded, but is of limited use for RT.	Potential to trace information related to requirements in all project phases. Tendency to focus on information derived from requirements in the RS in later phases, so less emphasis on production-related information about individual requirements. Often support the RT of versions, variants, and user-defined items.
(4) Tasks and job roles that RT can assist	Offer complete tailorability. RT can be provided to support any task and job role, though it is problematic to meet different needs simultaneously without any RT infrastructure in place.	RT is provided to assist the activity the tool supports, so the role of the tool user is predefined. Their task-specific frameworks constrain the domain of working, making them difficult to use for other purposes.	Support for a breadth of activities within the concern of the tool's domain (e.g., able to assist requirements checking, etc.). Supports specific jobs, but often configurable to support tasks for other project phases. RT workbenches tend to support managerial activities rather than the activities of RS producers.	RT can assist lifecycle-wide tasks and roles (e.g., those related to maintenance and management, such as impact analysis and progress reporting, etc.). More support for activities related to the use of requirements rather than production and refinement.
(5) Longevity of RT support	Configured for immediate needs. RT can degrade with quantities of information and time, as not usually integrated with lifecycle-wide tools, and poor at handling changes and evolution.	Provide RT at a snapshot in time to support a specific activity, so neglect requirements for on-going management. Longevity of support depends on both horizontal and vertical integration with other tools.	RT is provided for the duration of the activities supported. Predominantly forwards-engineering tools, so RT can deteriorate with progression to later phases, as it can be difficult to reflect any work here and account for iteration. Longevity of support depends on vertical integration with other tools.	Can provide RT for a project's life, though tends to start from a static baseline. RT tightness and granularity depends on the underlying repository and degree of internal integration. RT can deteriorate due to iteration problems and poor feedback.
(6) Support for the traceability of group activities	Promote individualistic working, as provide no common or consistent framework for RT, so encourage immediate and ad hoc solutions. Typically used, by a single user, to record activities after they have happened.	Most support individualistic working. Those which directly support group activities (like the brainstorming of requirements amongst stakeholders), increasingly tend to make both the process and its end results traceable.	RT workbenches tend to be used as after-the-event documentation tools by single users, as they can be difficult to adapt to working practices. Concurrent work is often difficult to coordinate, so the richness of information can be lost. Participative work is actively supported in some (generally not RT workbenches), but traceability of this work varies.	Multiple users are supported through shareable repositories and techniques to assist activity coordination and integration (e.g., workspaces). Often depends on an agreed RS and strict project partitioning, so RT can deteriorate when requirements are unstable and overall control is lacking.
(7) Main strengths	(i) Flexibility to provide customised RT to suit individual project and organisational needs. (ii) Often sufficient for the RT of small and short term projects.	(i) Can provide tight RT for the immediate needs of particular requirements-related activities. (ii) Those supporting group activity, often provide traceability of it.	(i) RT workbenches provide good RT from and back to information which is initially input to the tool, and through a breadth of related activities (i.e., fine-grained horizontal RT within requirements phases). (ii) Added value (e.g., RT checks, visibility, etc.).	(i) Ability to provide on-going RT (i.e., depth of coverage or vertical RT). (ii) Open environments (and meta-CASE), provide more flexibility in the choice of RE approach and in the RT of this.
(8) Main weaknesses	(i) Requires much work to initially configure, can involve mundane and repetitive activities for use, and often provides little more than an electronic version of paper-based RT. (ii) Poor control and integration, so no guarantee as to the usefulness, usability, and longevity of the RT provided.	(i) Only provides restricted forms of RT between limited types and amounts of requirements-related information, so has limited life and use. (ii) Typically suffer from a limited potential for integration and poor information management, as mainly stand-alone, preventing fuller and longer RT support.	(i) RT workbenches attempt to be holistic, but none support all activities. Typically enforce: a top-down approach; classification schemes; and pre-empt a relatively static baseline (without support for its development). As RT depends on correct use, the main concern can be RT rather than RS production. (ii) RT workbenches integrate poorly, so difficult to support the RT of early problem definition work, or to provide on-going RT with later changes (much manual intervention can be required to do so).	(i) RT is typically coarse-grained and dependent on step-wise development. As the tightness of RT varies, iteration and later requirements changes can prevent on-going RT (due to poor backwards RT, which rarely accounts for the occurrence of manual intervention or work-arounds). (ii) Increasing flexibility (with those tools open to external integration), is typically counterbalanced by poorer RT.

Table 1: Tool support for requirements traceability

development and use of tools to support RT: how can RT be coherently and consistently provided if each individual has his or her own understanding as to what RT is?

4.2: Conflicting underlying problems

Each practitioner also had his or her own understanding as to the main cause of the RT problem. This finding is reflected in the literature, where it has been attributed to: coarse granularity of traceable entities [47]; immature integration technology [3]; hidden information [52]; and project longevity [42]. The problems that improved RT were expected to address were just as diverse, a finding also reflected in the literature: to support RS evolvability [30]; to enable safety analysis, audits, and change control [24]; to understand systems from multiple viewpoints [14]; and to permit flexible process modelling [20].

These findings demonstrate that: (a) the phrase "RT problem" is commonly used to umbrella many problems; and that (b) RT improvements are expected to yield the solution to

further (and even ambitious or conflicting) problems. Complicating this was the observation that, underlying every situation in which RT is required in practice, different user, project, task, and informational requirements come into play. These cumulatively influence the problems experienced, which has further implications for any potential support: how can RT account for all these problems simultaneously?

5: A framework for addressing the problem

To provide a framework in which to locate and address the fundamental cause of RT problems, we first need to establish some shared and working definitions.

5.1: Defining requirements traceability

The definition most commonly cited in the literature is:
- *"A software requirements specification is traceable if (i) the origin of each of its requirements is clear and if (ii) it facilitates the referencing of each requirement in future*

development or enhancement documentation" (ANSI/IEEE Standard 830-1984) [26].

This definition specifically recommends *backward traceability* to all previous documents and *forward traceability* to all spawned documents. An alternative definition, derived from the word "trace" in the Oxford English Dictionary, is:

- The ability to *"delineate"* and *"mark out"* *"perceptible signs of what has existed or happened"* in the lifetime of a requirement to enable one to *"pursue one's way along"* this record.

Together, these suggest the following definition for RT:

- *"Requirements traceability refers to the ability to describe and follow the life of a requirement, in both a forwards and backwards direction (i.e., from its origins, through its development and specification, to its subsequent deployment and use, and through all periods of on-going refinement and iteration in any of these phases)."*

5.2: Pre-RS & post-RS traceability

Our investigations further suggest that RT is of 2 basic types:

- *"Pre-RS traceability, which is concerned with those aspects of a requirement's life prior to its inclusion in the RS (requirement production)."*
- *"Post-RS traceability, which is concerned with those aspects of a requirement's life that result from its inclusion in the RS (requirement deployment)."*

Figure 1 shows the typical setting of RT to illustrate these definitions. Note how requirements knowledge is distributed and merged in successive representations; note also the added complication of iteration and change propagation.

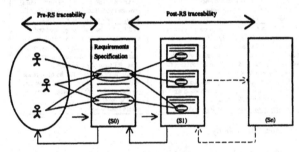

Figure 1: Two basic types of requirements traceability

Forwards and backwards RT are clearly essential. However, we emphasise the pre-RS and post-RS separation, because RT problems in practice were found to centre around a current lack of distinction here. Although both these types of RT are needed, it is crucial to understand their subtle differences, as each type imposes its own distinct requirements on potential support.

The main differences involve the information they deal with and the problems they can assist. Post-RS traceability depends on the ability to trace requirements from, and back to, a baseline (the RS), through a succession of artifacts in which they are distributed. Changes to the baseline need to be re-propagated through this chain. Pre-RS traceability depends on the ability to trace requirements from, and back to, their originating statement(s), through the process of requirements production and refinement, in which statements from diverse sources are

eventually integrated into a single requirement in the RS. Changes in the process need to be re-worked into the RS. Changes to the RS need to be carried out with reference to this process, so they can be instigated and propagated from their source. This requires visibility of the subtle interrelationships that exist between requirements early on.

5.3: Support for pre-RS & post-RS traceability

Existing support mainly provides post-RS traceability. Any problems here are an artifact of informal development methods. These can be eliminated by formal development settings, which automatically transform an RS into an executable, and replay transformations following change [18]. In contrast, the issues that pre-RS traceability are to deal with are neither well understood nor fully supported. Post-RS traceability support is not suitable. This generally treats an RS as a *black-box*, with little to show that the requirements are in fact the end product of a complex and on-going process. Rigid commitment to categories for recording information also make it difficult to represent this process and to account for the dynamic nature of the sources and environment from which requirements are drawn. It has been argued that pre-RS traceability problems will remain, irrespective of formal treatment, as this aspect of a requirement's life is inherently paradigm-independent [18].

5.4: The need for improved pre-RS traceability

Only recently have these issues been acknowledged [17]. Our empirical findings intensify this concern: most of the problems attributed to poor RT were found to be due to the lack of (or inadequate) pre-RS traceability. Practitioners require techniques to record and trace information related to RS production and revision. Pre-RS traceability was also required to:

- Yield improvements in quality, as previously closed issues (even decisions about how to conduct the RE exercise itself), could be made explicit, possible to re-open, and possible to re-work (so assisting auditing [6], repeatability [29], etc.).
- Provide more economic leverage, as to use and maintain an RS in practice, it is often necessary to reconstruct an understanding of how it was produced (to compensate for invisibility [11]), which is currently error-prone and costly.

6: Problems confronting pre-RS traceability

Having identified insufficient pre-RS traceability as the main contributor to continuing RT problems, and shown how it is likely to be the only contributor in formal development settings, our investigations were re-focused to determine: what improvements in pre-RS traceability would involve; and how these could be realised. These indicated that the main barrier is due to an *establish and end-use conflict*. By this, we mean that the 2 main parties involved (i.e., those in a position to make it possible and those who require it to assist their work), have conflicting problems and needs (as shown in Figures 2 and 3).

6.1: Problems faced by the providers

- Perceived as an optional extra (and of low priority), so the allocation of time, staff, and resources is often insufficient.
- No allocation and management of the different roles that practitioners need to assume to: obtain and document the required information; organise it; and maintain it.

- Imbalance between the work involved and benefits gained.
- Individual efforts are ad hoc and localised, whereas a combined and full-time responsibility by all is really needed.
- No agreement on the end-user requirements, resulting in a tendency to focus only on their immediate and visible needs.
- Concern for pre-RS traceability lessens, and concern for post-RS traceability increases, after the RS has been formally signed off. Concern must continue, but this is problematic as the activities are unpredictable, change cultures are immature, and it depends upon RT being present to do so.
- Information (e.g., tacit knowledge), cannot always be obtained, and the quality of that which is varies. Deliverable-driven cultures can discourage gathering certain information.
- The documentation of required information is no guarantee of its traceability. That which is structured, so it is traceable in many ways, provides no guarantee it will be up to date.
- Poor feedback regarding best practice, and little dedicated support (be this clerical, procedural, or computer support), perpetuates the same problems and restricts advances.

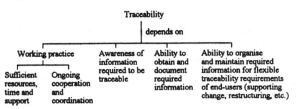

Figure 2: Deconstructing the RT problem for provision

6.2:Problems imposed by the end-users

- A stereotypical end-user cannot be predefined. Their requirements will differ and often be inconsistent.
- The quantity, heterogeneity, and depth of detail of the potential information required, precludes predefinition.
- Inability to predefine how any access to information, and its subsequent presentation, will be required.
- Reliance on personal contact, as there is always something that is out of date, undocumented, inaccessible, or unusable.
- Each end-use context exhibits unique requirements, so problems will exist if end-users do not have the ability to filter and access the information pertaining to RS production that they require under different circumstances.

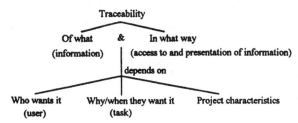

Figure 3: Deconstructing the RT problem for end-use

6.3:Addressing both parties

The challenge lies in satisfying both parties. For end-users, pre-RS traceability must be sensitive to contextual needs, but they cannot predefine their anticipated requirements for it. The providers must identify and document relevant information, in a (re)usable form (either as a by-product of other work or through more explicit support), but they cannot forsee and address all possible needs. Problems intensify when the same individuals assume both positions. The social nature of the activities involved suggests that technology alone will not provide a complete solution for pre-RS traceability.

7:Solutions to pre-RS traceability problems

An RS was produced to specify what is required to provide and make use of pre-RS traceability. The complexity of these requirements indicate that it would be premature to offer a comprehensive solution. It is a compound problem in need of improvements in many diverse areas. Here, we focus on those basic requirements for which some solutions already exist, and make recommendations for additional research.

7.1:Increasing awareness of information

Studies have revealed what project information is required by those involved in the different phases of development [35]. However, our investigations show that it is not possible to generalise, as both the amount and type required will remain subject to dispute. This issue is generally tackled by pre-specifying the types and structure of information required to assist focused activities, like the gIBIS argumentation scheme for design deliberation [7], but such schemes do not consider the wider informational requirements of all potential RE activities. RT models (as described in [50]), specifically aim to increase awareness of the various stakeholders' needs (primarily to inform the link types to maintain between different information), but use of such models will always be subjective. Problems like these could be assisted through the introduction of dedicated job roles (e.g., independent project documentalist, to augment and unify contributions, encourage objectivity, etc.).

7.2:Obtaining & recording information

Much progress has been made in the ability to obtain and record diverse types of RE information. For example: the history of requirements evolution (REMAP [49]); requirements trade-offs (KAPTUR [1]); explanations and justifications (XPLAIN [44]); a record of collaborative activities (Conversation Builder [33]); and multimedia information [45]. For comprehensive coverage, such tools could be amalgamated in an exploratory workbench (or requirements pre-processor), using suitable integration standards. With additional computer metaphors, so that more RE activities can be carried out on-line, more of this information could be produced as a by-product of main activities. Advances here can be informed through the use of ethnography, or ethnomethodology, to study and describe the details of requirements production, use, and manipulation.

7.3:Organising & maintaining information

To support iterative development, information requires flexibility of content and structure. Relevant work includes the use of: viewpoints as a structuring principle [19]; logical frameworks for modelling and analysing an RS to support gradual elaboration [13]; hypertext to provide explicit visibility of structure and maintain relations [22]; and change models [40]. More research is needed to deal with informal and unstable information. Much could also be gained from: guidelines to reconceptualise requirements as modular viable systems; the object-oriented representation of self-monitoring multimedia objects; various rollback strategies for persistent repositories; and the creation of explicit job roles to cover the responsibilities of: (a) project librarian (to collect, clean-up, and distribute information); (b) repository manager (to coordinate, control, and maintain information integrity); and (c) RT facilitator (to provide and ensure continual RT).

7.4: Access & presentation of information

RT is predominantly hardwired, predefining what can be traced, and its presentation [21]. Developments in areas such as information retrieval, artificial intelligence, and human computer interaction, are often pertinent. Focused research, like that separating the representation of requirements from flexible presentation, offers potential [31]. Programmable multimedia workstations for end-users would also enable: graphical and textual traces; sophisticated visualisation, to assist activities like impact analysis (i.e., presenting requirements dynamically, using animation, links which light up, etc.); concurrent (global and local) traces; and engaging methods of interrogation. To account for the context of end-use, research is needed to provide flexible RT, where traces can dynamically mature to queries.

8: A research agenda

The current research and recommendations concentrate on throwing increasing amounts and types of information at the pre-RS traceability problem. When such information is generated through adherence to methods, models, or guidelines, it will vary in reliability, as these are rarely used as intended. Any manually-provided information will suffer from subjectivity and incompleteness, as it is difficult to be reflexive, notions of relevance differ, classification schemes are rarely shared, and equal commitment to detail is unlikely. Furthermore, there will always be occasions when the information required will either: not be there; be tailored to a different audience; or not be entirely suited to the purposes at hand.

8.1: Location & access of pre-RS sources

In our investigations, we found that practitioners regularly encountered the above situation. When they do, their fall-back strategy involves identifying and talking to those who can assist. A statistically significant finding was the agreement that the most useful pieces of pre-RS information were: (a) the ultimate source of a requirement; and (b) those involved in the activities which led to its inclusion and refinement in the RS. RT problems (to date), have been solely attacked with techniques that aim to supplant human contact with information. However, even when suitable information is available, the ability to augment this with face-to-face communication was found to be desirable, often essential, and even a fundamental working practice. It is the inability to do just this which we found to underlie many of the continued RT problems.

This finding implies that both *eager* and *lazy* generation of project information is required. By eager, we mean whilst engaged in aspects of RS production. Such information is well suited to the immediate needs of those involved and useful as a later reference point. With time, this static snapshot is less suited to additional needs, and difficult to interrogate. Information generated on need (i.e., lazily and by those originally responsible), can be provided with hindsight, and targeted to specific needs. Both are essential. Without reference to information recorded at the time, to regain context, it would become increasingly difficult to reproduce the required details.

8.2: Location & accessibility: the crux of the problem

Surprisingly, the inability to locate and access the sources of requirements and pre-RS work was *the most commonly cited problem* across all the practitioners in our investigations. This problem was also reported to be a major contributor to others:

- An out of date RS, as an RS evolves poorly when those originally responsible are not involved in its evolution, or where it is impossible to regain the original context.
- Slow realisation (and deterioration as a result) of change, as the most time-consuming and erroneous part is often the identification of those to involve and inform.
- Unproductive conflict resolution, decision making, and negotiation, as most tools supporting these activities do not help to identify or locate the essential participants.
- Poor collaboration, as the invisibility of changing work structures and responsibilities makes it difficult to: transfer information amongst parties; integrate work; and assign work to those with relevant knowledge and experience.
- Difficulty in dealing with the consequences when individuals leave a project and with the integration of new individuals.
- Poor reuse of requirements, as reuse is mainly successful when those initially responsible for their production are either directly involved or readily accessible.

This problem was often reported to be due to politics, which prohibited any knowledge of, or access to, the original sources or requirements engineers. This can only be addressed by re-examining the policies of affected projects. The other reason behind this problem was reported to be the difficulty in keeping track of the original sources and subsequent traces of participation. The common approach, listing contributors to information in document fields, was felt insufficient. This cause of the problem can be tackled with suitable assistance.

Certain project characteristics were found to promote the occurrence of this problem. In projects consisting of individuals split into a number of teams, the location and access of sources was found to be either impossible, time consuming, or unreliable. This was due to: a lack of shared or project-wide commitment; information loss; inability to assess the overall state of work or knowledge; little cross-involvement; poor communication; minimal distribution of information; and changing notions of ownership, accountability, responsibility, and working structure (characteristics amongst those identified elsewhere as contributors to project failure). Characteristics that reduced its occurrence were found in projects consisting of few individuals, due to: a clear visibility of responsibilities and knowledge areas; clarity of working structures; team commitment and ownership; and individuals who acted as *common threads of involvement* (also contributors to success).

8.3: Related work

Many project management tools provide facilities to model organisational charts, role structures, work breakdown structures, work-flow, etc. Although these are often incorporated in CASE tools (e.g., the ProKit WORKBENCH [54]), they are not well suited to the location and access problem. They tend to be descriptive, prescriptive, or predictive, so used to model formal, static structures and predefined work plans. The drift between what is modelled, what took place, and what is the case in later project life, can be substantial. RS production and maintenance is a social accomplishment in which such structures are continuously created and recreated. Notions like ownership and responsibility are often only transient. The ability to locate relevant individuals therefore deteriorates as the volume and complexity of communication paths grow over time. Models which can reflect these dynamics and manage this complexity are critically needed.

Some recent models (e.g., DesignNet [37]), make initial attempts here, typically through the ability to restructure plans, and so forth. Models of the organisational environment in which a system is intended to operate are also relevant. These each tend to embed different views of an organisation. They focus on specific structures, such as the intentional structure [60] or the responsibility structure [55], so singularly lack an appreciation of the wider organisational context. Collective and more dynamic variants of these could help clarify the organisational structure of development projects. Process modelling research is of further interest here, as these models promise to provide a fuller understanding of the complete environment in which a system is developed (see [43]).

Following a comprehensive analysis of software errors, recommendations were made for modularising responsibility and promoting communication [39]. Our studies independently consolidate and particularise this: RT problems will persist when accurate responsibility cannot be located and these individuals cannot be accessed for the informal communication often necessary to deal with them. The remedy is to provide a continuously up to date picture which promotes and instigates these activities. Our current research is directed at exactly this.

9: Conclusions

We have illustrated the multifaceted nature of the so-called "requirements traceability problem" that many practitioners claim to experience. We have shown why little real progress has been made here, and how this can only be achieved if based on a thorough understanding of the actual problem. We have distinguished between pre-RS and post-RS traceability, demonstrated how advances in the former are needed and offer most opportunity, and made suggestions for progress here.

In conclusion, to achieve any order of magnitude improvement with the RT problem, there is a need to re-focus research efforts on pre-RS traceability. Of particular concern is the intrinsic need for the on-going ability to rapidly locate and access those involved in specifying and refining requirements, to facilitate their informal communication. Continuous and explicit modelling of the social infrastructure in which requirements are produced, specified, maintained, and used (reflecting all changes), is fundamental to this re-orientation.

Acknowledgements

Much of this work was carried out by the principle author, whilst at Oxford University, supported by a BT University Research Initiative. This author would also like to thank the States of Jersey for continued financial support. Both authors acknowledge the comments and assistance of colleagues, students, and anonymous referees. In particular: David Michael; Marina Jirotka; Matthew Bickerton; Joseph Goguen; Daniel Berry; Jeff Kramer; and Manny Lehman.

References

[1] Bailin, S.C., Moore, J.M., Bentz, R. & Bewtra, M. (1990). KAPTUR: Knowledge Acquisition for Preservation of Tradeoffs and Underlying Rationales, *Proceedings of the Fifth Conference on Knowledge-Based Software Assistant*, Liverpool NY, Sept.

[2] Bowen, J., O'Grady, P. & Smith, L. (1990). A Constraint Programming Language for Life-Cycle Engineering, *Artificial Intelligence in Engineering*, Vol. 5, No. 4, pp. 206-220.

[3] Brown, A.W., Earl, A.N. & McDermid, J.A. (1992). *Software Engineering Environments: Automated Support for Software Engineering*, McGraw-Hill.

[4] Brown, P.G. (1991). QFD: Echoing the Voice of the Customer, *AT&T Technical Journal*, March/April, pp. 21-31.

[5] CADRE. (1992). *Teamwork/RqT*, Marketing Brochure, CADRE Technologies, Inc.

[6] Chikofsky, E.J. & Rubenstein, B.L. (1988). CASE: Reliability Engineering for Information Systems, *IEEE Software*, March, pp. 11-16.

[7] Conklin, J. & Begeman, M.L. (1988). gIBIS: A Hypertext Tool for Exploratory Policy Discussion, *ACM Transactions on Office Information Systems*, Vol. 6, No. 4, pp. 303-331.

[8] Cooke, J. & Stone, R. (1991). A Formal Development Framework and its Use to Manage Software Production, in [25], pp. 10/1.

[9] Davis, A.M. (1990). *Software Requirements: Analysis and Specification*, Prentice-Hall, Inc.

[10] Davis, C.G. & Vick, C.R. (1977). The Software Development System, *IEEE Transactions on Software Engineering*, Vol. 3, No. 1, pp. 69-84.

[11] Devanbu, P., Brachman, R.J., Selfridge, P.G. & Ballard, B.W. (1991). LaSSIE: A Knowledge-Based Software Information System, *Communications of the ACM*, Vol. 34, No. 5, pp. 34-49.

[12] Dorfman, M. & Thayer, R.H. (1990). *Standards, Guidelines, and Examples on System and Software Requirements Engineering*, IEEE Computer Society Press Tutorial.

[13] Dubois, E. (1990). Logical Support for Reasoning About the Specification and the Elaboration of Requirements, *Artificial Intelligence in Databases and Information Systems*, Meersman, R.A., Shi, Z. & Kung, C.H. (Eds.), Elsevier Science Publishers B.V., pp. 79-98.

[14] Easterbrook, S. (1991). *Elicitation of Requirements from Multiple Perspectives*, Ph.D Thesis, Department of Computing, Imperial College of Science, Technology & Medicine, London University, June.

[15] European Space Agency. (1987). *ESA Software Engineering Standards*, ESA PSS-05-0, Issue 1, Jan., ESA Publications Division.

[16] Evans, M.W. (1989). *The Software Factory*, John Wiley and Sons.

[17] Finkelstein, A. (1991). A (Neat) Alphabet of Requirements Engineering Issues, in Van Lamsweerde, A. & Fugetta, A. (Eds.), *ESEC '91: 3rd European Software Engineering Conference*, Milan, Italy, Oct. 21-24, Springer-Verlag, pp. 489-491.

[18] Finkelstein, A. (1991). Tracing Back from Requirements, in [25], pp. 7/1-7/2.

[19] Finkelstein, A., Kramer, J., Nuseibeh, B., Finkelstein, L. & Goedicke, M. (1992). ViewPoints: A Framework for Integrating Multiple Perspectives in System Development, *International Journal of Software Engineering and Knowledge Engineering*, Vol. 2, No. 1, pp. 31-57.

[20] Fischer, W.E. (1991). CASE Seen From Both Sides of the Fence, in Van Lamsweerde, A. & Fugetta, A. (Eds.), *ESEC '91*, Milan, Italy, Oct. 21-24, Springer-Verlag, pp. 509-511.

[21] Flynn, R.F. & Dorfman, M. (1990). The Automated Requirements Traceability System (ARTS): An Experience of Eight Years, in *System and Software Requirements Engineering*, Thayer, R.H. & Dorfman, M. (Eds.), IEEE Computer Society Press Tutorial, pp. 423-438.

[22] Garg, P.K. & Scacchi, W. (1989). ISHYS: Designing and Intelligent Software Hypertext System, *IEEE Expert*, Fall '89, pp. 52-63.

[23] Gotel, O.C.Z. & Finkelstein, A.C.W. (1993). *An Analysis of the Requirements Traceability Problem*, Technical Report TR-93-41, Department of Computing, Imperial College.

[24] Hamilton, V.L. & Beeby, M.L. (1991). Issues of Traceability in Integrating Tools, in [25], pp. 4/1-4/3.

[25] IEE. (1991). *Tools and Techniques for Maintaining Traceability During Design*, IEE Colloquium, Computing and Control Division, Professional Group C1, Digest No.: 1991/180.

[26] IEEE. (1984). *IEEE Guide to Software Requirements Specifications*, ANSI/IEEE Standard 830-1984.

[27] Interactive Development Environments. (1991). *Software Through Pictures: Products and Services Overview*, IDE, Inc.

[28] Jackson, J. (1991). A Keyphrase Based Traceability Scheme, in [25], pp. 2/1-2/4.

[29] Jarke, M. & Pohl, K. (1992). Information Systems Quality and Quality Information Systems, in Kendall, K.E., Lyytinen, K. & DeGross, J.I. (Eds.), *The Impact of Computer Supported Technologies on Information Systems Development*, Elsevier Science Publishers B.V., pp. 345-375.

[30] Johnson, W.L., Feather, M.S. & Harris, D.R. (1991). Integrating Domain Knowledge, Requirements, and Specifications, *Journal of Systems Integration*, Vol. 1, pp. 283-320.

[31] Johnson, W.L., Feather, M.S. & Harris, D.R. (1992). Representation and Presentation of Requirements Knowledge, *IEEE Transactions on Software Engineering*, Vol.18, No.10, pp. 853-869.

[32] Kaindl, H. (1993). The Missing Link in Requirements Engineering, *ACM SIGSOFT Software Engineering Notes*, Vol. 18, No. 2, pp. 30-39.

[33] Kaplan, S.M. (1990). Conversation Builder: An Open Architecture for Collaborative Work, in Diaper, D., Gilmore, D., Cockton, G. & Shackel, B. (Eds.), *HCI Interact '90, Proceedings of the IFIP TC 13 3rd International Conference on HCI*, Cambridge, UK, Aug. 27-31, Elsevier Science Publishers B.V., North-Holland, pp. 917-922.

[34] Keys, E. (1991). A Workbench Providing Traceability in Real-Time System Development, in [25], pp. 3/1-3/2.

[35] Kuwana, E. & Herbsleb, J.D. (1993). Representing Knowledge in Requirements Engineering: An Empirical Study of What Software Engineers Need to Know, *Proceedings of the IEEE International Symposium on Requirements Engineering*, San Diego, California, Jan. 4-6, pp. 273-276.

[36] Lefering, M. (1993). An Incremental Integration Tool Between Requirements Engineering and Programming in the Large, *Proceedings of the IEEE International Symposium on Requirements Engineering*, San Diego, California, Jan. 4-6, pp. 82-89.

[37] Liu, L.C. & Horowitz, E. (1989). A Formal Model for Software Project Management, *IEEE Transactions on Software Engineering*, Vol. 15, No. 10, pp. 1280-1293.

[38] Lubars, M., Potts, C. & Richter, C. (1993). A Review of the State of the Practice in Requirements Modeling, *Proceedings of the IEEE International Symposium on Requirements Engineering*, San Diego, California, Jan. 4-6, pp. 2-14.

[39] Lutz, R.R. (1993). Analyzing Software Requirements Errors in Safety-Critical, Embedded Systems, *Proceedings of the IEEE International Symposium on Requirements Engineering*, San Diego, California, Jan. 4-6, pp. 126-133.

[40] Madhavji, N.H. (1992). Environment Evolution: The Prism Model of Changes, *IEEE Transactions on Software Engineering*, Vol. 18, No. 5, pp. 380-392.

[41] Marconi Systems Technology. (1992). *Requirements Traceability and Management Manual V1.2.4*, GEC Marconi Ltd.

[42] Mays, R.G., Orzech, L.S., Ciarfella, W.A. & Phillips, R.W. (1985). PDM: A Requirements Methodology for Software System Enhancements, *IBM Systems Journal*, Vol. 24, No. 2, pp. 134-149.

[43] Mi, P. & Scacchi, W. (1990). A Knowledge-Based Environment for Modeling and Simulating Software Engineering Processes, *IEEE Transactions on Knowledge and Data Engineering*, Vol. 2, No. 3, pp. 283-294.

[44] Neches, R., Swartout, W.R. & Moore, J.D. (1985). Enhanced Maintenance and Explanation of Expert Systems Through Explicit Models of Their Development, *IEEE Transactions on Software Engineering*, Vol. 11, No. 11, pp. 1337-1351.

[45] Palmer, J.D. & Fields, N.A. (1992). An Integrated Environment for Requirements Engineering, *IEEE Software*, May, pp. 80-85.

[46] Polack, A.J. (1990). Practical Applications of CASE Tools on DoD Projects, *ACM SIGSOFT Software Engineering Notes*, Vol. 15, No. 1, pp. 73-78.

[47] Ramamoorthy, C.V., Garg, V. & Prakash, A. (1986). Programming in the Large, *IEEE Transactions on Software Engineering*, Vol. 12, No. 7, pp. 769-783.

[48] Ramamoorthy, C.V., Garg, V. & Prakash, A. (1988). Support for Reusability in Genesis, *IEEE Transactions on Software Engineering*, Vol. 14, No. 7, pp. 1145-1153.

[49] Ramesh, B. & Dhar, V. (1992). Supporting Systems Development by Capturing Deliberations During Requirements Engineering, *IEEE Transactions on Software Engineering*, Vol. 18, No. 6, pp. 498-510.

[50] Ramesh, B. & Edwards, M. (1993). Issues in the Development of a Requirements Traceability Model, *Proceedings of the IEEE International Symposium on Requirements Engineering*, San Diego, California, Jan. 4-6, pp. 256-259.

[51] Reubenstein, H.B. & Waters, R.C. (1991). The Requirements Apprentice: Automated Assistance for Requirements Acquisition, *IEEE Transactions on Software Engineering*, Vol. 17, No. 3, pp. 226-240.

[52] Robinson, D. (1991). CASE Support for Large Systems, in Van Lamsweerde, A. & Fugetta, A. (Eds.), *ESEC '91*, Milan, Italy, Oct. 21-24, Springer-Verlag, pp. 504-508.

[53] Smithers, T., Tang, M.X. & Tomes, N. (1991). The Maintenance of Design History in AI-Based Design, in [25], pp. 8/1-8/3.

[54] Sodhi, J. (1991). *Software Engineering: Methods, Management, and CASE Tools*, McGraw-Hill.

[55] Strens, R. & Dobson, J. (1992). *On the Modelling of Responsibilities*, Computing Laboratory, University of Newcastle.

[56] Takeda, N., Shiomi, A., Kawai, K. & Ohiwa, H. (1993). Requirements Analysis by the KJ Editor, *Proceedings of the IEEE International Symposium on Requirements Engineering*, San Diego, California, Jan. 4-6, pp. 98-101.

[57] Texas Instruments. (1988). *A Guide to Information Engineering Using the IEF: Computer-Aided Planning, Analysis, and Design.*

[58] U.S. Department of Defense. (1988). *Military Standard: Defense System Software Development.* DOD-STD-2167A. Washington, D. C., Feb. 29.

[59] West, M. (1991). The Use of Quality Function Deployment in Software Development, in [25], pp. 5/1-5/7.

[60] Yu, E.S.K. (1993). Modelling Organizations for Information Systems Requirements Engineering, *Proceedings of the IEEE International Symposium on Requirements Engineering*, San Diego, California, Jan. 4-6, pp. 34-41.

Software Change Impact Analysis for Design Evolution

Shawn A. Bohner

611 West Poplar Road
Sterling, VA 22170-4733
(703) 450-7270

Abstract

Studies have shown that software system designs frequently experience degradation from continued changes during software maintenance activities. Much of this is caused by the change extent not being apparent or discernible with the tools and methods available to the software maintainer. Software change impact analysis offers considerable improvement to this situation. Since software maintenance process models have not fully addressed impact analysis and its potential for enhancing the productivity of software maintainers, this paper introduces a software maintenance process model that emphasizes impact analysis. Using directed graphs, this paper suggests traditional process and product metrics as well as new impact analysis metrics that address software workproduct traceability and inter-workproduct dependencies. Software staff can use these and other metrics to understand and control the changes to the software system design. As changes are requested, measurements can be made, impact assessed, and clarified design decisions made.

1 Introduction

During software development, software design typically reflects a functional view of the system for the purpose of communicating details of its construction. Software development is often performed without regard for how changes will be implemented after delivery. Even during post-deployment support, schedule and cost constraints frequently subvert efforts to properly address changes that promote (rather than degrade) software system maintainability. Software change *impact analysis* -- the assessment of the effect of changes -- provides techniques to address this problem by identifying the likely ripple-effect of software changes and using this information to re-engineer the software system design. By embodying impact analysis in the software maintenance process, the evolution of the software system design can be greatly enhanced.

Impact analysis aids the maintenance team in identifying software workproducts affected by software changes. Such analysis not only permits evaluation of the consequences of planned changes, it also allows trade-offs between suggested software change approaches to be considered. Since software maintenance process models seldom address this type of analysis and its potential for enhancing the productivity of software maintainers, this paper covers this in some detail.

Given the software maintenance perspective, an interesting impact analysis technique that can enhance software design is the use of change histories to guide the structure of the software system. That is, the partitioning and encapsulation of components (software modules and associated documentation) according to or derived from the experience base with software changes is used to direct the design along with traditional software design criteria. For example, if a software system normally receives many change requests associated with billing specifications (rates and tariffs), the software components associated with these changes should be structured to accommodate many such changes, enabling the system to be more responsive to change. This idea will be described in more detail later in the paper.

This paper outlines a software change impact analysis approach that supports software design evolution. It begins by reviewing the importance of controlling change during maintenance and examines existing models of maintenance to see how software change impact analysis is incorporated. Next, a new model of software maintenance that supports software change impact assessment is proposed. This model is used as a framework for suggesting the kinds of metrics needed during maintenance to perform impact analysis. Finally, the complex relationships among maintenance workproducts are discussed in support of software system design evolution.

2 Software Evolution

The traditional software lifecycle depicts software maintenance as starting after software is deployed. However, as Schneidewind points out, software maintenance begins with user requirements, and principles of good software development apply across both the development and maintenance processes [Sch89]. Since good software development supports software change, software change is a necessary consideration throughout the life of a software product. This section examines software change and process models that address software change activities.

2.1 Software Change

Unlike many other types of products, the software product is intended to be malleable. A solution is implemented in software when it is expected to evolve or change periodically; the software can be changed incrementally and adapted as the environment changes around it. Although software neither deteriorates nor changes with age, most of software maintenance involves change that potentially degrades the software unless it is proactively controlled [Leh80] [Leh85]. Rework represents almost 40 percent of the cost of maintenance [Boe87]. Thus, software change impact analysis can be very important in understanding and controlling the cost of software changes.

Otto Neurath's analogy about software change is appropriate in this regard: Changing software is like trying to rebuild boats on the open sea. Individual planks can be replaced only by using existing planks for support. The entire boat can be rebuilt over time as long as the process proceeds one plank at a time. If too much is changed too quickly, the boat sinks. [Bus88]

Adaptability, highly desirable in a system with a long life expectancy, is both a blessing and a curse: If software is easy to adapt, we adapt it quickly, frequently, and at relatively low cost. On the other hand, while we adapt the software, it can grow in size and complexity, with a concomitant decrease in understandability and adaptability. Only when the pain of making the next change becomes acute do we discard the system and replace it with an entirely new one. In the interest of cost and time, we attempt to postpone redevelopment through controlling software change.

Assuming that the software system design is not flawed due to shortcuts taken during development, software starts out well-designed; modifications are relatively localized with little overlap or collision during initial changes. As changes are applied to the software, the design can suffer significant augmentation, potentially degrading the maintenance characteristics of the system [Swa89]. A seemingly minor software change is often much more extensive (and therefore expensive to implement) than expected.

This phenomenon manifests itself in various forms of software complexity (some necessary due to system task complexity and others which are correctable) that drastically effect the change characteristics of the system. In this sense, change localization and the complexity of software dependencies determine the effectiveness of a software system design. For example, if the software is highly modular using encapsulation and information hiding techniques [Par81], then the anticipated changes should be relatively localized and not have ripple-effects to other non-related components. However, if the clusters of change effects become large with significant overlap, then we are likely to see an increase in the rate of errors, failures, and increased effort to make changes.

The effect of manifold changes can be seen in the resulting inadequate and/or out-of-date documentation, improperly or incompletely patched software, poorly structured design or code, artifacts that do not conform to standards, and more. The problem compounds itself by increasing complexity, increasing time for developers to understand code being changed, and increasing the ripple-effect of software changes. These problems often result in higher software maintenance cost. Effective software change impact analysis methods and tools are necessary for controlling the resulting escalation of software maintenance complexity and costs. In the next section, we examine whether such methods have been incorporated in existing models of software maintenance.

2.2 Software Maintenance Models

Over the years, several software maintenance models have been proposed, often to emphasize particular aspects of software maintenance. Among these models, there are common activities. The following is a brief summary of software maintenance models reported in the literature.

Boehm's model of maintenance [Boe76] consists of three major phases: understanding the software, modifying the software, and revalidating the software. The Martin-McClure model is similar, [Mar83], consisting of program understanding, program modification, and program revalidation. Parikh [Par82] has formulated a description of maintenance that emphasizes the identification of objectives before understanding the software, modifying the code, and validating the modified program. Sharpley's model [Sha77] has a different focus; it highlights the corrective maintenance activities through problem verification, problem diagnosis, reprogramming, and baseline reverification.

The Yau and Patkow models are most useful in evaluating the effects of change on the system to be maintained. Yau [Yau80] focuses on software stability through analysis of the ripple-effect of software changes. This model of software maintenance involves several steps:

69

- determining the maintenance objective
- understanding the program
- generating a maintenance change proposal
- accounting for the ripple-effect
- regression testing the program

A distinctive feature of this model is the post-change impact analysis provided by the evaluation of ripple-effect.

The Patkow model [Pat83] concentrates on the front-end maintenance activities of identifying and specifying the maintenance requirements. This model addresses change through diagnosis of the change followed by change localization. Then, the modification is designed and implemented, and the new system is validated. An important feature of this model is its emphasis on specification and localization of the change.

None of the maintenance models described here incorporates metrics explicitly as a method for assessing and controlling change. Rombach and Ulery [Rom89] propose a method of software maintenance improvement that complements this work by focusing the goals, questions, and specific measurements associated with activities in the context of a software maintenance organization. However, their method does not specify a framework for metrics that supports impact analysis in the software maintenance process. Lewis and Henry [Lew89] have addressed the need for metrics during development to help make the resulting product more maintainable, but their work has not extended into the actual maintenance process. To meet the need for understanding and control during maintenance, the next section proposes a new model of the maintenance process that depicts where and how metrics can be used to manage software evolution.

3 Software Maintenance Process

The software maintenance activities in this model are no different in principle from the other models described earlier. That is, understanding software, implementing the change, and retesting the new system are the basic building blocks of the maintenance process. A major distinction between development and maintenance is the set of constraints imposed on the maintainer by the existing implementation of the system. Information about system artifacts, relationships and dependencies can be obscure, missing, or incorrect as a result of continued changes to the system. This situation makes it increasingly difficult for the maintainer to understand the software system and the implications of a proposed software change.

Thus, a model of the maintenance process must indicate how a proposed change is evaluated and made. Figure 1 illustrates a simplified view of software maintenance activities using a simplified variant of Structured Analysis and Design Technique (SADT). Although the activities depicted emphasize software maintenance, it is important to recognize that these activities occur in any model of software development. That is, no matter whether a change is made before or after delivery of a product, the potential effects of the change should be analyzed and acted upon in a careful and controlled manner.

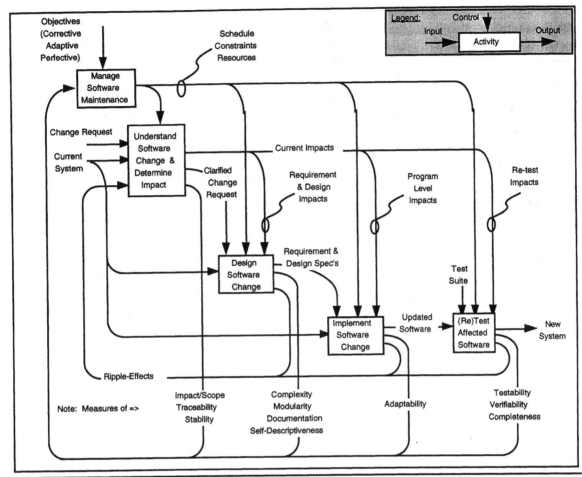

Figure 1: SADT Diagram of Software Maintenance Activities

The feedback paths at the bottom of the SADT diagram of maintenance indicate measurable attributes in the associated activity. The results are then assessed by management before the next activity is undertaken. Thus, the metrics act as a controlling mechanism in the (possibly iterative) progression from existing system and change requests to the new system. Each activity is discussed in turn.

Manage Software Maintenance controls the sequence of activities by receiving feedback and determining the next appropriate action. All activities are performed with the maintenance objective (*corrective, adaptive, or perfective*) in mind. It is important to note that management can make several decisions at this point: continue with the next activity and implement the change, repeat an activity to get more information, repeat an activity for an alternative implementation of the proposed change, or decide not to implement the change.

Understand Software Change and Determine Impact evaluates the proposed change request for clarification and determines possible effects of the change. This activity determines if the change can be made without perturbing the rest of the software. Although this activity is shown as a precursor to the other maintenance activities, it is clear that it transcends the entire process. *Current impacts* outputs provide valuable information to each of the subsequent activities for navigation and scoping within the workproduct set. *Impact/scope* of the change is an evaluation of the number and size of system artifacts that will be affected by the change. *Traceability* suggests the connectivity of the relevant workproducts

71

and whether the overall system will be easier or harder to navigate once the proposed change is made. If the impact is too large, or if the traceability will be severely hampered by the change, management may choose at this point not to implement the change. As a continuing process, this activity measures the stability of the software based on ripple-effect information provided by the other activities as changes occur. Software *stability* is defined as the resistance to the amplification of changes in software during maintenance [Yau80]. It, too, is a composite metric of attributes such as the coupling and cohesion of affected modules.

Design Software Change takes the clarified change request requirements and generates requirements and design specifications. Here, design is a creative process where the maintainer understands the constraints of the current system and models the system to meet the requirements of the change. The *complexity* and *volume* of relevant products, the *self-descriptiveness* of the source code, and the documentation quality all have a profound effect on the ability of a software maintainer to understand the software being changed. Moreover, the *complexity* of the relationships among products must be analyzed to determine if the overall maintainability of the system will be enhanced or degraded by the change. If the manager is unhappy with the likely degradation of these system characteristics, the necessity for the change may be reassessed, or the way in which the change is to be implemented may be reevaluated.

Implement Software Change generates the proposed change. The ability to make appropriate and accurate software changes is driven in part by the system's *adaptability*, a composite metric that indicates whether the system will be harder or easier to maintain as a result of the change. This activity also accounts for ripple-effect and provides the information to *Understand Software Change and Determine Impact* (that is, to analyze the propagation of changes to other code modules as a result of the change just implemented); this serves as an effectiveness check of the original impact analysis.

(Re)Test Affected Software is the final activity before delivery of the modified software. The modifications are tested to assure that they meet new requirements, and the overall system is subject to regression testing to verify that it meets existing ones. The *testability* of the software can be evaluated to determine whether the new changes have made the system easier or harder to test in the future. Where necessary, tests are designed to meet acceptance criteria for the new and modified requirements imposed by the change. Therefore, *completeness* and *verifiability* are also observed in this activity.

Impact analysis plays a key role in this software maintenance process. For the design software change activity, requirements and design impacts are provided. For the implement software change activity, program level impacts are identified. For the re-test affected software activity, re-test impacts identify the appropriate tests. The ripple-effects discovered during each of these activities augment the set of known impacts and furnish a more effective impact analysis.

Notice that all of the attributes fed back to management are aspects of overall software maintainability. The maintainability measures give management and customer an idea of the overall quality of the resulting product. Low software maintainability results in difficult and costly software maintenance activities. By monitoring product quality with each change, the model can be used to increase overall quality and enhance maintenance productivity. In general, the more maintainable our software systems are, the cheaper they will be to maintain. As is many time the case, up-front effort to understand the change pays considerable maintenance dividends in the long run.

4 Impact Analysis

This impact analysis-oriented model focuses on software change and its traceable consequences. Impact analysis is seldom considered prior to actually making a change to an existing system. Usually, only system source code is analyzed to reflect the ripple-effect after a change has been made [Yau88]. However, waiting until the change is made is far too late in the maintenance process to evaluate the effects of the change. A focus on code is inadequate in light of the litany of software workproducts needed for understanding and maintaining a system.

Some attempts have been reported at examining a change before its implementation. For example, requirements traceability has been extended beyond the traditional tracking of requirements to making predictions of the effects of changed requirements [RAD86]. Honeywell's Requirements to Test Tracking System (RTTS) tracks the Navy's documents specified by MIL-STD-1679. RTTS creates, analyzes, and maintains traceability links among software lifecycle documents. Other systems that allow requirements traceability include Sommerville's SOFTLIB, University of California at Berkeley's GENESIS, Rational's CMVT, Intermetric's Byron, and Sun's NSE. In all cases, the traceability perspective is helpful but is too narrow and at too high a level to be helpful during maintenance.

This approach offers instead a unified view of the maintenance process in terms of the software workproduct set as a graph of software lifecycle objects connected by horizontal and vertical traceability relationships. For each workproduct (e.g. requirements, design, code, test plans) *vertical traceability* expresses the relationships among the parts of the workproduct. For example, the vertical traceability of the requirements exhibits the interdependencies among the individual system requirements. Similarly, *horizontal traceability* addresses the relationships of these components across pairs of workproducts. For example, each design component is traced to the code components that implement that part of the design. Both types of traceability are necessary to understand the complete set of relationships to be assessed during impact analysis. The traceability information is initially obtained through static analysis of the software workproduct set and updated as more information about the software change is obtained through the software change process.

Some research has been conducted on capturing and depicting the horizontal traceability relationships. Impact analysis as discussed here, augments this by introducing the vertical traceability relationships in the analysis. In this section, the stage is set for software design evolution using software change impact analysis. Current research activities are discussed, the representation strategy used in this approach is detailed, and traceability measurements are analyzed.

4.1 Current Impact Analysis Research

Researchers have addressed dependency analysis (or vertical traceability) from a program-viewing perspective using incremental data flow techniques [Tah87]. Currently, this work is restricted to source code but shows promise for application to other workproducts. Similar principles are applied in research on improving retesting strategies for modified systems using a combination of data flow analysis and logic coverage techniques [Har90][Pod90]. Software dependency analysis is also part of the "Maintenance Assistant Project" at the Software Engineering Research Center [Wil87]. This project considers key relationships among program modules, data objects, pointer variables, and programmer notations. Program dependency classes are based on:

- Data flow - dependencies between data objects when the value held by an object may be used to calculate or set another value.
- Definition - dependencies where one program entity is used to define another.
- Calling - dependencies between two program modules where one calls the other.
- Functional - dependencies between program modules and global data objects that are created and/or updated by the module.

Software lifecycle objects (SLOs) are workproducts representing documents of one kind or another containing varied levels of software engineering information. In existing horizontal traceability tools, the granularity of SLOs is typically at the document level. This level is too high for accurate impact assessment of a software system change. If the SLO relationships are too coarse, they must be decomposed to understand complex relationships. On the other hand, if they are too granular, it is difficult to reconstruct them into recognizable, easily understood software workproducts.

The following is a brief survey of software engineering environments that have incorporated horizontal traceability as part of their overall approach to development.

ALICIA: The Automated Life Cycle Analysis System (ALICIA) [RAD86] was developed by Software Productivity Solutions for Rome Air Development Center to support impact analysis with a project database model of MIL-STD-2167. ALICIA addresses SLO granularity using information content rather than entire documents. It supports completeness and consistency checking of traceability relationships as well as navigation among SLOs in the project database.

SODOS: The Software Document Support (SODOS) environment [Hor86] was developed at the University of Southern California to support the development and maintenance of software documentation. SODOS manages software lifecycle objects using an object-oriented model and a hypermedia graph of relationships. The documents are defined in a declarative fashion using a structural hierarchy, information content, and intra/inter-document relationships. SODOS supports completeness and consistency checking of traceability relationships, and navigation among SLOs.

PMDB: The Project Master Database (PMDB) was developed at TRW [Pen84] to provide an automated and integrated software engineering environment database. The PWDB supports traceability, completeness and consistency checking as well as navigation mechanisms for browsing the database. The database does not support impact analysis directly, but the query capability of the DBMS allows views of relationships.

System Factory: The USC System Factory Project [Sca88] conducts research in alternative strategies for development of large-scale software development. Part of their prototype system is a hypertext-based documentation integration facility (DIF), created to provide a mechanism for developing and maintaining software documentation with its associated relationships. DIF enables visualization of objects in the software system, and hierarchy charts of software objects display the dependencies of related software objects.

Notice that although some of these systems facilitate horizontal traceability, none includes vertical traceability. Moreover, the granularity varies from one system to another, and none of the systems use the traceability information to control the process in any way. That is, the static analysis of the relationships among workproducts is not followed by a broad, dynamic analysis of how the process should proceed. For this reason, we incorporate traceability at a level of SLO granularity that allows us to measure process and product characteristics and make decisions based on them.

4.2 Traceability Graph Representation Approach

Both horizontal and vertical traceability can be depicted using directed graphs [Yau87][Cle88]. A *directed graph* is simply a collection of objects, called *nodes*, and an associated collection of ordered pairs of the nodes, called *edges*. The nodes represent information contained in documents, articles, and other workproducts. Each workproduct contains a node for each component. For example, the design is represented as a collection of nodes, with one node for each design module, and the requirements specification has one node for each requirement. The directed edges represent the relationships within a workproduct and between workproducts. The first node of the edge is called the *source node*, and the second is the *destination node*.

The graphs can be represented in a number of ways. In the past, matrices have stored the relationships among nodes, and graphs were generated from each matrix. Today, hypermedia technology offers new flexibility in working with the graphical relationships and representing them within the workproduct set [Big88]. The links provide structure and labeling capabilities. No matter how the graphical structure is implemented, the linkage captured in the graphical representation provides a basis for measurement and assessment of relationships within and across workproducts. At the same time, labeling and other attribute information offer contextual views of the software workproduct set.

Figure 2 illustrates how the graphical relationships and traceability links among related workproduct deliverables can be determined. Each requirement is examined, and a link is established between that requirement and the design components that implement it. In turn, each design component is linked with the code modules that implement it. Finally, each code module is linked with the set of test cases that test it. The resulting linkages form the underlying graph that exhibits the relationships among the workproducts.

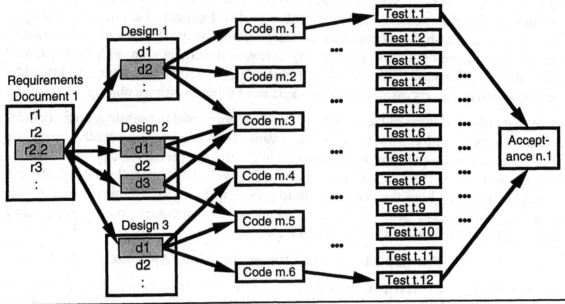

Figure 2: Traceability in Software Workproducts

The graph that results is a representation of the horizontal traceability of the system to be maintained. It can be thought of as a collection of nodes partitioned into four categories, one for each of requirements, design, code and test. Figure 3 illustrates how the graph might look. Each category is represented in the figure by a box around its constituent nodes. Notice that there are additional edges within a box; these edges represent the vertical traceability for the particular workproduct represented by the box. (There is evidence that the vertical traceability links can be generated with information from the compiler and other static analysis tools [Wil87].) For example, the design box shows within it the relationship among the design components.

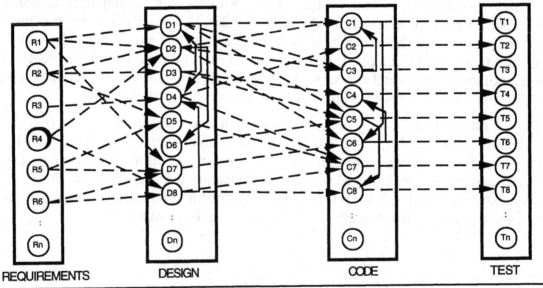

Figure 3: Underlying Graph for Maintenance

It is important to note that the edges are depicted differently. The solid lines are used for vertical traceability, while the dashed lines show horizontal traceability. In either case, (A,B) is ordered so that A provides input to B. Figure 4 shows the results of an example horizontal and vertical traceability SLO identification from Figure 3 on a change to requirement SLO 4.

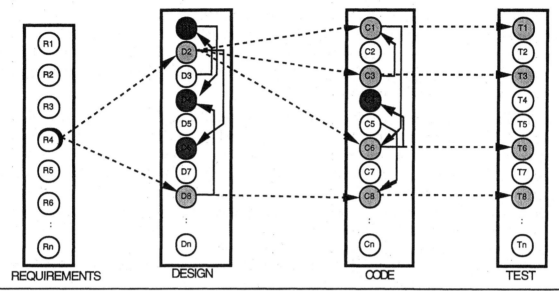

REQUIREMENTS   DESIGN   CODE   TEST

Figure 4: Determine Workproduct Impact

The lightly shaded circles are the horizontally traced objects while the darker shaded circle represent those objects that are vertically traced. The perspective is constrained to the software change for purposes of identifying potentially impacted workproducts and providing a reasonable foundation for a navigation tool.

5 Analyzing Software Change with Traceability

There is considerable evidence in the metrics literature that some measures of complexity and size are good indicators of likely cost and error rate [Car90], [Lew89], [Kaf87]. If the size and/or complexity of the graphs increases with the proposed change, there is reason to expect the size and complexity of the corresponding workproducts to increase as well. Using this information, software engineers may decide to implement the change in a different way or not at all.

The graphs proposed in this approach suggest a natural set of metrics to be used to evaluate the maintainability of the system whenever a change is proposed [Pfl90]. First, the change to vertical traceability for each workproduct can be assessed by examining the size and complexity of the vertical traceability graph within each "box". Complexity can be measured by examining the characteristics of the graph itself to determine how complex the resulting workproduct will be after a change. Size can be measured by counting the number of nodes, which correspond to the number of requirements, number of design components, and so on.

When considering vertical traceability, the goal is to keep node degrees small to minimize impact. For example, the in-degree of a node is the number of edges for which the node is the destination; the out-degree is the number of edges for which the node is the source. The out-degree of a node undergoing change indicates the number of nodes that are dependent on it and therefore likely to change as well. If this number is high, it may be prudent to partition the node such that the dependencies are more uniformly allocated across multiple nodes. Similarly, the in-degree represents the number of nodes that have a direct effect on a particular node. Keeping in-degree low may be a characteristic of good design.

The vertical traceability metrics are *product metrics* that reflect the effect of change on each workproduct being maintained. Examination of horizontal traceability requires the broader view of the maintenance process afforded by *process metrics*. To understand changes in horizontal traceability, the *relationships* among the workproducts and how they relate to the process as a whole must be understood.

The relationships among workproducts are represented by the dashed lines of the traceability graph. For each pair of adjacent workproducts, we can examine the subgraph formed by the nodes of the workproducts and the dashed lines that connect them to one another. In this way, we can form three graphs: one relating requirement to design, one relating design to code, and one relating code to testing. We then measure the each of the three relationship graphs for size and complexity, in the same way that we evaluated the workproduct graphs in the previous section. That is, we measure characteristics of the graph to tell us about the underlying workproducts and the effects of change. If a proposed change increases the size or complexity of the relationship between a pair of workproducts, the resulting system is likely to be more difficult to maintain.

Finally, we can use the entire horizontal traceability graph to tell us how overall traceability will be affected by a change. Measures such as cyclomatic complexity can be applied to the graph to determine if the overall system is likely to become more complex when the proposed change is made. Similarly, in-degree/out-degree, the number of nodes, and the number of edges can be used as indicators of decreasing maintainability.

Additional measures can aid software maintainers in deciding whether and how to make a change. For example, define a *tracing path* of the horizontal traceability graph to be a path from a requirement node to a design node to a code node to a test node. Thus, a tracing path traces the implementation of a requirement. A minimal set of tracing paths covers the horizontal traceability graph (that is, it includes every node of the graph). The *traceability* of a graph can be defined as the number of paths in the minimal set of tracing paths. Given a proposed change to the system, we can evaluate the impact of the change on the traceability metric. If traceability increases, the difficulty of maintaining the system should increase.

The next section discusses the use of impact analysis in design evolution. As software systems change, their traceability attributes can be monitored to determine if and when the changes are degrading the maintainability of the software. The impact analysis can steer the software design evolution clear of changes that disrupt the maintainability of the software.

6 Design Evolution

The software design of a system should respond to its anticipated changes. As changes are made to the system, the change dependencies or ripple-effect should be small and localized. Software change impact analysis provides a conduit for determining the change dependency information necessary to make design decisions, therefore supporting the software design with valuable information that ultimately leads to better design evolution.

The software change dependencies also provide useful information to guide the software maintainer through the design of the change so that the focus is on the relevant software workproducts and not the entire system. This reduces the complexity of the task as well as providing a roadmap of the change domain within the system.

Experiential data on the change history provides valuable information on how the software system can be designed. Assuming that a Pareto analysis discovers the twenty percent of the software that is effected by eighty percent of the changes, the software system design can be re-engineered accordingly. The changes can be categorized into related change clusters or domains to provide a basis for re-designing highly changed modules or objects. The clusters provide boundary information for partitioning the design so that changes are highly localized and the design remains relatively stable [Yau80]. Since past change histories often reflect future change trends, this clustering serves to reduce the complexity of the software system design with respect to anticipated changes. The result is that the software system design is more resilient to environmental changes (the ultimate goal of software design).

One simple but effective method of software change impact analysis used at Contel is the software change post-tracking. Essentially, changes are recorded along with the pertinent change dependencies during the change process. The change administrator receives these recorded change sets and places them in categories according to their characteristics. The result is a historical database of changes (and their impact information) that the maintenance staff uses to determine the most likely change dependencies associated with a current change request. Not only does this improve software change effort estimates by making visible the ramifications of the change, it also provides a mechanism to assess trends where the change extents are becoming large, where the partitioning of the software system design may be inappropriate, or when a part of the system may require re-engineering.

7 Conclusions

Software change is a key ingredient in the software maintenance activities. When impact of a software change is assessed, both horizontal and vertical dependencies must be integrated to yield a detailed impact analysis of the change. A software maintenance process that focuses on controlling changes from the beginning was proposed. This process provides a framework for impact analysis information to guide the maintainer through software changes. The impact analysis provides valuable information for the evolution of the software system design.

The maintenance process can be viewed from both a product and process perspective. In either case, traceability graphs are useful tools for impact analysis. The impact analysis presented here, including its graph representation and associated metrics, is algorithmic and automatable. That is, the graph representation is able to be analyzed with a host of techniques from graph theory. Additionally, the graph representation can be represented in the links of a hypermedia-based tool for navigating the software workproducts. The graphical presentation forms a communication and navigation paradigm for software maintenance activities. Just as abstraction helps us to analyze the key elements of the workproducts we create, so too does a graphical abstraction help us focus on the relationships among the components of the systems we maintain.

Software maintainers can use these and other metrics to understand and control software maintenance design evolution trends. As changes are requested, measurements can be made, impact assessed, and design decisions made. Moreover, the more we understand the impact, the less risk we take when making each change and the better that we can control software design degradation resulting from change.

8 References

[Big88]   J. Bigelow, "Hypertext and CASE", *IEEE Software*, March 1988.

[Boe76]   B. Boehm, "Software Engineering", *IEEE Transactions on Computers*, No. 25, Vol. 12, December 1976, pp. 1226-1242.

[Boe87]   B. Boehm, "Improving Software Productivity", *IEEE Computer*, September 1987, pp. 43-57.

[Bus88]   E. Bush, CASE for Existing Systems, *CASE Outlook*, Volume 2, No. 2, 1988, pp. 1, 6-15.

[Car90]   D. Card, and R. Glass, Measuring Software Design Quality, *Prentice-Hall, Englewood Cliffs, NJ*, 1990.

[Cle88]   L. Cleveland, "An Environment for Understanding Programs," *Proceedings of Conference on Software Maintenance*, 1988, pp. 500-509.

[Gar89]   P. Garg and W. Scacchi, "A Hypertext System to Manage Software Life Cycle Documents", *IEEE Software*, July 1989.

[Har69]   F. Harary, Graph Theory, *Addison-Wesley (Reading, MA)*, 1969.

[Har90]   J. Hartmann and D. Robson, ."Techniques for Selective Revalidation, *IEEE Software*, January 1990.

[Hen81]   S. Henry, and D. Kafura, "Software Structure Metrics Based on Information Flow," *IEEE Transactions on Software Engineering*, SE-7, September 1981, pp.509-518.

[Hor86]   E. Horowitz and R. Williamson, "SODOS: A Software Document Support Environment - Its Definition", *IEEE Transactions on Software Engineering*, VOl. SE-12 No.8, August 1986.

[Kaf87]   D. Kafura, and G. Reddy, "The Use of Software Complexity Metrics in Software Maintenance," *IEEE Transactions on Software Engineering*, SE-13(3) March 1987, pp. 335-343.

[Leh80]   M.M. Lehman, "Programs, Life Cycles, and Laws of Software Evolution", *Proceedings of the IEEE*, Vol. 68, No. 9, Sept. 1980, pp. 1060-1076.

[Leh85]   M.M. Lehman and L.A. Belady, "Program Evolution – Processes of Software Change," *Academic Press*, London, England, 1985.

[Lew89]   J. Lewis, and S. Henry, "A Methodology for Integrating Maintainability Using Software Metrics", *Proceedings of Conference on Software Maintenance*, October 1989, Miami Florida, pp. 32-39.

[Lie80]   B. P. Lientz and E. B. Swanson, Software Maintenance Management, *Addison-Wesley (Reading, MA)*, 1980.

[Mar83]   J. Martin and C. McClure, "Software Maintenance: The Problem and Its Solutions", *Prentice-Hall, [London]*, 1983.

[McC76]   T. J. McCabe, "A Complexity Measure," *IEEE Transactions on Software Engineering*, SE-2, December 1976, pp. 308-320.

[Par82]   G. Parikh, "Some Tips, Techniques, and Guidelines for Program and System Maintenance", Techniques of Program and System Maintenance, *Winthrop Publishers, [Cambridge, Mass.]*, 1982, pp. 65-70.

[Par85]   D. L. Parnas, P. C. Clements, and D. M. Weiss, "Modular Structure of Complex Systems", *IEEE Transactions on Software Engineering*, SE-II (3), March 1985.

[Pat83]   B. H. Patkau, "A Foundation for Software Maintenance", Ph.D. Thesis, Department of Computer Science, University of Toronto, December 1983.

[Pen84]   M. H. Penedo and E. D. Stuckle,"Integrated Project Master Database (PMDB), IR&D Final Report", TRW Technical Report, TRW-84-SS-22, December 1984, Released through Arcadia as Arcadia-TRW-89-008.

[Pfl87]   S. L. Pfleeger, Software Engineering, The Production of Quality Software, *MacMillian Publish Company (New York, NY)*, 1987.

[Pfl90]   S. L. Pfleeger and S. A. Bohner, "A Framework for Software Maintenance Metrics", *Proceedings of Conference on Software Maintenance*, November 1990.

[Pod90]   A. Podgurski and L. A. Clarke, "A Formal Model of Programming Dependencies and its Implications for Software Testing, Debugging, and Maintenance," *IEEE Transactions on Software Engineering*, Vol. 16, No. 9, September 1990, pp. 965-979.

[RAD86]   RADC-TR-86-197, "Automated Life Cycle Impact Analysis System", Rome Air Development Center, Air Force Systems Command, Griffiss Air Force Base, Rome, NY, December 1986.

[Rom89]   H. D. Rombach and B. T. Ulery, "Improving Software Maintenance through Measurement", *Proceedings of the IEEE*, No. 4, Vol. 77, April 1989, pp. 581-595.

[Sch89]   N. Schneidewind, "Software Maintenance: The Need for Standardization", *Proceedings of the IEEE*, No. 4, Vol. 77, April 1989, pp. 618-624.

[Sha77]   W. K. Sharpley, "Software Maintenance Planning for Embedded Computer Systems", *Proceedings of the IEEE COMPSAC*, November 1977, pp. 520-526.

[Swa89]   E. B. Swanson and C. M. Beath, Maintaining Information Systems in Organizations, *John Wiley and Sons, New York, NY*, 1989.

[Tah88]   A. Taha and S. Thebaut, "Program Change Analysis Using Incremental Data Flow Techniques", SERC-TR-26-F, Software Engineering Research Center, University of Florida, Gainesville, FL, January 1988.

[Wild87]   N. Wilde and B. Nejmeh, "Dependency Analysis: An Aid for Software Maintenance", SERC-TR-23-F, Software Engineering Research Center, University of Florida, Gainesville, FL, January 1987.

[Yau80]   S. S. Yau and J. S. Collofello, "Some Stability Measures for Software Maintenance", *IEEE Transactions on Software Engineering*, Vol. SE-6, No. 6, November 1980, pp. 545-552.

[Yau87]   S .S. Yau and J. J. Tsai, "Knowledge Representation of Software Component Interconnection information for Large-Sacle Software Modifications, *IEEE Transactions on Software Engineering*, Vol. SE-13, No. 3, March 1987, pp. 545-552.

[Yau88]   S. S. Yau and S. Liu, "Some Approaches to Logical Ripple Effect Analysis", SERC-TR-24-F, Software Engineering Research Center, University of Florida, Gainesville, FL, January 1988.

Configuration Management Survey

Gene Forte
CASE OUTLOOK Staff

In this article we review the range of capabilities and features now available in configuration management tools and relate these to the basic requirements for improved software development. An in-depth survey of leading CM products indicates how well the industry is currently satisfying developers' needs.

The role of configuration management (CM) has grown in importance over the years for a number of reasons. Software projects have grown larger resulting in many more components to be managed, which exponentially increases the difficulty of maintaining control. As projects expand, a point is reached at which CM without automation becomes infeasible. Unfortunately, if you fail to put CM in place at the start of a project, you can suddenly find that your project is out-of-control late in the schedule when you have the fewest options remaining. Failure to maintain configuration control typically accounts for many of the classic problems experienced during the testing and system integration phases of development, and perpetually throughout the maintenance life cycle. Here are some typical complaints:

- The latest version of a code module is lost
- System builds take too long to complete and are often repeated due to errors
- Bugs that were previously fixed reappear later in a subsequent application version
- Extensions or bug fixes are applied to the wrong version of a module
- There are synchronization problems among requirements documents, design representations, source code, executables, test data, test results, problem reports, etc.
- There is a low level of module reuse because developers can't find or don't trust the documentation
- There are general quality control and reliability problems and slow response to problem reports

The basic issues are becoming more acute due to the increasing size and complexity of software systems being built. Simultaneously, management is becoming more sensitive to growing backlogs and cost and schedule overruns because software is now more strategically important to the success of the enterprise. Software managers can no longer tolerate the delays and wasted effort caused by ineffective configuration management.

New Roles for Configuration Management

The sheer size of software applications is not the only factor contributing to the increased need for CM. New computing topologies, new application structures, changing division of responsibility between applications and system software, new design automation technology, and new relationships between information systems and the organization are all factors redefining the role of CM.

New Objects to Manage

The introduction of CASE tools has greatly increased the number of machine-readable objects that must be maintained in synchronization within the development environment. Data flow diagrams, E-R diagrams, structure charts, data dictionaries, state transition diagrams, database schemas, screen and report definitions all have to be related to each other and to specific source code and executable image versions. Many CASE tools guarantee consistency among the representations which they create and use explicitly; however, they do not guarantee consistency with external objects created by other tools, code created by hand, and so on. Consequently, a general-purpose CM facility is needed to serve in the role of a project-wide coordinator that extends across all tools and all phases of the life cycle.

Cooperative and Distributed Processing

The advent of cooperative (host-workstation) and distributed (peer-peer) processing introduces additional configuration complexities. Now we have to worry about synchronizing components of applications that may be developed, and will certainly be used, in different physical locations. Modifications to a subsystem on one platform may or may not affect the other subsystems, depending on how it affects the application interfaces. In the case of a central server, modifications may affect many different client applications (and many versions of those applications) that rely on it. Now we have a CM challenge that extends across time, space and different applications.

Enterprise Computing Environments

Even as computing systems are becoming architecturally more distributed, companies are looking for ways to enhance competitive advantage by integrating them more tightly in a functional sense. Companies are uniting divisions and business units by linking previously separate information systems and building "cross functional applications" that span the traditional boundaries. Again, this increases the complexity of the CM task by expanding the scope of dependency management across more software-related components. The impact of changing a software item, a data definition or a procedural policy can potentially spread across an entire organization. Not only do software developers need a comprehensive way to assess the impacts of change, but also a way to physically distribute changed components in an organized and timely manner.

Some companies are even experimenting with totally new application delivery modes in which they intro-

New computing topologies, new application structures, changing division of responsibility between applications and system software, new design automation technology, and new relationships between information systems and the organization are all factors redefining the role of CM.

duce new functionality in major releases across the entire corporation, rather than completing one application at a time. Such a strategy requires a very sophisticated and reliable CM mechanism that can identify the enterprise-wide impacts of change and keep track, not only of all versions of a software component, but also all the locations where versions exist and are in use.

Asset Management and Reusability

Traditionally, CM has played a role in software asset management at the source code level. Applications require good CM procedures to maintain their integrity over time as bug fixes and enhancements are introduced. A developer evaluating a module for reuse needs to have access to its documentation and feel confident that it accurately reflects the current state of the module. (S)he would also like access to design representations and test data to save time in making modifications and retesting. The traditional CM function needs enhancement in this area to provide efficient ways to automatically search through existing modules to find potentially reusable components.

With CASE tools we now have the potential to reuse designs as well as code modules, making CM an even more important aspect of a reuse strategy. We now need to manage data definitions, analysis and design diagrams, computational algorithms and policy rules that must be consistently applied. Under a reusability scenario, maintaining versions is not just a matter of replacing a component with an improved version, but of maintaining multiple variants that are derived from a common "generic" reusable component, and "tuned" for specific applications. Clearly, we would like a CM facility that not only recognizes that multiple versions exist and makes them accessible, but one that also provides information about the *content and purpose* of the variants.

In the area of asset management there appears to be significant overlap between an expanded CM role and the goal of a CASE repository. In a sense, the repository concept is the elaboration of the traditional role of the data dictionary to include many of the new items introduced by CASE technology. So far, the proper functionality for repositories versus CM facilities has not been completely sorted out. For example, IBM's Repository maintains information about the design objects in a CASE environment, including code modules, but does not directly perform the complete CM task itself with respect to source code maintenance. On the other hand, many CM systems can now manage virtually any type of object (diagrams, text, source code, etc.) at the file level but do not provide effective integration interfaces to CASE tools for on-line access. Where the needed capabilities ultimately reside will depend as much on market influences as technical priorities, and will differ from product to product. As an example, Figure 1 shows Softool's modular approach to integrating the CM function with the larger CASE environment. How the puzzle is assembled within a particular organization will be a primary challenge for those responsible for the firm's software development environment.

SOFTOOL'S LAYERED INTEGRATION ARCHITECTURE

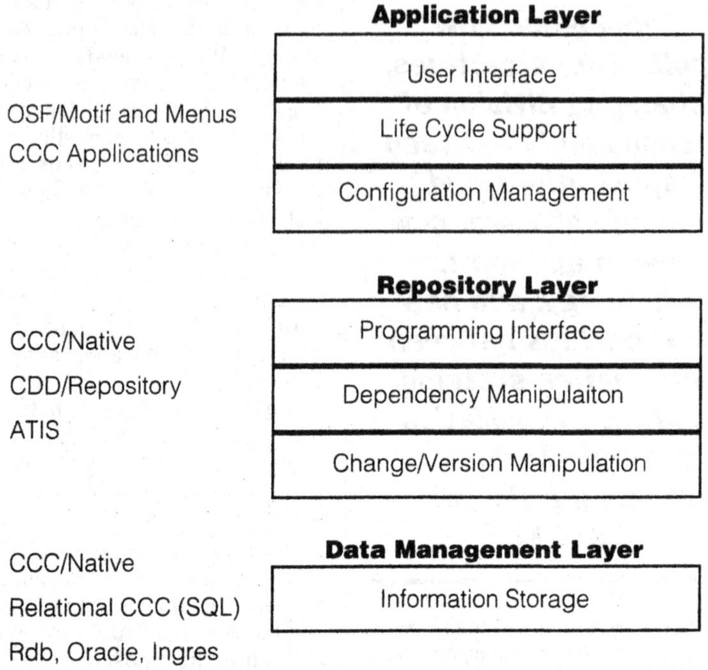

Application Layer

User Interface
Life Cycle Support
Configuration Management

OSF/Motif and Menus
CCC Applications

Repository Layer

Programming Interface
Dependency Manipulaiton
Change/Version Manipulation

CCC/Native
CDD/Repository
ATIS

Data Management Layer

Information Storage

CCC/Native
Relational CCC (SQL)
Rdb, Oracle, Ingres

Figure 1. Softool's layered architecture allows it to integrate with new software development technologies, such as CASE design tools and repositories.

CM and Software Maintenance

CM has always been a factor in software maintenance, since it provides the organizing mechanism for introducing new versions that extend capability or repair defects. With the tendency for software to operate on multiple platforms, CM becomes increasingly important since there may be many platform variants for each major release. In addition, software maintenance organizations often support multiple versions in the field, including alpha and beta test sites, and they are also responsible for testing new engineering releases. They must be able to recreate, on demand, both the latest and any previous release of an application (along with all its variants).

A major problem in such a scenario is maintaining synchronization between Software Problem Reports (which describe an observed defect), Software Change Requests (which define a fix to be applied), and the actual software artifacts. Consequently, some CM systems have been extended to incorporate a defect tracking facility that organizes the change-driving documents, provides a task assignment mechanism and monitors the current status of activity related to each request.

Configuration Management and Software Quality

Because effective CM can have an immediate effect on the quality and productivity of software without changing the design methodology in use, CM tools may be the logical first step for bringing software automation into an organization. In fact, the Software Engineering Institute (SEI) identifies basic configuration man-agement as a requirement for getting to the first stage of software development process maturity. At its most basic, CM eliminates much of the confusion of software versions evident in the common complaints we listed above. More sophisticated CM products go further by actually defining and enforcing a development model with well-defined stages, deliverables for each stage and transition criteria for moving between stages. In some cases, the CM product is flexible enough to permit the organization to model its own process, and to change it when needed to implement a Continuous Process Improvement program. Given this perspective, CM can play an important part at all five stages of process maturity defined by the SEI.

Because effective CM can have an immediate effect on the quality and productivity of software without changing the design methodology in use, CM tools may be the logical first step for bringing software automation into an organization.

Just as the CM function overlaps with the repository concept, it also relates to the notion of an Integrated Project Support Environment (IPSE) or Software Integration Framework (we use the terms interchangeably). Most existing IPSEs, such as Esprit's *PCTE*, Softlab's *Maestro*, and Atherton's *Software BackPlane*, have basic facilities that enable the CM function. Often there is a distribution of basic mechanisms; for example, there may be an underlying link management or object management facility that permits the definition

Key CM Issues in Software Development and Maintenance

Alex Lobba, Softool Corp.

With new approaches to software development such as rapid prototyping, distributed relational databases and CASE, the role of configuration management is changing. Here are some of the issues that are emerging as key drivers for CM technology and products.

Impact Analysis–Projects usually end up running over schedule. Software managers and engineers do not have up-front information to size the impact of a proposed change. As a project progresses it is necessary to ensure that all the needed components are tested and included in the released change package. A very high percentage of production "crises" are the result of incomplete testing and, given the way that systems keep evolving, hidden impact is more and more probable. Finally, there is the migration nightmare: how can a system be ported if even the isolation of a subsystem (or any part of it) is practically impossible without impact analysis?

Change Packaging–Typically, a fix or enhancement affects multiple components. Test and production re-runs are often caused by missing pieces. Change packaging groups together components modified for the same reason (e.g., a specific change request) and ensures that no items are left behind in the migration between stages of approval. This issue also relates to impact analysis: the change package can only be guaranteed (all impacted pieces included) if complete impact analysis is included.

Block Point Release–When a new release is due, things get very hectic, and there are always one or two fixes holding up everything else. Also, engineers work on multiple releases at the same time. Assigning change requests to a given release and being able to transfer all their changes from one release to the next eliminates last minute log jams and provides up-to-date status information.

Configuration Views vs. Individual Items–Managing an application from the perspective of different, dynamic views (e.g., development, test, approved, release 1, release 2).

Configuration Management vs. Dependency Management–Because of the lack of standards, configuration management is a very ill-defined term. The most ambitious goal of CM is to be able to maintain many views of a system as "snapshots" taken at different moments in time or in different states or stages. This concept has been confused in many cases with a related but simpler problem: the control of dependencies between components before and after a given event. This is equivalent to replacing a two-dimensional problem (that of representing any number of simultaneously existing snapshots of the system) with a linear one (taking two of them and concentrating on the differences between them).

Vendor Code–Most users of vendor code modify the source supplied with it, and then, when the new release shows up, they have no efficient way to include their existing modifications with the new release. The result is that they typically run versions of the system that are two or three releases behind the current one. The solution is to understand what changed in both "branches," create a view that will hold the new system, understand the impact of conflicting changes and apply changes across the systems. These steps are essentially the concepts of change management, configuration management, impact analysis and change application, respectively.

Parallel Development–A part of all systems is typically common across them (common code). Common code is usually the most frequently changed code precisely because it belongs to multiple systems. Access conflicts happen, and more than one developer needs to modify a component. Often they simply create a copy of the code and modify it, with the unwanted side effect that the latest change to be migrated overwrites a previous one. The CM solution is to keep branches isolated and to track them separately and automatically. The CM system constrains migration, prevents inadvertent overwrites and assists in the merging of variant branches. A related facility, called "life-cycle visibility," is to notify all parties affected by a change. In many ways, the parallel development problem is more a management problem than a technical one, although CM facilities can relieve the extensive bookkeeping task and minimize errors.

Role of PCs–More and more development is being done on PCs and workstations in cooperative mode due to the emergence of PC COBOL compilers and testing tools, emulators and bridges (e.g., CICS and DB2) and cooperative architectures (SAA, NAS, New Wave, etc.). PCs are used mainly in the initial design and coding phases where it is believed there are no big migration concerns. Sources "go out" to the PC-LAN (or stand-alone PCS) and after a while changed items are brought back into the mainframe-controlled area. Whatever happens in the middle is the "PC Black Hole," even if you have total control on the mainframe side. As PC development environments become more powerful, we are seeing a growing need for change and configuration control that is tightly integrated with the mainframe environment.

DB2–The most advanced relational DBMSs, such as (but not limited to) DB2, create a need for sophisticated, integral configuration management because of the separation of logical and physical layers which creates an additional binding step. In this environment, change and configuration control of DB2 objects must extend to all attributes that are important for the application's life cycle such as format and change history, data distribution, access authorization, indexes, field procedures and locking conditions.

Release and Distribution Management–It is becoming more and more common for development to be done in a single location with the actual production execution spread across multiple remote sites, not all of which are necessarily running identical hardware or operating system platforms. In this scenario how do you make sure that all (and only) the right changes are propagated to each and every production environment and that the changes are properly synchronized? This is just the start of a more global definition of configuration management, where the "configurations" do not necessarily reside exclusively within tightly connected environments. What is needed is multi-platform CM with tighter connectivity across heterogeneous environments.

Emergency Maintenance–Independently of how structured the normal life cycle is, emergencies happen (in many cases they are the only changes applied to very old systems). Facilities are required that permit urgent fixes and prevent those fixes from being inadvertently over-written by changes applied later. This is equivalent to feeding changes through the wrong end of the life cycle and making sure that they are not covered by changes coming the other way.

Buying Influences–There are several layers (and corresponding organizational layers) affected and involved with CM. On the one hand CM is an inherently technical issue, because it deals with the "entropy" or complexity of the system in a continuously changing environment. A lack of CM adversely affects technical developers, testers, migrators, and other technical staff. On the other hand, the benefits of CM can be capitalized in an optimal way only by putting its basic functionality to work serving cross life cycle support functions which are the main concern of project leaders, and mid-level managers concerned with development, QA and integration. Although the implementation of CM permeates many layers, including very technical ones, it requires substantial commitments from high level management to succeed. The challenge then is to relate an intrinsically technical problem to tangible benefits that high level management can (literally) buy in to.

and management of dependencies been objects in the environment. The mechanism may also generate notification events when objects are accessed or modified. Components that provide traditional CM capabilities may then be built on top and take advantage of the underlying mechanism, in effect plugging into the environment as a special-purpose tool, albeit one that is useful across the entire life cycle (i.e., a *cross life cycle* tool).

Besides keeping track of file versions and configurations, some CM systems overlap with CASE frameworks by providing elements of context management. This means that developers can create unique views or subsets of the total project file system that relate to their specific interests and responsibilities. This has the immediate advantage of reducing intellectual complexity by limiting the amount of information the developer has to contend with (i.e., directory structures are simplified). For example, name conflicts among developers are prevented since each name is unique to a specific context. When associated with security provisions, like passwords, context management can also be a mechanism for restricting access so that developers don't inadvertently "step on" each other's designs.

Context management also relates to parallel development strategies. For example, two developers might each be permitted to have copies within their own contexts of a module taken from a "project" context. The CM environment will determine under what circumstances either of the two versions may replace the project version, and also keep track of any conflicts resulting from the fact that the two versions differ.

The future relationship between CM products and IPSE products will, as in the case of repositories, evolve over time in response to technological and market influences. As a result, we'll see IPSEs that offer CM capabilities–such as Softlab's *Maestro*, Atherton Technology's *Configuration Management*

SoftBoard, and Benchmark Technologies' *ISPW*–as well as CM products that support tool integration, such as Softool's *CCC* and CaseWare's *Amplify Control (see Figure 2)*.

General requirements for CM

Given our general discussion of new CM challenges, let's define the specific capabilities that you might look for in a CM product. In the survey segment of this article, we'll describe features of the leading CM products in terms of these definitions. Because of the overlap with repositories and IPSEs mentioned above, and the expected rapid evolution anticipated in the CM field, we have created a very broad framework for evaluating CM products. Virtually no products address all the defined capabilities at the present time, although some come close. Hopefully, the framework will have some longevity as the field progresses.

Version Control

Basic version control maintains multiple versions of a source code file. File and directory naming or other schemes needed to keep the versions separate are handled by the CM system. The developer simply asks for the latest version or a specific earlier version using a common file name. The version control function includes the ability to track how a component of software arrived through successive generations to its present state. It allows the developer to isolate the changes between one version and the next, and to return to previous versions if desired. To save storage, a differencing mechanism is usually employed in which only a baseline (starting state) and changes from the baseline for each subsequent version are actually saved. Intermediate versions are regenerated from this information upon request.

AMPLIFY CONTROL ARCHITECTURE

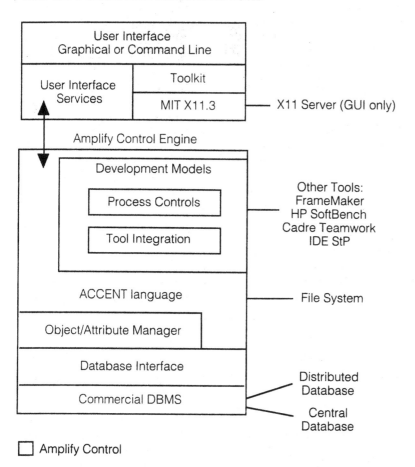

Amplify Control

Figure 2. CaseWare's Amplify Control architecture builds functionality on top of existing DBMS and windowing technology. Major components include process control and tool interfaces integrated with a development model definition facility based on the proprietary ACCENT language. An object management system is based on one of several underlying commercial databases. The graphical user interface is built on X-Windows for portability.

Version control has grown more sophisticated with the ability to support multiple derivatives from a common ancestor, a capability called *branching* or *variant versions*. This is useful for supporting multiple platforms or for trying several approaches to a design in parallel. If branching is supported, then the CM system must provide some type of *long transaction mechanism* to control when copies of a module may be checked out and checked back in without allowing developers to inadvertently destroy each others' changes.

Configuration Control

Basic configuration control expands on the version control idea by allowing sets of files to be associated with each other as a group or system. All the files that are part of an application can be associated with a *system baseline*. As the components of the system are modified, new system versions are created and the specific versions of each module that make up subsequent systems are automatically tracked. Thus, the CM hierarchy is extended to include the notion of a composite system object, which may also have parallel version branches, where each system version comprises a specific set of components, each having its own independent version.

System Building

To further automate the job of creating system versions, CM systems also incorporate build facilities that take responsibility for collecting all the required source files, compiling them and linking them into an executable object. First generation build facilities, like the UNIX Make tool, required the developer to build very explicit scripts to direct the building activity. Improvements on this scheme include automatic determination and location of the latest module version based on a generic script, and the incorporation of "rules" that can be interpreted at build time. For example, the build procedure may be instructed to use modules in the "released" state, which are not necessarily the latest versions in existence if development of the next version is in process. To improve the reliability and repeatability of system builds, the most sophisticated tools maintain information about the compiler and linker versions and the compiler and linker options used to generate the system.

Reporting and Query Capabilities

As the CM function is viewed more in terms of a quality management program, the reporting and querying capability of CM tools become increasingly important. A range of information can be derived from the CM system including:

• The specific version history of a module or a system (how often has it been changed and why)

• What specific changes occurred between one version of a module and the next

• Who changed a module, when and why

• How versions correspond to problem reports and change authorizations

• Which modules will be affected by a proposed change; which modules will have to be recompiled and linked

Such tracking information helps the development manager plan schedules and costs, helps the QA manager ensure that procedures are being followed consistently, and assists developers looking for possible sources of discrepancies in new software versions. Ideally, all of this information is available both on line in interactive mode and through printed reports.

Traceability

A specific type of "meta data" that relates directly to quality control is *requirements tracing* information. A fundamental premise of modern quality control is that quality means conformance to requirements. To make quality control a practical reality in software, requirements must be defined and measurable–and to measure how well a requirement is met, you must know where it is satisfied in the deliverable item (forward tracing). The flip side of conformance is that the product should not have features that were not specified. To ensure this you must be able to verify that every deliverable function was derived from a requirement (reverse tracing).

As it is currently implemented in most CM systems, requirements tracing allows developers to tag file versions with identifiers that are propagated with new versions of the file. New identifiers can be appended along the way and are also propagated forward. Subsequently, developers can report on which modules, and which versions of modules, satisfy specific requirements (forward tracing) or what requirements are satisfied by a given module (reverse tracing).

With the introduction of CASE tools, the traceability problem is complicated. Besides an expanding number of machine readable objects that are potentially traceable from requirements throughout the development life cycle, there is the added issue of *granularity*, or the size of the smallest unit of information that can be traced to a requirement. Whereas individual source code files tend to represent fairly small "chunks" of design information (ideally, single-function modules), this is not true of higher level representations like structure charts or dataflow diagrams. Many case tools save a complete high-level diagram (encompassing many objects and functions) as a single file, so traditional file-level traceability tools can only associate requirements with an entire diagram, which is generally too course a granularity to be very useful. Consequently, there is a growing need to permit requirements tracing at a level smaller than a file.

To accommodate this need, as well as providing other benefits, some CM systems are really more than file management systems, they are sophisticated database management systems that can deal with very small items of information, down to a single data element. Thus, a CM system might be able to tag a specific change in a source file (e.g., a single line of code) with related requirements information and allow traceability to that level.

Traceability is another area of overlap between CM tools and the repository concept, since a CASE repository allows design elements, such as a single transform or dataflow from a DFD, to be managed and related to requirements information individually, thus providing the level of traceability needed. The problem is that few existing CASE tools are interfaced with a project-wide repository and continue to manage their information in files, which CM tools cannot access internally. In addition, existing repositories are not designed to store entire files, such as source code modules, so the native file system or CM system is still used to actually perform file manipulation, although meta data about the file (file name, access path, version, associated requirements, etc.) may be stored in the repository itself. As in the case of context management, the ultimate solution may involve targeted CM functionality built on top of a more generalized object management system (with granularity smaller than the file level) provided by a CASE integration framework or IPSE.

Development Process Control

A final major area of support provided by advanced CM systems is development process control. CM systems contribute in several ways:

• By controlling who can make changes to the software

• By documenting the changes

• By requiring that development follow a defined process with explicit stages and transitions

• By automating the migration of controlled items through the development process

The process control functions of the CM system are built on top of the capabilities already described. For example, context management facilities can be used to define several separate file areas corresponding to the stages of a company-specific software life cycle. The areas might correspond to "development stage," "testing stage" and "production stage," for example. Access to each area is carefully controlled by the CM system so that, for example, after promotion to the testing stage, only QA personnel can access the component versions belonging to the system under test. However, new enhancements could be started simultaneously by modifying the latest version of the system kept in the development area.

Rather than having developers move files from one area to the next individually, a complete new system baseline is defined and automatically "moved" to the next stage by the CM system (actually, pointers to the original baseline and version "deltas" are often used to save space). Automatic checks may be included to determine that all required deliverables have been authorized for promotion before migration of the system to the next stage can occur.

The most flexible CM products allow the user organization to implement its own development process by defining company-specific stages, access policies, promotion criteria and tracking reports. Interfaces facilities can also allow the CM system to interact with other facilities such as electronic mail, project management and documentation systems.

Differentiating Features of CM Products

In selecting a CM system for your organization, the first criteria is that it run in your operating environment. The major groupings here are IBM mainframe (MVS, VM), VAX/VMS, UNIX and PC. Most UNIX-targeted products are highly portable across the various "flavors," and several products offer equivalent functionality under VMS and UNIX. The mainframe products tend to be highly tailored to a specific operating system and DBMS in order to automate more of the complex details of building systems in these environments. For example, the complexities of database binding (DB2), library access, timesharing, transaction processing and job control are largely hidden by products such as Benchmark Technologies' ISPW (see Figure 3).

User Interface

The user interface can be command line driven, forms driven or graphical. The forms approach, such as that used by Softool's *CCC*, can help customize the CM tasks to a specific job role, e.g., developer, QA specialist, manager, project librarian, and so on. Graphical interfaces can help users understand the version history of a system and how it is constructed from modules. For example, CaseWare's *Amplify* and HP/Apollo's *DSEE* show version branch trees and configuration diagrams as shown in Figure 4.

Variety of Object Types

Originally, CM meant source code control, and all CM systems are adept at managing text files. Some store the original file (baseline) and all differences (difference sets) that comprise later versions, a technique sometimes referred to as the *sequential model*. Most products save the latest version and differences that are used to regenerate previous versions on the assumption that this will save processing time in the majority of cases. An alternative approach, called the *integrated model*, is to save all the code elements (e.g., source lines) that were ever present in the file in a database, and to build each source version on the fly from the individual elements. The integrated approach was invented to deal with the complexities of parallel development and multiple

MANAGING COMPLEX BUILD ENVIRONMENTS

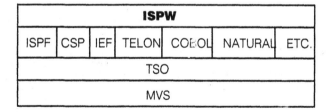

Source: Benckmark Technologies

Figure 3. Products targeted for the mainframe environment must be able to handle very complex build processes and a wide variety of application development objects. Benchmark Technologies' ISPW provides a simplified interface between the developer and many of the tools and activities involved in mainframe development, including change control, regeneration, migration and delivery, audit compliance, status tracking, space management and change impact reporting.

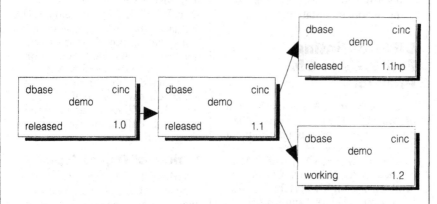

Figure 4. CaseWare's Amplify Control provides a graphical view of the version history of a particular component (in this case, a source file). Graphical renditions are also provided to represent configurations and the system build process.

version branches. It is particularly effective for the case where a developer wants to merge branches or apply a change across several branches at the same time.

With the expanding array of development work products introduced by CASE, many CM products have been extended to control a variety of object types, including:

- Source code
- Data definitions
- Database schema and procedures
- Screen and report definitions
- Design diagrams and models
- Test data and results
- Textual documentation
- System configuration information
- Job control language

Most products, however, still rely on a text comparison "differencing algorithm" to save disk space. Consequently, they cannot provide the degree of storage efficiency for diagrams and other non-textual objects–they merely save each version as a complete file. A few products also employ binary compaction schemes that can operate on any type of file, but they are usually less efficient than text differencing applied to text files.

Granularity of Objects and Object Relationships

CM products are beginning to offer management capabilities for objects other than native operating system files. In one approach, a CM database is associated with the file system so that "meta data" can be linked with file versions, and composite objects consisting of multiple files (e.g., an application system) can be defined and tracked. Dependencies and relationships between files are maintained in the database. This is essentially the same as providing hooks from a repository by which it can manage files stored externally by the native file system. Softool's *CCC*, HP/Apollo's *DSEE*, Legent's *Endevor* and Benchmark Technologies' *ISPW* represent such an approach. The advantage is that the CM system can manage the files used by other CASE tools without any modification to those tools.

A more fundamental approach is to provide a true object management system, that is, an object-oriented database facility that can directly manage a wide variety of user-defined object types, not just those recognized by the native file system. This has the advantage of providing a direct link management facility between objects supporting advanced features such as require-

ments traceability at arbitrary levels of granularity (e.g. by data element or process), type-specific compaction techniques and more dynamic process control functionality. The disadvantage of this approach is that all the development tools whose work products are managed by the object management system must be directly connected to the object interface, i.e., their internal code must be modified so they input and output objects rather than files. Products that offer object-oriented capabilities (although they can also operate at the file level) include Atherton Technology's *Software BackPlane* and Sun's *NSE*.

User-Defined Attributes and Reporting

Besides the typical information tracked by a CM product, it is often desirable to append other company-specific information to the CM records. This might include defect information, labor and cost statistics, approvals, textual annotation, and so on. A common feature is a CM user interface for custom meta data that appears as a relational database with an extensible schema so the user can configure the system to suite her/his needs. A general-purpose report writer is also a useful adjunct to help the user create customized documentation of the development process.

Besides a batch-oriented report capability, it is helpful to have as much of the information available online as possible, accessible through a standard query language such as SQL or a "query-by-example" facility. Many of the CM products surveyed allow the user to "navigate" through the CM database in a number of ways, for example, by version, by system baseline, by change set, by Problem Report or Change Authorization number, and so on.

Parallel Development Support

Many CM products provide support for parallel development by supporting multiple projects simultaneously, giving each project a completely separate file area and by tracking the development process (e.g., the promotion sequence) independently. Of course, any product that operates in a mainframe or LAN environment must support multi-user access. Access mechanisms vary, but the two main approaches are check-in/check-out and copy-modify-merge. The *check-in/check-out* approach is the simplest—when a component is checked out for modification, it is locked and no one else is allowed to modify it, although other team members may view the component or make copies. However, once a file is locked, none of the subsequent copies can be checked back into the controlled area.

The *copy-modify-merge* approach permits parallel development of a module, perhaps to try alternate solutions to a bug, or to create vari-ants for different target platforms. More than one copy of the module can be taken and modified, and maintained in separate version branches. Later, all descendents from a common source can be merged, usually with automatic detection of conflicts (i.e., changes to the same source code line in more than one file). Resolution of conflicts is the responsibility of the person doing the merge.

CM Models and Model Definition Facilities

CM products differ most widely in their adoption of various software development models, and in their ability to define custom models. Some products deal primarily with version histories, i.e., they are essentially file oriented. Others allow most functions—such as reporting, archiving, promotion to the next stage of development, or rolling back to a previous version–to be performed on groups of files alternately called a system, collection, model or assembly. Differences between system versions may be captured as "change sets" which consolidate all the variations across all components from one system version to the next.

Some models view the software development process as a sequence of states through which a system passes toward production status *(see Figure 5)*. In some cases, roles are associated with each of the states so that only certain tasks and options are presented via the user interface, depending on the current state and the identity of the user. The possible transition paths between states are defined and specific enabling criteria may be associated with the transitions, such as requiring authorizations or certain checks to be

A CM DEVELOPMENT MODEL

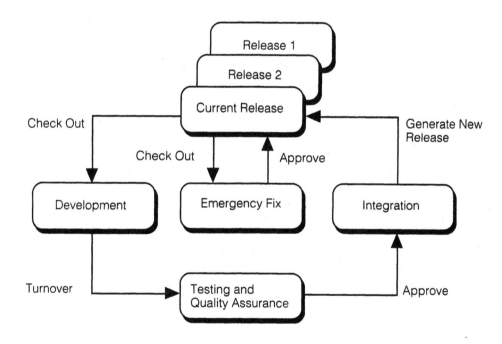

Source: Softool Corporation.

Figure 5. Configuration management products can help manage the software development process by supporting and enforcing a well-defined development model with specific stages, transition paths and transition criteria.

91

performed. When transitions occur, as when a system is promoted from development to testing, triggers associated with the transition may invoke other actions, such as the notification, via e-mail, of anyone who needs to know about the event.

CM tools are now emerging that can incorporate sophisticated process models defined by the user through a customization language. Often the language can also be used to integrate the CM system with other tools and facilities in the environment. For example, CaseWare's *Amplify* has as associated language called *Accent* used to define a development model with states such as "Working," "Testing," "In QA" and "Released," and to establish standards for version control, configuration control, automated builds, security and access control, and tool integration. Using Accent, the user can define permissible status levels for components and define what actions can be performed by individuals based on both the component status and the user's group and role.

Problem Tracking

An area of opportunity for integrating CM with other functions is in the area of testing and problem tracking. By integrating a problem tracking system with the CM facility, the task of determining which bugs have been fixed and what feature requests have been implemented in a given release are greatly simplified. This is particularly important for maintaining software programs in the field, whether commercial products or in-house applications distributed throughout the corporation. For example, Softool's *CCC* provides an interface to their *Kinsman* product, a "help desk" tool designed to support a phone-based support function by managing software trouble reports and their resolution.

Distributed Operation

Except for mainframe-only products, most CM tools operate in a multi-user environment under UNIX, VMS or a PC-based LAN. Using network file-access protocols such as NFS, a CM tool can easily manage file versions located on a central file server. More advanced tools can manage a project with files located in multiple physical locations, and can build systems from files distributed across the network. HP/Apollo's *DSEE* product can also employ the distributed computing environment by automatically initiating parallel compile operations on multiple platforms during a system build in order to reduce elapsed time.

Tool Integration Facilities

Several CM products provide interfaces to other tools that provide a measure of integration between the CM function and other development activities such as, design, testing and project management. The interfaces range in sophistication from simple data export facilities to integration facilities approaching that of a full-scale IPSE. Integration capabilities include:

• Invoking other tools from the CM user interface, e.g., starting up an editor when a source file is checked out

• Initiating CM procedures from other CASE products, e.g., automatically checking out a dataflow diagram by opening it within a CASE analysis tool

• Initiating action in other tools automatically, e.g., starting a design rule checker automatically when a file is checked in or sending mail when a baseline is promoted to the next stage of development

• Sharing information between the CM system and other tools, e.g., providing the project tracking system with information about task completions and module status, or sending current version information to a librarian tool

Many CM systems already have turnkey interfaces to a variety of popular CASE tools.

CM Vendor Contacts

Advanced Technology International, 212-354-8280

Atherton Technology, 408-734-9822

Benchmark Technologies, Ltd., 403-269-7499

Cadre Technologies, 401-351-5950

CaseWare, Inc., 714-754-0308

Computer Associates, 201-874-9000 or local sales office

Digital Equipment Corp., 508-467-6780 or local sales office

Expertware, 408-746-0706

HP/Apollo, 408-746-5601 or local sales office

IBM, local sales office

Legent Corp., BST Division, 508-366-8100

Pansophic Systems, 800-323-7335 or local sales office

Sage Software, Polytron Division, 503-645-1150

Softlab, 415-957-9175

Softool, 805-683-5777

Software Maintenance & Development Systems, Inc., 508-369-7398

Sun Microsystems, 415-960-1300 or local sales office

Team One Systems, 800-442-6650

Yard Software Systems (U.K.), 44-249-656194

Survey

In our survey of configuration management products we have included not only products positioned squarely in the CM niche, but also those with CM functionality added to other capabilities, as in the case of Cadre's *Teamwork* product which is primarily a design workbench. We have also included CASE frameworks that incorporate CM features, such as Atherton's *Software BackPlane.*

Table 1 on page 38 consolidates the results of our survey conducted in August 1990. The entries are based on the definitions found in the following sidebar. The column titled "Lexicon" provides a list of common features found among CM products in each capability category to give the reader a better feeling for what functionality is being identified. A comparison of the product feature list to the lexicon is not necessarily a measure of completeness, since in some cases the choices in the lexicon are mutually exclusive or express tradeoff alternatives.

///

Chapter 3
Automated Support for Impact Analysis

Purpose

Automated support is essential for effective impact analysis. There is considerable work in identifying change impacts in the many software artifacts produced during development and maintenance. This chapter gives you examples of impact-analysis tools and environments.

The Papers

In the first paper, "The Integrated CASE Manifesto," Alan Simon outlines his predictions for integrated computer-assisted software-engineering technology. Integration – the "I" in I-CASE – is described in terms of data, control, presentation, process, and platform. Simon discusses the 10 "must haves" of I-CASE, of which the first two are bidirectional traceability across tools and life-cycle steps and bidirectional impact analysis. These must haves give a reasonable case for impact analysis being at the core of future CASE tools and their repositories.

The next paper, "A Practical Software Maintenance Environment," consolidates dependency-analysis concepts and software change. In a discussion of software-maintenance environments, James Collofello and Mikael Orn discuss automation to support software-maintenance tasks. These include understanding software, changing software, tracing ripple-effects, releasing changed software, documenting acquired knowledge, and planning/scheduling maintenance tasks. In ripple-effect analysis, the authors' descriptions of relationships is particularly interesting because they describe the use of impact analysis during maintenance.

In the next paper, "Intelligent Support for Software Development and Maintenance," Gail Kaiser, Peter Feiler, and Steven Popovich apply artificial intelligence to make a software-engineering environment sensitive to the changes done within it. Their project, Professor Marvel (or Marvel for short), supports two aspects of an intelligent assistant.

First, it models some system structure and relationships in the software product to make developers aware of the consequences of the tasks being performed. Marvel's model of relationships is interesting from the impact-analysis perspective because it addresses the dependencies of evolving software artifacts. Second, Marvel participates in development activities through "opportunistic" processing. Marvel detects jobs that it can do and does them so that the developer is relieved of some of the burden.

The final paper is "Maintenance Support for Object-Oriented Programs" by Norman Wilde and Ross Huitt. This paper is based on the authors' exploration of dependency-analysis tools and their application to object-oriented programs. It builds on work they presented in earlier papers [Wilde 1987], [Wilde 1989]. In one of those [Wilde 1989], they broadly discuss the capabilities necessary for tracing program dependencies and visualizing programs. They examine the context in which dependency-analysis tools can be used and give some perspectives on commercial tools to support software analysis. The focus in this paper is on issues in object-oriented programs such as inheritance and polymorphism.

References

[Wilde 1987]   N. Wilde and B. A. Nejmeh, "Dependency Analysis: An Aid for Software Maintenance," Tech. report SERC-TR-23-F, Software Eng. Research Center, Univ. of Florida, Gainsville, Fla., Jan. 1987.

[Wilde 1989]   N. Wilde, R. Huitt, and S. Huitt, "Dependency Analysis Tools: Reusable Components for Software Maintenance," Tech. report SERC-TR-26-F, Software Eng. Research Center, Univ. of Florida, Gainsville/Purdue Univ., West Lafayette, Ind., Jan. 1989; also in *Proc. of Conf. on Software Maintenance*, IEEE CS Press, Los Alamitos, Calif., 1989, pp. 126-131.

The Integrated CASE Manifesto

by Alan Simon

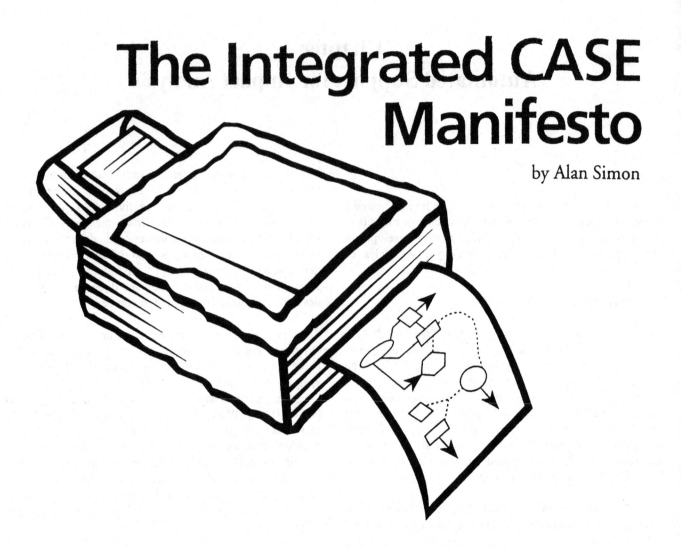

Almost from the inception of CASE technology, there has been a demand for integration and interoperability among tools. From the sharing of design information to varying degrees of control integration and notification, the desire for integration has been directed not only at products and tools from a single vendor, but also at cooperative software engineering support through products from different software companies and even home-grown tools.

PROMISES, PROMISES

During the late 1980s and early 1990s, a great deal of talk — some would say "hype" — regarding integrated CASE (or I-CASE) focused on almost magical integration frameworks into which tools from many different vendors could not only share data but also be automatically notified of each and every change within the enterprise that affected them. The software industry in general was carried away by the visions and promise of the I-CASE movement, from common user interfaces to massive, monolithic, and finely granular repositories storing gigabytes or even terabytes of CASE-oriented data.

Alas, it wasn't as easy as we had thought . . . or at least hoped. Neither standardization efforts nor vendor-sponsored frameworks nor any other base technologies were sufficient to bring about the wonderful world of integrated CASE we envisioned being just around the corner.

"The Integrated CASE Manifesto" by A. Simon from *American Programmer*, July 1994, pp. 3–7.

But all is not lost. Vendors have renewed their efforts, in some cases stepping back from integration strategies of the recent past and considering new integration and interoperability models. As CASE-specific standardization efforts such as ANSI X3H6 (CASE control integration) and the Portable Common Tools Environment (PCTE) trudge forward, the "survivors" in the CASE industry have pursued new avenues of integrating their tools with others — a trend that will no doubt continue.

We must ask one question, though, as the vendor community moves ahead with integration and interoperability: What exactly *is* integrated CASE?

On the surface, the five points of integration espoused by Tony Wasserman of Interactive Development Environments, Inc., of San Francisco (referenced in [1]) are representative of the different forms of integration that should be considered. These integration points are:

1 Data — the ability of one tool to share data with another

2 Control — the ability of one tool to send control information to another and to receive and service control requests from other tools

3 Presentation — a common user interface

4 Process — the ability to participate in the same methodology

5 Platform — the ability to run on the same platform or communicate with one another across heterogeneous platforms through basic connectivity and interoperability services (e.g., messaging, remote procedure calls)

THE 10 "MUST HAVES" OF I-CASE

One could argue that the five integration points listed above are more *categories* into which integration might fall than they are features users must have in order for tool integration and interoperability to be of real value to them. I would offer instead the following list of 10 requirements as a manifesto for CASE integration for the rest of the 1990s.

Given the rapid changes in the CASE community, particularly in the past year or so, it is of little value to point out that such-and-such a vendor offers several of these features but not others, while some other software company provides other features but not those provided by the first. Rather, use this manifesto as both a checklist and a wish list against which you can compare tool suites and pairs and from which you can make requests (read "demands") of CASE tool vendors and providers of tools that integrate those tools.

1. Bidirectional Traceability Across Tools and Life-Cycle Steps

One of the most time-consuming tasks systems developers face, especially those involved in migration and transition programs, is developing traceability matrices and charts manually. Particularly when legacy systems are involved in the process, there is a genuine worry about ensuring that all the necessary source data elements are transitioned into the target environment, that all source business processes that are to survive business process reengineering do so, and so on. Of course, as we'll see in the examples below, traceability doesn't necessarily have to deal with the legacy system transition space. It can also apply to the systems development life cycle, from requirements and business needs analysis through implementation and operation.

By "bidirectional" I mean that two classes of questions must be answered. The first class deals with source-to-target traceability, while the second class is for target-back-to-source linkages. Examples of questions from the two classes include:

Forward Traceability

★ "Of all the source data elements in subject area CUSTOMERS within my legacy environment, how many are currently included in the target environment CUSTOMERS subject area, and what is their current relational form?"

★ "Of all the requirements collected during the business needs analysis phase of our methodology, which ones have been implemented and fully tested? Which ones have been designed but have not yet been implemented? Which ones have been implemented but are awaiting testing?"

Reverse Traceability

★ "I'm looking at target environment subject area STORES. What was the source of these data elements in the legacy environment, and exactly what mappings were used to establish the target data?"

★ "What requirements are supposed to be fulfilled by the module I'm designing?"

Note that questions in both categories above cannot be answered from within the tool space of a single product. For example, the second question in the Forward Traceability category requires — at the very least — that some requirements collection tool share data with testing tools. Ideally, the integrated environment user's request to answer the second question should be met with some degree of control integration, permitting the user to invoke the requirements collection tool to browse through and dig for information about the requirements that he or she is seeking.

I believe that traceability (along with impact analysis, which I discuss next) is one of the most important "horizontal CASE" functions — that is, a CASE function that spans multiple life-cycle phases, unlike a tool that is intended to operate exclusively at the design stage. The inability to ask and receive answers for traceability-oriented questions can lead to lost information or costly retrofitting of forgotten data or functionality. Therefore a CASE integration environment should support traceability.

2. Bidirectional Impact Analysis

As with traceability, impact analysis is an extremely important hori-

zontal CASE function. And again drawing a parallel with traceability, the bidirectional nature is a necessary attribute. Questions that must be answered from the CASE environment include:

Forward Impact Analysis

★ "I need to change this design feature. What programs, screens, database stored procedures, test suites, documentation modules, and backup utilities are affected by my change?"

Reverse Impact Analysis

★ "I had to do an emergency code patch on the operational system, and it was a feature that had been designed incorrectly, not just a programming bug. What designs are affected by this change, and are the requirements correct?"

Data sharing — the minimum requirement — should ideally be augmented by a control notification mechanism that can be used to invoke the tools against which the impact analysis is occurring.

3. An Open Environment

Openness . . . perhaps *the* most overused of the many overused terms of the past decade in the information systems arena. With respect to CASE integration, openness simply means that through one or more integration mechanisms, enough interoperability can occur among tools to present the user with an integrated picture of his or her environment. Whether this is based on standards or a number of

point-to-point interoperability mechanisms is, at least initially, less important than *having* the interoperability in the first place. As long as the capability to integrate the tools within the environment actually exists, the CASE environment can probably be categorized as "open."

4. An Awareness of Client-Server, Open Systems, and Enterprise Computing Technology

Nearly every computer professional is aware of the overwhelming trend away from centralized computing toward distributed computing solutions. As a result, client-server computing, open systems, and enterprise computing technologies are becoming more and more pervasive in the target information systems being developed today and those that will be developed tomorrow.

Therefore an integrated CASE environment must be "aware" of these three distinct yet overlapping "movements," and that awareness must be from two different points of view. The CASE environments themselves should, ideally, be architected primarily to support the client-server paradigm, with additional support for open systems. But at the same time, it may be necessary to support a pervasive "enterprise computing" discipline that requires, for example, corporate standards for data names, enterprise repositories, and so forth. This could mean that client-side tools communicate with servers over open communications mechanisms and, if necessary, across the span of an organization's enterprise. (For example, a developer working on a PC-based design tool in New York may share information over the enterprise network with another developer working on a workstation-based tool in London.)

On the other side, though, the integrated CASE environments should be capable of creating open, client-server applications that use "enterprise computing" facilities for directory services, repository services, and so on. The three movements should be attributes of both the I-CASE environment itself and the systems that are created from the use of that environment.

5. Notification Facilities

Regardless of the implementation, it is imperative that tools be able to notify one another of events and other important occurrences that are likely to be of interest or importance across the tool space. Whether this occurs through messaging or remote procedure calls, via a notification server or active database [1], and regardless of other attributes of the particular scheme, notification is every bit as important as the ability to share data.

6. Support Both Forward and Reverse Engineering

The tremendous interest in recent years in legacy system migration has brought to light one of the glaring weaknesses of early CASE environments. Rarely do development projects begin from scratch; more likely there is some need to deal with existing applications. Even when rehosting and migration are not factors, CASE

often comes into play long after a system has been first developed, when there are no CASE-based requirements and designs from which to proceed with subsequent versions of the application environment.

Thus reverse engineering of environments back into design stages is a must for integrated CASE environments. While not a trivial undertaking, it is much easier to reverse engineer data than business processes, which may be represented and scattered throughout the programmed logic of the applications. Products that aid the process reengineering function have begun to appear, and as these mature, a greater reverse engineering capability will be available to users.

7. Tool Selection

Quite simply, users should be free to select tools within various spaces as they wish without sacrificing integration. The desire to use a particular data modeling tool, for example, should not preclude integration of the data and control from that tool with products that fit other spaces in the life cycle.

8. Multiple-Tool, Multiple–Life-Cycle Verification and Validation

The verification and validation (V&V) process must be able to cross tool boundaries and different life-cycle stages. Questions such as the following must be answered:

★ "Are all of my data flows from the data flow diagrams (DFDs)

accounted for in my data model?"

★ "Are all conceptual data objects handled within the work flow architecture of the applications?"

As with impact analysis and traceability, both data and control integration are important for achieving integrated V&V functionality.

9. Sufficient Granularity

The degree of granularity supported by an integrated environment determines the level of detail against which cross-tool traceability, impact analysis, and V&V can be performed. That is, repository or dictionary information must be detailed enough to assess the relationships of data flows to entities and attributes, rather than DFD designs to entity-relationship (ER) diagrams.

Of course, the finer the level of granularity, the greater the storage impact. For departmental-class applications, this is not much of a problem. At the enterprise level, though, sufficient granularity can be a major impediment to both system storage and performance. Nevertheless, without granularity to as fine a level of detail as possible, it will be nearly impossible to support I-CASE era functionality.

10. Multiple Models, Multiple Methodologies

The integrated CASE environment must be capable of supporting multiple modeling techniques and multiple methodologies without "breaking." In the modeling space, for example, one team might be using classical ER modeling while another might be using IDEF1x. The integrated environment should allow for the mapping of models from these spaces against one another and the sharing of information as necessary . . . as well as the eventual merger of these models.

With respect to methodologies, one team might be focused on a rapid prototyping approach, while another group might be using a classic waterfall methodology for a relatively small project. At some point, the efforts of these two teams need to touch and be integrated, and the environment should not preclude that.

A FINAL WORD

The 10 items discussed above may be implemented in a variety of ways, and as information systems technology marches forward, even more "I-CASE enablers" will likely emerge. The foregoing list should be viewed more from the "what must be done" point of view than the "how to do it" point of view. Whether data integration is provided by a monolithic common repository or via message sharing among the data dictionaries of multiple tools is less important (though, of course, not totally irrelevant) than the fact that there is sufficient data integration and granularity to support traceability and impact analysis.

Perhaps the methodology to follow with respect to CASE integration should be, "Let's get it working first, then we'll look at the best way to do it." What is important is that the 10 points described above become com-

monplace in CASE-based development. Until they are, there will be some very large holes that will need to be plugged.

REFERENCE

1   Simon, A. *The Integrated CASE Tools Handbook*. New York: Van Nostrand Reinhold–Intertext, 1993.

Alan Simon is the author of 19 professional and career-oriented computer books, including The Integrated CASE Tools Handbook *(Van Nostrand Reinhold–Intertext, 1993). He has worked in a variety of consulting, vendor community, and user organization positions and specializes in distributed databases, CASE technology, and systems migration and transition.*

Mr. Simon can be reached at 447 Matthews Lane, Jackson, NJ 08527 (908/905-4492; CompuServe: 70714,2517; Internet: 70714.2517@compuserve.com). ★

A Practical Software Maintenance Environment

James S. Collofello

Computer Science Department
Arizona State University
Tempe, AZ 85287

Mikael Orn

GTE Communication Systems Corporation
2500 W. Utopia Road
Phoenix, AZ 85027

Abstract

This paper provides an update of a research project at Arizona State University whose objective is the development of a practical software maintenance environment. The existing functional capabilities of the environment are described as well as research currently in progress.

Background

The need for effective and practical software maintenance tools has been well documented. This paper describes an ambitious research project at Arizona State University (ASU) that started in 1983 and whose objective has been to develop a software maintenance environment. This maintenance environment is being developed to support both managerial and technical maintenance tasks. These tasks include:

- understanding software
- changing software
- tracing ripple effect
- retesting changed software
- documenting acquired knowledge
- planning and scheduling maintenance tasks

The major components of this environment are the maintenance personnel, the maintenance tools, and the software syntactic and semantic data bases. Maintenance personnel are included as they provide information for updating the semantic data bases. The information provided by the maintenance personnel includes the various undocumented assumptions that are made during software implementation as well as other semantic information that has not been recorded. The realization that this unrecorded knowledge exists is especially important in light of the high turnover rate experienced by the software industry. In many cases when an employee quits, the organization not only loses an employee but also much of the knowledge laboriously obtained about the respective software. The design of a maintenance environment must provide a means for saving this information, thereby, shortening the learning curve for replacement personnel. Any practical maintenance environment must therefore heavily emphasize a powerful and convenient interface for maintenance personnel.

The ASU software maintenance environment project has already produced initial research results which identify a set of syntactic and semantic information. This information is crucial for maintainers to understand software and account for ripple effects as a consequence of modifying the software. These results have been documented elsewhere [1–6]. In the remainder of this paper, the existing functional capabilities of the maintenance environment will be described as well as the current research projects in progress to expand and enhance these capabilities.

Existing Functional Capabilities

Currently, the ASU software maintenance environment (tool) operates on compiler error-free Pascal code. It provides facilities to understand code, document code, and analyze code for ripple effects.

The current implementation is a menu driven system which is based on a syntactic parser. The main menu consists of the following options:

1. Structure Chart
2. Import/Export Data
3. Module Specification
4. Detailed Design
5. Testing Strategy
6. Data Dictionary
7. Module Code
8. Ripple Effect Analyzer
9. Help
10. Exit

The ASU tool breaks the Pascal code down into components called modules. A module simply is either a Pascal procedure, a Pascal function, or the main Pascal body itself. The user can analyze the Pascal program by selecting any module and then request the information that corresponds to that module. The tool keeps track of the current module. The tool also allows the user to analyze the structure and documentation of the Pascal program described below.

Understanding and Documentation Features

The *structure chart* is a graphic representation of the calling hierarchy of the Pascal code. The user can use the arrow keys to traverse the calling hierarchy. The module in the center of the screen is always the "current" module. When the user wants to take a closer look at a particular module, he/she can exit the structure chart and choose any of the other options from the main menu.

The *import/export data* will display the parameters used in the module call and the global variables referenced in the current module. It will also display the type that each variable is declared as (utilizing the standard Pascal scope rules) and whether a parameter is passed by value or reference.

The next four options of the main menu allow the user to create, view, or edit the current module's *specification*, *detailed design, testing strategy*, or *data dictionary*. The documentation can be accessed through the VAX/VMS screen editor. The tool keeps track of the text files and the appropriate read/write modes.

The *module code* option allows the user to view the current module's code. The user has access to edit commands such as search and scroll to help while browsing the code.

The system also has a *help* utility that can be invoked from the main menu. The help utility, like the rest of the program, is menu driven.

The Ripple Effect Analyzer

The most powerful utility in the current implementation is its *ripple effect analyzer*. It has been implemented as part of a research project described in [7]. Before the implementation is described, it is necessary to present some of the fundamental definitions that the ripple effect analyzer is based upon.

Ripple effect can be defined as the phenomenon where a change in one piece of a software system affects at least one other area of the same software system. Software in this context includes both the source code and any documentation such as specifications, designs, and test strategies.

Two distinct types of ripple effect can be identified [8]. One aspect of this ripple effect is *logical* or functional in nature. It involves identifying other affected areas of the software to ensure they are logically and functionally consistent with the initial change. Another aspect of the ripple effect concerns the *performance* of the various parts of the system. It involves analyzing how the performance in other areas in a system is affected by an initial change. The current implementation at ASU assists the user in the logical aspect of ripple effect analysis.

Ripple effects may be divided into two levels: direct and indirect [9]. The *direct ripple effect* occurs when the change of one variable directly affects the definition of another variable. *Indirect ripple effect* occurs when the affected variable in turn affects yet other variables. The same line of thought applies to dependencies between modules. The ASU tool facilitates both direct and indirect ripple effects.

Finally, we need to clarify the difference between syntactic and semantic knowledge. *Syntactic knowledge* is that basic information that is derivable from the source code. This "basic information" includes data flow, control flow, and calling hierarchy. In addition to syntactic knowledge, semantic knowledge is necessary to find the probable ripple effects. *Semantic knowledge* consists of programming knowledge and domain knowledge. Semantic knowledge is more difficult to derive and more difficult to verify. Analysis based on syntactic information alone may implicate many sections of code not truly affected; whereas semantic analysis can pinpoint effects more accurately at the cost of being incomplete.

Fig. 1 shows a typical scenario of error flow after a source code modification. The big bubbles each symbolize a module. The little gray area in the upper left hand corner is where the change was made. The arrows within each module show the possible intramodular ripple effects while the arrows between modules show the possible intermodular ripple effects.

One approach to limit the possible ripple effects is to add and use the semantic information. In Fig. 1, the gray circles are examples of where these "filters" can be applied. The filters consist of semantic information that is presented in such way that it can be used to decide whether a possible ripple is probable.

The second and third types of filters are ones that have been applied in the ASU tool. They both attempt to limit the possible ripple effects at the perimeter of each module. Filter type two acts as a ripple effect is about to enter a module and start a new wave of intramodular ripples. Filter type three acts as a ripple effect is about to propagate beyond the current module. Examples of these kinds of ripple effects are procedure calls and the use of global variables. Notice that all the filters are associated with a

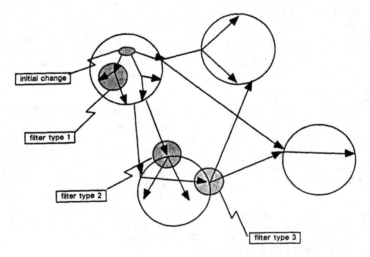

Fig. 1. The error flow after a software modification.

Relations: **calls**
                is_called_by

    Attributes: actual parameter name
                formal parameter name
                passing mode   (reference, value, or name)
                type

    Comments: *Each relation may have zero or more attribute lists*
                For each parameter, there is one attribute list

Relations: **declares_variable_used_in**
                uses_variable_declared_in

    Attributes: variable name
                type

    Comments: *Each relation may have one or more attribute lists*
                For each variable, there is one attribute list

Fig. 2. The syntactic relations and their attributes.

particular module rather than with a particular syntactic relation (arrow). This is an important design decision that makes the ASU implementation different from previous tools.

The ASU tool tracks the errorflow between modules. This is done through the use of syntactic relations. Since the syntactic relations are easy to maintain (they can be machine generated), they create the base for a network consisting of both syntactic relations and semantic templates. A semantic template is the implementation of a "filter" in Fig. 1.

The goal of the ASU tool was to create a tool that could be kept consistent in an environment that changes frequently. Since the syntactic relations can be updated automatically through the use of a syntactic parser, the key is to create a network of semantic templates that can be kept up to date with a minimal amount of interaction from the users.

The syntactic relations cover the intermodular errorflow. There are two mechanisms of intermodular communication -- global variables and parameter passing [10]. This motivates the definition of the following syntactic relations:

- calls
- is_called_by
- declares_variable_used_in
- uses_variable_declared_in

Note that the first two and the last two relations are the reverse of each other. In other words, if A calls B then B is_called_by A and if A declares_variable_used_in B then B uses_variable_declared_in A. Therefore, the set of relations shown above really represents only two bidirectional relations.

These relations are not unique to the ASU tool. However, they are used differently than other tools (see [7] for a literature review of related tools). First, notice that both the source and the destination of each relation always is the name of a module rather than a variable. This reflects the modular approach that was taken in this tool implementation. This modular approach gives the user the ability to switch between two levels of ripple effect analysis: A high level view of intermodular ripple effect, and a lower level of intramodular ripple effect (the latter is yet to be implemented in the ASU tool).

The other difference in the use of the syntactic relations is the addition of several attributes with each relation. The attributes represent the variables and parameters that are involved in the syntactic relationships. Fig. 2 shows the syntactic relations and their attributes. For each parameter that is passed along in the call, the following information is kept as attributes: The actual name, the formal name, the passing mode (by name, by reference, by value), and the type. All this information is available from the syntactic parser.

The relations declares_variables_used_in and uses_variable_declared_in also have attributes containing additional information. Each relation has a list of the variables that are actually referenced in the relation. The type of each variable is also specified.

A further discussion on why the syntactic relations described above were picked and their ability to cover logical ripple effect is given in [7] pp. 72–76.

The semantic templates have been implemented to be attached to a particular module rather than a particular syntactic relation. This modular approach promotes the consistency and flexibility by making the semantic documentation of each module somewhat independent of other modules. Any module and its semantic templates can now be updated without risking the introduction of erroneous semantic information elsewhere. For example, a particular variable may change roles locally in one module, but not in others. This new role can now be documented for future ripple effect analysis in that particular module, other modules may keep their original semantic information about the original role. Of course, this inconsistency in the role of the variable could cause problems in the program. However, a ripple effect analysis would point out this inconsis-

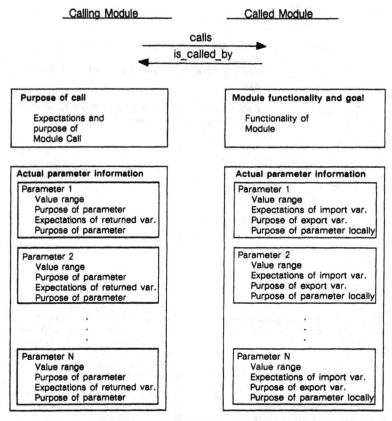

Fig. 3. Templates associated with calls and is_called_by.

tency. It is then up to the user to decide whether the inconsistency is acceptable.

Six different semantic templates were implemented in the ASU tool:

1. Module functionality and goal
2. Purpose of call
3. Variable usage information
4. Variable declaration information
5. Formal parameter information
6. Actual parameter information

Any module may have all six types of templates at any time. Templates number one and five can only exist in one copy per module. The other four templates can exist in any number of copies in any given module.

Templates number one, two, five, and six all exist in connection with module calls. When the ripple effect analyzer is invoked, templates two and six line up on the calling module's side against templates one and five on the called module's side (see Fig. 3).

Fig. 3 also shows how the content of each of the templates line up with its counterpart. Using this method of comparing semantic templates, it does not matter if two different programmers are responsible for modules A and B. It is possible to check the assumptions made by each programmer against each other.

Keeping the templates separate from the syntactic relations promotes flexibility: Each template is kept independently from others, and more than one template may be used together with the same syntactic relation. In addition, more than one syntactic relation may use the same semantic template. Fig. 4 shows how two sets of syntactic relations share templates.

In Fig. 4, modules A and B both make a call to module C. Module C's templates 1, 5a, 5b, and 5c are reused for both sets of syntactic relations. By lining up the templates against each other, it makes it very easy for the user of the ripple effect analyzer to compare any assumptions that may be inconsistent.

Templates number three and four are used in a similar manner as the previously described templates, but in connection with the syntactic relations declares_variable used in and uses variable declared in (see Fig. 5).

Initializing the Ripple Effect Analyzer

Most of the consistency checks are done by the tool. When a new session is started, the user is asked for the name of the file where the Pascal code is kept. The tool then runs its parser and generates all the syntactic relations.

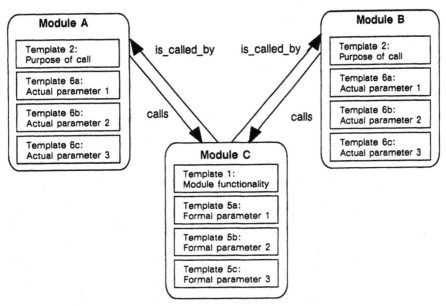

Fig. 4. The flexibility of the semantic templates.

Since the semantic templates cannot be generated automatically, it is important to be able to reuse them. The user is asked if he/she wants to use the semantic templates from a previous session. Unless it is the first time this particular Pascal program has been analyzed, the user would probably like to reuse the semantic information.

The tool now loads the semantic templates from a file into run-time memory. The tool searches the semantic templates in the file and looks for a field containing which state the template was in last time. The possible states are empty, new, old, or okay. See Fig. 6 for the legend of what they are and how the states can be transferred.

As the tool loads a template, it checks to see if it has "okay" status. All templates with "okay" status are transferred to "old." All other templates are initialized to empty.

Next, each "old" state templates is either transferred to okay or empty depending on whether the syntactic relations that used them still exist or not (if a procedure call has been removed since the last time the ripple effect analyzer was used, all semantic templates connected with that call exclusively will be removed).

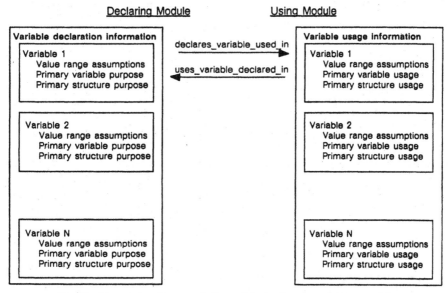

Fig. 5. Templates in association with declares_variable_used_in
and uses_variable_declared_in.

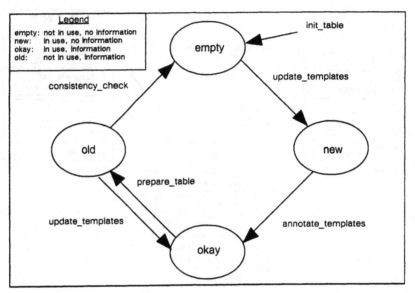

Fig. 6. The four template states.

Finally, the tool creates any new semantic templates that may be needed by transferring them from "empty" to "new." For each "new" template, the user is prompted to fill out the necessary information in it. If the user chooses to enter the information, the state is transferred to "okay." If the user chooses to wait with the semantic documentation until he/she is actually performing the analysis, the template remains in the "new" state.

Using the Ripple Effect Analyzer

After the initialization is done, the tool is ready to be used. The user chooses a module (usually the main program or the module where changes were last made) as a starting point. This becomes the "current" module. The tool now lists all the syntactic relations that start or end at the current module. The user uses the arrow keys to pick one of the relations he/she would like to investigate.

The tool now displays the syntactic relation and the corresponding semantic templates. The templates belonging to the current module are listed on the left side of the screen, and the templates of the targeted module are displayed on the right side of the screen (with the corresponding fields matching each other). See Fig.'s 3 and 5. The user can now decide whether the semantic assumptions are consistent. When the user is done investigating the syntactic relation; the targeted module becomes the current module.

The user can now either backtrack to where he/she came from (the tool keeps track of where the user came from) or pick another syntactic relation from the current module's list. The tool marks each syntactic relation that has been investigated with an asterisk, so the user will not investigate the same ripple twice by mistake.

The user can trace both direct and indirect ripple effects through any of the modules. As the user runs across semantic templates that are marked as "new," he/she is asked to document them. If the user wants to change any documentation in a template, that can be done on the fly as well.

Current Research

The ASU software maintenance environment project is currently staffed with five master's level students and two Ph.D. students under the direction of Professor James S. Collofello. The following paragraphs present a brief description of the efforts currently in progress in expanding both the technical and managerial capabilities of this environment.

Semantic Data Base Integrity

One of the problems with maintaining a semantic data base is preserving the integrity of the information contained due to constant program modifications. As code changes are made to the software, a practical maintenance environment must provide an efficient method for maintenance personnel to update corresponding semantic information. One approach currently under research and development is the integration of a configuration management tool with the maintenance environment which maps code changes to the sections of the semantic data base affected.

Display of Maintenance Information

Considerable research must be performed as to the best method to display information to the maintenance programmers. Although multiple windows appears to be a popular approach, several questions remain concerning exactly what should be displayed, how it should be displayed, and the degree of interaction necessary by the maintenance programmers. The ideal blend of textual and graphical information as well as color must also be further investigated.

Expansion to Modern Language Capabilities

An effective software maintenance environment for the future must take into account the powerful features found in the newer programming languages such as Ada™. Ways of communicating and documenting knowledge concerning such programming constructs as packages, generics and tasks must be researched. For example, in most current understanding tools some form of a structure chart is utilized to represent the relationship of modules in the program. This approach is inadequate for representing packages or the relationship of interactive tasks.

Management Information Systems

An important functional capability of a maintenance environment should be the provision of support for maintenance managers. This involves the collection of relevant project information to facilitate educated maintenance decisions.

Our current research in this area involves the definition of this relevant project information, the specification of how this information can be acquired by the maintenance environment, and the determination of the optimal way of communicating this information to the maintenance managers. One aspect of this research involves the scheduling of maintenance personnel and assigning tasks. Another aspect involves estimating the cost of a new product release based on data collected from previous releases. A third aspect concerns the collection of metrics which might lead to decisions concerning release content.

Summary

The ASU software maintenance environment project has been described. First, the background to this project and the objectives of the project were stated. Second, the current status and the existing functional capabilities were described. The current implementation of the tool provides primarily extensive understanding and documentation capabilities and a powerful ripple effect analysis capability. Finally, the current research topics that will enhance the software maintenance environment were presented.

™ Trademark of the U.S. Department of Defense

References

[1] S. J. Bortman, "Display of Maintenance Information," Master's thesis, Arizona State University, 1984.

[2] J. W. Blaylock, "A Syntactic Knowledge Base for ME2," Master's thesis, Arizona State University, 1984.

[3] J. S. Collofello and S. J. Bortman, "An Analysis of the Technical Information Necessary to Perform Effective Software Maintenance," Proc. Phoenix Conf. Computer and Communications, 1986.

[4] J. S. Collofello and J. W. Blaylock, "Syntactic Information Useful for Software Maintenance," Proc. AFIPS National Computer Conference, Vol. 54, 1985, pp. 547–553.

[5] V. Walker, "A Proposed Data File Documentation Scheme," Master's thesis, Arizona State University, 1986.

[6] J. S. Collofello and D. A. Vennergrund, "Ripple Effect Analysis based on Semantic Information," Proc. AFIPS National Computer Conference, 1987, pp. 675–682.

[7] M. G. Orn, "A Ripple Effect Analysis and Control Tool (REACT)," Master's thesis, Arizona State University, 1987.

[8] S. S. Yau, J. S. Collofello, and T. MacGregor, "Ripple Effect Analysis of Software Maintenance," Proc. IEEE COMPSAC, 1978, pp. 60–65.

[9] S. S. Yau and S. Chang, "Estimating Logical Stability in Software Maintenance," Proc. IEEE COMPSAC, 1984, pp. 109–119.

[10] A. Pizzarello, Development and Maintenance of Large Software Systems, Belmont, CA: Lifetime Learning Publications, 1984.

Intelligent Assistance for Software Development and Maintenance

Gail E. Kaiser, *Columbia University*
Peter H. Feiler, *Software Engineering Institute*
Steven S. Popovich, *Columbia University*

Using relatively simple technology, Marvel understands the user's actions and their consequences. In many cases it will do tasks automatically, lightening the workload.

In a 1973 article, Terry Winograd wrote of his dream of an intelligent assistant for programmers.[1] The fundamental requirement for an intelligent assistant, he wrote, is that it understand what it does. That is, it should be based on an explicit model of the programming world.

Winograd described an imaginary programming environment that would provide early error checking, answer questions about the program and the interactions among program parts, handle trivial programming problems, and automate simple debugging tasks.

We have developed an environment that handles the first two duties, early error checking and answering questions about programs. Our environment has a certain understanding of the systems being developed and how to use tools to produce software. It aids individual programmers and helps coordinate programmer teams.

Our assistant's knowledge is described in a model and achieves intelligence by in-

terpreting the model. We have not yet applied the model of this environment to other project aspects, such as project management, which are handled by some integrated project support environments.

Our model draws from research into software engineering and artificial intelligence. From software-engineering research, we gained experience in building and using particular tools and environments in specific development processes. From artificial-intelligence research, we discovered suitable structures to represent knowledge about software entities and the role of tools in the development process.

The result is Professor Marvel — Marvel for short — an environment that supports two aspects of an intelligent assistant: It provides *insight* into the system and it actively participates in development through *opportunistic processing*. Like its fictional counterpart, the Kansas magician who turned out to be the wizard in *The*

Wizard of Oz, Marvel can produce impressive results with relatively simple technology.

Marvel's roots and the prototype implementation is described in the box on p. 43. A more elaborate implementation that will extend Marvel's concepts to nonprogramming activities is under way.

Key components

To fulfill Winograd's fundamental requirement, an intelligent assistant must understands what it does. However, there is a spectrum of intelligent systems. Most software tools are moronic assistants that know what to do but do not understand the purpose of the objects they manipulate or how their tasks fit into the development process. In other words, they know the *how* but do not understand the *why.*

A development environment cannot understand why it performs an activity unless it knows

- the properties of the objects it manipulates,
- the system's tools and activities, and the objects they manipulate,
- the preconditions under which a tool or activity can be activated, and
- the results or postconditions of each activity (the state of development after an activity terminates).

Object base. Marvel has two key components. The first is a database that stores data represented as objects, as in object-oriented languages. This object base maintains all the entities that are part of the evolving system, all the information about the history and status of the project, and all the tools used in development and maintenance.

The object base defines the object classes and the relationships among objects (such as one object is a component of another and when applied to another object will produce a third). The object base

is active: Accessing objects may trigger action.

Process model. The second key component is a model of the development process that imposes a structure on programming activities. The model is an extensible collection of rules that specify the conditions that must exist for particular tools to be applied to particular objects. Some rules are relevant only when a user invokes a tool, others apply when the environment initiates tool processing, and still others apply equally to both cases.

Interpretation through forward and backward chaining lets the environment perform activities automatically when it knows the results of these activities will

---

Most software tools are moronic assistants that know the how but do not understand the why.

---

soon be required by the user.

Rather than add intelligence to individual tools, the model encapsulates all the intelligence in the environment, so it is not necessary to modify the tools. The box on p. 47 illustrates the potential for intelligent assistance by describing how an object base and a development model enhance two well-known programming tools.

Insight

Marvel has insight, which means it is aware of the user's activities and can anticipate the consequences of these activities based on an understanding of the development process and the produced software.

Insight lets individual programmers become informed more quickly about the

structure and relationships in the software product, to be aware of the consequences and side effects of their tasks, and to be guided in the job of making even major changes to a system and getting it back into a consistent state.

Insight also helps coordinate the activities of multiple programmers so they can accomplish their tasks without interfering with each other, knowing that the results of simultaneous work will be combined in a controlled way.

The two key elements that support insight are a rich, structured information repository and a set of mechanisms that make appropriate information available at appropriate times. The information repository is the object base. The access mechanisms fall into two categories, those that support direct access or browsing, and those that support retrieval.

Object base. Marvel's object base is conceptually related to object-oriented programming languages, in that each object is an instance of a class that defines its type. The object base contains a set of objects that represent both the system and its development history. Object types include module, procedure, type, design description, user manual, and development step. Typing lets Marvel provide an object-oriented user interface: The environment makes available only those commands that are relevant to the object under consideration, within the context of the user's recent activities.

However, unlike most object-oriented languages, Marvel's object base is persistent: It retains its state across invocations of the environment. This lets Marvel provide a file-less environment. Marvel exposes its users only to the logical entities comprising the target system, not to the physical storage organization of directories and files. Other knowledge-based environments offer similar capabilities in their database support.[2]

Each class defines certain properties of an object and inherits other properties from its superclass or superclasses. Some properties, called attributes, define the contents and status of objects. Other properties, called methods, define the development activities applicable to the objects of a class. Attributes may be simple values (integers and strings) or they may represent relationships with other objects.

Simple attribute values include object names, object status (such as if it has been analyzed for static semantic errors), and string entities (such as pieces of source text or binary object code). Attributes that represent relationships include the logical, syntactic structure (for example, a module is composed of procedures, types, and variables), semantic dependencies (such as intended use — indicated by the import clauses of modules — or actual use as demonstrated by the invocation of a procedure). Relationships are bidirectional by default, which permits more flexible querying. A user can ask for all uses of procedure p as well as all uses of other procedures by procedure p.

All information about objects is maintained in the object base, and inferred or derived by Marvel where possible. Users are spared the tedium of entering redundant information.

Information access. Information in the object base is accessed for two reasons: (1) viewing and querying and (2) modification. Both users and tools may access information.

Users generally modify the structural hierarchy, the names of objects, and source-text attributes through a view of the object base. A view is the subset of information in the object base that is currently relevant. Other attributes (analysis status or use relationships) are maintained by tools to reflect the current state of the target system. Users can also browse and query this auxiliary information.

Browsing. Browsing takes place according to views. The default view is the logical structure (the library-module-component hierarchy) of the target system. For example, the user sees program libraries containing modules, which in turn contain other modules or indivisible compo-

nents (procedures, types, variables, and so on).

The user navigates through this structural hierarchy just as he navigates through directory structures in file systems. However, limited bandwidth prohibits exposing the user to the complete structure at once (unless we use very small fonts!), which is generally all right in any case because of information overload.

Views can be displayed and browsed many ways. In Marvel, objects and their parts have selectable textual representations. By selecting such an entity, the user specifies the current focus and by doing so determines processing and command selection. Hence, Marvel has an object-oriented interface.

Marvel tries to balance the amount of information presented to the user. One view displays a single level of the structural hierarchy. If the user selects an object to edit, it can be opened for viewing if the component represents a reference to another object. The newly opened object can be viewed in the current window or in another window.

Another view shows multiple levels of the hierarchy at once. This lets Marvel respond to user requests for more context information, reducing the need for repeated user queries or browsing operations. For example, a view of a module's content contains the names of the component objects and their type (whether they are procedures or documents). Similarly, Marvel provides visual feedback of values for certain essential attributes (if a module contains an error, for example), thus eliminating additional queries while still avoiding information overload.

Marvel also lets the user navigate by following cross-references, such as opening the specification of a module referenced in the import list of another module. Such cross-link browsing capabilities make it easier for the user to get an impression of the context of a piece of software.

In summary, the browsing capability lets the user manually navigate through the object base, changing the focus. This lets Marvel track user actions, anticipate consequences, and help the user cope with the consequences. However, manual navigation is inadequate for general search tasks.

For example, if the user maintains a system with 150 modules, trying to find the three modules with outstanding errors can be a tedious task if done by browsing. A general querying capability combined with a browsing capability solves this problem.

Queries. A general answering capability supports searches of the object base according to conditions phrased in a stylized command language: "Retrieve all software objects with proper name x," for example, or "Retrieve all modules that contain errors."

The search space can be constrained several ways. One way is through particular search conditions, such as by object type or attribute value. Another way is to limit the the search to a particular substructure, such as searching a procedure in a particular library. Marvel also prunes the search space by using dependency information, such as import and actual procedure use.

Queries may be explicit or implicit. Explicit queries are initiated by the user. Marvel has predefined, short forms of common queries, such as:

• What components use a particular function?

• Are certain components not used at all? (Useful during maintenance and cleanup.)

• Which components (or modules) have errors?

• Which components have a particular error? and

• Is anybody else intending to or modifying a particular component (or module)?

Such queries let the user get an impression of the structure and connectivity of the software to be modified or maintained.

Implicit queries are initiated by Marvel for several reasons. It does so when it encounters an exceptional condition and needs essential information to repair the problem. For example, if the user wants to edit procedure p, but procedure p is not in the module currently in focus, Marvel queries the object base for a procedure named p. If the query returns a unique element, Marvel can change the focus; if there are many procedures named p, Marvel asks the user to choose one.

A second reason for Marvel to generate implicit queries is to present a query result

Marvel: Past, present, and future

Marvel's concepts are based on our experience with another environment that provided assistance to users. We extracted the properties that made that environment an active assistant into Marvel's model.

The concepts of this model have been validated through a first prototype implementation, based on the earlier environment, that supports the rules and strategies. This prototype has been followed by an implementation with full object base support and dynamic extension of the object base structure and the set of rules and strategies.

Marvel's ancestry. In the late 1970s and early 1980s, we and other members of the Gandalf project developed a multiuser, software-engineering environment called Smile.[1] Smile, which supports programming in C and runs on Unix, has been used on the Gandalf[2] and Gnome[3] projects at Carnegie Mellon University and by the Inscape project[4] at AT&T Bell Laboratories, and has been distributed to at least 40 sites.

Smile passes the crucial test of supporting its own maintenance. It has supported the simultaneous activities of seven to 10 programmers. The largest system developed and maintained in Smile has about 61,000 lines of source code.

Smile is a relatively intelligent assistance. It supports insight and opportunistic processing. It provides a file-less environment to its users, answers queries, coordinates the activities of multiple programmers, and automatically invokes tools. It hides the particulars of the Unix file system and utilities and presents its own model of the programming world. Smile's object base is implemented through a combination of file system and in-core object structure that is kept persistent in a file. Smile's knowledge of software objects and the programming process is hard-coded into the environment.

Marvel's proof of concept. We chose first to validate Marvel's concept of rules and strategies. We started with Smile for the prototype implementation. This lets us concentrate on the implementation of the rule-processing facility with minimal extensions to Smile's simple object base, yet still gave us an operational environment prototype. It also let us compare the prototype with the original Smile system, which has been in use for several years.

This implementation of Marvel replaced Smile's hard-coded knowledge about the software-development process with rules. Rules and strategies are written using a text editor, and the text file is parsed by a rule compiler.

The rule compiler translates rule preconditions and postconditions into (1) a "fast-load" syntax tree and (2) symbol-table structures that link each occurrence of a predicate or a relation in a precondition with a potentially satisfying postcondition and vice versa, and also link these predicates and relations to each relevant rule.

A rule set and strategy can be loaded at start-up and additional strategies can be loaded later, but there is no checking among simultaneously used strategies. Individual rules can be separately turned on and off.

Forward chaining, backward chaining, and the ability to turn strategies on and off are implemented through an interpreter that works directly with the structures produced by the rule compiler. This rule interpreter takes a simple approach for processing rules rather than employing a match network mechanism; the entire condition of every applicable rule is rechecked whenever a relevant predicate or relation is asserted or negated. To support the rule interpretation, we added some attributes and relations to Smile's hard-coded object base.

The performance resulting from this simple-minded approach is unacceptable for large numbers of rules and large object bases, but was satisfactory for processing the rules describing Smile's behavior. Forward chaining proceeds breadth-first using a queue of rules whose preconditions are satisfied. Backward chaining is depth-first, attempting to derive the desired postconditions of one candidate rule before trying an alternative rule.

Once the object base and the rule compiler and interpreter were in place we were able to capture Smile's knowledge about programming activities and their automation in rules and strategies and replace the hard-coded knowledge. The working prototype provided us with feedback for improvement in a number of areas. These were taken into account in a second implementation of Marvel.

Looking into the future. After the concept prototype of Marvel was completed at SEI, an implementation of Marvel that is independent of the Smile implementations was begun.

One version of this implementation is operational. It includes enhancement of the rule interpreter and an extensible object base. In this implementation, the rule interpreter supports consistency checking and merging of strategies as they are loaded dynamically, as well as dynamic unloading of strategies. The new object base supports object-class hierarchies and dynamic extensibility of structures stored in the object base. We have published details of this object-base implementation.[5]

Our work is progressing in several areas. We are adding multiple-user support to the new object-base implementation. We are investigating concurrency and recovery support through long transactions. To support Smile's capability of background processing, we are considering extending the rule interpreter to allow concurrent rule firing.

References

1. G.E. Kaiser and P.H. Feiler, "Intelligent Assistance without Artificial Intelligence," *Proc. Compcon*, CS Press, Los Alamitos, Calif., 1987, pp. 236-241.
2. A. Nico Habermann, D. Notkin, "Gandalf: Software-Development Environment," *IEEE Trans. Software Eng.*, May 1985.
3. D.B. Garlan and P.L. Miller, "Gnome: An Introductory Programming Environment Based on a Family of Structure Editors," *SIGPlan Notices*, May 1984, pp. 65-72.
4. D.E. Perry, "Software Interconnection Models," *Proc. Int'l Conf. Software Eng.*, CS Press, Los Alamitos, Calif., 1987, pp. 61-69.
5. G.E. Kaiser et al., "Database Support for Knowledge-Based Engineering Environments," *IEEE Expert*, Summer 1988.

to the user automatically. For example, say a user gives the command to edit the specification of a module component that is being exported. Marvel informs the user of the expected extent of the consequences and requests confirmation to go ahead with the editing. Marvel can use the same information to check if the affected components are accessible (have been reserved by the user) for modification. The result of this query can again be presented to the user, or Marvel can attempt to reserve and/or add new editing tasks to the user's agenda.

Implicit queries are made when the result of the query provides insight into expected activities, making the user aware of the potential consequences of his actions.

Opportunistic processing

Marvel performs opportunistic processing, which means it undertakes simple development activities so programmers need not be bothered with them. In our model only menial activities are automated, such as determining when the source code has changed, invoking the compiler, and recording errors found during compilation.

Marvel performs an activity when the opportunity arises, between the time a user's action causes additional processing and the time the user requests the results of the action. This form of assistance differs from intelligent assistants such as the Programmer's Apprentice (also known as KBEmacs[3]), which focuses on automatic program construction.

In addition to objects, the object base maintains the process model that helps Marvel decide when to apply tools on the user's behalf. The process model is an extensible collection of rules consisting of a precondition, an activity, and many postconditions.

Marvel carries out its actions by interpreting the rules in different ways. Forward chaining lets Marvel invoke tools as soon as their preconditions are satisfied; backward chaining lets it find the tools whose postconditions satisfy the preconditions of other tools that have been activated.

The extent of this automation is controlled through strategies. Each strategy specifies a certain degree of assistance that is appropriate for a type of user or law of programming activity. For example, Marvel automatically performs different functions for an long-term user than it would for a novice. Similarly, Marvel may report on the use of undefined variables less frequently when new code is written than during test and debugging.

It is important to realize two facts about the use of rules in Marvel. First, Marvel consists of a generic kernel. An instance of Marvel is created by supplying a description of the object base structure and the process model to the kernel. Second, only systems managers need to write object base descriptions, rules, and strategies. Users select from strategies defined for them to choose a desired behavior of Marvel. They can extend the set of strategies if desired.

Rules. Marvel rules are based on condition/action pairs. When the condition is true or satisfied, the action is applied to working memory (in this case, the object base). However, these so-called production rules are inadequate because they do not separate the invocation of a tool from the results produced by the tool, which we must do to integrate existing tools without modification. Therefore, we divide a rule into three parts: a precondition, an activity, and a postcondition.

Figure 1 shows a compile rule that illustrates the properties of these three parts.

Preconditions. A precondition is a Boolean expression that must be true before an activity can be performed. The operands of a precondition are objects and their attributes.

In Figure 1, notcompiled(module) is a precondition for the compile-module activity. Assuming that static semantic analysis and code generation are separate activities, the precondition also requires all semantic analysis to have completed successfully. This takes the form of "for all components c such that in(module, component c): analyzed(component c)," where analyzed(c) is true only if the analysis of component c did not find any errors.

Activities. The activity part of a rule represents an integral development task, such as compile module and edit procedure. Activities are medium-grained: Low-level editing commands applied during the course of an edit-procedure activity are not considered activities. Nor are high-level commands, such as "fix bug," because they involve many tasks and perhaps many users.

In the object base, each activity is associated with a tool that carries it out. Each tool has an attribute that determines if it can be invoked by the environment without human intervention. For example, the compile-module activity is associated with the compiler, which can be invoked automatically; the edit-procedure activity is associated with an editor, which requires human interaction.

Postconditions. A postcondition is an assertion that becomes true when an activity is completed. A postcondition can consist of several alternative assertions. Each alternative reflects a different result of the activity. For example, the compile rule in Figure 1 shows compiled(module) and errors(module) as the two possible assertions, capturing the fact that compilation may succeed or fail. The postcondition alternatives are mutually exclusive — only one gets asserted, based on the result of the activity. Both preconditions and postconditions are written as well-formed formulas in first-order, predicate calculus.

Our rules are similar syntactically to Hoare's assertions,[4] where a programming language construct is associated with its preconditions and postconditions. If the preconditions are true before the language construct is executed, the postconditions will be true afterward. However, the semantics of Marvel's postconditions differ from Hoare's in that the purpose of the postcondition is not verification, but to update the object base.

Controlled automation. Forward and backward chaining contribute to oppor-

```
notcompiled(module) and
    for all components c such that in(module, component c):
        analyzed(component c)
    { compile module }
compiled(module) |
errors(module);

in(module, component c)
    {edit component c}
notanalyzed(component) and
    notcompiled(module);
```

Figure 1. Compile rule and edit rule.

tunistic processing by letting Marvel use rules to determine what needs to be done and what can be done automatically.

Forward chaining. If the preconditions of an activity are satisfied and the activity is one that it can perform, Marvel does so without human intervention. This behavior is similar to language-oriented editors, which automatically perform actions like type checking and code generation when a user makes a subtree replacement in a program's abstract syntax tree.

Marvel would interpret the rule in Figure 1 to mean that the assistant may compile all modules M if all the components of M have been analyzed successfully and M has not yet been compiled. If a module was previously unsuccessful at compiling, the postcondition errors(module) will be true. The compile-module activity will not be reported unnecessarily while errors(module) is true, because the precondition notcompiled(module) cannot be satisfied. If the user edits a component to fix the error, the edit activity will cause notcompiled(module) to be true again, and compilation can be attempted.

Forward chaining means Marvel can perform this second attempt at compilation when that precondition is satisfied. It does not have to perform the activity as soon as the preconditions are true or at any particular time thereafter. However, it may go ahead and apply the tool, and use forward chaining to determine additional activities whose preconditions are now satisfied as new postconditions are generated, using otherwise idle computing resources.

Backward chaining. If a user invokes an activity whose preconditions are not satisfied (execute program, for example), Marvel looks for activities it can perform to generate postconditions that would satisfy the preconditions. It uses backward chaining to do so; this is similar to Make.

When a user requests regeneration of an executable system after changes have been made to its source code, Marvel uses dependency information it maintains in the object base to determine which modules must be recompiled. Of course, it may not be possible to satisfy all the preconditions, and in this case the user is informed of the

```
not reserved(module) and saved(module)
  { reserve module }
reserved(module, userid);

reserved(module, userid)
  { change component }
notanalyzed(component) and notcompiled(module);

for all components k such that in(module, component k)
  and uses(component k, component c):
    reserved(module, userid)
  { change component c }
```

Figure 2. Change rules and reserve rule.

problem. Marvel is not expected to find and repair bugs, for example. In general, Marvel will not automatically perform activities that invoke tools requiring human intervention.

Consider the case of a large programming team where multiple users are not permitted to change the same module at the same time. This might be handled with a rule like that in Figure 2, which requires each user to reserve a module before changing it. The preconditions for the reserve-module activity are (1) the module has not been reserved (not reserved(module)) and (2) the module has been saved by the version-control tool (saved(module)).

The second rule in Figure 2 states that the change-component activity cannot be done unless the module that contains the component is reserved. The change-component activity lets the user modify the specification of a component, as opposed to edit component, which lets the user modify the component's body only.

The third rule in Figure 2 states that not only should the containing module be reserved, but the user must reserve any other modules whose components use the component that will be changed (c and k are two objects of the same type). Backward chaining lets Marvel automatically reserve any modules whose components may be modified to remain consistent with the changed component. It also prevents the user from modifying the specification of a component when other modules cannot be reserved (according to the first rule), which means that someone else is currently working on them. Thus, the user does not start a job he may not be able to finish.

Hints and strategies. When Marvel per-

forms opportunistic processing, it must choose the degree of automation wisely. In other words, it must adapt to the user's current goals. To do this, Marvel selects appropriate points on the spectrum between the earliest and latest time an activity can be performed automatically and disables automatic processing when it gets in the user's way. We have provided Marvel with hints and strategies to help it make these decisions.

A hint is a rule with no postconditions. The preconditions of a hint are used to help Marvel decide when to apply a tool whose preconditions are satisfied.

For example, it makes sense that Marvel should delay recompiling a module automatically even when preconditions are satisfied if a user with modification rights is browsing the module. The rationale is that the user may decide to edit some components, and the generation of code will have been wasted. This is captured in a hint shown in Figure 3, giving this precondition for the compile-module activity. When Marvel follows a strategy that includes this hint, compilation is delayed until the user changes his focus to another module.

Of course, the user must be allowed to invoke the compiler without changing focus to another module. That is why this precondition is stated as a hint, not as part of a rule. Hints apply only to the opportunistic processing of the environment, not to user-initiated activities. In other words, hints are considered during forward chaining; ignored during backward chaining.

A strategy is a collection of hints and rules that apply only when the strategy is in force. Marvel employs strategies by combining their rules and hints. One or more strategies may be employed at the same

```
not reserved(module) or
  < reserved(module, userid) and
    not equals(module, focus
    (userid) ) >
  { compile module }
```

Figure 3. Compile hint.

time. When this results in more than one rule for the same activity, all their preconditions must be satisfied, but only one member of the set of postconditions may be asserted.

Marvel cannot choose its own strategies. Instead, the user selects appropriate strategies by telling the environment something about his intentions: for example, that he is a manager versus a programmer, developing a new software system versus maintaining an old software system, or making major changes versus making a minor revision. A strategy whose rules and hints result in automatic type checking immediately after each component is edited would be appropriate for a minor revision, but not for a major change involving many interrelated components.

Handling side effects

Using a tool often causes side effects. For example, the analysis tool invoked for the analyze-component activity may change the values of several component attributes. Setting the value of an attribute is considered an activity, resulting in a situation where one action of Marvel is embedded inside another rather than being a consequence of forward or back-

ward chaining. This case demonstrates a limitation of Marvel's rules: Secondary actions whose arguments are not simple derivatives of the arguments of the preconditions or the activity cannot easily be expressed as postconditions.

Instead, potential side effects are indicated by tool attributes. In such cases, the secondary activities are often described by their own rules, and these must be considered for further processing.

Figure 4 shows some rules related to a component's uses attribute. The uses attribute lists the other components the component depends on. The first rule gives the obvious preconditions and postconditions for the analyze-component activity. The second rule states that a component c cannot use another component k unless component k is in the same module or is imported into the module. The third rule states that a component cannot be imported by a module M unless it is exported by another module N. The fourth rule states that a component cannot be exported by a module unless it is in that module.

Consider what happens when the analysis tool finds that procedure p (a component) calls procedure q (another component) and tries to set the uses attribute of procedure p to include procedure q. If q is in the same module as p, there is no prob-

lem — the attribute is set and the analysis continues.

If q is not in the same module, Marvel checks if it is imported. If q is not already imported, Marvel notes that imports(module, component) is a postcondition of the import-component activity (the third rule) and further realizes it can perform the import-component activity.

So it considers the preconditions of the import-component activity. Marvel queries its object base to find the module that does contain q. If q is already exported from this module, Marvel imports it. If not, backward chaining lets Marvel follow the preconditions of this activity given in the fourth rule, add q to the exports of its module, import q into the original module, and finally allow the analysis tool to set the uses attribute of p.

This is only one possible strategy. It ignores the possibility that distinct procedures named q might be found in more than one module. Sometimes language-specific typing information can narrow the possibilities, but Marvel usually must interrupt the user to explain its dilemma and ask which q is intended.

Another possibility is that there is no component named q in the object base. If so, Marvel considers the add-component-q activity, whose postcondition is, of course, the existence of q. If permitted by the current strategy, Marvel could carry out this activity on its own by creating a stub for the procedure within the module where the use occurs. Or Marvel could ask the user to create the procedure (or its stub) before continuing the analysis, but this might be intrusive.

The preferred solution is to inform the analysis tool of the problem and prevent it from performing the procedure-p-uses-procedure-q activity. This causes the analysis tool to terminate unsuccessfully, generating the errors(p) predicate among its postconditions.

In the above discussion, import component and export component do not require human interaction, so Marvel can carry out the repairs. An alternative strategy requires the assistant to take the imports and exports as given. This might be appropriate for languages such as Ada that include their own module constructs, where reference to an external compo-

```
notanalyzed(component)
  { analyze component }
analyzed(component) |
errors(component);

in(module, component c) and
  < in(module, component k) or imports(module, component k) >
  { component c uses component k }
uses(component c, component k);

exports(module N, component) and
  not equal(module M, module N)
  { import component }
imports(module M, component);

in(module, component)
  { export component }
exports(module, component);
```

Figure 4. Analyze rule, uses rule and import/export rules.

114

nent without the appropriate With clause should be detected as an error. A second alternative would require Marvel to ask the programmer if q is a typographical error before carrying out all the previously described actions.

Over time the modular structure of systems degenerates. For systems written in languages with explicit export/import declarations, such as Ada, the number of these declarations tends to increase, even though some imported components are no longer used.

Marvel can maintain such old code by providing both rigid and flexible strategies in the same environment. Flexible strategies let it reflect the actual usage of components automatically in the export/import lists, removing unnecessary exports/imports and adjusting exports/imports as the code is being reorganized. Rigid strategies provide stability during development phases such as testing and integration by taking the export/import declarations as givens to be checked against.

In Figure 4, Marvel implicitly queried its object base to locate procedure q. Implicit queries are necessary to determine if preconditions are satisfied and to find the next rules to be applied in forward and backward chaining. Implicit queries are also used to anticipate the postconditions of activities. This lets Marvel notify the user as soon as a user action is likely to lead to adverse results.

Consider the two rules in Figure 5. Through forward chaining, changing a component will lead to semantic analysis, which may result in errors. When a user invokes the editor on a particular component with the change-component command, he indicates to Marvel his intention to modify the component specification. Marvel notices that forward chaining after the completion of the editing activity would propagate to other components based on the used-by attribute, whose reprocessing might result in error.

Instead of letting the user edit the component specification blindly, Marvel can query the object base and inform the user of the potentially affected sites. This lets the user abort his change-component command if he was not aware of the potential damage caused by the intended change.

Adding knowledge to tools

Make[1] has a simplistic world model consisting of files and command lines. A Make file defines dependencies among files and gives the command lines for restoring consistency among dependent files. Make's notion of consistency is based entirely on files and time: If the time stamp of an input file is later than the time stamp of an output file, then the indicated command line is passed to the Unix shell. Make is widely used for generating a new executable version of a system after one or more source files have been modified.

However, Make's knowledge is primitive. Its object base consists of files that have a single attribute, their time stamp. Make does not know anything about applying tools to files; it just handles command lines as indivisible strings. Make does not have any understanding of source versus object files, of modules versus systems, of programmers or of programming.

How can we add this knowledge to Make?

First, a notion of an object is defined, where each object belongs to a class. One class might be system, while another might be module. Each class defines the attributes, or properties, of its objects. For example, a module-object-code object might have a history attribute that describes how it was generated and a derivation-of attribute that points to the object representing the corresponding source code.

Rules would then be added to model the part of the development process relevant to Make. One rule might be that a programmer object can modify a module object; another might state that after such a modification, the module object is no longer consistent with its derivation attribute and there is an obligation to restore this consistency. A third rule might state that a precondition for a programmer to test a system is that all module object code objects that are components of the corresponding executable system must be consistent with their module.

If Make were armed with this knowledge, then it would be more intelligent than it is now. It would then be easier to integrate Make with other tools that support configuration management, version control, and task management, assuming all these tools were similarly augmented with knowledge of software objects and with understanding of their roles in the development process.

The Cornell Program Synthesizer[2] also has a simplistic world model, consisting of nodes in a parse tree. The nodes have types, such as program and identifier.

When an identifier node is inserted as a child of an expression in the parse tree, the Synthesizer compares the identifier's name with the names defined in the symbol table. If not found, the part of the display corresponding to the new node is highlighted; the highlighting is removed when a matching identifier node is inserted as a child of a declaration.

The immediate feedback provided by the Synthesizer makes it easy to correct static semantic errors while the programmer is still in the context of editing a program.

The primitive knowledge of the Synthesizer has been somewhat improved in the Synthesizer Generator.[3] The Synthesizer Generator uses a knowledge base that defines classes of nodes such as expression, attributes of nodes such as type, and equations that specify dependencies among attributes.

The language-based editors produced by the Synthesizer Generator automatically reevaluate the attribute equations whose input attributes have changed in value. However, these editors do not know that the purpose of updating attributes is to provide immediate feedback to programmers about static semantic errors and to incrementally generate the object code needed to test the program. With this understanding, the editors could, for example, separate error detection from error reporting according to whether the programmer is making many changes or only one; in the first case, the programmer is unlikely to want to hear about errors after every keystroke.

This knowledge could be added to the Synthesizer Generator and the language-based editors it produces via rules that model the part of the development process relevant to program editing. One rule might be that a programmer object can modify the parse tree represented by a program object. A second rule might state that the editor has an obligation to notify the programmer of any errors in the program; another might say that a precondition for a programmer to resume execution of program is that no substantive changes have been made to any procedure already on the runtime stack.

Adding this kind of knowledge to the Synthesizer Generator would make its editors relatively intelligent. For example, they could then simulate attribute reevaluation at appropriate points to obtain insight into the consequences of the programmer's actions and warn the programmer about changes that invalidate the internal execution state of the debugger.

References

1. S.I. Feldman, "Make: A Program for Maintaining Computer Programs," *Software Practice and Experience*, April 1979, pp. 255-265.
2. T. Teitelbaum and T. Reps, "The Cornell Program Synthesizer: A Syntax-Directed Programming Environment," *Comm. ACM*, Sept. 1981; reprinted in *Interactive Programming Environments*, D.R. Barstow, H.E. Shrobe, and E. Sandewall, eds., McGraw-Hill, New York, 1984.
3. T. Reps and T. Teitelbaum, "The Synthesizer Generator," *SIGPlan Notices*, May 1984, pp. 41-48.

```
reserved(module, userid)
   { change component }
notanalyzed(component) and notcompiled(module);

notanalyzed(component)
   { analyze component }
analyzed(component) |
errors(component);
```

Figure 5. Change and analyze rules.

A sample session

Figure 6 shows a snapshot of Marvel in the middle of a procedure edit. The screen has two windows: In the large window is a transcript of a session in which the user is interacting with the Marvel command interpreter. The window is scrollable, so the complete transcript is accessible. In the small window Marvel presents an item in the object base for the user to edit using his favorite editor; in this case, Emacs. The bottom of the screen shows icons that are part of the X Windows system.

The transcript in the large window shows interactions between the user and Marvel that demonstrate some of Marvel's behavior. At the beginning of the session, the user enters an existing workspace to modify a system, in this case an interactive program for fractional arithmetic. This work-space is a Marvel database that is private to the user. It is connected to a public database, where the baseline version of the software resides.

One module has previously been reserved from the public database and made available for modification in the private workspace. All other parts of the system that physically reside in the public database are accessible transparently for reading.

The user's attention is focused on the object that represents the whole program, which is indicated by the prompt showing the system name — Fractions. First, the

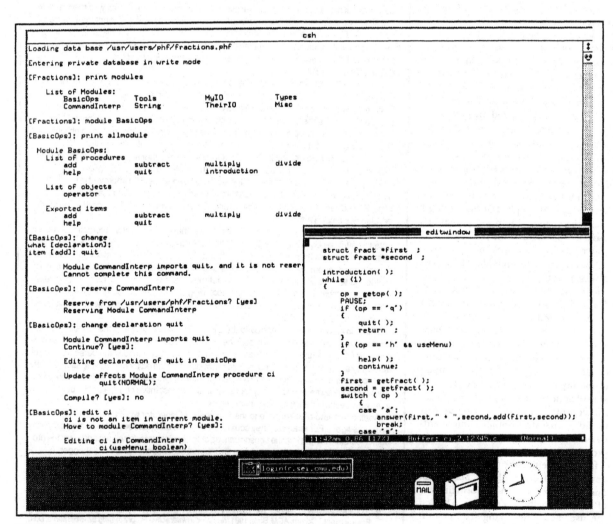

Figure 6. A Marvel screen.

116

user requests a view of the system, namely, its list of modules. The user then focuses on the BasicOps module, and the prompt changes.

Now the user requests another view, in this case a more detailed view of a particular module. Because the user did not specify a module name, the system chose the module in the current focus. The result is a view showing all the components of the module (several procedures and an object; the module does not contain data-type definitions), and a list of components that are available externally as part of the module specification (exported items).

With the Change command, the user attempts to modify the Quit procedure's specification. The system prompts for missing command parameters, providing defaults. Marvel first performs an implicit query to determine the consequences of the planned change. The user is informed that the Quit procedure is used by another module for which the user does not have modification rights. Under the default strategy, chosen by the user, Marvel does not reserve the module, but aborts the command.

The user then explicitly reserves the module. Marvel confirms that the module is to be reserved from the public database, and a second modification attempt succeeds. The user is informed which components are potentially affected before the actual editing, and is asked after the modification if the affected compo-

nents should be analyzed and compiled as well. Because the user expects to correct the affected procedure, he declines the offer.

The modified component is analyzed and compiled in the background, while the user issues the Edit command to make a local modification to the Ci procedure. Marvel changes the focus to the appropriate module, displays the procedure specification, and presents the user with the procedure body in the editor window.

The model embodied in the Marvel environment formalizes the concepts of insight and opportunistic processing by

• maintaining all knowledge about both the specific development effort and the general development process in the object base,

• making multiple views of the object base available both to users and tools,

• modeling the development process as rules that define the preconditions and postconditions of development activities, and

• gathering collections of rules into strategies.

This lets Marvel provide software-engineering environments that intelligently assist development and maintenance efforts by individuals and teams of users through controlled automation, using available development tools.   ❖

Acknowledgments
Dave Ackley, Naser Barghouti, Susan Dart, Mark Dowson, Bob Ellison, David Garlan, Dan Miller, John Nestor, Gavin Oddy, Cecile Paris, Colin Tully, Nelson Weiderman, Ursula Wolz, and the anonymous referees reviewed drafts of this article and made many useful criticisms and suggestions. Purvis Jackson assisted us with technical editing.

This work was started while Kaiser was a visiting computer scientist at the SEI. The first prototype implementation was done at the SEI. Research on Marvel continues at Columbia University, supported in part by Kaiser's Digital Equipment Corp. faculty award, in part by a grant from Siemens Research and Technology Laboratories, and in part by the Defense Dept.

References
1. T. Winograd, "Breaking the Complexity Barrier (Again)," *Proc. ACM SIGPlan-SIGIR Interface Meeting on Programming Languages — Information Retrieval,* ACM, New York, 1973, pp. 13-30; reprinted in *Interactive Programming Environments,* D.R. Barstow, H.E. Shrobe, and E. Sandewall, eds., McGraw-Hill, New York, 1984.

2. D.S. Wile and D.G. Allard, "Worlds: An Organizing Structure for Object-Bases," *SIGPlan Notices,* Jan. 1987, pp. 16-26.

3. R.C. Waters, "KBEmacs: Where's the AI?" *AI Magazine,* Spring 1986, pp. 47-56.

4. C.A.R. Hoare, "An Axiomatic Approach to Computer Programming," *Comm. ACM,* Oct. 1969, pp. 576-580, 583.

Maintenance Support for Object-Oriented Programs

Norman Wilde and Ross Huitt

Abstract—This paper describes some of the difficulties that may be expected in the maintenance of software developed using the new object oriented languages. The concepts of inheritance and of polymorphism provide the great strengths of these languages, but they also introduce difficulties in program analysis and understanding. The paper analyzes problems of dynamic binding, object dependencies, dispersed program structure, control of polymorphism, high-level understanding, and detailed code understanding. Examples are presented based on code from a PC Smalltalk environment and from studies of two systems under development at Bell Communications Research. Recommendations are made for possible tool support, particularly using the concepts of dependency analysis, external dependency graphs, and clustering methodologies.

I. Introduction

THE SOFTWARE paradigm of object-oriented programming (OOP) has become increasingly popular in recent years. More and more organizations are introducing object-oriented methods and languages into their software development practices. Claimed advantages of OOP include extensive reuse of software objects and easier maintenance through better data encapsulation [1]. Some evidence has begun to appear that these benefits may be achieved in practice [18].

To achieve these gains, object-oriented languages such as C++, Objective C, Smalltalk, and Eiffel have introduced the concepts of an object class inheritance hierarchy and of polymorphism. Each object class may either implement a needed method itself, or else rely on an implementation from one of its superiors in the hierarchy. Different object classes respond to messages having the same name to do similar tasks, even though the code implementing the methods may be quite different for the different classes.

Although maintenance may turn out to be easier for programs written in such languages, it is unlikely that the maintenance burden will completely disappear. Maintenance, in its widest sense of "post deployment software support," is likely to continue to represent a very large fraction of total system costs. Accordingly, the Florida/Purdue Software Engineering Research Center in collaboration with Bell Communications Research (Bellcore) has been studying the im-

Manuscript received April 27, 1992; revised July 23, 1992. This work was supported by Bell Communications Research and the Florida/Purdue Software Engineering Research Center (SERC). SERC is an industry–university research center with support from 13 industrial sponsors, the Florida High Technology and Industry Council, and the National Science Foundation under Grants ECD 861 4385 and ECD 914 6148. Recommended by V. Rajlich.
N. Wilde is with the Department of Computer Science, University of West Florida, Pensacola, FL 32514.
R. Huitt is with Bell Communications Research (Bellcore), RRC 1H-206, Piscataway, NJ 08854.
IEEE Log Number 9204090.

pact of object orientation on the software maintenance task. This study has included discussions with practitioners of object oriented programming at Bellcore and the collection of statistics on several object oriented systems as well as a brief review of some existing commercial object oriented environments.

Inheritance and polymorphism represent complications as well as benefits for the maintenance process. This paper identifies some of the main difficulties that we foresee and describes tool capabilities that would seem to be needed to provide more effective support for the maintenance of object oriented programs. Examples are presented from a PC Smalltalk environment and from two Bellcore systems. We will look for types of tools that can be applied to an existing body of source code; thus there will be no assumption that a particular documentation methodology or CASE tool was used in system development. In any case maintenance programmers have a well-founded distrust of any external documentation not derivable from the code itself. Recommendations for tool support make use of the concepts of dependency analysis, external dependency graphs, and statistical clustering.

II. The Problem of Dynamic Binding

Many maintenance tools depend on tracing dependencies within programs. Object-oriented languages such as Smalltalk complicate the tracing process considerably by allowing dynamic binding of messages to specific methods. A given variable may refer to an object of any class so, using polymorphism, the method to be executed when a given message is sent to it will be determined at run time by the class of the object it represents at that instant. Similarly in C++, object pointers and references may refer not only to objects of their declared class but also to descendants of that class. When an operation is performed on the object, a function declared as virtual will dynamically bind to the implementation of the function that is appropriate to the object's underlying class at runtime.

While dynamic binding provides much of the flexibility of object-oriented languages, it may also greatly complicate the tracing of dependencies. Specifically, when a message is sent to a variable holding an object, the actual method implementation that will be called depends on the object's class. Since different implementations will establish different dependencies, static analysis will not always be able to identify precisely the dependencies in the program.

```
Object ‹at:put:›
  .
  .
┌ Collection
│ ┣ Bag ‹at:put:›
│ ┣ IndexedCollection
│ │ ┣ FixedSizeCollection
│ │ │ ┣ Array
│ │ │ │ ┗ CompiledMethod
│ │ │ ┣ Bitmap
│ │ │ ┣ ByteArray
│ │ │ ┣ Interval ‹at:put:›
│ │ │ ┣ String ‹at:put:›
│ │ │ ┃ ┗ Symbol ‹at:put:›
│ │ ┗ OrderedCollection ‹at:put:›
│ │   ┣ Process
│ │   ┗ SortedCollection ‹at:put:›
│ ┗ Set ‹at:put:›
│   ┣ Dictionary ‹at:put:›
│   │ ┣ IdentityDictionary ‹at:put:›
│   │ ┃ ┗ MethodDictionary ‹at:put:›
│   │ ┗ SystemDictionary ‹at:put:›
│   ┗ SymbolSet
  .
  .
┣ DisplayObject
│ ┗ DisplayMedium
│   ┗ Form ‹at:put:›
  .
  .
┗ MType
    │ .
    │ .
    ┗ ListRec ‹at:put:›
      .
      .
```

Fig. 1.   Smalltalk/V partial object hierarchy showing **at:put:** methods.

For example, the Smalltalk/V[1] system provides a large body of reusable object classes organized in a hierarchy as shown in Fig. 1 [5]. Fourteen of these object classes implement the **at:put:** message, which generally is used to place an object at a particular place within a collection of objects. Encountering an unfamiliar **at:put:** message while trying to understand a Smalltalk/V program, a maintainer would normally use a cross-reference browser to look at the code being invoked by the message. However, it may be difficult for the maintainer to decide which of the 14 methods must be examined. A more sophisticated tool, such as a program slicer [27], would have even greater difficulty in tracing the data flow of the message since it would not be able to use the maintainer's background knowledge to limit its search to a few object classes.

Broadly speaking there would seem to be four approaches to the problem.

1) Perform a "worst case" analysis in which the possible effects of the message are taken to be the union over all the relationships set up by any of the method implementations. This method might be adequate for C++ programs that use the virtual directive sparingly; it will be less satisfactory for systems such as Fig. 1 that have many implementations of a given message.

[1] Bellcore does not provide comparative analysis or evaluation of products or suppliers. Any mention of products or suppliers in this paper is done where necessary for the sake of scientific accuracy and precision or for background information to a point of technical analysis, or to provide an example of a technology for illustrative purposes, and should not be construed as either positive or negative commentary on that product or vendor. Neither the inclusion of a product or a vendor, nor the omission of a product or vendor, should be interpreted as indicating a position or opinion of that product or vendor on the part of the authors or of Bellcore. Bellcore does not make any purchasing recommendations.

2) Use dynamic analysis, in which the program is run for several test cases with probes inserted to detect the real classes of the objects of interest. The problem, of course, is that the test cases may not detect all the behavior that the program is capable of exhibiting, and thus incorrect conclusions may be drawn.

3) Allow human input to identify the possible classes of objects. We are exploring a design for a more sophisticated Dependency Analysis Tool Set that would allow the user to describe the expected classes of the objects that the program is manipulating. In several cases that we have studied, it would seem that the user can limit the scope of a query to obtain much more focused results. Again, however, the obvious problem is that the human may give the wrong constraints, leading again to incorrect analysis of the system.

4) It may be possible to analyze each message to reduce greatly the number of possible classes for each object. For example some of Graver's work on type analysis of Smalltalk has shown promising results in this area [8]. If types are declared for a relatively small number of objects in the program, the types of many of the remaining objects can be deduced. Even if it is not possible to make a precise determination, it may often be feasible to reduce greatly the number of possibilities.

We would suggest that environments for object-oriented maintenance should provide support for several of these approaches. Debugging environments could usefully store information about the classes of each object that have been encountered at run-time. Analysis tools should be able to make use of such information, as well as human input, to limit the scope of analysis. When no other information is available, tools should default to showing all the potential dependencies in the system using the first approach mentioned above. It may be useful to maintain the distinction between the set of potential relationships and the more limited set of probable relationships found after pruning using one of the mentioned approaches. The first set would be used by tools checking for subtle ripple effects or bugs but the second would probably be sufficient for general program understanding tasks.

III. DEPENDENCIES IN OBJECT-ORIENTED SYSTEMS

A dependency in a software system is, informally, a direct relationship between two entities in the system $X \rightarrow Y$ such that a programmer modifying X must be concerned about possible side effects in Y. Earlier reports ([28]–[30]) analyzed the dependencies in conventional software systems. The main kinds of entity considered were data items (or variables), processing modules, and data types. Dependencies were classified as follows:

- data dependencies between two variables;
- calling dependencies between two modules;
- functional dependencies between a module and the variables it computes;
- definitional dependencies between a variable and its type.

119

To deal with object oriented languages, we need to add the following kinds of entities:[2]

- object classes;
- methods (which are specific code segments);
- messages (which may be thought of as "names" of methods).

Variables may now represent instances of an object class instead of, or in addition to, conventional data values. Object classes may be thought of as special kinds of types while methods are special kinds of processing module. However the use of polymorphism and hierarchy creates an explosion in the kinds of dependencies that need be considered:

Class-to-Class Dependencies:
— C1 is a direct super class of C2
— C1 is a direct sub class of C2
— C1 inherits from C2
— C1 uses C2 (which may be subclassified as "uses for interface", and "uses for implementation")

Class to Method:
— method M returns object of class C
— C implements method M
— C inherits method M

Class to Message:
— C understands message

Class to Variable:
— V is an instance of class C
— V is a class variable of C
— V is an instance variable of C
— V is defined by class C

Method to Variable:
— V is a parameter for method M
— V is a local variable in method M
— V is imported by M (ie, is a nonlocal variable used in M)
— V is defined by M
— M refers to V

Method to Message:
— message M' is name of method M
— method M sends message M'

Method to Method:
— method M1 invokes method M2
— method M1 overrides M2

Environments for maintaining OOP's need to provide ways of browsing these different kinds of relationships. The multi-dimensional nature of the interconnections will make it very difficult to use listing or text screen based systems for program understanding. Multi-window displays would seem to be a minimum requirement to display enough information.

IV. THE STRUCTURE OF OOP's

There is a general impression among practitioners that OOP's may tend to be structured rather differently than

[2] In the absence of a standard object oriented terminology, we have adopted Smalltalk's terms; in C++ the corresponding terms would be classes, member functions, and member function names.

TABLE I
SIZES OF METHODS IN THREE OBJECT-ORIENTED SYSTEMS

System and Domain	Language	Number of Methods	Median Method Size
Bellcore: Interactive network design aid	C++	1280	1 executable statement
Bellcore: Prototype of noninteractive task planning system	Smalltalk	477	2 noncomment lines
Smalltalk/V: Sample from the environment's class library	Smalltalk	2224	3 noncomment lines

conventional programs. For many tasks very brief methods may be written that simply "pass through" a message to another method with very little processing. Thus a system may consist of a large number of very small modules rather than a relatively smaller number of larger ones.

We know of no large-scale study of the metrics of object-oriented systems. However we have collected data on the three systems shown in Table I [31]. The small sizes of the methods are striking. Although the three systems are for very different problem domains, in all three cases 50% of the methods are less than 2 C++ statements or 4 Smalltalk lines long.

This sample may not, of course, be typical of OOP practices in other systems and languages. However, some of the work on good object oriented programming style would seem to encourage the use of many small methods [11]. The Law of Demeter proposed by Lieberherr and Holland would restrict a method from " . . . retrieving a subpart of an object that lies deep in that object's Part-of hierarchy" [14]. Such prohibited accesses would probably be eliminated by encapsulating the work in specialized methods of the supplier class, with the effect of taking code out of one client method and distributing it through several small methods in the supplier. Lieberherr and his associates have proposed a language of propagation patterns that a programmer could use to reduce the number of methods that need to be constructed [15] and have suggested a way of abstracting out the propagation patterns from existing code to facilitate understanding [26].

If this pattern of a large number of rather small methods does turn out to be typical, there are significant implications for maintenance tool support. The code for any given task would be very widely dispersed [20]. Understanding of a single line of code may require tracing a chain of method invocations through several different object classes and up and down the object hierarchy to find where the work is really getting done (see Fig. 2). Such searching is both time-consuming and error prone. Most existing browsers would have the maintainer walk down the links in the chain one by one, opening a new browse window at each step. However, the result is likely to be a clutter of overlaid windows that adds little to program understanding.

We would suggest that tools for OOP need to address specifically the problem of finding chains of relationships rather than simply cross-referencing the links in a chain. Finding such chains may be complicated by the dynamic

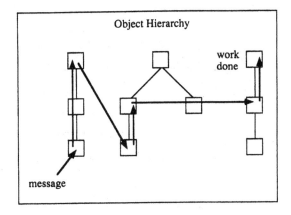

Fig. 2. Typical chain of message invocations.

binding problems discussed in Section II. Also, more interface design work is needed to find better ways of displaying such chains in a comprehensible way without unnecessary clutter. While such displays may be difficult to design, the task of developing them would be considerably eased by the relatively small size of the methods at each link of the chain.

V. HIGH-LEVEL SYSTEM UNDERSTANDING

High level system understanding is chiefly needed when a maintainer is coming to grips with a system for the first time. The maintainer needs some way to sort out the components and perceive the overall architecture of the system. A high-level understanding will give a maintainer a framework to help make sense of the more detailed information acquired as specific maintenance tasks are undertaken.

There is little tool support for high-level system understanding even for conventional (i.e., nonobject oriented) systems. Several researchers have suggested using clustering methods of different kinds to identify system structure (e.g., [2], [17], [10], [24], [25]). However, we know of no generally available tools implementing these ideas.

The module calling hierarchy or structure chart can be generated by several existing tools (e.g., [12]). Calling hierarchies are a useful tool for understanding systems designed using functional decomposition approaches in which the main packaging unit is the processing module (e.g, a function or procedure). In such systems the top level "main module" will likely be a good place to start in system understanding and, if the modules subordinate to it are reasonably cohesive, examining them may give a quick overview of system functions.

But in OOP, the calling hierarchy would be a hierarchy of methods, which has several disadvantages. First, the dynamic binding problem mentioned in Section II may make the hierarchy difficult to compute. Second, there may be no real "main" method in the system [19]. This is one of the facts about object oriented design that beginners tend to find disconcerting. Finally, a hierarchy of methods loses sight of the grouping of methods in objects, which is presumably the most important aspect of the design. An obvious understanding aid would be the object class hierarchy, but because it groups

objects with similar methods, it fails to show how the objects combine to provide the different functional capabilities of the program. For example, in Smalltalk/V the `Pane` objects work together with `Dispatcher` objects to provide windows for text editing. But these objects are in different class hierarchies. Helm, Holland, and Gangopodhyay have suggested that object oriented systems should really be described using *contracts* that specify the relationships among such cooperating objects [9].

One possible high-level understanding tool would be a display of the graph of the "Class Uses Class" dependency described in Section III. However the result will be a graph not a hierarchy; graphs are notoriously more difficult to display and comprehend than trees. In a medium scale system with hundreds of object classes the graph may not be particularly comprehensible.

Environments for object-oriented maintenance should probably provide several alternative clustering methods that can be chosen by the user during system exploration. The "Class Uses Class" dependency could provide the links for clustering but some experimentation will be needed to find the most useful methodologies. As suggested by Hutchens and Basili (in [10]) it would probably be necessary to first identify and remove utility classes such as `String`, `Integer`. etc. that will have connections to a large number of classes and will thus turn the graph into a spiderweb.

VI. LOCATING SYSTEM FUNCTIONALITY

In the object-oriented paradigm, the location of methods may be more crucial than in conventional programs. The location problem arises partly from the cornucopia of objects and methods offered by systems like Smalltalk. It has been observed that it may be quite difficult to find, for example, the right class to use for a group of objects out of Smalltalk's many different classes of `Collection` [20]. Another source of the problem is that it may not always be easy to determine which of two or three object classes should be the "host" for a given function. In a library information system, did the designer decide that checking out a book was a method on class `Book`, class `LibraryUser`, or class `Library`?

Thus the maintainer of an OOP may have some difficulty in finding where different functions are carried out, either to reuse them or to modify them. While locating code can also be difficult in conventional programs the dispersion of functionality into different object classes may make the problem more serious for OOP. At a minimum, if the reuse benefits of OOP are to be achieved it must be possible to locate the code to be reused fairly efficiently.

Dynamic analysis may be the best solution. A test case is needed that causes the system to exercise the functionality that is being sought. Debugging environments allow the maintainer to trace or step through the execution of the code, identifying the object classes and methods that are involved. Unfortunately, if little prior information is available to aid in setting breakpoints, it may be necessary to step through a great deal of code to find the code segments of interest.

We would suggest experimenting with statistical analysis of traces of programs. Traces of method invocations could be made of test cases that exercise the functionality in question and compared to traces of other cases where that functionality is expected to be absent. One could imagine a graphic display of the object hierarchy showing only those methods that appear in the first set of traces and not in the second.

VII. UNDERSTANDING POLYMORPHISM

Polymorphism requires consistent use of method names within a system. In theory, a given message name should mean "the same thing" to any object that responds to it. In the example in Fig. 1 the `at:x put:y` message is implemented differently by many different classes, but it should always place the object `y` at the specified location within the receiving collection. The maintainer of such a system knowing what the message means, need not investigate its implementation anew for each implementing class. The use of such *standard protocols* has been identified as one of the strengths of object-oriented methodology [11].

If, however, method naming is not done consistently, subtle errors may be introduced. For example, if a system contains several implementations of the same message with significantly different effects, a maintainer may be misled in interpreting the code and introduce errors when changes are made. Practicing programmers have told us of finding cases of naming confusions; an example from the Smalltalk/V library is given below.

A maintainer who imperfectly understands the naming conventions used by the designers is particularly likely to introduce these kinds of errors, at considerable cost to later maintainers. While problems of inconsistent use of naming conventions are also found in conventional systems, in OOP more reliance is placed on correct naming. In many conventional languages the compiler or linker would complain if two modules had the same name; in OOP such duplicate naming is actively encouraged!

No totally automatic solution would seem to be possible for keeping similar the semantics of similarly named methods. However, some automatic support might be possible using the concept of the *external dependency graph* of each method. External dependency graphs were introduced to represent the effects of execution of a module in a conventional programming language [29]. The graph, which may often be calculated automatically using data flow methods, shows the dependencies between data items that are created by the module.

The different implementations of a message may be categorized into equivalence classes based on their external dependency graphs. As an example consider Smalltalk/Vs 14 implementations of `at:x put:y` shown in Fig. 1. It will be remembered that these methods place the object `y` at location `x` within the receiver. The result of a simplified hand calculation of their external dependency graphs is shown in Fig. 3. As can be seen, there are four equivalence classes of the graphs, which hint at four different kinds of semantic behavior of these 14 methods. Dependency Pattern A seems to be the standard case and is, presumably, the pattern desired by the original

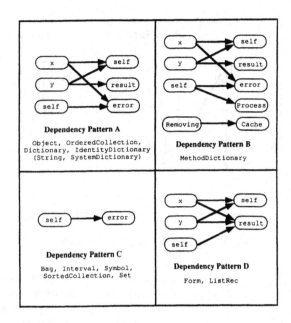

Fig. 3. External dependencies of the Smalltalk/V `at:x put:y` methods.

designers of the system. Each of these methods uses the value of `self` (the receiver) and `x` (the location) to check that the operation can be performed; in other words, there is a valid location `x` within object `self`. (For simplicity we represent the error checking by a graph node called `error`. The actual processing involves calling error handling routines in the Smalltalk/V environment.) The value of `y` is placed at location `x` in `self`, thus changing `self`. Finally, the parameter `y` is returned as the result of the operation. This pattern of dependencies is created by the methods in the classes `Object`, `OrderedCollection`, `Dictionary`, `IdentityDictionary` while very similar patterns, with slightly more error checking, are found in `String` and `SystemDictionary`.

Dependency Pattern B shows more complicated processing since, when the `MethodDictionary` is changed, the Smalltalk/V environment must be updated to make sure that any future message sends will find the new method, not the old. The use of the `at:x put:y` message name is reasonable, but maintainers may need to be aware of this special processing. Dependency Pattern C shows methods which are simple error stubs, since `Bag`, `Interval`, `Symbol`, `SortedCollection` and `Set` do not allow values to be placed at a specified location.

The most interesting case is Dependency Pattern D, for the `Form` and `ListRec` classes. Some external dependencies are similar to those of the standard case but these methods return `self` instead of returning parameter `y`. It would seem likely that these methods were added by a different coder who did not respect the implicit naming conventions of the system. The methods constitute a potential trap for any maintainer who uses them without careful study of their code. We would suggest that projects that use polymorphism heavily should consider comparing the external dependency graphs of methods to detect such problems before they cause trouble.

VIII. Detailed Code Understanding

Detailed code understanding is at the heart of the maintenance process. Maintainers spend a large fraction of their time doing code reading tasks to understand precisely the module that they are going to modify. The typical question at this point is: "What exactly is this line of code doing?" In conventional programs the answer is normally found by studying the function calls and the data items in the code and then reading the function implementations and searching out the definitions and uses of the data. Cross referencers and browsers aid in this process (e.g., [3], [6], [22]). Such tools have been implemented in many programming environments. Other tools that have been proposed, but more rarely implemented, include ripple effect analyzers [32] and program slicers [27].

The class hierarchy and polymorphism seem to introduce two kinds of complications to detailed code understanding. First, as mentioned in Section IV, the code that must be examined to understand a given method may be quite widely dispersed. Second, as indicated in Section III, hierarchy and polymorphism multiply the number of kinds of relationships that may need to be considered in planning a specific change to an OOP. One approach that may be fruitful would be querying tools and browsers built around the concept of Dependency Analysis given in [29]. Dependency Analysis provides a uniform method of viewing the different kinds of relationship in the system and so can more easily handle the multiple kinds of dependencies of object oriented programs. It also focuses on identifying chains of relationships instead of simple cross-references, and thus may be useful in tracing through widely dispersed code fragments. Browsers may be constructed that display information in multiple windows based on the output of a dependency query [30]. We are currently working on the design of a generalized Dependency Analysis toolset intended to address the problems of OOP.

IX. Some Existing Object-Oriented Environments

This paper does not pretend to be a review of OOP environments, but during its preparation we have seen literature or demonstrations of several of the current commercial products. The products studied include:

- Smalltalk/V with its Application Manager package, from Digitalk, Inc.;
- Objectworks, from ParcPlace Systems;
- Objective-C, from The Stepstone Corp.; and
- Saber C++, from Saber Software, Inc.

Several interesting academic tools have also been described in the literature [13], [23]. It should be remembered that new products are appearing very rapidly and new features are constantly being added to old ones, so our impressions may be out of date.

From the point of view of maintenance, the main kind of static analysis provided by these tools is *cross-reference browsing*. Typically the user can look at the code of one method, select a message or a variable, get a "pick list" of methods implementing the message or of references to the variable, and pop open a window on the corresponding code. Browsing is typically supported using several different kinds of dependencies, such as the class inheritance structure, methods implementing a message, variable references, file locations of definitions, etc.

The dynamic debugging tools provided by several of the products should also be very useful for detailed code understanding during maintenance. Facilities provided include the insertion of breakpoints, various levels of execution stepping and tracing, insertion of test data, monitoring of test coverage, etc. A most important feature is the ability to examine and manipulate objects and their contents easily so that the user can view the actual state of the complex data structures that are established by an OOP. Graphic displays of object relationships would seem to be very useful.

X. Conclusions

This paper has attempted to outline some of the main difficulties that can be expected in maintaining OOP's and has proposed directions for possible tool support of the maintenance process. Some of the main proposals may be summarized as follows.

- Environments for object-oriented maintenance need to address the problem of *dynamic binding*. It is unlikely that any single strategy will be appropriate for all cases so tools could be designed to incorporate multiple sources of information about bindings, ranging from dynamic analysis to human input.
- Statistical clustering tools would form a very useful component of an object oriented maintenance environment. Such tools would aid the maintainer in understanding the high level structure of the system. Similarly, tools for analyzing and comparing traces of system behavior might aid the maintainer in identifying the classes and methods associated with a particular functionality.
- The storage and analysis of external dependency information for methods could aid in controlling some of the semantic problems of polymorphism.
- Designers of several different kinds of tools could find an appropriate paradigm in the concept of Dependency Analysis with its emphasis on tracing chains of relationships.

Acknowledgment

The authors would like to thank P. Matthews of Bell Communications Research both for originally directing our attention to the problems of maintaining object oriented systems and for many ideas contributed during discussions of this topic.

Authors' note: The Florida/Purdue Software Engineering Research Center is supported by Andersen Consulting, Inc., Bell Communications Research, Bell Northern Research, Community Sciences Corporation, Digital Equipment Corporation, GTE Data Services, Harris Corporation, IBM, Magnavox Electronics Co., Northrop Electronics Systems, Sun Microsystems, Inc., The United States Army, and Westinghouse Savannah River Co.

REFERENCES

[1] G. Booch, "Object-oriented development," *IEEE Trans. Software Eng.*, vol. SE-12, pp. 211–221, Feb. 1986.

[2] S.C. Choi and W. Scacchi, "Extracting and restructuring the design of large systems," *IEEE Software*, vol. 7, pp. 66–71, Jan. 1990.

[3] L. Clevland, "A program understanding support environment," *IBM Systems J.*, vol. 28, pp. 324–344, 1989.

[4] B.J. Cox, *Object-Oriented Programming: An Evolutionary Approach.* Reading, MA: Addison Wesley, 1986

[5] Digitalk, Inc., Smalltalk/V Mac Tutorial and Programming Handbook, Digitalk Corp., Los Angeles, CA, 1989.

[6] J. Foster and M. Munro, "A documentation method based on cross-referencing," in *Proc. IEEE Conf. Software Maintenance*, pp. 181–185, Sept. 1987.

[7] A. Goldberg D. Robson, *Smalltalk-80: The Language and Its Implementation.* Reading, MA: Addison Wesley, 1985.

[8] J. Graver and R. Johnson, "A type system for Smalltalk," in *Proc. 17th Annual ACM Symp. Principles of Programming Languages*, pp. 136–150, 1990.

[9] R. Helm *et al.*, "Contracts: Specifying behavioral compositions in object-oriented systems," in *Proc. ECOOP/OOPSLA 90-SIGPLAN Notices*, vol. 25, pp. 169–180, Oct. 1990.

[10] D. Hutchens and V. Basili, "System structure analysis: Clusteing with data bindings," *IEEE Trans. Software Eng.*, vol. SE-11, pp. 749–757, Aug. 1985.

[11] R.E. Johnson and B. Foote, "Designing reusable classes," *J. Object-Oriented Programming*, vol. 1, pp. 25–35, June/July 1988.

[12] D.R. Kuhn, "A source code analyzer for maintenance," in *Proc. IEEE Conf. Software Maintenance*, pp. 176–180, Sept. 1987.

[13] M. Lejter *et al.*, "Support for maintaining object-oriented programs," in *Proc. IEEE Conf. Software Maintenance*, pp. 171–178, Oct. 1991.

[14] K.L. Lieberherr and I.M. Holland, "Assuring good style for object-oriented programs," *IEEE Software*, vol. 6, pp. 38–48, Sept. 1989.

[15] K. Lieberherr *et al.*, "Graph-based software engineering: Concise specifications of cooperative behavior," *Tech. Rep. NU-CCS-91-14*, College of Computer Science, Northeastern University, Sept. 1991.

[16] B.P. Lientz and B. Swanson, *Software Maintenance Management.* Reading, MA: Addison-Wesley, 1980.

[17] S.-S. Liu and N. Wilde, "Identifying objects in a conventional procedural language: An example of data design recovery," in *Proc. IEEE Conf. Software Maintenance*, pp. 266–271, Nov. 1990.

[18] D. Mancl and W. Havanas, "A study of the impact of C++ on software maintenance," in *Proc. IEEE Conf. Software Maintenance*, pp. 63–69, Nov. 1990.

[19] B. Meyer, *Object-Oriented Software Construction.* Englewood Cliffs, NJ: Prentice Hall, 1988.

[20] J. Nielsen and J. Richards, "Experience of Learning and Using Smalltalk", IEEE Software, pp. 73–77, May 1989.

[21] D. Perry and G. Kaiser, "Adequate testing and object-oriented programming," *J. Object Oriented Programming*, vol. 2, pp. 13–19, Jan./Feb. 1990.

[22] V. Rajlich *et al.*, "Visual support for programming-in-the-large," in *Proc., IEEE Conf. Software Maintenance*, pp. 92–99, Oct. 1988.

[23] J. Sametinger, "A tool for the maintenance of C++ programs," in *Proc. IEEE Conf. Software Maintenance*, pp. 54–59, Nov. 1990.

[24] R.W. Schwanke and M.A. Platoff, "Cross references are features," in *Proc. 2nd Int. Workshop on Software Con Fig. Management*, pp. 86-95, Oct. 1989.

[25] R.W. Selby and V. Basili, "Error localization during software maintenance: Generating hierarchical system descriptions from the source code alone," in *Proc. IEEE Conf. Software Maintenance*, pp. 192–197, Oct. 1988.

[26] I. Silva-Lepe, "Abstracting graphed-based specifications of object-oriented programs," *Tech. Rep. NU-CCS-92-4*, College of Computer Science, Northeastern University, Mar. 1992.

[27] M. Weisner, "Program slicing," in *Proc. 5th Int. Conf. Software Engineering*, pp. 439–449, Mar. 1981.

[28] N. Wilde and B. Nejmeh, "Dependency analysis: An aid for software maintenance," *SERC-TR-13-F*, Software Engineering Research Center, Univ. Florida, Gainesville, FL, Sept. 1987.

[29] N. Wilde, R. Huitt, and S. Huitt, "Dependency analysis tools: Reusable components for software maintenance," in *Proc. IEEE Conf. Software Maintenance*, pp. 126–131, Oct. 1989.

[30] N. Wilde and R. Huitt, "A reusable toolset for software dependency analysis," *J. Systems and Software*, vol. 14, pp. 97–102, Feb. 1991.

[31] N. Wilde *et al.*, "Describing object oriented software: What maintainers need to know," *SERC-TR-54-F*, Software Engineering Research Center, Univ. Florida, Gainesville, FL, Dec. 1991.

[32] S.S. Yau, "Ripple effect analysis of software maintenance," in *Proc. COMPSAC-78*, IEEE Computer Society, pp. 60–65, 1978.

Chapter 4

Dependency-Analysis Approaches

Purpose

This chapter examines dependency modeling, including the techniques and formalisms for representing program dependencies. The papers describe some of the key issues in analyzing source-code dependencies from the data, control, and component perspectives. The descriptions of data and control dependencies expose you to program dependence graphs. The treatment of component dependencies gives you insight into change propagation. Much of the material is presented in considerable detail.

The Papers

Dependency analysis is an effective way to identify the impacts of software change. Although programming languages are intended to express instructions to the computer, they frequently do little to convey (or enforce) design information to the software engineer (although this can vary with the language used). Programming languages provide a reasonable structure to capture information about data definition and use as well as logic- and control-flow information. With this data, a programmer can make reasonable decisions as to what statements, modules, and data elements might be affected by a software change.

The chapter begins with a paper that ties control-and data-dependence concepts together. In "Using Dependence Analysis to Support Software Maintenance," Joseph Loyall and Susan Mathisen present a language-independent definition of interprocedural dependency analysis and describe its implementation in a prototype tool that supports software maintenance.

The description of the prototype is a good transition from the previous chapter on automated support for impact analysis. The authors formally define and discuss data, control, and syntactic dependence. They also outline how software maintainers can use these concepts to evaluate the appropriateness of a software change and its effects on

regression testing and to determine the vulnerability of critical source-code sections.

Next, Susan Horwitz, Thomas Reps, and David Binkley present an in-depth treatment of data and control dependence in program slicing across program procedures. In "Interprocedural Slicing Using Dependence Graphs," they introduce the notion of a *system dependence graph* to account for multiple procedures in a program, extending the view of a program dependence graph. The thrust of this paper is an algorithm for interprocedural program slicing that uses the system dependence graph to account for transitive dependencies involved in procedure calls within a program.

In the third paper, "Data Dependency Graphs for Ada Programs," Louise Moser describes a compositional method for constructing data dependency graphs for Ada programs. This method combines composition rule techniques with data dependency graphs to construct larger aggregate units. The author examines composition rules for iteration, recursion, exception handling, and tasking. Many of the ideas presented parallel the use of dependency information in impact analysis.

In the next paper, "Data Flow Analysis and Its Application to Software Maintenance," James Keables, Katherine Robertson, and Anneliese von Mayrhauser describe an incremental data-flow analysis approach. Data-flow analysis, like transitive closure, is a way to determine the impacts of change. An understanding of data-flow analysis is a good foundation for grasping the technical details behind many impact-analysis approaches.

One problem in general for maintaining program-dependency information is that, when a program is modified, this information may have to be generated from scratch. The time to do this is negligible for small programs (usually), but can take hours for large, incremental programs. The authors describe techniques for maintaining this information that do not require from-scratch regeneration.

In the last paper, "Change Impact Identification in Object Oriented Software Maintenance," D. Kung, J. Gao, P. Hsia, F. Wen, Y. Toyoshima, and C. Chen introduce an object-oriented model for identifying change impacts as they pertain to software maintenance. The authors discuss the types of code changes in an object-oriented class library and suggest various automated approaches to identifying different kinds of code changes and their respective impacts. They also describe an object-oriented software-maintenance environment that implements the resulting impact-analysis techniques. This paper offers an object-oriented perspective to analyzing software-change impacts by examining encapsulation, aggregation, inheritance, polymorphism, and dynamic binding.

Using Dependence Analysis to Support the Software Maintenance Process

Joseph P. Loyall Susan A. Mathisen

TASC
Reading, Massachusetts 01867

Abstract

Dependence analysis is useful for software maintenance because it indicates the possible effects of a software modification on the rest of a program. This helps the software maintainer evaluate the appropriateness of a software modification, drive regression testing, and determine the vulnerability of critical sections of code. This paper presents a definition of interprocedural dependence analysis and its implementation in a prototype tool that supports software maintenance.

1 Introduction

One of the major challenges in software maintenance is the need to determine the effects of modifications made to a program. During a survey we performed in which we interviewed several software maintainers involved in the maintenance of three different avionics software applications, each maintainer expressed the desire for automated *change management*. In other words, they wanted the ability to determine the possible semantic effects of a software modification for three reasons:

- To evaluate the appropriateness of a proposed modification. If a change is proposed that has the possibility of affecting large, disjoint sections of a program, the change might need to be re-examined to determine whether a safer change is possible.
- To drive regression testing, i.e., to determine the parts of a program that need to be retested after a change is made.
- To indicate the vulnerability of critical sections of code. If a procedure that provides critical functionality is dependent on many different parts of a program, its functionality is susceptible to changes made in these parts.

Dependence analysis has been proposed as a tool in software maintenance and debugging [10] because it aids the software maintainer in examining and understanding a program. Specifically, dependence analysis is useful for software maintenance to indicate the possible effects of a software modification on the rest of a program [7].

We have developed a notion of interprocedural dependence analysis that indicates the conditions under which a statement of one procedure[1] is dependent on a statement of another procedure. A procedure of a program is considered dependent on another procedure if and only if a statement of the first procedure is dependent on a statement of the second.

Our definitions extend intraprocedural dependence graph concepts presented in [1] and [7]. These definitions of dependence analysis represent a program as one large control flow graph (CFG), with procedures substituted in-line. Our definitions represent a procedural program as a set of CFGs, each representing a procedure, and sets of edges representing procedure calls and returns between them. Our definitions produce the same dependences as those in [7] but utilize smaller graphs and only require computation of dependences for the statements in the body of a procedure once.

Other definitions of interprocedural dependences have been presented in the context of producing *slices* of programs, i.e., a set of statements in a program related by dependences. The interprocedural slices in [10] do not consider the calling context of a procedure and, therefore, produce a less precise set of dependences than our definitions. Horwitz et al. presented definitions of interprocedural dependences that do consider the calling context of procedures, but the definitions are based upon a restricted language [2]. Our definition is language independent and therefore more general.

As part of this research, we have developed a prototype software maintenance environment that provides dependence analysis to indicate the possible effects of software modifications. The prototype also provides automated regression testing, result checking, and test coverage analysis. The prototype implements interprocedural procedure-level dependence analysis based upon the definitions presented in this paper. Procedure-level dependences provide an abstract view that is often closer to the software maintainer's view of large systems. Our survey of software

[1] We use procedure to mean either a procedure, a function, or a main program. A function can be viewed as a procedure with an extra parameter through which a value can be returned.

Reprinted from *Proc. Conf. on Software Maintenance*, IEEE CS Press, Los Alamitos, Calif., 1993, pp. 282–291. Copyright © 1993 by The Institute of Electrical and Electronics Engineers, Inc. All rights reserved.

maintainers indicated that maintainers often have a functional view of the system being maintained, understanding the behavior of particular procedures better than the individual statements and data items implementing a procedure's function. Software maintainers often perform testing based upon this view of the system, choosing tests to exercise particular functions or requirements associated with procedures of the system [9].

This paper is structured as follows: The next section summarizes the relevant definitions of intraprocedural dependences presented by Podgurski and Clarke in [7]. Section 3 presents our definitions of interprocedural dependences, i.e., dependences between statements of different procedures, and a notion of procedure-level dependences based upon interprocedural statement-level dependences. Section 4 describes our prototype software maintenance tool and our implementation of interprocedural procedure-level dependence analysis to support software maintenance. Finally, Section 5 presents conclusions and describes future research.

2 Intraprocedural dependence analysis

This section summarizes the notion of dependences between statements within a program procedure, defined formally in [7]. These definitions are language-independent and presented in terms of characteristics of control flow graphs and def/use graphs. We will expand these definitions in Section 3 to define dependences between procedures.

2.1 Background

The following basic definitions are necessary to define dependence analysis.

Definition 1 A *directed graph* G is a set $G = (N_G, E_G)$ consisting of a nonempty set N_G of nodes, a set $E_G \subseteq (N_G \times N_G)$ of edges. For each $(u, v) \in E_G$, u is the source of (u, v) and v is the target.

Definition 2 A *walk* in a graph G is a finite non-null sequence of nodes $W = n_1 n_2 \cdots n_k$ with each $n_i \in N_G$ for $i = 1 \ldots k$ and each $(n_j, n_{j+1}) \in E_G$ for $j = 1 \ldots k-1$. W is called a walk from n_1 to n_k or a n_1-n_k walk; k is called the length of W.

Definition 3 A *control flow graph (CFG)* G for a procedure of a program is a directed graph that satisfies the following conditions:

1. G contains two distinguished nodes: an initial node $n_{IG} \in N_G$ (which represents the procedure's entry point), and a final node $n_{FG} \in N_G$ (which represents the procedure's exit point).

2. Every node of G occurs on some n_{IG}-n_{FG} walk.

Each node of a CFG represents a simple statement in the procedure represented by the CFG. Each edge represents a possible flow of control from the statement represented by its source node to the statement represented by its target node. There is a designated initial node and a designated final node for each procedure's CFG. This restriction is made for simplicity only. For example, if a procedure has several return statements, the node for each return statement would have an edge to n_{FG} in the CFG for the procedure.

Definition 4 A *def/use graph* is a set $\mathbf{G} = (G, \Sigma, D, U)$, where G is the CFG for a procedure, Σ is a finite set of symbols, $D : N_G \rightarrow \mathcal{P}(\Sigma)$, and $U : N_G \rightarrow \mathcal{P}(\Sigma)$.

The set of symbols Σ is the set of identifiers naming variables that occur in the procedure represented by G. The functions D and U map a node of G to the set of variables *defined* and *used*, respectively, in the statement represented by the node. $\mathcal{P}(\Sigma)$ represents the powerset, i.e., the set of all sets, of Σ.

2.2 Forward dominators

Dependence relations between statements in a procedure are described in [7] in terms of forward dominance.

Definition 5 Let G be a CFG. A node $u \in N_G$ *forward dominates* a node $v \in N_G$ iff every v-n_{FG} walk in G contains u. The node u *properly forward dominates* v iff $u \neq v$ and u forward dominates v. The node u *strongly forward dominates* v iff u forward dominates v and there is an integer $k \geq 1$ such that every walk in G beginning with v and of length $\geq k$ contains u. A node $u \in N_G$ is the *immediate forward dominator* of a node $v \in (N_G - \{n_{FG}\})$ iff u is the first node that properly forward dominates v on every v-n_{FG} walk in G.

2.3 Control dependence

There are two notions of control dependence, *strong* and *weak* control dependence. Strong control dependences occur when the execution of a statement in a procedure can determine which of several alternative control paths are executed, thereby bypassing some statements. For example, the condition of a branch statement determines which branch is executed, and the condition of a loop determines whether the body of the loop is executed.

Weak control dependence includes both strong control dependence and the case where execution of a statement can indefinitely delay the execution of certain statements. For example, the condition of a loop can cause the body of the loop to be executed an infinite number of times, thereby indefinitely delaying execution of any statements following the loop. Strong and weak control dependence are defined formally in the following definitions.

Definition 6 Let G be a CFG and let $u, v \in N_G$. Node u is *directly strongly control dependent* on v iff v has successors v' and v'' such that u forward dominates v' but does not forward dominate v''. Node u

is *strongly control dependent* on v iff there exists a v-u walk not containing the immediate forward dominator of v.

Definition 7 Let G be a CFG and let $u, v \in N_G$. Node u is *directly weakly control dependent* on v iff v has successors v' and v'' such that u strongly forward dominates v' but does not strongly forward dominate v''. Node u is *weakly control dependent* on v iff there exists a sequence of nodes, $n_1, n_2, \ldots, n_k$, $k \geq 2$, such that $u = n_1$, $v = n_k$, and n_i is directly weakly control dependent on n_{i+1} for $i = 1, 2, \cdots, k-1$.

2.4 Data dependence

A data dependence exists when one statement provides a value subsequently used by another statement either directly or through a chain of data definitions and references.

Definition 8 Let $\mathbf{G} = (G, \Sigma, D, U)$ be a def/use graph and let $u, v \in N_G$. Node u is *directly data dependent* on node v iff there is a walk vWu in G such that $(D(v) \cap U(u)) - D(W) \neq \emptyset$. Node u is *data dependent* on v iff there exists a sequence of nodes, $n_1, n_2, \ldots, n_k$, $k \geq 2$, such that $u = n_1$, $v = n_k$, and n_i is directly data dependent on n_{i+1} for $i = 1, 2, \cdots, k-1$.

$D(W)$ denotes the union of all $D(n_i)$, where n_i is a node in the sequence W.

2.5 Syntactic dependence

A statement in a procedure is syntactically dependent on another statement of the procedure if there is a chain of control and data dependences between the two statements.

Definition 9 Let $\mathbf{G} = (G, \Sigma, D, U)$ be a def/use graph and let $u, v \in N_G$. Node u is *weakly syntactically (strongly syntactically) dependent* on node v iff there is a sequence of nodes, $n_1, n_2, \ldots, n_k$, $k \geq 2$, such that $u = n_1$, $v = n_k$, and either n_i is *weakly (strongly) control dependent* on n_{i+1} or n_i is data dependent on n_{i+1} for $i = 1, 2, \cdots, k-1$.

3 Interprocedural dependence analysis

This section extends the definitions in Section 2 to define dependence relations between procedures of a program. Informally, a procedure A is considered to be dependent on a procedure B if and only if at least one statement in A is dependent on a statement in B. First, we define dependence relations between statements of different procedures. Our definitions of interprocedural statement-level dependence analysis are language independent because they are based upon CFGs and def/use graphs, extending the definitions in [7] (summarized in Section 2). Finally, we formally define dependence relations between procedures of a program based upon dependence relations between their statements.

3.1 Background

The following basic definitions are necessary to define interprocedural dependence analysis.

Definition 10 An *interprocedural control flow graph* for a program is a set $\mathcal{G} = (G_1, \ldots, G_k, C, R)$, consisting of control flow graphs $G_1, \ldots, G_k$ representing procedures in the program, a set C of *call* edges, and a set R of *return* edges. An interprocedural control flow graph $\mathcal{G}$ satisfies the following conditions:

1. There is a one-to-one onto mapping between C and R. Each call edge is of the form $(u, n_{IG_j}) \in C$ and the corresponding return edge is of the form $(n_{FG_j}, u) \in R$, where $u \in N_{G_i}$ for some $G_i \in \mathcal{G}$ and n_{IG_j} and n_{FG_j} are the initial and final nodes, respectively, of some $G_j \in \mathcal{G}$.

2. $\mathcal{G}$ contains two distinguished nodes: an initial node $n_{I\mathcal{G}} = n_{IG_i}$ and a final node $n_{F\mathcal{G}} = n_{FG_i}$, $G_i \in \mathcal{G}$.

An interprocedural CFG is a set of CFGs for procedures linked together by call and return edges[2]. Each call edge is an edge from a node representing a procedure call to the initial node of the CFG for the called procedure. There is a corresponding return edge for each call edge from the final node of the called procedure's CFG back to the node representing the procedure call. For simplicity, we assume that there is a designated initial node and a designated final node for the interprocedural CFG and that there are no unstructured halts within procedures. We will show how to relax these restrictions in Section 3.6.

Figure 1 illustrates an interprocedural CFG $\mathcal{G}$ representing a program that searches an array of trees. $\mathcal{G} = (G_{\text{main}}, G_{\text{search}}, C, R)$ where $C = \{(5, \text{search}_I), (11, \text{search}_I), (12, \text{search}_I)\}$, $R = \{(\text{search}_F, 5), (\text{search}_F, 11), (\text{search}_F, 12)\}$, $n_{I\mathcal{G}} = \text{main}_I$, and $n_{F\mathcal{G}} = \text{main}_F$. The solid arrows represent edges in the CFGs for **main** (G_{main}) and **search** (G_{search}). The dashed lines represent call and return edges.

Definition 11 An *interprocedural def/use graph* is a set $\Theta = (\mathcal{G}, \Sigma, D, U)$, where $\mathcal{G} = (G_1, \ldots, G_k, C, R)$ is an interprocedural CFG, Σ is a finite set of symbols, $D : (N_{G_1} \cup \cdots \cup N_{G_k}) \rightarrow \mathcal{P}(\Sigma)$, $U : (N_{G_1} \cup \cdots \cup N_{G_k}) \rightarrow \mathcal{P}(\Sigma)$.

The set of symbols Σ is the set of identifiers naming variables that occur in the set of procedures represented by $\mathcal{G}$. We assume uniqueness of identifiers. This is simply a conceptual distinction, since different variables with identical identifiers can be given unique tags. The functions D and U represent the definitions and uses, respectively, of variables at nodes in $\mathcal{G}$. They include the definitions and uses of actual and formal parameters at nodes representing procedure calls.

---

[2]Our definition of interprocedural control flow graphs differs only slightly from the definition of ICFGs in [4], which has explicit call and return nodes for each procedure call.

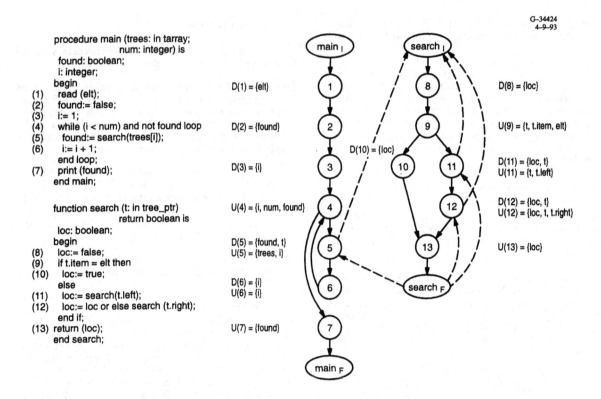

```
procedure main (trees: in tarray;
                num: integer) is
    found: boolean;
    i: integer;
    begin
(1)    read (elt);
(2)    found:= false;
(3)    i:= 1;
(4)    while (i < num) and not found loop
(5)       found:= search(trees[i]);
(6)       i:= i + 1;
       end loop;
(7)    print (found);
    end main;


function search (t: in tree_ptr)
                 return boolean is
    loc: boolean;
    begin
(8)    loc:= false;
(9)    if t.item = elt then
(10)      loc:= true;
       else
(11)      loc:= search(t.left);
(12)      loc:= loc or else search (t.right);
       end if;
(13)   return (loc);
    end search;
```

$D(1) = \{elt\}$

$D(2) = \{found\}$

$D(3) = \{i\}$

$U(4) = \{i, num, found\}$

$D(5) = \{found, t\}$
$U(5) = \{trees, i\}$

$D(6) = \{i\}$
$U(6) = \{i\}$

$U(7) = \{found\}$

$D(8) = \{loc\}$

$U(9) = \{t, t.item, elt\}$

$D(10) = \{loc\}$

$D(11) = \{loc, t\}$
$U(11) = \{t, t.left\}$

$D(12) = \{loc, t\}$
$U(12) = \{loc, t, t.right\}$

$U(13) = \{loc\}$

Figure 1: **Trees search program and its interprocedural def/use graph**

Formally, let $G_i, G_j \in \mathcal{G}$ be CFGs in the interprocedural def/use graph Θ. For each $n_c \in N_{G_i}$, such that $(n_c, n_{IG_j}) \in C$ (and, therefore, $(n_{FG_j}, n_c) \in R$), $D(n_c)$ includes

- formal parameters of the called procedure into which values are passed

- actual parameters into which values are returned (including variables into which function values are returned).

$U(n_c)$ includes

- actual parameters from which values are passed

- formal parameters of the called procedure through which values are returned.

Figure 1 illustrates the D and U sets for each node of the trees search program. Empty sets are omitted.

Definition 12 An *interprocedural walk*, $\mathcal{W}$, in an interprocedural CFG $\mathcal{G} = (G_1, G_2, \ldots, G_k, C, R)$ is a sequence of nodes $n_1 n_2 \ldots n_l$ where $n_i \in (N_{G_1} \cup N_{G_2} \cup \cdots \cup N_{G_k})$, $i = 1 \ldots l$, and $(n_j, n_{j+1}) \in (E_{G_1} \cup E_{G_2} \cup \cdots \cup E_{G_k} \cup C \cup R)$. $\mathcal{W}$ satisfies the following conditions:

1. $\mathcal{W}$ contains the sequence $u n_{IG} \mathcal{Y} n_{FG} v$, where $G \in \mathcal{G}$, $\mathcal{Y}$ is a sequence of nodes, and $u \neq v$, iff $\mathcal{Y}$ contains the subsequence $v n_{IG}$.

2. $\mathcal{W}$ cannot contain the sequence $n_{FG} v n_{IG}$, for any $G \in \mathcal{G}$, $v \in (N_{G_1} \cup N_{G_2} \cup \cdots \cup N_{G_k})$.

3. $\mathcal{W}$ contains the sequence uvw, where $(v, n_{IG}) \in C$ and $u \neq n_{FG}$ for some $G \in \mathcal{G}$, iff $w = n_{IG}$.

An interprocedural u-v walk $\mathcal{W}$ in $\mathcal{G}$ represents a valid execution path from u to v in $\mathcal{G}$. Not every path in a program's interprocedural CFG represents a valid execution path of the program. This is because a procedure call in a program causes the procedure to be executed exactly once and then returns to the point of the call. However, in the interprocedural CFG for a program there might be several return edges leading from the final node in a procedure. Therefore, there is often a path that enters a procedure from one node and returns from the procedure to a different node, although such a path does not correspond to a valid execution of the program. For example, in Figure 1 the CFG for **search** has three return edges, therefore there is a path that enters the **search** procedure from node 5 and returns to node 12, an invalid execution path. Condition 1 of Definition 12 ensures that an interprocedural walk remembers its "calling context" so that it must return to the node that called it[3].

---

[3] This ensures that our definitions of interprocedural dependences are more precise than those presented in [10] which do not consider the calling context. Our definitions are as powerful

Condition 2 ensures that an interprocedural walk does not immediately reenter a procedure's CFG after leaving it. Condition 3 ensures that an interprocedural walk that includes a procedure call node proceeds into the procedure's CFG, unless it just returned from it. These conditions are necessary because a procedure call represents exactly one execution of the procedure; when it is encountered, the procedure must be executed and upon return from the call, the statement following the calling statement must be executed.

For example, the walk

$$\mathcal{W} = 4, 5, \text{search}_I, 8, 9, 10, 13, \text{search}_F, 5$$

is a valid interprocedural walk in the interprocedural CFG of Figure 1. However,

$$\mathcal{W}' = 4, 5, \text{search}_I, 8, 9, 10, 13, \text{search}_F, 12, 13, \text{search}_F, 5$$

is not because $\mathcal{W}'$ contains the subsequence

$$5, \text{search}_I, \mathcal{Y}, \text{search}_F, 12$$

where $\mathcal{Y} = 8, 9, 10, 13$, but

$$12, \text{search}_I \not\subseteq \mathcal{Y}$$

(condition 1 of Definition 12). Likewise, the sequences

$$13, \text{search}_F, 5, \text{search}_I$$

and

$$4, 5, 6$$

are not valid interprocedural walks (conditions 2 and 3 of Definition 12).

Definition 13 Let $\mathcal{G}$ be an interprocedural CFG and let G_i and G_j be CFGs in $\mathcal{G}$. Let $u \in N_{G_i}$ and $v \in N_{G_j}$. Node u *forward dominates* node v iff every v-$n_{F\mathcal{G}}$ interprocedural walk in $\mathcal{G}$ contains u. The node u *properly forward dominates* v iff $u \neq v$ and u forward dominates v. The node u *strongly forward dominates* v iff u forward dominates v and there is an integer $k \geq 1$ such that every interprocedural walk in $\mathcal{G}$ beginning with v and of length $\geq k$ contains u. The node u is the *immediate forward dominator* of the node v iff u is the first node that properly forward dominates v on every v-$n_{F\mathcal{G}}$ interprocedural walk in $\mathcal{G}$.

By this definition, a node is only involved in an interprocedural forward dominance relation if there is a path from the node to the final node of its interprocedural CFG. Since Definition 3 requires that every node in a procedure's CFG must occur on a walk from the initial node of the CFG to the final node of the CFG and every call edge in an interprocedural CFG has a corresponding return edge, every node in an interprocedural CFG $\mathcal{G}$ lies on a $n_{I\mathcal{G}} - n_{F\mathcal{G}}$ interprocedural walk as long as there is a call to the node's procedure along the walk. If there is no call to a procedure along any $n_{I\mathcal{G}} - n_{F\mathcal{G}}$ interprocedural walk, the procedure

as those in [2] which do consider the calling context, but more general because they are language independent.

is never executed. Therefore, there can be no dependences between it and other, executed procedures of the program. There are still dependences among statements within the unexecuted procedure, according to the definitions in Section 2. However, there are no forward dominance or dependence relations between statements of the unexecuted procedure and executed procedures of the program.

3.2 Interprocedural control dependence

A statement in one procedure is strongly control dependent on a statement in another procedure when execution of the second statement is necessary to determine whether the first statement is executed. Likewise, a statement in a procedure is weakly control dependent on a statement in another procedure if the first statement is strongly control dependent on the second or if the second statement can cause execution of the first to be indefinitely delayed.

Definition 14 Let $\mathcal{G}$ be an interprocedural CFG and let G_i and G_j be CFGs in $\mathcal{G}$. Let $u \in N_{G_i}$ and $v \in N_{G_j}$. Node u is *directly strongly control dependent* on v iff v has successors v' and v'' such that u forward dominates v' but does not forward dominate v''. Node u is *strongly control dependent* on v iff there exists a v-u interprocedural walk not containing the immediate forward dominator of v.

For example, node 10 in Figure 1 is directly strongly control dependent on node 9 because 10 forward dominates itself but not node 11. Likewise, node 5 and node 8 are both directly strongly control dependent on node 4. Node 8 is strongly control dependent on node 9 because there is a 9-8 interprocedural walk, $9, 11, \text{search}_I, 8$, that does not contain the immediate forward dominator, 13, of node 9.

Definition 15 Let $\mathcal{G}$ be an interprocedural CFG and let G_i and G_j be CFGs in $\mathcal{G}$. Let $u \in N_{G_i}$ and $v \in N_{G_j}$. Node u is *directly weakly control dependent* on v iff v has successors v' and v'' such that u strongly forward dominates v' but does not strongly forward dominate v''. Node u is *weakly control dependent* on v iff there exists a sequence of nodes, $n_1, n_2, \ldots, n_k$, $k \geq 2$, such that $u = n_1$, $v = n_k$, and n_h is directly weakly control dependent on n_{h+1} for $h = 1, 2, \cdots, k - 1$.

For example, node 7 in Figure 1 is directly weakly control dependent on node 4 because node 7 strongly forward dominates itself but not node 5. Notice that node 7 is not strongly control dependent on node 4 because node 7 is the immediate forward dominator of node 4.

3.3 Interprocedural data dependence

A statement in one procedure is data dependent on a statement in another procedure if the second statement provides data that the first statement subsequently uses.

Definition 16 Let $\Theta = (\mathcal{G}, \Sigma, D, U)$ be an interprocedural def/use graph and let $G_i, G_j \in \mathcal{G}$. Let $u \in N_{G_i}$ and $v \in N_{G_j}$. Node u is *directly data dependent* on node v iff there is an interprocedural walk $v \mathcal{W} u$ in Θ, such that $(D(v) \cap U(u)) - D(\mathcal{W}) \neq \emptyset$. Node u is *data dependent* on v iff there exists a sequence of nodes, $n_1, n_2, \ldots, n_k, k \geq 2$, such that $u = n_1$, $v = n_k$, and n_h is directly data dependent on n_{h+1} for $h = 1, 2, \ldots, k-1$.

For example, node 9 in Figure 1 is directly data dependent on node 1 because of the global variable `elt`. Node 9 is also data dependent on node 5 because statement 5 defines the formal parameter t which is then used by statement 9.

3.4 Interprocedural syntactic dependence

A syntactic dependence between statements of different procedures occurs because of a chain of control or data dependences between the statements.

Definition 17 Let $\Theta = (\mathcal{G}, \Sigma, D, U)$ be an interprocedural def/use graph and let $G_i, G_j \in \mathcal{G}$. Let $u \in N_{G_i}$ and $v \in N_{G_j}$. Node u is *weakly (strongly) syntactically dependent* on node v iff there is a sequence of nodes, $n_1, n_2, \ldots, n_k, k \geq 2$, such that $u = n_1$, $v = n_k$, and n_h is weakly (strongly) control dependent on n_{h+1} or n_h is data dependent on n_{h+1} for $h = 1, 2, \ldots, k-1$.

For example, node 10 in Figure 1 is strongly syntactically dependent on node 1 because node 10 is directly strongly control dependent on node 9 and node 9 is directly data dependent on node 1.

3.5 Procedure-level dependence

A procedure is considered dependent on another procedure iff at least one statement of the first procedure is dependent on a statement of the second.

Definition 18 Let P_i and P_j be two procedures with CFGs G_i and G_j, respectively. P_i is *weakly control (strongly control, data, syntactically) dependent* on P_j iff there exists $n_i \in N_{G_i}$ and $n_j \in N_{G_j}$, such that n_i is weakly control (strongly control, data, syntactically) dependent on n_j.

Theorem 1 *The definitions of interprocedural dependences (Definitions 14, 15, 16, and 17) subsume the intraprocedural dependence definitions (Definitions 6, 7, 8, and 9).*

Proof: This is trivially demonstrated by setting $G_i = G_j$ in each of Definitions 14, 15, 16, and 17. □

3.6 Dependence analysis for nonprocedural and unstructured programs

For simplicity of presentation, our definitions of interprocedural dependence analysis in this paper have assumed that programs are procedural and structured,

i.e., each program consists of well-defined procedures and has a single entry and single exit point. In this section, we relax those assumptions.

Our definitions apply to non-procedural programs by representing a structured non-procedural program as a single CFG of the form described in [7] and Section 2. Treating this CFG as an interprocedural CFG with one procedure and empty sets C and R, the definitions apply and equal the definitions in [7] (Theorem 1).

Supporting programs with unstructured halts requires the following amended definition of interprocedural CFGs.

Definition 10(Amended) An *interprocedural control flow graph* for a program is a set $\mathcal{G} = (G_1, \ldots, G_k, C, R, H)$, consisting of control flow graphs $G_1, \ldots, G_k$ representing procedures in the program, a set C of *call* edges, a set R of *return* edges, and a set H of *halt* edges. An interprocedural control flow graph $\mathcal{G}$ satisfies the following conditions:

1. There is a one-to-one onto mapping between C and R. Each call edge is of the form $(u, n_{IG_j}) \in C$ and the corresponding return edge is of the form $(n_{FG_j}, u) \in R$, where $u \in N_{G_i}$ for some $G_i \in \mathcal{G}$ and n_{IG_j} and n_{FG_j} are the initial and final nodes, respectively, of some $G_j \in \mathcal{G}$.

2. $\mathcal{G}$ contains two distinguished nodes: an initial node $n_{I\mathcal{G}} = n_{IG_i}$ and a final node $n_{F\mathcal{G}} = n_{FG_i}$, $G_i \in \mathcal{G}$.

3. Every edge in H is of the form $(n_H, n_{F\mathcal{G}})$, where n_H represents an unstructured halt of the program and n_H is not the source of any other edges.

Every unstructured halt of the program is represented by a node in the program's interprocedural CFG with an edge in H to the final node of the program's interprocedural CFG. Every interprocedural walk containing a halt node, n_H, must therefore be of the form $\mathcal{Y} n_H$ or $\mathcal{Y} n_H n_{F\mathcal{G}}$, where $\mathcal{Y}$ contains no halt nodes and $(n_H, n_{F\mathcal{G}}) \in H$. Definitions 11 through 18 require no changes; they hold for the unstructured interprocedural CFG of the amended Definition 10.

This changes the conditions of procedural CFGs in Definition 3 slightly when they are present in an interprocedural CFG. The CFG, G, for a procedure still has a single distinguished entry node, n_{IG}. It might have several exit nodes, however: n_{FG} and any number of *halt* nodes. Every node of G occurs on some walk from n_{IG} to one of the exit nodes. When computing the forward dominance relations and dependences between statements within the procedure, each halt node is treated as the source of an edge to n_{FG} (thereby fulfilling the single exit node requirement). When computing the forward dominance relations and dependences between statements in different procedures, halt nodes are treated as the source of an edge to the final node of the interprocedural CFG.

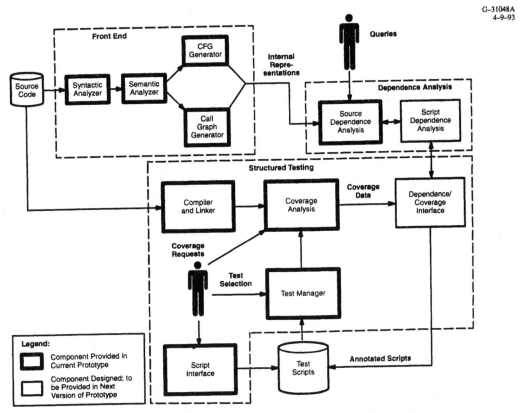

Figure 2: **Architecture of the software maintenance prototype.**

4   A prototype system to support software maintenance

We have developed a prototype system, illustrated in Figure 2, that provides automated support for the software maintenance process. The system provides the following capabilities:

- Dependence analysis to determine the possible effects of software modifications, thereby indicating the portions of a program that need to be regression tested

- Automated test execution to perform regression testing

- Automated result checking to verify test results with the results of previous tests

- Coverage analysis to measure the thoroughness of testing

The prototype implements selected portions of a methodology we developed to provide automated support for verification and validation (V&V) throughout the software life cycle [6]. The prototype supports the maintenance of Ada programs and is hosted in the DEC ULTRIX environment with OSF/MOTIF user interfaces. The Front End incorporates the Arcadia

language processing tools [3]. The Structured Testing component interfaces with commercial test management and coverage tools. The Dependence Analysis component implements conservative but safe approximations of some of the interprocedural procedure-level dependences defined in Section 3.

The rest of this section discusses our implementation of interprocedural procedure-level dependence analysis. More detailed discussion of other components of the maintenance prototype can be found in [5].

4.1   Implementation of procedure-level dependence analysis

Our implementation of procedure-level dependence analysis builds upon the ProDAG analysis system [8]. ProDAG provides statement-level dependence analysis within a single procedure based on Podgurski and Clarke's intraprocedural definitions in [7] (summarized in Section 2). We have extended ProDAG to support interprocedural procedure-level dependence analysis.

The maintenance prototype utilizes ProDAG software to generate the following graphs for each procedure of an Ada program ([8] describes the implementation of these routines):

- a *control flow graph (CFG)* consisting of nodes

representing simple statements and edges representing the flow of control between statements

- a *def/use graph* created by annotating each node of a CFG with the variables defined and used at the node

- a *forward dominator graph* which contains a node corresponding to each node in the procedure's CFG and contains an edge from a node u to a node v iff u forward dominates v.

In addition to these graphs, the maintenance prototype builds a *call graph* for the complete program and annotates each node of the call graph with summary def/use information for the node's procedure. The summary def/use information is used in determining data dependences between procedures based upon global variables, so local variables are pruned from each procedure's *def* and *use* sets.

Each dependence graph is implemented as a set of relationships (i.e., a type of pointer) between nodes in the call graph. For example, to indicate that a procedure P_i is directly data dependent on a procedure P_j, a relationship from the call graph node representing procedure P_i to the node representing procedure P_j is created and added to the direct data dependence set. The following paragraphs describe the algorithms to detect dependences and add relationships to the sets representing dependence graphs. Because of time constraints on development of the initial software maintenance prototype, we have not implemented weak control or weak syntactic dependence and some of the algorithms produce conservative but safe approximations of dependences between procedures of a program. In other words, the algorithms indicate all the procedure-level dependences that exist based on the definitions in Section 3 but also indicate some dependences that do not actually exist. Each paragraph includes an informal justification for the conservative and safe nature of the algorithm.

The procedure-level direct strong control dependence graph. Our direct control dependence algorithm detects only direct *strong* control dependences. First, the CFG, G_i, for each procedure P_i is traversed and two lists are built:

- DOM(P_i) contains an entry for every P_j such that there is a node $u \in N_{G_i}$ that represents a call to P_j and u forward dominates the initial node of G_i (determined by examination of the forward dominator graph for G_i).

- NDOM(P_i) contains an entry for every P_j such that there is a node $u \in N_{G_i}$ that represents a call to P_j and u does not forward dominate the initial node of G_i.

DOM(P_i) represents every procedure call that must occur during execution of P_i. NDOM(P_i) represents procedure calls that might or might not occur during execution of P_i.

A list, $L(P_i)$, of procedures strongly control dependent on a procedure P_i is built using the following algorithm:

1. $L(P_i)$ is initially equal to NDOM(P_i).

2. Starting at the beginning of $L(P_i)$, examine each procedure, P_j, in $L(P_i)$ in order. Any procedures in DOM(P_j) that are not already in $L(P_i)$ are appended to the end of $L(P_i)$. Stop when every procedure in $L(P_i)$ has been examined.

An edge is added to the direct control dependence graph from the node representing each procedure in $L(P_i)$ to P_i. In addition, if P_i has any node u that does not forward dominate the initial node of G_i, an edge is added to the direct control dependence graph from P_i to P_i (Definition 14).

By Definition 5, each member P_j of NDOM(P_i) has a corresponding node $u \in N_{G_i}$, representing a call of P_j, such that there is a walk from the initial node, n_{IG_i}, of G_i to the final node, n_{FG_i}, of G_i that does not contain u. Since, by definition 3, u lies on some n_{IG_i}-n_{FG_i} walk, there exists a branch node, v, in G_i with two successors v' and v'', such that u forward dominates v' but not v''. By Definition 6, u is directly strongly control dependent on v and by Definition 12, n_{IG_j} is also directly strongly control dependent on v. Therefore, by Definition 18, P_j is strongly control dependent on P_i.

Likewise, every node that forward dominates n_{IG_j} is also directly strongly control dependent on v. Therefore, every $P_k \in$ DOM(P_j) is also directly strongly control dependent on P_i.

For example, consider the CFGs in Figure 3. Procedure B is directly strongly control dependent on procedure A because node 2 has successors 3 and 4, such that node 7 (and 8 and 9) forward dominates 4 but not 3. Likewise, procedure C is directly strongly control dependent on procedure A, because node 14 forward dominates node 4 but not 3. However, procedure D is not directly strongly control dependent on procedure A even though it is also called in procedure B, because node 16 does not forward dominate node 4 or 3 (a path through B can bypass the call to D). In addition, since nodes 3 and 4 are both control dependent on node 2, procedure A is directly strongly control dependent on itself. DOM$(A) = \emptyset$, NDOM$(A) = \{B\}$, DOM$(B) = \{C\}$, and NDOM$(B) = \{D\}$. Therefore, the algorithm correctly computes $L(A) = \{A, B, C\}$ and $L(B) = \{B, D\}$.

The procedure-level direct data dependence graph. The direct data dependence graph considers both global data usage and parameter passing between procedures. To determine direct data dependences based on global variables, the *def* and *use* lists for all nodes in the call graph are pairwise compared. If a variable appears on the *def* list for a procedure P_i and also on the *use* list for a procedure P_j, an edge is added to the direct data dependence graph from P_j to P_i. This is a conservative but safe approximation. By Definitions 16 and 18, there is a data dependence (based on global variables) from a procedure P_j to a procedure P_i whenever there is an interprocedural walk vWu such that v represents a statement in P_i that defines a global variable x, u represents a

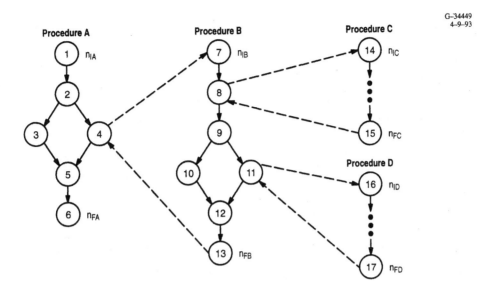

G–34449
4–9–93

Figure 3: **Example:** B and C are directly strongly control dependent on A. B, C, and D are control dependent on A.

statement in P_j that uses x, and x is not redefined anywhere along $\mathcal{W}$. Our algorithm detects such a dependence because it recognizes that v defines x and that u uses x. However, it also indicates a dependence even if the $v\mathcal{W}u$ walk doesn't exist or if $\mathcal{W}$ exists but x is redefined along $\mathcal{W}$.

For every edge from a node n_i to a node n_j in the call graph, the formal parameter list of the procedure, P_j, corresponding to n_j is examined to detect dependences based on parameter passing and function returns. If P_j has an actual parameter qualified as an IN parameter, an edge is added to the direct data dependence graph from P_j to P_i. If P_j has an actual parameter qualified as an OUT parameter or if P_j is a function, an edge from P_i to P_j is added to the direct data dependence graph. If P_j has an IN OUT parameter, an edge from P_i to P_j and an edge from P_j to P_i are both added. Any statements in P_i or P_j using values defined during the procedure call or return clearly lie in an interprocedural walk containing the node representing the procedure call and the resulting direct data dependence (Definition 16) is detected. However, the algorithm does not examine whether statements in the body of P_j actually use values passed in or whether statements in P_i use values that are returned, so the algorithm might indicate dependences that don't exist.

The procedure-level control and data dependence graphs. The strong control dependence graph is built by computing the transitive closure of the direct strong control graph. This indicates all strong control dependences between procedures because any interprocedural walk v-u not containing the immediate forward dominator of v (Definition 14) implies that either u is directly strongly control dependent on v or there is a chain of direct strong control

dependences $n_1, \ldots, n_k$, where $u = n_1$, $v = n_k$, and n_i is directly strongly control dependent on n_{i+1} for $i = 1 \ldots k - 1$.

Likewise, the data dependence graph is built by taking the transitive closure of direct data dependence graphs (Definition 16). This is a conservative and safe approximation because the direct data dependence graphs are conservative and safe.

The procedure-level strong syntactic dependence graph. The strong syntactic dependence graph is built by taking the union of the direct strong control and direct data graphs and then taking the transitive closure of the result. The strong syntactic dependence graph is conservative because of the conservativeness of the direct graphs.

5   Conclusions and future research

We have presented definitions of dependence relations between procedures of a program, both at the statement- and at the procedure-level. The definitions extend the intraprocedural definitions given in [7]. Because our definitions are defined in terms of CFGs, def/use graphs, and dominators, they are language-independent and thereby more general than the interprocedural dependence definitions in [2] which are defined in terms of a simple language. Furthermore, our definitions consider the calling context of a procedure call, requiring that a procedure call return to the place from which it was called. This results in more precise dependence analysis than that in [10], in which an interprocedural *slice*, i.e., a section of a program chosen based on data and control dependences, can include a procedure call that returns to a point other than that from which it was called ([2] also considers calling context). Our definitions are presented in the context of procedural, structured programs, but are straightforward to extend to non-procedural and unstructured programs, as explained in Section 3.6.

We have developed a prototype system that uses dependence analysis to support software maintenance. The prototype indicates direct strong control, direct data, strong control, data, and strong syntactic dependences between procedures of a program. The procedure-level dependences indicated by the prototype are often closer to the software maintainer's functional view of a system than statement- or variable-level dependences. The dependences indicate to a software maintainer the possible effects of software modifications and can be used to judge the appropriateness of a modification, to drive regression testing, and to determine the vulnerability of critical sections of code. The prototype incorporates and builds upon several of the software tools of the Arcadia consortium, including their language processing tools and the ProDAG system. A detailed discussion of the prototype system can be found in [5].

The prototype provides a graphical query interface and dependence results are presented to the user both graphically and textually. The prototype is being demonstrated on avionics Ada software of modest size (approximately 2000 lines of code, 8 procedures). We are currently enhancing the prototype to provide better support for large programs and enhanced graphical interfaces.

The prototype currently provides a conservative but safe approximation of the effects of software modifications based upon dependence analysis. For example, assume that a procedure makes three consecutive calls, to procedures A, B, and C. Also, assume that A and B each define the global variable x and C uses x. Currently, our system would indicate a direct data dependence from C to A because of x. However, because of the intervening definition by B, the assignment to x from A cannot directly affect C's use of x and is a false dependence. Future research will improve our algorithms, improving the approximation of the actual definitions and eliminating some of the false dependences indicated. For example, data dependences will examine possible interprocedural walks in a program. Future research will also investigate the implementation of weak control and weak syntactic dependence.

We also plan to investigate the use of dependence information in conjunction with test coverage information for automated test selection. During structured testing, information about the parts of a program executed by a set of test data is collected and stored in a test coverage database. When the software maintainer makes a change to a program, dependence analysis indicates the parts of the program that could be affected. A test selection tool would use this information and extract test sets from the coverage database that have previously executed the affected parts of the program.

Finally, we plan to provide statement- and variable-level system-wide dependence information in addition to procedure-level. Since this will increase the number of indicated dependences, an enhanced graphical user interface will be developed to effectively manage and present the large amounts of information and to allow the software maintainer to navigate through it.

Acknowledgements

We are grateful to Lori Clarke, who read and commented on an early draft of this paper.

References

[1] J. Ferrante, K.J. Ottenstein, and J.D. Warren. The program dependence graph and its use in optimization. *ACM Transactions on Programming Languages and Systems*, 9(3):319–349, July 1987.

[2] S. Horwitz, T. Reps, and D. Binkley. Interprocedural slicing using dependence graphs. *ACM Transactions on Programming Languages and Systems*, 12(1):26–60, January 1990.

[3] R. Kadia. Issues encountered in building a flexible software development environment. In *Fifth Symposium on Software Development Environments*, McLean, Virginia, December 9-11 1992.

[4] William Landi and Barbara G. Ryder. Pointer-induced aliasing: A problem classification. In *Proceedings 18th ACM Symposium on Principles of Programming Languages*, pages 93–103, Orlando, Florida, January 21-23 1991.

[5] J.P. Loyall, S.A. Mathisen, P.J. Hurley, and J.S. Williamson. Automated maintenance of avionics software. In *Proceedings IEEE NAECON*, Dayton, OH, May 24-28 1993.

[6] J.P. Loyall, S.A. Mathisen, P.J. Hurley, J.S. Williamson, and L.A. Clarke. An advanced system for the verification and validation of real-time avionics software. In *Proceedings 11th IEEE Digital Avionics Systems Conference*, pages 370–375, Seattle, WA, October 5-8 1992.

[7] A. Podgurski and L.A. Clarke. A formal model of program dependences and its implication for software testing, debugging, and maintenance. *IEEE Transactions on Software Engineering*, 16(9):965–979, September 1990.

[8] Debra J. Richardson, T. Owen O'Malley, Cynthia Tittle Moore, and Stephanie Leif Aha. Developing and integrating ProDAG into the Arcadia environment. In *Fifth Symposium on Software Development Environments*, McLean, Virginia, December 9-11 1992.

[9] C.P. Satterthwaite. The maintenance of operational flight programs. In *Proceedings 11th IEEE Digital Avionics Systems Conference*, pages 388–393, Seattle, WA, October 5-8 1992.

[10] Mark Weiser. Program slicing. *IEEE Transactions on Software Engineering*, SE-10(4):352–357, July 1984.

Interprocedural Slicing Using Dependence Graphs

SUSAN HORWITZ, THOMAS REPS, and DAVID BINKLEY
University of Wisconsin–Madison

The notion of a *program slice*, originally introduced by Mark Weiser, is useful in program debugging, automatic parallelization, and program integration. A slice of a program is taken with respect to a program point p and a variable x; the slice consists of all statements of the program that might affect the value of x at point p. This paper concerns the problem of interprocedural slicing—generating a slice of an entire program, where the slice crosses the boundaries of procedure calls. To solve this problem, we introduce a new kind of graph to represent programs, called a *system dependence graph*, which extends previous dependence representations to incorporate collections of procedures (with procedure calls) rather than just monolithic programs. Our main result is an algorithm for interprocedural slicing that uses the new representation. (It should be noted that our work concerns a somewhat restricted kind of slice: rather than permitting a program to be sliced with respect to program point p and an *arbitrary* variable, a slice must be taken with respect to a variable that is *defined* or *used* at p.)

The chief difficulty in interprocedural slicing is correctly accounting for the calling context of a called procedure. To handle this problem, system dependence graphs include some data dependence edges that represent *transitive* dependences due to the effects of procedure calls, in addition to the conventional direct-dependence edges. These edges are constructed with the aid of an auxiliary structure that represents calling and parameter-linkage relationships. This structure takes the form of an attribute grammar. The step of computing the required transitive-dependence edges is reduced to the construction of the subordinate characteristic graphs for the grammar's nonterminals.

Categories and Subject Descriptors: D.3.3 [**Programming Languages**]: Language Constructs—*control structures, procedures, functions, and subroutines*; D.3.4 [**Programming Languages**]: Processors—*compilers, optimization*

General Terms: Algorithms, Design

Additional Key Words and Phrases: Attribute grammar, control dependence, data dependence, data-flow analysis, flow-insensitive summary information, program debugging, program dependence graph, program integration, program slicing, subordinate characteristic graph

An earlier version of this paper appeared in abridged form in the *Proceedings of the ACM SIGPLAN 88 Conference on Programming Language Design and Implementation*, (Atlanta, Ga., June 22–24, 1988), *ACM SIGPLAN Not. 23*, 7 (July 1988) [10].

This work was supported in part by a David and Lucile Packard Fellowship for Science and Engineering, by the National Science Foundation under grants DCR-8552602, DCR-8603356, and CCR-8958530, by the Defense Advanced Research Projects Agency, monitored by the Office of Naval Research under contract N00014-88-K-0590, as well as by grants from IBM, DEC, and Xerox.

Authors' address: Computer Sciences Department, University of Wisconsin–Madison, 1210 W. Dayton St., Madison, WI 53706.

1. INTRODUCTION

The *slice* of a program with respect to program point p and variable x consists of all statements and predicates of the program that might affect the value of x at point p. This concept, originally discussed by Mark Weiser in [22], can be used to isolate individual computation threads within a program. Slicing can help a programmer understand complicated code, can aid in debugging [17], and can be used for automatic parallelization [3, 21]. Program slicing is also used by the algorithm for automatically integrating program variants described in [11]; slices are used to compute a safe approximation to the change in behavior between a program P and a modified version of P, and to help determine whether two different modifications to P interfere.

In Weiser's terminology, a *slicing criterion* is a pair $\langle p, V \rangle$, where p is a program point and V is a subset of the program's variables. In his work, a slice consists of all statements and predicates of the program that might affect the values of variables in V at point p. This is a more general kind of slice than is often needed: rather than a slice taken with respect to program point p and an *arbitrary* variable, one is often interested in a slice taken with respect to a variable x that is *defined* or *used* at p. The value of a variable x defined at p is directly affected by the values of the variables used at p and by the loops and conditionals that enclose p. The value of a variable y *used* at p is directly affected by assignments to y that reach p and by the loops and conditionals that enclose p. When slicing a program that consists of a single monolithic procedure (which we will call in*tra*procedural slicing), a slice can be determined from the closure of the directly-affects relation. Ottenstein and Ottenstein pointed out how well suited *program dependence graphs* are for this kind of slicing [19]; once a program is represented by its program dependence graph, the slicing problem is simply a vertex-reachability problem, and thus slices may be computed in linear time.

This paper concerns the problem of in*ter*procedural slicing—generating a slice of an entire program, where the slice crosses the boundaries of procedure calls. Our algorithm for interprocedural slicing produces a more precise answer than that produced by the algorithm given by Weiser in [22]. Our work follows the example of Ottenstein and Ottenstein by defining the slicing algorithm in terms of operations on a dependence graph representation of programs [19]; however, in [19] Ottenstein and Ottenstein only discuss the case of programs that consist of a single monolithic procedure, and do not discuss the more general case where slices cross procedure boundaries.

To solve the interprocedural-slicing problem, we introduce a new kind of graph to represent programs, called a *system dependence graph*, which extends previous dependence representations to incorporate collections of procedures (with procedure calls) rather than just monolithic programs. Our main result is an algorithm for interprocedural slicing that uses the new representation.

It is important to understand the distinction between two different but related "slicing problems:"

Version 1. The slice of a program with respect to program point p and variable x consists of all statements and predicates of the program that might affect the value of x at point p.

Version 2. The slice of a program with respect to program point p and variable x consists of a reduced program that computes the same sequence of values for x at p. That is, at point p the behavior of the reduced program with respect to variable x is indistinguishable from that of the original program.

For *intra*procedural slicing, a solution to Version 1 provides a solution to Version 2, since the "reduced program" required in Version 2 can be obtained by restricting the original program to just the statements and predicates found in the solution for Version 1 [20].

For *inter*procedural slicing, restricting the original program to just the statements and predicates found for Version 1 may yield a program that is syntactically incorrect (and thus certainly not a solution to Version 2). The reason behind this phenomenon has to do with multiple calls to the same procedure: it is possible that the program elements found by an algorithm for Version 1 will include more than one such call, each passing a different subset of the procedure's parameters. (It should be noted that, although it is imprecise, Weiser's algorithm produces a solution to Version 2.)

In this paper we address Version 1 of the interprocedural slicing problem (with the further restriction, mentioned earlier, that a slice can only be taken with respect to program point p and variable x if x is defined or used at p). The algorithm given in the paper identifies a subgraph of the system dependence graph whose components might affect the sequence of values for x at p. A solution to Version 2 requires either that the slice be extended or that it be transformed by duplicating code to specialize procedure bodies for particular parameter-usage patterns.

Weiser's method for interprocedural slicing is described in [22] as follows:

> For each criterion C for a procedure P, there is a set of criteria $UP_0(C)$ which are those needed to slice callers of P, and a set of criteria $DOWN_0(C)$ which are those needed to slice procedures called by P. ... $UP_0(C)$ and $DOWN_0(C)$ can be extended to functions UP and DOWN which map sets of criteria into sets of criteria. Let CC be any set of criteria. Then
>
> $$UP(CC) = \bigcup_{C \in CC} UP_0(C)$$
> $$DOWN(CC) = \bigcup_{C \in CC} DOWN_0(C)$$
>
> The union and transitive closure of UP and DOWN are defined in the usual way for relations. $(UP \cup DOWN)^*$ will map any set of criteria into all those criteria necessary to complete the corresponding slices through all calling and called routines. The complete interprocedural slice for a criterion C is then just the union of the intraprocedural slices for each criterion in $(UP \cup DOWN)^*(C)$.

However, this method does not produce as precise a slice as possible because the transitive-closure operation fails to account for the calling context of a called procedure.[1]

---

[1] For example, the relation $(UP \cup DOWN)^*(\langle p, V \rangle)$ includes the relation $UP(DOWN(\langle p, V \rangle))$. $UP(DOWN(\langle p, V \rangle))$ includes all call sites that call procedures containing the program points in $DOWN(\langle p, V \rangle)$, not just the procedure that contains p. This fails to account for the calling context, namely the procedure that contains p.

Example. To illustrate this problem, and the shortcomings of Weiser's algorithm, consider the following example program, which sums the integers from 1 to 10. (Except in Section 4.3, where call-by-reference parameter passing is discussed, parameters are passed by value-result.)

```
program Main          procedure A(x, y)      procedure Add(a, b)      procedure Increment(z)
   sum := 0;             call Add(x, y);         a := a + b               call Add(z, 1)
   i := 1;               call Increment(y)    return                   return
   while i < 11 do    return
      call A(sum, i)
   od
end
```

Using Weiser's algorithm to slice this program with respect to variable z and the **return** statement of procedure *Increment*, we obtain everything from the original program. However, a closer inspection reveals that computations involving the variable *sum* do not contribute to the value of z at the end of procedure *Increment*; in particular, neither the initialization of *sum*, nor the first actual parameter of the call on procedure A in *Main*, nor the call on *Add* in A (which adds the current value of i to *sum*) should be included in the slice. The reason these components are included in the slice computed by Weiser's algorithm is as follows: the initial slicing criterion "⟨end of procedure *Increment*, z⟩", is mapped by the DOWN relation to a slicing criterion "⟨end of procedure *Add*, a⟩". The latter criterion is then mapped by the UP relation to *two* slicing criteria—corresponding to *all* sites that call *Add*—the criterion "⟨call on *Add* in *Increment*, z⟩" and the (irrelevant) criterion "⟨call on *Add* in A, x⟩". Weiser's algorithm does not produce as precise a slice as possible because transitive closure fails to account for the calling context (*Increment*) of a called procedure (*Add*), and thus generates a spurious criterion (⟨call on *Add* in A, x⟩).

A more precise slice consists of the following elements:

```
program Main          procedure A(y)         procedure Add(a, b)      procedure Increment(z)
   i := 1;               call Increment(y)       a := a + b               call Add(z, 1)
   while i < 11 do    return                  return                   return
      call A(i)
   od
end
```

This set of program elements is computed by the slicing algorithm described in this paper.

The chief difficulty in interprocedural slicing is correctly accounting for the calling context of a called procedure. To address the calling-context problem, system dependence graphs include some data dependence edges that represent *transitive* dependences due to the effects of procedure calls, in addition to the conventional edges for direct dependences. The presence of transitive-dependence edges permits interprocedural slices to be computed in two passes, each of which is cast as a reachability problem.

The cornerstone of the construction of the system dependence graph is the use of an attribute grammar to represent calling and parameter-linkage relationships among procedures. The step of computing the required transitive-dependence edges is reduced to the construction of the subordinate characteristic graphs for the grammar's nonterminals. The need to express this step in this fashion (rather than, for example, with transitive closure) is discussed further in Section 3.2.

The remainder of the paper is organized as follows: Section 2 defines the dependence graphs used to represent programs in a language without procedure calls. Section 2 also defines the operation of intraprocedural slicing on these dependence graphs. Section 3 extends the definition of dependence graphs to handle a language that includes procedures and procedure calls. The new graphs are called *system dependence graphs*. Section 4 presents our slicing algorithm, which operates on system dependence graphs and correctly accounts for the calling context of a called procedure. It then describes how to improve the precision of interprocedural slicing by using interprocedural summary information in the construction of system dependence graphs, how to handle programs with aliasing, how to slice incomplete programs, and how to compute *forward slices* (i.e., the program elements potentially *affected by* a given variable at a given point). Section 5 discusses the complexity of the slicing algorithm. We have not yet implemented this algorithm in its entirety; thus, Section 5 provides an analysis of the costs of building system dependence graphs and of taking interprocedural slices rather than presenting empirical results. Section 6 discusses related work.

With the exception of the material on interprocedural data-flow analysis employed in Section 4.2, the paper is self-contained; an introduction to the terminology and concepts from attribute-grammar theory that are used in Section 3.2 may be found in the Appendix.

2. PROGRAM-DEPENDENCE GRAPHS AND PROGRAM SLICES

Different definitions of program dependence representations have been given, depending on the intended application; they are all variations on a theme introduced in [16], and share the common feature of having an explicit representation of data dependences (see below). The "program dependence graphs" defined in [7] introduced the additional feature of an explicit representation for control dependences (see below). The definition of program dependence graph given below differs from [7] in two ways. First, our definition covers only a restricted language with scalar variables, assignment statements, conditional statements, while loops, and a restricted kind of "output statement" called an *end statement*,[2] and hence is less general than the one given in [7]. Second, we omit certain classes of data dependence edges and make use of a class introduced in [8, 11]. Despite these differences, the structures we define and those defined in [7] share the feature of explicitly representing both control and data dependences; therefore, we refer to our graphs as "program dependence graphs," borrowing the term from [7].

---

[2] An end statement, which can only appear at the end of a program, names one or more of the variables used in the program; when execution terminates, only those variables will have values in the final state; the variables named by the end statement are those whose final values are of interest to the programmer.

2.1 The Program Dependence Graph

The program dependence graph for program P, denoted by G_P, is a directed graph whose vertices are connected by several kinds of edges.[3] The vertices of G_P represent the assignment statements and control predicates that occur in program P. In addition, G_P includes three other categories of vertices:

(1) There is a distinguished vertex called the *entry vertex*.

(2) For each variable x for which there is a path in the standard control-flow graph for P on which x is used before being defined (see [1]), there is a vertex called the *initial definition of x*. This vertex represents an assignment to x from the initial state. The vertex is labeled "$x := \text{InitialState}(x)$".

(3) For each variable x named in P's end statement, there is a vertex called the *final use of x*. It represents an access to the final value of x computed by P, and is labeled "$\text{FinalUse}(x)$".

The edges of G_P represent *dependences* among program components. An edge represents either a *control dependence* or a *data dependence*. Control dependence edges are labeled either **true** or **false**, and the source of a control dependence edge is always the entry vertex or a predicate vertex. A control dependence edge from vertex v_1 to vertex v_2, denoted by $v_1 \rightarrow_c v_2$, means that, during execution, whenever the predicate represented by v_1 is evaluated and its value matches the label on the edge to v_2, then the program component represented by v_2 will eventually be executed if the program terminates. A method for determining control dependence edges for arbitrary programs is given in [7]; however, because we are assuming that programs include only assignment, conditional, and while statements, the control dependence edges of G_P can be determined in a much simpler fashion. For the language under construction here, the control dependences reflect a program's nesting structure; program dependence graph G_P contains a *control dependence edge* from vertex v_1 to vertex v_2 of G_P iff one of the following holds:

(1) v_1 is the entry vertex and v_2 represents a component of P that is not nested within any loop or conditional; these edges are labeled **true**.

(2) v_1 represents a control predicate and v_2 represents a component of P immediately nested within the loop or conditional whose predicate is represented by v_1. If v_1 is the predicate of a while-loop, the edge $v_1 \rightarrow_c v_2$ is labeled **true**; if v_1 is the predicate of a conditional statement, the edge $v_1 \rightarrow_c v_2$ is labeled **true** or **false** according to whether v_2 occurs in the **then** branch or the **else** branch, respectively.[4]

---

[3] A *directed graph* G consists of a set of *vertices* $V(G)$ and a set of *edges* $E(G)$, where $E(G) \subseteq V(G) \times V(G)$. Each edge $(b, c) \in E(G)$ is directed from b to c; we say that b is the *source* and c the *target* of the edge.

[4] In other definitions that have been given for control dependence edges, there is an additional edge from each predicate of a **while** statement to itself, labeled **true**. This kind of edge is left out of our definition because it is not necessary for our purposes.

A data dependence edge from vertex v_1 to vertex v_2 means that the program's computation might be changed if the relative order of the components represented by v_1 and v_2 were reversed. In this paper, program dependence graphs contain two kinds of data dependence edges, representing *flow dependences* and *def-order dependences*.[5] The data dependence edges of a program dependence graph are computed using data-flow analysis. For the restricted language considered in this section, the necessary computations can be defined in a syntax-directed manner.

A program dependence graph contains a flow dependence edge from vertex v_1 to vertex v_2 iff all of the following hold:

(1) v_1 is a vertex that defines variable x.

(2) v_2 is a vertex that uses x.

(3) Control can reach v_2 after v_1 via an execution path along which there is no intervening definition of x. That is, there is a path in the standard control-flow graph for the program by which the definition of x at v_1 reaches the use of x at v_2. (Initial definitions of variables are considered to occur at the beginning of the control-flow graph; final uses of variables are considered to occur at the end of the control-flow graph.)

A flow dependence that exists from vertex v_1 to vertex v_2 is denoted by $v_1 \rightarrow_f v_2$.

Flow dependences can be further classified as *loop carried* or *loop independent*. A flow dependence $v_1 \rightarrow_f v_2$ is carried by loop L, denoted by $v_1 \rightarrow_{lc(L)} v_2$, if in addition to (1), (2), and (3) above, the following also hold:

(4) There is an execution path that both satisfies the conditions of (3) above and includes a backedge to the predicate of loop L.

(5) Both v_1 and v_2 are enclosed in loop L.

A flow dependence $v_1 \rightarrow_f v_2$ is loop-independent, denoted by $v_1 \rightarrow_{li} v_2$, if in addition to (1), (2), and (3) above, there is an execution path that satisfies (3) above and includes *no* backedge to the predicate of a loop that encloses both v_1 and v_2. It is possible to have both $v_1 \rightarrow_{lc(L)} v_2$ and $v_1 \rightarrow_{li} v_2$.

A program dependence graph contains a def-order dependence edge from vertex v_1 to vertex v_2 iff all of the following hold:

(1) v_1 and v_2 both define the same variable.

(2) v_1 and v_2 are in the same branch of any conditional statement that encloses both of them.

(3) There exists a program component v_3 such that $v_1 \rightarrow_f v_3$ and $v_2 \rightarrow_f v_3$.

(4) v_1 occurs to the left of v_2 in the program's abstract syntax tree.

A def-order dependence from v_1 to v_2 with "witness" v_3 is denoted by $v_1 \rightarrow_{do(v_3)} v_2$.

Note that a program dependence graph is a multigraph (i.e., it may have more than one edge of a given kind between two vertices). When there is more than one loop-carried flow dependence edge between two vertices, each is labeled by a

---

[5] For a complete discussion of the need for these edges and a comparison of def-order dependences with anti- and output dependences see [9].

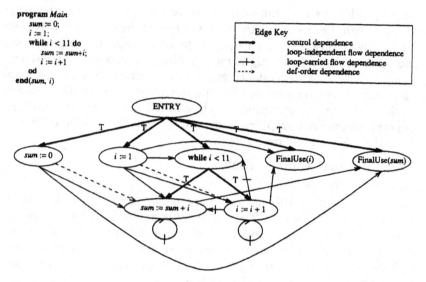

```
program Main
    sum := 0;
    i := 1;
    while i < 11 do
        sum := sum+i;
        i := i+1
    od
end(sum, i)
```

Edge Key

⟶ (bold)	control dependence
⟶	loop-independent flow dependence
—+→	loop-carried flow dependence
⤏	def-order dependence

Fig. 1. An example program, which sums the integers from 1 to 10 and leaves the result in the variable *sum*, and its program dependence graph. The boldface arrows represent control dependence edges, solid arrows represent loop-independent flow dependence edges, solid arrows with a hash mark represent loop-carried flow dependence edges, and dashed arrows represent def-order dependence edges.

different loop that carries the dependence. When there is more than one def-order edge between two vertices, each is labeled by a vertex that is flow-dependent on both the definition that occurs at the edge's source and the definition that occurs at the edge's target.

Example. Figure 1 shows an example program and its program dependence graph.

The boldface arrows represent control dependence edges; solid arrows represent loop-independent flow dependence edges; solid arrows with a hash mark represent loop-carried flow dependence edges; dashed arrows represent def-order dependence edges.

2.2 Program Slices (of Single-Procedure Programs)

For vertex s of program dependence graph G, the *slice* of G with respect to s, denoted by G/s, is a graph containing all vertices on which s has a transitive flow or control dependence (i.e., all vertices that can reach s via flow and/or control edges): $V(G/s) = \{w \mid w \in V(G) \land w \rightarrow^*_{c,f} s\}$. We extend the definition to a set of vertices $S = \bigcup_i s_i$ as follows: $V(G/S) = V(G/(\bigcup_i s_i)) = \bigcup_i V(G/s_i)$. Figure 2 gives a simple worklist algorithm for computing the vertices of a slice using a program dependence graph.

The edges in the graph G/S are essentially those in the subgraph of G induced by $V(G/S)$, with the exception that a def-order edge $v \rightarrow_{do(u)} w$ is included only if G/S contains the vertex u that is directly flow-dependent on the definitions at

```
procedure MarkVerticesOfSlice(G, S)
declare
    G: a program dependence graph
    S: a set of vertices in G
    WorkList: a set of vertices in G
    v, w: vertices in G
begin
    WorkList := S
    while WorkList ≠ ∅ do
        Select and remove vertex v from WorkList
        Mark v
        for each unmarked vertex w such that edge w →_f v or edge w →_c v is in E(G) do
            Insert w into WorkList
        od
    od
end
```

Fig. 2. A worklist algorithm that marks the vertices in G/S. Vertex v is in G/S if there is a path along flow and/or control edges from v to some vertex in S.

v and w. In terms of the three types of edges in a program dependence graph, we define

$$
\begin{aligned}
E(G/S) = \quad & \{(v \to_f w) \mid (v \to_f w) \in E(G) \wedge v, w \in V(G/S)\} \\
\cup \ & \{(v \to_c w) \mid (v \to_c w) \in E(G) \wedge v, w \in V(G/S)\} \\
\cup \ & \{(v \to_{do(u)} w) \mid (v \to_{do(u)} w) \in E(G) \wedge u, v, w \in V(G/S)\}.
\end{aligned}
$$

The relationship between a program's dependence graph and a slice of the graph has been addressed in [20]. We say that G is a *feasible* program dependence graph iff G is the program dependence graph of some program P. For any $S \subseteq V(G)$, if G is a feasible program dependence graph, the slice G/S is also a feasible program dependence graph; it corresponds to the program P' obtained by restricting the syntax tree of P to just the statements and predicates in $V(G/S)$ [20].

Example. Figure 3 shows the graph that results from taking a slice of the program dependence graph from Figure 1 with respect to the final-use vertex for i, together with the one program to which it corresponds.

The significance of an intraprocedural slice is that it captures a portion of a program's behavior in the sense that, for any initial state on which the program halts, the program and the slice compute the same sequence of values for each element of the slice [20]. In our case, a program point may be (1) an assignment statement, (2) a control predicate, or (3) a final use of a variable in an end statement. Because a statement or control predicate may be reached repeatedly in a program by "computing the same sequence of values for each element of the slice," we mean: (1) for any assignment statement the same *sequence* of values are assigned to the target variable; (2) for the predicate the same *sequence* of Boolean values are produced; and (3) for each final use the same value for the variable is produced.

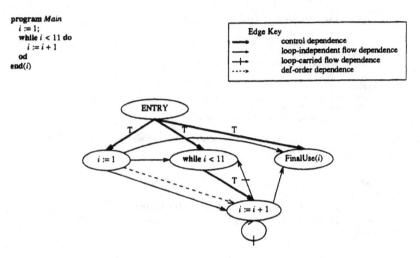

```
program Main
    i := 1;
    while i < 11 do
        i := i + 1
    od
end(i)
```

Edge Key

- ———▶ control dependence
- ——▶ loop-independent flow dependence
- —+—▶ loop-carried flow dependence
- ----▶ def-order dependence

Fig. 3. The graph and the corresponding program that result from slicing the program dependence graph from Figure 1 with respect to the final-use vertex for i.

3. THE SYSTEM DEPENDENCE GRAPH: AN INTERPROCEDURAL DEPENDENCE GRAPH REPRESENTATION

We now turn to the definition of the *system dependence graph*. The system dependence graph, an extension of the dependence graphs defined in Section 2.1, represents programs in a language that includes procedures and procedure calls.

Our definition of the system dependence graph models a language with the following properties:

(1) A complete system consists of a single (main) program and a collection of auxiliary procedures.

(2) Procedures end with **return** statements instead of **end** statements (as defined in Section 2). A **return** statement does not include a list of variables.

(3) Parameters are passed by value-result.

We make the further assumption that there are no call sites of the form $P(x, x)$ or of the form $P(g)$, where g is a global variable. The former restriction sidesteps potential copy-back conflicts. The latter restriction permits global variables to be treated as additional parameters to each procedure; thus, we do not discuss global variables explicitly in this paper.

It should become clear that our approach is not tied to the particular language features enumerated above. Modeling different features will require some adaptation; however, the basic approach is applicable to languages that allow nested scopes and languages that use different parameter-passing mechanisms. Section 4.3 discusses how to deal with systems that use call-by-reference parameter passing and contain aliasing.

A system dependence graph includes a *program dependence graph*, which represents the system's main program, *procedure dependence graphs*, which represent the system's auxiliary procedures, and some additional edges. These

146

additional edges are of two sorts: (1) edges that represent direct dependences between a call site and the called procedure, and (2) edges that represent transitive dependences due to calls.

Section 3.1 discusses how procedure calls and procedure entry are represented in procedure dependence graphs and how edges representing dependences between a call site and the called procedure are added to connect these graphs together. Section 3.2 defines the *linkage grammar*, an attribute grammar used to represent the call structure of a system. Transitive dependences due to procedure calls are computed using the linkage grammar and are added as the final step of building a system dependence graph.

In the sections below, we use "procedure" as a generic term referring to both the main program and the auxiliary procedures when the distinction between the two is irrelevant.

3.1 Procedure Calls and Parameter Passing

Extending the definition of dependence graphs to handle procedure calls requires representing the passing of values between procedures. In designing the representation of parameter passing, we have three goals:

(1) It should be possible to build an individual procedure's procedure dependence graph (including the computation of data dependences) with minimal knowledge of other system components.

(2) The system dependence graph should consist of a straightforward connection of the program dependence graph and procedure dependence graphs.

(3) It should be possible to extract a precise interprocedural slice efficiently by traversing the graph via a procedure analogous to the procedure Mark-VerticesOfSlice given in Figure 2.

Goal (3) is the subject of Section 4.1, which presents our algorithm for slicing a system dependence graph.

To meet the goals outlined above, our graphs model the following slightly nonstandard, two-stage mechanism for runtime parameter passing: when procedure P calls procedure Q, values are transferred from P to Q by means of intermediate temporary variables, one for each parameter. A different set of temporary variables is used when Q returns to transfer values back to P. Before the call, P copies the values of the actual parameters into the call temporaries; Q then initializes local variables from these temporaries. Before returning, Q copies return values into the return temporaries, from which P retrieves them.

This model of parameter passing is represented in procedure dependence graphs through the use of five new kinds of vertices. A call site is represented using a *call-site* vertex; information transfer is represented using four kinds of *parameter* vertices. On the calling side, information transfer is represented by a set of vertices called *actual-in* and *actual-out* vertices. These vertices, which are control dependent on the call-site vertex, represent assignment statements that copy the values of the actual parameters to the call temporaries and from the return temporaries, respectively. Similarly, information transfer in the called procedure is represented by a set of vertices called *formal-in* and *formal-out* vertices. These vertices, which are control dependent on the procedure's entry vertex, represent assignment statements that copy the values of the formal parameters from the call temporaries and to the return temporaries, respectively.

Using this model, data dependences between procedures are limited to dependences from actual-in vertices to formal-in vertices and from formal-out vertices to actual-out vertices. Connecting procedure dependence graphs to form a system dependence graph is straightforward, involving the addition of three new kinds of edges: (1) a *call* edge is added from each call-site vertex to the corresponding procedure-entry vertex; (2) a *parameter-in* edge is added from each actual-in vertex at a call site to the corresponding formal-in vertex in the called procedure; (3) a *parameter-out* edge is added from each formal-out vertex in the called procedure to the corresponding actual-out vertex at the call site. (Call edges are a new kind of control dependence edge; parameter-in and parameter-out edges are new kinds of data dependence edges.)

Another advantage of this model is that flow dependences can be computed in the usual way, using data-flow analysis on the procedure's control-flow graph. The control-flow graph for a procedure includes nodes analogous to the actual-in, actual-out, formal-in and formal-out vertices of the procedure dependence graph. A procedure's control-flow graph starts with a sequence of assignments that copy values from call temporaries to formal parameters and ends with a sequence of assignments that copy values from formal parameters to return temporaries. Each call statement within the procedure is represented in the procedure's control-flow graph by a sequence of assignments that copy values from actual parameters to call temporaries, followed by a sequence of assignments that copy values from return temporaries to actual parameters.

An important question is *which* values are transferred from a call site to the called procedure and back again. This point is discussed further in Section 4.2, which presents a strategy in which the results of interprocedural data-flow analysis are used to omit some parameter vertices from procedure dependence graphs. For now, we assume that all actual parameters are copied into the call temporaries and retrieved from the return temporaries. Thus, the parameter vertices associated with a call from procedure P to procedure Q are defined as follows (G_P denotes the procedure dependence graph for P):

> In G_P, subordinate to the call-site vertex that represents the call to Q, there is an actual-in vertex for each actual parameter e of the call to Q. The actual-in vertices are labeled $r\_in := e$, where r is the formal parameter name.
>
> For each actual parameter a that is a variable (rather than an expression), there is an actual-out vertex. These are labeled $a := r\_out$ for actual parameter a and corresponding formal parameter r.

The parameter vertices associated with the entry to procedure Q and the return from procedure Q are defined as follows (G_Q denotes the procedure dependence graph for Q):

> For each formal parameter r of Q, G_Q contains a formal-in vertex and a formal-out vertex. These vertices are labeled $r := r\_in$ and $r\_out := r$, respectively.

Example. Figure 4 repeats the example system from the Introduction and shows the corresponding program and procedure dependence graphs connected with parameter-in edges, parameter-out edges, and call edges.

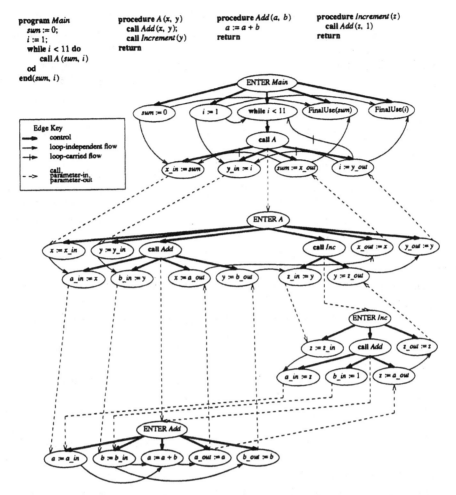

```
program Main          procedure A (x, y)      procedure Add (a, b)     procedure Increment (z)
   sum := 0;             call Add (x, y);         a := a + b              call Add (z, 1)
   i := 1;               call Increment (y)       return                  return
   while i < 11 do     return
      call A (sum, i)
   od
end(sum, i)
```

Fig. 4. Example system and corresponding program and procedure dependence graphs
connected with parameter-in, parameter-out, and call edges. Edges representing control
dependences are shown (unlabeled) in boldface; edges representing intraprocedural flow
dependences are shown using arcs; parameter-in edges, parameter-out edges, and call
edges are shown using dashed lines.

(In Figure 4, as well as in the remaining figures of the paper, def-order edges
are not shown. Edges representing control dependences are shown unlabeled; all
such edges in this example would be labeled **true**.)

3.2 The Linkage Grammar: An Attribute Grammar that Models
   Procedure-Call Structure

Using the graph structure defined in the previous section, interprocedural slicing
could be defined as a graph-reachability problem, and the slices obtained would
be the same as those obtained using Weiser's slicing method. As explained in the
Introduction, Weiser's method does not produce as precise a slice as possible
because it fails to account for the calling context of a called procedure.

Example. The problem with Weiser's method can be illustrated using the graph shown in Figure 4. In the graph-reachability vocabulary, the problem is that there is a path from the vertex of procedure *Main* labeled "$x\_in := sum$" to the vertex of *Main* labeled "$i := y\_out$", even though the value of i after the call to procedure A is independent of the value of sum before the call. The path is as follows:

$$Main: "x\_in := sum" \rightarrow A: "x := x\_in" \quad \rightarrow A: "a\_in := x" \quad \rightarrow Add: "a := a\_in"$$
$$\rightarrow Add: "a := a + b" \quad \rightarrow Add: "a\_out := a" \rightarrow Inc: "z := a\_out"$$
$$\rightarrow Inc: "z\_out := z" \quad \rightarrow A: "y := z\_out" \quad \rightarrow A: "y\_out := y"$$
$$\rightarrow Main: "i := y\_out"$$

The source of this problem is that not all paths in the graph correspond to possible execution paths (e.g., the path from vertex "$x\_in := sum$" of *Main* to vertex "$i := y\_out$" of *Main* corresponds to procedure *Add* being called by procedure A, but returning to procedure *Increment*).

To overcome this problem, we add an additional kind of edge to the system dependence graph to represent transitive dependences due to the effects of procedure calls. The presence of transitive-dependence edges permits interprocedural slices to be computed in two passes, each of which is cast as a reachability problem. Thus, the next step in the construction of the system dependence graph is to determine such transitive dependences. For example, for the graph shown in Figure 4, we need an algorithm that can discover the transitive dependence from vertex "$x\_in := sum$" of *Main* to vertex "$sum := x\_out$" of *Main*. This dependence exists because the value of sum after the call to A depends on the value of sum before the call to A.

One's first impulse might be to compute transitive dependences due to calls by taking the transitive closure of the graph's control, flow, parameter, and call edges. However, this technique is imprecise for the same reason that transitive closure (or, equivalently, reachability) is imprecise for interprocedural slicing, namely that not all paths in the system dependence graph correspond to possible execution paths. Using transitive closure to compute the dependence edges that represent the effects of procedure calls would put in a (spurious) edge from vertex "$x\_in := sum$" of *Main* to vertex "$i := y\_out$" of *Main*.

For a language without recursion, this problem could be eliminated by using a separate copy of a procedure dependence graph for each call site; however, to handle a language *with* recursion, a more powerful technique is required. The technique we use involves defining an attribute grammar, called the *linkage grammar*, to model the call structure of each procedure as well as the intraprocedural transitive flow dependences among the procedure's parameter vertices. Interprocedural transitive flow dependences among a system dependence graph's parameter vertices are determined from the linkage grammar using a standard attribute-grammar construction: the computation of the *subordinate characteristic graphs* of the linkage grammar's nonterminals.[6]

In this section we describe the construction of the linkage grammar and the computation of its subordinate characteristic graphs. It should be understood that the linkage grammar is used *only* to compute transitive dependences due to

---

[6] A summary of attribute-grammar terminology can be found in the Appendix.

150

calls; we are not interested in the language defined by the grammar, nor in actual attribute values.

The context-free part of the linkage grammar models the system's procedure-call structure. The grammar includes one nonterminal and one production for each procedure in the system. If procedure P contains no calls, the right-hand side of the production for P is ϵ; otherwise, there is one right-hand side nonterminal for each call site in P.

Example. For the example system shown in Figure 4, the productions of the linkage grammar are as follows:

$$Main \rightarrow A \qquad A \rightarrow Add\ Increment \quad Add \rightarrow \epsilon \qquad Increment \rightarrow Add$$

The attributes in the linkage grammar correspond to the parameters of the procedures. Procedure inputs are modeled as inherited attributes, procedure outputs as synthesized attributes. For example, the productions shown above are repeated in Figure 5, this time in tree form.

In Figure 5, each nonterminal is annotated with its attributes; a nonterminal's inherited attributes are placed to its left; its synthesized attributes are placed to its right.

More formally, the program's linkage grammar has the following elements:

(1) For each procedure P, the linkage grammar contains a nonterminal P.

(2) For each procedure P, there is a production $p: P \rightarrow \beta$, where for each site of a call on procedure Q in P there is a distinct occurrence of Q in β.

(3) For each actual-in vertex of P, there is an inherited attribute of nonterminal P.

(4) For each actual-out vertex of P, there is a synthesized attribute of nonterminal P.

Attribute a of nonterminal X is denoted by "$X.a$".

Dependences among the attributes of a linkage-grammar production are used to model the (possibly transitive) intraprocedural dependences among the parameter vertices of the corresponding procedure. These dependences are computed using (intraprocedural) slices of the procedure's procedure dependence graph as described in Section 2.2. For each grammar production, attribute equations are introduced to represent the intraprocedural dependences among the parameter vertices of the corresponding procedure dependence graph. For each attribute occurrence a, the procedure dependence graph is sliced with respect to the vertex that corresponds to a. An attribute equation is introduced for a so that a depends on the attribute occurrences that correspond to the parameter vertices identified by the slice. More formally:

> For each attribute occurrence of $X.a$ of a production p, let v be the vertex of the procedure dependence graph G_P that corresponds to $X.a$. Associate with p an attribute equation of the form $X.a = f(\ldots, Y.b, \ldots)$ where the arguments $Y.b$ to the equation consist of the attribute occurrences of p that correspond to the parameter vertices in G_P/v.

151

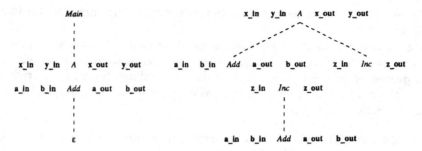

Fig. 5. The productions of the example linkage grammar shown in tree form. Each nonterminal is annotated with its attributes; a nonterminal's inherited attributes are placed to its left; its synthesized attributes are placed to its right.

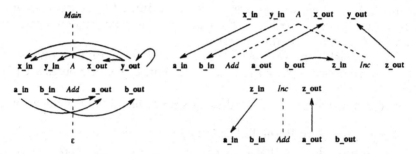

Fig. 6. The productions of Figure 5, augmented with attribute dependences.

Note that the actual function f on the right-hand side of the equation is completely irrelevant because the attribute grammar is *never* used for evaluation; all we need is that the equation induce the dependences described above.

Example. Figure 6 shows the productions of the grammar from Figure 5, augmented with attribute dependences.

The dependences for production *Main* → *A*, for instance, correspond to the attribute-definition equations

$$A.x\_in = f1(A.x\_out, A.y\_out)$$
$$A.y\_in = f2(A.y\_out)$$
$$A.x\_out = f3(A.y\_out)$$
$$A.y\_out = f4(A.y\_out)$$

It is entirely possible that a linkage grammar will be a circular attribute grammar (i.e., there may be attributes in some derivation tree of the grammar that depend on themselves); additionally, the grammar may not be well formed (e.g., a production may have equations for synthesized attribute occurrences of right-hand side symbols). This does not create any difficulties as the linkage grammar is used *only* to compute transitive dependences and *not* for attribute evaluation.

Example. The equation $A.y\_out = f4(A.y\_out)$ makes the example attribute grammar both circular and not well formed. This equation is added to the attribute grammar because of the following (cyclic) path in the graph shown in Figure 4:

Main: "$i := y\_out$" $\rightarrow$ *Main*: "**while** $i < 11$"
$\rightarrow$ *Main*: "**call** A" $\rightarrow$ *Main*: "$i := y\_out$"

Transitive dependences from a call site's actual-in vertices to its actual-out vertices are computed from the linkage grammar by constructing the subordinate characteristic graphs for the grammar's nonterminals. The algorithm we give exploits the special structure of linkage grammars to compute these graphs more efficiently than can be done for attribute grammars in general. For general attribute grammars, computing the sets of possible subordinate characteristic graphs for the grammar's nonterminals may require time exponential in the number of attributes attached to some nonterminal. However, a linkage grammar is an attribute grammar of a restricted nature. For each nonterminal X in the linkage grammar, there is only one production with X on the left-hand side. Because linkage grammars are restricted in this fashion, for each nonterminal of a linkage grammar there is one subordinate characteristic graph that covers all of the nonterminal's other possible subordinate characteristic graphs. For such grammars it is possible to give a polynomial-time algorithm for constructing the (covering) subordinate characteristic graphs.

The computation is performed by an algorithm, called ConstructSubCGraphs, which is a slight modification of an algorithm originally developed by Kastens to construct approximations to a grammar's transitive dependence relations [13]. The covering subordinate characteristic graph of a nonterminal X of the linkage grammar is captured in the graph TDS(X) (standing for "Transitive Dependences among a Symbol's attributes"). Initially, all the TDS graphs are empty. The construction that builds them up involves the auxiliary graph TDP(p) (standing for "Transitive Dependences in a Production"), which expresses dependences among the attributes of a production's nonterminal occurrences.

The basic operation used in ConstructSubCGraphs is the procedure "AddEdgeAndInduce(TDP(p), (a, b))", whose first argument is the TDP graph of some production p and whose second argument is a pair of attribute occurrences in p. AddEdgeAndInduce carries out three actions:

(1) The edge (a, b) is inserted into the graph TDP(p).

(2) Any additional edges needed to transitively close TDP(p) are inserted into TDP(p).

(3) In addition, for each edge added to TDP(p) by (1) or (2), (i.e., either the edge (a, b) itself or some other edge (c, d) added to reclose TDP(p)), AddEdgeAndInduce may add an edge to one of the TDS graphs. In particular, for each edge added to TDP(p) of the form ($X_0.m$, $X_0.n$), where X_0 is the left-hand side occurrence of nonterminal X in production p and ($X.m$, $X.n$) $\notin$ TDS(X), an edge ($X.m$, $X.n$) is added to TDS(X).

An edge in one of the TDS graphs can be *marked* or *unmarked*; the edges that AddEdgeAndInduce adds to the TDS graphs are unmarked.

```
procedure ConstructSubCGraphs(L)
declare
    L: a linkage grammar
    p: a production in L
    Xᵢ, Xⱼ, X: nonterminal occurrences in L
    a, b: attributes of nonterminals in L
    X: a nonterminal in L
begin
    /* Step 1: Initialize the TDS and TDP graphs */
    for each nonterminal X in L do
        TDS(X) := the graph containing a vertex for each attribute X.b but no edges
    od
    for each production p in L do
        TDP(p) := the graph containing a vertex for each attribute occurrence Xⱼ.b of p but no edges
        for each attribute occurrence Xⱼ.b of p do
            for each argument Xᵢ.a of the equation that defines Xⱼ.b do
                Insert edge (Xᵢ.a, Xⱼ.b) into TDP(p)
                let X be the nonterminal corresponding to nonterminal occurrence Xⱼ in
                    if i = 0 and j = 0 and (X.a, X.b) ∉ TDS (X) then Insert an unmarked edge (X.a, X.b) into TDS(X) fi
                ni
            od
        od
    od
    /* Step 2: Determine the sets of induced transitive dependences */
    while there is an unmarked edge (X.a, X.b) in one of the TDS graphs do
        Mark (X.a, X.b)
        for each occurrence X̂ of X in any production p do
            if (X̂.a, X̂.b) ∉ TDP (p) then AddEdgeAndInduce(TDP (p), (X̂.a, X̂.b)) fi
        od
    od
end
```

Fig. 7.   Computation of a linkage grammar's sets of TDP and TDS graphs.

The TDS graphs are generated by the procedure ConstructSubCGraphs, given in Figure 7, which is a slight modification of the first two steps of Kasten's algorithm for constructing a set of evaluation plans for an attribute grammar [13].

ConstructSubCGraphs performs a kind of closure operation on the TDP and TDS graphs. Step 1 of the algorithm—the first two for-loops of Construct-SubCGraphs—initializes the grammar's TDP and TDS graphs; when these loops terminate, the TDP graphs contain edges representing all direct dependences that exist between the grammar's attribute occurrences, and the TDS graphs contain unmarked edges corresponding to direct left-hand-side-to-left-hand-side dependences in the linkage grammar's productions. Our construction of attribute equations for the linkage grammar ensures that the graph of direct attribute dependences is transitively closed; thus, at the end of Step 1, TDP(p) is a transitively closed graph. In Step 2 of ConstructSubCGraphs, the invariant for the **while**-loop is

If a graph TDP(p) contains an edge e' that corresponds to a marked edge e in one of the TDS graphs, then e has been induced in all of the other graphs TDP(q).

When all edges in all TDS graphs have received marks, the effects of all dependences have been induced in the TDP and TDS graphs. Thus, the TDS(X) graphs computed by ConstructSubCGraphs are guaranteed to cover the transitive dependences among the attributes of X that exist at any occurrence of X in any derivation tree.

154

Put more simply, because for each nonterminal X in a linkage grammar there is only a single production that has X on the left-hand side, the grammar only derives one tree. (For a recursive grammar it will be an infinite tree.) All marked edges in TDS represent transitive dependences in this tree, and thus the $\text{TDS}(X)$ graph computed by ConstructSubCGraphs represents a subordinate characteristic graph of X that covers the subordinate characteristic graph of any partial derivation tree derived from X, as desired.

Example. The nonterminals of our example grammar are shown below annotated with their attributes and their subordinate characteristic graphs.

x_in y_in *A* x_out y_out   a_in b_in *Add* a_out b_out   z_in *Inc* z_out

3.3 Recap of the Construction of the System Dependence Graph

The system dependence graph is constructed by the following steps:

(1) For each procedure of the system, construct its procedure dependence graph.

(2) For each call site, introduce a call edge from the call-site vertex to the corresponding procedure-entry vertex.

(3) For each actual-in vertex v at a call site, introduce a parameter-in edge from v to the corresponding formal-in vertex in the called procedure.

(4) For each actual-out vertex v at a call site, introduce a parameter-out edge to v from the corresponding formal-out vertex in the called procedure.

(5) Construct the linkage grammar corresponding to the system.

(6) Compute the subordinate characteristic graphs of the linkage grammar's nonterminals.

(7) At all call sites that call procedure P, introduce flow dependence edges corresponding to the edges in the subordinate characteristic graph for P.

Example. Figure 8 shows the complete system dependence graph for our example system.

4. INTERPROCEDURAL SLICING

In this section we describe how to perform an interprocedural slice using the system dependence graph defined in Section 3. We then discuss modifications to the definition of the system dependence graph to permit more precise slicing and to extend the slicing algorithm's range of applicability.

4.1 An Algorithm for Interprocedural Slicing

As discussed in the Introduction, the algorithm presented in [22], while safe, is not as precise as possible. The difficult aspect of interprocedural slicing is keeping track of the calling context when a slice "descends" into a called procedure.

The key element of our approach is the use of the linkage grammar's characteristic graph edges in the system dependence graph. These edges represent transitive data dependences from actual-in vertices to actual-out vertices due to

155

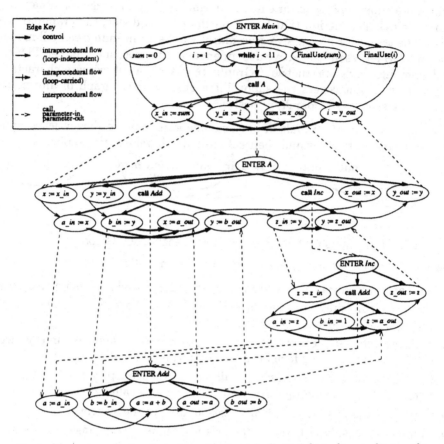

Fig. 8. Example system's system dependence graph. Control dependences, shown unlabeled, are represented using medium-bold arrows; intraprocedural flow dependences are represented using arcs; transitive interprocedural flow dependences (corresponding to subordinate characteristic graph edges) are represented using heavy, bold arcs; call edges, parameter-in edges, and parameter-out edges (which connect program and procedure dependence graphs together) are represented using dashed arrows.

procedure calls. The presence of such edges permits us to sidestep the "calling context" problem; the slicing operation can move "across" a call without having to descend into it.

Our algorithm for interprocedural slicing is given in Figure 9.

In Figure 9, the computation of the slice of system dependence graph G with respect to vertex set S is performed in two phases. Both Phases 1 and 2 operate on the system dependence graph using essentially the method presented in Section 2.2 for performing an intraprocedural slice—the graph is traversed to find the set of vertices that can reach a given set of vertices along certain kinds of edges. The traversal in Phase 1 follows flow edges, control edges, call edges, and parameter-in edges, but does *not* follow def-order edges or parameter-out edges. The traversal in Phase 2 that follows flow edges, control edges, and parameter-out edges, but does *not* follow def-order edges, call edges, or parameter-in edges.

156

```
procedure MarkVerticesOfSlice(G, S)
declare
   G: a system dependence graph
   S, S': sets of vertices in G
begin
   /* Phase 1: Slice without descending into called procedures */
      MarkReachingVertices(G, S, {def-order, parameter-out})

   /* Phase 2: Slice called procedures without ascending to call sites */
      S' := all marked vertices in G
      MarkReachingVertices(G, S', {def-order, parameter-in, call})

end

procedure MarkReachingVertices(G, V, Kinds)
declare
   G: a system dependence graph
   V: a set of vertices in G
   Kinds: a set of kinds of edges
   v, w: vertices in G
   WorkList: a set of vertices in G
begin
   WorkList := V
   while WorkList ≠ ∅ do
      Select and remove a vertex v from WorkList
      Mark v
      for each unmarked vertex w such that there is an edge w → v whose kind is not in Kinds do
         Insert w into WorkList
      od
   od
end
```

Fig. 9.   The procedure MarkVerticesOfSlice marks the vertices of the interprocedural slice G/S. The auxiliary procedure MarkReachingVertices marks all
vertices in G from which there is a path to a vertex in V along edges of kinds
other than those in the set Kinds.

Suppose the goal is to slice system dependence graph G with respect to some
vertex s in procedure P; Phases 1 and 2 can be characterized as follows:

Phase 1. Phase 1 identifies vertices that can reach s, and are either in P itself
or in a procedure that calls P (either directly or transitively). Because parameter-
out edges are not followed, the traversal in Phase 1 does not "descend" into
procedures called by P. The effects of such procedures are not ignored, however;
the presence of *transitive flow dependence edges* from actual-in to actual-out
vertices (subordinate-characteristic-graph edges) permits the discovery of vertices
that can reach s only through a procedure call, although the graph traversal does
not actually descend into the called procedure.

Phase 2. Phase 2 identifies vertices that can reach s from procedures (transitively) called by P or from procedures called by procedures that (transitively)
call P. Because call edges and parameter-in edges are not followed, the traversal
in Phase 2 does not "ascend" into calling procedures; the transitive flow
dependence edges from actual-in to actual-out vertices make such "ascents"
unnecessary.

Figures 10 and 11 illustrate the two phases of the interprocedural slicing
algorithm. Figure 10 shows the vertices of the example system dependence graph
that are marked during Phase 1 of the interprocedural slicing algorithm when
the system is sliced with respect to the formal-out vertex for parameter z in

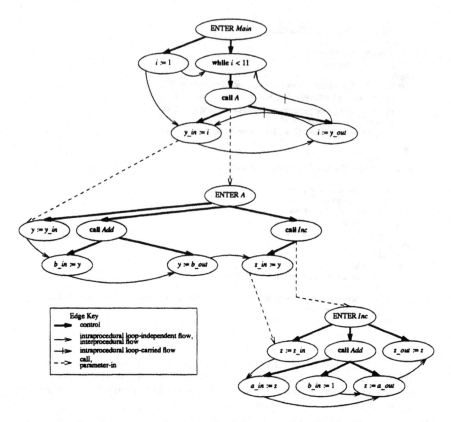

Fig. 10. The example program's system dependence graph is sliced with respect to the formal-out vertex for parameter z in procedure *Increment*. The vertices marked by Phase 1 of the slicing algorithm as well as the edges traversed during this phase are shown above.

procedure *Increment*. Edges "traversed" during Phase 1 are also included in Figure 10.

Figure 11 adds (in boldface) the vertices that are marked and the edges that are traversed during Phase 2 of the slice.

The result of an interprocedural slice consists of the sets of vertices identified by Phase 1 and Phase 2 and the set of edges induced by this vertex set. Figure 12 shows the completed example slice (excluding def-order edges.)

4.2 Using Interprocedural Summary Information to Build Procedure Dependence Graphs

The slice shown in Figure 12 illustrates a shortcoming of the method for constructing procedure dependence graphs described in Section 3. The problem is that including both an actual-in and an actual-out vertex for *every* argument in a procedure call can affect the precision of an interprocedural slice. The slice shown in Figure 12 includes the call vertex that represents the call to *Add* from A; however, this call does not in fact affect the value of z in *Increment*. The problem is that an actual-out vertex for argument y in the call to *Add* from A is

Fig. 11. The example program's system dependence graph is sliced with respect to the formal-out vertex for parameter z in procedure *Increment*. The vertices marked by Phase 2 of the slicing algorithm as well as the edges traversed during this phase are shown above in boldface.

included in A's procedure dependence graph even though *Add* does not change the value of y.

To achieve a more precise interprocedural slice, we use the results of interprocedural data-flow analysis when constructing procedure dependence graphs, in order to exclude vertices like the actual-out vertex for argument y.

The appropriate interprocedural summary information consists of the following sets, which are computed for each procedure P [4]:

GMOD(P): The set of variables that might be *modified* by P itself or by a procedure (transitively) called from P.

GREF(P): The set of variables that might be *referenced* by P itself or by a procedure (transitively) called from P.

GMOD and GREF sets are used to determine which parameter vertices are included in procedure dependence graphs as follows: for each procedure P, the parameter vertices subordinate to P's entry vertex include one formal-in vertex

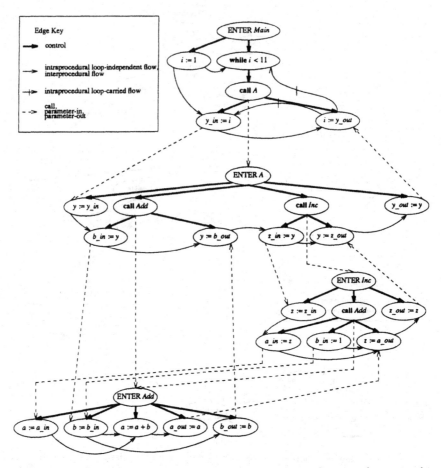

Fig. 12. The complete slice (excluding def-order edges) of the example program's system dependence graph sliced with respect to the formal-out vertex for parameter z in procedure *Increment*.

for each variable in GMOD(P) ∪ GREF(P) and one formal-out vertex for each variable in GMOD(P). Similarly, for each site at which P is called, the parameter vertices subordinate to the call-site vertex include one actual-in vertex for each variable in GMOD(P) ∪ GREF(P) and one actual-out vertex for each variable in GMOD(P). (It is necessary to include an actual-in and a formal-in vertex for a variable x that is in GMOD(P) and is not in GREF(P) because there may be an execution path through P on which x is *not* modified. In this case, a slice of P with respect to the final value of x must include the initial value of x; thus, there must be a formal-in vertex for x in P and a corresponding actual-in vertex at the call to P.)

Example. The GMOD and GREF sets for our example system are:

Procedure	GMOD	GREF
A	x, y	x, y
Add	a	a, b
Inc	z	z

160

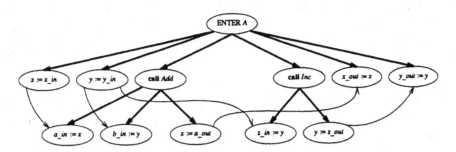

Fig. 13. Procedure A's procedure dependence graph built using interprocedural summary information. The actual-out vertex for argument y of the call to Add has been omitted, and the flow edge from that vertex to the vertex "$z\_in := y$" has been replaced by an edge from the vertex "$y := y\_in$" to the vertex "$z\_in := y$".

Because parameter b is not in GMOD(Add), Add's procedure dependence graph should not include a formal-out vertex for b, and the call to Add from A should not include the corresponding actual-out vertex.

Figure 13 shows A's procedure dependence graph as it would be built using GMOD and GREF information.

The actual-out vertex for argument y of the call to Add is omitted, and the flow edge from that vertex to the actual-in vertex "$z\_in := y$" is replaced by an edge from the formal-in vertex "$y := y\_in$" to the actual-in vertex "$z\_in := y$". The new edge is traversed during Phase 1 of the interprocedural slice instead of the (now omitted) flow edge from "$y := a\_out$" to "$z\_in := y$", thus (correctly) bypassing the call to Add in procedure A.

4.3 Interprocedural Slicing in the Presence of Call-By-Reference Parameter Passing and Aliasing

Our definitions of system dependence graphs and interprocedural slicing have assumed that parameters are passed by value-result. The same definitions hold for call-by-reference parameter passing in the absence of aliasing; however, in the presence of aliasing, some modifications are required. This section presents two approaches for dealing with systems that use call-by-reference parameter passing and contain aliasing. The first approach provides a more precise slice than the second, at the expense of the time and space needed to convert the original system into one that is alias-free. (These costs may, in the worst case, be exponential in the maximum number of parameters passed to a procedure.) The second approach avoids this expense by making use of a generalized notion of flow dependence that includes flow dependences that exist under the possible aliasing patterns.

Our first approach to the problem of interprocedural slicing in the presence of aliasing is to reduce the problem to that of interprocedural slicing in the *absence* of aliasing. The conversion is performed by simulating the calling behavior of the system (using the usual activation-tree model of procedure calls [4]) to discover, for each instance of a procedure call, exactly how variables are aliased at that instance. (Although a recursive system's activation tree is infinite, the number of different alias configurations is finite; thus, only a finite portion of the activation tree is needed to compute aliasing information.) A new copy of the procedure (with a new procedure name) is created for each different alias configuration; the procedure names used at call sites are similarly adjusted. Within each procedure, variables are renamed so that each set of aliased variables is replaced by a single variable.

This process may generate multiple copies of the vertex v, with respect to which we are to perform a slice. If this happens, it is necessary to slice the transformed system with respect to *all* occurrences of v. The slice of the original system is obtained from the slice of the transformed system by projecting elements in the slice of the transformed system back into the original system; a vertex is in the slice of the original system if any of its copies are in the slice of the transformed system.

Example. Figure 14 shows a system with aliasing, and the portion of the system's activation tree that is used to compute alias information for each call instance.

We use the notation of [4], in which each node of the activation tree is labeled with the mapping from variable names to memory locations. The transformed, alias-free version of the system is shown below.

program *Main*	**procedure** $P1(x, y)$	**procedure** $P2(xy)$
$a := 1$;	**if** $y = 0$ **then**	**if** $xy = 0$ **then**
$b := 0$;	**call** $P2(x)$	**call** $P2(xy)$
call $P1(a, b)$;	**fi**;	**fi**;
$z := b$	$y := y + 1$	$xy := xy + 1$
end	**return**	**return**

If our original goal had been to slice with respect to the statement "$y := y + 1$" in procedure P, we must now slice with respect to the set of statements {"$y := y + 1$", "$xy := xy + 1$"}.

Our second approach to the problem of interprocedural slicing in the presence of aliasing is to generalize the definition of a flow dependence to include dependences that arise under the possible aliasing patterns. A procedure dependence graph has a flow dependence edge from vertex v_1 to vertex v_2 iff all of the following hold:

(1) v_1 is a vertex that defines variable x.
(2) v_2 is a vertex that uses variable y.
(3) x and y are potential aliases.
(4) Control can reach v_2 after v_1 via a path in the control-flow graph along which there is no intervening definition of x or y.

Note that clause (4) does not exclude there being definitions of other variables that are potential aliases of x or y along the path from v_1 to v_2. An assignment to a variable z along the path from v_1 to v_2 only overwrites the contents of the memory location written by v_1 if x and z refer to the same memory location. If z is a potential alias of x, then there is only a *possibility* that x and z refer to the same memory location; thus, an assignment to z does not necessarily overwrite the memory location written by v_1, and it may be possible for v_2 to read a value written by v_1.

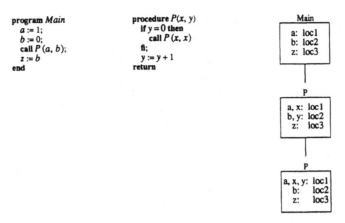

```
program Main          procedure P(x, y)
   a := 1;               if y = 0 then
   b := 0;                  call P(x, x)
   call P(a, b);         fi;
   z := b                y := y + 1
end                    return
```

```
Main
┌──────────┐
│ a: loc1  │
│ b: loc2  │
│ z: loc3  │
└──────────┘

P
┌──────────────┐
│ a, x:  loc1  │
│ b, y:  loc2  │
│ z:     loc3  │
└──────────────┘

P
┌────────────────┐
│ a, x, y:  loc1 │
│ b:        loc2 │
│ z:        loc3 │
└────────────────┘
```

Fig. 14. A program with aliasing and the portion of its activation tree needed to compute all alias configurations.

The notion of a def-order edge must also be generalized in the presence of aliasing. A procedure dependence graph has a def-order dependence edge from vertex v_1 to vertex v_2 iff all of the following hold:

(1) v_1 and v_2 define variables x_1 and x_2, respectively.

(2) x_1 and x_2 are potential aliases.

(3) v_1 and v_2 are in the same branch of any conditional statement that encloses both of them.

(4) There exists a program component v_3 such that $v_1 \rightarrow_f v_3$ and $v_2 \rightarrow_f v_3$.

(5) v_1 occurs to the left of v_2 in the procedure's abstract syntax tree.

The interprocedural slice of a system dependence graph containing dependence edges as defined above is computed by the same two-phase algorithm used to compute the interprocedural slice of a system in the absence of aliasing. The data dependences in a procedure provide a safe approximation to the true dependences required for each alias configuration. Because these edges cover all possible alias configurations, the resulting slice may contain unnecessary program elements.

Example. Consider again the system shown in Figure 14. The possibility of aliasing between formal parameters x and y of procedure P gives rise to flow dependences from the actual-out vertices "$x := x\_out$" and "$x := y\_out$" of the call $P(x, x)$ to the vertex "$y := y + 1$". Because of these dependences, the slice with respect to the statement "$z := b$" in the main program yields the entire system, even though the statement "$a := 1$" in *Main* and the conditional statement in P have no effect on the value computed for z. The approach based on replicating procedures determines a more precise slice that does not include the statement "$a := 1$" or the conditional statement, as shown below:

```
program Main      procedure P1(y)
   b := 0;           y := y + 1
   call P1(b);     return
   z := b
end
```

163

4.4 Slicing Partial System Dependence Graphs

The interprocedural slicing algorithm presented above is designed to be applied to a complete system dependence graph. In this section we discuss how to slice *incomplete* system dependence graphs.

The need to handle incomplete systems arises, for example, when slicing a program that calls a library procedure that is not itself available, or when slicing programs under development. In the first case, the missing components are procedures that are called by the incomplete system; in the second case, the missing components can either be not-yet-written procedures called by the incomplete system (when the program is developed top-down), or possible calling contexts (when the program is developed bottom-up).

In either case, information about the possible effects of missing calls and missing calling contexts is needed to permit slicing. This information takes the form of (safe approximations to) the subordinate characteristic graphs for missing called procedures and the superior characteristic graphs for missing calling contexts.

When no information about missing program components is available, subordinate characteristic graphs in which there is an edge from each inherited attribute to each synthesized attribute, and superior characteristic graphs in which there is an edge from each synthesized attribute to each other attribute (including the other synthesized attributes), must be used. This is because the slice of the incomplete system should include all vertices that could be included in the slice of some "completed" system, and it is always possible to provide a call or a calling context that corresponds to the graphs described above.

For library procedures, it is possible to provide precise subordinate characteristic graphs even when the procedures themselves are not provided. For programs under development, it might be possible to compute characteristic graphs, or at least better approximations to them than the worst-case graphs, given specifications for the missing program components.

4.5 Forward Slicing

Whereas the *slice* of a program with respect to a program point p and variable x consists of all statements and predicates of the program that might affect the value of x at point p, the *forward slice* of a program with respect to a program point p and variable x consists of all statements and predicates of the program that might be affected by the value of x at point p. An algorithm for *forward* interprocedural slicing can be defined on system dependence graphs, using the same concepts employed for (backward) interprocedural slicing. As before, the key element is the use of the linkage grammar's characteristic graph edges in the system dependence graph to represent transitive dependences from actual-in vertices to actual-out vertices due to the effects of procedure calls.

An algorithm for forward interprocedural slicing is given as procedure MarkVerticesOfForwardSlice of Figure 15.

In Figure 15, the computation of the forward slice of system dependence graph G with respect to vertex set S is performed in two phases. The traversal in Phase 1 follows flow edges, control edges, and parameter-out edges, but does *not* follow call edges, def-order edges, or parameter-in edges. Because call edges

```
procedure MarkVerticesOfForwardSlice(G, S)
declare
    G: a system dependence graph
    S, S': sets of vertices in G
begin
    /* Phase 1: Slice forward without descending into called procedures */
        MarkVerticesReached(G, S, {def-order, parameter-in, call})

    /* Phase 2: Slice forward into called procedures without ascending to call sites */
        S' := all marked vertices in G
        MarkVerticesReached(G, S', {def-order, parameter-out})

end

procedure MarkVerticesReached(G, V, Kinds)
declare
    G: a system dependence graph
    V: a set of vertices in G
    Kinds: a set of kinds of edges
    v, w: vertices in G
    WorkList: a set of vertices in G
begin
    WorkList := V
    while WorkList ≠ ∅ do
        Select and remove a vertex v from WorkList
        Mark v
        for each unmarked vertex w such that there is an edge v → w whose kind is not in Kinds do
            Insert w into WorkList
        od
    od
end
```

Fig. 15. The procedure MarkVerticesOfForwardSlice marks the vertices of the forward interprocedural slice G/S. The auxiliary procedure Mark-VerticesReached marks all vertices in G to which there is a path from a vertex in V along edges of kinds other than those in the set Kinds.

and parameter-in edges are not followed, the traversal in Phase 1 does not descend into called procedures. The traversal in Phase 2 follows flow edges, control edges, call edges, and parameter-in edges, but does *not* follow def-order edges or parameter-out edges. Because parameter-out edges are not followed, the traversal in Phase 2 does not ascend into calling procedures.

5. THE COMPLEXITY OF THE SLICING ALGORITHM

This section discusses the complexity of the interprocedural slicing algorithm presented in Section 4.1. In the absence of aliasing, the cost is polynomial in (various) parameters of the system. In the presence of aliasing, the cost remains polynomial if we use the generalized definitions of data dependences given in Section 4.3 (at the price of somewhat less precision in taking slices). Alternatively, if we follow the approach of transforming the system to one that is alias-free, more precise slices can be obtained, but the cost can increase by an exponential factor that reflects the blow-up in size that can occur due to the number of aliasing patterns in the program. The measures of system size used below are those associated with the system dependence graph created according to one or the other of these approaches. In particular, if the approach of transforming to an alias-free system is used, the measures of system size used below are those associated with the alias-free system.

165

5.1 Cost of Constructing the System Dependence Graph

The cost of constructing the system dependence graph can be expressed in terms of the parameters given in the following tables:

Parameters that measure the size of an individual procedure	
V	The larest number of predicates and assignments in a single procedure
E	The largest number of edges in a single procedure dependence graph
$Params$	The largest number of formal parameters in any procedure
$Sites$	The largest number of call sites in any procedure

Parameters that measure the size of the entire system	
P	The number of procedures in the system (= the number of productions in the linkage grammar)
$Globals$	The number of global variables in the system
$TotalSites \le P \cdot Sites$	The total number of call sites in the system

Interprocedural data-flow analysis is used to compute summary information about side effects. Flow-insensitive interprocedural summary information (e.g., GMOD and GREF) can be determined particularly efficiently. In particular, in the absence of nested scopes, GMOD and GREF can be determined in time $O(P^2 + P \cdot TotalSites)$ steps by the algorithm described in [6].

Intraprocedural data-flow analysis is used to determine the data dependences of procedure dependence graphs. For the structured language under consideration here, this analysis can be performed in a syntax-directed fashion (for example, using an attribute grammar) [8]. This involves propagating sets of program points, where each set consists of program points in a single procedure. This computation has total cost $O(V^2)$.

The cost of constructing the linkage grammar and computing its subordinate characteristic graphs can be expressed in terms of the following parameters:

Parameters that measure the size of the linkage grammar	
$R = Sites + 1$	The largest number of nonterminal occurrences in a single production
$G = P + TotalSites$	The number of nonterminal occurrences in the linkage grammar
$\le P \cdot R$ $= P \cdot (Sites + 1)$	
$X = Globals + Params$	The largest number of attributes of a single nonterminal
$D \le R \cdot X$	The largest number of attribute occurrences in a single production
$= (Sites + 1)$ $\cdot (Global + Params)$	

To determine the dependences among the attribute occurrences in each production, its corresponding procedure is sliced with respect to the linkage vertices that correspond to the attribute occurrences of the production. The cost of each slice is linear in the size of the procedure dependence graph; that is, the cost is bounded by $O(V + E)$. Consequently, the total cost of constructing the linkage grammar is bounded by $O(G \cdot X \cdot (V + E))$.

It remains for us to analyze the cost of computing the linkage grammar's subordinate characteristic graphs. Because there are at most D^2 edges in each TDP(p) relation, the cost of AddEdgeAndInduce, which recloses a single TDP(p) relation, is $O(D^2)$. The cost of initializing the TDP relations with all direct dependences in ConstructSubCGraphs is bounded by $O(P \cdot D^2)$.

In the inner loop of Step 2 of procedure ConstructSubCGraphs, AddEdge-AndInduce is called once for each occurrence of nonterminal N. There are at most X^2 edges in each graph TDS(N) and G nonterminal occurrences where an edge may be induced. No edge is induced more than once because of the marks on TDS edges; thus, the total cost of procedure ConstructSubCGraphs is bounded by $O(G \cdot X^2 \cdot D^2)$ [13].

5.2 Slicing Costs

An interprocedural slice is performed by two traversals of the system dependence graph, starting from some initial set of vertices. The cost of each traversal is linear in the size of the system dependence graph, which is bounded by $O(P \cdot (V + E) + \textit{TotalSites} \cdot X)$.

6. RELATED WORK

In recasting the interprocedural slicing problem as a reachability problem in a graph, we are following the example of [19], which does the same for intraprocedural slicing. The reachability approach is conceptually simpler than the data-flow equation approach used in [22], and is also much more efficient when more than one slice is desired.

The recasting of the problem as a reachability problem does involve some loss of generality; rather than permitting a program to be sliced with respect to program point p and an *arbitrary* variable, a slice can only be taken with respect to a variable that is defined or used at p. For such slicing problems the interprocedural slicing algorithm presented in this paper is an improvement over Weiser's algorithm because our algorithm is able to produce a more precise slice than the one produced by Weiser's algorithm. However, the extra generality is not the source of the imprecision of Weiser's method; as explained in the Introduction and in Section 3.2, the imprecision of Weiser's method is due to the lack of a mechanism to keep track of the calling context of a called procedure.

After the initial publication of our interprocedural-slicing algorithm [10], a different technique for computing interprocedural slices was presented by Hwang et al. [12]. The slicing algorithm presented in [12] computes an answer that is as precise as our algorithm, but differs significantly in how it handles the calling-context problem. The algorithm from [12] constructs a *sequence* of slices of the system—where each slice of the sequence essentially permits there to be one additional level of recursion—until a fixed-point is reached (i.e., until no further elements appear in a slice that uses one additional level of recursion). Thus, each slice of the sequence represents an approximation to the final answer. During each of these slice approximations, the algorithm uses a stack to keep track of the calling context of a called procedure. In contrast, our algorithm for interprocedural slicing is based on a two-phase process for propagating marks on the system dependence graph. In Phase 1 of the algorithm, the presence of the linkage grammar's subordinate-characteristic-graph edges (representing transitive dependences due to the effects of procedure calls) permits the entire effect of a call to be accounted for by a single backward step over the call site's subordinate-characteristic-graph edges.

Hwang et al. do not include an analysis of their algorithm's complexity in [12], which makes a direct comparison with our algorithm difficult; however, there are several reasons why our algorithm may be more efficient. First, the algorithm from [12] computes a sequence of slices, each of which may involve reslicing a procedure multiple times; in contrast, through its use of marks on system-dependence-graph vertices, our algorithm processes no vertex more than once during the computation of a slice. Second, if one wishes to compute multiple slices of the same system, our approach has a significant advantage. The system dependence graph (with its subordinate-characteristic-graph edges) need be computed only once; each slicing operation can use this graph, and the cost of each such slice is linear in the size of the system dependence graph. In contrast, the approach of [12] would involve finding a new fixed point (a problem that appears to have complexity comparable to the computation of the subordinate characteristic graphs) for each new slice.

In [18], Myers presents algorithms for a specific set of interprocedural data-flow problems, all of which require keeping track of calling context; however, Myers's approach to handling this problem differs from ours. Myers performs data-flow analysis on a graph representation of the program, called a *super graph*, which is a collection of control-flow graphs (one for each procedure in the program), connected by call and return edges. The information maintained at each vertex of the super graph includes a *memory component*, which keeps track of calling context (essentially by using the name of the call site). Our use of the system dependence graph permits keeping track of calling context while propagating simple marks rather than requiring the propagation of sets of names.

It is no doubt possible to formulate interprocedural slicing as a data-flow analysis problem on a super graph and to solve the problem using an algorithm akin to those described by Myers to account correctly for the calling context of a called procedure. As in the comparison with [12], our algorithm has a significant advantage when one wishes to compute multiple slices of the same system. Whereas the system dependence graph can be computed once and then used for each slicing operation, the approach postulated above would involve solving a new data-flow analysis problem from scratch for each slice.

The vertex-reachability approach we have used here has some similarities to a technique used in [5], [6], and [15] to transform data-flow analysis problems to vertex-reachability problems. In each case, a data-flow analysis problem is solved by first building a graph representation of the program and then performing a reachability analysis on the graph, propagating simple marks rather than, for example, sets of variable names. One difference between the interprocedural slicing problem and the problems addressed by the work cited above, is that interprocedural slicing is a "demand problem" [2] whose goal is to determine information concerning a specific set of program points rather than an "exhaustive problem" in which the goal is to determine information for all program points.

APPENDIX: ATTRIBUTE GRAMMARS AND ATTRIBUTE DEPENDENCES

An attribute grammar is a context-free grammar extended by attaching *attributes* to the terminal and nonterminal symbols of the grammar and by supplying *attribute equations* to define attribute values [14]. In every production $p: X_0 \to X_1, \ldots, X_k$, each X_i denotes an *occurrence* of one of the grammar symbols; associated with each such symbol occurrence is a set of *attribute occurrences* corresponding to the symbol's attributes.

Each production has a set of attribute equations; each equation defines one of the production's attribute occurrences as the value of an *attribute-definition function* applied to other attribute occurrences in the production. The attributes of a symbol X are divided into two disjoint classes: *synthesized* attributes and *inherited* attributes.

An attribute grammar is *well formed* when the terminal symbols of the grammar have no synthesized attributes, the root nonterminal of the grammar has no inherited attributes, and each production has exactly one attribute equation for each of the left-hand side nonterminal's synthesized attribute occurrences and for each of the right-hand side symbols' inherited attribute occurrences. (The grammars that arise in this paper are potentially *not* well formed, in that a production may have equations for synthesized attribute occurrences of right-hand side symbols. The reason that this does not cause problems is that the "linkage grammar" of the interprocedural slicing algorithm is used *only* to compute transitive dependences due to calls; we are not interested in the language defined by the grammar, nor in actual attribute values.)

A derivation tree node that is an instance of symbol X has an associated set of *attribute instances* corresponding to the attributes of X. An *attributed tree* is a derivation tree together with an assignment of either a value or the special token **null** to each attribute instance of the tree.

Ordinarily, although not in this paper, one is interested in analyzing a string according to its attribute-grammar specification. To do this, one first constructs the string's derivation tree with an assignment of **null** to each attribute instance and then evaluates as many attribute instances as possible, using the appropriate attribute equation as an assignment statement. The latter process is termed *attribute evaluation*.

Functional dependences among attribute occurrences in a production p (or attribute instances in a tree T) can be represented by a directed graph, called a *dependence graph*, denoted by $D(p)$ (respectively, $D(T)$), and defined as follows:

(1) For each attribute occurrence (instance) b, the graph contains a vertex b'.
(2) If attribute occurrence (instance) b appears on the right-hand side of the attribute equation that defines attribute occurrence (instance) c, the graph contains the edge $b' \to c'$.

An attribute grammar that has a derivation tree whose dependence graph contains a cycle is called a *circular* attribute grammar. (The grammars that arise in this paper can be circular grammars.)

A node's *subordinate* and *superior characteristic graphs* provide a convenient representation of transitive dependences among the node's attributes. (A *transitive dependence* exists between attributes that are related in the transitive closure of the tree's attribute dependence relation, or, equivalently, that are connected by a direct path in the tree's dependence graph.) The vertices of the characteristic graphs at node r correspond to the attributes of r; the edges of the characteristic graphs at r correspond to transitive dependences among r's attributes.

The subordinate characteristic graph at r is the projection of the dependences of the subtree rooted at r onto the attributes of r. To form the superior characteristic graph at node r, we imagine that the subtree rooted at r has been pruned from the derivation tree, and project the dependence graph of the remaining tree onto the attributes of r. To define the characteristic graphs precisely, we make the following definitions:

(1) Given a directed graph $G = (V, E)$, a *path* from vertex a to vertex b is a sequence of vertices, $[v_1, v_2, \ldots, v_k]$, such that $a = v_1$, $b = v_k$, and $\{(v_i, v_{i+1}) \mid i = 1, \ldots, k-1\} \subseteq E$.

(2) Given a directed graph $G = (V, E)$ and a set of vertices $V' \subseteq V$, the *projection* of G onto V' is defined as

$$G//V' = (V', E')$$

where $E' = \{(v, w) \mid v, w \in V'$, and there exists a path $[v = v_1, v_2, \ldots, v_k = w]$ in G such that $v_2, \ldots, v_{k-1} \notin V'\}$. (That is, $G//V'$ has an edge from $v \in V'$ to $w \in V'$ when there exists a path from v to w in G that does not pass through any other elements of V'.)

The subordinate and superior characteristic graphs of a node r, denoted $r.C$ and $r.\bar{C}$, respectively, are defined formally as follows. Let r be a node in tree T, let the subtree rooted at r be denoted T_r, and let the attribute instances at r be denoted $A(r)$, then the subordinate and superior characteristic graphs at r satisfy:

$$r.C = D(T_r)//A(r)$$
$$r.\bar{C} = (D(T) - D(T_r))//A(r).$$

A characteristic graph represents the projection of attribute dependences onto the attributes of a single tree node; consequently, for a given grammar, each graph is bounded in size by some constant.

REFERENCES

1. AHO, A. V., SETHI, R., AND ULLMAN, J. D. *Compilers: Principles, Techniques, and Tools,* Addison-Wesley, Reading, Mass., 1986.
2. BABICH, W. A., AND JAZAYERI, M. The method of attributes for data flow analysis: Part II. Demand analysis. *Acta Inf. 10,* 3 (Oct. 1978), 265–272.
3. BADGER, L., AND WEISER, M. Minimizing communication for synchronizing parallel dataflow programs. In *Proceedings of the 1988 International Conference on Parallel Processing* (St. Charles, IL, Aug. 15–19, 1988). Pennsylvania State University Press, University Park, PA, 1988.
4. BANNING, J. P. An efficient way to find the side effects of procedure calls and the aliases of variables. In *Conference Record of the Sixth ACM Symposium on Principles of Programming Languages* (San Antonio, Tex., Jan. 29–31, 1979). ACM, New York, 1979, pp. 29–41.
5. CALLAHAN, D. The program summary graph and flow-sensitive interprocedural data flow analysis. In *Proceedings of the ACM SIGPLAN 88 Conference on Programming Language Design and Implementation* (Atlanta, Ga., June 22–24, 1988). *ACM SIGPLAN Not. 23,* 7 (July 1988), 47–56.

6. COOPER, K. D., AND KENNEDY, K. Interprocedural side-effect analysis in linear time. In *Proceedings of the ACM SIGPLAN 88 Conference on Programming Language Design and Implementation* (Atlanta, Ga., June 22–24, 1988). *ACM SIGPLAN Not. 23*, 7 (July 1988), 57–66.

7. FERRANTE, J., OTTENSTEIN, K., AND WARREN, J. The program dependence graph and its use in optimization. *ACM Trans. Program. Lang. Syst. 9*, 3 (July 1987), 319–349.

8. HORWITZ, S., PRINS, J., AND REPS, T. Integrating non-interfering versions of programs. TR-690, Computer Sciences Dept., Univ. of Wisconsin, Madison, March 1987.

9. HORWITZ, S., PRINS, J., AND REPS, T. On the adequacy of program dependence graphs for representing programs. In *Conference Record of the Fifteenth ACM Symposium on Principles of Programming Languages* (San Diego, Calif., Jan. 13–15, 1988). ACM, New York, 1988, pp. 146–157.

10. HORWITZ, S., REPS, T., AND BINKLEY, D. Interprocedural slicing using dependence graphs. In *Proceedings of the ACM SIGPLAN 88 Conference on Programming Language Design and Implementation* (Atlanta, Ga., June 22–24, 1988). *ACM SIGPLAN Not. 23*, 7 (July 1988), 35–46.

11. HORWITZ, S., PRINS, J., AND REPS, T. Integrating non-interfering versions of programs. *ACM Trans. Program. Lang. Syst. 11*, 3 (July 1989), 345–387.

12. HWANG, J. C., DU, M. W., AND CHOU, C. R. Finding program slices for recursive procedures. In *Proceedings of the IEEE COMPSAC 88* (Chicago, Oct. 3–7, 1988). IEEE Computer Society, Washington, D.C., 1988.

13. KASTENS, U. Ordered attribute grammars. *Acta Inf. 13*, 3 (1980), 229–256.

14. KNUTH, D. E. Semantics of context-free languages. *Math. Syst. Theor. 2*, 2 (June 1968), 127–145.

15. KOU, L. T. On live-dead analysis for global data flow problems. *J. ACM 24*, 3 (July 1977), 473–483.

16. KUCK, D. J., MURAOKA, Y., AND CHEN, S. C. On the number of operations simultaneously executable in FORTRAN-like programs and their resulting speed-up. *IEEE Trans. Comput. C-21*, 12 (Dec. 1972), 1293–1310.

17. LYLE, J., AND WEISER, M. Experiments on slicing-based debugging tools. In *Proceedings of the First Conference on Empirical Studies of Programming* (June 1986).

18. MYERS, E. A precise inter-procedural data flow algorithm. In *Conference Record of the Eighth ACM Symposium on Principles of Programming Languages* (Williamsburg, Va., Jan. 26–28, 1981). ACM, New York, 1981, pp. 219–230.

19. OTTENSTEIN, K. J., AND OTTENSTEIN, L. M. The program dependence graph in a software development environment. In *Proceedings of the ACM SIGSOFT/SIGPLAN Software Engineering Symposium on Practical Software Development Environments* (Pittsburgh, Pa., April 23–25, 1984). *ACM SIGPLAN Not. 19*, 5 (May 1984), 177–184.

20. REPS, T., AND YANG, W. The semantics of program slicing. TR-777, Computer Sciences Dept., Univ. of Wisconsin, Madison, June 1988.

21. WEISER, M. Reconstructing sequential behavior from parallel behavior projections. *Inf. Process. Lett. 17* (Oct. 1983), 129–135.

22. WEISER, M. Program slicing. *IEEE Trans. Softw. Eng. SE-10*, 4 (July 1984), 352–357.

Received April 1988; revised August 1989; accepted August 1989

Data Dependency Graphs for Ada Programs

LOUISE E. MOSER, MEMBER, IEEE

Abstract—We present a novel compositional method of constructing data dependency graphs for Ada programs. These graphs are useful in a program development environment for analyzing data dependencies and tracking information flow within a program. Graphs for primitive program statements are combined together to form graphs for larger program units. Composition rules are described for iteration, recursion, exception handling, and tasking, as well as for simpler Ada constructs. The correctness of the construction and the practicality of the technique are discussed.

Index Terms—Ada, data dependency analysis, data dependency graphs, programming language constructs.

I. INTRODUCTION

DATA dependency analysis has been used extensively for a variety of purposes, including program optimization [5], [10], parallelization and vectorization [1], [12], [16], security analysis and validation [3], [9], and software reliability validation and analysis [6], [15]. In data dependency analysis, a data structure is constructed to represent the flow of information within a program so that inferences can be made about the effects of one part of the program on other parts of the program.

Traditionally, dependency analysis has been performed with so-called data dependence graphs [4], [11], unfortunately misnamed since the nodes of the graph represent statements of the program while the edges represent dependencies between statements. Thus, the graphs make no reference to data. Data dependence graphs normally represent every statement of the program with all of its dependencies. They are typically two to three times the size of the program itself. Consequently, problems of storage and analysis of the graphs can arise.

Furthermore, the construction of existing data dependence graphs is usually incremental and sequential [15], [19], rather than compositional. Yet, modern programming languages, such as Ada, are designed to support structured programming and to allow program units to be composed. Moreover, program development environments for Ada provide extensive support for combining together such units. Although some researchers have investigated interprocedural data dependency analysis [2],

[8], [14] and others have considered high-level dependency analysis [18], no one has given a compositional method of constructing data dependency graphs. Thus, modern techniques of program composition and information hiding are precluded.

In this paper, we introduce composition rules for constructing data dependency graphs. The nodes of these graphs represent variables and constants, and the edges represent the dependence of a variable, after execution of a program statement or unit, on other variables and constants prior to that execution. Our elegant compositional method combines together data dependency graphs for individual program statements into graphs that represent data dependencies for larger program units. When individual graphs are composed, nodes and arcs needed for local variables and intermediate steps of the calculation can be removed. Thus, for well-structured programs with relatively few global variables, the graphs are smaller, and less costly to analyze, than the more detailed full graph.

Of course, these graphs contain less information than the conventional graphs. They are thus unsuitable for local code optimization and for vectorization, but are much more suitable for security analysis and validation and for software reliability validation and analysis than are conventional data dependence graphs. In particular, these graphs are useful in multilevel security applications for certifying information flow and for checking confinement with respect to storage channels, and they can also be used in software reliability analysis to identify uninitialized variables as well as unused variables and constants.

Moreover, in contrast to the graphs of [5], [7], there is no intention of fully capturing the semantics of a program in these dependency graphs. Thus, analysis of the graphs could indicate a possible dependency where semantic analysis would show that none exists. For example, in the absence of information as to which branch of a conditional is executed, the construction assumes that both are possible. Because these graphs represent flow of information between variables and not the values of variables, analysis is easier than symbolic execution [17], but it is also more conservative.

In what follows, we provide composition rules for iteration, recursion, exception handling, and tasking, as well as for simpler Ada constructs. These composition rules can easily be adapted to other structured languages, such as Pascal, Modula II, and C. The composition rules for simple sequential statements are quite straightforward but, when the flow of control is broken by an exit

Manuscript received February 10, 1988; revised December 18, 1988, May 28, 1989, and December 3, 1989. Recommended by T. Ichikawa. This work was supported in part at California State University, Hayward, by the National Science Foundation under Grant DCR-8408544 and by the National Security Agency, Office of Cryptographic Research, under Grant MDA904-84-H-0009.

The author is with the Department of Electrical and Computer Engineering, University of California, Santa Barbara, CA 93106.

IEEE Log Number 9034385.

from a loop, a return from a procedure, or an exception raised in a block, they must be modified. Additional complication is introduced by tasks that are executed concurrently and asynchronously. Meaningful data dependency graphs for concurrent units can be constructed, but a choice must be made between complicated analyses or, alternatively, some extra dependencies in the graphs. For practical reasons, we choose the latter. We assume that the names of variables provided by the Ada scope, type, and generic mechanisms have been resolved. We exclude aliasing which has been studied in detail in [2], [14] and access types which are reserved for treatment in a subsequent paper. Variables that are shared by tasks in concurrent units are also excluded, although the composition rule for tasks can easily be modified to accommodate them.

II. CONSTRUCTION OF THE GRAPHS

We now describe the composition rules for constructing the data dependency graphs; these rules correspond to language constructs of Ada. A *graph* G is a pair $< V(G)$, $E(G) >$, where $V(G)$ is the set of vertices, or nodes, of G and $E(G)$ is the set of edges, or arcs, of G. The *arcs* of G are ordered pairs (u, v), where $u, v \in V(G)$. The nodes of these graphs correspond to program variables and constants, and the arcs indicate information flow between them. The nodes are labeled with program identifiers that have been suitably disambiguated.

A node that represents a constant or a variable prior to execution of a program unit is referred to as an *input node* and is qualified by a prime. All other nodes represent variables after execution of the program unit and are referred to as *noninput nodes*. An arc (u, v) indicates that the variable whose identifier labels node v depends, after execution of the program unit, on the constant or variable whose identifier labels node u, where u may or may not be an input node. In these graphs there is only one arc from u to v; insertion of a second arc from u to v has no effect.

An *in-arc* to v is an arc of the form (u, v); an *out-arc* from v is an arc of the form (v, u). In these dependency graphs, if a node corresponding to a variable has no in-arcs, the variable does not depend upon any variable or constant. We may expect this situation for the graph representing a program statement, but if it persists into the graph for a full program it may indicate an error. A node is *isolated* if it has no in-arcs or out-arcs. These dependency graphs contain no isolated nodes because input nodes are deleted when dependencies on those nodes cease to exist.

A *box* is an auxiliary structure that is used to identify a subgraph of a graph. The subgraph inside a box is composed with the graph that represents the dependencies when the flow of control is broken by a handling of an exception, an exit from a loop, a return from a procedure, or the termination of a task. The subgraph outside a box represents the unbroken flow of control of the program.

We commence by considering the graphs for the primitive program statements: the read and write statements, the constant declaration and assignment statements, the exit, return, raise, and terminate statements, and the procedure or function call. In what follows, b represents a variable and $d(d_j)$ represents an expression (which may be a variable or a constant) that contains data upon which b depends following execution of the program statement.

A. Read and Write Statements

For the read statement

read(d, b);

d represents the source (file) of the data read in. To construct the graph G we create a new node b, a new node d', and an arc (d', b), as shown in Fig. 1. For the write statement

write(b, d);

d is an expression with operands $d_1, \cdots, d_k$ and b represents the destination (file) to which the data are written. To construct the graph G we create a new node b, new nodes $d'_1, \cdots, d'_k$, and arcs $(d'_1, b), \cdots, (d'_k, b)$.

B. Assignment Statement

$b := d$;

Here d is an expression with operands $d_1, \cdots, d_k$. To construct the graph G we create a new node b, new nodes $d'_1, \cdots, d'_k$, and arcs $(d'_1, b), \cdots, (d'_k, b)$, as shown in Fig. 2. If b is an array element $b[i]$, we create a new node b', a new node i', an arc (b', b), and an arc (i', b). These dependency graphs do not distinguish between elements of arrays. An assignment to an array element is an assignment to the entire array, and a use of an array element is a use of the entire array and also of the index expression. The treatment of records is similar to that of arrays. Also, the graph constructions for the constant declaration and assignment statements are similar.

C. Exit, Return, Raise, and Terminate Statements

For the exit statement, we create a node and a box labeled exit L, where L is the loop to which the exit applies; a copy of the node is placed inside and outside the box. Such a node is referred to as an *exit node*, and the box is referred to as an *exit box*. Similarly, for the return statement, we create a *return node* and a *return box* labeled return S, where S is the subprogram (procedure or function) to which the return applies. In the case of a function, if the expression d being returned has operands $d_1, \cdots, d_k$, we create new nodes $d'_1, \cdots, d'_k$, and arcs (d'_j, S). For the raise statement, we create an *exception node* and an *exception box* labeled raise X, where X is the exception being raised. Similarly, for the terminate statement we create a *terminate node* and a *terminate box* labeled terminate T, where T is the task being terminated. A graph for a program fragment, each execution of which ends in an exit, return, raise or terminate statement, is referred to as a *terminal graph*.

Fig. 1. Graph for a read or write statement.

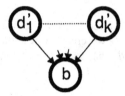

Fig. 2. Graph for an assignment statement.

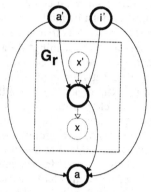

Fig. 3. Graph for a procedure call.

D. Procedure or Function Call

The graph G_r constructed for a procedure (see Section II-H) has nodes corresponding to global variables and formal parameters. To construct the graph G for a procedure call, we must consider the in, out, and in/out parameters.

1) In Parameters: If there is an input node x' for a formal in parameter with arcs to nodes v_l and if the corresponding actual parameter is an expression with operands $d_1, \cdots, d_k$, we create new nodes $d'_1, \cdots, d'_k$, and arcs (d_j, v_l). We then delete the node x' and the arcs (x', v_l). In particular, if the actual parameter is an array element $a[i]$, we create new nodes a' and i' and insert the arcs (a', v_l) and (i', v_l). If the expression is a field of a record, the treatment is similar.

2) Out Parameters: If there is a noninput node x for a formal out parameter, we create a new node d for the corresponding actual parameter, insert the arc (d, x), and eliminate x. If the actual parameter is an array element $a[i]$, we insert additional arcs from the input nodes a' and i' that may have been created in 1) to the noninput node a. If the actual parameter is a field of a record, the treatment is similar.

3) In/Out Parameters: If there is an input node x' for a formal in/out parameter, we apply 1) for in parameters. Similarly, if there is a noninput node x for the formal parameter, we apply 2) for out parameters, as illustrated in Fig. 3.

The construction for a function call is similar except that there are no out or in/out parameters and the return node for the function is treated as a node for an out parameter and is not deleted.

Now we consider the graphs for composite program units. The composition rules described below are based on the simpler graph operations of subsumption, elimination, merger, and reduction. These operations remove nodes and arcs from the graphs when data are no longer relevant and dependencies no longer exist, for example, when a variable is assigned a new value. For procedures and functions, the nodes of the graph represent parameters, global variables, and constants; thus, the paths between input and noninput nodes are generally short, easing the analysis of the graph.

E. Statement Composition

$S_r; S_t;$

Here, S_r and S_t are compositions of zero or more statements, and G_r and G_t are their respective dependency graphs. We let m'_r (m'_t) denote an arbitrary input node of G_r (G_t) and n_r (n_t) an arbitrary noninput node of G_r (G_t). Initially, we assume that S_r and S_t contain no exit, return, raise, terminate, call, or accept statements. The graph construction for statement composition is then performed in two steps:

1) For each input node m'_t of G_t, if its label appears on a noninput node n_r of G_r then, for each out-arc from m'_t to n_t, we delete that arc, insert an arc from n_r to n_t, and delete the node m'_t. Similar operations are performed if the label of m'_t appears only on an input node m'_r of G_r. This process is referred to as the *subsumption* of the nodes m'_t by the nodes n_r or m'_r and yields an intermediate graph $\overline{G}$, as shown in Fig. 4.

The justification for the subsumption step is that it replaces input nodes of G_t by similarly labeled nodes of G_r that represent constants and variables after execution of S_r and before execution of S_t.

2) For each noninput node n_t of G_t, if its label appears on a noninput node n_r of G_r then, if the corresponding node n_r of $\overline{G}$ has in-arcs from nodes u_i and out-arcs to nodes v_j, we insert the arcs (u_i, v_j) into $\overline{G}$. Then we delete from $\overline{G}$ the arcs (u_i, n_r) and (n_r, v_j), the node n_r, and each input node m'_r that has become isolated. This process is referred to as the *elimination* of the nodes n_r and yields the graph G, as shown in Fig. 4.

The justification for the elimination step is that a dependency graph should contain only a single noninput node for each label. If the graph $\overline{G}$ contains a pair of such nodes, the same variable has been assigned twice, once in each statement, and only the second assignment determines the value of the variable after execution of the composite statement. Thus, the earlier node n_r of G_r is eliminated, but the dependencies to which it contributed are

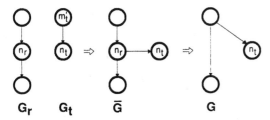

Fig. 4. Graph construction for statement composition, where G_r is the graph of S_r, G_t is the graph of S_t, and G is the graph of $S_r; S_t$. Here we assume that $n_r \in G_r$ and $m_t', n_t \in G_t$ and that these three nodes have the same label. First m_t' is subsumed by n_r and then n_r is eliminated.

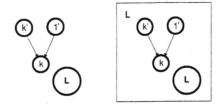

Fig. 5. Example 1. Composition with an exit statement.

preserved, i.e., each pair of arcs consisting of an in-arc to n_r and an out-arc from n_r is replaced by a single arc.

When the statements being composed contain an exit, return, raise, or terminate statement L that breaks the flow of control of the program, the statement composition rule must be extended. In particular, if S_r (S_t) is the null statement, then G_r (G_t) is the empty graph and composition of G_r with G_t yields G_t (G_r). If G_r is a terminal graph, composition of G_r with G_t yields the terminal graph G_r, whereas if G_t is a terminal graph and G_r is not, composition of G_r with G_t yields a terminal graph (which, in general, is different from G_t), since the corresponding program statements can terminate only through a nonsequential flow of control.

More generally, to extend the composition rule, we let n^L denote the exit, return, raise, or terminate node labeled L, H_r (H_t) the subgraph of G_r (G_t) outside the boxes, and $\{K_r^L\}$ ($\{K_t^L\}$) the set of subgraphs of G_r (G_t) inside the boxes. (These sets may be empty.) As above, we compose H_r with H_t and introduce arcs from each node n^L of H_r to each noninput node n_t of H_t to obtain the subgraph H of G outside the boxes. Likewise, for each box labeled L of G_t, we compose H_r with K_t^L, introduce arcs from each node n^L of H_r to each noninput node n_t of K_t^L, and then merge (see Section II-F for a description of the merge operation) the results with K_t^L to obtain the subgraph K^L of G inside the box labeled L. If there does not exist a box labeled L for G_t, then K^L is K_r^L. If G_r does not contain a box labeled L and S_t consists solely of an exit, return, raise, or terminate statement L, the graph for the composition consists of a copy of G_r and the raise node inside and outside the box labeled L, as shown in Fig. 5. A more complex example of composition is illustrated in Fig. 10.

Example 1.

$k := k + 1;$
exit L;

The subgraph H of G outside the boxes will subsequently be composed with the graph for the statement that follows the composite statement. For an exception, the subgraph K^L inside the box labeled L will be composed with the graph for the handler and then merged with the subgraph H to allow for the two possibilities that the raise may or may not occur. For a loop, the subgraph H, which represents the complete executions of the loop body, will

be composed with the subgraph K^L, which represents the final partial execution of the body of the loop. For a procedure, the subgraph H will be merged with the subgraph K^L to allow for the two possibilities that the return may or may not occur, and similarly for a task. A modification of the subsumption and elimination operations for call and accept statements is given in Section II-K.

F. Alternative Statement

    if d **then**
        S_r;
    else
        S_t;
    end if;

Initially, we assume that S_r and S_t contain no exit, return, raise, terminate, call, or accept statements. We let G_r and G_t denote their respective dependency graphs. For each noninput node n_r of G_r that does not also appear as a noninput node of G_t, we create an input node m_r' with the same label as n_r (if it does not already exist) and insert an arc from m_r' to n_r, as shown in Fig. 6. Similar nodes and arcs are created for each noninput node n_t of G_t that does not also appear as a noninput node of G_r. These additional arcs are necessary to cover the possibility that the values of variables remain unchanged if the other alternative is chosen.

If the condition d is an expression with operands $d_1, \cdots, d_k$, we create new nodes d_j' and arcs from the d_j' to each node of G_r (G_t) that is not an input node, as shown in Fig. 6. These arcs correspond to control dependencies and indicate that the noninput nodes of G_r and G_t depend upon the operands of the conditional expression. At this intermediate stage of the construction, there may be multiple nodes with the same label; these nodes must now be merged.

If there are nodes among the d_j', m_r', and m_t' that have the same label, we merge those nodes. That is, if m_r' and m_t' have the same label then, for each out-arc from m_t' to n_t, we delete that arc, insert an arc from m_r' to n_t, and delete the node m_t'. Similarly, if two noninput nodes n_r and n_t have the same label, we merge those nodes. That is, if n_r has in-arcs from nodes u_i and out-arcs to nodes v_j, then for all i, j we insert the arcs (u_i, v_j) and delete the arcs (n_r, v_j). If n_t has in-arcs from nodes w_i and out-arcs to nodes z_j, then for all i, j we insert the arcs (w_i, z_j) and (w_i, n_r), delete the arcs (w_i, n_t) and (n_t, z_j), and delete the node n_t. This process is referred to as *merger*. The

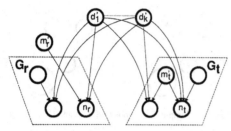

Fig. 6. Intermediate stage of the graph construction for an if statement.

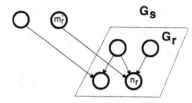

Fig. 7. Graph construction for zero or one iteration of a loop.

justification for merger is that it constructs a graph that contains all of the dependencies of both branches of the alternative statement.

If the alternative statement contains an exit, return, raise, or terminate statement, the operation of merger must be extended. In particular, if G_r (G_t) is the empty graph, the result of merging G_r (G_t) with G_t (G_r) is the graph G_t (G_r). If G_r and G_t are both terminal graphs, their merger is a terminal graph, whereas if G_r (G_t) is a terminal graph and G_t (G_r) is not, their merger is not a terminal graph.

More generally, to extend the rule for merger we let n^L denote the exit, return, raise, or terminate node labeled L, H_r (H_t) the subgraph of G_r (G_t) outside the boxes, and $\{K_r^L\}$ ($\{K_t^L\}$) the set of subgraphs of G_r (G_t) inside the boxes. If H_r(H_t) is a terminal graph and H_t(H_r) is not, we *reduce* H_r (H_t) by eliminating all noninput nodes other than exit, return, raise, and terminate nodes. Then we merge H_r and H_t to obtain the subgraph H of G outside the boxes and, for each box labeled L, we merge K_r^L and K_t^L to obtain the subgraph K^L of G inside the box. See the graph G_2 of Fig. 9. The justification for the reduction step is that if the graph H_r (H_t) is a terminal graph then the corresponding branch of the alternative statement can only terminate with the broken flow of control represented by the graph K_r^L (K_t^L).

A modification of the merge operation for call and accept statements is described in Section II-K. The construction for the case statement is an obvious extension of that for the if statement.

G. Iterative Statement

loop
   S_r;
end loop;

Initially, we assume that S_r contains no exit, return, raise, terminate, call, or accept statements. We construct the graph G_s for zero or one iteration of the loop from the graph G_r that represents the loop body S_r. For each non-input node n_r of G_r, we create an input node m_r' with the same label as n_r (if it does not already exist) and insert an arc from m_r' to n_r, as shown in Fig. 7. These additional arcs allow for the possibility that the statements of the loop body are not executed.

The graph G_s represents zero or one iteration of the loop. The graph for an arbitrary number of iterations is formed by composing the graph G_s with itself, using the rule for statement composition. The composition must be repeated until the graph becomes invariant. For a graph G_s with i noninput nodes, at most i iterations of the loop can occur before this happens. The graph G_s^i represents the dependency structure for 0 through i iterations and can be constructed using $\lceil \log_2 i \rceil$ compositions. Termination of a loop must be induced by an exit, raise, return, or terminate statement. If the loop does not terminate, no dependency graph exists for the loop as a whole. The data dependency analysis does not address the question of whether the loop terminates.

We now consider a loop L that contains an exit L statement. The *exit when d* statement is equivalent to **if** d **then exit** L; **end if** and is treated as such. If the exit is not subject to a condition, the statements following the exit are never executed and, although the loop may be syntactically correct, it is semantically equivalent to a loop in which the exit occurs at the end.

Thus, we let H_r denote the subgraph of G_r outside the exit L box (H_r may include other boxes) and K_r^L the subgraph of G_r inside the exit L box (K_r^L represents the computation if the exit is taken). As above, we construct the graph H_s and compose it with itself i times to obtain the graph H_s^i that represents 0 through i iterations of the loop. We then compose H_s^i and K_r^L. Finally, we delete the exit node, its in-arcs, and the exit L box to obtain the graph G, which represents 0 or more iterations followed by a partial execution of the loop body.

Similar constructions are required for loops that terminate through raise, return, or terminate statements. The **while** and **for** loops are special cases of the loop in which the **exit when** occurs at the beginning of the loop.

H. Block

The graph G_r for the body of a block is constructed using the composition rules. It should not contain any input nodes corresponding to variables local to the block; such a node indicates the use of an uninitialized variable and constitutes an error. To construct the graph G for the block, we eliminate nodes that correspond to variables local to the block.

1) Procedure or Function: In particular, if the block is a procedure or function that calls, or is called by, other procedures or functions, then there is an order in which the calls are made and in which the graphs can be constructed. First we assume that the procedure or function is nonrecursive. The graph construction for recursive procedures and functions is described below.

Thus, we let S denote a subprogram (procedure or function) that contains a return S statement and let G_r denote the graph for the body of that subprogram. If the return is not subject to a condition, the statements following it are never executed and, although the subprogram may be syntactically correct, it is semantically equivalent to a subprogram in which the return occurs at the end.

We let H_r denote the subgraph of G_r outside the return S box and K_r^S the subgraph of G_r inside that box. To construct the graph G for the subprogram S, we merge H_r with K_r^S and delete the box. If S is a function and the return node depends on nodes $d_j'(d_j)$, we insert arcs from the $d_j'(d_j)$ to the node for the function. Finally, we delete the return node along with its in-arcs to obtain the graph G.

I. Recursion

In constructing the graphs for recursive procedures and functions, a method of successive approximations is used, i.e., a sequence of graphs is constructed, each of which is a better approximation to the final graph. Thus, if $\Re$ is a set of mutually recursive procedures (or functions) and if the recursion terminates, then there is at least one procedure in $\Re$ that contains a base case and there is some order in which base case graphs for the procedures in $\Re$ can be constructed. Also, in a sequence of recursive calls to procedures in $\Re$, there is at least one call in an alternative or iterative statement. For the iterative statement, the base case is a loop that executes zero times.

First we consider an innermost alternative or iterative statement of a procedure R in $\Re$ that contains a recursive call. We construct the graph K for the base case of the iterative statement as follows. For each variable or formal parameter x to which an assignment is made in a procedure in $\Re$, we create new nodes x' and x and an arc (x', x). If the condition d of the alternative or iterative statement has operands $d_1, \cdots, d_k$, we create new nodes $d_1', \cdots, d_k'$ and insert the arcs (d_j', x) into the graph K. For the alternative statement, we construct the graph for the branch that contains the base case using the composition rules and then create the additional nodes and arcs as for the iterative statement.

For a procedure R in $\Re$, we now construct the graph G_R^0 for the base case of R using the composition rules and the graphs K for the innermost alternative and iterative statements. Next we construct the graph G_R^1 using the composition rules and the graphs G_P^0 for each recursive call in R to a procedure P. In general, the graph G_R^{i+1} is constructed using the graph G_P^i (or G_P^{i+1} if it has already been constructed) for each recursive call in R to a procedure P. The graph G_R^i contains nodes for global variables and formal parameters, and represents the computation after exit from a particular invocation of R. As we show in [13], the graphs G_R^i converge to a graph G_R^n that represents the data dependencies for the procedure R. We now consider an example that illustrates the graph construction for mutually recursive procedures (Fig. 8).

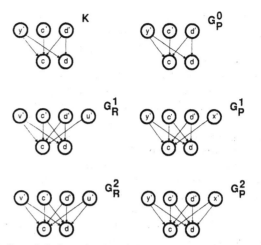

Fig. 8. Example 2. Dependency graphs for mutually recursive procedures.

Example 2:

```
procedure P(x, y: in integer);
begin
    d := y + d;
    if d <> y then
        R(x, c);
    end if;
end;

procedure R(u, v: in integer);
begin
    c := c + u;
    P(d, v);
end;
```

J. Exception Handling

In previous sections, the composition rules were extended to allow for an exception to be raised. Now we consider the construction for a block in which an exception is handled.

```
exception
    when X => S^X;
    . . .
    when others => S^A;
```

We let G_r denote the graph constructed for the statements preceding the exception handler in the block and let H denote the subgraph of G_r outside the boxes. If a raise statement in the block is not subject to a condition, the statements following the first such raise and preceding the handler are never executed and, although the block may be syntactically correct, it is semantically equivalent to a block that contains the statements preceding the first raise followed by the corresponding handler statements.

For each exception X that is raised and handled in the block, we compose K^X and G^X, where K^X is the subgraph of G_r inside the raise box and G^X is the graph for the handler statement S^X. We insert arcs from each $d_j'(d_j)$ upon which the exception node depends to each noninput node of G^X. Then, we delete the exception node, its in-arcs, and the raise X box. Finally, we merge the result with the graph H to obtain a new graph, which we also refer to as H.

If the block provides a handler for anonymous exceptions, the same construction applies, but the graph G for the block now consists of H and the boxed subgraphs of G_r that represent exceptions not handled within the block. If an exception is reraised (i.e., S^X contains a raise statement), again the same construction applies but the graph G for the block now contains a graph in a box labeled X (the box of G^X). This graph will subsequently be composed with the graph for a handler for **others** exceptions in an outer scope if such a handler exists.

If an exception is raised but not handled within a block, the exception node and the box remain a part of the graph for the block. The exception then becomes anonymous and can be handled by an others handler in an outer scope. If there is no such handler, the exception will be propagated to the last statement of the program and the final graph that is constructed will contain an exception node and a box. In this case, the program is represented by the subgraph outside the box, since the subgraph inside the box corresponds to an aborted or invalid execution.

Example 3:

```
b := a;
d := c;
if d then
    f := e;
else
    h := e + 2 * g;
    raise X;
end if;
b := c + 1;
exception
    when X => h := g; k := g;
```

In Fig. 9, G_1 is the graph for the statements $b := a$; $d := c$, G_2 is the graph for the if statement, G_3 is the graph for the statement $b := c + 1$, and G_4 is the graph for the handler statements $h := g$; $k := g$. We compose the graphs G_1, G_2, and G_3 using the extended composition rule given in Section II-E to obtain the graph in Fig. 10. Then we apply the rule for a block that contains an exception handler. We compose the graph in the box for the raised exception with the graph for the corresponding handler and then merge this graph with the graph for the rest of the block, as shown in Fig. 11.

K. Tasking

For Ada programs with tasks, we assume that variables are not shared by different tasks of a block. Thus, the only data that flows between tasks is via parameters in a rendezvous. If shared variables are necessary, the graph construction can be modified to accommodate them. Initially, we assume that the rendezvous are nonreciprocal, i.e., that calls and accepts are not nested within accept bodies

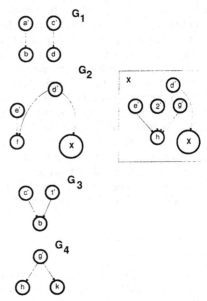

Fig. 9. Example 3. Component graphs G_1, G_2, G_3, and G_4.

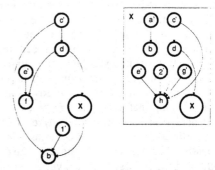

Fig. 10. Example 3. Composition of G_1, G_2, and G_3.

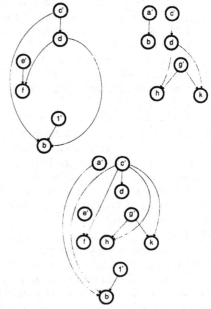

Fig. 11. Example 3. Exception handling: composition with G_4 before and after merger.

178

in such a way that a cycle of rendezvous may exist. Reciprocal rendezvous are discussed below.

Because of the inherent nondeterminism of Ada tasking, the graphs we construct must represent all of the possible interleavings of statements in different tasks of a block. Furthermore, because of the dependencies introduced by the rendezvous, the graphs for the tasks of a block are not independent but intersect in the nodes that represent parameters in a rendezvous. Thus, the graphs for the tasks are only intermediate graphs that contain partial information—the graph of importance and interest is the graph for the block that contains the tasks.

1) Graph for Entry: In constructing the graph for a block, we must take into account all of the possible rendezvous between calls and accepts for each entry declared in a task of the block. Thus, we consider all calls and accepts for a particular entry simultaneously rather than sequentially. Instead of constructing a separate graph for each call and accept, we construct a single graph for each entry E, which we refer to as the *graph for entry E*. The graph for entry takes into account all calls for each accept and all accepts for each call of the entry and is, in some sense, a "product" graph.

To construct the graph for entry, first we construct the graph for the body of each accept for the entry. Then we construct a graph for each instance of the accept provided by a call to the entry of the accept. Thus, for the statement

accept $E(\cdot\cdot\cdot)$ **do**
  S_r;
end accept;

we let G_r denote the graph corresponding to the body S_r of the accept. For each call to the entry E, we construct a graph G_{rj} from the graph G_r by identifying actual and formal parameters, as for a procedure call. Thus, for each call to the entry of the accept, we replicate the graph G_r and use these graphs to construct the graphs G_{rj}. Next, we merge the nodes of the graphs G_{rj} that represent variables (but not parameters) of the accept to obtain a graph G_R for each accept. Finally, we merge the nodes of the graphs G_R that represent the actual parameters of the corresponding calls to obtain the graph G_E for entry E.

Since one or more calls or accepts for an entry may be subject to a condition in an alternative, iterative, or select statement, we create a special node, referred to as an *entry node*, which depends upon the nodes of each condition and upon which each noninput node of the entry graph depends. These entry nodes are not merged in the graph for the body of the block in which the entries are declared, but they are eliminated from the graph for the block as a whole.

In the graphs for entry, the nodes corresponding to formal parameters are eliminated. If an actual parameter appears in more than one call, the graph for entry will contain more than one input (noninput) node for that actual parameter. Similarly, if a variable appears in more than one accept, the graph for entry will contain more than one input (noninput) node for that variable. To distinguish these nodes, the calls and accepts for each entry are enumerated and their nodes are tagged with these numbers so that appropriate nodes of the graph for entry can be distinguished until they are subsumed, eliminated, or merged. The set of nodes corresponding to the actual parameters (variables) of a particular call (accept) is referred to as an *interface*.

Thus, the nodes of the graph of a composite statement are tagged with the numbers of the calls and accepts contained within it. During composition the tags ensure that nodes of the interfaces are not affected if the variables they represent are not within the statements being composed. Consider the following example for which the graph for entry is shown in Fig. 12.

Example 4:

```
          task A;
          task body A is
            a, b: integer;
          begin
            . . .
<<L1>>    E(a, b);
          end A;

          task B;
          task body B is
            d: bool; e, f: integer;
          begin
            . . .
          if d then
<<L2>>      E(e, f);
          end if;
          end B;

          task C is;
            entry E(x, y: in out integer);
          end;
          task body C is
            u, v: integer;
          begin
            . . .
<<L3>>    accept E(x, y: in out integer);
          do
            x := x + u;
            v := y + v;
          end accept;
            . . .
<<L4>>    accept E(x, y: in out integer);
          do
            x := x + u;
            v := y + v;
          end accept;
          end C;
```

2) Select Statement: The **select** statement is somewhat similar to the case statement except that for the select statement the alternatives are chosen asynchronously from those that are open. In the select statement

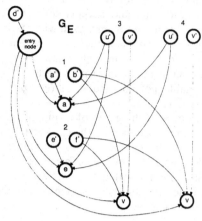

Fig. 12. Example 4. Tasking: a graph for entry.

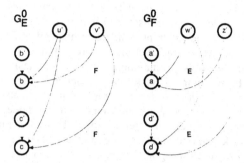

Fig. 13. Example 5. Graph construction for reciprocal rendezvous.

```
select
    when d₁ => S_{r1};
        · · ·
    when d₁ => S_{ri};
        · · ·
    else S_{r,l+1};
end select;
```

if S_{ri} is protected by a guard d_i with operands $d_{i1}, \cdots,$ d_{ik} and S_{ri} contains an accept with entry E_{ri}, we create new nodes d'_{ij} and insert arcs from the d'_{ij} to the entry node of the graph for entry E_{ri}, as well as to the noninput nodes of G_{rj}, where $1 \leq j \leq l + 1$. Furthermore, for each noninput node n_{ri} of G_{ri} that does not appear as a noninput node of the graphs of the other alternatives, we create an input node m'_{ri} with the same label as n_{ri} (if it does not already exist) and insert an arc from m'_{ri} to n_{ri}. Finally, for each pair of graphs G_{ri} and G_{rj}, we merge the nodes $d'_{ij}, m'_{ri},$ and m'_{rj} in the same interface graph that are labeled with the same identifier. Similarly, we merge the noninput nodes n_{ri} and n_{rj}.

3) Tasks and Blocks that Contain Tasks: Using the graphs for entry and the other composition rules, we now construct the graphs for tasks and blocks that contain tasks. Thus, for each entry E we enumerate the calls and accepts for that entry and construct the graph for entry E (only one copy is required). In the case of nonreciprocal rendezvous, there is an order in which the graphs for entry can be constructed. We commence by constructing the graph for an "innermost" nested call or accept.

The graph for a task is constructed from the graphs for the entries in the calls and accepts of the task. If the task does not contain a terminate statement, the usual composition rules apply. If the task contains a terminate statement, the construction is similar to that for a procedure with a return statement. After elimination of nodes for local variables in the tasks, the nodes in the graphs for entry that represent variables referenced in the same task will have the same tag, whereas nodes that represent variables in different tasks will have different tags since there are no shared variables. Like the graph for a task,

the graph for the body of a block is constructed by composition with the graphs for entry.

The graph G for the block as a whole consists of the graphs for the tasks contained in the block and the graph for the body of the block. These graphs may intersect in the graphs for entry. No further composition or merger is necessary because variables are not shared. However, the entry nodes and the nodes representing local variables are deleted and the tags of the remaining nodes are removed.

The graphs constructed from the graphs for entry are more conservative and less accurate than if they had been constructed by analyzing all of the possible interleavings of statements in a task. Determining the actual interleavings is a difficult problem, because the number of possibilities is exponential. For that reason, we have assumed that for a particular entry every call matches every accept, and we have merged together the graphs for accepts corresponding to different calls. As a result, the graphs may contain dependencies that are not actual dependencies, but the alternative is a depth of analysis inappropriate to data dependency graphs.

4) Reciprocal Rendezvous: Now we let $\mathfrak{R}$ be a set of entries of reciprocal rendezvous, i.e., a set of entries for which a syntactic analysis reveals the possible existence of a cycle of calls and accepts of the entries of $\mathfrak{R}$ in different tasks. In Example 5, entries E and F form a set of reciprocal rendezvous, since the body of an accept of E contains a call of F and vice versa. Such a potential cycle may not actually be realized when the program is executed, because the calling task in a rendezvous is suspended until the rendezvous completes.

For each entry E of $\mathfrak{R}$, we construct a graph G_E^0 similar to the graph for entry E constructed previously except that for each call or accept of an entry F of $\mathfrak{R}$ that is contained in the body of an accept of E we use the empty graph, as shown in Fig. 13. Similarly, we construct the graph G_E^1 except that for each call or accept of an entry F of $\mathfrak{R}$ that is contained in the body of an accept of E we use the graph G_F^0. In general, the graph G_E^{i+1} is constructed using the graphs G_F^i for the calls and accepts of the entries F of $\mathfrak{R}$ that are contained in the body of an accept of E. It can be demonstrated that, unless the program inevitably deadlocks, the graphs G_E^i converge in a graph G_E^n that represents the necessary dependency relationships. The graph G_E^n is the graph for entry E for reciprocal rendezvous.

Example 5:

```
                task A is
                   entry E(x: in out integer);
                end;
                task body A is
                   a, u, v: integer;
                begin
                   . . .
<<L1>>          accept E(x: in out integer) do
                   x := x + u;
                end accept;
                   . . .
<<L2>>          accept E(x: in out integer) do
                   x := x + v;
<<L3>>             F(a);
                end accept;
                end A;

                task B is
                   entry F(y: in out integer);
                end;
                task body B is
                   b, w, z: integer;
                begin
                   . . .
<<L4>>          accept F(y: in out integer) do
<<L5>>             E(b);
                   y := w;
                end accept;
                   . . .
<<L6>>          accept F(y: in out integer) do
                   y := y + z;
                end accept;
                end B;

                task C;
                task C is
                   c, d: integer;
                begin
                   . . .
<<L7>>             E(c);
                   . . .
<<L8>>             F(d);
                end C;
```

III. Correctness of the Construction

The proof of correctness of the graph construction involves showing that the graph for each type of program statement represents the correct dependency relationships and that composition of program statements preserves those relationships. In particular, we must show that no data dependencies are lost and no data dependencies are introduced by subsumption and elimination.

That no erroneous dependencies are introduced by subsumption and elimination follows from the fact that these operations introduce no arcs from nodes of G_l to nodes of G_r. However, subsumption may introduce arcs from nodes of G_r to nodes of G_l, and elimination may introduce arcs from nodes of G_r to nodes of G_l but, by the definition of subsumption and elimination, such arcs just represent the transitivity of the dependency relationship.

To see that no dependencies are lost, we observe that subsumption may result in deletion of arcs of G_l and elimination may result in deletion of arcs of G_r. Nevertheless, the construction is such that, if a dependency exists between two nodes before subsumption and elimination, and the nodes remain in the composite graph, then the dependency still exists between the two nodes after these operations are performed. Again, the proof is based on transitivity of the dependency relationship.

Similarly, we can show the correctness of the graph construction for the other types of program statements. However, we note that dependency in these graphs is a syntactically defined property and that extraneous dependencies may be introduced, as for conditional statements and tasking. The complete proof of correctness, while not difficult, is lengthy due to the many different program statement types. The details can be found in [13].

IV. Practicality of the Technique

In practical applications, the data dependency graphs constructed by our technique depend on the nature of the program and on the use that is made of the graphs. At one extreme, the dependency graph for the entire program can be constructed. Since programs generally involve only a few input and output files, the graph for the entire program is quite small and simple, and of little use. At the other extreme, the graphs for individual statements without composition can be constructed. The aggregate of those graphs is large, comparable in size to the program text, and also of little use. The utility of these data dependency graphs derives from the construction by composition of graphs for program units that are of interest to the programmer, software engineer, or other user.

A typical unit of interest is the procedure and, thus, we now compare the size of data dependency graphs for procedures against the size of the uncomposed component graphs. A procedure with few parameters and few references to global variables, but with many local variables, will have a data dependency graph that is much smaller than the aggregate of the graphs for its component statements. In contrast, consider a less probable procedure with a single local variable that depends on all of its in parameters and on which all of its out parameters depend. The dependency graph for such a procedure will be larger than the aggregate of the graphs for its component statements if there are at least two in parameters, at least two out parameters, and a total of five or more parameters.

As an example of what typically happens in practice, we considered five Ada programs extracted from a communications network experiment at the University of California, Santa Barbara. Each of these programs is composed of several thousand Ada statements, and all of them make extensive use of tasking, exception handling, and other Ada language constructs. Examination of the programs reveals that the programmers made extensive use of the Ada package facility for implementing abstract data types; indeed, about 75% of the code can be regarded as the definition of abstract data types. In these programs, the abstract data types are quite simple and their definitions are shallow, seldom more than two levels deep. In larger programs, the abstract data types might be more complex and might comprise a smaller proportion of the program.

The abstract data types are typically declared as record types, and the functions and procedures are quite simple, consisting of five to ten statements on average. The procedures seldom declare many local variables, although use is often made of variables global to the procedure but local to the package. The data dependency graphs for these procedures often show a reduction in size from the aggregate of the graphs for individual statements, because a record variable is represented as a single node in the graph and, thus, successive manipulations of different fields of the record are subsumed into a single data dependency.

The objective of abstract data types is to hide the details of the representation of the data, and their use in these programs is quite successful; the major units of the programs are much shorter and clearer than they would have been without the use of abstract data types. It is equally important to achieve a similar clarification in the data dependency graphs if they are to be useful. Here the composition rules for data dependency graphs are quite effective. The data dependency graphs for statements in the major program units, with the composition rules combining together the hidden dependencies within the abstract data types, are at an appropriate level of abstraction.

Other Ada language constructs are also used quite extensively in these programs. Most rendezvous are of a very simple structure with an exact match between a single call statement and a single accept statement, although a few accept statements are called from several parts of the program. The graph construction involving rendezvous is thus relatively simple, but the graphs themselves involve several tasks and are quite complex. It is clear from the graphs that the various tasks in these programs are highly interdependent. Exception handlers in these programs are also quite simple, perhaps closer to premature exits than to handlers. They add relatively little to the complexity of the graphs, but are useful in that they provide an explicit representation of the variables that may have been modified prior to an exception being raised.

In summary, the data dependency graphs constructed by our method clearly depend on the application, the programming style, and the program units under consideration. Because of subsumption due to repeatedly referenced variables, composition generally reduces the size of the dependency graphs from that of the aggregate of the component graphs for the individual program statements. Our limited experience shows that these data dependency graphs are substantially more tractable and more useful for program development and program validation than are conventional data dependence graphs. It also indicates that, to make extensive use of these dependency graphs in a program development environment, mechanical support is desirable.

V. CONCLUSION

We have presented a novel compositional method of constructing data dependency graphs based on composition rules. These rules match other composition-based program development techniques, and enable data dependency graphs for complex programs to be constructed from the simpler graphs for the units of which they are composed. The graphs constructed by this method are useful in a program development environment for analyzing data dependencies and tracking information flow within a program. These dependency graphs are generally quite compact with relatively few nodes and arcs and, thus, are less costly to store and analyze, which can be a significant advantage, particularly for nontrivial Ada programs.

REFERENCES

[1] F. E. Allen and J. Cocke, "A program data flow analysis procedure," *Commun. ACM*, vol. 19, no. 3, pp. 137–147, Mar. 1976.
[2] M. Burke and R. Cytron, "Interprocedural dependence analysis and parallelization," *ACM SIGPLAN Notices (Proc. SIGPLAN 86 Symp. Compiler Construction)*, vol. 21, no. 7, pp. 162–175, July 1986.
[3] D. E. Denning and P. J. Denning, "Certification of programs for secure information flow," *Commun. ACM*, vol. 20, no. 7, pp. 504–513, July 1977.
[4] R. Farrow, K. Kennedy, and L. Zucconi, "Graph grammars and global program data flow analysis," in *Proc. 17th IEEE Symp. Foundations of Computer Science*, Oct. 1976, pp. 42–56.
[5] J. Ferrante, K. Ottenstein, and J. D. Warren, "The program dependence graph and its use in optimization," *ACM Trans. Program. Lang. Syst.*, vol. 9, no. 3, pp. 319–349, Aug. 1987.
[6] L. D. Fosdick and L. J. Osterweil, "Data flow analysis in software reliability," *Comput. Surveys*, vol. 8, no. 3, pp. 305–330, Sept. 1976.
[7] S. Horwitz, J. Prins, and T. Reps, "On the adequacy of program dependence graphs for representing programs," in *Conf. Rec. Fifteenth Annu. ACM Symp. Principles of Programming Languages*, ACM, New York, Jan. 1988.
[8] S. Horowitz, J. Prins, and T. Reps, "Integrating non-interfering versions of programs," in *Conf. Rec. Fifteenth Annu. ACM Symp. Principles of Programming Languages*, ACM, New York, Jan. 1988, pp. 133–145.
[9] A. K. Jones and R. J. Lipton, "The enforcement of security policies for computation," *Oper. Syst. Rev. Proc. Fifth Symp. Operating System Principles*, vol. 9, no. 5, pp. 197–206, Nov. 1975.
[10] G. A. Kildall, "A unified approach to global program optimization," in *Conf. Rec. First ACM Symp. Principles of Programming Languages*, ACM, New York, Oct. 1973, pp. 194–206.
[11] D. J. Kuck, *The Structure of Computers and Computations*. New York: Wiley, 1978.
[12] D. J. Kuck, R. H. Kuhn, D. A. Padua, B. Leasure, and M. Wolfe, "Dependence graphs and compiler optimization," in *Conf. Rec. Eighth ACM Symp. Principles of Programming Languages*, ACM, New York, Jan. 1981, pp. 207–218.
[13] L. E. Moser, "Composition rules for data dependency graphs," Dep. Comput. Sci., Univ. California, Santa Barbara, Tech. Rep. TRCS87-17, Oct. 1987.
[14] E. W. Myers, "A precise inter-procedural data flow algorithm," in *Conf. Record Eighth Annu. ACM Symp. Programming Languages*, ACM, New York, Jan. 1981, pp. 219–230.
[15] K. J. Ottenstein and L. M. Ottenstein, "The program dependence

182

graph in a software development environment," *ACM SIGPLAN Notices*, vol. 19, no. 5, pp. 177–184, May 1984.

[16] D. A. Padua and M. J. Wolfe, "Advanced compiler optimizations for supercomputers," *Commun. ACM*, vol. 29, no. 12, pp. 1184–1201, Dec. 1986.

[17] J. H. Reif and H. R. Lewis, "Symbolic evaluation and the global value graph," in *Conf. Rec. Fourth ACM Annu. Symp. Principles of Programming Languages*, ACM, New York, Jan. 1977, pp. 104–118.

[18] B. K. Rosen, "High-level data flow analysis," *Commun. ACM*, vol. 20, no. 10, pp. 712–724, Oct. 1977.

[19] B. G. Ryder and M. C. Pauli, "Incremental data-flow analysis," *ACM Trans. Program. Lang. Syst.*, vol. 10, no. 1, pp. 1–50, Jan. 1988.

Data Flow Analysis and its Application to Software Maintenance

James Keables, Katherine Roberson, Anneliese von Mayrhauser

Illinois Institute of Technology, Department of Computer Science

Abstract

Data flow analysis has long been a useful aid in analyzing programs under development. It may be even more useful during maintenance. Most realistic maintenance situations require understanding the impact of introducing data flow anomalies and the errors associated with them increase during maintenance. At the same time, it is undesirable to re-analyze an entire product which consist of thousands of lines of code. This paper presents algorithms that limit the scope of recalculation of data flow information for representative program changes. A prototype data flow analysis program has been developed for a subset of the ADA™ language. an example, analyzed by the prototype shows its possible use by program maintenance personnel.

I. Introduction

Data flow analysis has great potential for software maintenance. Its benefits are:

1) help in understanding software. This is one of the most crucial aspects of software maintenance. Most errors introduced during maintenance stem from lack of understanding of the software. Therefore, the impact of changes cannot be assessed correctly. Data flow analysis sheds light on usage of data and variables throughout the code, helps to assess the impact of changes to data and variables and thus contributes to better understanding of the code.

2) identification of possible problems. As changes are made in the code, the possibility of introducing anomalies increases (dead code, unused variables, unintentional modification of variables, improper or missing initialization of variables.) Data flow analysis is able to pinpoint many such problems.

3) guidance in regression testing. By knowing the effects of changes on data flow, it becomes possible to focus regression testing on those parts of the system that have been identified through data flow analysis.

These potential benefits can only be realized if there are efficient algorithms that do not require re-analyzing the code in its entirety. Section III presents algorithms that limit the scope of such recalculation as changes are made in the code. Examples illustrate the use of partial data flow analysis to bring data flow information up to date. Section IV identifies some common problems facing software maintenance personnel and shows how data flow analysis can be used to provide information leading to the solution of these problems. Section V describes a collection of maintenance tool prototypes for the analysis of Ada programs. This tool kit combines data flow analysis with test path generation and program text perusal/editing tools. Section VI describes limitations and further work that is underway to extend the scope of analysis.

II. Data Flow Analysis
A. Terms and Notation

Data flow analysis is based on a control flow graph. It is common for this graph, G, a connected, directed graph with a single entry node, n_0. G contains a set of

184

nodes, $N = \{ n_0 , n_1 , \ldots , n_m \}$, which represent sequences of program instructions and a set, E, of ordered pairs indicating the edges (i.e., the flow of control) between nodes in G.

A path is a sequence of nodes $(n_1 , \ldots , n_k)$ where for each n_i and n_{i+1}, (n_i , n_{i+1}) is in E. With this notion of a path, the predecessors, Pred(n), of a given node are defined as those nodes for which there is a path to the given node. The successors of n, Succ(n), are similarly defined. The immediate predecessors of a node n_i, denoted P(n_i), are all nodes, n_j, such that (n_j , n_i) is in E. The immediate successors of a node n_i, S(n_i), are similarly defined.

A path is said to be definition-clear (or simply clear) with respect to a given variable if the path contains no assignment to that variable. A variable is live at a given point in a program if there is a clear path from that point to a use of the variable in question. There are many uses of live variable analysis in optimizing compilers, among them redundant subexpression elimination. Applications of live variable analysis to software maintenance include identifying possible program errors, as we shall see in a later section.

A definition of a program variable is any expression that modifies the variable. A definition made at node n_i is said to reach node n_j if n_j is a successor of node n_i and there is at least one clear path (one which does not contain a node that redefines the given variable) from n_i to n_j. [1] The identification of reaching definitions has clear application for software maintenance personnel as we shall see in Section IV.

B. Global Data Flow Analysis

Global data flow is concerned with the calculation and propagation of data flow information throughout a computer program. Much of the research that has been done in this area involves defining intervals as subgraphs of the control flow graph that describes a computer program. By combining intervals (and the information pertaining to each interval), a series of increasingly simpler flow graphs results in the collection of all of the data flow relations for the program being analyzed. This information is then propagated back to the initial intervals. [1]

As an alternative to the interval approach, data flow information may be collected by traversing the nodes in the control flow graph, propagating the data flow information as the nodes are visited. The procedure iterates until the data flow information identified with each node does not change. [3] It is this iterative procedure that is implemented in the software maintenance tool kit described in Section IV.

Before showing how the iterative data flow analysis algorithm is applied to an example program, the issue of subroutine calls in computer programs must be examined. Algorithms for collecting summary information for subroutine calls can be used to identify interprocedural data flow relationships. This allows subroutine calls to be treated a simple statements for the purpose of global data flow analysis. [5]

III. Algorithms for Analyzing Software Changes

In order to investigate the usefulness of data flow analysis for software maintenance personnel, we must consider how the data flow for a given program changes as the result of modifications of statements in the code (nodes in the flow graph.) In particular, we would like to identify the other nodes that will be affected by the change, limiting the scope of the recalculation of live variables and reaching definitions. In the algorithms that follow, we will consider the following changes to the data flow:

a) the deletion of a node from the control flow graph (a statement is deleted),

b) the insertion of a node into the control flow graph (a statement is added),

c) the modification of an existing node (a statement is modified.)

These three categories suffice to describe any change activity to the program represented by the control flow graph. When nodes are moved from one place in the control flow graph to another, the movement may be considered as a deletion followed by an insertion. The following paragraphs describe algorithms that may be used to identify the scope of a change to a node in the control flow graph with respect to live variables and reaching definitions. Then we shall see how these algorithms work together to drive the recalculation of data flow information following a program change corresponding to an arbitrary control flow graph node, n. We assume that at node n we can identify the following sets of variables:

nu (new uses) - set of variables, x, such that x is used at node n, and x is not live at the nodes in Pred(n).

nm (new mods) - set of variables, x, such that x is modified at node n.

du (deleted use) - set of variables, x, such that x is no longer used at node n and x is not live at the nodes in Succ(n).

dm (deleted modification) - set of variables, x, such that x is no longer modified at node n.

These sets are used in appropriate combinations for determining the scope of changes to live variables and reaching definitions.

A. Live Variables

Given that a change has been made to node n, we would like to identify other nodes in the flow graph where we need to recalculate live variables. In general, these are all predecessors between n and the next previous node containing uses or modifications of the variables whose use characteristics changed at node n.

Before presenting a general algorithm for identifying nodes where live variables must be recalculated, the following figures demonstrate some changes in live variables due to additions and deletions of variable uses and modifications.

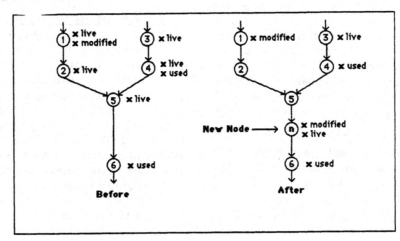

Figure 1(a) Effects of a new definition on live variables. The new definition of x at node n screens nodes 1, 2, 4, and 5 from "seeing" the use of x at node 6.

186

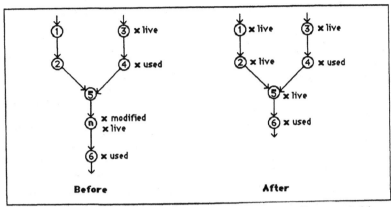

Figure 1(b) Effects of deleting a definition on live variables. The deleted definition of **x** at node **n** no longer screens nodes 1, 2, 4, and 5 from "seeing" the use of **x** at node 6.

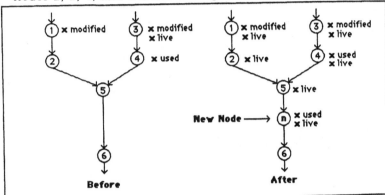

Figure 1(c) Effects of a new use on live variables. The new use of **x** at node **n** makes **x** live at nodes 1, 2, 4, and 5.

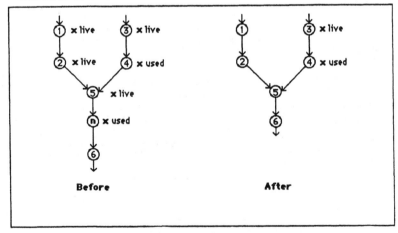

Figure 1(d) Effects of deleting a use on live variables. The deleted use of **x** at node **n** means **x** is no longer live at nodes 1, 2, 4, and 5.

In the algorithm that follows, LVout[n] denotes the set of variables which are live at node n. XUSE[n] and MOD[n] denote, respectively, the sets of variables that are used or modified at node n. In general, the change information for the modified node is passed up the flow graph until we have identified all nodes for which live variables must be recalculated.

Live variable scope algorithm:

```
LiveMod ( node, vars)
   /* node is the node where the */
   /* recalculation will begin vars is */
   /* the set of variables causing the */
   /* recalculation */
   recalc ← recalc + {node}
   LVout[node] ← ∅
   for each x ∈ vars
      if x ∈ XUSE[node] or x ∈ MOD[node]
         /* x cannot affect live */
         /* variables at any */
         /* predecessor of node */
         vars ← vars - {x}
   if vars = ∅
   then
      /* the effects of the changed */
      /* variables have been exhausted */
      return
   else
      /* pass information to each */
      /* predecessor */
      for each pnode in P(node) do
         LiveMod(pnode, vars)
end LiveMod
```

B. Reaching Definitions

Given that a change has been made to node n, we would like to identify other nodes in the flow graph where we need to recalculate reaching definitions. In general, these are the successor nodes between n and the next node containing a definition of the variables whose modification characteristics at n were changed. Before presenting an algorithm to identify the nodes where we need to recalculate the reaching definitions, the following figures demonstrate some of the changes in the reaching definitions due to additions or deletions of variable modifications (definitions):

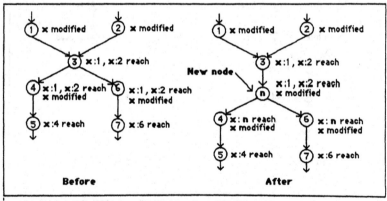

Figure 2(a) Effects of a new definition on reaching definitions. The new definition of **x** at node n blocks the definitions of **x** at nodes 1 and 2 from reaching nodes 4 and 6.

188

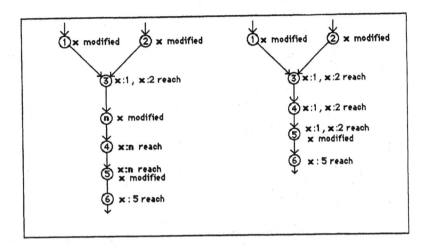

Figure 2(b) Effects of deleting a definition on reaching definitions. The deletion of node n allows the definitions of **x** at nodes 1 and to reach nodes 4 and 5.

In the following algorithm, REACH[*n*] denotes the set of variable definitions that reach *n* . In general, the change information for node *n* is passed down the tree until we have identified all of the nodes for which the reaching definitions must be recalculated.

Reaching definition scope algorithm:
ReachMod (node, vars)
   /* node is where the recalculation will
   /* begin vars is the set of variables */
   /* involved in the recalculation */
   /* recalc is the set of nodes for which*/
   /* reaching definitions will be */
   /* recalculated */
   recalc ← recalc + {node}
   REACH[node] ← ∅
   for each x ∈ vars
     if x ∈ MOD[node]
       vars ← vars - {x}

  if vars = ∅
  then
    /* effects of the variables in vars */
    /* have been exhausted */
    return
  else
    /* pass information to each */
    /* successor */
    for each snode in S(node) do
      ReachMod(snode, vars)
end ReachMod.

C. Insertion, Deletion, and Modification of Nodes

The following algorithms tie together those presented above defining the changes in the data flow following the modification, insertion, or deletion of a given control flow graph node. For the sake of completeness, an algorithm describing the change to the data flow following the movement of a node is included as well.

When the use/modification characteristics of one or more variables at a particular node changes:
   ChangeNode(n)
     recalc ← ∅
     lvars ← nu ∪ nm ∪ du ∪ dm
     LiveMod(n, lvars)
     recalculate live vars for nodes in recalc
     recalc ← ∅
     rvars ← nm ∪ dm
     ReachMod(n, rvars)
     recalculate reaching defs for nodes
          in recalc

When a node is inserted into the control flow graph:

```
InsertNode(n)
    insert node n into the flow graph
    recalc ← ∅
    lvars ← nu ∪ nm
    LiveMod( n, lvars )
    recalculate live vars for nodes in recalc
    recalc ← ∅
    rvars ← nm
    ReachMod( n, rvars )
    recalculate reaching definitions for
                nodes in recalc
```

When a node is deleted from the control flow graph:

```
DeleteNode(n)
    /* remember which nodes are */
    /* predecessors/successors */
    pn ← P(n)
    sn ← S(n)
    delete node n from the flow graph
    recalc ← ∅
    lvars ← du ∪ dm
    for each node in pn do
                LiveMod( n, lvars )
    recalculate live vars for nodes in recalc
    recalc ← ∅
    rvars ← dm
    for each node in sn do
                ReachMod( n, rvars )
    recalculate reaching definitions for
                nodes in recalc
```

Moving a node from one place to another can be treated as a deletion followed by an insertion:

```
MoveNode(n)
    DeleteNode(n)
    determine where the node is to be
                inserted
    InsertNode(n)
```

IV. Application to Software Maintenance

The remainder of this paper is concerned with the use of the information provided by data flow analysis in support of software maintenance personnel. The example program shown in Figure 3 will be used (the numbers in parentheses indicate nodes in the control flow graph that represent the given source statements):

Figure 3.

```
 1 (1)   procedure main is
 2
 3           mainvar1 , mainvar2 , mainvar3 :
                    INTEGER;
 4
 5 (2)       procedure init is
 6           begin   -- initialize global variables
 7 (3)          mainvar1 := const1;
 8 (4)          mainvar2 := const2;
 9           end init ;
10
11 (5)       procedure level1 (lev1prm :
                        in out INTEGER) is
12              l1var : INTEGER;
13
14 (6)          procedure level2(lev2prm :
                        in out INTEGER) is
15                 l2var : INTEGER;
16
17              begin -- level 2
18 (7)              case lev2prm is
19 (8-9)                when mainvar2 =>
                            mainvar2 := mainvar2 / 2;
20 (10-11)              when others =>
                            mainvar2 := mainvar2 * 2;
21                  end case ;
22
23 (12)             lev2prm := mainvar2 + 35 ;
24              end level2;
25
26          begin   -- level1
27
28 (13)         l1var := 3.14159 * lev1prm;
29 (14)         mainvar2 := 2 * l1var ;
30 (15)         level2(lev1prm);
31
32          end level1;
33
34      begin -- main
35
36 (16)     init ();        -- initialize global variables
37
38 (17)     while mainvar3 < mainvar2 loop
39
40 (18)         level1( mainvar1 );
41
42          end loop ;
43
44 (19)     if mainvar3 > mainvar2
45 (20)     then
46 (21)         mainvar3 := 100;
47 (22)         level2( mainvar1 );
48 (23)         mainvar3 := mainvar1;
49 (24)     else
50 (25)         level2( mainvar1 );
51          end if;
52
```

190

```
53 (26)        PUT(mainvar1);
54 (27)        PUT(mainvar2);
55 (28)        PUT(mainvar3);
56
57      end main ;
```

This program may be represented by the control flow graph shown in Figure 4:

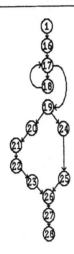

Figure 4. Control Flow Graph

The use of interprocedural data flow algorithms allows us to treat the subroutine calls at nodes 16, 18, 22, and 25 as simple statements with their respective modification and use characteristics. Thus, separate control flow representations for the subroutines themselves are not necessary. One drawback to this approach is that the algorithms specify what variables <u>might</u> be used or modified as the result of a call to a particular subroutine rather than identifying uses and modifications that <u>must</u> occur. Applying the above mentioned data flow analysis to the example program establishes the following data flow relationships. At each node, L indicates the live variables, M the variables which may be modified, U the variables that might be used, A the variables which are available (for which there is at least one reaching definition), and R the definitions that reach the given node:

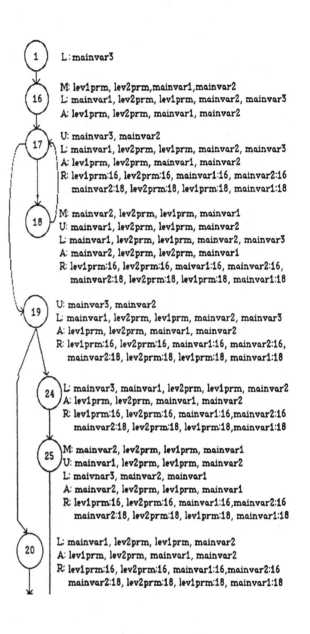

```
 ┌────┐   M: mainvar3
 │ 21 │   L: mainvar1, lev2prm, lev1prm, mainvar2
 └────┘   A: lev1prm, lev2prm, mainvar1, mainvar2, mainvar3
    │     R: lev1prm:16, lev2prm:16, mainvar1:16, mainvar2:16,
    │        mainvar2:18, lev2prm:18, lev1prm:18, mainvar1:18
    ▼
 ┌────┐   M: mainvar1, lev2prm, lev1prm, mainvar1
 │ 22 │   U: mainvar1, lev2prm, lev1prm, mainvar2
 └────┘   L: mainvar2, mainvar1
    │     A: mainvar3, mianvar2, lev2prm, lev1prm, mainvar1
    │     R: lev1prm:16, lar2prm:16, mainvar1:16, mainvar2:16,
    │        mainvar2:18, lev2prm:18, lev1prm:18, mainvar1:18
    ▼
 ┌────┐   M: mainvar3
 │ 23 │   U: mainvar1
 └────┘   L: mainvar3, mainvar2, mainvar1
    │     A: mainvar2, lev2prm, lev1prm, mainvar1, mainvar3
    │     R: mainvar3:21, mainvar2:22, lev2prm:22,
    │        lev1prm:22, mainvar1:22
    ▼
 ┌────┐   U: mainvar1
 │ 26 │   L: mainvar3, mainvar2
 └────┘   A: mainvar2, lev2prm, lev1prm, mainvar1, mainvar3
    │     R: mainvar2:25 lev2prm:25, lev1prm:25, mainvar1:25,
    │        mainvar2:22, lev2prm:22, lev1prm:22, mainvar1:22.
    │        mainvar3:22
    ▼
 ┌────┐   U: mainvar2
 │ 27 │   L: mainvar3
 └────┘   A: mainvar2, lev2prm, lev1prm, mainvar1, mainvar3
    │     R: mainvar2:25 lev2prm:25, lev1prm:25, mainvar1:25,
    │        mainvar2:22, lev2prm:22, lev1prm:22, mainvar1:22.
    │        mainvar3:22
    ▼
 ┌────┐   U: mainvar3
 │ 28 │   A: mainvar2, lev2prm, lev1prm, mainvar1, mainvar3
 └────┘   R: mainvar2:25 lev2prm:25, lev1prm:25, mainvar1:25,
          mainvar2:22, lev2prm:22, lev1prm:22, mainvar1:22,
          mainvar3:22
```

A. Detection of Data Flow Anomalies

Data flow analysis algorithms can be used to gather information concerning data flow anomalies which are symptomatic of programming errors. [4] For instance, if in examining the data flow of a program, it is detected that a variable may not have been assigned a value before it is used in a calculation, an _undefined reference_ exists. Another anomaly that may be identified using data flow analysis is the _useless_ _definition_. (If the value of a variable is not used between assignments, then the earlier assignment might just as well not have been made.)

Four categories of information provided by data flow analysis (Mods, Uses, Live, and Avail) help to identify these two data flow anomalies, should they exist in the program. First, consider the set of variables for which definitions are not available at a given node.

An attempt to use any such variable constitutes a reference to an undefined variable. In our example, the variable mainvar3 is used on line 38 (node 17) and on line 44 (node 19) before it is defined.

Second, if a variable is modified (defined) at a given node, but is not live on exit from that node, there must be another definition between the given node and the next use of that variable. Thus, this definition of the variable is useless. In our example program, the definition of variable mainvar3 at line 46 (node 21) is useless, since mainvar3 is defined again at line 48 and the call to level2() does not involve any use of mainvar3. We note that we could not have made this determination without the summary data flow information concerning the call to level2().

The following table summarizes the data flow characteristics that point to data flow anomalies:

mod	use	live	avail	anomaly
-	T	-	F	undefined reference
T	-	F	-	useless definition

As we shall see in the next section, pointing out data flow anomalies can play a significant role in support of program maintenance. Here is the output of the data flow analysis program pointing out these two anomalies:

Data Flow Anomalies:

The possible use of variable [MAINVAR3] at line [38] may constitute an undefined reference.

The possible use of variable [MAINVAR3] at line [44] may constitute an undefined reference.

The possible definition of variable [LEV2PRM] at line [50] may constitute an unnecessary definition.

The possible definition of variable [LEV1PRM] at line [50] may constitute an unnecessary definition.

The possible definition of variable [MAINVAR3] at line [46] may constitute an unnecessary definition.

The possible definition of variable [LEV2PRM] at line [47] may constitute an unnecessary definition.

The possible definition of variable [LEV1PRM] at line [47] may constitute an unnecessary definition.

There are several aspects of software maintenance that can benefit from the information that data flow analysis provides: understanding the program that must be maintained, identifying existing program errors, and (most importantly) making program modifications and testing them.

B. Understanding Programs

A primary activity in software maintenance involves evolving the existing software system to satisfy the changing needs of users. In other words, the software maintainer must find out where the desired system differs from the actual system. This requires an understanding of the actual system on the part of the software maintainer. This understanding is not something that should be taken for granted, since it is not at all uncommon for the maintenance personnel to be different from the people who originally developed the system. In fact, one survey of software maintenance personnel [9] indicates that between 18 and 25 percent of the time involved in the software change process goes into defining and understanding a given change. An additional 23 to 33 percent is taken up tracing through the logic of the existing system. In this area of the software change process, data flow analysis can be used to provide the software maintainer with information about the existing (and possibly unfamiliar) program text.

In our example program, if the software maintainer needs to know which variables may be used or modified by a given subroutine, say level1(), it is not necessary to trace through the text of the subroutine to find out. The summary relations calculated using Barth's algorithms contain this information. In the case of level1(), mainvar1, mainvar2, lev1prm, and lev2prm are identified as variables that may be used and modified.

C. Identifying Existing Program Errors

We have already described how data flow analysis can point out data flow anomalies in a program. Since data flow anomalies tend to point out possible programming errors, their identification provides support to software maintenance personnel as they seek to find existing program errors. In our example program, a data flow anomaly alerts the software maintainer that the variable mainvar3 is used before it is defined.

Another important piece of information available from data flow analysis is the set of definitions that reach a particular node. This information is of interest to the software maintainer who can identify the source line where a certain variable has an unexpected (and possibly erroneous) value. The knowledge of where that value may have come from (i.e., the definitions that reach the given node) gives the software maintainer important clues in identifying cause of the program error. In our example program, the software maintainer considering the subroutine call at node 22 may find it important to know that the definitions of mainvar1 from both node 16 and node 18 reach node 22. That is, the value of mainvar1 as it is passed to level2() may come from either the call to init() or from the call to level1().

D. Modifications to Programs

Software maintenance activity involves modification software. Data flow analysis provides important information in the support of this activity as well. Before the change is made, data flow information may be used as input to decisions concerning what should be changed. After the fact, data flow information can be used to verify that data flow anomalies (and the programming errors that they identify) have been removed by the software modification. In addition, data flow analysis provides a way to indicate when a maintenance activity has introduced new data flow anomalies into the code. Let's consider these three cases individually.

1) Before a proposed change is made, the software maintainer needs to know what impact that change will have on the rest of the program. The information concerning which variables get used at a given node and what definitions reach that node provide important information for conducting this impact analysis. Imagine that the person maintaining our example program is contemplating a change to the value that is assigned to mainvar2 in the subroutine init(). The data flow information provided indicates that nodes 17, 18, 19, 22, and 25 all have uses of mainvar2 and that the definition from node 16 (the call to init()) reaches each of those nodes. Thus, the software maintainer must determine whether or not the new value assigned to mainvar2 is compatible with each of those uses. Thus, the summary information provided by the interprocedural data flow algorithms and the calculation of reaching definitions aid the software maintainer in assessing the impact of a change before is made.

2) After a modification to a program has been made, data flow analysis can be used to help verify that the change had the desired result. In our example program, the software maintainer may add an initialization to mainvar3 in the init() routine. If the data flow of the program is analyzed after such a change, it can be verified that the "undefined reference"

anomalies have been removed. Here is a condensation of the output from the data flow analysis program verifying the change that was made (since a line of program text has been added, the node numbers have changed slightly):

Node: 17 (represents the call to init())
Mods: LEV1PRM LEV2PRM MAINVAR1
    MAINVAR2 MAINVAR3
Live: MAINVAR1 LEV2PRM LEV1PRM
    MAINVAR2 MAINVAR3
Avail: LEV1PRM LEV2PRM MAINVAR1
    MAINVAR2 MAINVAR3

Node: 18 (represents the condition for the while loop)
Successors: 20 19
Mods:
Uses: MAINVAR3 MAINVAR2
Avail:LEV1PRM LEV2PRM MAINVAR1
    MAINVAR2 MAINVAR3
Reaching Defs: LEV1PRM:17 LEV2PRM:17
    MAINVAR1:17 MAINVAR2:17
    MAINVAR3:17 MAINVAR2:19
    LEV2PRM:19 LEV1PRM:19 MAINVAR1:19

Node: 20 (represents the condition for the if statement)
Uses: MAINVAR3 MAINVAR2
Avail: LEV1PRM LEV2PRM MAINVAR1
    MAINVAR2 MAINVAR3
Reaching Defs: LEV1PRM:17 LEV2PRM:17
    MAINVAR1:17 MAINVAR2:17
    MAINVAR3:17 MAINVAR2:19
    LEV2PRM:19 LEV1PRM:19 MAINVAR1:19

Data Flow Anomalies:
  The possible definition of variable [LEV2PRM] at line [51] may constitute an unnecessary definition.
  The possible definition of variable [LEV1PRM] at line [51] may constitute an unnecessary definition.
  The possible definition of variable [MAINVAR3] at line [47] may constitute an unnecessary definition.

The possible definition of variable [LEV2PRM] at line [48] may constitute an unnecessary definition.

The possible definition of variable [LEV1PRM] at line [48] may constitute an unnecessary definition.

The fact that the data flow anomalies no longer list the undefined reference to mainvar3 indicates that the program modification has removed the data flow anomaly. Furthermore, the information collected about nodes 18 and 20 indicate that mainvar3 is used at each of those nodes and that the definition of mainvar3 at node 17 reaches nodes 18 and 20. So data flow information can be used to indicate the disappearance of data flow anomalies.

3) It is possible that, in making a change to a program, the software maintainer will introduce new data flow anomalies. This is where the data flow analysis program assumes the role as the "powerful, thorough, and tireless critic" [4], pointing out new data flow anomalies. Suppose, for example that our example program must be modified to output the value of mainvar1 before and after all processing. If the software maintainer mistakenly adds the PUT(mainvar1) statement before the call to init() rather than after, she or he will have introduced an undefined reference, as is shown by the following messages:

Data Flow Anomalies:

The possible use of variable [MAINVAR1] at line [37] may constitute an undefined reference.

The possible definition of variable [MAINVAR3] at line [48] may constitute an unnecessary definition.

E. Testing Software Modifications

The last section showed how information pertaining to variable use and definition reaches can be used before a software modification is made to gauge the impact of the modification. The same information can also be used to identify existing regression test cases that should be run to exercise the code that was affected by the modification. For instance, the software maintainer making the change in the definition of

mainvar2 described above can use the data flow information provided to determine that test cases in the regression tests for the modification should exercise both branches of the if statement. The modified definition reaches both branches and both branches call level2(), which has been determined through the summary data flow information to contain possible uses of mainvar2.

V. Data Flow Analysis of Ada Programs

A toolkit to aid in the maintenance of Ada applications has been proposed [6]. A prototype of the toolkit has been implemented using the Icon programming language [10]. The data flow analysis algorithms described above are included in the toolkit. As was mentioned earlier, an iterative approach to global data flow analysis was taken, using the algorithms described in [3]. Interprocedural data flow information was gathered according to the algorithms provided in [5]. This summary information allows subroutine calls to be treated as simple program statements for the purpose of global data flow analysis. Work is underway to extend the scope of partial data flow analysis to include concurrency, access types, and a more detailed treatment of complex data types. The algorithms will be further developments of [11, 13] and use a heuristic knowledge base to overcome limitations of static analysis.

Besides data flow analysis, the toolkit provides facilities to display program text in its various representations, including the ability to view the program at varying levels of detail. Displaying the program as a tree allows the user to view the program at a high-level and then "zoom in" on sections of the code that are of particular interest. This capability is particularly useful to software maintenance personnel. By allowing the maintainer to begin with a less detailed view of the program, it provides support for the activity of understanding the code that must be maintained. And when the software maintainer is making an actual modification to the program, the display program, working hand in hand with the data flow information described previously, allows the maintainer to "step back a bit" in the code and examine some of the effects of the given change.

A third important area of the toolkit generates test paths through the program text. This capability is of great importance to the software maintainer who would like to know how to test code modifications. Coupled with the display program and the data flow analysis, the test path generator allows the maintainer to "see" which paths must be covered for regression testing.

VI. Conclusions

This paper presented algorithms that provide efficient, partial re-analysis of data flow in programs as they are modified during maintenance. These algorithms can contribute significantly to program maintenance as they facilitate understanding of the code and of proposed changes, help to perform a formal impact analysis and drive the selection of test cases for regression testing.

To demonstrate the usefulness of the algorithms, they were implemented as part of a prototype toolkit for maintaining ADA™ programs. Extensions to current limitations are underway.

References:

1. Kennedy, K., A Survey of Data Flow Analysis Techniques, *Program Flow Analysis: Theory and Applications*. (Edited by Muchnick, S., and Jones, N.) Prentice-Hall, Englewood Cliffs, N.J., 1980.

2. Allen, F.E., and Cocke, J. A Program Data Flow Analysis Procedure. *Communications of the ACM*, Vol. 19, No. 3 (March 1976), 137-147.

3. Hecht, M.S., and Ullman, J.D., A Simple Algorithm for Global Data Flow Analysis Problems, *SIAM Journal of Computing*, Vol. 4, No. 4, (December 1975), 519-532.

4. Fosdick, L.D., and Osterweil, L.J., Data Flow Analysis in Software Reliability, *Computing Surveys*, Vol. 8, No. 3, (September 1976), 305-330.

5. Barth, J.M., A Practical Interprocedural Data Flow Analysis Algorithm, *Communications of the ACM*, Vol. 21, No. 9, (September 1978), 724-736.

6. Roberson, K. A., "A Toolkit for Analyzing and Maintaining ADA™ Programs," M. S. Thesis, Illinois Institute of Technology, Dec. 1987.

7. Zvegintzov, N., "What life? What Cycle?", *AFIPS Conference Proceedings*, 51, 1982.

8. Fjelstad, R. K., Hamlen, W. T., "Application Program Maintenance Study: Response to Our Respondents", *Proceedings GUIDE* 48, Philadelphia, PA, 1979.

9. Brooks, R., "Using an Behavioral Theory of Program Comprehension in Software Engineering", *Third International Conference on Software Engineering Proceedings,* 1978, pp. 196-201.

10. Griswold, R. E., Griswold, M. T., *The Icon Programming Language,* Prentice-Hall, Englewood Cliffs, New Jersey, 1983.

11. Wilson, C., Osterweil, L. J., "Omega - A Data Flow Analysis Tool for the C Programming Language", *IEEE Transactions on Software Engineering,* Vol. SE-11, No. 9, September 1985.

12. Taylor, R. N., and Osterweil, L. J., "Anomaly Detection of Concurrent Software by Static Data Flow Analysis", *IEEE Transactions on Software Engineering,* Vol. SE-6, No. 3 (May 1980), pp. 265-278.

13. Taylor, R. N., "A General-Purpose Algorithm for Analyzing Concurrent Programs," *Communications of the ACM*, Vol. 26, No. 5 (May 1983), pp. 362-376.

Change Impact Identification in Object Oriented Software Maintenance

D. Kung, J. Gao, P. Hsia, F. Wen

The Univ. of Texas at Arlington
P. O. Box 19015
Arlington, TX 76019-0015

Y. Toyoshima, and C. Chen

Fujitsu Network Transmission Systems, Inc.
3099 North First Street
San Jose, CA 95134-2022

Abstract

In the object-oriented (OO) paradigm, new features (such as encapsulation, aggregation, inheritance, polymorphism and dynamic binding) introduce new problems in software testing and maintenance. One of them is the difficulty of identifying the affected components (such as classes) when changes are made in object-oriented class libraries or programs. This paper discusses the types of code changes in an object-oriented class library, and provides an automated solution to identify different kinds of code changes and their impact. In addition, an OO software maintenance environment that implements the research result is described. Our experience with the environment prototype shows promising results.
Key words and phrases: software maintenance, object oriented programming, change analysis, impact identication, regression testing, environment, tool

1 Introduction

One important activity of software maintenance is regression testing, which ensures that the modified software still satisfies its intended requirements. To save effort, regression testing should retest only those parts that are affected by the modifications. In traditional function-oriented programming, only control dependencies exist between the modules; hence, it is relatively easy to identify the affected modules. In the object-oriented (OO) paradigm, a number of new features is supported, such as encapsulation, information hiding, inheritance, aggregation, polymorphism, and dynamic binding. These new features introduce new problems in the maintenance phase, including difficulty of identifying the affected components when changes are made.

Encapsulation and information hiding imply the so-called "delocalized plan" [19], in which several member functions from possibly several object classes are invoked to achieve an intended functionality. This phenomenon means that changes to a member function of a class may affect many classes. Inheritance and aggregation imply structure and state dependent behavior reuse, i.e., the data members, function members, and state dependent behavior of a class are re-used

by another class. Thus, there are data dependencies, control dependencies, and state behavior dependencies between the two classes. Moreover, since the inheritance and aggregation relations are transitive relations, the above dependencies also are transitive dependencies. Polymorphism and dynamic binding imply that objects may take more than one form, and the form which an object assumes is unknown until run time. This makes the identification of the affected components much more difficult.

The maintenance complications introduced by the OO features can be summarized as follows: 1) although it is relatively easy to understand most of the data structures and member functions of the object classes, understanding of the combined effect or combined functionality of the member functions is extremely difficult; 2) the complex relationships between the object classes make it difficult to anticipate and identify the ripple effect[1] [6] of changes; 3) the data dependencies, control dependencies, and state behavior dependencies make it difficult to prepare test cases and generate test data to "adequately" retest[2] the affected components; 4) the complex relations also make it difficult to define a cost-effective test strategy to retest the affected components.

This paper discusses types of changes that can be made to an OO library. It also describes a method for identifying the affected classes due to structure changes to an object class library. The method is based on a reverse engineering approach designed to extract the classes and their interrelationships. This information is represented in a multigraph, which is used to automatically identify the changes and the effects of those changes. The method has been implemented in the integrated testing and maintenance environment. The architecture and functionality of the relevant part will be presented.

---

[1]The ripple effect refers to the phenomenon that changes made to one part of a software system ripple throughout the system.

[2]We use this term loosely to mean retesting the software with a certain degree of confidence. We choose not to give a formal definition of adequacy in this paper.

The organization of this paper is as follows: In section 2, a brief review of related work on maintenance of conventional software as well as OO software is given. In section 3, we discuss types of changes and change identification. A formal model is presented to facilitate change identification and impact identification, which is described in section 4. In section 5, we describe a support system for OO testing and maintenance. In section 6, we report our experience on OO software maintenance and in section 7, we present the conclusions and future work.

2 Related Work

Hartmann and Robson examined several regression testing strategies, including methods for capturing the program portion which may be affected by maintenance modifications to a conventional program [8]. A similar study was conducted by Leung and White [14] using a formally defined cost model. Laski and Szermer described an algorithm for identifying the affected parts in conventional program maintenance [11]. The algorithm is based on differentials between the control flow graphs for the original program and the modified program. In [13], impact of data and function changes is addressed using a dynamic approach.

Some conventional program maintenance systems have been reported in the literature. The VIFOR (Visual Interactive FORtran) [17] were developed for FORTRAN programs, the MasterScope [20] for Interlisp, and the CIA (C Information Abstractors) [3] for C. These systems provide editing, browsing, and database supports to a maintainer. In particular, the VIFOR system also provides graphical display and transformations between the textual representation and the graphical representation.

Wilde and Huitt [23] analyzed problems of dynamic binding, object dependencies, dispersed program structure, control of polymorphism, high level understanding and detailed code understanding. The authors then provided a general list of recommendations, including the use of dependency analysis [22] and clustering methods [4] [15], for possible tool support.

Crocker and Mayrhauser addressed problems relating to class hierarchy changes, class signature changes, and polymorphism [5]. The authors then proposed a list of tools to help solve some of the problems. The tools provide information collection, storage, analysis, inference, and display capabilities.

An early system for maintaining C++ programs was reported by Samethinger in [18]. The system utilized the inheritance relation and containment relations (e.g., a class is contained in a file, or a method belongs to a class, etc.) to provide text-based browsing facilities to an OO software maintainer.

The C++ Information Abstractors [7] used program analyzers to extract cross-reference information

Components		Changes
data changes	1	change data definition/declaration
	2	change data access scope/mode/uses
	3	add/delete data
method interface changes	4	add/delete external data usage
	5	add/delete external data updates
	6	add/delete/change a method call
	7	change its signature or messages
method structure changes	8	add/delete a sequential segment
	9	add/delete/change a branch/loop
method component changes	10	change a control sequence
	11	add/delete/change local data
	12	change a sequential segment
class component changes	13	change a defined/redefined method
	14	add/delete a defined/redefined method
	15	add/delete/change a defined datum
	16	add/delete a virtual abstract method
	17	change an attribute access mode/scope
class relationship changes	18	add/delete a superclass
	19	add/delete a subclass
	20	add/delete an object pointer
	21	add/delete an aggregated object
	22	add/delete an object message
class library changes	23	change a class (defined attributes)
	24	add/delete a relation between classes
	25	adde/delete a class and its relations
	26	add/delete an independent class

Figure 1: Different Types Of Code Changes

and stored the information in a database. A maintainer could query the data base to obtain the desired knowledge to maintain a C++ program.

Lejter, Meyers, and Reiss discussed the difficulty of maintaining an OO software system due to the presence of inheritance and dynamic binding [12]. The authors then described the XREF/XREFDB prototype system that provided text editing and relational data base querying support to facilitate OO software maintenance. A similar system was described in [16].

Our system is similar in many aspects to the above systems. It uses program analyzers to collect information and stores the information in a data base. It provides both graphical and textual display and browsing, whereas most of the existing systems provide only textual display and browsing (with VIFOR as an exception). It is capable of automatically identifying the changes to an OO program and deriving the affected parts from the changes. Another difference is that our system is integrated with testing capabilities to facilitate regression test case and test data reuse and generation, result analysis, and report generation.

3 Change Identification

One of the major difficulties in software maintenance is to identify changes and their impact automatically since it is very difficult to keep track of the changes when a software system is modified extensively by several persons. This capability becomes even more crucial when the modifications are performed by one group of persons and regression testing is performed by another group of persons. In this section, we first discuss the different types of code changes. We then describe how to identify the various types of code changes.

3.1 Types Of Code Changes

Figure 1 provides a classification of code changes in an OO class library. These change types are explained as follows:

Data change: Any datum (i.e., a global variable, a local variable, or a class data member) can be changed by updating its definition, declaration, access scope, access mode and initialization. In addition, adding new data and/or deleting existing data are also considered as data changes.

Method change: A member function can be changed in various ways. Here we classify them into three types: *component changes, interface changes,* and *control structure changes.* Component changes include: 1) adding, deleting, or changing a predicate, 2) adding, deleting a local data variable, and 3) changing a sequential segment. Structure changes include: 1) adding, deleting, or modifying a branch or a loop structure, and 2) adding, or deleting a sequential segment. The interface of a member function consists of its signature, access scope and mode, its interactions with other member functions (for example, a function call). Any change on the interface is called an interface change of a member function.

Class change: Direct modifications of a class can be classified into three types: *component changes, interface changes* and *relation changes.* Any change on a defined/redefined member function or a defined data attribute is known as a component change. A change is said to be an interface change if it adds, or deletes a defined/redefined attribute, or changes its access mode or scope. A change is said to be a relation change if it adds, or deletes an inheritance, aggregation or association relationship between the class and another class.

Class library change: These include: 1) changing the defined members of a class, 2) adding, or deleting a class and its relationships with other classes. 3) adding, or deleting a relationship between two existing classes[3], 4) adding, or deleting an independent class.

---

[3]Changing a relationship R1 (between two classes) into a relationship R2 is considered as deleting R1 and adding R2.

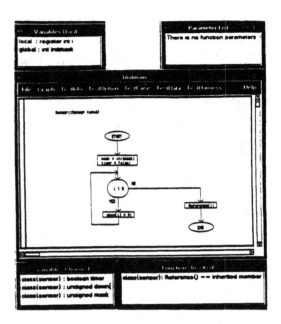

Figure 2: A BBD for a member function in the Inter-Views Library

3.2 Method Change Identification

A directed diagram, called block-branch diagram (BBD) is used to facilitates the understanding of the member functions and their interfaces and relationships to the global data, class data, and other member functions. Figure 2 shows a BBD for a member function of the InterViews library. The various components of a BBD is explained as follows:

- The large window displays the BBD body, denoted B; it encapsulates the program graph for the member function[4].

- The upper left window displays the global and class data that are used by the member function; this is denoted by Du;

- The upper right window displays the input/output parameters, denoted P, of the member function;

- The bottom left window displays the global and class data that are defined (i.e., updated) by this member function; this is denoted by Dd;

- The bottom right window displays functions that are called by this member function; this is denoted by Fe;

Formally, the block branch diagram for a member function f is a quintuple

$$BBD_f = (D_u, D_d, P, F_e, B)$$

where the components are as defined above. When no confusion can arise, we will omit the subscript f

---

[4]The program graph can be used, among others, to generate basis path test cases and test data [2]. However, it is beyond the scope of this paper to explore this issue.

from BBD_f. A BBD body is formally defined by a directed graph $B = (V, E)$, where V denotes the set of program graph vertices and $E \subset V \times V$ the directed edges representing the control flows. For more details the reader is referred to [kung93b].

Let $BBD = (D_u, D_d, P, F_s, B)$, and $BBD' = (D'_u, D'_d, P', F'_s, B')$ be the BBDs for a member function C::f(...) and its modified version C::f'(...) respectively. Recall that $B = (V, E)$ (or $B' = (V', E')$) is a directed graph which represents the control structure of C::f(...)(or C::f'(...)). Method structure and/or component changes are identified as follows:

- if $V - V' \neq \emptyset$ then any $v \in (V - V')$ is a deleted block node.

- if $V' - V \neq \emptyset$ then any $v \in (V' - V)$ is an added block node.

- if $E - E' \neq \emptyset$ then any $e \in (E - E')$ is a deleted control edge.

- if $E' - E \neq \emptyset$ then any $e \in (E' - E)$ is an added control edge.

A member function interface change is identified as follows:

- if $D_u - D'_u \neq \emptyset$, then some data uses are removed.

- if $D'_u - D_u \neq \emptyset$, then some data uses are added.

- if $D_d - D'_d \neq \emptyset$, then some data definitions are removed.

- if $D'_d - D_d \neq \emptyset$, then some data definitions are added.

- if $F_s - F'_s \neq \emptyset$, then some function calls are removed[5].

- if $F_s - F'_s \neq \emptyset$, then some function calls are added.

3.3 Data Change Identification

Data change identification is easy since the needed information is captured by the BBD's (and the internal representation) for the member functions[6]. In particular, information about each data item's access scope, type, access mode, update set (i.e., functions that define the data item), and use set (i.e., functions that use the data item). To identify data change, this information is compared with the information for the original software. If any of the above information is different, the corresponding type of change is identified.

---

[5]Signature change is treated as deleting and then adding a function.

[6]Functions not belong to any class are treated as member functions of a dummy system class in our approach.

3.4 Class Change Identification

A class is a pair $C = (D_{def}, F_{def})$, where D_{def} is a set of defined/redefined data attributes, F_{def} is a set of defined/redefined member functions. Let $C' = (D'_{def}, F'_{def})$ be a modified version of a class C. Then class code change is identified as follows:

- if $D_{def} - D'_{def} \neq \emptyset$, then any $d \in (D_{def} - D'_{def})$ is a deleted data attribute.

- if $D'_{def} - D_{def} \neq \emptyset$, then any $d \in (D'_{def} - D_{def})$ is an added data attribute.

- if any $d \in D'_{def} \cap D_{def}$ is changed, then a residual data attribute is changed.

- if $F_{def} - F'_{def} \neq \emptyset$, then any f in $(F_{def} - F'_{def})$ is a deleted member function.

- if $F'_{def} - F_{def} \neq \emptyset$, then any f in $(F'_{def} - F_{def})$ is an added member function.

- if any $f \in F'_{def} \cap F_{def}$ is changed, then a residual defined/redefined member function is changed.

3.5 Class Library Change Identification

A class library L is a collection of ORDs. An ORD is an edge labeled directed graph $ORD = (V, L, E)$, where V is the set of nodes representing the object classes, $L = \{I, Ag, As\}$ is the set of edge labels (for inheritance, aggregation, and association), and $E = E_I \bigcup E_{AG} \bigcup E_{AS}$ is the set of edges. For a detailed definition and how to reverse code to yield an ORD, the reader is referred to [9]. As mentioned earlier, Figure 3 shows the screen dump of an ORD for part of the InterViews library. In the figure, the inheritance and aggregation relationships are shown using Rumbaugh et al's notation, while association is shown using directed arcs. The figure says that World is associated with OptionDesc, and hence dependent on OptionDesc. MonoScene is a part of Sensor, and hence Sensor is dependent on MonoScene. The figure also shows that World is a derived class of Scene, and hence, it is dependent on Scene.

Modifications to a library can be classified into three basic cases, i.e., adding an ORD, deleting an ORD, and changing an ORD[7]. In the first two cases, there is no impact to the other ORD's, therefore, we will consider only the last case. An ORD can be changed in several ways: changing the defined members of a class, adding/deleting a relation between two existing classes, and adding/deleting a class and its relations. Change identification for a single class has been discussed in the previous subsection. Here, we focus on structure change of a class library.

Let $ORD = (V, L, E)$ and $ORD' = (V', L', E')$ be the ORD's for two versions of the same software. A structure change in an ORD is

---

[7]Note an isolated class is an ORD.

200

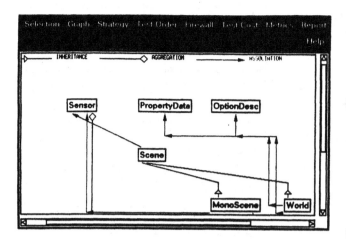

Figure 3: An ORD for a part of the InterViews Library

- if $V' - V \neq \emptyset$ then any $v \in (V' - V)$ is an added class node.

- if $V - V' \neq \emptyset$ then any $v \in (V - V')$ is a deleted node.

- if $E' - E \neq \emptyset$ then any $e \in (E' - E)$ is an added new edge.

- if $E - E' \neq \emptyset$ then any $e \in (E - E')$ is a deleted edge.

- if any v in $V \cap V'$ is changed, then a residual class is changed.

To facilitate understanding, Figure 4 shows the different types of structure changes for an ORD[8]. Figures 4(a) and (b) show the two cases in which a new class node is added into the original ORD by inserting a new relation with an residual class. Two cases of a class deletion are given in Figures 4(c) and (d). Notice that if a class node is removed from an ORD, then all relation edges between the class node and other classes must be deleted. In Figure 4(e), an existing relation edge is removed from two residual classes. In Figure 4(f), a new relation edge between two residual classes is added.

4   Change Impact Identification

After change identification, it is very important to detect the ripple effects of the changes because these changes may affect the software in different aspects, including functions, structures, behavior, and performance. Clearly understanding these effects not only reduces the cost of software maintenance but also saves the regression test effort. For example, if we

---

[8]An independent single class in a class library is considered as an ORD. Thus, adding (or deleting) an independent single class adds (or deletes) an ORD.

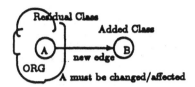

(a) Add a new "superclass"

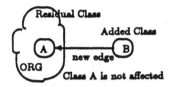

(b) Add a new dependent class

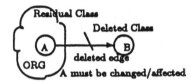

(c) Delete a "superclass"

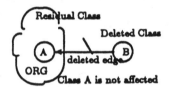

(d) Delete a relation between classes

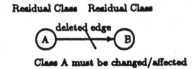

(e) Delete a dependent class

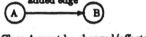

(f) Add a relation between classes

Figure 4: Different Structural Changes In An ORD

can find all the affected components in the given software, the testers need only to retest these components instead of all of the components in the software. Thus, it is very important to identify and enclose all the affected components after changing a software.

Change impact identification includes data change impact identification, method change impact identification, class change impact identification, and class library change (i.e., class relation change) impact identification. Existing results, e.g., [13], can be used to identify data and method change impacts. A class firewall concept is introduced in [10] to enclose all possible affected classes after some changes are made in a class. In this paper, we focus on changes of classes and their relationships. An automated solution is given to identify the change impact due to changes of classes and their relationships.

4.1 Class Library Change Impact Identification

The major task of class library change impact identification is to find all the affected classes due to changes of interclass relationships. We use a class firewall concept introduced in [10] to enclose all affected classes. The computation of a class firewall is based on the ORDs for the class library.

As shown in Figure 4, there are six types of structure changes in an ORD. Taking into consideration the differences in treating the inheritance, aggregation and association relationships, the impact on a residual class is identified as follows:

1. Adding a new "superclass":

   (a) If the new edge is an inheritance edge, then it expands A's members. According to Weyuko's *antidecomposition* axiom[9], we should retest these new inherited members in the context of class A [24]. In addition, integration testing of class A's new inherited members and its other members is needed to make sure that they work well together.

   (b) If the edge is an inheritance or aggregation edge, then it expands A's state space in terms of state behavior (see Figure 4.1a). That is, its states and transitions are extended by its inherited members from class B. According to Weyukos's *anticomposition* axiom[10], we should retest the state behaviors of class A.

---

[9]There exists a program P and component Q such that T is adequate for P. T' is the set of vectors of values that variables can assume on entrance to Q for some t of T, and T' is not adequate for Q. [21]

[10]There exist program P and Q, and test set T, such that T is adequate for P, and the set of vectors of values that variables can assume on entrance to Q for inputs in T is adequate for Q, but T is not adequate for P;Q.[P;Q is the composition of P and Q. [21]

   (c) If the edge is an association edge, then at least one method of class A must be changed, and hence, A is affected in this sense.

2. Adding a new dependent class.

   Class A is not affected and hence does not need to be retested.

3. Deleting a "superclass".

   This changes class A by removing class B from class A's superclass or component class list:

   (a) If the edge is an inheritance edge, then it reduces the inherited members. This only affects class A's test cases which related to those removed members.

   (b) If the edge is an inheritance or aggregation edge, then it reduces the states and transitions of class A (see Figure 4.1b). According to Weyuko's antidecomposition axiom, we should retest the state behaviors of the modified class A.

   (c) If the edge is an association edge, then at least one method of class A must be changed, and hence, A is affected in this sense.

4. Deleting a dependent class.

   Class A is not affected.

5. Deleting a relationship between existing classes.

   This is similar to (c) above.

6. Adding a relationship between existing classes.

   This is similar to (a) above.

We have discussed the different types of structure changes of an OO library. We have shown how some of the changes affect a residual class A even though its defined attributes were not changed at all. Thus, class A should be retested. A residual class like class A is called an *addition affected class* if it is directly affected by any edge addition (or class addition) in an ORD (cases (a) and (f) above). Similarly, a residual class is called a *deletion affected class* if it is directly affected by any edge deletion (or class deletion) in an ORD (cases (c) and (e) above).

4.2 Class Firewall Generation

The basic idea of computing a class firewall is described in [10]. A class firewall is a set of affected classes when some changes are made in a class library or an object-oriented program. A binary relation R, derived from an ORD $= (V,L,E)$, is introduced to compute the class firewall.

$$R = \{< C_j, C_i > | C_i, C_j \in V \wedge < C_i, C_j, l > \in E)\}$$

where R is the dependence relation which defines the dependence between classes, according to the inheritance, aggregation, and association relations.

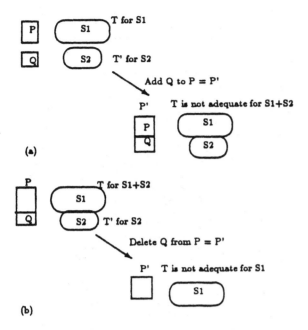

(a)

(b)

Figure 5: Changes in Object State Space

In [10], we have proved that for an ORD, if the modification a class library changes a class C without altering the structure of the ORD, then a class firewall for C, denoted CCFW(C), can be computed as follows:

$$CCFW(C) = \{C_j | < C, C_j >\in R^*\}$$

where R^* is the transitive closure of R. That is, if $< C_i, C_j >\in R$ and $< C_j, C_k >\in R^*$, then $< C_i, C_k >\in R^*$. The transitive closure of R can be computed by the famous Warshall algorithm [1].

Let L be a class library and L' its modified version. Assume that ORD = (V, L, E) is an ORD in L and that ORD' = (V', L', E') its modified version. We define a binary relation R_r as

$$R_r = R \cap (V \times V) \cap (V' \times V')$$

where $\times$ is the Cartesian product operation. In other words, R_r is the relation which defines the dependencies between the residual classes. The class firewalls are generated as follows:

- The class firewall for a changed class C is computed as follows:

$$CCFW(C) = \{Cj | < C, Cj >\in R_r^*\}$$

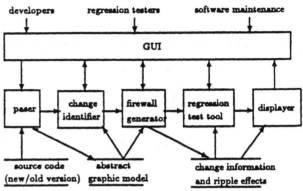

Figure 6: The Architecture Of OOTME

- The class firewall for addition affected classes is computed as follows:

$$CCFW = \{C_j | (\exists C)(\exists k)((< C_j, C, k >\in E' - E) \wedge < C, C_j >\in R'^*\}$$

where R' is the dependence relation for the modified ORD.

- The class firewall for deletion affected classes is computed as follows:

$$CCFW = \{Cj | ((\exists C)(\exists k)((< C_j, C, k >\in E - E') \wedge < C, C_j >\in R'^*\}$$

5 Support System

The objective of a software maintenance system is to help a software maintainer in: understanding a given software, identifying code changes, supporting software updates and enhancement, and detecting change effects. Therefore, any software maintenance system has to fulfill four important requirements: 1) it has to be able to provide the various information about the software, including its structures, and the interfaces and relationships between different components at the different levels; 2) it has to provide an efficient and user-friendly interface to present the various information about software and support maintenance activities; and 3) it has to be able to identify code changes between different software versions and their effects. Figure 5 depicts the architecture of an OO testing and maintenance environment we are currently developing. The components of the environment are described as follows:

- *GUI*: The GUI is constructed based on Motif and X window software; therefore it is user-friendly.

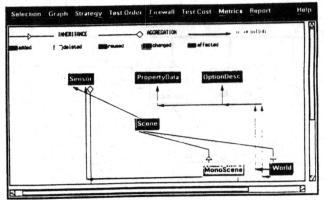

Figure 7: Change impact identification

- *Parser*: There are three different parsers: the ORD parser, the BBD parser, and the OSD parser. The user can use them to extract information from a class library.

- *Displayer*: There are three Displayers: the ORD Displayer, the BBD Displayer, and the OSD Displayer. The user can use them to display the ORDs, BBDs, and OSDs, respectively.

- *Change identifier*: The change identifier can be used to to find the code changes between two different versions of the same class library. It can also be used to automatically identify the impact of a planned code change to help a maintainer to determine whether the change shall be carried out.

- *Firewall generator*: The firewall generator can be used to identify a class firewall to enclose all the possible affected classes in a class library when it is modified.

- *Regression test tool*: The regression test tool consists of a test strategy generator and a test case generator. The test strategy generator produces a cost-effective test order for each class in the library [10]. This test order will be used as a re-test sequence in class unit testing and re-integration testing. The test case generator is used to generate new test cases.

We have applied this tool to many applications, including the Interviews library. Figure 7 shows an example listing of the firewall information for a subset of the InterViews library. We have also compared the two versions (3.0 and 3.1) of the Interviews library using the OOTME. It lists all of the differences between these two versions, including 68 added classes, 76 deleted classes, and 46 residual classes (reused

classes). In addition, it also identifies 26 changed residual classes, 16 affected classes, and 4 unaffected classes. The detailed results are given in tables 1 – 3.

6 Experience

Aids to understand an OO software system, anticipate and identify the effects of change, and facilitate regression testing are desirable capabilities of an OO software maintenance environment. Our experience indicates that it is extremely time consuming and tedious to test and maintain an OO software system. This problem becomes even more acute when documentation is either missing or inadequate. Consider, for example, the InterViews library originally developed by Stanford University. An early version of the library consisted of 146 files, more than 140 classes, more than 400 relationships, and more than 1,000 member functions. We felt that it was difficult to obtain a high level of understanding of the classes, member functions, and their relationships. Our initial experiment showed that it took an average of two hours for a C++ programmer to understand a small member function (ranging from a few lines to less than 20 lines) that invokes other member functions. Without tool support, it is almost impossible to anticipate and identify the effect of change because a class can be instantiated by another class which can then use the capabilities of the former. To ensure quality of our products, we often had to retest the entire library when major changes were made.

Software engineers in the industry consider the system useful for testing, maintenance, and reengineering. The application of the system to the InterViews library, an elevator library, and a PBX program shows that it facilitates understanding, test ordering [9][10], test case generation (for which automatic support will be available in the future), and effort estimation (in terms of extended cyclomatic complexity and CO-COMO model).

The application of the automatic change and change effect identification capabilities to the InterViews library has produced promising results. However, our experience is too limited to draw any conclusions. We anticipate that these capabilities will be particularly useful in the maintenance phase. Without tool support, one has to document each change and identify its impact according to one's knowledge of the system. This is both time consuming and inaccurate. The tool will reduce costs significantly and improve productivity in documentation and regression testing by automatically identifying the changes and their impact, thus eliminating many errors. Although the system is still in its prototyping stage, several companies have expressed interests in experimenting with the system and we are porting it to more companies.

7 Conclusion and Future Work

We have described the various types of code changes of an OO system and a formal model for capturing and inferencing on the changes to identify affected components. The model and the inference capabilities have been implemented in a tool prototype. Experience with an earlier version of the tool shows promising results. As reported elsewhere [10][9], the changed and affected classes can be tested in a cost-effective order to avoid extensive construction of test stubs.

Identification of changes and their impact is only one aspect of software maintenance. We are currently extending the capabilities to include various metrics, such as complexity, object-orientedness, and effort, to facilitate the maintenance work. The system is being expanded with these new features and integrated with a test environment to provide retesting support.

8 Acknowledgment

The material presented in this paper is based on work supported by the Texas Advanced Technology Program (Grant No. 003656-097), Fujitsu Network Transmission Systems, Inc., Hewlett-Packard Company, and the Software Engineering Center for Telecommunications at UTA.

9 References

[1] A. V. Aho, J. E. hopcroft and J. D. Ullman, Data Structures and Algorithms, Addison-Wesley Publication Company, 1983.

[2] B. Beizer, "Software Testing Techniques," 2nd ed., Van Hostrand Reinhold, 1990.

[3] Y.-F. Chen, M. Y. Nishimoto, and C. V. Ramamoorthy, "The C information abstract system," IEEE Trans. Software Eng., Vol. 16, pp. 325 – 334, Mar. 1990.

[4] S. C. Choi and W. Scacchi, "Extracting and restructuring the design of large systems," IEEE Software, Vol. 17, No. 1, pp. 66 – 71, Jan. 1990.

[5] R. T. Crocker and A. v. Mayrhauser, "Maintenance Support Needs for Object – Oriented Software," Proc. of COMPSAC'93, pp. 63 – 69, 1993.

[6] T. Gane and C. Sarson, "Structured System Analysis," McDonnell Douglas, 1982.

[7] J. E. Grass and Y.-F. Chen, "The C++ information abstractor," in UNSENIX C++ Conference. Proc., pp. 265 – 277, 1990.

[8] J. Hartmann and D. J. Robson, "Revalidation During the Software Maintenance Phase," Proc. IEEE Conference on Software Maintenance, pp. 70 – 80, 1989.

[9] D. Kung, J. Gao, P. Hsia, J. Lin and Y. Toyoshima, "Design Recovery for Software Testing of Object-Oriented Programs," Proc. of the Working Conference on Reverse Engineering, pp. 202 – 211, IEEE Computer Society Press, 1993.

[10] D. Kung, J. Gao, P. Hsia, Y. Toyoshima, and C. Chen, "Firewall, regression testing, and software maintenance of object oriented systems," to appear in Journal of Object Oriented Programming, 1994.

[11] J. Laski and W. Szermer, "Identification of Program Modifications and its Applications in Software Maintenance," Proc. IEEE Conference on Software Maintenance, pp. 282 – 290, 1992.

[12] M. Lejter, S. Meyers, and S. P. Reiss, "Support for maintaining object-oriented programs, " IEEE Transactions on Software Engineering 18:1045 – 52 Dec 1992.

[13] H. K. N. Leung and L. White, "A study of integration testing and software regression at the integration level," Proc. IEEE Conf. on Software Maintenance, pp. 290 – 301, 1990.

[14] H. K. N. Leung and L. White, "A Cost Model to Compare Regression Test Strategies," Proc. Conf. Software Maintenance, pp. 201 – 208, 1991.

[15] S. Liu and N. Wilde, "Identifying Objects in a Conventional Procedural Language: An Example of Data Design Recovery", Proceedings of IEEE Conference on Software Maintenance, pp. 266 – 271, 1990.

[16] P. D. O'Brien, D. D. Halbart, and M. F. Kilian, "The Trellis programming environment," in Proc. 1987 Conf. Object-Oriented Programming Systems, Languages and Applications (OOPSLA'87), pp. 91 – 102, Oct. 1987.

[17] V. Rajlich, N. Damaskinos, and P. Linos, "VIFOR: a tool for software maintenance," Software: Practice & Experience Vol. 20 pp. 67 – 77, Jan 1990.

[18] J. Sametinger, "A tool for the maintenance of C++ programs," Proc. IEEE Conf. on Software Maintenance, pp. 54 – 59, 1990.

[19] E. Soloway et al, "Designing documentation to compensate for delocalized plans," CACM Vol. 31, No. 11, pp. 1259 – 1267, Nov. 1988.

[20] W. Teitelman and L. Masinter, "The Interlisp programming environment," IEEE Computer, Vol. 14, No. 4, pp. 25 – 34, Apr. 1981.

[21] E. J., Weyuker, "The evaluation of program-based software test data adequacy criteria," CACM, Vol. 31, No. 6, pp. 668 – 675, 1988.

[22] N. Wilde, R. Huitt and S. Huitt, "Dependency Analysis Tools: Reusable Components for Software Maintenance", Proc. IEEE Conference on Software Maintenance, pp. 126 – 131, October 1989.

[23] N. Wilde and R. Huitt, "Maintenance support for object-oriented programs," IEEE Trans. on Software Eng., Vol. 18, No. 12, pp. 1038 – 1044, Dec. 1992.

[24] Dewayne E. Perry and Gail E. Kaiser, "Adequate Testing and Object-Oriented Programming," January/February JOOP, 1990.

class name	class name	class name	class name	class name
ActiveHandler	Adjustable	AllocationInfo	AllocationTable	AllocationTableImpl
BoxImpl	CoordinateSpace	DebugGlyph	Dialog	DialogHandler
DialogKitImpl	Drag	DragZone	DragZoneSink	FieldButton
FieldEditorImpl	FieldStringEditor	FileBrowserImpl	FileChooserImpl	FontBoundingBox
GLContext	InputHandler	InputHandlerImpl	LayoutKit	LayoutKitImpl
LayoutLayer	MFDialogKitImpl	MFKitForeground	MFKitFrame	MFKitImpl
MFKitInfo	MFKitMenuItem	MenuImpl	MonoKitForeground	MonoKitFrame
MonoKitImpl	MonoKitInfo	MonoKitMenuItem	OLKitImpl	OL_AbbrevMenuButton
OL_Anchor	OL_Button	OL_Cable	OL_Channel	OL_CheckBox
OL_CheckMark	OL_Dragbox	OL_Elevator	OL_ElevatorGlyph	OL_FieldEditor
OL_Frame	OL_Gauge	OL_Indicator	OL_MenuMark	OL_Mover
OL_Pushpin	OL_PushpinLook	OL_Scrollbar	OL_Setting	OL_Slider
OL_Specs	OL_Stepper	OL_Tick	OL_ToLimit	Observable
Observer	WidgetKitImpl	WidgetKitOverlay		

Table 1: New added classes in InterViews3.1

class name	class name	class name	class name	class name
ApplicationWindow	BMargin	BoxAllocation	BoxComponent	BreakSet
Center	DeckInfo	FixedSpan	HCenter	HGlue
HMargin	HRule	HitTarget	HitTargetList	IconWindow
LMargin	LRBox	Listener	ManagedWindow	Margin
OptionDesc	Overlay	PSFont	PSFontImpl	Page
PageInfo	Patch	Pattern	PointerHandler	PopupWindow
PossibleHitTarget	Printer	PrinterInfo	PrinterRep	PropertyData
RMargin	Raster	Regexp	ReqErr	Resource
ResourceImpl	Rule	Sensor	Session	SessionIOHandler
SessionRep	Shadow	SimpleCompositor	Stencil	Style
StyleAttribute	StyleRep	StyleWildcard	StyleWildcardInfo	StyleWildcardMatchQuality
Superpose	TBBox	TIFFRaster	TIFFRasterImpl	TMargin
Target	TeXCompositor	Tile	TileReversed	TopLevelWindow
TransformSetter	Transformer	TransientWindow	VCenter	VGlue
VMargin	VRule	ValueString	Window	World
XYMarker				

Table 2: Deleted classes from InterViews3.0

class name	class name	class name	class name	class name
(C)Aggregate	(C)Allocation	(C)Background	(C)Bitmap	(C)Border
(C)Box	(C)Break	(C)Brush	(C)Canvas	(C)Color
(C)Composition	(C)Deck	(C)Display	(C)Event	(C)Extension
(C)Font	(C)FontFamily	(C)Glyph	(C)Handler	(C)Hit
(C)HitImpl	(C)Image	(C)LRComposition	(C)MonoGlyph	(C)Requisition
(C)TBComposition	(A)AggregateInfo	(A)Align	(A)Character	(A)CompositionComponent
(A)Cursor	(A)Discretionary	(A)Glue	(A)Group	(A)HStrut
(A)LRMarker	(A)Label	(A)Layout	(A)ShapeOf	(A)Space
(A)Strut	(A)VStrut	(U)Allotment	(U)ArrayCompositor	(U)Compositor
(U)Requirement				

Table 3: Reused classes in InterView3.1

Chapter 5
Traceability Approaches

Purpose

The papers in this chapter introduce the traceability technology used to determine the effects of software changes. Advances in software-development environments and repository technology have enabled software engineers to trace the impacts of software changes. The papers in this chapter will familiarize you with issues about determining impacts from relationships among types of software artifacts. Much of the material is from the perspective of development environments and documentation systems.

The Papers

Unlike the more mature field of source-code analysis, there has been little direct research in determining impacts from traceability relationships. Most traceability work has been accomplished as part of work in software-development environments, often part of federal or corporate initiatives, with little exposure in the open literature.

There are some good sources of information on traceability systems that are too long to include here. One such work describes Alicia (the Automated Life Cycle Analysis System), which was developed for the U.S. Air Force's Rome Laboratories to support impact analysis with a software project database [RADC 1986]. Alicia represents a comprehensive traceability impact-analysis system. We describe it, along with other interesting traceability systems, in more detail in our introduction to this book.

Traceability relationships are often represented in a graph structure that is amenable to navigation with a hypertext system. In "A Hypertext System to Manage Software Life Cycle Documents," Pankaj Garg and Walt Scacchi describe the Document Integration Facility, an experiment that is part of the Software Factory project. DIF, which uses hypertext mechanisms to manage software artifacts, addresses traceability through the use of hypertext links and navigation mechanisms. The authors present DIF as an alternative to project-database approaches and demonstrate its usefulness in development and maintenance environments.

In "SODOS: A Software Document Support Environment – Its Definition," Ellis Horowitz and Ronald Williamson examine traceability from the documentation perspective. They explore the mechanisms necessary to support an automated software-documentation system using Smalltalk-80, a relational database-management system, and a graph model of software documentation. The graph model and support for traceability are of particular interest because they are the basis for impact analysis at the software-artifact level. The authors describe how they constructed the Sodos prototype and how it was to be used.

The next traceability paper, "Traceability Based on Design Decisions," presents a view of the software structure as conceptual models that connect source code with design decisions and map the result onto the target model. Aniello Cimitile, Filippo Lanubile, and Giuseppe Visaggio discuss this process in terms of software conversion from Pascal to Ada. Conceptual models, including essential design and language-oriented design, are represented in a graph model. These models are used by the Traceability Support System, a system that connects different views on software-system structure with design decisions and assists in evaluating the effects of changes.

Guillermo Arango, Eric Schoen, and Robert Pettengill conclude the chapter with "A Process for Consolidating and Reusing Design Knowledge," in which they examine traceability from the perspectives of evolution and reuse. Although the focus is on reuse, not on traceability directly, the authors effectively demonstrate how developers can use traceability information to evolve software systems. They present a validated process for constructing work spaces to support the design and evolution of a product family.

References

[RADC 1986]   Rome Air Development Center, "Automated Life Cycle Impact Analysis System," Tech. report RADC-TR-86-197, Rome Laboratories, U.S. Air Force Systems Command, Griffiss Air Force Base, Rome, N.Y., Dec. 1986.

A Hypertext System to Manage Software Life-Cycle Documents

Pankaj K. Garg and *Walt Scacchi*, *University of Southern California*

Traditional systems don't handle the documentation requirements of large-scale, multiproject software development. But this hypertext-based system does.

Documenting software systems is a necessity, since not all relevant information about the system can be embodied in a system's source code. The larger the system, the more critical the problems of documents' consistency, completeness, traceability, revision control, and retrieval efficiency.

For the next generation of operating systems, Robert Balzer has envisioned an environment[1] based on objects and relationships between objects, as opposed to the conventional file-based systems. Using this philosophy, we have constructed the Documents Integration Facility for the development, use, and maintenance of large-scale systems and their life-cycle documents.

The philosophy underlying DIF is twofold. First, it is necessary for an effective engineering-information system to prescribe the information that must be stored, to ensure the completeness and preciseness of the information. Second, for the engineering-information system to be generally applicable, it should be possible to change the information requirements prescribed by the system according to the needs of different settings.

DIF helps integrate and manage the documents produced and used throughout the life cycle — requirements specifications, functional specifications, architectural designs (structural specifications), detailed designs, source code, testing information, and user and maintenance manuals. DIF supports information management in large systems where there is much natural-language text.

DIF has been used to integrate and manage the life-cycle documents of more than a dozen systems (in the System Factory) totaling more than 200,000 lines of code, developed by more than a dozen teams of three to seven people each. More

Garg is now at Hewlett-Packard Laboratories. An earlier version of this article appeared in *Proc. 21st Hawaii Int'l Conf. on System Sciences*, CS Press, Los Alamitos, Calif., 1988, pp. 337-346.

than 40 Mbytes of life-cycle descriptions have been managed by DIF. The results of this experiment suggest DIF's potential usefulness for larger systems (those of more than a million lines of code).

In a typical project's life cycle, information about the process and the product is diffused among several individuals, and it is easy both for information to be lost and for information bottlenecks to be created. DIF encourages the easily accessible storage of relevant information about the process and the product.

In DIF, we consider segments of software documents as the objects to be stored, processed, browsed, revised, and reused. Links explain the relationship between the objects. DIF stores the objects in files and the relationships between the objects in a relational database, resulting in a persistent object base. This eases the reuse of documents.

DIF also provides software-engineering tools to process the information in the objects. By judiciously using links, keywords, and information structure, DIF users can alleviate problems of traceability, consistency, and completeness. Through the Unix RCS revision-control facility, DIF provides revision control. Through interfaces to the browsing mechanisms of the Ingres database system, DIF provides efficient document retrieval. Through the Unix mail system, DIF lets project participants exchange structured messages. Through language-directed editors, DIF eases the development of software descriptions in several formal languages. And through software-engineering tools for functional and architectural specifications, DIF aids the analysis of formal descriptions.

Documents in hypertext

Through the development process, DIF stores all relevant information about the target system in textual objects as nodes of hypertext. Hypertext is a storage structure where information is stored in the nodes of a graph. Links between hypertext nodes allow efficient browsing of the information. Attributes attached to nodes and links provide information filtering.

No restriction is put on the nature of information in the nodes, so the same hypertext may contain a node of natural-language text and a node of program code. This is the main advantage that hypertext systems have over conventional database-management systems, document bases, and knowledge bases.

Through the development process, DIF stores all relevant information about the target system in textual objects as nodes of hypertext.

Documentation method

To effectively manage the documents in a large-scale software process, you must first understand what needs to be documented. To this end, we use the System Factory documentation method, which is an eight-year-old laboratory project at the University of Southern California set up to experiment with novel ways of software-project management and with the development, use, and maintenance of innovative software technologies. The uniqueness of the System Factory method of documentation is the blend of organizational and technical concerns that it advocates.

In the System Factory, the software process is broken into activities, where each activity culminates in the production of a document. The eight documents that emerge from the System Factory method are:

• Requirements specification. This document describes both the operational and nonoperational requirements of the system being developed.

Operational (testable) requirements outline the system's performance characteristics, interface constraints, quality-assurance standards, and human factors. The operational requirements are defined so you can trace them through design and implementation.

Nonoperational requirements outline the organizational resources available to support system development, the package of resources being built into the target system, forethoughts about the system's development life cycle, assumptions about the system's operation in its target environment, and expected changes in the system's operational requirements over its lifetime.

The requirements-specification document is written in a natural language, for which DIF provides an interface to text-editing and -formatting systems. DIF provides mechanisms like keyword association and linking that help you browse through the requirements. By defining a form for the requirements document, the manager of several projects can standardize the contents of the requirements document at the level of sections and subsections. By judiciously choosing keywords and links, the manager can set up the requirements to ease the tracing of operational requirements through the system's design and implementation.

• Functional specification. This document details the computational functions the target system will perform in terms of the computation objects, their attributes, attribute-value ranges, object and attribute relationships, the actions that manipulate them, constraints on the actions, global stimulus/response monitors, and the system agents that organize and

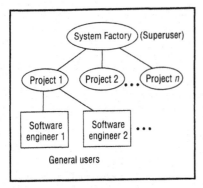

Figure 1. System Factory structure.

embed these into a system environment.

You write these formal functional specifications in the specification language Gist,[1] which promotes the incremental development, refinement, and rapid prototyping of operational system specifications.

In incremental development, you first give an informal, narrative specification. Next, you describe the objects (both active and passive) in the target system and its environment in a graphical form. Finally, you give the formal description of the objects and agents in Gist.

DIF recognizes the formal Gist text and lets you send it for processing through the Gist specifications analyzer and simulator. It also automatically activates the Gist language-directed editor.

• Architectural specification. This document describes the system modules' interconnection structure with defined data-resource interfaces, arranged to facilitate parallel detailed design and implementation. You use the NuMIL module-interconnection language[2] to descibe this document. You can also formally define system-timing and concurrency constraints in this document.

DIF provides access to the NuMIL editor and processing environment, which lets you define modules and their resource dependencies as well as check and track changes in the modules. It also provides access to a structure visualizer that graphically displays the module interconnections.

• Detailed-design specification. This document describes (in Gist and NuMIL) the behavioral algorithms and system-dependent operations consistent with the computational modules and resource interfaces defined in the architectural specification.

• Source-code document. This contains the target system's source code and reflects the system structure as detailed in the earlier documents.

• Testing and quality-assurance document. This document stores test cases that specify how you can trace the operational requirements to test-case runs to validate the system's performance. You can use keywords and links in DIF to link the test cases to the operational requirements.

• User manual. This document describes the commands, error messages, and example uses of the system in a standard user-manual format.

• System-maintenance guide. This document describes how the system can be enhanced, how its performance can be better tuned, known system bugs, and porting constraints.

Coupling this documentation method with DIF lets you produce, organize, and

---

Interfaces to Latex, spell checkers, and other tools provide a text-processing environment akin to the Unix documenter's workbench.

---

store encyclopedic volumes of life-cycle information for subsequent browsing, reuse, and revision.

DIF structure

Figure 1 shows the organizational structure supported by DIF in the System Factory. In the System Factory, the project manager prescribes what needs to be described in each document. There are potentially several projects in the factory at the same time, and several software engineers work on each project.

Operation modes. Corresponding to the type of users in the System Factory, DIF allows two modes of operations: a superuser mode and a general-user mode. The two modes are comparable to the database administrator and the user, respectively. In superuser mode, you define the factory structure (what projects

are in the factory and who is responsible for each one) and the structure of the documents (what needs to be documented). In general-user mode, you create, modify, and browse through the hypertext base. The general user can operate at two levels: the information level and information-structure level.

Forms and basic templates. The superuser defines the forms and the basic templates in the factory. One concern of the System Factory was to ensure that all the projects have a standard document structure. Thus, each document is defined as a *form*, which is a tree-structured organization of basic templates to be instantiated with project-specific information. Figure 2 shows an example requirements-specifications form. Such forms provide a way of defining the process that is to be followed by the project members.

The superuser defines each form only once; *all* projects inherit that form. This allows standardization of documents across projects. It also lets the software engineers concentrate on the *content* of the documents without being bothered about their structure.

When defining the basic templates, the superuser also defines the nature of information that needs to be given in each basic template. This entails providing the type of the basic template (narrative, graphical, NuMIL, Gist, C code, executable code, or object code) and a text template that the general user can use to enter information in the instances for that basic template.

General users can define additional project-specific basic templates, but they cannot modify the basic templates defined by the superuser. Instead, they create instances of the superuser-defined basic templates and enter information in those instances. In a project, a basic template can have many instances.

Project information. The superuser provides project information. Project-related information in DIF consists of a list of projects and the software engineers working on them. This information lets DIF check users' read and write privileges. There is no restriction on who may read the information of any project. The superuser has read and write privileges for all information.

A general user can add links, keywords, and annotations to other users' and other projects' basic templates. (The links, keywords, and annotations are tools that allow easier later browsing of the project information — something we call "information trailblazing.")

Adding more project information like tasks, schedules, and progress reports is a natural extension to DIF hypertext. We have described this issue at length elsewhere.[3]

Information level. DIF facilities let users enter, modify, and use the information required by the forms as dictated by the superuser. DIF provides language-directed editors for all the formal languages used in the System Factory. The general user need not worry about the files that must be created when entering information in basic templates because DIF automatically generates a file name based on the project and the basic template.

For backup, DIF can store entire forms in RCS. DIF lets you check forms in to and out of RCS. Options like retrieving revisions through user-defined identifiers and cut-off dates are available through the DIF interface.

You can request that a software tool process the information in a basic template from within DIF itself, without entering the operating system. For example, if a basic template contains C code, you can request that the code be compiled.

Interfaces to Latex, spell checkers, and other tools provide a text-processing environment akin to the Unix documenter's workbench.

Information-structure level. The information-structure lets the general user navigate through the information hypertext stored in DIF. (This level is different from a database schema because, in a schema, the structure does not change with the information. Here, the structure depends on the currently defined links.) DIF provides these navigation mechanisms:

• Links. The user (either superuser or general user) can define links between basic templates. You can link the system's operational requirements to the code

Section number	Section heading
1.	Overview and summary
2.	Problem definition
2.1.	Technology in use
2.2.	System diagram
2.3.	Theory of system operation
2.4.	Intended application
2.5.	User skills
3.	Operational requirements
3.1.	Performance characteristics
3.2.	Standard interfaces
3.3.	Software quality-assurance plans
3.4.	Software portability
3.5.	User orientation
4.	Nonoperational requirements
4.1.	Resources available for development
4.2.	Package of resources built into the system
4.3.	Forethoughts about the system's life cycle
4.4.	Assumptions about system operation
4.5.	Expected changes in operational requirements
Basic-template number	**Basic-template heading**

Figure 2. Requirements-specification form.

modules that support the capability. Links may be *operational* links, which readily support situations where executable descriptions must be linked to the source code. For example, you can link a C-code basic template to the executable basic template derived from that code. Visiting that operational link results in the execution of the linked basic template. Future versions of DIF will support arbitrary shell-procedure attachments.

DIF supports two types of links: node-to-node links, which are relationships between the definition of two basic templates, and point-to-point links, which link one point in a basic template to a point in another basic template.

• Keywords. For each basic template, you can define keywords that describe the semantics of the information contained in that basic template. DIF stores the keywords associated with basic templates in a relation maintained in the Ingres database. This lets you use the Ingres querying facilities to navigate through documents.

For example, you can look for all basic templates (within and across projects) that have a particular keyword, list the keywords of a basic template, or search for basic templates that have keywords satisfying a pattern. DIF also has standard browsing functions for users not trained in the Ingres mechanisms.

In creating DIF, we were mainly concerned with the efficient storage and usage of keywords, not how they are derived. You can attach automatic keyword-generation tools to DIF if you want.

DIF lets a document's readers create keywords of their own. This lets new personnel in a project team quickly tune the documents to their needs.

• Forms and compositions. Forms are a convenient way to view the documents related to each life-cycle activity.

To fully use the potential of the hypertext information in DIF, you can define your own composition of basic templates. A composition is similar to a form, except that it is not enforced on all projects but is associated with the user who is browsing the documents. You define compositions, as you do forms, by defining the constituent basic templates. You can also define compositions on the basis of the trail you have followed while browsing through the hypertext.

You use compositions to print hardcopy documents, much like the path facility in a typical hypertext system. We have developed special-purpose tools to correctly compose different types of basic templates and to generate appropriate markup code for the Latex text-formatting system. You can also use compositions to generate make files for different system configurations.

Document integration and parallel development. DIF provides several features that let you view system information in an integrated manner within and across projects. The documents are organized in a tree of Unix directories and files, as Figure 3 shows. Although you enter information in DIF at the file level, DIF invisibly handles all the routine file-management functions (like creating directories for related

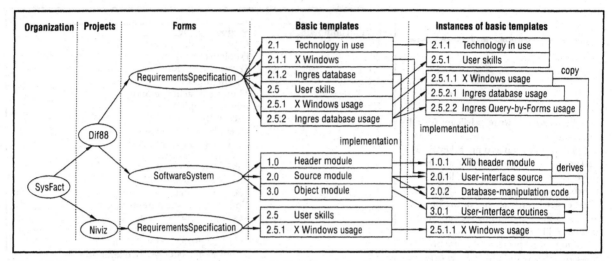

Figure 3. Hypertext structure for life-cycle documents. At the far left is an organization (System Factory) with two projects (Dif88 and Niviz). Each project has forms like Requirement Specifications and Software System. Each form has basic templates defined by the superuser (common to all projects) or general user (specific to one project). Each basic template may have more than one instance in a project. Objects in ovals are mapped to Unix directories, while those in rectangles are mapped into Unix files.

documents).

For example, when entering information for the system's operational requirements, you do not have to create the file to store the text associated with the operational requirements; DIF does it automatically. You need only be concerned with creating or manipulating software descriptions. This provides an object-oriented environment of persistent descriptions rather than simply a loose collection of files and directories.

DIF lets the engineers in the System Factory develop parts of documents in parallel without worrying about integration issues. Thus, one person could be writing the target system's operational requirements while another person is writing its nonoperational requirements. The individual efforts are automatically merged in the same hypertext document.

File structure. At the heart of DIF's implementation are the Unix file system and the Ingres database system. The file system provides a repository for the textual and graphical information; Ingres stores information-structure-level and project-level information. DIF builds a file structure (on Unix) that models the System Factory structure (see Figure 1). Figure 3 shows an example file structure.

At the root of this file structure is the System Factory directory that contains directories for each project. Under every project directory is a directory for each form defined in the factory. Under the directory for each form are files for the basic templates in the form. For example, Fig-

ure 3 shows part of the requirements-specifications directory in the System Factory. Files in this directory represent basic templates, like 2.1 (Technology in Use) and 2.5 (User Skills).

User-defined instances of basic templates are also maintained as files. For example, in Figure 3's Dif88 project, basic template 2.0 (Source Module) has at least two instances: User-Interface Code and Database-Manipulation Code.

Using DIF

Figure 4 shows DIF's top-level interface, which shows a snapshot of the system with the user editing three basic templates. The workstation screen is divided into three main window types: command, status, and workspace. You issue commands to DIF by clicking one of the command windows. DIF handles textual I/O through pop-up windows. The status window shows information like the current project, the number of basic templates visited in this session, the version numbers of the systems being used, the current user, and the current mode. DIF creates all browsing windows in the workspace window.

In Figure 4, Editor Window 1 shows an annotation example. The basic template (2.5 User Skills) in Editor Window 2 is linked to the basic template (2.5.1 X Windows) in Editor Window 3 with the link ElaboratedIn. Editor Window 3 was opened by clicking the Target File part of the link window that in turn was obtained by clicking the link icon in Editor Window 2.

Hypertext editing. We have extended the X Windows editor to provide two kinds of hypertext functions: the capabilities to annotate the text at any point and to link two points in two basic templates.

To add an annotation at a point in the text, you place the mouse pointer at the point and press F2. This opens a dialogue window with an editor window in which you can enter an annotation.

In the text, annotations are marked with a special character icon. Any user can look up an annotation by placing the mouse at this icon and pressing the F1 key. You can have multiple annotations at a single point; this supports group discussions. DIF automatically records attributes like the annotation's creation date and author.

To add a link from one basic template to another, you open the two templates in two separate editor windows. You then position the mouse pointer at the link's source position and press F3. DIF asks for the link name to be added. After entering the name, you position the mouse pointer at the second template and press F4. As with annotations, DIF displays links in the text as special character icons (the icon is different from the annotation icon).

To display the details of a link, you position the mouse at the link icon and press F5. To follow a link, you click the Target File item in this display of link details; DIF then opens another window that contains an editor for the link target. You can associate link names with special-purpose scripts that will be executed when the link is traced.

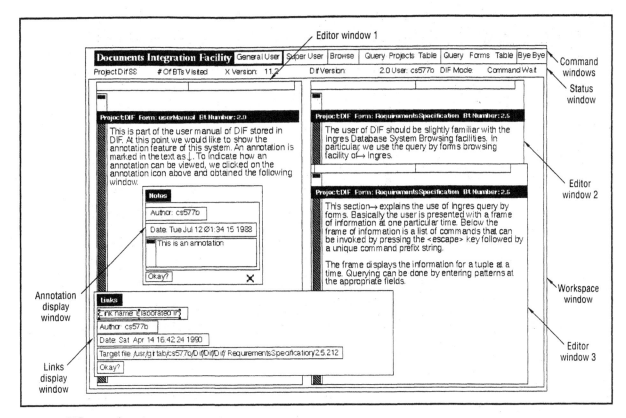

Figure 4. DIF screen layout.

Command modes. There are six modes available in DIF's command-windows title bar: general-user, superuser, browse, projects-table query, form-table query, and session-end (the Bye Bye window).

General-user mode. By clicking the general-user command window, you get a menu as shown in Figure 5a. This provides functions at the general-user level like creating or deleting an instance of a basic template, creating or deleting a project-specific basic template, editing the information contained in a basic template, processing the information in a basic template through a software-engineering tool, mailing a basic template to another project participant, and various operations on compositions of basic templates.

To edit a basic template, you select the Edit Bt item from the menu. DIF presents a menu of available forms and basic templates. Once you select the appropriate form and its constituent basic template, DIF opens a window with an editor process to edit the corresponding file. This reflects the buffering that DIF provides

Create an Instance of a BT	Add Project	Browse Links Table
Delete an Instance of a BT	Delete Project	Browse Keywords Table
Create a BT	Rename Project	List Keywords of Current Project
Delete a BT	Add Project Users	List Keywords of Another Project
Edit a BT	Delete Project Users	List BTs having a Keyword, within project
Invoke a Tool	Create Form	List BTs having a Keyword, across projects
Define a Composition	Delete Form	List Forms having a Keyword, within project
Add a BT to a Composition	Delete BT	List Forms having a Keyword, across projects
Delete a BT from a Composition	Add BT	List Keywords of a Compositions
Show a Composition Definition	Change Password	List Projects having a Keyword
Print a Composition	Clear Database	Step through Links of a BT
Delete a Composition	Print a Screen Dump	HELP
Change Project	HELP	
HELP		
(a)	**(b)**	**(c)**

Figure 5. Menus for **(a)** general-user, **(b)** superuser, and **(c)** browse functions.

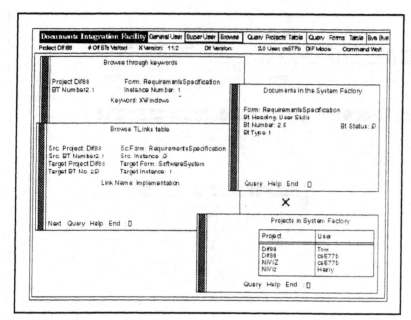

Figure 6. Browsing through Query Forms Table.

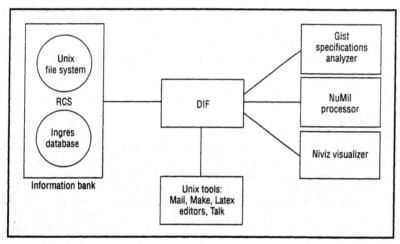

Figure 7. DIF's organization.

from the operating system's file-management facilities. You can change the default editor through a parameter supplied to DIF on its invocation. While you are editing a basic template, you can choose to edit another basic template in another window by either the same selection mechanism or by following a link from any of the previous basic templates being edited.

Superuser mode. By clicking the superuser command window, you are presented with the menu shown in Figure 5b that lets you act as the administrator of the hypertext document, providing functions to create, modify, and delete forms, projects, and project members. When defining forms, the superuser can define the process model that is to be followed in the life cycle of the various projects.

Browsing. The next three command windows — Browse, Query Projects Table, and Query Forms Table — provide browsing facilities for the hypertext storage structure. The Query Projects Table and Query Forms Table command windows provide interfaces to Ingres query-by-forms facility, which gives you access to several methods to make queries about the projects and the forms' structure.

Figure 6 shows a typical usage of this facility. The windows in the workspace were created per user requests. For example, when you click the Query Projects Table command, the window labeled Projects In The System Factory opens. In this window,

you can query the database about the projects in the System Factory by specifying patterns for either projects or users. The position and sizes of the windows are always under user control, a feature provided by X Windows.

The Browse command window provides many predefined browsing facilities for the hypertext document. Figure 5c shows the menu of these facilities. You can create, delete, or browse through links between basic templates. Using keywords, you can search for appropriate projects, forms, compositions, or basic templates.

DIF environment

Because DIF can accommodate all life-cycle activities, we consider it to be a software-engineering environment. With the progress of the target system through the various life-cycle activities, DIF offers a uniform interface to access the appropriate tools, like a functional specification analyzer and an architectural design processor, at each phase. In the interfaces to these tools, it supports the notion of interface *transparency*. DIF provides unobtrusive use of the tool that it interfaces to while providing mechanisms that the tool itself lacks.

Figure 7 shows the organization of DIF with respect to the other tools in the System Factory. The basic set of tools, described in detail elsewhere,[4] contains

• a Gist specification analyzer and simulator that aids the development and use of the formal functional specifications of (sub)systems under development,

• a module-interconnection and interface-definition processor that supports the design and evolution of multiversion system configurations described in the NuMIL language,

• an Emacs-like language-directed editing environment for constructing and revising structured documents and system description languages like Gist, NuMIL, and C,

• a systems visualizer that graphically presents system configurations, and

• Unix tools like RCS, Make, Spell, Nroff/Troff, Talk, and Mail. The interface to the mailing system helps people coordinate their activities via structured messages consisting of basic templates.

Design issues

In designing DIF, several issues concerned us, including tools interface, consistency and completeness, reuse, scaling up, on-line information, multiproject support, and revision control:

• Tools interface. Although the Unix philosophy of providing loosely coupled tools and using them either independently or coupled through piping mechanisms has been fruitful, the plethora of tools now commonly available has thwarted their efficient use. Developers need a structured way to access the tools. Systems like DIF that organize the tools according to their usage will improve the utility of the underlying tools and thus software engineers' productivity. The ease of adding tools to DIF is also an advantage to engineers.

• Consistency, completeness, and traceability. A natural concern for document management is to provide mechanisms that help maintain documents' consistency and completeness over time and that provide traceability mechanisms across different life-cycle documents.

DIF addresses consistency through its keyword and link mechanisms. You can use keywords to locate related documents to propagate changes. You can use automated links to define how changes in the source basic template should be propagated to the target basic template.

DIF addresses completeness through the notion of forms for defining the life-cycle documents. They let the superuser ensure that critical system aspects have been documented at the appropriate places.

DIF addresses traceability through the use of links and of keyword-searching and navigation mechanisms.

• Reuse. System documentation is a time-consuming process, and it is imperative that we find ways to reuse documents. DIF is a first step in this direction, since it provides a hypertext-based persistent repository of document objects with facilities for efficient browsing and retrieval. Thus, you can locate and reuse basic templates. In an empirical study done in the System Factory, we found DIF to be used frequently to retrieve and convert old documents into new ones, especially when the

old documents were from a closely related project.

• Scaling up. To support large-scale systems engineering, we tried to choose wisely between what information goes into the database and what information goes into the file system. Most of the textual information (except keywords) is stored in the Unix file system. In fact, we exploited the Unix file system's structural mechanisms to encode some of the documents' structural information.

The information stored in the database is therefore minimal. Throughout the System Factory experiment, we have found that the size of information in the database system is no greater than 1 percent of

the information in the file system. This requires further experimentation but if the results are at all indicative, DIF has been able to achieve the kind of storage distribution that we wanted — and it did so with existing file and database systems.

• On-line information. One thrust of the DIF philosophy is to shift the medium of information exchange in the software process from paper to on-line form. This has the obvious advantage of being a dynamic medium, since documents can be modified very easily. On the other hand, paper documents have advantages like physical feel, the ability to be written on, and ability to be read almost anywhere. DIF has covered both bases by providing

---

Other hypertext systems

DIF is in some ways similar to current hypertext systems, including commercial systems like Guide[1] and research projects like Sodos,[2] Textnet,[3] Planetext,[4] Notecards,[5] and Neptune.[6] All share the goal of managing textual information.

But DIF differs from most other hypertext systems in that it is geared toward facilitating information management in the software process. It can define the activities of a software process so that you can easily produce, use, and revise the appropriate information.

We have integrated DIF with several tools in the System Factory to provide an integrated software-engineering environment. For example, you can enter a system's functional specifications through a Gist editor that is syntactically tuned for the Gist specification language. Through an interface with RCS, DIF provides a revision-management facility. As such, DIF can serve as a basis for configuring several software-engineering (CASE) tools. The other hypertext systems cannot, since they are mostly closed systems.

DIF lets you store the documentation for multiple projects in the same hypertext base. It allows manipulation of links between documents across and within projects. It maintains project-user information for access control. Keywords associated with the nodes in the hypertext let you browse documents within and across projects.

The project most similar to DIF is the Sodos system designed by Ellis Horowitz and Ronald Williamson. Sodos was implemented in Smalltalk and, like DIF, managed life-cycle documents in an object-oriented fashion. But key differences set the two systems apart: Sodos manages documents for single projects only. Its revision mechanism is limited to letting you define the revision numbers for parts of the documents stored. Sodos was not built as part of a software-engineering environment and thus did not provide interfaces to any development tools.

Textnet, Notecards, and Planetext support the notion of building hypertext systems to support the management of textual information. Because they are not oriented toward software documents, their concern for relevance and completeness of information, maintaining different versions concurrently, and providing access to other tools to process the information contained in the nodes is minimal.

The Dynamic Design environment built on top of Neptune is designed as an engineering-information system. The concepts of basic templates and compositions in DIF are similar to the concepts of project components and contexts in Dynamic Design. However, Dynamic Design does not support multiple projects and does not support concepts similar to forms and instances of basic templates, which are very important in DIF.

References

1. P.J. Brown, "Presenting Information on Workstation Screens," in *Workstation and Publication Systems*, R.A. Earnshaw, ed., Springer-Verlag, New York, 1987, pp. 122-128.
2. J. Conklin, "Hypertext: An Introduction and Survey," *Computer*, Sept. 1987, pp. 17-41.
3. R.H. Trigg and M. Weiser, "Textnet: A Network-Based Approach to Text Handling," *ACM Trans. Office Information Systems*, Jan. 1986, pp. 1-23.
4. J. Bigelow, "Hypertext and CASE," *IEEE Software*, March 1988, pp. 23-27.
5. F.G. Halasz, "Reflections on Notecards: Seven Issues for the Next-Generation Hypermedia Systems," *Comm. ACM*, July 1988, pp. 836-855.
6. E. Horowitz and R. Williamson, "Sodos: A Software-Documentation Support Environment: Its Definition," *IEEE Trans. Software Eng.*, Aug. 1986, pp. 849-859.

sophisticated mechanisms for hard-copy rendition of documents and hypertext mechanisms for on-line text management. With DIF, you can potentially get the best of both worlds by not having to worry about storing paper documents and at the same time being able to use paper documents when convenient.

• Multiproject support. DIF is unique among the current hypertext systems for software documents in that it provides support for multiple projects through the same hypertext base. (The box on p. 97 describes some other hypertext-based systems.) This is an advantage in large project environments where related subsystems are developed almost independently and the efforts must later be merged. Through the use of appropriate attribute links and keywords, you can use the information-structure-level information in DIF to tie together otherwise independently developing projects.

• Revisions. The interface to the RCS revision-management facility lets you manage revisions on complete forms. Only one revision of a form is active at a time, and the database reflects the information structure for that form. However, DIF does not provide mechanisms to manage revisions of the information in the database. This means that the information in the file system has revision trees but the database system has no such corresponding structure. We are planning to remedy this deficiency by offering revision management for both the database and file systems in future versions of DIF.

Experience with the prototype usage in the System Factory has convinced us of DIF's utility. DIF, as an active medium, lets you capture much of the information related to a system's design, development, use, and maintenance. You can change the process model built into DIF. You can easily manage several project documents and even exchange information across projects.

But DIF is not complete. We are now investigating the issues of incorporating into the system more knowledge about the activities that the participants in a project perform. The granularity at which DIF considers activities is very coarse; for example, as requirements specifications and functional specifications. If we could determine finer grained actions, we could support them better.

For example, after defining a new requirement, the user of the target system normally wants to communicate the definition to the developers. If this knowledge is precoded in the support environment, the communication act does not have to be carried out explicitly by the users but can be carried out by the support environment as soon as the requirement is defined. Similarly, the users can subscribe to events. For example, if someone has subscribed to the event Change Bt X, every time someone else changes basic template X, that person can be informed of the change. Our group is pursuing efforts in this direction. ❖

References

1. R. Balzer, "Living in the Next-Generation Operating System," *IEEE Software*, Nov. 1987, pp. 77-85.
2. K. Naryanaswamy and W. Scacchi, "Maintaining Configurations of Evolving Software Systems," *IEEE Trans. Software Eng.*, March 1987, pp. 324-334.
3. P. Garg and W. Scacchi, "Ishys: Designing an Intelligent Hypertext System," *IEEE Expert*, Fall 1989, pp. 52-62.
4. W. Scacchi, "The System Factory Approach to Large-Scale Software Engineering," *Proc. MCC University Research Symp.*, Microelectronics and Computer Technology Corp., Austin, Texas, 1987.

Acknowledgments

We thank Salah Bendifallah for extensive comments on earlier versions of this article and the design of DIF. Comments from the anonymous reviewers have clarified some misconceptions and helped improve the presentation. We thank Amitabh Agrawal and John Leggett for their comments on the article. We thank Abdulaziz Jazzar for his contributions to DIF. We acknowledge the contribution of all those people who helped develop and use DIF in the system-factory class at USC in the 1985-86 and 1986-87 academic years.

The work reported here has been supported by AT&T through research grants and contracts, Hughes Radar Systems Group under contract KSR576195-SN8, Pacific Bell, and Eastman Kodak. Garg was also supported in part by the USC graduate school through the All-University Predoctoral Merit Fellowship.

Address questions about this article to Garg at Hewlett-Packard Laboratories, 1501 Page Mill Rd., Palo Alto, CA 94303; Internet garg@ hplabs.hp.com.

SODOS: A Software Documentation Support Environment—Its Definition

ELLIS HORQWITZ AND RONALD C. WILLIAMSON

Abstract—This paper describes the data abstraction mechanisms used in SODOS (Software Documentation Support), a computerized system which supports the definition and manipulation of documents used in developing software. Our purpose is to show the generic definition of a document, to define precisely the operations of consistency, completeness, and traceability, and finally to show how the generic document and associated operations are mapped onto the relational model. The SODOS system differs from others in that it is built on top of a database management system (DBMS) and an object-based model of the Software Life Cycle (SLC). One advantage of this model is that it supports software documentation *independent* of any fixed methodology that the developers may be using. Another advantage of the system is that it permits *traceability* through all phases of the Software Life Cycle, thus facilitating the testing and maintenance phases. In this paper we define the document representation in terms of a graph model mapped into a relational data model.

Index Terms—Database, documentation, object programming, Smalltalk-80, software.

I. INTRODUCTION

SODOS (Software Documentation Support) is a computerized environment which supports the definition and manipulation of documents used in developing software. The central idea is to have all information generated at the specification and development phases available to the maintenance personnel in a complete, structured, and traceable form. The environment differs from others [1]–[10] in that it is built on top of a database management system (DBMS) and an object-based model of the Software Life Cycle (SLC). In this paper we present the data abstraction mechanisms used in SODOS. The document representation is described in terms of a tree structured model and the associated operations are defined accordingly. For a user oriented view of SODOS see [12] and for a discussion of its implementation see [13].

The process of developing software involves refinement of an abstract definition of a problem solution into an implementation of the solution. First, from the initial concept of the solution a set of requirements are developed.

The requirements are then decomposed function by function with a definition of the data and processing requirements for each function. The realization of each function begins with a modular decomposition of the major functions, then data structures and algorithms are developed for each function. The data structure definitions and the algorithms are next translated into a computer processible description. This description is then debugged and functionally tested producing a validated implementation.

The model we use of the software development process consists of a sequence of temporal phases each dependent on the other. There is continual feedback among all of the phases leading to a cyclic structure. We refer to this sequence as the Software Life Cycle [14]. The SLC definition used for our research consists of seven phases:

1) Conceptual/System Requirements Definition phase
2) Functional Requirements phase
3) Architectural or Preliminary Design phase
4) Implementation phase
5) Integration and Test phase
6) Maintenance phase
7) Configuration Management.

We assume that each phase in the SLC overlaps considerably. The information produced at the Requirement Specification phase is accessed through to the final Test and Integration phase. The design documents are referred to up to and including the Implementation and Maintenance phases. The information needed to manage the effort grows continuously throughout the SLC.

Viewing the development of software as an information management problem, the solution used in SODOS is to define all information entering the system to be part of a structured database. The information and the relationships with other information in the system is entered into the database and is structured according to the predefined model of the SLC.

In SODOS, the descriptions from each SLC phase are organized and managed as structured documents. The document is represented, not as a sequential file but as a complex object with an internal structure and well defined relationships with other objects in the SLC model. The set of objects and the relationships among the objects are analyzed using a formal graph model. The graph model provides a means by which we can define basic SLC operations that we consider important. The operations studied in this context include document structure consist-

Manuscript received December 28, 1984; revised January 31, 1986. This work was supported in part by the Hughes Aircraft Company Fellowship Program and by the Air Force Office of Scientific Research under Grant 82-0232.

E. Horowitz is with the Department of Computer Science, University of Southern California, Los Angeles, CA 90089.

R. C. Williamson was with the Department of Computer Science, University of Southern California, Los Angeles, CA 90089. He is now with Hughes Aircraft Company, Software Engineering Division, AI Technology Department, El Segundo, CA 90245.

IEEE Log Number 8607942.

ency, document completeness, and document traceability. These operations and the document representation itself are defined in more detail in later sections.

II. Modeling the SLC to Determine the Documentation Requirements

The method we use to determine the information or documentation requirements for the SLC involves building a model of the SLC. The model consists of

1) the objects,
2) the attributes of the objects,
3) the relationships among the objects, and
4) the set of actions, called the behavior, performed on the objects.

The first three components represent the static nature of the SLC and the behavior represent the dynamic interaction within the SLC.

The objects in the system are models of reality and when they exist they have a set of properties, and the objects may be created, destroyed, or modified by changing their properties. The objects with similar properties are grouped in sets called *classes*. When objects are created, we say that we have created an instance of a class within which the object is defined. When objects are destroyed we delete all references to the instance and the data values are released.

The class defines a set of operations that can be performed on the objects, and a set of data values within the object. The operations and data values are defined for both the object class and the instances of the class. For example, we can view a document as an instance of a document class, and a subset of the operations which can be performed on the document is: modify, delete, copy, and print. The attributes can either be pointers to other objects or descriptions of the kind of information the object holds. The attributes along with the operations form the properties of the objects. The attributes are defined at the class level and each instance inherits the attributes definition of the class. The attribute definition within the class basically form a data template, each instance when created defines the values of the attributes within the template.

The relationships connect the objects within the model based on the semantic context. For example, a system requirement is related to a functional requirement by the "derived from" relationship. The functional requirement in turn is related to a design module by the "required by" relationship. These relationships are categorized as

1) 1-1
2) 1-many (possibly null).

The 1-1 relationship is the simplest. It defines a correspondence between a unique pair of instances. For example, if one person is responsible for writing a document, then there is a relationship between one AUTHOR instance and the instance of the document. This relationship is 1-1. The 1-1 relationship is used to define subsets within the environment. In the above example, the author

or authors of the document is a subset of all the authors in the environment.

The 1-many relationship defines a correspondence between one object instance and a set of object instances. For example, the Preliminary User Manual (PUM) contains a reference to a set of user commands. The instance of the PUM is related to a set of command description instances in the COMMAND object. The 1-many relationship is also used to define hierarchies within the environment. For example, a document is structured in terms of chapters, sections, and components. This structure forms a natural hierarchy that is represented as a set of 1-many relationships, i.e., a 1-many relationship between the section and the components contained in the section.

III. Document Representation

The primary uses of documentation in software development projects are management reporting and communication among project personnel. The documentation usually takes the form of memos, notes, tutorials, formal documents, manuals, and the source code and associated data. At each phase of the SLC a set of formal documents is produced that describes the analysis and activities of that phase. A companion paper describes the interface to SODOS that allows creation, updating, deletion and querying of the SLC documents. The purpose of this section is to present and discuss the definition and representation of the SLC documents.

A. Defining Documents

In SODOS each of the SLC documents are represented as instances of a DOCUMENT class such as that categorized as in Fig. 1. Each subclass of the DOCUMENT class provides a template to construct an instance of the document. This template consists of the type of the information to be stored in each specific kind of document, its structure, the operations that may be performed on the document and the relationships between the document and other documents in the current SLC phase or other phases. It is the responsibility of a Document Administrator on each project to determine the appropriate document definitions based on the project standards and guidelines. The definition of each document may be taken from existing standard document structures or may have to be defined anew. The Document Administrator defines a new document by subclassing (inserting) the new document definition within an existing document class, such as the Requirement Document class, and describes the structure and interrelationships of the documents using a set of relational schemas.

Once the document classes have been defined and the database of document classes have been loaded the individual system engineers, designers and programmers create new documents by instantiating the appropriate document class. An instance of the DOCUMENT class has a general structure as shown in Fig. 2. A standard structure is used consisting of sections, appendixes, components, and figures. The components consist of text and keywords

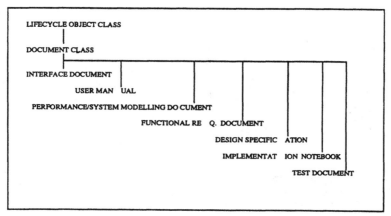

Fig. 1. The software life cycle object class.

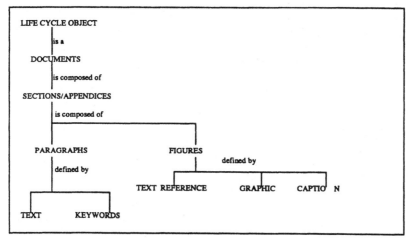

Fig. 2. The DOCUMENT class.

and the figures consist of a text reference, a graphic, and a caption. Composing the documents consists of creating instances of each of these components. Each document instance is represented internally as a set of relations that form the view of the document. The document is the union of these relations and does not exist as a text file elsewhere. Specific subclasses of the DOCUMENT class for each phase of the SLC are described in more detail in later sections.

Creating an instance of a document adds an entry to the DOCUMENT relation that maintains a collection of all the documents in the system. The columns of the DOCUMENT relation are the attributes of each document instance. The "instance" attribute references the instance of the document that maintains another set of relations representing the structure and content of the document. Fig. 3 illustrates the DOCUMENT relation in the context of representing a subset of the software system hierarchy. In the DOCUMENT relation each document has an entry that consists of its document identification, the document title, its type or class, the revision identification, the date last updated, the document's author(s), a status (new, incomplete, under review, complete, approved), and the

document instance. Each document instance is represented internally as a set of STRUCTURE, TEXT, FIGURE, and KEYWORD relations.

B. Document Structure

Documents are structured by a sectional hierarchy with each section containing a sequence of components and figures. For example, each instance of a User Manual subclass may be structured by the sections:

Section 1.0	—Introduction
Section 2.0	—Commands
Section 3.0	—Error Recovery
Section 4.0	—Performance Monitoring
References	—a table
Appendix A	—Commands sorted by function
Appendix B	—Commands sorted alphabetically

The subclass definition of User Manual contains a description of this structure in terms of a relational schema. The schema represents the hierarchical and sequential relationships among the components, that is sections, components, and figures, of the document. Fig. 3 shows the

219

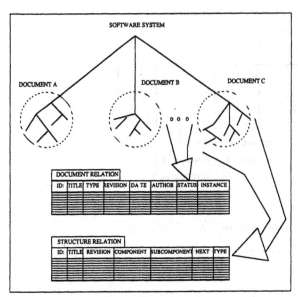

Fig. 3. Representing document instances and document structure.

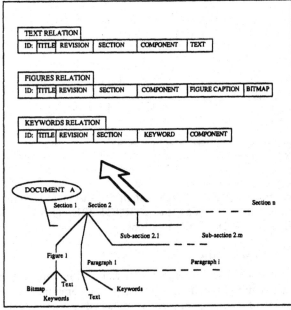

Fig. 4. Representing document content.

STRUCTURE relation in correspondence with the hierarchical nature of the document structure.

C. Document Content

The relations, which represent the content of a document, are also contained in the class definition of the document. The content consists of the text for each component, the set of keywords associated with the text, and the graphics, text reference, and caption associated with each figure. Fig. 4 shows the content relations as they relate to the hierarchical structure of the document. The text of the document is maintained in the TEXT relation which

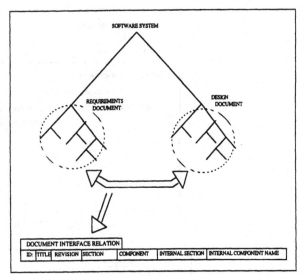

Fig. 5. Representing document interfaces.

maintains the association between the document identification, document title component name, and the component text. The component text itself consists of a set of paragraphs.

The figures in the document are represented by a FIGURE relation that maintains the association between the document identification, document title, figure name, the text reference, the figure caption, and the figure's graphics.

The associations between keywords and the components or figures are also maintained as part of the content schema. The KEYWORD relation includes the keyword, the component name, and the document structure attributes.

D. Interrelating Documents

The documents are associated with each other based on predefined relationships which depend on the semantic context of the documents. For example, a system requirement is related to a functional requirement by the "derived-from" relationship. The functional requirement in turn is related to a design module by the "required-by" relationship.

Each Document class and subclass contains a schema that defines the relationships of each document instance with other document instances. Fig. 5 shows the relation that represents the interface among the documents. The simplest relationship represented is that between components. Continuing the example above, a component in a Functional Requirements document may define a specific requirement. This requirement is related to Design document components, both components and figures, which define the design modules and the module structure. The design module descriptions are in turn related to the code that implements the requirement. The code is also organized hierarchically and each piece of code is mapped into a structural component which is related back to the original requirement.

220

IV. A Formal Description of the Document Representation

A formal graph model, as defined in [15], is used to define the structure of each document and the relationships among the components of the documents. In the SODOS representation the graph structure is mapped into the Relational Data Model [16], and all of the graph operations are mapped into an extension of the standard relational algebra operations. The extension consists of graph traversal, clipping, pruning, and updating operations defined using the relational algebra in combination with the implementation languages control structures. Three additional operations that check consistency, completeness, and traceability of the documents are formally defined for the graph model and are also mapped into a set of extended relational algebra based operations. These operations are described in detail in R. Williamson's dissertation [11].

A. Document Graph Model Definition

The graph model for the set of documents used in the Software Life Cycle consists of a representation of the structure, content, and interrelationships of all the documents. Each node in the graph represents a component of each document, such as a requirement, a design module, a segment of code, or a test description. Each arc in the graph represents a relationship among the components, such as structural association, a requirement to design a module association or a design module to code segment association. We will call this type of association, a structure link. (In SODOS the structure links are entered by the user.) Traversal through the graph is made in order to search for information satisfying queries against the document components, to check completeness of the structure of the documents, or to check for consistency of the document structure or the relationships among each document's components.

The formal representation of the documents as a graph is now presented.

Definition: A graph G is defined as $G = (N, A)$ where

N is a set of nodes $\{n_1, n_2, \cdots\}$ and

A is a set of arcs $\{a_1, a_2, \cdots\}$;

where each arc a_i is incident to an unordered arc $\{a, b\}$, $a, b \subset N$.

Definition: A path is defined as a sequence of arcs a_1, $a_2, \cdots$ such that

1) a_i and a_{i+1} have a common endpoint, and
2) both end nodes of a_i are not the same node and if a_i is not the first or last arc then it has one of its end nodes in common with a_{i-1}, and the other end node with a_{i+1}.

For our present purposes we define a document instance D as follows.

Definition: A *document graph structure* is a graph

$$D = (N, A = (A_N, A_S))$$

where A is composed of two disjoint sets of edges, A_N, A_S, where $A = (A_N \cup A_S)$. Each element of N represents

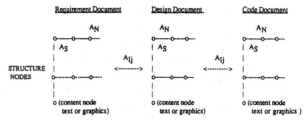

Fig. 6. The documents graph.

the components of the document and each element of A represents the structure links.

The elements of A_N represent the sequence or "next component" links and the elements of A_S represent the hierarchy or "subcomponent" links. The documentation used in the SODOS1 environment consists of a collection of SLC documents. Each document is related to another based on the association between the individual components of the document. Components of a document correspond to the nodes in the document graph representation D and the structure of the document is represented by the arcs A which form the document tree. The structure of the document must be consistent with the document class definition and since each document is built within the framework of SODOS the documents would normally be inherently consistent. However, in converting documents, which were generated outside of the SODOS environment, to the SODOS framework the structural consistency must be checked. Determining structural consistency of the document involves showing connectedness and searching for circuits within the graph (from [15, p. 22]). The consistency operation is discussed in the next section. Each node of the document must have a path through the A_S nodes to a node that has a "content" attribute. This means that every component in a final document must have some graphic or text associated with it, otherwise the document is incomplete. The check for completeness involves searching through each node and finding a "subcomponent" path leading to a component that is either text or a figure. The completeness operation is also discussed in the next section.

The associations between document components connect each of the document graph structures such that the collection of the structures are transformed into a single connected graph. The definition of the resulting directed graph F (shown in Fig. 6) is as follows.

Definition: A collection of *document graph structures* is a forest,

$$F = (N, A = (A_N \cup A_S \cup A_{I1} \cup A_{I2} \cup \cdots \cup A_{Im}))$$

where N, A_N, and A_S are defined as before and A_{Ij} are arcs representing the interrelationships among the document components.

Querying and updating a set of related documents involves traversing the graph representation of all documents based on selected arcs. The definition and analysis of the query operation are presented in the next section.

B. Document Graph Model Operations

Accessing and validating the documents in SODOS gives rise to several ways of traversing through the directed graph representation of the set of documents. Four classes of operations are now defined and discussed: determination of consistency, verification of completeness, traceability, and the query operation.

The graph representation of the document instance structure S is defined as being *structure-consistent* as follows.

Definition: A graph $S = (N, A = (A_N, A_S))$ is *structure-consistent* iff there exists a node n_r in N such that there is a unique path with arcs in A to every node in N from n_r (i.e., S is a directed tree).

To verify that a graph representation of a document is *structure-consistent* the result in is used. This result states that to determine if a graph S is a directed tree, it must be shown that:

The underlying undirected graph is connected and S has one node n_r which has no incoming arcs, and all other nodes have exactly one incoming arc.

To check *structure-consistency* of the document structure graph involves determining if the root node for the document exists. Next the graph is searched to determine that there is exactly one incoming structure arc for each component node. The search through the document graph is restricted to only the structure arcs contained in the sets, A_S and A_N.

The graph representation of the document instance structure S is defined as being *structure-complete* as follows.

Definition: A graph $S = (N, A = (A_N, A_S))$ is *structure-complete* iff S is *structure-consistent* and for every component node in N there exists a path P to a component node in N, which has a "content," where "content" is an attribute of the components meaning either text or a figure graphic.

To check *structure-completeness* of the document structure graph, basically works as follows. A set of all document components is initially defined. The CONTENT and STRUCTURE relation tables are then searched for matching components. When a structure component has a match with a content component the component is deleted from the document component set. For each remaining component, we search for a path of length two, using the subcomponent arcs, which connects the original component to a component matching a content component. If such a path is found the component is deleted from remaining set of document components.

The graph representation W of the collection of software documents' instance structure and component interrelationships is defined as follows.

Definition: Let $W = (N, A = (A_N, A_S, A_{N1}, A_{N2}, \cdots, A_{Nm}))$ be a graph. A document W_{doc1}, a subgraph of W, is defined as *traceable* with respect to W_{doc2}, a subgraph of W, iff for every content component node, n_{doc1} in W_{doc1}, there exists a path P_i containing arcs in A_{Ni} to a content component node, n_{doc2} in W_{doc2} and also there exists a path P_j containing arcs in A_{Nj} from n_{doc2} to n_{doc1}.

The *traceability* relationship among components is an equivalence relation that partitions both documents into equivalence classes. Each component satisfying the traceability relation is a member of an equivalence class. The equivalence classes consisting of a single content component node represent those nodes, which are not traceable, and the remaining equivalence classes represent the traceable components.

To determine *traceability* of the graphs representing a pair of software documents and the component interrelationships, the sets of content components and interrelationship arcs for each of two documents are maintained during the search of both document graphs. Each content component is matched as an endpoint to one or more of the interrelationship arcs. If their is a match in both interrelationship sets the content component is added with the related component to a set representing the equivalence class of related components. If no match or a match in only one document is found the component is tagged as a nontraceable component within a degenerate equivalence class.

A *query* Q_E, against the graph W, and with the query expression E, is defined as follows.

Definition:

Q_E = the set of components contained in the path.

$P = \{a_i | a_i$ is in A and the end nodes of a_i satisfying the expression $E\}$.

A structure query traverses only the arcs contained in A_S and A_N. A traceability query traverses the arcs A_{Ni} across documents and the arcs A_S within the documents. The maximum cost of a given query is the sum of the weights assigned to each type of arc within a query path. Specific queries are addressed in [11].

V. MAPPING A GENERIC DOCUMENT ONTO THE RELATIONAL MODEL

Software requirement, specification and development documents include both structured and loosely structured data related in a hierarchical manner. The pure Relational Model does not fully support

1) loosely structured information, such as outline formatted text,

2) tree representation and tree traversal operations, or

3) complex structural operations, such as comparing similarity.

Our goal here is to describe the mapping of generic document characteristics onto an extended Relational Model. This model provides an information structure which is powerful enough to represent hierarchies and support complex structural operations while maintaining the benefits of the Relational Model. In addition, the structure is flexible enough to represent the loosely structured textual information, e.g., requirement specifications, module descriptions, module structure descriptions, procedures, expressions, and data values. This section concerns the representation of such information in a structured, hierarchical relational form.

The interaction with this structure involves a set of questions, commands or queries which entails searching through the structure to find or modify specific life cycle objects. For example, we may want to find

1) all subfunctions of a given function,

2) all design modules which satisfy a given function,

3) all procedures in a given module which have a given data object as input or output,

4) a set of tests related to a given function and the results of those tests.

Software system design is structured according to the mechanism used to manage the software development project. Several documents are produced during the development process which describe the system to be developed at various stages of conceptualization.

The requirement document is the basis for the design specification document and this document in turn forms the basis for the implementation's documentation. The design is structured hierarchically with the system design split into several modules. Each module is further broken down into design submodules and each submodule represents a set of procedures or functions. At each stage data types, values and the data flow among the components is defined. Each module and submodule is assigned an import/export list which defines the inputs and outputs of the unit. Both this structure and the dataflow is represented in the information structure.

A. Definition of the Structure

The basic kinds of information found in the Software Life Cycle phases are statements, keywords, simple data types (such as character strings, numeric), complex objects (abstract data types), graphical structures, etc. Attributes of this information must also be maintained, e.g., the relationships among the set of requirement's statements, keywords and data specifications and corresponding design information.

The optimum representation at each phase is one in which the data are accessed most efficiently. However, if each phase uses a different representation, very little sharing or traceability of information can take place. In addition such issues as consistency and integrity of information among phases is not adequately addressed.

The extended Relational Model structure proposed here is a set of relations $R = (R_1, R_2, \cdots, R_n)$. Each relation has m columns with each column having a Domain D_j. The instances of the domains may be simple data types or another life cycle structure, i.e., another set of relations. The definition of such a structure is recursive in the sense that a life cycle structure is defined in terms of life cycle structures. Traversing such a structure involves recursive operations. The structure then resembles a tree-like representation in a relational form. The recursive operations must be added to the relational algebra to provide adequate traversal through the tree structure.

The tree structure is represented in the relations by two related columns which define the links in the tree. A tree node corresponds to a row in the relation and the node's father link is defined by an entry in the appropriate column. A tree is defined by specifying which two columns in the relation are to define the structure. The columns must be updated with the tree structure in mind.

The tree structure can be represented in this manner but additional operations are required to effectively traverse and update the tree structure. The set of operations, not shown to be complete at this stage, are as follows:

1) Define new tree structure on an existing relation.

2) Specify which columns define the tree structure.

3) Start a query at a specified node and traverse the subtree.

4) Prune the tree structure.

5) Clip the tree structure (copy a subtree and delete).

6) Copy the tree structure (copy a subtree with no deletion).

Defining a new tree structure on an existing relation involves expanding the relation with at least one column with entries related to an existing column. This requires updating the new column entries with values based on values in the existing column entry.

Pruning the tree structure is represented in the corresponding relation by deletion of a set of tuples which represent the subtree to be pruned. Clipping the tree structure involves the same operation as pruning on the original relation with the resulting tuples forming a new relation representing the clipped subtree. The root of the clipped subtree must be distinguished in the resulting relation by inserting the nil value in the appropriate column. Copying the tree structure is similar to clipping but with no deletion in the original relation.

B. The Relational Database Representation

This section describes a conceptual relational database management system extension to the Smalltalk-80 environment. The Smalltalk-80 environment is extended to include functions for creation, deletion, updating, and querying of relational data structures. The content of a specific database is defined by a set of relations structured according to a formal definition or schema. The structure follows from Rochkind's [20] work in extending the Unix Operating System, S. Weyl's work [21] in extending Interlisp with a database support system, and Baroody and DeWitt's work [22] in defining an approach to an object oriented database implementation.

We chose to design to the Relational Model to illustrate and take advantage of the data abstraction mechanisms of the Smalltalk-80 language and to take advantage of the Relational Model's simplicity and concise nonprocedural set of operators.

The relational DBMS extension is partitioned into two functional areas:

1) the conceptual database system (Conceptual Level), and

2) the database file system (Internal Level).

The conceptual database system performs the following functions:
1) Relational data model definition,
2) Query/Update interface, and
3) Management of the relationships and constraints.

The conceptual database models (e.g., Network, Hierarchical, Relational) [23] vary in the way the information is defined, accessed, interrelated, and managed. This is reflected in the operations defined in implementing each model.

The database file system performs the following functions:
1) Stores individual records or pages,
2) Implements the access method,
3) Controls access to the records or pages,
4) Management of primary and secondary keys, and
5) Journals the updates to enable recovery after a system crash.

The database file system supports any of the conceptual database models such as Relational [19], hierarchical [23], network [23], entity-relationship, or event model [24]. At this point in the research we are investigating the conceptual level interface to the relations from the SODOS system. Access to the file system is abstracted in the present research, but the design and implementation of the access itself involves other difficult research problems.

One major problem not addressed in our research is that of mapping the complex Smalltalk object structure onto the secondary access storage. When storing an instance of a Smalltalk-80 class in a tuple of a relation, the main memory representation within each column domain is a reference to the object pointer. The object itself resides in main memory. In order to design the database file system to support the storage of objects, a complex mapping must be made between the internal object representation and the sequential nature of secondary access storage. Research at Xerox Corporation [17], [18] focused on the mapping of objects residing in main memory onto secondary storage. This research involves a large virtual object memory spanning main memory and secondary storage media.

1) The DATABASE Class: The Database management system and the file system consist of a reference to a new Smalltalk-80 Class: DATABASE. Each Database is a particular subclass of a FileStream class. Each set of relations is assumed to be part of an instance of the Class DATABASE. This will be explained in detail in the following sections. The FileStream class performs the actual transfer of a byte stream organized in pages to the physical storage medium.

The DATABASE class consists of a message protocol or set of functional capabilities and a directory for manipulating and managing the physical storage of the individual relations in the database. Each relation defined within the Database can be represented at the conceptual level in at least two ways. A relation may be
1) An instance of the Class: RELATION, or
2) A subclass of the Class: RELATION with tuples of the relation being instances of the subclass.

The choice of either of the above representation affects the internal storage representation of the relation and the message structure for creating and modifying the relation at the conceptual level. Examples of the first approach will be presented here and is used in the design. Each relation subclass or instance has a message protocol for combining, accessing and updating the information stored in the relation.

When viewing a relation as an instance of the Class RELATION, each relation (e.g., the STUDENT relation in a student database example) is created by sending the Class RELATION the message template

new: #(list of attribute or column names)

Tuples or rows in the relation are created by sending the relation the message

addtuple: # (list of values)
or
union : aRelation

2) The Conceptual Database System Design: The conceptual level and the model at that level is an abstract representation of the information in a database. There are several definitions of a conceptual model of a database. The one used here is the Relational Model definition of C. J. Date [23]; we define *"the Relational Model of a database as a user's view of that database as a collection of time varying, normalized relations of assorted degrees"* where a relation has a very specific definition. A relation is a set of n-tuples where n is the degree of the relation. Each element in the tuple belongs to a predefined domain or data type and each tuple in the relation is unique with respect to that relation. An identification of a tuple or a set of tuples is called the "key." A "key" which uniquely identifies an individual tuple can be a "primary key" and a "key" and a "key" which identifies a set of tuples is called a "secondary key." In the Smalltalk-80 design of a Relational conceptual model the Class RELATION is a subclass of the Class COLLECTION, predefined within the language. As a subclass a relation inherits all of the COLLECTION operations and characteristics. Additional operations must be defined for the Class RELATION to override or create new functions for the special characteristics of the relation.

The data model is defined in terms of a schema, where the schema is a definition of the information content of the database. The relational schema includes a definition of
1) Domains
2) Relations
3) Constraints.
Domains are defined in terms of data types such as integer, character string, floating point, fixed point, or any other abstract data type. Relations are defined in terms of a ordered tuple of column names and column domains. The constraints are defined as restrictions against relations and/or domains.

In the Smalltalk-80 model of the Relational Database, each instance of the DATABASE Class is a set of schemas, and domains. The schema in turn is a set of relations and definitions. We create a schema as follows.

schema__name ← userDatabase schema:
                    #(set of relation instances).

The userDatabase is an instance of the DATABASE class and keeps track of the schemas and the relations defined within the schema, schema__name. A domain is created by

domain__name ← userDatabase domain:6aDataType.

A Relation class definition in the Smalltalk-80 model consists of
1) a collection of tuples;
2) internal representation of
       number of columns,
       column names,
       column domains,
       key fields;
3) a set of integrity and consistency constraints;
4) a storage structure representation;
5) an access method; and
6) a physical storage representation.

The Smalltalk-80 expressions for creating instances of relations involve messages which define the column names, domains, keys, new tuples to be added to the relation and/or a sequential input file. The expressions take the form:

Relation new: #('name1' 'name2' · · ·)
       domain: #(a set of domain names).

"The following expression assumes the domain associated with the values 'val1' etc."

(Relation new: #('name1' 'name2' · · ·))
                       addTuple: #('val1' 'val2'
                       · · ·).

(Relation new: #('name1' 'name2' · · ·))
   primaryKey:#(a set of column names)
                       "if not specified or the set of column names is empty a default primary key is used."
   secondaryKey: #(a set of column names).
           domain: #(a set of domain names).

Relation readFrom: 'input.file'.
                       "The 'input file' contains the number of columns, column names column domains, key fields, and the tuple values."

The result of the above expressions is a relation instance which may be assigned a variable name as follows.

relation__instance ← Relation readFrom: 'input.file'.

In addition to the definition and creation operations, operators are necessary to
1) list schemas within a database:

userDatabase listSchemas. "Smalltalk-80 expression"

2) list relations within a schema or database:

userDatabase listRelations. "Smalltalk-80 expression"
or
userDatabase listrelations: aSchemaName.

3) list definitions of relations:

userDatabase listRelationDefinitions: #(a set of relation names).

4) list definitions of domains:

userDatabase listDomainDefinitions: #(a set of domains).

Relation instance messages modify, retrieve, store, and create new tuples within the relation and perform set and relational functions on the relation instances. The set and relational operators include union, intersect, difference, select, project, and join. The set operators are binary operators and require that both relation arguments be of the same degree and each corresponding column must be over the same domain. In the following expressions "rel" "rel__union" "rel__intersect" "rel__minus" "rel__select" "rel__project" "rel__equijoin" are all references to instances of relations.

The union of two relations is the set of all tuples belonging to either to either or both relations. The Smalltalk-80 union: message sent to a relation instance with a relation instance as an argument takes the form

rel__union ← rel union: aRelation.

where aRelation can be a relation instance variable, a relation instance expression, or any other nested set/relational operator expression.

The intersection of two relations is the set of all tuples belonging to both relations. The Smalltalk-80 intersect: message sent to a relation instance with a relation instance as an argument takes the form

rel__intersect ← rel intersect: aRelation.

The difference of two relations is the set of all tuples belonging to one relation and not the other. The Smalltalk-80 minus: message sent to a relation instance with a relation instance as an argument takes the form

rel__minus ← rel minus: aRelation.

The combination of the union: and minus: messages allows updating of a relation. We add the "**update: to: where:**" message for convenience.

rel__update ← rel update: #(a set of column names)
                       to: #(a set of corresponding values)
                       where:[a predicate on any of the column values].

The "**update:**" template takes a list of column names and associates it with the "**to:**" template's list of new values. The "**where:**" template contains a predicate on values in the relation and selects a set of tuples to which the "**update: to:**" template arguments are applied.

The relational operators are also implemented in the extended Smalltalk-80 system. The form of the expressions follows that of the relational algebra and allows nesting of relational operations.

The select operation returns a relation which contains a subset of the tuples in the original relation satisfying a predicate on the values of the specified columns in the relation. The Smalltalk-80 expression takes the form

rel__select ← rel select: [a predicate].

The project operator returns a relation which contains a subset of the columns of the original relation. The Smalltalk-80 expression takes the form

rel__project ← rel project: #(a set of column names).

Several joins can be defined based on the comparison operation used =, #, <, >, <=, >=. We implement the equijoin here (i.e., using the = comparator). The equijoin returns a relation based on the equality of values in corresponding columns in two relations. The corresponding columns in each relation must be defined over the same domain. The Smalltalk-80 expression takes the form

rel__equijoin ← rel equijoin: aRelation
over: aColumnName.

3) The Database and Relation Object Classes: The Class **Database**, which is a subclass of the Smalltalk-80 system class **Object**, contains all the operations necessary to define and manage new schemas and domains at the conceptual level. The mechanism used to manage the relations is the Data Dictionary which is keyed by relation and maintains the definition of each relation and its mapping onto secondary storage. The internal model of the database requires operations to define and maintain primary and secondary keys on each relation, and operations to access the physical database. The messages to the instances of the Class Database for conceptual level functions include the following.

1) schema: defines a new schema as a set of relations.

2) domain: defines a new domain as a specific data type.

3) listRelations: lists all relations and their column names and dom.

4) listSchemas: lists all schemas and the relations they represent.

5) listDomains: lists all domains and the data types they represent.

Messages associated with the internal model functions include the following.

- PutRecord: aRecord atKey: akey in: aFile—adding a record to physical storage.

- GetRecordAt: aKey in: aFile—retrieving a record from the physical storage.
- DeleteRecordAt: aKey in: aFile—deleting a record from the physical storage.
- GetNextRecordIn: aFile.
- OpenFile: aFile.
- CloseFile: aFile.
- SavedFile: aFile—opens and closes aFile.
- IsKey: aKey in: aFile—determines if the key provided is valid for this file.
- FileStatus: aFile—returns whether the file is open or closed.

The relation data structure was implemented as a separate class **Relation** as a subclass of the Smalltalk-80 system class, **Collection**. The internal representation for the tuples resident in main memory is a set of dictionaries, or keyed tables. The "Primary Dictionary" and "Secondary Dictionaries" maintain the cross references between the tuple contents, the primary key and the secondary keys associated with each relation. Each tuple is represented as an instance of the **Tuple** class which is a subclass of the Smalltalk-80 system class, **OrderedCollection**. The mapping of the main memory resident and secondary storage resident tuples is performed by the Database class which maintains the data dictionary for all of the **Relation** class instances.

VI. CONCLUSIONS

The objective of SODOS is to combine object oriented representation and database technology with a "user-friendly" interface to produce an integrated software development environment that significantly decreases software life cycle costs. The main focus of this paper is the representation of a document as a complex object with SODOS. The document is stored as a set of structured components within an extended relational data model context. The components and the relationships among the components can then be queried without significantly burdening the software documentation process. We provided a formal definition of *consistency*, *completeness*, and *traceability* of the software documentation.

REFERENCES

[1] B. W. Boehm, "Software engineering—As it is," in *Proc. 4th Int. Conf. Software Eng.*, 1979, pp. 11–21.
[2] M. S. Deutsch, "An industrial software engineering methodology supported by an automated environment," in *Proc. Nat. Comput. Conf.*, 1982, vol. 51, 1982, pp. 301–307.
[3] H. L. Hausen, and M. Mullerburg, "Conspectus of software engineering environments," in *Software Development Environments: A Tutorial*. Washington, DC: IEEE Comput. Soc. Press, 1981, pp. 462–476.
[4] A. I. Wasserman, "Tutorial: Software development environments," in *Proc. COMPSAC 1981, IEEE Comput. Soc.*, EHO 187-5.
[5] W. E. Howden, "Contemporary software development environments," *Commun. ACM*, vol. 25, no. 5, pp. 318–329, 1982.
[6] R. W. Mitze, "The UNIX system as a software engineering environment," *Software Eng. Environments*, pp. 345–357, 1981.
[7] P. S. Newman, "Towards an integrated development environment," *IBM Syst. J.*, vol. 21, no. 1, pp. 81–107, 1982.
[8] T. A. Standish, "The importance of Ada programming support en-

vironments,'' in *Proc. Nat. Comput. Conf.*, vol. 51, 1982, pp. 333–339.

[9] V. Stenning *et al.*, ''The Ada environment: A perspective,'' *Computer*, vol. 6, pp. 26–36, 1981.

[10] M. Bayer *et al.*, ''Software development in the CDL2 laboratory,'' Technische Universitat, Berlin, Germany, Tech. Rep., 1981.

[11] R. Williamson, ''SODOS—A software documentation support environment,'' Doctoral dissertation, Dep. Comput. Sci., Univ. Southern California, Los Angeles, pp. 1-210, 1984.

[12] E. Horowitz and R. Williamson, ''SODOS—Its use,'' Dep. Comput. Sci., Univ. Southern California, Los Angeles, Tech. Paper TR-84-313, pp. 1-30, 1984.

[13] —, ''SODOS—Its implementation,'' Dep. Comput. Sci., Univ. California, Los Angeles, Tech. Paper TR-84-315, pp. 1–40, 1984.

[14] A. I. Wasserman, ''Toward integrated software development environments,'' in *Proc. Int. Seminar Software Eng., Applications*, 1980, pp. 1–21.

[15] S. Even, *Graph Algorithms*. Rockville, MD: Computer Science Press, 1979.

[16] E. F. Codd, ''A relational model for large shared data banks,'' *Commun. ACM*, vol. 13, no. 1, pp. 377–385, 1970.

[17] A. Goldberg, *Smalltalk-80: The Language and its Implementation*. Reading, MA: Addison-Wesley, 1983.

[18] —, ''Smalltalk-80: The interactive programming environment,'' Xerox Corp., Tech. Rep., 1982.

[19] E. F. Codd, ''A relational model for large shared data banks,'' *Commun. ACM*, vol. 3, pp. 377–385, 1970.

[20] M. J. Rochkind, ''Structure of a database file system for the UNIX operating system,'' *Bell Syst. Tech. J.*, vol. 61, pp. 2387–2405, 1982.

[21] S. Weyl, ''An Interlisp relational data base system,'' Stanford Res. Inst., Tech. Note, pp. 1–35, 1975.

[22] A. J. Baroody and D. J. DeWitt, ''An object-oriented approach to database system implementation,'' *ACM Trans. Database Syst.*, pp. 576–601, 1981.

[23] C. J. Date, *An Introduction to Database Systems*. Reading, MA: Addison-Wesley, 1977.

[24] D. McLeod and R. King, ''The event model,'' Univ. Southern California, Los Angeles, Tech. Rep., 1982.

Traceability Based on Design Decisions

A. Cimitile(*), F. Lanubile(**), and G. Visaggio(**)

(*) Dipartimento di Informatica e
Sistemistica, University of Naples,
via Claudio 21, 80125, Naples, Italy
fax: +39/81/7683186

(**) Dipartimento di Informatica,
University of Bari,
via G.Amendola 173, 70126, Bari, Italy
fax: +39/80/243196 email:giuvis@vm.csata.it

Abstract[1]

In this paper, we model the different points of view which exist on a software structure as distinct conceptual models. The mapping among models of the same software structure is made through the assumption of design decisions. We represent these mapping as a graph, the model dependency descriptor, which connects components of source models with those in the target models. A traceability relation is set between components by making the transitive closure of the model dependency descriptor. The traceability relation which we propose links objects and also tracks decisions having a role in the transformation.

A Traceability Support System incorporates a number of design databases and implements the model dependency descriptor. Its use enables the management of systems, which were developed by using different design methods and different programming environments, and the capturing of the assumptions set during both development and maintenance.

1: Introduction

Changeability is an inherent property of modern software systems together with complexity, conformity and invisibility [4]. A useful software system is required to evolve in order to incorporate new functional and data requirements which come from experiencing the system itself. Laws, regulations and habits change, by forcing software to adapt to the new social environment. Requests of change come also from the need to conform to the new technologies, programming environments and design methods.

The high development costs cause changes to be incorporated into the existing systems by lengthening the system life cycle. Significant papers about software evolution, such as [13] and [14], state that the most important aspects to take under control are: the system complexity, the available documentation, the informal knowledge acquired through experience, and the accessibility both to documentation and knowledge. Our research on software maintenance [6], [10], [11], [12], aims to investigate these critical factors and to improve the methods which limit the risks related to the intrinsic entropy of system evolution.

The variety of processors, peripheral devices, operating systems, database management systems, graphical user interfaces, and programming languages brings programmers to implement a same software system on different target platforms, or build an heterogeneous system upon components of different hardware and software technologies. This heterogeneity complicates the maintenance process ever further.

Several databases, such as [5], [8] and [15], have been proposed which hold all the relevant information of a software system to perform the maintenance tasks. While these proposals deal with a unique point of view on the software structure, in [11] we have proposed a multidatabase environment, which is composed of a set of database schemes related to different representations of a same software structure. There is a source model, called Essential Design, which represents a normalized specification of software design, and one or more target models, called Language-Oriented Designs, which represent the software structure in the form imposed by the programming environment. The set of models allows the designer to specify a software system as a program family [2], [17].

[1]This work has been partially supported by "Progetto Finalizzato Sistemi Informatici and Calcolo Parallelo" of CNR (Italian National Research Council) under grant no. 90.00785.PF69

The current paper focuses on the integration of the different representation models of a same software system. Traceability between different views of a software system is assured by a web of decisions, which define the alternatives, individuate the choices, and supply the relative justifications. The refinement of an element in the Essential model is a problem which is solved through a chain of design decisions until to obtain the corresponding elements in the Language-Oriented model.

The traceability relation, which we propose in this paper, differs from related work on traceability [9], [16], [19], because in addition to the links among objects, we also track the decisions which have a role in the transformation. The paper differs from related work on design decisions [1], [7], [18], [20], because the design artifacts which we link belong to specific conceptual models of software design. In fact the design decisions are used to enrich the traceability relation with the assumptions which arise during both development and maintenance.

The different representation of a software system and the related decisions are incorporated into a tool, the Traceability Support System, which enables the maintenance and reuse of heterogeneous systems.

The present paper aims to describe the use of design decisions to capture the links between different models of software structure. In order to understand our approach, we first discuss in section 2 the use of multiple views on a software design. Section 3 defines the model dependency descriptor, representing the decision web, and the traceability relation between structure models. Section 4 describes the Traceability Support System and shows its use. The last section suggests some conclusions and describes the future work.

2: Software structure representation

Many aspects exist in a software solution which are independent of the limitations imposed by the adopted programming system (programming language plus run-time environment). The required services and the need for quality attributes tend to survive to the technological innovation, while the hardware and software technologies are subject to frequent changes which bring a system to exist in different versions and variants. In order to reduce the cost of development and maintenance, we must capitalize the knowledge which is produced during the design and implementation of a software system, by saving the core of the solution and excluding the insignificant details. Brooks in [4] describes the core as follows:

The essence of a software system is made of data objects, functions, algorithms, invocations of functions. Its conceptual constructs are applied without regards a particular representation.

We propose separating the initial specification of the software structure, called Essential Design, from the final specification, called Language-Oriented Design, which reflects the final configuration imposed by the programming and run-time environment. First, the software engineer produces the Essential Design, by applying the principles of software engineering (separation of concerns, modularity, abstraction, generality and anticipation of change) on the basis of the program objectives, and the required quality attributes. After having evaluated the hardware-software platform, he then produces the Language-Oriented Design by means of a specialization of the Essential Design.

The Essential Design aims to fit the desired functional characteristics with a suitable model of software quality. It considers the programming environment as technologically perfect and therefore is thus the best solution which the designer can achieve. Each adaptation to the implementation platform, which determines the form of a Language-Oriented Design, must tend towards the same levels of quality.

The two most common design methods, functional decomposition and object-oriented decomposition, are taken into account in the Essential Design. The former, Essential Design via Functional Decomposition (EDFD), is still the dominant design method in the software industry and it is used for building most currently running programs. The latter, Essential Design via Object-Oriented Decomposition (EDOOD), evolved over the 80s and it will gain increasing weight in the future.

The EDFD model contains the entity types "module", "parameter", "global data structure" and relationships such as "module calls module", or "module uses global data structure", while the EDOOD model contains the entity types "class", "object", "operation", "attribute" and relationships such as "class inherits from class", or "class offers operation".

The Language-Oriented design models are specialized according to the language and their entity types recall the syntactic constructs typical of the programming language. So, the Pascal-Oriented Design model (PascalOD) defines the entity types "procedure" and "function" as subtypes of "routine", while the Ada-Oriented Design model (AdaOD) defines the entity types "subprogram", "variable", "type", "constant", as subtypes of "importable/exportable component".

For the sake of brevity, we omit in this paper the Enhanced ER diagrams which specify the conceptual models. However, they can be found in [11] together with further details about the Essential and Language-Oriented Design models.

3: The decision web

The derivation of a Language Oriented Design from the Essential Design can be viewed as an iterative refinement of design components, where each refinement reflects an explicit choice in a set of alternative solutions.

We use a model dependency descriptor to specify the dependencies between two different design models. The former is the source from which the transformation starts and the latter is the target refinement. When developing in a forward direction, the sources may be either a EDFD or a EDOOD model, while a target can be any Language Oriented model, such as PascalOD or AdaOD.

3.1: The model dependency descriptor

A *model dependency descriptor* G is an acyclic directed graph

$$G = (V, E)$$

The set of vertices V is composed of three disjoint subsets

$$V = S \cup T \cup D$$

where S is the set of objects of the source design model, including instances of both entity types and relationships, T is the set of objects of the target design model, and D represents the set of decisions which are involved in the transformation. Like in [20], a decision d_i is 4-tuple:

$$d_i = (p_i, A_i, a_{ik}, j_i),$$

where p_i contains the description of the problem, A_i is the set of available alternatives, a_{ik} shows the alternative selected as solution, and j_i justifies the reason for the choice.

The edges E are divided in four disjoint subsets:

$$E = I \cup O \cup C \cup R$$

The subset I represents *Input relations* between source design objects and decisions:

$$I \subseteq S \times D$$

The subset O represents *Output relations* between decisions and target design objects:

$$O \subseteq D \times T$$

The subset C represents *Cause relations* connecting decision nodes whose problems have been caused by previous decisions:

$$C \subseteq D \times D$$

A refinement for which there are no alternatives to take into account is represented through direct links between source and target design objects, because there are no decisions to record. In this case, the traceability among components is reduced to the subset R, which represents *deRivation relations*:

$$R \subseteq S \times T$$

A graphic representation of the model dependency descriptor is shown in fig.1.

3.2: The traceability relation

The *traceability relation* G^* is defined to be the transitive closure of the model dependency descriptor G. It links each component of a source design model to one or more components of a target design model, through a path whose intermediate nodes are the decisions involved in the transformation.

The traceability relation has a great importance for the evolution of a software system, because it makes it possible to cross the gap between different design models of a same software system. For example, given a system S which has been designed by functional decomposition and implemented in Pascal language as version v, we have two sets of design objects, respectively denoted $S_v(EDFD)$ and $S_v(PascalOD)$. Both sets are linked by a decision web, the traceability relation, which is expressed as a mapping below:

$$G^*: S_v(EDFD) \rightarrow S_v(PascalOD)$$

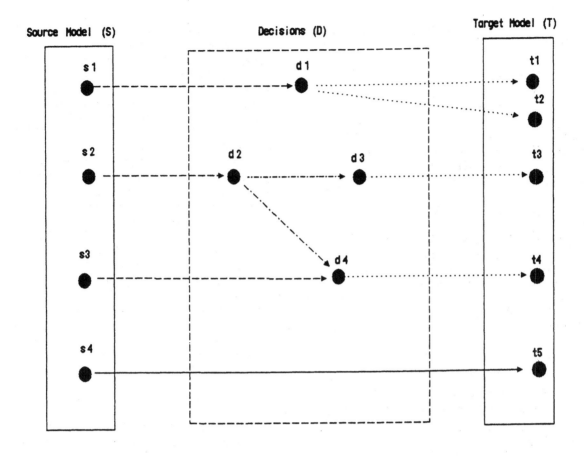

Legend

- - - - →   Input relations (I)   -·-·-·→   Cause relations (C)

··········→   Output relations (O)   ———→   deRivation relations (R)

Figure 1: The model dependency descriptor

If the system S is modified, producing the version $v+1$, the change will reverberate both on the Essential Design and on the Language-Oriented Design, by means of a couple of new model dependency descriptors:

$$S_v(EDFD) \to S_{v+1}(EDFD) \to S_{v+1}(PascalOD)$$

Obviously, several decisions in the first traceability relation G* may be reused in the final transformation.

Modifying the development approach to system S_v, by changing the design method from functional to object-oriented, and the programming language from Pascal to Ada, for example, will result in the following transformations:

$$S_v(EDFD) \to S_{v+1}(EDOOD) \to S_{v+1}(AdaOD)$$

The same software system might be implemented in two programming languages, for example C and

Pascal. In this case the transformations are the following:

$$S_V(EDFD) \left\langle \begin{array}{l} \rightarrow S_V(PascalOD) \\ \\ \rightarrow S_V(COD) \end{array} \right.$$

The inverse of the traceability relation, $G^{*-1} \subseteq TxS$, may be used to support a design recovery process which has as key objective the development of structures useful for understanding a system [3]

$$G^{*-1}: S_V(languageOD) \rightarrow S_V(EDFD)$$

where *languageOD* is instantiated by the programming language of the current implementation.

Reengineering the old system S in a new system S_r involves the following transformations:

$$S(languageOD) \rightarrow S(EDFD) \rightarrow S_r(EDFD) \rightarrow$$
$$\rightarrow S_r(languageOD)$$

4: The Traceability Support System

The model dependency descriptor has been implemented in a system called *Traceability Support System*. The current release is intended to explore problems arising from the integration of well structured information, such as design models, and partially structured information, represented by the decisions. Fig.2 shows the functional architecture of the Traceability Support System.

Because populating the design databases by manual data entry involves an expensive overhead, we have included the tools Extractor and Translator, which are part of the System Quality Monitor, a prototype shown in [11]. The Extractor tool automatically produces design information according to a Language-Oriented Design schema, starting from source code. The initial prototype analyzes Pascal programs. On the contrary, Essential Design information may be supplied in a forward direction, starting from the repository of a CASE tool used for design specification. The Translator tool maps information from the repository schema to an Essential Design schema, either EDFD or EDOOD. At the moment, the prototype translates the repository of a widespread CASE tool into an Essential via Functional Decomposition schema.

After the design database has been loaded, the Decision Editor allows the user to enter and store decisions in the system. Fig.3 shows the template

which is structured as the 4-tuple (problem, Alternatives, solution, justification).

Once a decision has been entered, the user then interacts with the Dependency Editor, which makes it possible to build or modify the model dependency descriptor, by adding, removing or checking the existence of input, output, cause and derivation relations (by means of the primitives AddIRelation, RemoveIRelation, IsIRelation, AddORelation, RemoveORelation, IsORelation, AddCRelation, RemoveCRelation, IsCRelation, AddRRelation, RemoveRRelation, IsRRelation). Fig.4 shows the use of the primitive AddIRelation to connect the module "Getword" to the related decision.

When the user wants to examine the model dependency descriptor, the Dependency Browser makes it possible to trace design objects and decisions along a dependency link (by means of the primitives: SelectSNode, SelectTNode, SelectDNode, NextNode, PreviousNode). From the current source object, the primitive TraceForward retrieves all the decisions and target objects, which are the in the transitive closure of the model dependency descriptor, while from the current target object, the primitive TraceBackward implements the inverse relation. From the current decision, a user can view the description of the problem. Starting from it, as shown in fig.5, he may request the related solution, the alternatives, the reason of choice, the nodes influenced by the choice, and the nodes which have caused the problem (respectively by means of the primitives Solution, Alternatives, Why, ScopeOfEffect, History).

With the Dependency Browser we can make questions as the following: "what are the AdaOD objects corresponding to the module *GetWord*?", "what alternatives have been evaluated for hiding the internal representation of the type *Word*?", "why the Ada Limited Private keyword has been selected?", "what are the consequences of using a package *HandleWords*?". In order to answer, the Dependency Browser has access to the design objects acting as a database front end.

The design objects are stored in separate database schemes, one for each design model. A user can interface to any design database through both a logical layer and semantic layer. The logical interface layer requires the knowledge of the relational schemes which have been derived from the Enhanced ER models. A user can write a symbolic expression using SQL (Structured Query Language), or fill a two-dimensional grid using QBE (Query By Example). We make provision for these two query languages because they are popular among DBMS's users.

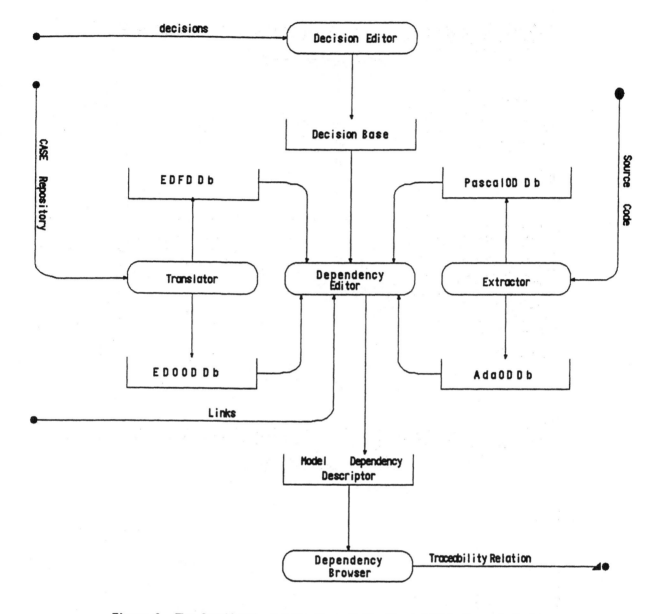

Figure 2 The functional architecture of the Traceability Support System

The semantic layer provides an easier interface to the design databases which take advantage of the conceptual abstraction and the graphical representation of the Enhanced ER models. A user can browse through a design database, by selecting an entity and choosing to examine the entity itself or a relationship starting from it. All the requests specified in the conceptual layer are mapped into queries at the logical level.

We have used the Informix relational DBMS to manage the design databases at the logical and physical levels, and the Informix 4GL for building the semantic layer. The Decision Editor, Dependency Editor and Dependency Browser have been implemented using Toolbook, a construction set for developing Microsoft Windows applications. In order to query the design databases from the Dependency Browser, we have built a Dynamic Link Library, containing the functions which interface with Informix DBMS.

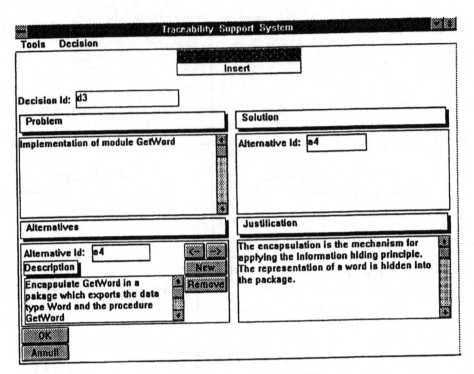

Figure 3: The Decision Editor

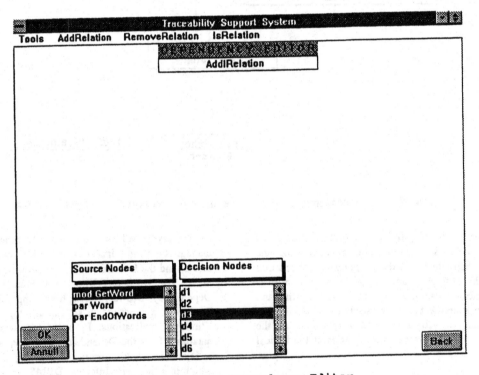

Figure 4: The Dependency Editor

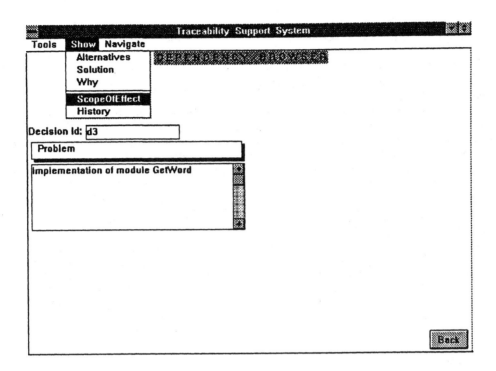

Figure 5: The Dependency Browser

4: Conclusions

We proposed the modeling of a software structure in accordance with two different points of view, whereby one is dependent on a given programming language while the other one is completely independent. This duality makes it possible to manage systems which were developed by using different design methods and different programming languages.

We suggested the integration of the design decisions with the design models in a graph, the model dependency descriptor, and their use to assure traceability between different representations of the same software structure. A traceability relation is defined as the transitive closure of the model dependency descriptor. The traceability relation links objects in different design models and enables the preservation of the assumptions set during both development and maintenance.

Using a Traceability Support System, which connects the different views on system structure with design decision, helps to evaluate the effects of changes, choose between design alternatives, and verify the weakness or strength of the machine platform and the programming environment

A number of design case studies have been used to test the adequacy of the Traceability Support System. The resulting programs, going from 2000 to 7000 LOCs, were written in Pascal code by students of a software engineering course. The successful application of the model dependency descriptor has encouraged us to extend the test in an industrial environment, for experimenting the actual implications of decision reuse in the maintenance process.

In the future research, we want also investigate a metric-based approach on the evaluation of design decisions. This approach will require the integration of the Traceability Support System with the System Quality Monitor.

References

[1] G.Arango, L.Bruneau, J.Cloarec, and A.Feroldi, "A Tool Shell for Tracking Design Decisions", *IEEE Software*, vol.8, no.2, 1991, pp.75-83.

[2] L.A.Belady, and P.M.Merlin, "Evolving Parts and Relations - A Model of System Families", in M.M.Lehman and L.A.Belady, *Program Evolution - Processes of Software Change*, Academic Press, 1985.

[3] T.J.Biggerstaff, "Design Recovery for Maintenance and Reuse", *IEEE Computer*, July 1989, pp.36-49.

[4] F.P.Brooks, "No Silver Bullet: Essence and Accidents of Software Engineering", *IEEE Computer*, April 1987.

[5] Y.Chen, M.Nishimoto, and C.V.Ramamoorthy, "The C Information Abstraction System", *IEEE Transactions on Software Engineering*, vol.16, no.3, March 1990, pp.325-334.

[6] A.Cimitile, F.Lanubile, and G.Visaggio, "A Decision Model for Controlling Software Evolution", *Proceedings of the ERCIM Workshop on Software Quality Principles and Techniques*, Pisa, 1992.

[7] V.Dhar, and M.Jarke, "Dependency Directed Reasoning and Learning in Systems Maintenance Support, *IEEE Transactions on Software Engineering*, vol.14, no.2, 1988, pp.211-227.

[8] S.W.Dietrich, and F.W.Calliss, "The Application of Deductive Databases to Inter-Module Code Analysis", in *Proceedings of the Conference on Software Maintenance*,1991, pp.120- 128.

[9] E.Horowitz, and R.C.Williamson, "SODOS: A Software Documentation Support Environment - Its Definition", *IEEE Transactions on Software Engineering*, vol.SE-12, no.8, August 1986, pp.849-859.

[10] F.Lanubile, and G.Visaggio, "Maintenance of Heterogeneous Systems", in *Proceedings of the Workshop on Software Evolution*, Bari, 1992.

[11] F.Lanubile, and G.Visaggio, "Maintainability via Structure Models and Software Metrics", in *Proceedings of the 4th International Conference on Software Engineering and Knowledge Engineering*, 1992.

[12] F.Lanubile, and G.Visaggio, "Software Maintenance by Using Quality Levels", in *Proceedings of the Workshop on Software Quality: Measurement and Practice*, Naples, 1992.

[13] M.M.Lehman, "Uncertainty in Computer Application and its Control Through the Engineering of Software", *Software Maintenance: Research and Practice*, vol.1, 1989, pp.3-27.

[14] M.M.Lehman, and L.A.Belady, *Program Evolution - Processes of Software Change*, Academic Press, 1985.

[15] M.Lejter, S.Meyers, and S.P.Reiss, "Support for Maintaining Object-Oriented Programs", in *Proceedings of the Conference on Software Maintenance*, 1991, pp.171-178.

[16] Luqi, "A Graph Model for Software Evolution", *IEEE Transactions on Software Engineering*, vol.16, no.8, August 1990, pp.917-927.

[17] D.L.Parnas, "On the Design and Development of Program Families", *IEEE Transactions on Software Engineering*, vol.SE-2, no.1, March 1976.

[18] C.Potts, and G.Bruns, "Recording the Reasons for Design Decisions", in *Proceedings of the 10th International Conference on Software Engineering*, 1988, pp.418-427.

[19] C.V.Ramamoorthy, Y.Usuda, A.Prakash, W.T.Tsai, "The Evolution Support Environment System", *IEEE Transactions on Software Engineering*, vol.16, no.11, November 1990, pp.1225-1234.

[20] C.Wild, K.Maly, and L.Liu, "Decision-Based Software Development", *Software Maintenance: Research and Practice*, vol.3, 1991, pp.17-43.

A Process for Consolidating and Reusing Design Knowledge

Guillermo Arango, Eric Schoen, and Robert Pettengill
Schlumberger Laboratory for Computer Science
Austin, Texas 78720-0015, USA—B.P. 620-05, 92542 Montrouge, France

Abstract

Significant improvements in design quality and productivity are possible when designers operate in a domain-specific information workspace with low-cost access to relevant application, design, and technology information. We present a validated process for constructing such workspaces to support product family design and evolution. The process involves three related efforts: (i) techniques to consolidate critical analysis and design information from different projects and different engineering sites—domain analysis; (ii) on-line representation of the information in structured form—technology books; and (iii) methods and tools to reuse information. We have already benefitted from applying the process and methodology described in this paper with minimal computer support. As the volume of information grows, we will require computer-based tools to manage design knowledge. We have learned a useful lesson: a process for consolidating and reusing design knowledge is powerful by itself.

1 Design as Evolution and Reuse

Design evolution and maintenance—rather than design synthesis— is the dominant activity in many software development organizations. General industry data suggests that design evolution accounts for 70% to 90% of the cost of a software system and that lack of understanding accounts for 50% to 90% of evolution costs. Thus, lack of understanding is responsible for 35% to 80% of evolution costs and for most of the risk involved [22]. Our own experience confirms this; most of the risk and from one to two thirds of the cost of design evolution projects can be traced to designers' and maintainers' lack of understanding of the consequences of incremental change. This situation is especially serious in the case of long-lived systems, highly-constrained designs, and in concurrent design of systems involving electronic, mechanical, and software components.

1.1 Strategy

Significant improvements in design quality and productivity are possible if engineers operate in a domain-specific information workspace with low-cost access to the best information available in the organization. This information workspace must include knowledge about the domain of applications, about specific products, and about design and implementation technologies. The major elements of our strategy are:

1. Techniques to consolidate critical analysis and design information for product families—*domain analysis*;

2. Representation of reusable information in structured form—*technology books*;

3. Methods and tools to reuse information.

We have already benefited from applying the process and methodology described in this paper with minimal computer support. As the volume of information grows, so will increases in the need for computer-based tools to manage design knowledge. We have confirmed that: (*i*) a process for consolidating and reusing design knowledge is powerful by itself, and (*ii*) in our engineering domains, the reuse of analyses and designs is, by far, more useful than the reuse of software.

1.2 Technology Books and Product Books

The process can be supported by a range of technologies, from conventional paper-based documentation to databases and tools that mediate between designers and between designers and their designs. In this paper, we describe how we moved from existing documentation practices, to structured documentation, to databases.

We have adopted an organization for design information workspaces consisting of two kinds of databases—*technology books* and *product books*—that are analogous to engineering handbooks lining the shelves of hardware designers' offices. Technology books consolidate the best knowledge available in the organization about a *class of problems* (e.g., some class of signal processing problems, data acquisition, measurement techniques, error detection in data communications). Because acquiring the knowledge to explain and solve these problems is difficult, the information in each technology book is narrowly defined.

The analysis and design of any software system draws knowledge from a number of application and technology domains [13]; larger and/or more complex systems draw upon larger numbers of domains. Our objective is to provide designers with a collection of technology books for those domains that are relevant to the generation of specific product families. Our experience suggests that a medium size embedded system of perhaps 32K lines of assembly code may require from 10 to 20 technology books. Because many products in a family implement common functionality, and hence rely upon one or more common technology domains, a technology book may be reused across a product family.

Product books consolidate knowledge that is specific to individual system instances. They include specialized versions of analyses drawn from technology books, standard work products of the design process (the domain of most commercial CASE tools), histories of deliberations (the domain of commercial design rationale capture tools [3]), and histories of documentation (the domain of most commercial version control systems).

In their present form, technology books are object-oriented databases whose objects capture typed information about analyses, designs, and code in a variety of notations. Relations with well-defined semantics link objects; these can be used to navigate through the technology book, and to reason about the information it contains. The balance of this paper focuses on technology books.

1.3 Applicability

When does it make sense to consolidate and reuse design knowledge?

1. When working on systems that are inherently difficult to understand. These include: very large systems [4] and highly-constrained systems—including real-time embedded systems and systems with tightly-coupled interactions between software, electrical, and mechanical design.

2. When working on projects with high probability of design information being reused. These include the evolution of systems with a stable technology base, systems with long lives, and systems belonging to families with variants customized for different clients, national markets, etc.

3. When engineering organizations have short product development cycles, operating under challenging regulatory systems, or with high product-maintenance costs.

The process discussed in this paper is applied in the context of projects involving four to six engineers with design cycles of 6 to 12 months. The designs qualify as highly constrained, with firmware, electronic, and mechanical components evolving concurrently. The resulting product families

have lives of approximately 20 years during which large numbers of custom variants are generated. The cost of changing firmware in products after release is very high (*e.g.*, the cost of replacing ROMs on thousands of installed devices).

Outline

In the next section, we discuss the process of consolidating analysis and design knowledge. In Section 3 we elaborate on the structure of technology books and in Section 4 we discuss some examples of their use. Section 5 provides an overview of current tools. Section 6 summarizes our experiences in transferring and applying the process.

2 Consolidation of Analysis and Design Knowledge

The process of analysis and design knowledge consolidation has several objectives:

1. Define a language for problem specification.

2. Produce formal models of solutions to those problems.

3. Demonstrate that the models explain our systems.

4. Identify good designs that map solutions to selected implementation technologies.

5. Explicitly specify issues, assumptions, constraints, and dependencies in those designs.

6. Explicitly specify how (reusable) software modules relate those designs.

Technology books collect and organize the results of this process. Their contents include language definitions (*i.e.*, jargon), formal models, demonstrations, designs, issues, assumptions, constraints, dependencies, and software modules (Figures 2 and 3).

2.1 Domain Analysis

Our process is a form of domain analysis [18]. In general, domain analysis identifies and organizes knowledge about some class of problems—the problem domain—to permit a designer to describe and solve problems in that domain. We have extended these techniques to produce more than the usual definition of vocabulary and of canonical problem specifications. Technology books include analytical models of classes of solutions, computational design models for these analyses, and implementations of these designs. They further contain rigorous explanations that justify the implementations in terms of the designs, and the designs in terms of the underlying analytic models. These explanations are formal in the same sense that mathematical proofs are formal.

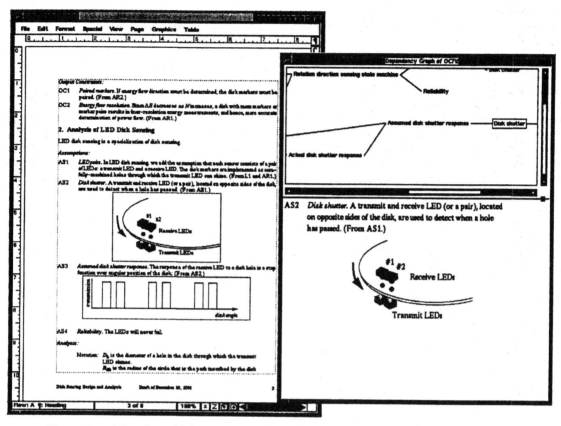

Figure 1: Migration of information from structured documents to technology books.

We choose the problem domain to investigate according to the needs and priorities of current or future projects. We then identify sources of information (*e.g.*, available technical literature, industrial standards, documentation from previous projects), relevant systems, experts, and consultants.

The steps in the process at the problem analysis level are:

1. Define the basic concepts in the problem domain. Specify the meaning of those concepts and their relationships unambiguously.

2. Produce rigorous definitions of typical problems using those concepts and relationships.

3. Develop analytical models of solutions and demonstrate that those models do indeed produce solutions.

4. Investigate the possibility of unifying these models. Propose new concepts if necessary.

5. Explicitly specify how existing systems implement the formalized solutions.

The steps in the process at the design analysis level are:

1. Generalize common designs from existing samples and identify the critical design issues.

2. Explicitly specify the assumptions, imported, and exported constraints in each design.

3. Based on knowledge from (1) and (2), investigate the possibility of unifying those abstract designs by classifying assumptions and relaxing constraints. Propose new architectures as needed.

4. Demonstrate how existing designs are specializations or adaptations of the abstract designs and formalize those adaptations that seem reusable.

5. Make explicit how (reusable) software models relate to specialized designs.

Recovering analytic models from implemented systems is expensive. In one instance, for example, recovering the mathematical model governing a signal processing task from 12,000 lines of assembly code took two scientists four months of work. The synthesis of rigorous derivations and explanations—called formal rationales in this paper—is expensive as well. On occasions it may be as difficult as proving theorems in physics or mathematics. The high cost of recovering critical knowledge motivates our formalizing it for reuse.

The process usually takes place during a period of from six months to one year, with the direct participation of approximately a half-dozen persons—domain experts, experienced designers, and modeling researchers—and other experts or designers participating as correspondents or reviewers. The process starts with a "kick-off" meeting to develop a common understanding of: the boundaries of the problem domain, the business context, the basic vocabulary, product variants, and application scenarios. This meeting may take from two to three days. Subsequent meetings focus on merging and reviewing the result of the work done by individuals. Most participants devote only part of their time to domain analysis activities. Domain analysis becomes a background activity because it is important to take the time necessary to allow ideas to mature.

2.2 Evolution of the technology book medium

Different levels of tool support are possible, from conventional paper-based documentation to on-line databases. During the past two and a half years, we have progressed through four levels.

1. *Informal documentation.* Our engineering colleagues used paper-based implementations of the techniques. (The first technology books they produced were actual books.) This demonstrated to us that the much of the strength of the approach is not based on technology, but rather on the methodology for knowledge consolidation, analysis, and reuse. But the methodology lends itself to gradual improvement in the technology dimension.

2. *Structured documentation.* From recording design knowledge informally, we progressed to a semiformal approach using template documents and commercial document preparation systems (Word and FrameMaker). We trained designers to organize their analysis and design documents using a small number of basic concepts. Structured documentation in this context does not mean adopting the notations of specific commercial CASE tools. The engineers stored information in tagged paragraphs to facilitate its identification and reuse. Example paragraphs tags were: requirement, analysis issue, position, argument, formal analysis, assumption, design constraint, and software module. The cross-reference facilities allowed encoding dependencies between related paragraphs. On the left side of Figure 1, we see a page from a technology book organized as a structured document. Paragraphs in the document are tagged with labels displaying the type and identification number of each item of information. "OC" paragraphs, for example, contain information on output constraints of a design, "AS" paragraphs contain information about assumptions.

In practice, the use of structured documentation was a powerful educational and technology transfer mechanism. It made explicit the categories of information used during the process, and it facilitated reviewing documents produced during the process. It was also a prerequisite for formalizing the representation of information in technology books.

3. *On-line object-oriented repository.* The paragraph types from structured documents became object types in an object-oriented repository (ObjectStore [14]). The paragraphs from structured documents became the contents of "text" attributes of objects in the repository. We developed software tools to parse existing documents into the repository and to generate publication-quality documents from the repository. Interactive tools operating on the repository (Figure 1, right side) facilitated inspecting the information stored in objects, visualizing dependencies between objects, and mechanically generating custom documents on different topics by navigating relationships (*e.g.*, "depends on", "is part of") between objects. Relationships include: classification, aggregation, IBIS-like deliberation networks [3], and others used in composing a design rationales (Figures 2 - 5).

4. *RADIO—an interactive modeling environment.* The suite of RADIO tools (Section 5.1) support interactive definition of new modeling objects and relations allowing user extension of the domain and documentation models. Attributes and relations may be entered and manipulated by task-specific entry, visualization, or simulation tools.

3 Using a Technology Book

In this section, we discuss the kinds of information typically found in technology books. In Section 4, we illustrate how information in technology books is used to compose rationales.

3.1 Technology book structure

Technology books use a small number of semantic and syntactic tags. These tags represent a careful compromise between usability and formality [12, 20]. The semantic tags include, for example: issue, definition, assumption, imported constraint, exported constraint, position, design decision, unresolved, and result. Syntactic tags identify, for example, authors, headings, equations, enumerations, etc. We store information in typed nodes and in relations between nodes. A typical information node may include encapsulated documents or information fragments, and other attributes. The information nodes are organized into taxonomies according to their types. The major hierarchies include domain entities, project entities, work products, resources, statements, and analyses. Relationships between information nodes are organized into a taxonomy based on their semantics and their use in building rationales. The general categories of relations

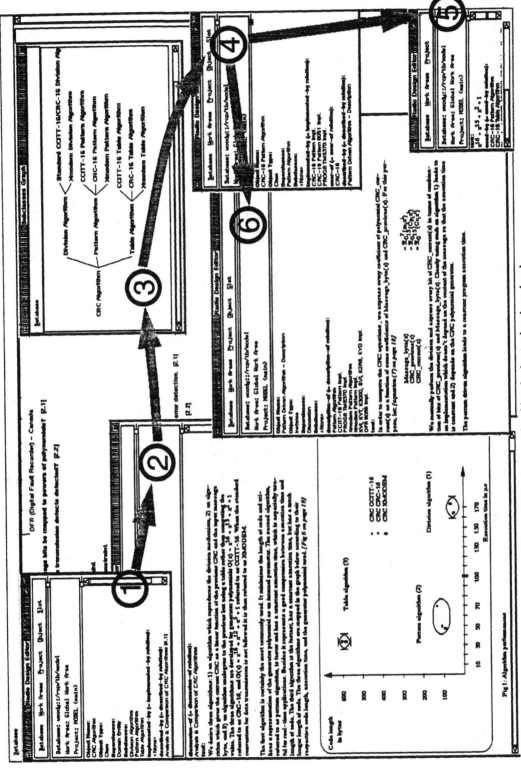

Figure 2: Finding an algorithm in the technology book

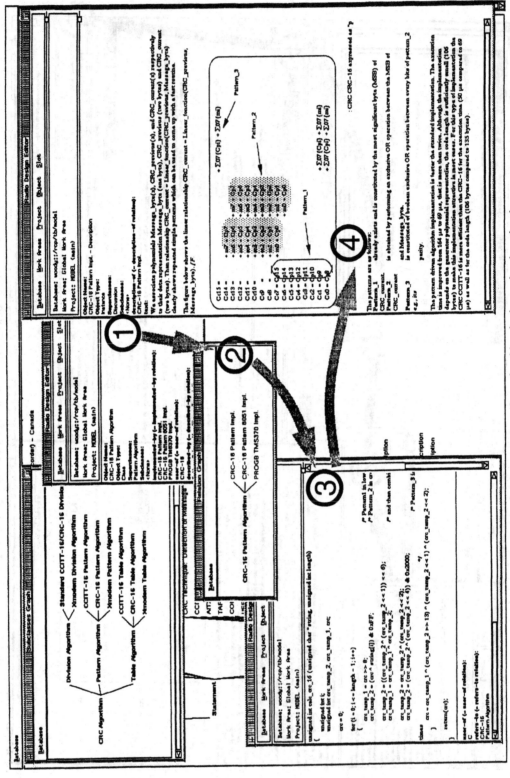

Figure 3: Finding an implementation of an algorithm in the technology book

242

include: history, taxonomy, derivation, aggregation, use, justification, interconnection, and ownership. The choice of relationship types in a particular technology book is determined by analysis of the domain. Figures 2-5 offer examples of relationship types. These can be created interactively with technology book editing tools (Section 5.1).

Atomic rationales are represented by text associated with an object. These rationales may be further combined by following task specific relations to form structured rationales.

3.2 Example

Software reusability is enabled by the reuse of analyses and design. A common barrier to software reuse is the difficulty of understanding the design assumptions and constraints embedded in a piece of code. Technology books store enough information to help designers decide whether to reuse a software module. If they so decide, the information further helps them to understand how to adapt the model to the context of reuse. In [2], we discuss a specific method for design reuse in the context of technology books.

In Figures 2 and 3, we illustrate interactions with a technology book describing error detection techniques for data transmission. The designer is trying to find a suitable implementation for Cyclic Redundancy Check (CRC). The designer first uses the justification relations in the problem domain model to confirm her understanding of the applicability of CRC to her problem. In Figure 2, she finds that there are three choices of algorithm for computing the CRC ① using the taxonomic relationship. She then follows an analysis relationship to access a comparison of the time and space performance properties of the algorithms ②. The designer decides that a pattern algorithm will combine good runtime execution and storage performance based on the comparison. Next, in a taxonomic graph of the family of known CRC algorithms ③, she identifies multiple combinations of generator polynomials and algorithms. Following derivation and constraint relationships for a previous model of her product, she determines that she must use the CRC-16 polynomial to maintain backwards compatibility; therefore, she then inspects the CRC-16 Pattern Algorithm ④. She finds the required polynomial coefficients via a uses relationship ⑤, and inspects a mathematical description of the algorithm ⑥ found via a documentation link.

In Figure 3, the designer, having selected a specific algorithm ①, is now free to explore known implementations. A graph of the implementation relation ② reveals that there are three implementations of the CRC-16 pattern algorithm. The designer selects a C-language implementation ③ and browses the source code. She also views the detailed documentation for this implementation ④.

4 Composition of design rationales

Design rationales or explanations are the response to "how" or "why" queries [1, 8, 9]. Rationales may be composed by extracting information from related technology book objects. Figure 4 illustrates a partial graph of technology book objects that are used to compose a rationale for explaining the propagation of a change. The objects are drawn from a technology book concerned with data acquisition techniques. Boxed text represents object instances. The "tags" attached to the objects indicate their types. Gray lines represent relations.

To answer the question, "How do changes in data representation from binary to floating-point actually translate into performance changes?" a designer must extract from the design model (Figure 4) relevant information to provide a complete explanation. Here are some of the explanation steps from an actual evolution case:

- Measured quantities are used in pulse generation; thus, a change affecting measured quantities may affect pulse generation computations.

- The choice of the pulse thresholding technique imposes a specific performance constraint on the execution time of the implementation.

- The requirement that pulse generation software run on a M68HC11 microprocessor implies that floating-point arithmetic in hardware is not available.

- Execute_time_op must then be computed based on the execution times of routines in the floating-point arithmetic library.

- The other values required to compute Execute_time_pulse_generation are retrieved from specification and design objects in the model.

- The value for Execute_time_pulse_generation with floating-point arithmetic is computed and the result is compared with the value for binary arithmetic.

- The difference is added to the current execution time for the code module implementing the P-type pulse-generation component.

- The resulting value must be compared with execution constraints associated with that module. These can be found encoded as constraints associated with the detailed design of the object, or may be derived from global constraints for the control loop that schedules the execution of the pulse-generation component.

At each step in the explanation process, the designer searches for appropriate bits of information. If the information is not directly recorded, she must ask additional questions. Insights gained during this process may lead to additions to the product model for future reuse.

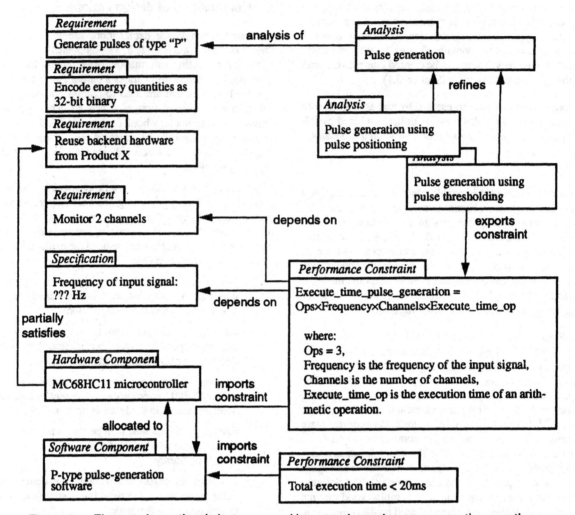

Figure 4: Elements in a rationale instance used in answering a change-propagation question.

Different forms of explanations or rationales can be composed from technology and product books:

1. Design history—the chronological sequence of states in a design.

2. Trace of deliberations or negotiation [3, 11, 17, 19]—the issues, position, arguments, and trade-offs that the team has considered.

3. Traces of work product development—work product defined by the software process in the organization (*e.g.*, marketing-requirements, specifications, high-level design, detailed-design, code), or work product parts that are explicitly linked [16] (see Figure 5). Requirements-to-code traces are an example of these type of structures.

4. Formal rationales (explanations)—basic principles, assumptions, and analytical derivations.

The first three kinds of rationales are often regarded as a side-effect—in the form of a record or trace—of a process whose purpose is to advance the state of a design. In contrast, formal rationales are a product in themselves with a role similar to that of analytical derivations found in engineering textbooks.

5 Tool environment

We are currently developing RADIO, an environment with which designers contribute to and access technology books. In the following, we describe the tools that comprise RADIO, the important issues in designing such tools, and the relationship between RADIO and similar electronic

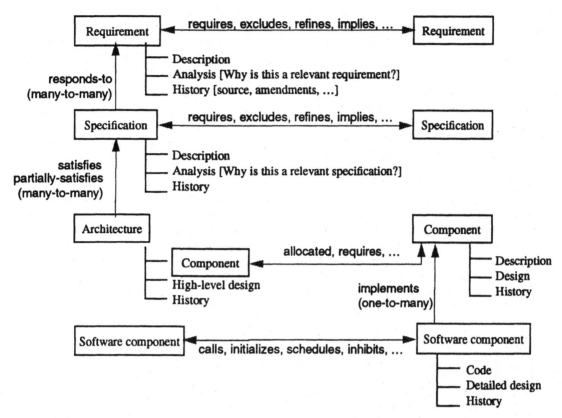

Figure 5: Abstract rationale graph for answering questions about software structure. The boxed text stands for "objects" in the rationale structure. Gray lines indicate relations that can exist between objects; arrowheads indicate directionality of the relations (doubled-headed arrows indicate potential relations in either direction). Different object pairs can be related by different relation types.

notebook projects.

5.1 Implementation Framework

The RADIO environment consists of an object-oriented database, a modeling language, user interfaces for acquiring and presenting technology book information, commercial tools as needed to support specific documentation requirements, and a number of ancillary support tools. RADIO 1.0 consists of approximately 75,000 lines of C++ custom code that glue together the functionality of commercial packages and implement editor and browser interfaces. Code for visualization and interaction is the fastest growing component as we experiment with task-oriented interfaces.

Database

The master repository for technology books is a commercial object-oriented database system (ObjectStore).The database system provides an efficient medium for storing and retrieving information in arbitrarily complex formats. RADIO tools access the database in a client–server architecture. ObjectStore provides transactions and concurrency control, which are needed to coordinate the activities of simultaneous technology book users. We also make use of ObjectStore's version facility to allow multiple designers to work simultaneously for extended periods of time without interfering with one another. (To help our designers to understand it, the versioning model is similar to that of file-oriented source code control systems, such as RCS [23].)

Modeling Language

Technology books contain semiformal information. The formal portion of the information structures knowledge about the domain (*e.g.*, the domain model, analyses of problems and designs). We store this information in objects defined by a simple, self-describing modeling language (called DOLL), which is in turn built atop C++ and Object-Store. The language allows designers to create and modify objects interactively. The language also allows designers to define relations that can exist between objects; these definitions allow it to maintain logical consistency as the designer asserts and retracts such relations [21].

DOLL differs from object-oriented languages such as C++, which emphasize runtime efficiency and storage compactness; DOLL instead emphasizes descriptiveness and runtime flexibility. This allows a designer to evolve descriptions in objects as her understanding evolves. Given the performance of current OODB technology, our emphasis on flexibility does not translate into real-time performance penalties. Response times are in the sub-second range.

The informal portion of a technology book consists of text, pictures, tables, and equations. We use FrameMaker, a commercial document preparation system, to acquire this information from designers, which we then store as sequences of paragraphs attached to DOLL objects. DOLL can also generate files from the contents of the technology book, which allows us to produce publication-quality documents for printing or for casual online examination.

User Interface

The RADIO user interface depicts technology book contents, allows the designer to navigate through a technology book, and helps her to add information to it. The interfaces are constructed with Motif, and use a custom, extensible, object-oriented library to structure the display of, and interaction with, technology book information within the windows Motif creates. RADIO's interfaces also embody some intelligence about the domain modeling task, which allows them to actively assist designers. These capabilities are presented in [21]. We are currently creating custom interfaces to allow designers to interact more intuitively with technology book contents.

Open Architecture

There is a limitless number of forms of expression of technology book information. Clearly, we cannot implement tools to acquire and present each one; instead, we are designing RADIO with an open architecture to allow us to integrate public domain and commercial tools as needed. Presently, we support a remote procedure call interface to other tools. Eventually, we will adopt PCTE [6] or CORBA [5] as a common communications substrate for RADIO tools.

RADIO Mail System

RADIO explicitly models its user community. Each RADIO installation contains a user database that keeps track of user-specific information. (We anticipate this facility will be used to help customize RADIO's user interfaces on a per-user basis.) The user database already supports a "mail" system (and a mail user interface similar to the widely available

xmh program) to help users to communicate with one another. Users construct messages using FrameMaker, which are then imported into the user database and distributed to recipients' mailboxes. FrameMaker provides a simple means for users to send richly-formatted messages—containing pictures, tables, and equations—in addition to plain text.

5.2 RADIO and Electronic Design Notebooks

One can view technology books as electronic design notebooks [7, 10, 24]. This is certainly true; technology books contain text and graphics that document product designs and design histories. However, they also contain more. A technology book is domain specific, not product specific. It contains the results of a domain analysis, structured in a manner that allows the analysis to be reused to provide rationale for the design of many products that operate in the domain. Similarly, it contains design information, which can also be reused across product boundaries [2].

6 Summary of Experiences

6.1 Validation

We have applied this process in the context of an ongoing, multi-year collaboration with a Schlumberger engineering center producing firmware for real-time embedded systems. We have developed technology books for problem domains in signal processing, data acquisition, and communications. Consequently, we regard the knowledge consolidation process as effective. The reuse techniques have been smoothly integrated with complementary software process improvements made at the same engineering center. The engineering group is currently applying the methods to the design of actual systems. Anecdotal evidence collected during the past year includes:

- The structured documentation techniques developed to organize contributions to technology books have been adopted to document the analyses and designs of products. We found the popular belief that engineers do not like to document is untrue, if by documentation we mean the formalization of knowledge and the derivation of rigorous explanations. Designers find this activity intellectually challenging and satisfying. In this context, documentation is not what we assign to junior engineers; on the contrary, it is a reward for expertise.

- Technology books are informally shared across engineering sites. The reuse of designs from technology books in sites other than the site of origin have been credited for the discovery of at least one major product-design flaw, accuracy improvements in one product, and firmware speed-up improvements in two other products.

- Reduction to one-third the number of design iterations for a product release in a recently completed project with respect to comparable past projects. Designers of a follow-on project estimate that approximately 70% of the design will be reused from technology books developed during the previous year.

- Technology books are being used to disambiguate marketing requirements between engineers and marketing personnel.

These results are promising. It will take more time to collect statistically significant data on productivity and quality improvements, and on the impact on software maintenance.

6.2 Technology Transfer

We consider our approach to transferring methods and tools from the laboratory to the engineering organizations to be effective. The following factors have helped:

- Techniques and tools customized to complement existing process-improvement initiatives.

- Emphasis on the transfer of methodology rather than technology.

- Continuous involvement of researchers in the normal engineering process.

- Adaptation to the notations and tools used by designers.

- Simplification of concepts, techniques, and vocabulary.

6.3 Conclusions

This paper outlines a validated discipline for the consolidation and reuse of design knowledge. The paper does not include sufficient detail on methods and tools to enable duplicating these experiences. A companion paper [2] provides additional detail on a design evolution method. We are engaged in a process of methodology extension, refinement, and empirical validation and we continue to investigate the reuse design rationales, improved means to visualize design information, and the integration of technology books with analysis and simulation tools.

Acknowledgments

We are grateful to Remi St. Martin, Brad Kitterman, Farrokh Abadi and to the engineers in the Electricity Management Division of Schlumberger Industries for their contributions to the evolution and validation of technology book and design methods. Michel Boissard authored the technology book on error-correction techniques from which we drew examples for this paper. Annie Anton assisted in populating it.

Bibliography

[1] G. Arango and E. Schoen. Using product models to compose rationales. In *AAAI-92 Workshop on Design Rationale Capture and Use*, pages 1–8, San Jose, California, July, 1992. American Association for Artificial Intelligence.

[2] G. Arango, E. Schoen, R. Pettengill, and J. Hoskins, The Graft-Host method for design evolution. In *Proceedings of the 15th International Conference on Software Engineering*, Baltimore, MD, 1993. IEEE Computer Society.

[3] E.J. Conklin and K.C. Burgess Yakemovic, A process-oriented approach to design rationale, *Human-Computer Interaction*, 1991, Vol. 6, pp. 357-391.

[4] P. Devanbu, R. Brachman, P. Selfridge, and B. Ballard, LaSSIE: A knowledge-based software information system, *Communications of the ACM*, Vol. 34, No. 5, pp. 3549, May 1991.

[5] Digital Equipment Corp., Hewlett-Packard Co., HyperDesk Corp., NCR Corp., Object Design, Inc., and SunSoft, Inc. *The Common Object Request Broker: Architecture and Specification*, OMG Doc. No. 91.12.1, Rev. 1.1, Object Management Group, Inc., December 1991.

[6] European Computer Manufacturers Association. *Standard ECMA-149 Portable Common Tool Environment (PCTE) Abstract Specification*, Geneva, December, 1990, ECMA.

[7] G. Fischer, A. Girgensohn, K. Nakakoji, and D. Redmiles. Supporting software designers with integrated domain-oriented design environments. *IEEE Transactions on Software Engineering*, 18(6):511–522, June, 1992.

[8] T. R. Gruber and D. M. Russell. Beyond the record and replay paradigm for design rationale support. In *AAAI-92 Workshop on Design Rationale Capture and Use*, pages 111–118, San Jose, California, July, 1992. American Association for Artificial Intelligence.

[9] J. M. Carroll and T. P. Morgan, editors. Special issue of *Human-Computer Interaction*. 6(3&4). 1991.

[10] F. Lakin, J. Wambaugh, L. Leifer, D. Cannon, and C. Sivard. The Electronic Design Notebook: Performing

medium and processing medium. In R. Makkuni, editor, *Visual Computer: International Journal of Computer Graphics*. August, 1989.

[11] J. Lee. Extending the Potts and Bruns model for recording design rationale. *Proc. of 13th International Conference on Software Engineering*, pages 114-125. 1991. IEEE Computer Society.

[12] J. Mylopoulos, L. Chung, and B. Nixon. Representing and using nonfunctional requirements: A process-oriented approach. *IEEE Transactions on Software Engineering*, SE18(6):483–497, June, 1992.

[13] J. M. Neighbors. Draco: A method for engineering reusable software systems. In T. Biggerstaff and A. Perlis, editors, *Software Reusability*, pages 295–319. ACM Press. 1989.

[14] Object Design, Inc. *ObjectStore User Guide*, DU 1002-100, Object Design, Inc., Burlington, Mass., October, 1992.

[15] D. L. Parnas (1979). Designing software for ease of extension and contraction. In *IEEE Transactions on Software Engineering*, Vol. SE5(2):128–138.

[16] D. E. Perry (1987). Software interconnection models. In *Proceedings of the Ninth International Conference on Software Engineering*, pages 61–69. Monterey, California. IEEE Computer Society.

[17] C. Potts and G. Bruns, Recording the Reasons for Design Decisions. *Proc. of 10th International Conference on Software Engineering*, pages 418-427. 1988. IEEE Computer Society.

[18] R. Prieto-Díaz and G. Arango, editors. *Domain Analysis and Software Systems Modeling*, IEEE Computer Society Press, 1991.

[19] B. Ramesh and V. Dhar. Supporting systems development by capturing deliberations during requirements engineering. *IEEE Transactions on Software Engineering*. SE18(6):498–510, June, 1992.

[20] C. Rich and Y. A. Feldman. Seven layers of knowledge representation and reasoning in support of software development. *IEEE Transactions on Software Engineering*, SE18(6):451–469, June 1992.

[21] E. Schoen. Active assistance for domain modeling. In *Proceedings of the Sixth Annual Knowledge-Based Software Engineering Conference*, pages 26–35, Syracuse, New York, September, 1991. IEEE Computer Society.

[22] T. A. Standish. An essay on software reuse. *IEEE Transactions on Software Engineering*, SE10(5):494–497. September, 1984.

[23] W. F. Tichy. Design, implementation, and evaluation of a revision control system. In *Proceedings of the Sixth International Conference on Software Engineering*, Tokyo, Japan, 1982. IEEE Computer Society.

[24] W. H. Uejio. An electronic design notebook for the DARPA Initiative in Concurrent Engineering. In *Proceedings of the CERC Conference on Concurrent Engineering*, February, 1990.

Chapter 6

Impact Representation

Purpose

The papers in this chapter describe how developers can represent software-change dependencies for analysis. Information about dependencies can show how objects relate to one another, making it easier to determine the potential impacts of a change. There are several ways, some formal, that developers can define or describe dependencies — from simple marks on program statements to sophisticated truth-maintenance rules to be evaluated by a production rule system. Often graphs are used.

Reading this chapter is good preparation for the next chapter on impact determination, since impact-determination techniques often operate on dependency representations such as those described here.

The Papers

Often software professionals perceive changes to a software system as beginning with a change request and affecting only software components. More often than not, the system housing the software also has considerable influence over the software-change process.

This aspect of change is reflected in the first paper, "The Prism Model of Changes," in which Nazim Madhavji presents a change taxonomy suitable for a broad range of artifacts. The taxonomy incorporates change structure and dependency representations to analyze changes to the artifacts, including people, policies, laws, resources, processes, and results. Madhavji underlines the complexity of change by showing the necessary expansion to other environmental factors. He distinguishes changes to the artifacts from changes to the environment that houses them. Prism has two facilities. Its Dependency Structure aids in describing items and their interdependencies as well as identifying the possible effects of changes. Its Change Structure aids in classifying, recording, and analyzing change-related data from a qualitative perspective.

In the next paper, "A Unified Interprocedural Program Representation for a Maintenance Environment," Mary Jean Harrold and Brian Malloy detail how to represent source-code dependencies using a graph technique for representing interprocedural program dependencies. *Unified interprocedural graphs* combine existing program dependency graphs with interprocedural dependency information to efficiently represent interactions among code procedures. UIGs are designed to save storage space and access times in their representations, making the dependency analysis of large programs more feasible.

The next paper, "A Formal Model of Program Dependencies and Its Implications for Software Testing, Debugging, and Maintenance," outlines a formal model of program dependencies. Andy Podgurski and Lori Clarke present a general model of program dependencies that include control- and data-flow dependence information in terms of strong and weak syntactic dependence. They then relate this information to semantic dependence models to examine how a program statement can affect the execution of other statements. Finally, they solidify these concepts by discussing them in terms of software-maintenance activities.

To conclude the chapter, Luqi describes a representation of software change in "A Graph Model for Software Evolution." The graph model formally describes dependencies among software artifacts. Luqi seeks to formalize the objects and activities involved in software evolution in sufficient detail to enable automated software-change updates. This model of software evolution serves as a foundation for program-change semantics, which describe the meaning of the change with respect to program properties.

The Prism Model of Changes [*]

Nazim H. Madhavji

McGill University, School of Computer Science
3480 University Street, Montreal, PQ, CANADA H3A 2A7
email: madhavji@opus.cs.mcgill.ca

ABSTRACT: A software development environment supports a complex network of items of at least the following major types: people, policies, laws, resources, processes, and results. For various predictable and unpredictable reasons, such items may need to be changed on an on-going basis. This problem of change, however, has not as yet been surmountable and is therefore currently of fundamental importance in software environment research. In an attempt to overcome this problem, we have designed a model of changes and its supporting two change-related environment infrastructures with the following key or unique features: (1) a separation of concern between changes to the described items and changes to the environmental facilities housing these items; (2) a facility, called the Dependency Structure, for describing various items and their inter-dependencies, and for identifying the items affected by a given change; (3) a facility, called the Change Structure, for classifying, recording and analysing change related data, and for making qualitative judgements of the consequences of a change; (4) identification of the many distinct properties of a change; and (5) a built-in mechanism for providing feedback. This paper describes our approach to the problem of change in the Prism project and gives a rationale for the design of the model of changes as well as that of the two change related environment infrastructures.

Keywords: model of changes, process model, Dependency Structure, Change Structure, infrastructures, software process, change management, project management, feedback, multi-type environment, Prism.

"A state without the means of some change is without the means of its conservation."

-- Edmund Burke[†]

1. Introduction

Prism is an experimental *multi-type* software environment research project. The term, multi-type, implies the many types of items which are explicitly represented in an environment, and are possibly subject to change. The Prism project began with its primary focus on software processes (item type processes) [1], as indeed have many other well-known process-oriented environments, such as Arcadia [2], Marvel [3], E-L [4], IPSE 2.5 [5], SPM [6] and ESF [7]. However, through subsequent research described in this paper, we have broadened our focus to include items of other types, such as people, policies, laws, other processes, resources and results.

[*]This research was in part funded by the Natural Science and Engineering Research Council of Canada.

[†] Edmund Burke: *Reflections on the Revolution in France*, Oxford Dictionary of Quotations, Oxford University Press, London, 1941.

This paper addresses one of the challenging problems in the field of software engineering, that of managing changes to items of various types in a multi-type software environment. In order to have an improved understanding of the problem of change, and design an appropriate solution to this problem, we have built a *model* of changes supported by two environment *infrastructures* [2], called the Dependency Structure and the Change Structure. These three features (i.e., the model and the two infrastructures) are the primary novel points of this paper. The detailed results of this research are described in three recent reports on the problem of change [8, 9, 10]. This paper is a synthesis of the key results from these reports.

The Prism model of changes is an abstract description of the part of the Prism software environment that is specialised to handle the problem of change within a software project. Among the several main benefits of this model is that it provides an insight into the characteristics of the main components of the environment that are necessary to cope with changes. One such component is the Dependency Structure, which permits the representation of items of various types (e.g., people, policies, laws, processes, resources, results, etc.) and their inter-dependencies, and simplifies identification of the items affected by a given change. The other component is the Change Structure, which facilitates the classification, recording and analysis of change related data. These two environment infrastructures operate side-by-side in order to support change management processes in a software environment.

1.1. Problem Definition and Background

The problem of change can be defined as: (a) identifying the need to make a change to an item in the environment, (b) acquiring adequate change related knowledge about the item, (c) assessing the impact of a change on other items in the environment, (d) selecting or constructing a method for the process of change, (e) making changes to all the items and their inter-dependencies involved satisfactorily, (f) recording the details of the changes for future reference, and (g) releasing the changed item back into the environment.

The problem of change, especially that related to software products (item of type results), has long been recognised as a key issue in software environment research. This has led to different ways of supporting systematic evolution of a software product through configuration management and version control [11, 12, 13, 14].

More recently, changes to programmed software processes have received significant attention [15], including changes to dynamic, or enacted, software processes [16, 17]. Osterweil has pressed for rigorous descriptions of software process through process programming [18], so that changes can be accurately specified and assessed. Similarly, Perry has recognised the need for extensive knowledge of the places where changes must be made [19]. In addition, Redwine [16] has pointed out the scale of changes in the process model life-cycle: changing instances, types, type systems, etc.

The problem of change in a software environment, however, is not limited to items of types "results" and "(software) processes"; it extends far beyond these. For example, there can be changes to items such as: (i) policies for: developing software, using hardware and software resources, constructing or serving processes, making and obeying laws, dealing with humans, and indeed making new policies; (ii) laws applied to items of different types; (iii) humans of a certain class who create policies, laws, processes, provide resources and order products to be built; (iv) humans of another class who follow these policies, laws and processes, use resources, and build software; (v) processes for creating software and other processes, policies, laws, etc.; (vi) resources of all sorts in the environment, including time; and of course (vii) different kinds of products. This wide variety of different items in a multi-type environment is further complicated by various levels of abstraction that can exist in an environment. Example levels include: individual, group, project, organisation, and so on.

The breadth of the item types and the depth of the hierarchy in an environment implies a highly complicated network of relationships amongst the different items in the environment. Furthermore, none of the items described above are static when in actual use, and hence they need to be maintained. This implies that changes to items of the described types is an inherent property of a software environment[†]. This galactic view of changes to items of different types in an environment should be clearly contrasted to the atomic view of changes to variables, expressions, declarations and statements in a system of code modules. Of course, it is the changes to the former that require changes to be made to the latter.

Thus, an important question that needs answering is that how does one know precisely the impact of a change, or non-change, to an item of any type whatsoever on the rest of the items in the environment? For example, what is the impact of changing a management policy on the development of a product? Of course, there are many such questions that need to be answered by a software environment aimed at solving the problem of change. An important related question is, what means does the environment have to facilitate such changes on an on-going basis? This problem is so critical that any environment builder must address in its design. In fact, adapting Edmund Burke's quote to software environments: *an environment without the means of some change is without the means of its conservation.*

Another major problem of change not widely recognised is changes to the means of change, implying: (a) the different kinds of changes that may be required to those environment facilities specialised to handle the problem of change, and (b) the ways of accommodating such changes on an on-going basis. This meta level of changes is important because the quality of change related environment facilities has a direct impact on the quality of items in the environment. Perry also supports this

view in [19], where he discusses a two-way relationship between a software environment and the supported process model.

1.2. Solution Approach

The Prism model of changes incorporates a two-tier approach to designing, implementing and controlling changes to the items in an environment. The first aspect deals with identifying the set of items affected due to a given change; and the second aspect deals with classifying and recording analytical data related to the change. These aspects also include feedback mechanisms to instigate changes to items and provide projection for future changes. In addition, there is a built-in mechanism in the model for supporting (meta) changes to change related environment facilities. The net effect of this approach is that it is a structured approach to accommodating changes, on an on-going basis, to the items as well as the change related environment facilities. In all, this approach to accommodating changes entails: (a) describing dependencies amongst the different items in the environment; (b) providing feedback concerning the use of items; (c) identifying an item to be changed, based on received feedback or otherwise; (d) performing impact analysis; (e) designing or selecting a methodology for the change; (f) carrying out the change; (g) classifying and recording data related to the change; (h) performing deviation analysis between projected and factual values; (i) providing immediate feedback concerning the change; (j) performing post analysis; (k) making future projections; (l) providing meta feedback concerning environment facilities; (m) performing meta feedback analysis; and (n) incorporating meta changes.

1.3. Problems Addressed and Research Contributions

In this paper, we address the following fundamental problems of change: (i) identifying the need to make a change to an item in the environment, (ii) assessing the impact of a change, (iii) acquiring adequate change related knowledge concerning an item, and (iv) changes to the means of making changes to items. Note, however, that suitable methodologies for accommodating changes and the detailed syntax and semantics for describing the different types of items are outside the scope of this *model-based* paper. Despite this, the problems addressed in this paper form a significant component of the total problem of change.

The primary contributions of this paper are:

(1) an explicit model of changes;

(2) an environmental facility, called the Dependency Structure, for describing items and their inter-dependencies, and for identifying items of change affected by a given change;

(3) an environmental facility, called the Change Structure, for classifying, recording and analysing change related data, and for making qualitative judgements of the consequences of a change;

(4) identification of the many properties of a change;

(5) a built-in mechanism in the environmental facilities for providing feedback; and

(6) a comparison of some selected models of change.

1.4. Organisation of the Paper

The next section describes the Prism model of changes and its key properties. Section three and four describe the Dependency Structure and the Change Structure, respectively. Section five focuses on the problem of incorporating infrastructural changes. Section six makes comparisons with related

---

[†] Note that this is also recognised by Lehman in his recent Uncertainty Principle for computer applications [20], which, although intended for the item type results, carries over to other types of items such as people, polices, laws, etc.

work, and section seven draws some conclusions.

2. The Prism Model of Changes

Two terms which can help clarify this paper are:

(1) *Infrastructures*: unless otherwise stated, this means environmental facilities provided by an environment (e.g., the Dependency Structure and the Change Structure).

(2) *Items of change*: as stated earlier this includes such items as people, policies, laws, processes, etc., which may need to be changed in the environment. They do not include infrastructures. Changes to infrastructures are considered separately from changes to items of change.

Below, we first describe an overview of the Prism model of changes, followed by an analysis of its key properties.

2.1. Model Overview

Figure 1 shows the Prism model of changes. The model depicts the levels of operation where change is implemented; the key change related infrastructures; and the processes carried out during the use and the maintenance of the infrastructures. Thus, in a sense Figure 1 is a (change) process model. For simplicity, the model does not show any processes that *govern* the use of the infrastructures, and which may evolve with changes to the infrastructures.

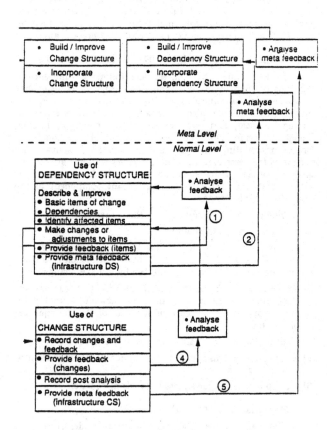

Figure 1 - The Prism model of changes

There are two levels of operation in this model: (a) the normal level (below the horizontal broken line), and (b) the meta level (above the broken line). At the normal level there exists the *use* of the two environment infrastructures [2], called the Dependency Structure and the Change Structure. It is at this level where changes can occur to the items of change.

The Dependency Structure represents items of different types such as those mentioned above (not shown in Figure 1). These items have dependencies, which are also represented explicitly in the Dependency Structure. The items of change of the described types can occur at various levels of abstraction (shown later in Figure 2) during the operation of an environment: individual level, group level, project level, organisation level, and so on. Together, the types of items and the levels of abstraction can represent a comprehensive set of items concerning a software project. This has been kept implicit in the model so as to maintain simplicity. The items in the Dependency Structure can be variant [2] and their dependencies can be used to identify the set of affected items due to a given change.

Also, there is a mechanism to provide feedback concerning the use of the items of change (see the arrow labelled 1 in Figure 1). There is another mechanism to provide meta feedback concerning the use of the Dependency Structure (see the arrow labelled 2).

While updating an item, the Change Structure can be used to classify and record change related data for the item (see the arrow labelled 3), according to the properties of the change at hand and certain change substructures. Example change properties include: the decision whether to make the change, method of change, change benefits, etc. Example change substructures include: projection, factual, deviation analysis, feedback, post analysis, etc. Together, the change properties and associated substructures can capture a considerable amount of classified data concerning changes in a software project. Again, this has been kept implicit in the model so as to maintain simplicity.

There is a feedback cycle back to the Dependency Structure (see the arrow labelled 4), in order to test and validate the change made. The post analysis of the change provides ammunition for future changes to the item; whereas the meta feedback provides suggestions for improvements to the Change Structure (see the arrow labelled 5).

At the meta level (above the broken line in Figure 1), the meta feedback is used to improve the infrastructures. These modified infrastructures are then incorporated appropriately into the environment.

It is normally the case that changes to the infrastructures are much less frequent at the meta level than changes to the items of change at the normal level. The view taken in Prism is that infrastructures are *decreasingly* variant in the early part of their life-cycle, and eventually reach a point where they may become stable. The model in Figure 1 supports this view by incorporating explicitly the meta level of changes, and this differs from most other environments, where the infrastructures are treated as fixed parts of the environment.

2.2. Key Properties of the Model

Among the key properties of the proposed model of changes are that: (i) the model is *explicit*, (ii) the model is *incremental*, (iii) the model has a *continuous* use, and (iv) the model has *two levels* of change: normal and meta levels.

Firstly, the model illustrated in Figure 1 is explicit. It shows the key components and their interactions. Such a model is useful in several significant ways: (1) it helps to direct the focus of research on the problem of change, and the development of an associated environment; (2) it can be used as a yardstick to measure and analyse the relative strengths and weaknesses of other models of change; (3) it can help reason about the models of change; and (4) it can be used to build tailored models of change from the generic model in order to suit particular circumstances.

Secondly, the Prism model is incremental in that as a software project progresses, new items of change, their inter-dependencies, and new change related data and feedback information, are all incrementally captured within the model. This property of the model is significant because information is generally not required or produced in big batches in an environment. It may also occur that certain information (e.g., analytical data resulting from monitoring changes over a period of time) cannot be produced at one time, and so recording of this information must be interleaved with other activities in the environment. Thus, this property suggests the incremental character of certain software tools to support changes in an environment.

Thirdly, the proposed model has a continuous use in that: (i) its use begins when a software project is undertaken, (ii) it is used actively throughout the life-cycle of the project, and (iii) it is used passively during the life-cycles of other parallel and subsequent projects. This property of the model is important because discontinuous use of the model implies that for certain phases of the life-cycle of a software project there would be no representation of the items of change and their inter-dependencies, no record of the changes made, and no post analysis. Consequently, the quality of change related decisions made in the environment may be low due to the lack of adequate history of changes.

Finally, the model has two levels of operation: normal and meta levels of change. This separation of concern here is important because matters concerning change at the normal level are entirely different from those at the meta level. At the normal level, issues are *domain sensitive*, meaning that the items of change, their properties, methods of change, etc., all concern the elements of the software project supported by the environment. On the other hand, at the meta level the issues are *domain free*, meaning that they concern the change related infrastructures.

3. The Dependency Structure

The Dependency Structure, supports the model of changes by facilitating the description of the items of change and their inter-dependencies. It propagates and feeds back change information concerning these items the infrastructure in a structured manner. The key components of the Dependency Structure are: (a) levels of abstraction of the items of change, and (b) basic types of items of change at each level of abstraction.

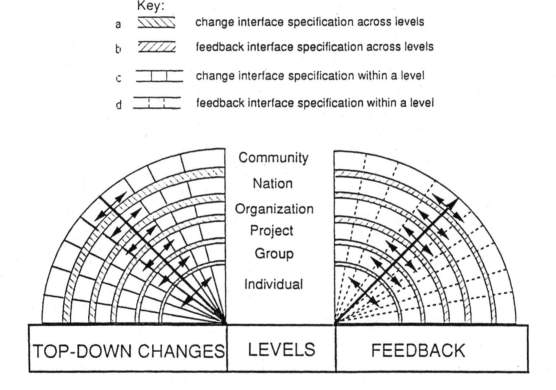

Key:

a   change interface specification across levels

b   feedback interface specification across levels

c   change interface specification within a level

d   feedback interface specification within a level

Figure 2 - Levels of abstraction of the items of change

3.1. Levels of Abstraction

Figure 2 shows example levels of abstraction of the items of change: Individual, Group, Project, Organisation, Nation, and Community (of nations). The downward arrow across the levels of abstraction in the left half of Figure 2 shows that *changes* can be propagated downwards; whereas, the upward arrow in the right half of the figure shows that *feedback* information can be propagated upwards. Changes and feedback can also be propagated within a level of abstraction. This is shown in Figure 2 by pairs of small arrows emanating from the upward and downward arrows. However, note that not all changes in the hierarchy start at the root and terminate at the leaves, and vice versa for the feedback information. This allows for autonomy at any given level of abstraction.

In order to accommodate changes appropriately, making changes to items and passing feedback information should not be carried out in an ad hoc manner. This structured view is depicted by the shaded areas at each level of abstraction in Figure 2 which represent (i) in the left half of the figure: *change interface specifications*, and (ii) in the right half of the figure: *feedback interface specifications*, for propagating changes and feedback information across the level, respectively (see the key in the figure for additional clarity). As will be seen later, these specifications play an important role in tackling the problem of change in an environment. Similarly, the solid lines and the broken lines within a level of abstraction represent specifications for change and feedback propagation within the level, respectively.

There are many significant advantages of the hierarchical organisation for handling the problem of change:

(a) there is a clean separation of concern for each level of abstraction in an environment [15],

(b) the concept of change and feedback interface specifications introduces a formal basis for tackling the dynamics of change in a software project;

(c) specific levels of abstraction may be selected for implementing formal support for changes (e.g., levels Individual and Group), while leaving other levels for informal treatment; and

(d) desired sub-structures at a given level of abstraction may be selected for implementing formal support for changes (e.g., for the level Group: requirements engineering group, software design group, and the software maintenance group), while leaving other sub-structures for informal treatment.

The levels of abstraction shown in Figure 2 should not be confused with Perry and Kaiser's model of environments based on a sociological metaphor [21]. Their classification of environments into individual, family, city and state models focuses on the scale of problems addressed by state of the art environments. It provides insight into the environmental requirements for software projects of different size, duration and complexity. This should be clearly contrasted with the homogeneity in Prism of the basic types of items of change that exist at any level of abstraction.

Similarly, while the layered behaviour model of software development processes used by Curtis, Krasner and Iscoe [22] shares some of the abstractions of Figure 2, their purpose is to analyse problems experienced in developing large software systems. In particular, they propose behavioural analysis of software development and the factors that control its productivity and quality. They view this as a way of overcoming the key problems encountered when the software development process is analysed with models that focus on stages of transforming the artifact.

Our central concern in this section is to identify: (i) items of change, (ii) where in the environment they exist, (iii) what dependencies exist among these items, and (iv) how changes and feedback information can be propagated within the environment. Collectively, these issues present a key problem that must be addressed in the design of a software environment. The Dependency Structure is an important step towards overcoming the problem of tracking change.

3.2. Basic Types of Items

The basic types of items of change at each level of abstraction include: (a) people involved in a software project, (b) project policies, (c) associated laws that must be obeyed, (d) processes supporting the policies, (e) resources, and (f) the results produced. All types of items in a software environment may change from time to time.

The primary reason for classifying items of change into types is to break down the global problem of change in an environment into manageable sub-problems. It is by separation of concern for each type that considerable simplicity may be achieved in: (i) reasoning about changes, (ii) choosing or devising methods of change, and (iii) managing changes. The classification aids in understanding and controlling: dependencies amongst the change items of different types; feedback information about the use of items and changes to them; propagation of change across and within the levels of abstraction in an environment; a history of changes; detailed analysis of the result of change; the information base concerning their attributes; and the selection of the change properties. The classification is supported in Prism by explicit representation of the items of different types in the Dependency Structure and their change related data in the Change Structure.

3.3. Inter-dependencies

At a given level of abstraction, there are usually many sets of tightly related items of change. Each such set is called a *sheet*, and it encapsulates desired items of change and their inter-dependencies. In a software environment there are usually many interacting sheets, forming a system of sheets as shown in Figure 3. We note here that this is in marked contrast to the Darwin software environment [23], where laws enforced for regulating the operation and evolution of a software system are described separately from other possibly related types of items in the environment.

In a system of sheets, items of various types encapsulated within a sheet can be exported (shown as solid arrows in Figure 3) by the sheet (say, D at the level Group) to affect, or impose upon, sibling and lower level sheets (say, E, G, H, and I). Similarly, feedback information concerning the use of an imported item can be propagated from a user-sheet to the supplier-sheet (shown as broken arrows in Figure 3).

The Prism model of changes ensures that the propagation of change and feedback information across sheets is not arbitrary or ad hoc. Individual sheets include formal change and feedback interface specifications. These specifications identify *item-sheet* pairs. Each such pair denotes (i) a particular item of change concerning which change or feedback information might be generated, and (ii) the sheet to which this information should be directed.

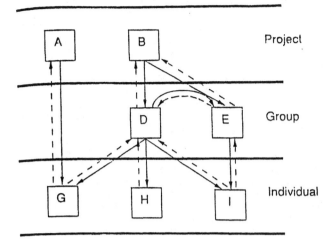

Figure 3 - A system of interacting sheets

3.4. An Example Sheet Program

Consider for example: (i) the sheet D at the level Group in Figure 3; (ii) assume that there are three individuals (i.e., human resources) in the programming group denoted by sheet D: Joe and Tom as programmers and John as a module tester, with children sheets at the level Individual labelled G, H and I respectively; and (iii) assume that the group leader has established a group policy, associated laws and processes:

Policy-1:
To build reliable and readable software modules.

Law-1: *All the given test cases associated with a module must be demonstrated to have been satisfactorily carried out prior to releasing the module into the common pool of binary modules.*

Law-2: *The code of a tested module should have meaningful identifiers and should be indented using the tool INDENT prior to releasing the module into the common pool of source modules.*

Process-1:
Robustness inspection of a module prior to depositing the binary in the common pool.

Process-2:
Quality inspection of a module prior to depositing the source in the common pool.

These items are described as follows within sheet D:

(Level of abstraction: Group *)*
SHEET D;

(Feedback concerning non-local human resources *)*
FEEDBACK
    Joe, Tom, John P-SHEET B;

(Exported Items *)*
EXPORT
    Law-1, Process-1 C-SHEET I;
    Law-2, Process-2 C-SHEET G, H;
    Policy-1 S-SHEET E;

(Declaration of items*)*
POLICIES
    Policy-1 = *(* reliable, readable modules *)*
    POLICY
      object-type: module-code;

```
        process: coding;
        object-result1: reliable;
        object-result2: readable;
      END;
    LAWS
      Law-1 = (* module testing *)
        test(m) → for t in m.testcases ensure t.status=tested;
      Law-2 = (* coding style *)
        ids(m) → m.identifiers = meaningful;
        indentation(m) → m.indent-tool=INDENT;

PROCESSES
    (* binary pool: reliability inspection *)
    Process-1(m, binpool) =
        if test(m) then binpool +:= m;

    (* source pool: quality inspection *)
    Process-2(m, srcpool)=
        if ids(m) & indentation(m) & test(m) then
          srcpool +:= m;

    (* manual readability inspection *)
    ids(m) = manual return m.identifiers = meaningful;

(* Designated human resources (sheets) *)
RESOURCES-HUMAN
    G, H, I;

BEGIN

(* Create children sheets for the human resources *)
CreateSheet (G); CreateSheet (H); CreateSheet (I);

(* Assign human resources to children sheets *)
G := Joe; H := Tom; I : = John;

(* Law-1, Law-2 dependent on Policy-1 *)
Law-1 ← Policy-1.object-result1; (* reliable *)
Law-2 ← Policy-1.object-result2; (* readable *)

(* Process-1 & 2 dependent on Policy-1 *) Process-1 ← Policy-1.object-result1; (* reliable *)
Process-2 ← Policy-1.object-result2; (* readable *)
END-SHEET D.
```

In the code description above, there are: (i) interface specifications for passing back feedback information and for exporting items of change, (ii) declarations of locally defined policies, laws, processes and resources, and (iii) a statement part. In the statement part, the group leader (i.e., owner of sheet D) needs to create positions (by the CreateSheet procedure) for the programmers in the group, i.e., sheets G, H and I (see Figure 3). These positions are filled with the programmers who have been allocated to this group (i.e., imported by virtue of the feedback specification): Joe, Tom and John. This establishes ownerships of the lower level sheets where items of change can be exported from sheet D. Dependencies between parts of Policy-1 and Law-1, Law-2, Process-1 and Process-2 are also described in the statement part.

Policy-1 in the declaration part has been broken down into sub-components: the type of object (object-type), the process concerned (process), and the results desired (object-result1 and object-result2). This enables precise specification of the dependencies between parts of the policy and the associated laws and processes in the statement part of the sheet. Law-1 and Law-2 use specific attributes of a module in stating the reliability and readability laws, e.g., m.testcases, t.status, m.identifiers, and m.indent-tool. Process-1 describes the process of depositing a module in the pool of binary modules. This process is carried out only if Law-1 (reliability) is not violated. Similarly, in Process-2, the source code of the tested module is deposited in the source pool provided that Law-2 is obeyed (module's identifiers are inspected manually, the required tool

INDENT should have been used and, of course, the module has been tested).

In the interface part, Law-1 and Process-1 (module testing) are imposed upon John (child-sheet I) who is a module tester; Law-2 and Process-2 (module coding) are imposed upon Joe (child-sheet G) and Tom (child-sheet H) who are both programmers; and Policy-1, is exported to the sibling sheet E. This ensures that the development processes carried out by the module tester and coders meet the objectives set out in Policy-1 by the group leader. The feedback specification states that any feedback concerning the human resources (i.e., Joe, Tom and John) should be sent to the parent sheet B (broken arrow from D to B in Figure 3). Notice that the distinction between the child, sibling and the parent sheets, in the interface specifications above, is made explicit by the keywords C-SHEET, S-SHEET and P-SHEET respectively. This distinction can be useful to the person assigned to a given sheet (say, the group leader designated by sheet D), especially when assessing the impact of a change to an item or generating some feedback information.

Such change and feedback interface specifications support the process of change management because:

(i) they are formal, or programmable, and hence computing power can be used to: (a) check the consistency between interacting sheets, and (b) help identify affected items of change or automatically propagate feedback information concerning a given item to the responsible party;

(ii) they promote re-use and standardisation of items, such as software policies, laws and processes, within a software project; and

(iii) they are a tool or mechanism for organising items of change according to the levels of abstraction, sub-groups within any given level of abstraction, life-cycle phases, and other structures of a software project.

It is interesting to note that these points address concerns expressed by Osterweil [18], Balzer [24], Perry [19], Humphrey [25], and Dowson [15].

We have examined a number of other issues pertaining to the Dependency Structure which, due to lack of space here, are not presented in this paper; they appear in detail in [9]. These issues include the assessment of the impact of change, different types of feedback, and feedback views and uses.

4. The Change Structure

The Change Structure, supports the described model of changes by facilitating the classification, recording and analysis of change related data. It can propagate feedback information concerning items of change as well as the infrastructure, all in a structured manner. There are three primary features of the Change Structure: (a) integration with the Dependency Structure, (b) a framework for changes, and (c) an information base. Integration with the Dependency Structure permits switching back and forth between an item of change in the Dependency Structure and its change related data in the information base; the framework is a classification scheme which simplifies the structuring of the decisions made for a given change to an item; and the information base provides the necessary data to support the process of making change related decisions. In this paper, we focus on only the aspects integration and framework; information base is outside the scope of this paper.

4.1. Integration with the Dependency Structure

An item of change, such as a software policy, an associated law, a resource, etc., that is declared in a sheet in the Dependency Structure is associated with a set of components in the Change Structure each of which is called a *CS-sheet*. So as to avoid confusion, a sheet in the Dependency Structure is hereafter referred to as a DS-sheet. A CS-sheet describes a particular change in the history of changes to a given item.

Clearly, a DS-sheet has as many associated *sets* of CS-sheets as there are local items of change declared in the DS-sheet. Also, because DS-sheets occur at different levels of abstraction, such as Individual, Group, Project, Organisation, Nation and Community, this implies that CS-sheets also exist at such levels in the environment.

Figure 4 shows (through two broken arrows) a DS-sheet with local items A and B associated with their histories in the form of CS-sheets. Item D in the DS-sheet is a non-local item and hence its history of changes is accessible through its definition in the exporting DS-sheet.

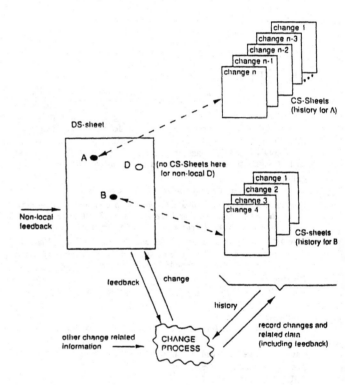

Figure 4 - Integration of CS-sheets with a DS-sheet

A change to an item in a DS-sheet can be instigated by local or non-local feedback, the latter propagated using feedback interface specifications in the DS-sheet. Every time a change is made to an item in a DS-sheet, all the details of the change and related data are recorded in a new CS-sheet associated with the item. Also, any received non-local feedback concerning the item that might have instigated the change, or have been taken into account in the change, should be recorded in this new CS-sheet. Thus, all change related data concerning a particular change to an item are encapsulated in one place.

During the process of making a change, it may be necessary to access previously recorded history of changes made to the item, including possibly of other items via appropriate cross-links (not shown in the figure), in order to obtain an improved understanding of the problem of change. The resultant interactions are shown in Figure 4 as five solid arrows at the bottom of the figure.

An important point about the Prism model of changes is that not only are those decisions that result in changes to an item recorded in a CS-sheet but also those that result in non-changes. This is important because a record of negative decisions may influence future change requests to the item.

The integration of CS-sheets with DS-sheets has two significant aspects to it:

(1) every item of change in the Dependency Structure has a simple connection to the history of previous changes to the item (and other related data such as non-local feedback), and

(2) the history of all the changes that have occurred in an environment is categorised according to the levels of abstraction and substructures that exist in a software project.

These two aspects of integration culminate in simplified access to, and storage of, change related data while accommodating changes in an environment.

4.2. Framework for Changes

The framework of a change is a rich classification scheme that is specialised to capture change related data specific to a given change. In fact, the framework forms the basis for the design of a CS-sheet. The framework itself is not an information base; nor should the framework be confused with a *methodology* for making changes. Rather the framework is an infrastructural support within which changes can be carried out by following one or more methodologies. The framework is in fact methodology independent, implying that it is versatile enough to be used in varying situations. For example, there may be a need to use different methodologies for making changes depending on the type of the item of change (e.g., person, policies and results) and the constraints acting on the change (e.g., availability of resources for making changes). Thus the generality of the proposed framework is one of the strong points of the Change Structure.

4.2.1. Organisation of the Framework

The framework for a change is a quintuple: (i) *type* of the item of change, (ii) *location* of the item in the environment, (iii) *DS-feedback* concerning the item, (iv) *properties* of a change, and (v) *substructures* of a change. The type of an item of change is one of: people, policies, laws, processes, resources, and results; the location of an item of change is the precise DS-sheet in the Dependency Structure where the item is declared; and the DS-feedback is the non-local and the local feedback information concerning the item that is gathered in the Dependency Structure and that which instigated the current process of change or non-change. These three aspects should be well known from the earlier sections. In the CS-sheet describing a change, the type and location of the item associated to the CS-sheet can be known through an infrastructural pointer. This is shown in Figure 4 as the broken arrow from the history of CS-sheets, for say A, to item A in the DS-sheet.

On the other hand, the properties of a change and some substructures form a two-dimensional view of change related data. For example, among the many properties of a change include (i) *decision* of whether to make a proposed change, and (ii) the *person* responsible for the change; and among the change substructures include the categories (i) *predicted* and (ii) *actual*. Thus, from this simple example, it is possible to obtain the following four views of change related data: (a) the predicted decision of whether a change will be made at a later time, (b) the person who is predicted to make this (predicted) decision, (c) the actual decision of change, and (d) the person who actually made this decision. Such views can be useful for many reasons, e.g., predicting aspects of future changes and making actual decisions based on past predicted and actual changes. Below we treat the properties and change substructures in more detail.

4.2.2. Properties of a Change

One of the key problems in accommodating changes in an environment is knowing: (a) all the factors that affect a given change, and (b) the consequencies of this change. The severity of the effect of this problem, however, can depend on the significance of the item of change in the environment. For example, changing a software policy at the level of abstraction Project can affect many project groups working on different aspects of the system under development; whereas changing a software process at the level Individual may not have the same impact on these project groups.

It is nonetheless important to have as clear an understanding as possible of any given change to an item in order to maintain the quality of the environment at all levels of abstraction. For this reason, there is a need to enumerate explicitly the various properties, or characteristics, of a change and consider them while making a change.

There is another reason to state the properties of a change explicitly, and that is that changes in an environment are not a one time activity. Thus, recording the different changes to an item, classified according to the various properties, permits the growth of a classified history of changes which may be used profitably in the decision making process during subsequent changes.

For any given property there are one or more numeric or descriptive values associated with it. These values depend on the item to which the property belongs. For example, the value of the property *person* (i.e., the name of the person who is going to make a change) can be Joe for a software module and Tim for a software policy. Clearly then, in an environment for a complex system where there can be a large number of items of change, there can be a considerably higher number of property values in total. This is yet another reason to state the properties of a change explicitly.

Table 1 gives a list of many properties of change that we have identified. This list is not meant to be exhaustive, and for the construction of an operating Change Structure there would be a need to extend this list. Our purpose here is only to illustrate the kind of properties that do exist for a given change.

Below we exemplify only two of these properties because of the lack of space. Each property has a name, description, and values, following which there is a brief discussion.

(1) *Name*: Method.

Description: The way of carrying out a change.

Values: A list of steps or actions; or a procedure or an

EXAMPLE PROPERTIES OF A CHANGE	

Criteria for deciding whether to make the change
Source of change
  - local feedback in the Dependency Structure (eager change)
  - non-local feedback in the Dependency Structure (demand change)
Decision of whether to make the change
Advantages of carrying out the decision taken
Disadvantages of carrying out the decision taken
Reason for the change or non-change
	Structure of the change process used: meta life cycle
	  - requirements, specifications
	  - design and code
	  - testing and simulation
	  - make changes
	  - maintenance
	Method for carrying out the change
	  - batch style, incremental style
	Resources needed to make the change

What aspect of the item the decision is about
Type of Change
  - static, dynamic
  - corrective, adaptive, perfective
	Reliability of the change process
	Repeatability of the change process
	Extensibility of the change process
	  - including contractability
	Re-usability of the change process
	  - portability, generality supports re-usability
	Efficiency of the change process

Size of change (to this item)
Impact of a change on the entire system
  - qualitative, quantitative along with the degree of each
  - can involve cost analysis, etc.
Cost of obeying decision
Cost of not obeying decision
	Person responsible for the decision
	Reviewer of change
	  - quality control person, process program

Quantitative coupling with other changes
  - prevalence of this kind of changes
Qualitative coupling with other changes
Relation with a previous change (to this item)
  - how new is this change
Explicit constraints acting on the change
  - policy, law
  - sequencing of changes or activities
  - maximum, minimum changes permitted
  - cost, method, etc.
Compromises made in the change
  - includes agreements made with other parties
Conflict caused by the change
  - other people, functioning of other processes, etc.
	Phase of the project in which the decision is made
	Schedule of the change
	Schedule of the review process for this change
	
	Anticipation of the change
	  - anticipated, unanticipated
	Ease of change
	  - trivial, ..., not possible
	Absorption of change
	  - how much change can be sustained by the item
	Reversibility of the change

Table 1 - Example properties of a change

instantiated process program [18, 26, 27], that describes the method used in accomplishing the change.

Discussion: The method used to carry out a change should not be ad hoc or arbitrary. In general, there should be a life-cycle for the way to perform changes. Such a process life-cycle is extensively discussed by Boehm and Belz in [28], Kellner in [29] and by Madhavji et al. in [1]. The requirements for the change method, their specifications, test results, etc., also become properties of a change to an item (see the property *Structure* in Table 1).

(2) *Name*: Impact.

Description: The effect or the consequences of a change [17, 18, 19].

Values: Quantitative and qualitative effect of the change on other items, together with the degree of impact.

Discussion: The identification of the set of items that might be affected by a change can be obtained mechanically by processing the change interface specifications of

the DS-sheets concerned. Nevertheless, it is important to record this information in the CS-sheet describing the change because on future occasions the set of items affected by a change to the same item may differ.

The history of the CS-sheets belonging to the affected items describe qualitative and analytical data. The impact of a change then is a suitable synthesis of the quantitative and qualitative data.

The history of changes to the affected items may provide a profile of how other items have been affected over a period of time.

The classification of the properties, as described in Table 1, helps make a change manageable, because the change related data captured under a given property is generally not large and is in significant contrast to that captured under other properties.

It should be noted that the framework does not enforce that all the properties such as those listed in Table 1 need to be used for each change to each item at each level of abstraction in the environment. For certain practical reasons, it may be necessary to limit or restrict the use of the framework in its various dimensions. This is possible for example by selecting: (i) certain levels of abstraction only (see Figure 2), (ii) parts of a level of abstraction, (iii) particular phases of a software project, (iv) certain types of items only, or (v) only those properties of change that are most relevant to a given item. The fact that this is possible is one of the salient features of the proposed framework.

4.2.3. Overview of Change Substructures

Figure 5 shows the composition of the change substructures that is used, along with the change properties already described, in the design of a CS-sheet. There are three main kinds of substructures: (a) Source Analysis, (b) Post Analysis, and (c) Meta Feedback. The Source Analysis substructure provides a framework for classifying: (i) the projected values and (ii) the factual values of the properties of a given change; (iii) the deviation of the actual values from the projected values; and (iv) the feedback information concerning the change. The projected and factual values yield deviation analysis data, which can then be used to record any immediate feedback. This feedback is provided to the change process (see arrow labelled 4 in Figure 1) for re-adjusting the items in the Dependency Structure.

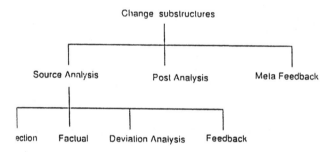

Figure 5 - Change substructures

If appropriate at this time, a post analysis of the aspects of the change can be incrementally carried out and recorded in the Post Analysis substructure. The post analysis is based on source analysis, and has two key aspects: (a) analysis of the change just made to the item and any future recommendations, and (b) analysis of the use of the Source Analysis substructure. The first aspect is used to make future projections; whereas the second aspect is used to recommend, to the Meta Feedback substructure, concrete suggestions for infrastructural improvements.

The meta feedback information is passed on, for analysis, to the party responsible for the maintenance of the Change Structure. This is shown in Figure 1 as a meta feedback loop (arrow labelled 5) from the Change Structure at the normal level of changes to the meta level activities.

A notable characteristic of the framework described above is that there are implicit dependencies between the substructures: Source Analysis, Post Analysis and Meta Feedback.

For example, deviation analysis is based on projection and factual values; feedback information is based on deviation analysis; post analysis is based on feedback; and meta feedback is based on post analysis. Each stage may also make a reference to the other previous stages. Thus, a key benefit of this organisation is that there is a structured approach to making (i) predictions for future changes, and (ii) recommendations for the improvement of the Change Structure.

Another notable characteristic is that all the decisions and analytical data concerning changes to all the items in an environment are explicitly recorded. Thus, for any given change to be made one can circumspectly consider the strong base of information that may help in making the change. Incidently, the recording of all the details of change may also help to mitigate the problems due to turnover of staff, who form perhaps the most important component of an environment.

There are a considerable number of other substructures and related details which, due to lack of space here, are not presented in this paper; they appear in [10]. In particular, this report describes a further breakdown of the Source Analysis, Post Analysis and Meta Feedback substructures.

5. Incorporating Infrastructural Changes

The meta feedback concerning the Dependency Structure, or the Change Structure, (see arrows labelled 2 and 5 in Figure 1) can originate in any DS-sheet, or CS-sheet, at any level of abstraction, and like the feedback concerning items of change, is continuous during the life-cycle of a project. It is, however, expected to be less frequent than the latter type of feedback, and perhaps more frequent in the early phases of the life-cycle of the infrastructures than in the later phases, simply because the infrastructures get stabilised with increased use.

Even so, an important question that needs to be addressed is how to incorporate any infrastructural changes (see Figure 1 above the broken line). Two of the key issues involved in this problem are: (1) whether the information from the old DS-sheets and CS-sheets needs to be transferred into the corresponding new sheets, and (2) the methodology for carrying out a transfer if the transfer should become necessary.

The first of the above two issues focuses on maintaining the compatibility between the old and the new version of the infrastructure, such that no transfer of information from the old to the new sheets, or instantiation, is necessary. While this approach would save a considerable amount of effort associated with instantiation, there is a danger of being drawn into making a compromise in the design of the new infrastructure.

The second issue deals with at least the following two approaches: (i) *eager instantiation*, and (ii) *lazy instantiation*. In the eager instantiation approach, we instantiate new sheets as soon as the new infrastructure is ready for release. Advantages of this approach are (a) retaining homogeneity of the sheets in the infrastructures, and (b) early detection of incompatibility problems. Disadvantages of this approach include the possibly large effort needed in the instantiation of the new sheets at one time.

In the lazy instantiation approach, we instantiate a new sheet upon demand. Advantages of this approach include the minimum amount of effort needed at any given time to carry out instantiation. Disadvantages include (a) long term heterogeneity of the sheets in the infrastructure, and (b) lazy identification of the incompatibility problems.

In the final analysis, it should be clear that the need to accommodate infrastructural changes in an environment is a real one. In an evolving environment, the neglect of such changes often leads the infrastructure to obsoleteness or unfriendliness. On the other hand, continuous and orderly maintenance of the infrastructure gives it longevity and possibly relative efficiency. The Prism model of changes facilitates such maintenance by providing a meta feedback scheme that is built into the infrastructures.

6. Related Work and Comparisons

The problem of change in software processes, including the wider aspect of dynamism, has recently been recognised as a key issue in the design of software environments. Among the points of concern expressed are (i) the evolution of programmed processes, and (ii) promotion of common technology across processes.

Redwine [16], points out several degrees of change in the process model life-cycle: changing instances, types, type systems, etc. On the other hand, Osterweil [18], has pressed for rigorous descriptions of software process code, so that changes can be accurately specified and assessed. In a similar vein, Perry [19] recognises the need for extensive knowledge of the places where changes must be made and the way these changes interact with various process instantiations and customisations. Humphrey, in his definition of a software process architecture [25], and Perry in [19], suggest the benefits of standardisation across projects, thereby simplifying changes across these projects.

The Prism model of changes addresses these issues, and more, in a direct and a specific way. Firstly, the levels of abstraction in the Dependency Structure (see Figure 2) provides a way of categorising items of change in an environment. This issue was one of the several key points in Dowson's summary report on the 3rd international software process workshop [15]. In a manner, this is an architectural point which can bring about standardisation of policies, laws, processes, resources, etc., within and across the levels of abstraction, while allowing for particular needs in unusual circumstances.

Secondly, it can be said that the Dependency Structure and the Change Structure provide a much broader and deeper view of the items of change in an environment than purely the software process view. Much of the extant literature focuses on software process models and programs in so far as changes are concerned; whereas, in our work we have attempted to centre changes explicitly around multiple items (i.e., people, policies, laws, processes, resources and results) and their interdependencies in the Dependency Structure, and around change properties and substructures in the Change Structure.

Thirdly, the change interface specifications encourage re-use of items in an environment. The subject of re-use of software processes was in fact one of the main points of Osterweil's keynote speech [18], and has also been pointed out by Balzer [24] and Kellner [29], among others. Our work on the Dependency Structure automatically extends re-usability to other items of change, such as policies and laws. This is a significant improvement over the current technology where policies, laws, processes, etc., are often re-invented in an ad hoc manner in different phases and parts of a software project.

Fourthly, change interface specifications and the change classification scheme solve a major part of the problem of assessing the impact of a change. More specifically, they help identify the items affected by a given change and enable qualitative analysis of change related data.

Fifthly, an important issue that is not significantly addressed in existing systems is the aspect of feedback [26]. In the design of change related infrastructures, we have incorporated mechanisms for communicating feedback information. Various feedback views [9] are therefore possible from the perspectives of the generator and receiver of this information, which may help in assessing items of change.

Sixthly, extending the idea of feedback even further, there is support for meta feedback concerning the infrastructures. A fundamental assumption underlying this mechanism is that the design of the infrastructures may not be right the first time; it rarely is, and therefore an escape mechanism is necessary where the users of the infrastructures can provide valuable input for improvements.

Finally, we have made extensive comparisons of the Prism model of changes (see Figure 1) with state-of-the-art research on changes in a number of systems: IPSE 2.5 [5], model of the Navy F-14A software support process [30], HFSP model [31], E-L system [4], Marvel [3], System Factory Project [32], and Arcadia [2]. The detailed comparisons, including tabulated findings, are presented in [8]; here we give a synopsis of this study.

The aspects of the Prism model used in the comparisons include: meta and normal levels of changes, infrastructures supporting changes, meta feedback, levels of abstraction, explicit dependencies between items of change, the types of items of change, the types of feedback information, recording of changes and of post analysis, and existence of an explicit model of changes.

The comparative study points out several issues concerning existing work on changes: focus is on the normal level changes; meta-level changes [19, 33] are briefly sketched; existence of explicit dependencies amongst the items of change supported; popular items of change are software products, processes and resources; items of change such as people, policies [19] and laws [23] are not widespread; weak focus on the levels of abstraction [19] where changes take place; feedback concerning a comprehensive set of items of change [34, 5] is not widely recognised; extensive classification scheme for changes is non-existent; and there is a lack of explicit models of change.

7. Conclusions

We have developed a model of changes in the Prism project [1, 8, 9, 10], with the following key or unique features: (a) separation between normal and meta levels of changes; (b) a comprehensive coverage of the types of items of change: people, policies, laws, processes, resources, and results; (c) explicit representation of the items of change and their interdependencies; (d) levels of abstraction in the environment where changes can occur; (e) classification of the different types of changes, together with post analysis; (f) normal and meta level feedback information; (g) integrated and complementary infrastructures specialised to support changes (i.e., the Dependency Structure and the Change Structure); and (h) being incremental and continuous. This adds significantly to the state-of-the-art research on the issue of changes described in [27].

The Prism model of changes is a strong basis for a practical system which may be used in industrial and other environments. In particular, our model suggests the use of infrastructures such as the Dependency Structure and the

Change Structure, without which accommodating changes in a software environment would be considerably more difficult and ad hoc. So as to have a practical feel for the model presented in this paper, we are currently experimenting with process descriptions and our process modelling methodology [1]. This should give us the much needed feedback in our approach to handling changes.

Acknowledgements

Nashira Keshavjee was the continuous source of countless thought provoking discussions throughout this research on the problem of change [8, 9, 10]. She suggested substantial improvements to earlier reports and made a number of editorial comments. Manny Lehman and Hausi Müller gave copious constructive criticisms on the earlier version of this paper. Kamel Toubache and Michael Timm provided several helpful comments. Herbert Schippers suggested pertinent changes to [8, 9, 10], and Udo Kelter and Michael Goedicke gave helpful remarks on [8]. To all these individuals the author is deeply thankful.

8. References

[1] N. H. Madhavji, et al., "Prism = Methodology + Process-oriented Environment," *Proc. 12th Int. Conf. on Soft. Eng.*, pp. 277-288, IEEE Computer Society Press, Nice, France, March 1990.

[2] R. N. Taylor, et al., "Foundations for the Arcadia Environment Architecture," *Proc. of the ACM Sym. on Soft. Dev. Env., ACM SIGPLAN Notices*, vol. 24, no. 2, pp. 1-13, Boston, MA., Nov. 1988.

[3] G. E. Kaiser, "Rule-Based Modeling of the Software Development Process," *in [27]*, pp. 84-86.

[4] T. Cheatham, "Activity Coordination Programs," *in [27]*, pp. 57-60.

[5] C. Roberts and A. Jones, "Dynamics of Process Models in PML ," *Proc. 5th Int. Workshop on the Software Process, ACM SIGSOFT*, ACM Press, Kennebunkport, Maine, USA, October 1989.

[6] L. G. Williams, "Software Process Modelling: A Behavioural Approach," *Proc. 10th Int. Conf. on Softw. Engineering* , pp. 174-186, IEEE Computer Society Press, Singapore, April 1988.

[7] C. Fernström and L. Ohlsson, "The ESF Vision of a Software Factory," in *Int. Conf. on System Development Environments and Factories*, ed. Madhavji, N. H., Schäfer, W., and Weber, H., pp. 91-98, Pitman Publishing, Berlin, May 1989.

[8] N. H. Madhavji, "The Prism Model of Changes - Part 1: Introduction," Technical Report TR-SOCS-90.15, p. 24, School of Computer Science, McGill University, Montreal, July 1990.

[9] N. H. Madhavji, "The Prism Model of Changes - Part 2: Dependency Structure," Technical Report TR-SOCS-90.16, p. 21, School of Computer Science, McGill University, Montreal, July 1990.

[10] N. H. Madhavji, "The Prism Model of Changes - Part 3: Change Structure," Technical Report TR-SOCS-90.17, p. 23, School of Computer Science, McGill University, Montreal, July 1990.

[11] W. Babich, in *Software Configuration Management*, Addison-Wesley, Reading, MA., 1986.

[12] S. I. Feldman, "MAKE- A Program for maintaining Computer Programs," *Soft.-Prac. and Exp.*, vol. 9, pp. 225-265, 1979.

[13] M.J. Rochkind, "The source code control system," *IEEE Transactions on Software Engineering*, vol. SE-1, pp. 364-370, Dec. 1975.

[14] W. F. Tichy, "RCS - A system for version control," *Software - Practice and Experience*, vol. 15, no. 7, pp. 637-654, 1985.

[15] M. Dowson, "Iteration in the Software Process: Review of the 3rd International Software Process Workshop," *Proc. 9th Int. Conf. on Soft. Eng.*, pp. 36-39, IEEE Computer Society Press, Monterey, California, April 1987.

[16] S.T. Redwine, "Constructing Enactable Models (or Process Models for Process Models): Session Summary," *in [27]*, pp. 17-22.

[17] L. G. Williams, "Emerging Issues: Session Summary," *in [27]*, pp. 29-31.

[18] L. Osterweil, "Software Processes are Software Too," *Proc. 9th Int. Conf. on Soft. Eng.*, pp. 2-13, IEEE Computer Society Press, Monterey, California, April, 1987

[19] D. E. Perry, "Problems of Scale and process Models," *in [27]*, pp. 126-128.

[20] M. M. Lehman, "Uncertainty in computer application and its control through the engineering of software," *Journal of Software Maintenance*, vol. 1, no. 1, pp. 3-27, September 1989.

[21] D. E. Perry and G. E. Kaiser, "Models of Software Development Environments ," *Proc. 10th Int. Conf. on Soft. Eng.*, pp. 60-68, IEEE Computer Society Press, Singapore, April 1988.

[22] B. Curtis, et al., "On Building Software Process Models Under the Lamppost," *Proc. 9th Int. Conf. on Soft. Eng.*, pp. 96-103, IEEE Computer Society Press, Monterey, California, April 1987.

[23] N. Minsky and D. Rozenshtein, "A Software Development Environment for Law-Governed Systems," *Proc. of the ACM Symp. on Soft. Development Environments, ACM SIGPLAN Notices*, vol. 24, no. 2, pp. 65-75, Boston, MA., Nov. 1988.

[24] R. Balzer, "Process Programming: Passing into a new Phase," *in [27]*, pp. 43-45.

[25] W.S. Humphrey, "The Software Engineering Process: Definition and Scope," *in [27]*, pp. 82-83.

[26] Dowson, M., ed., "Iteration in the software process," *Proc. 3rd Int. Software Process Workshop*, IEEE Computer Society Press, Breckenridge, Colorado, US, November 1986.

[27] C. Tully, ed., "Representing and Enacting the Software Process," *Proc. 4th Int. Software Process Workshop, ACM SIGSOFT*, vol. 14, no. 4, ACM Press, Moretonhampstead, Devon, UK, May 1988.

[28] B. Boehm and F. Belz, "Applying Process Programming to the Spiral Model," *in [27]*, pp. 46-56.

[29] M.I. Kellner, "Representation Formalisms for Software Process Modeling," *in [27]*, pp. 93-96.

[30] M.I. Kellner, "Experience with Enactable Software Process Models," *Proc. 5th Int. Workshop on the Software Process, ACM SIGSOFT*, ACM Press, Kennebunkport, Maine, USA, October 1989.

[31] T. Katayama , "A Heirarchical and Functional Software Process Description and Its Enaction," *Proc. 11th Int. Conf. on Soft. Eng.*, pp. 343-352, IEEE Computer Society Press, Pittsburgh, Pennsylvania, May 1989.

[32] W. Scacchi, "Modelling Software Evolution: A Knowledge-Based Approach," *in [27]*, pp. 153-155.

[33] L. Osterweil, "Automated Support for the Enactment of Rigorously described Software Processes," *in [27]*, pp. 122-125.

[34] V. R. Basili and H. D. Rombach, "Tailoring the Software Process to Project Goals and Environments," *Proc. 9th Int. Conf. on Soft. Eng.*, pp. 345-357, IEEE Computer Society Press, Monterey, California, April 1987.

A Unified Interprocedural Program Representation for a Maintenance Environment

Mary Jean Harrold, *Member, IEEE,* and Brian Malloy

Abstract—Modifying and then validating a program with many interacting modules, such as procedures, is an expensive and complex task: maintenance activities must be performed for changed procedures and for those procedures that directly or indirectly interact with the changed procedure. The problem is further compounded because the maintainer is rarely the author of the code and usually lacks an understanding of the program. Thus, a maintenance environment containing an efficient program representation and tools that access the representation to assist the user in understanding, modifying, analyzing, reengineering, testing, and debugging a program are needed. This paper presents our *unified interprocedural graph*, UIG, that extracts the important features of existing program representations, and adds new information, to provide an integrated representation for maintenance tasks. We adapt previous interprocedural techniques to use the UIG, and we provide sufficient information to accommodate development of new interprocedural techniques. Algorithms that were developed for previous representations were adapted to use the UIG by identifying the subset of nodes and edges in the UIG required for that computation. Newly developed algorithms can use the UIG since it contains data flow, control flow, data dependence, and control dependence information. The main benefits of our approach are the reduction in storage space since individual representations are not kept, the savings in maintenance time of a single representation over the individual representations, and the convenience of accessing a single program representation without increase in access time. A single program representation also assists in program understanding since relationships among program elements are incorporated into one graph.

Index Terms—Interprocedural program representation, maintenance environment, maintenance tools, program understanding.

I. INTRODUCTION

PROGRAM maintenance is an expensive process where an existing program is modified for a variety of reasons, including correcting errors, adapting to different data or processing environments, enhancing to add functionality or altering to improve efficiency. For programs with many interacting modules, such as procedures, modifying and then revalidating a program is complex: analysis, testing, and debugging may be required for each procedure individually (*intra*procedural) and for the interaction among procedures (*inter*procedural). The problem is further compounded because the maintainer is rarely the author of the code and usually lacks an understanding of the program. Thus, a maintenance

Manuscript received April 27, 1992; revised November 30, 1992. This work was supported in part by the National Science Foundation under Grant CCR-9109531 to Clemson University. Recommended by Vaclav Rajlich.

The authors are with the Department of Computer Science, Clemson University, Clemson, SC 29634-1906.

IEEE Log Number 9208630.

environment containing an efficient program representation, along with tools to access that representation to assist the user with maintenance tasks such as understanding, modifying, analyzing, reengineering, testing, and debugging at both the intraprocedural and interprocedural levels, is needed.

Currently, techniques do exist to assist in intraprocedural and interprocedural activities during maintenance, and all of them require information such as data flow, control flow, data dependence and control dependence. Complete reanalysis of a modified program's source code is avoided by incrementally updating the program's representation, including data flow information, to reflect changes [7], [16], [19]. For program understanding and assistance in locating the sources of errors, existing techniques use both data dependence and control dependence information to identify all statements in a program, including those that reach across procedure boundaries, that affect a given statement [9], [10]. This subset of all program statements is also used to identify those statements that can be scheduled in parallel [12], [13] and may assist in the generation of test cases. To determine whether iterations of a loop containing a call statement can be executed in parallel, both control flow and data flow information are used to determine the effects of the call on reference parameters and global variables [2]. This information permits an existing program to be adapted for parallel processing. For testing individual procedures or interfaces among interacting procedures, incremental data flow analysis techniques identify data dependencies [7], [16], [19], and incremental testing techniques [6], [8], [15], [20] assist in regression testing.

One approach to building an environment for maintenance is to incorporate each of the existing representations into a maintenance environment and use the associated algorithms to develop program maintenance tools. However, with this approach, the environment includes several independent program representations resulting in redundant information. For example, the code statements, the parameter information, and the program structure are repeated for each representation of the program. Additionally, with this approach, important program information, including control flow, data flow, control dependence and data dependence, is contained in different representations, which requires that new algorithms that use a different combination of this information access several representations. Our approach is to develop a unified interprocedural program representation that integrates information necessary for maintenance, and then adapt existing algorithms and develop new algorithms to use this unified representation. The main benefits of this approach are the reduction in storage space for the individual representations and the convenience of accessing a single program representation. Storage space is reduced for the individual representations since redundant information is eliminated. Implementations that require information previously provided by the individual program representations must only access a single representation to acquire the needed information. However, access time is not increased by using the single representation instead of the individual representations. Further, a single integrated representation that contains necessary program information can easily accommodate new techniques for maintenance tools. Another important benefit is the savings realized when a program is modified since our approach requires updating only one program representation instead of many different representations. Finally, a single program representation also assists in program understanding since relationships among program elements are contained in one graph.

This paper presents our unified interprocedural program representation, the *unified interprocedural graph* or UIG, that extracts the necessary features of existing program representations to permit access to information for maintenance tasks. The existing algorithms developed for each of these independent program representations are adapted to use this unified representation by identifying the subset of nodes and edges required for that computation. The complexity of the algorithms on the UIG is the same as on the program representations for which they were originally developed. The UIG is the program representation for our maintenance environment where the associated algorithms are used to build program maintenance tools. In the next section, we discuss the issues involved in developing a program maintenance environment. Section III presents a brief overview of the graph representations on which the UIG is based and illustrates them with an example. The algorithms that use these graphs to gather the interprocedural information are described but details are omitted from this presentation. More detailed discussions can be found in Ryder [17], Callahan [2], Harrold and Soffa [7], and Horwitz, Reps, and Binkley [9]. We present the details for handling reference parameters; global variables can be handled similarly. In Section IV, the UIG is presented, including details of its construction and adaptations of the existing interprocedural algorithms. Section V presents an overview of our maintenance tools, Section VI discusses our implementation and concluding remarks are given in Section VII.

II. Developing a Unified Program Representation

Fig. 1 illustrates the layered structure of our program maintenance environment. The outermost layer contains some of the classes of program maintenance tools. This outermost layer is built on top of primitive operations. In Fig. 1, we show a representative set of primitives such as *GetSlice()* and *GetDUPairs()*. Only the primitive operations access the innermost layer of the environment, the UIG. The design of the program maintenance environment uses an object-oriented approach that encapsulates the data and primitive operations. Program maintenance tools access the UIG only through these primitive operations. For example, a data flow tester accesses the *GetDUPairs()* and a viewer accesses the *GetCallGraph()*.

The first task in the development of our maintenance environment is to design a program representation that contains sufficient precision about both the individual procedures and the interaction among the procedures to permit computation of the necessary information for maintenance activities. Such a program representation contains control and data flow information along with control and data dependence information. We considered many different program representations and chose those four that contain the aspects of a program that must be included in our unified interprocedural graph. Construction of the UIG incorporates the required features of these existing program representations, resolves their differences and eliminates redundant information.

The next task is to design the environment's primitives by adapting existing interprocedural algorithms to use the UIG. These algorithms were originally designed to perform computations using other program representations. To adapt an algorithm for use with the UIG, we identify a subset of the nodes and edges in the UIG that are necessary for that computation, and show that the complexity of the algorithm does not increase when it is performed on this subset. The final task is to design program maintenance tools that use the primitive operations on the UIG to compute information about the program.

III. Interprocedural Representations

Since we extract information from four different program representations for the UIG, we overview details of each of the different representations.

A. The Call Graph

Existing interprocedural program representations are variations of a program's *call graph*. In a call graph, nodes represent individual procedures and edges represent call sites. Each edge is labeled with the actual parameters associated with that call site. Since one procedure may call another at many points, a call graph may be a multigraph with more than one edge connecting any two nodes. Fig. 2 presents a simple program *Sums*, that computes the sums of the first n positive integers, and *Sums'* call graph. Statements in the program are numbered for reference. The call graph contains nodes for *Sums* and for each of the three procedures *Acc*, *Add*, and *Inc*. Edge (*Sums, Acc*), labeled with actual parameters *sum* and *i*, represents the call to procedure *Acc* at line 6. Other call sites are represented by edges (*Acc, Add*), (*Acc, Inc*), and (*Inc, Add*) and correspond to lines 14, 15, and 19 respectively.

A program's call graph can be constructed efficiently [17] and used for many different applications. Since a call graph represents the procedural structure of a program and illustrates the calling relationships among procedures, it is useful during maintenance for program understanding. A call graph is also useful for interprocedural data flow analysis. Interprocedural data flow analysis algorithms that use a call graph are *flow-insensitive* since they do not consider the control flow of individual procedures [1], [3], [18], [21]. However, flow-insensitive interprocedural data flow analysis algorithms can determine information such as whether an actual reference parameter may be modified by a call to a procedure. For

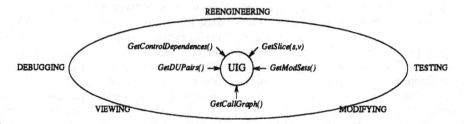

Fig. 1. Our program maintenance environment with the Unified Interprocedural Graph as the program representation. Representative "primitive" operations such as *GetSlice(s,v)* and *GetCallGraph()* are illustrated. Classes of program maintenance tools are shown on the outer layer of the environment.

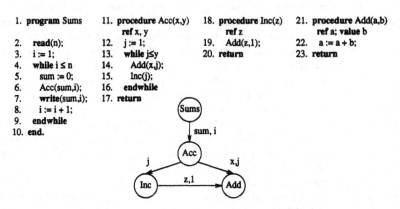

```
1. program Sums          11. procedure Acc(x,y)    18. procedure Inc(z)    21. procedure Add(a,b)
                             ref x, y                   ref z                  ref a; value b
2.   read(n);            12.  j := 1;              19.  Add(z,1);          22.  a := a + b;
3.   i := 1;            13.  while j≤y            20. return              23. return
4.   while i ≤ n        14.      Add(x,j);
5.     sum := 0;        15.      Inc(j);
6.     Acc(sum,i);      16.  endwhile
7.     write(sum,i);    17. return
8.     i := i + 1;
9.   endwhile
10. end.
```

Fig. 2. *Sums*, which computes the sums of the first *n* positive integers, and *Sums'* Call Graph. Nodes in the Call Graph represent procedures and edges represent procedure call sites. Edges are labeled with the actual parameters associated with the call site.

example, flow-insensitive data flow analysis of program *Sums* using its call graph in Fig. 2 determines that in procedure *Acc*, variable *x* may be modified by the call to procedure *Add*. This information is required for safe code optimization and parallelization.

B. The Program Summary Graph

Although a call graph is useful for many types of interprocedural analyses, it contains insufficient precision for many important applications. For example, a call graph contains no information about either the procedure returns or the flow of control in individual procedures. Thus, a call graph is not sensitive enough to answer questions such as whether a value of a reference parameter may remain unchanged over a procedure call. This *flow-sensitive* analysis must incorporate both the procedure returns and the flow of control of individual procedures. Such flow-sensitive information is essential for some optimizations and for register allocation across procedure boundaries.

To provide this data flow information, variations of the call graph have been developed that are sensitive to the control flow in individual procedures. One variation of the call graph is the *program summary graph* [2]. The program summary graph and the algorithms that use it for flow-sensitive data flow analysis were developed to reengineer existing programs for parallel environments. For example, more precise information about the behavior of reference parameters and global variables across call sites in Fortran **do** loops is required to permit greater parallelization of the iterations of the loops. A program summary graph contains information about actual reference parameters and global variables at call sites, and formal reference parameters and global variables at procedure entry and exit points. In a program summary graph, call and return nodes represent call and return sites for actual reference parameters, and entry and exit nodes represent procedure entry and exit points for formal reference parameters. Similar information is represented for global variables. First, we discuss the technique to handle reference parameters; later, we briefly discuss the handling of global variables.

In a program summary graph, for each procedure, there are entry and exit nodes for each formal reference parameter. At each call site, there are call and return nodes for each actual reference parameter. Fig. 3 depicts the program summary graph for program *Sums* of Fig. 2. In Fig. 3, circles represent call and return nodes and double circles represent entry and exit nodes. Nodes 1 and 2 represent the call and return sites, respectively, for actual parameter *sum* at the call to procedure *Acc* in line 6 of program *Sums*. Likewise, node pairs {3,4}, {11,12}, {9,10}, and {15,16} represent actual reference parameters at call and return sites on lines 6, 14, 15, and 19 respectively. Note that actual parameter *j* on line 14 of procedure *Acc* is passed by value and since we are only propagating reference parameters, there is no associated call/return pair for the call site in *Acc* nor is there an associated entry/exit pair in procedure *Add*. Nodes 5 and 6 represent the entry and exit points, respectively, in procedure *Acc* for formal reference parameter *x*. Node pairs {7,8}, {13,14} and {17,18} also represent entry and exit points for formal reference parameters on lines 11 and 17, 18 and 20, 21 and 23, respectively.

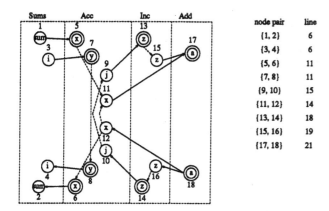

node pair	line
{1, 2}	6
{3, 4}	6
{5, 6}	11
{7, 8}	11
{9, 10}	15
{11, 12}	14
{13, 14}	18
{15, 16}	19
{17, 18}	21

Fig. 3. The program summary graph for *Sums* in Fig. 2. Circles represent call/return nodes, double circles represent entry/exit nodes, solid lines represent call/return binding edges and dashed lines represent reaching edges. Node numbers facilitate presentation and do not correspond to the line numbers of Fig. 2. The correlation between node pairs and lines is shown in the table to the right of Fig. 3.

There are two kinds of edges in the program summary graph: 1) binding edges that relate actual and formal reference parameters and 2) reaching edges that summarize the flow of data between procedure control points such as entry, exit, call and return for formal and actual parameters. In Fig. 3, solid lines represent binding edges and dashed lines represent reaching edges. For example, binding edges (1,5) and (6,2) relate actual parameter *sum* in *Sums* with formal parameter x in *Acc*. Other binding edges relating formal and actual parameters are (3,7) and (8,4), (9,13) and (14,10), (11,17) and (18,12), and (15,17) and (18,16). Reaching edge (5,11) indicates that any value of x that reaches the beginning of procedure *Acc* also reaches the call site in line 14, represented by node 11, where it is used as an actual parameter. Reaching edge (10,9) indicates that the value of j that reaches the return site in line 15, represented by node 10, also reaches back to the call site in line 15, represented by node 9. This reaching edge is a backedge in the program summary graph since the call site is in a loop in the program. Other reaching edges are (7,8), (13,15), (16,14), (12, 6), and (12,11).

Iterative algorithms [2] use the program summary graph to determine information such as whether the values of actual reference parameters *may-be-preserved* over a procedure call. The value of a variable may-be-preserved over a procedure call if there is some execution path through the procedure on which it is not redefined. An actual reference parameter may-be-preserved over a procedure call if there is a path in the program summary graph from the call node to the return node representing that parameter at that call site. In Fig. 3, there is a path from node 3, representing actual parameter i at the call to procedure *Acc*, to node 4, representing actual parameter i at the return. This path through nodes 3,7,8,4 means that there is some path through procedure *Acc* on which the associated formal parameter y is not redefined and thus, the value of i may-be-preserved over the call to procedure *Acc*.

Since the scope of global variables is the entire program, they are handled differently than reference parameters in the program summary graph. In the program summary graph, there is a single global node representing all global variables at each entry, exit, call and return site. Binding edges connect these global nodes across procedure boundaries. There is a reaching edge for each (entry, call), (entry, exit), (return, call) and (return, exit) pair. Associated with each of these reaching edges is a bit vector indicating which global variables are not redefined in that region of the program. For example, if there is a path from the beginning of a procedure to a call site where global variable g is not redefined, the bit in the (call, entry) vector corresponding to g is set. Iterative algorithms compute may-be-preserved information for global variables by considering paths through the program.

C. The Interprocedural Flow Graph

While the program summary graph provides flow-sensitive data flow information about reference parameters and global variables, it contains no information about the locations of the definitions and uses[1] of these variables that is required to test the interfaces among the procedures. For example, in Fig. 3, the program summary graph cannot be used directly to determine the locations of uses of actual parameter *sum* that can be reached from the call site in line 6 of program *Sums*. However, a variation of the program summary graph, the *interprocedural flow graph* and its associated data flow analysis algorithm [7], provides information at each node about the locations of definitions and uses of reference parameters and global variables that can be reached across procedure boundaries. The data flow analysis algorithm gathers intraprocedural data flow information at each node in the interprocedural flow graph and then propagates it throughout the program guided by the edges in the graph. The result is a set of definitions that reach each node in the graph (*reaching definitions*). A similar algorithm computes the set of uses that can be reached from each node in the graph (*reachable uses*). Using the local definitions that reach the call and exit nodes, the algorithm identifies pairs of definitions and uses for interface testing. The propagation algorithm must consider the calling context of called procedures so that traversal of the interprocedural flow graph continues correctly according to the way in which the procedure was called. A new edge, the *interprocedural reaching* edge connecting call and return nodes, ensures that data flow information is propagated only over possible execution paths in the program.

Fig. 4 depicts the interprocedural flow graph along with the reachable use sets that are attached to some of its nodes. The nodes are the same as those for a program summary graph and thus, identical to those in Fig. 3; binding and reaching edges are also the same. Interprocedural reaching edge (3,4) illustrates one difference between an interprocedural flow graph and a program summary graph. This edge summarizes the effects of the procedure call in line 6 of Fig. 2 on parameter i at the call site: the value of i may-be-preserved over the call. A second difference between the program summary graph and the interprocedural flow graph is the reachable use sets that

---

[1] A *definition* of a variable is a point in the program where the value of the variable is stored or changed, and a *use* of a variable is a point in the program where the value of the variable is fetched.

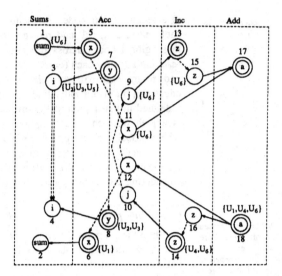

Fig. 4. The interprocedural flow graph for *Sums* in Fig. 2. Circles represent call/return nodes, double circles represent entry/exit nodes, solid lines represent binding edges, dashed lines represent reaching edges, and double dashed lines represent interprocedural reaching edges. Uses reachable across procedure boundaries are listed to the right of the graph and reachable use sets are attached to call and exit nodes.

are attached to nodes in the interprocedural flow graph. For program *Sums*, the use of variable a in line 22, U_6, is reachable from nodes 1, 9, 11, and 15 and is attached to those nodes. Thus, the definitions of the associated actual parameters that reach nodes 1, 9, 11, and 15 also reach the use of a in line 22. These definitions are: the definition of *sum* in line 5 since it reaches node 1 and the definition of j in line 12 since it reaches node 9. Other uses that can be reached over procedure boundaries are attached to call and exit nodes. Use sets are also computed for entry and return nodes, but are omitted from Fig. 3 since they are not used to compute the definition-use pairs for testing.

For data flow testing [5], [11], [14], the definition-use pairs are computed using the interprocedural flow graph and propagation algorithm described above [8]. Then, test cases are generated to traverse subpaths from the definitions to the uses during program execution. A subpath must contain no redefinition of the variable. To illustrate, consider reachable use U_6, consisting of the use of a in line 22, that can be reached from definitions in lines 5 and 12 of program *Sums* in Fig. 2. This reachable use of a, along with the two definitions, defines definition-use pairs (5, 22) and (12, 22) for a. These two definition-use pairs must be traversed during execution of the program. Other definition-use pairs, identified by considering the data dependencies, are also tested.

D. The System Dependence Graph

Although the interprocedural flow graph contains sufficient information to permit the computation of interprocedural data dependencies, it lacks information about control dependencies in the program. Such information is required for debugging and identifying the statements that can execute in parallel. A variation of the call graph that models a program's control dependencies is the *system dependence graph* [9]. The system dependence graph combines dependence graphs for individual procedures [4] with additional nodes and edges to permit the

computation of an interprocedural slice of the program. A *dependence graph* for an individual procedure [4] represents a procedure as a graph in which the nodes are statements and predicate expressions and the edges incident to a node represent both the data values on which the node's operations depend and the control conditions on which the execution of the operations depends. A *slice* of a program with respect to program point p and variable x consists of all statements and predicates in the program that might affect the value of x at point p [9]. Control and data dependencies provided by a dependence graph have many uses including exposing parallelism in a program and enabling optimizations; slicing is useful in testing and debugging.

To construct the system dependence graph, nodes are added to a procedure's dependence graph to model parameter passing. Parameter passing is represented by a call-site node and by four types of parameter nodes: actual-in, actual-out, formal-in, and formal-out. Control edges are added between the call-site nodes and the four types of parameter nodes. Parameter-in edges connect actual-in with formal-in nodes and connect formal-out with actual-out nodes. Intraprocedural data flow information allows the creation of flow dependence edges to represent the data dependencies among the statements.

The problem of preserving procedure calling context when computing a slice is similar to that observed for data flow set propagation in the interprocedural flow graph. For the system dependence graph, an *interprocedural flow* edge models the transitive flow dependencies, including both control and data dependencies, across a procedure call. This edge permits a more precise computation of a slice across procedure boundaries.

Fig. 5 shows the partial system dependence graph for program *Sums* in Fig. 2 where only procedures *Acc*, *Add*, and *Inc* are illustrated. In Fig. 5, double squares represent proc-entry nodes and thus, nodes 1, 16, and 23 are the proc-entry nodes in the graph. Squares represent call-site nodes

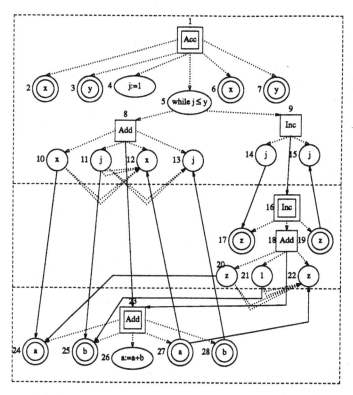

Fig. 5. Partial system dependence graph for *Sums* in Fig. 2, showing only procedures *Acc*, *Add*, and *Inc*. Double squares represent proc-entry nodes, squares represent call-site nodes, double circles represent formal-in/formal-out nodes, circles represent actual-in/actual-out nodes, solid lines represent parameter-in/parameter-out edges, dotted lines represent control edges, and double dotted lines represent interprocedural flow edges. Flow edges are omitted.

and there is one for every procedure call. Nodes 8, 9, and 18 are call-site nodes and represent procedure calls on lines 14, 15, and 19, respectively, in program *Sums*. Dotted lines are control edges and indicate the control dependencies between the statements. Control edges (1,2), (1,3), (1,4), (1,5), (1,6), and (1,7) indicate that statements corresponding to nodes 2, 3, 4, 5, 6, and 7 have the same control conditions for execution. Solid lines are parameter-in and parameter-out edges and associate formal and actual parameters. In Fig. 5, edges (10,24) and (27,12) bind actual parameter *x* at the call site in line 14 in procedure *Acc* to the formal parameter *a* in procedure *Add*. Finally, double dotted lines represent interprocedural flow edges. Edges (10,12), (11,12), (11,13), (20,22), and (21,22) are interprocedural flow edges that summarize the data flow over the procedure calls. For example, interprocedural flow edge (10, 12) indicates that the returned value of *x* from the call to procedure *Add* on line 14 in *Acc* is dependent on the value of *x* at the call. Likewise, interprocedural flow edge (11, 12) indicates that the returned value of *x* at that same call site is also dependent on the value of *j* at the call. An interprocedural slice of the partial program shown in Fig. 5 computed with respect to the formal-out parameter *z* represented by node 22 consists of all nodes except 2, 6, 10, and 12 and all edges except (1,2), (1,6), (10,24), (10,12), and (27,12).

IV. A Unified Interprocedural Representation

Although each of the interprocedural program representations described above is useful for its intended purpose,

none of them can be used to compute all of the information necessary for program maintenance. Clearly, the call graph contains insufficient precision to compute either flow-sensitive interprocedural data flow information or a slice of the program. While the program summary graph provides flow-sensitive data flow information about reference parameters and global variables, it contains insufficient information about the locations of definitions and uses of variables for either interprocedural data flow computation or interprocedural slicing. The interprocedural flow graph provides the precision needed for the interprocedural data flow computation but contains inadequate control information for slice computation. Likewise, the system dependence graph is useful for slice computation but cannot be used to propagate data sets since it lacks the interprocedural data flow information provided by the interprocedural reaching edge. Thus, a program representation that incorporates the features of each of the other graphs to provide control flow, data flow, control dependence, and data dependence is sufficient for the computation of all of the required information.

Since all of the interprocedural graphs described above are variations of the call graph, there is much redundancy in the information stored in the graphs. Node redundancy exists throughout the four graphs. For example, nodes in the call graph (Fig. 2) represent the same information about the program as the entry nodes in the system dependence graph (Fig. 5). Call/return nodes in the program summary graph (Fig. 3) and the interprocedural flow graph (Fig. 4) represent the same information about the parameters as the actual-in/actual-out nodes in the system dependence graph (Fig. 5). To emphasize this similarity, call/return and actual-in/actual-out nodes are depicted as circles in both graphs. Likewise, since the entry/exit nodes in the interprocedural flow graph and the formal-in/formal-out nodes in the system dependence graph represent the same information about the formal parameters in a procedure, they are shown as double circles in both graphs. There is also redundancy in the edges in the graphs. Parameter-in/parameter-out edges in the system dependence graph (Fig. 5) model the binding of the formal and actual parameters like the binding edges in both the program summary graph (Fig. 3) and the interprocedural flow graph (Fig. 4).

The UIG is designed to eliminate redundancies and to extract features of the call graph, the program summary graph, the interprocedural flow graph, and the system dependence graph. Additionally, algorithms developed for each of these program representations are adapted to use a subset of the nodes and edges in the UIG for their computations.

A. Constructing the Unified Interprocedural Graph

The UIG is constructed in two steps where subgraphs containing information about each procedure are first built and then connected to form the UIG. In Step 1, a UIG subgraph is constructed for each procedure in the program. Each UIG subgraph consists of the procedure's dependence graph along with additional nodes and edges to represent the flow of data for reference parameters. Intraprocedural data flow analysis is performed and information is gathered about formal and actual reference parameters and attached to nodes in the subgraph. In Step 2, the UIG subgraphs are connected by creating binding edges for formal and actual parameters and computing interprocedural control and data flow information to create the interprocedural reaching and interprocedural flow edges. Fig. 6 presents our algorithm BuildUIG that constructs the UIG.

Step 1: Constructing the UIG Subgraphs. In the first step of UIG construction, a UIG subgraph is created for each procedure P_i in the program. P_i's dependence graph is constructed where nodes in the graph represent statements in the procedure and control edges represent the control dependencies. In a procedure's dependence graph, there are nodes for every statement in the program, including a node for the procedure entry and nodes for all procedure calls. The entry nodes are replaced with a proc-entry node to represent the procedure entry and an entry/exit pair is created for each formal parameter in the procedure. Each call node is replaced with a call-site node to represent the call and a call/return pair for each actual parameter. New control edges are added to reflect the flow of control between the new nodes.

Intraprocedural data flow analysis is then performed on P_i's flow graph. The results of this analysis are used to create the flow-dependence edges and the reaching edges, and to compute the local use sets for each of the nodes in the UIG subgraph. If we consider each occurrence of a formal or actual parameter as a definition of the variable, a reaching edge is the same as a flow edge. At this point in the algorithm, the UIG subgraph for

```
algorithm BuildUIG(P)                    /* restricted to reference parameters */

input    P: a collection of procedures
output   G: a UIG for P

begin
/* Step 1: construct UIG subgraphs for each procedure */
     for each P_i ∈ P do          /* process each procedure */
          Construct the dependence graph for each procedure P_i
          for statement s representing procedure entry for P_i do
               Replace s with
                         a proc-entry node
                         an entry/exit pair for each formal parameter
          for each statement s containing a procedure call in P_i
               Replace s with
                         a call-site node for the procedure call
                         a call/return pair for each actual parameter
          Update control edges
          Perform intraprocedural data flow analysis on P_i
          Using intraprocedural data flow information
                    Create flow-dependence edges
                    Create reaching edges
                    Compute local use sets and attach to nodes
/* Step 2: constructing the UIG */
     Create binding edges for formal and actual parameters
     Create interprocedural flow edges
     Create interprocedural reaching edges
     Create call edges
end BuildUIG.
```

Fig. 6. Algorithm BuildUIG that constructs the unified interprocedural graph G for a collection of procedures P. In Step 1, UIG subgraphs are constructed for each procedure P_i in P. The UIG subgraphs are connected in Step 2 by the addition of the interprocedural edges.

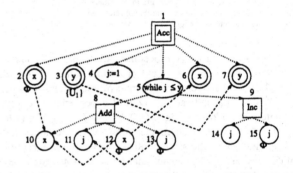

Fig. 7. UIG subgraph for procedure Acc in Fig. 2. Double squares represent proc-entry nodes, squares represent call-site nodes, double circles represent entry/exit nodes for formal parameters, circles represent call/return nodes for actual parameters, dotted lines represent control edges and dashed lines represent reaching edges. Flow edges between the nodes are omitted. Use sets that are gathered intraprocedurally for later propagation throughout the UIG are attached to the entry and return nodes. The use of y in line 13 of Sums, U_5, is the only nonempty use set and is attached to node 3. Note that use set numbering agrees with that given in Fig. 4.

each procedure is completed. Fig. 7 depicts the UIG subgraph for procedure Acc of Fig. 2.

Step 2: Connecting the UIG Subgraphs. The second step connects the individual UIG subgraphs at call sites by creating binding edges between call and entry nodes and between exit and return nodes. These binding edges represent the associations between formal and actual parameters. The interprocedural control information at call sites is determined using an algorithm by Horwitz, Reps, and Binkley [9] and used to create the interprocedural flow edges. May-be-preserved information is computed for each actual parameter using an

268

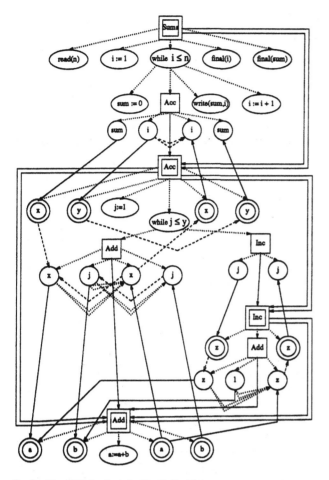

Fig. 8. The UIG for *Sums* in Fig. 2. Double squares represent proc-entry nodes, squares represent call-site nodes, double circles represent entry/exit nodes, circles represent call/return nodes, solid lines represent binding edges, double solid lines represent call edges, dashed lines represent reaching edges, double dashed lines represent interprocedural reaching edges, dotted lines represent control edges, and double dotted lines represent interprocedural flow edges. Flow edges and use sets are omitted.

iterative algorithm developed by Callahan [2]. When an actual parameter's value may-be-preserved over a procedure call, an interprocedural reaching edge is created to connect the call and return nodes associated with the call site. Finally, to permit efficiency in traversing the call graph, call edges are created to connect proc-entry nodes. Fig. 8 depicts the UIG for program *Sums* in Fig. 2.

B. Adapting the Algorithms

The features that are incorporated into each of the individual interprocedural representations are integrated into the UIG. Thus, each of the computations performed on the individual program representations can be accomplished through use of a primitive that accesses some subset of nodes and edges in the UIG. One such primitive is *GetDUPairs()* that computes the interprocedural definition-use pairs in the program. *GetDU-Pairs()* uses the call, return, entry and exit nodes, and the binding and reaching edges. Another primitive is *GetSlice(s, v)* for program statement s and variable v, which requires

information about all statements, control flow, and data flow in a program. A program slice is computed using a subset of the UIG consisting of all nodes and binding, flow, control, and interprocedural flow edges. Other examples of primitives and the subset of the UIG required are listed in Table I.

The UIG permits computing the same information as the individual program representations with the same time complexity. Since the subset of nodes and edges accessed using the UIG for each computation is the same as the corresponding nodes and edges accessed in the associated individual representation, the time complexity of each algorithm remains the same. Although the UIG combines information from four graphs, we achieve efficient space complexity by eliminating redundant information. The dominant space consideration in the UIG is the system dependence graph. The only relevant space considerations in the UIG that are not in the system dependence graph are the interprocedural reaching edges and the use sets. In the worst case, the number of interprocedural reaching edges is the same as the number of interprocedural flow edges and the size of the use sets attached to the nodes in the UIG is proportional to the number of statements in the program.

V. Maintenance Tools

A representative set of tools in our maintenance environment is shown in Fig. 1 and includes classes of tools for viewing, modifying, reengineering, testing, and debugging a program. The class of viewing tools accesses primitives such as *GetCallGraph()* that returns the information needed to allow the VIEWER to graphically display the structure of the program. Other functions in the VIEWER display the structure of a particular procedure and the locations of definitions and uses of global variables and parameters.

Tools to change the program operate on a copy of the UIG to determine the effects of the changes before they are made by the MODIFIER. Interaction with the viewer permits the user to graphically examine various views of the program using this copy of the UIG. If the user decides to accept the changed program, the original version of the UIG is replaced with this copy; otherwise the copy is discarded.

An important reengineering tool schedules a sequential program for parallel execution. Currently, our environment includes a parallelizer that schedules a sequential program for parallel execution on a shared memory asynchronous multiprocessor. Other planned tools in our environment include reengineering tools to parallelize on vectorizing and VLIW machines and tools to assist the user with tasks such as documenting and restructuring the program.

The class of testing tools includes program based, specification based, unit and integration TESTERs. Currently, we have incorporated both unit and integration data flow testers into our maintenance environment. The testing tools interact with the VIEWER to permit the user to graphically view the test case coverage of the program. Additionally, a graphical view of the program assists the user in generating test cases.

If errors are detected during testing, our debugging tools assist the user in locating the source of the errors. Our tools provide a type of static debugging since a static slice can be

TABLE I

	Correspondence between Computations and UIG Nodes/Edges	
Primitives	*Nodes*	*Edges*
GetControlDependences()	all nodes	binding, control, interprocedural flow
GetDUPairs()	call, return, entry, exit	binding, reaching, interprocedural reaching
GetModSets()	proc-entry	call
GetCallGraph()	proc-entry	call
GetSlice(s,v)	all nodes	binding, flow, control, interprocedural flow

The nodes in the UIG are proc-entry, call-site, entry, exit, call, return, and statement. Edges in the UIG are call, binding, reaching, control, interprocedural reaching, and interprocedural flow.

computed by the DEBUGGER and displayed by the VIEWER. We also plan to provide source level debugging of the program using either the UIG or a copy being modified.

VI. IMPLEMENTATION

We have implemented our UIG construction and several tools for our maintenance environment in the C programming language. The system constructs the UIG for a specified group of procedures and does not require that all of the procedures in the program be included. The system first constructs the UIG subgraphs using a modified version of the GNU C compiler[2] *gcc* and binds them together as indicated by the procedure calling structure. The remainder of the UIG is computed on demand by the user whenever it is needed for a particular tool. Further, the UIG is constructed incrementally since information computed for one tool is not recomputed when needed by another tool.

Currently, we have several tools implemented in our environment. The first tool is a viewer for the call graph. When the user requests the call graph, the information is computed by the primitive and used by the viewer to display the call graph of the procedures. A similar tool graphically represents the control flow graph for a single procedure. A third tool displays the source code with marked program slice when the user requests a backward slice on a statement in the program. Another tool assists in program testing. The def-use pairs are computed by the system and displayed to the user. For each test case provided by the user, the system determines the def-use coverage and displays the unsatisfied def-use pairs.

VII. CONCLUSION

In this paper, we have presented our unified interprocedural graph, or UIG, that combines the features of existing interprocedural program representations to permit understanding, modifying, analyzing, reengineering, testing, and debugging. Redundancies in existing program representations are eliminated and algorithms developed for each of these existing representations are adapted to use the UIG. We have incorporated this single program representation into a maintenance environment, used the associated algorithms to build primitives, and designed program maintenance tools that access the UIG only through the primitives. The main benefits of this approach are the reduction in storage space for the

individual representations, the savings in maintenance of a single program representation over the individual representations without loss in access time, and the convenience of accessing a single program representation. Another benefit is that a single program representation relates program elements to assist in program understanding. We are presently designing additional tools for our environment and completing our implementation.

REFERENCES

[1] F. E. Allen, M. Burke, P. Charles, R. Cytron, and J. Ferrante, "An overview of the PTRAN analysis system for multiprocessing," in *Proc. First Int. Conf. Supercomput.*, June 1987, pp. 194–211.
[2] D. Callahan, "The program summary graph and flow-sensitive interprocedural data flow analysis," in *Proc. SIGPLAN '88 Conf. Programming Language Design and Implementation*, June 1988, pp. 47–56.
[3] K. Cooper and K. Kennedy, "Fast interprocedural alias analysis," in *Proc. Sixteenth Annu. ACM Symp. Principles of Programming Languages*, Jan. 1989, pp. 49–59.
[4] J. Ferrante, K. J. Ottenstein, and J. D. Warren, "The program dependence graph and its use in optimization," *ACM Trans. Programming Languages and Systems*, vol. 9, no. 3, pp. 319–349, 1987.
[5] P. G. Frankl and E. J. Weyuker, "An applicable family of data flow testing criteria," *IEEE Trans. Software Eng.*, vol. 14, no. 10, pp. 1483–1498, Oct. 1988.
[6] M. J. Harrold, "An approach to incremental testing," Tech. Rep. 89–1, Dep. Comput. Sci., Ph.D. dissertation, Univ. Pittsburgh, Jan. 1989.
[7] M. J. Harrold and M. L. Soffa, "Computation of interprocedural definition and use dependencies," in *Proc. IEEE Comput. Soc. 1990 Int. Conf. Comput. Languages*, New Orleans, LA, Mar. 1990, pp. 297–306.
[8] ——, "Selecting data for integration testing," *IEEE Software*, special issue on testing and debugging, pp. 58–65, Mar. 1991.
[9] S. Horwitz, T. Reps, and D. Binkley, "Interprocedural slicing using dependence graphs," *ACM Trans. Programming Languages and Syst.*, vol. 12, no. 1, pp. 26–60, Jan. 1990.
[10] J. C. Hwang, M. W. Du, and C. R. Chou, "Finding program slices for recursive procedures," in *Proc. IEEE COMPSAC 88*, Oct. 1988.
[11] B. Korel and J. Laski, "A tool for data flow oriented program testing," *ACM Softfair Proc.* pp. 35–37, Dec. 1985.
[12] B. Malloy, R. Gupta, and M. L. Soffa, "Shape matching approach for scheduling fine-grained parallelism," in *Proc. 25th Annu. Int. Symp. Microarchitecture (MICRO-25)*, Dec. 1992.
[13] B. Malloy, E. L. Lloyd, and M. L. Soffa, "A fine grained approach to scheduling asynchronous multiprocessors," in *Proc. 4th Int. Conf. Comput. and Inform (ICCI)*, May 1992.
[14] S. C. Ntafos, "An evaluation of required element testing strategies," *Proc. 7th Int. Conf. Software Eng.*, Mar. 1984, pp. 250–256.
[15] T. J. Ostrand and E. J. Weyuker, "Using data flow analysis for regression testing," in *Proc. Sixth Annu. Pacific Northwest Software Quality Conf.*, Sept. 1988, pp. 58–71.
[16] L. L. Pollock and M. L. Soffa, "An incremental version of iterative data flow analysis," *IEEE Trans. Software Eng.*, vol. SE-11, no. 12, pp. 1537–1549, Dec. 1989.
[17] B. G. Ryder, "Constructing the call graph of a program," *IEEE Trans. Software Eng.*, vol. SE-5, no. 3, pp. 216–225, May 1979.
[18] ——, "An application of static program analysis to software maintenance," in *Proc. 20th Hawaii Int. Conf. Syst. Sci.*, Jan. 1987, pp. 82–91
[19] B. G. Ryder and M. C. Paull, "Incremental data-flow analysis," *ACM*

Trans. Programming Languages and Syst., vol. 1, no. 1, pp. 1–50, Jan. 1988

[20] A. M. Taha, S. M. Thebut, and S. S. Liu, "An approach to software fault localization and revalidation based on incremental data flow analysis," in *Proc. COMPSAC 89,* Sept. 1989, pp. 527–534.

[21] L. Torczan and K. Kennedy, "Efficient computation of flow insensitive interprocedural summary information," in *Proc. SIGPLAN '84 Symp. Compiler Construction, SIGPLAN Notices,* vol. 19, no. 6, June 1984.

A Formal Model of Program Dependences and Its Implications for Software Testing, Debugging, and Maintenance

ANDY PODGURSKI AND LORI A. CLARKE

Abstract—A formal, general model of program dependences is presented and used to evaluate several dependence-based software testing, debugging, and maintenance techniques. Two generalizations of control and data flow dependence, called weak and strong syntactic dependence, are introduced and related to a concept called semantic dependence. Semantic dependence models the ability of a program statement to affect the execution behavior of other statements. It is shown, among other things, that weak syntactic dependence is a necessary but not sufficient condition for semantic dependence and that strong syntactic dependence is a necessary but not sufficient condition for a restricted form of semantic dependence that is finitely demonstrated. These results are then used to support some proposed uses of program dependences, to controvert others, and to suggest new uses.

Index Terms—Data flow testing, program analysis, program dependences, program slicing, software debugging, software maintenance, software testing.

I. INTRODUCTION

PROGRAM dependences are relationships, holding between program statements, that can be determined from a program's text and used to predict aspects of the program's execution behavior. There are two basic types of program dependences: "control dependences," which are features of a program's control structure, and "data flow dependences," which are features of a program's use of variables. Informally, a statement s is control dependent on the branch condition c of a conditional branch statement if the control structure of the program indicates that c potentially decides, via the branches it controls, whether s is executed or not. For example, in the program of Fig. 1, statements 3 and 4 are control dependent on the branch condition at line 2. Informally, a statement s is data flow dependent on a statement s' if data potentially propagates from s' to s via a sequence of variable assignments. For example, in the program of Fig. 1, statement 5 is data flow dependent on statement 1, since data potentially propagates from statement 1 to statement 5. *Dependence analysis*, the process of determining a program's dependences, combines traditional control flow analysis

and data flow analysis [2], and hence can be implemented efficiently.

Until recently, most proposed uses of program dependences have been justified only informally, if at all. Since program dependences are used for such critical purposes as software testing [15], [16], [19], [22], debugging [3], [28], and maintenance [23], [28], code optimization and parallelization [8], [20], and computer security [7],[1] this informality is risky. This paper supplements other recent investigations of the semantic basis for the uses of program dependences [4], [13], [25] by presenting a formal, general model of program dependences and by using it to evaluate several dependence-based software testing, debugging, and maintenance techniques. The results support certain proposed uses of program dependences, controvert others, and suggest new ones.

One example of our results involves the use of program dependences to find "operator faults" in programs. An *operator fault* is the presence of an inappropriate operator[2] in a program statement. For instance, accidental use of the multiplication operator "*" instead of the addition operator "+" in the assignment statement "X := Y * Z" results in an operator fault. It would be useful to be able to automatically detect and locate operator faults; unfortunately, as with many other semantic questions about programs, the question of whether a program contains an operator fault or not is undecidable. This paper shows, however, that there is an algorithm, in fact an *efficient* one, that detects *necessary conditions* for an operator fault at one statement to affect the execution behavior of another statement. These necessary conditions are expressed in terms of program dependences. Consequently, dependences can be used to help locate the statements that might be affected by an operator fault at a given statement.

To determine some of the implications of program dependences, we relate control and data dependence to a concept called "semantic dependence." Informally, a program statement s is semantically dependent on a statement s' if the semantics of s', that is, the function computed by s', potentially affects the execution behavior of s. The significance of semantic dependence is that it is a

Manuscript received October 15, 1989; revised May 1, 1990. Recommended by N. G. Leveson.

A. Podgurski is with the Department of Computer Engineering and Science, Case Western Reserve University, Cleveland, OH 44106.

L. A. Clarke is with the Software Development Laboratory, Department of Computer and Information Science, University of Massachusetts, Amherst, MA 01003.

IEEE Log Number 9037077.

[1] The term "dependence" is not used in all the references given.

[2] The term "operator" refers to both the predefined operators of a programming language and to user-defined procedures and functions.

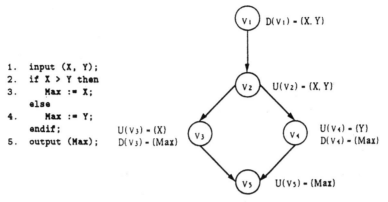

```
1.  input (X, Y);
2.  if X > Y then
3.      Max := X;
    else
4.      Max := Y;
    endif;
5.  output (Max);
```

$U(v_3) = (X)$
$D(v_3) = (Max)$

$D(v_1) = (X, Y)$

$U(v_2) = (X, Y)$

$U(v_4) = (Y)$
$D(v_4) = (Max)$

$U(v_5) = (Max)$

Fig. 1. Max program and its def/use graph.

necessary condition for certain interstatement semantic relationships. For example, if s and s' are distinct statements, then s must be semantically dependent on s' for an operator fault at s' to affect the execution behavior of s. Similarly, some output statement must be semantically dependent on a statement s for the semantics of s to affect the output of a program.

Three main results are presented in this paper:

1) A generalization of control and data dependence, called "weak syntactic dependence," is a necessary condition for semantic dependence.

2) A commonly used generalization of control and data dependence, which we call "strong syntactic dependence," is a necessary condition for semantic dependence only if the semantic dependence does not depend in a certain way on a program failing to terminate.

3) Neither data flow, weak syntactic, nor strong syntactic dependence is a sufficient condition for semantic dependence.

We use these results to evaluate several dependence-based testing, debugging, and maintenance techniques.

Section II defines some necessary terminology and Section III defines control, data, and syntactic dependence. Semantic dependence is informally defined in Section IV and then related to syntactic dependence in Section V. In Section VI, the implications of the results of Section V for software testing, debugging, and maintenance are described. In Section VII, related work not already considered in Section VI is surveyed. Section VIII presents a summary and discussion of possible future research directions. In the Appendix, the formal definition of semantic dependence is presented, and the proofs of the two most significant results of Section V are sketched.

II. TERMINOLOGY

In this section we define control flow graphs, some dominance relations, and def/use graphs.

A *directed graph or digraph* G is a pair $(V(G), A(G))$, where $V(G)$ is any finite set and $A(G)$ is a subset of $V(G) \times V(G) - \{(v, v) | v \in V(G)\}$. The elements of $V(G)$ are called *vertices* and the elements of $A(G)$ are called *arcs*. If $(u, v) \in A(G)$ then u is *adjacent to* v and v is *adjacent from* u; the arc (u, v) is *incident to* v and *incident from* u. A *predecessor* of a vertex v is a vertex adjacent to v, and a *successor* of v is a vertex adjacent from v. The *indegree* of a vertex v is the number of predecessors of v, and the *outdegree* of v is the number of successors of v.

A *walk* W in G is a sequence of vertices $v_1 v_2 \cdots v_n$ such that $n \geq 0$ and $(v_i, v_{i+1}) \in A(G)$ for $i = 1, 2, \cdots, n - 1$. The *length* of a walk $W = v_1 v_2 \cdots v_n$, denoted $|W|$, is the number n of vertex occurrences in W. Note that a walk of length zero has no vertex occurrences; such a walk is called *empty*. A nonempty walk whose first vertex is u and whose last vertex is v is called a $u-v$ *walk*. If $W = w_1 w_2 \cdots w_m$ and $X = x_1 x_2 \cdots x_n$ are walks such that either W is empty, X is empty, or w_m is adjacent to x_1, then the *concatenation* of W and X, denoted WX, is the walk $w_1 w_2 \cdots w_m x_1 x_2 \cdots x_n$.

All the types of dependence considered in this paper are directly or indirectly defined in terms of a "control flow graph," which represents the flow of control in a sequential, procedural program.

Definition 1: A *control-flow graph* G is a directed graph that satisfies each of the following conditions:

1) The maximum outdegree of the vertices of G is at most two[3].

2) G contains two distinguished vertices: the *initial vertex* v_I, which has indegree zero, and the *final vertex* v_F, which has outdegree zero.

3) Every vertex of G occurs on some $v_I - v_F$ walk.

A vertex of outdegree two in a control flow graph is called a *decision vertex*, and an arc incident from a decision vertex is called a *decision arc*. The set of decision vertices of G is denoted $V_{dec}(G)$.

Here, the vertices of a control flow graph represent simple program statements (such as assignment statements and procedure calls) and also branch conditions, while the arcs represent possible transfers of control between these. The program's entry point and exit point are represented by the initial vertex and final vertex, respectively. A de-

---

[3]This restriction is made for simplicity only.

273

```
1.   input (N);
2.   Fact := 1;
3.   while not N = 0 loop
4.      Fact := Fact * N;
5.      N := N - 1;
     end loop;
6.   output ("The factorial is ");
7.   output (Fact);
```

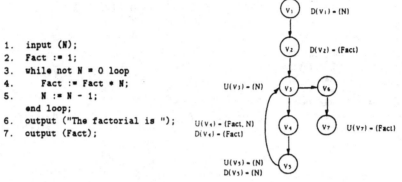

Fig. 2. Factorial program and its def/use graph.

cision vertex represents the branch condition of a conditional branch statement. The definition given here of a control flow graph is somewhat restricted, to simplify the presentation of results. This definition can be used to represent any procedural program, however, by employing straightforward representation conventions involving the use of dummy vertices and arcs.

The control flow graph of the program in Fig. 1 is shown alongside the program; the annotations to this graph are explained subsequently.

The next three definitions are used in defining types of control dependence.

Definition 2: Let G be a control flow graph. A vertex $u \in V(G)$ *forward dominates* a vertex $v \in V(G)$ iff every $v-v_F$ walk in G contains u; u *properly forward dominates* v iff $u \neq v$ and u forward dominates v.

Definition 3: Let G be a control flow graph. A vertex $u \in V(G)$ *strongly forward dominates* a vertex $v \in V(G)$ iff u forward dominates v and there is an integer $k \geq 1$ such that every walk in G beginning with v and of length $\geq k$ contains u.

In the control flow graph of Fig. 1, v_5 (strongly) forward dominates each vertex, whereas v_3 and v_4 forward dominate only themselves. In the control flow graph of Fig. 2, v_5 strongly forward dominates v_4, but v_6 does not strongly forward dominate v_4, because there are arbitrarily long walks from v_4 that do not contain v_6.

While control dependence has been defined in terms of forward dominance before [7], [8], the use of strong forward dominance for this purpose is apparently new.

We state the following theorem without proof.

Theorem 1: Let G be a control flow graph. For each vertex $u \in (V(G) - \{v_F\})$, there exists a proper forward dominator v of u such that v is the first proper forward dominator of u to occur on every $u-v_F$ walk in G.

The "immediate forward dominator" of a decision vertex d is the vertex where all walks leaving d first come together again. More formally:

Definition 4: Let G be a control flow graph. The *immediate forward dominator* of a vertex $v \in (V(G) - \{v_F\})$, denoted $ifd(v)$, is the vertex that is the first proper forward dominator of v to occur on every $v-v_F$ walk in G.

For example, in the control flow graph of Fig. 1, v_5 is the immediate forward dominator of v_2, v_3, and v_4. In the control flow graph of Fig. 2, v_6 is the immediate forward dominator of v_3.

Data, syntactic, and semantic dependence are defined in terms of an annotated control flow graph called a "def/use graph." For each vertex v in a def/use graph, $D(v)$ denotes the set of variables defined (assigned a value) at the statement represented by v, and $U(v)$ denotes the set of variables used (having their values referenced) at that statement. A def/use graph is similar to a program schema [11], [17] and is essentially the program representation used in data flow analysis [2].

Definition 5: A *def/use graph* is a quadruple $G = (G, \Sigma, D, U)$, where G is a control flow graph, Σ is a finite set of symbols called *variables*, and $D: V(G) \to \mathcal{P}(\Sigma)$, $U: V(G) \to \mathcal{P}(\Sigma)$ are functions.[4]

The def/use graphs of the programs in Figs. 1 and 2 are shown alongside the programs.

Definition 6: Let $G = (G, \Sigma, D, U)$ be a def/use graph, and let W be a walk in G. Then

$$D(W) = \bigcup_{v \in W} D(v).$$

For example, referring to the def/use graph of Fig. 1, $D(v_1 v_2 v_3 v_5) = \{ \mathbf{Max}, \mathbf{X}, \mathbf{Y} \}$.

As usual in the static analysis of programs, exactly what constitutes a variable, definition, or use is sometimes a subtle issue [2]. In the model of computation we adopt (see Section IV), values are associated with the variables (names) in Σ, and a vertex v can interrogate only the values of variables in $U(v)$ and modify only the values of variables in $D(v)$. In representing a program with our formalism, this means that if the statement represented by a vertex v reads or writes a storage element, or if this is *uncertain*, then a variable name that denotes the potentially accessed storage element should be included in $U(v)$ or $D(v)$, respectively. When the accessed storage element cannot be determined until runtime, it is permissible to include either a distinct name for each storage element that might be accessed or one name denoting all

---

[4]We denote the power set (set of all subsets) of a set S by $\mathcal{P}(S)$.

274

such elements, provided the same representation is used consistently. When the same storage element is accessed via different names in the program, all of these names can be included or a single name can be used in place of them. These are the conventions usually adopted in static analysis, where, for example, an access through a pointer is often treated as an access to all the objects that might be pointed to, and an access to an array element is often treated as an access to the entire array. These conventions are conservative, in that they may indicate data flow that cannot actually occur, but are safe, in that they will not fail to indicate any data flow that does occur.

III. CONTROL, DATA, AND SYNTACTIC DEPENDENCE

A. Control Dependence

The concept of control dependence is used to model the effect of conditional branch statements on the behavior of programs. Control dependence is a property of a program's control structure alone, in that it can be defined strictly in terms of a control flow graph. Various formal and informal definitions of control dependence are given in the literature. Usually these are expressed in terms of "structured" control statements of a particular language or class of languages. Such definitions have limited applicability, because control statements vary across languages and because "unstructured" programs occur in practice. Indeed, even judicious use of the *goto* statement or the use of restricted branch statements such as Ada's *exit*, *raise*, and *return* statements can result in programs that are, strictly speaking, unstructured. It is therefore desirable to have a language-independent definition of control dependence that applies to both structured and unstructured programs. Two definitions that satisfy these requirements are those of "weak control dependence" and "strong control dependence."

Strong control dependence was originally defined in the context of computer security [7][5], and this definition has been used by several authors [15], [20], [28]. To our knowledge, it was the first graph-theoretic, language and structure-independent characterization of control dependence to appear in the literature.

Definition 7: Let G be a control flow graph, and let u, $v \in V(G)$. Then u is *strongly control dependent* on v iff there exists a $v - u$ walk vWu not containing the immediate forward dominator of v.

For example, in the control flow graph of Fig. 1, the immediate forward dominator of the decision vertex v_2 is v_5; therefore v_3 and v_4 are strongly control dependent on v_2. In the control flow graph of Fig. 2, the immediate forward dominator of the decision vertex v_3 is v_6; therefore v_3, v_4, and v_5 are strongly control dependent on v_3. Note that the statements that are strongly control dependent on the branch condition of a structured *if-then* or *if-then-else* statement are those in its "body." The statements that are strongly control dependent on the branch condition of a structured *while* or *repeat-until* loop are the

[5]In [7] the concept is called "implicit information flow."

branch condition itself and the statements in the loop's body.

Weak control dependence [21] is a generalization of strong control dependence in the sense that every strong control dependence is also a weak control dependence.

Definition 8: Let G be a control flow graph, and let u, $v \in V(G)$. Vertex u is *directly weakly control dependent* on vertex v iff v has successors v' and v'' such that u strongly forward dominates v' but does not strongly forward dominate v''; u is *weakly control dependent* on v iff there is a sequence $v_1, v_2, \cdots, v_n$ of vertices, $n \geq 2$, such that $u = v_1$, $v = v_n$, and v_i is directly weakly control dependent on v_{i+1} for $i = 1, 2, \cdots, n - 1$.

Informally, u is directly weakly control dependent on v if v has successors v' and v'' such that if the branch from v to v' is executed then u is necessarily executed within a fixed number of steps, while if the branch from v to v'' is taken then u can be bypassed or its execution can be delayed indefinitely.

The essential difference between weak and strong control dependence is that weak control dependence reflects a dependence between an exit condition of a loop and a statement outside the loop that may be executed after the loop is exited, while strong control dependence does not. For example, in the control flow graph of Fig. 2, v_6 is (directly) weakly control dependent on v_3 (because v_6 strongly forward dominates itself, but not v_4), but not strongly control dependent on v_3 (because v_6 is the immediate forward dominator of v_3). In addition, v_3, v_4, and v_5 are (directly) weakly control dependent on v_3, because each strongly forward dominates v_4 but not v_6. The additional dependences of the weak control dependence relation are relevant to program behavior, because an exit condition of a loop potentially determines whether execution of the loop terminates.

The weak and strong control dependence relations for a control flow graph G can be computed in $O(|V(G)|^3)$ time [21].

B. Data Flow Dependence

Although several other types of data dependence are discussed in the literature, we require only data flow dependence [8], [20].

Definition 9: Let $G = (G, \Sigma, D, U)$ be a def/use graph, and let u, $v \in V(G)$. Vertex u is *directly data flow dependent* on vertex v iff there is a walk vWu in G such that $(D(v) \cap U(u)) - D(W) \neq \varnothing$; u is *data flow dependent* on v iff there is a sequence $v_1, v_2, \cdots, v_n$ of vertices, $n \geq 2$, such that $u = v_1$, $v = v_n$ and v_i is directly data flow dependent on v_{i+1} for $i = 1, 2, \cdots, n - 1$.

Note that if u is data flow dependent on v then there is a walk $v_1 W_1 v_2 W_2 \cdots v_{n-1} W_{n-1} v_n$, $n \geq 2$, such that $v = v_1$, $u = v_n$, and $(D(v_i) \cap U(v_{i+1})) - D(W_i) \neq \varnothing$ for $i = 1, 2, \cdots, n - 1$. Such a walk is said to *demonstrate* the data flow dependence of u upon v.

Referring to the def/use graph of Fig. 1, v_3 is directly data flow dependent on v_1, because the variable X is defined at v_1, used at v_3, and not redefined along the walk

$v_1 v_2 v_3$; v_5 is directly data flow dependent on v_3, because the variable **Max** is defined at v_3, used at v_5, and not redefined along the walk $v_3 v_5$. It follows that v_5 is data flow dependent on v_1; the walk $v_1 v_2 v_3 v_5$ demonstrates this dependence.

The direct data flow dependence relation for a control flow graph can be computed efficiently using a fast algorithm for the "reaching definitions" problem [2]. The data flow dependence relation can then be efficiently computed using a fast algorithm for transitive closure [1].

C. Syntactic Dependence

To evaluate uses of control and data dependence, it is necessary to consider *chains* of such dependences, that is, sequences of vertices in which each vertex except the last is either control dependent or data dependent on the next vertex. Informally, there is a "*weak* syntactic dependence" between two statements if there is a chain of data flow and/or *weak* control dependences between the statements, while there is a "*strong* syntactic dependence" between the statements if there is a chain of data flow dependences and/or *strong* control dependences between them. Weak syntactic dependence apparently has not been considered before in the literature; the notion of strong syntactic dependence is implicit in the work of several authors [3], [7], [8], [13], [15], [20], [28].

Definition 10: Let $G = (G, \Sigma, D, U)$ be a def/use graph, and let $u, v \in V(G)$. Vertex u is *weakly syntactically dependent* (*strongly syntactically dependent*) on vertex v iff there is a sequence $v_1, v_2, \cdots, v_n$ of vertices, $n \geq 2$, such that $u = v_1$, $v = v_n$, and for $i = 1, 2, \cdots, n - 1$, either v_i is weakly control dependent (strongly control dependent) on v_{i+1} or v_i is data flow dependent on v_{i+1}.

Since the weak and strong control dependence and data flow dependence relations for a def/use graph can be computed efficiently, the weak and strong syntactic dependence relations can be computed efficiently by using a fast algorithm for transitive closure.

Referring to the def/use graph of Fig. 2, v_6 is weakly syntactically dependent on v_5, because v_6 is weakly control dependent on v_3 and v_3 is data flow dependent on v_5; v_5 is strongly syntactically dependent on v_1, because v_5 is strongly control dependent on v_3 and v_3 is data flow dependent on v_1. Note that v_6 is not strongly syntactically dependent on v_5.

IV. SEMANTIC DEPENDENCE

Recall that, informally, a statement s is semantically dependent on a statement s' if the function computed by s' affects the execution behavior of s. In this section, a more precise but still informal description of semantic dependence is given. The formal definition is presented in the Appendix.

We first informally define the auxiliary terms necessary to define semantic dependence. A sequential procedural program can be viewed abstractly as an *interpreted* def/use graph. An *interpretation* of a def/use graph is an as-

signment of partial computable functions to the vertices of the graph. The function assigned to a vertex v is the one computed by the program statement that v represents; it maps values for the variables in $U(v)$ to values for the variables in $D(v)$ or, if v is a decision vertex, to a successor of v. An interpretation of a def/use graph is similar to an interpretation of a program schema [11], [17]. An operational semantics for interpreted def/use graphs is defined in the obvious way, with computation proceeding sequentially from vertex to vertex along the arcs of the graph, as determined by the functions assigned to the vertices. A *computation sequence* of a program is the sequence of states (pairs consisting of a vertex and a function assigning values to all the variables in the program) induced by executing the program with a particular input. An *execution history* of a vertex v is the sequence whose ith element is the assignment of values held by the variables of $U(v)$ just before the ith time v is visited during a computation. An execution history of a vertex is an interpreted def/use graph abstracts the "execution behavior" of a program statement.

A more precise description of semantic dependence can now be given.

Definition 11 (Informal): A vertex u in a def/use graph G is *semantically dependent* on a vertex v of G if there are interpretations I_1 and I_2 of G that differ only in the function assigned to v, such that for some input, the execution history of u induced by I_1 differs from that induced by I_2.[6]

For example, if the branch condition $X > Y$ in the program of Fig. 1 were changed to $X < Y$, then the program would compute the *Min* function instead of the *Max* function. Hence, for all unequal values of X and Y, this change demonstrates that vertex v_5 of the def/use graph of Fig. 1 is semantically dependent on vertex v_2. As another example, if the statement $N := N - 1$ in the program of Fig. 2 were changed to $N := N - 2$, the *while*-loop would fail to terminate for the input $N = 5$, preventing statement 6 from executing. Hence, this change demonstrates that vertex v_6 of the def/use graph of Fig. 2 is semantically dependent on vertex v_5.

Note that a pair of execution histories that demonstrate a semantic dependence can differ in two ways: a) the histories have corresponding entries that are unequal and b) one history is longer than the other. Informally, the semantic dependence is said to be *finitely demonstrated* if either:

1) Condition a) holds; or

2) Condition b) is demonstrated by finite portions of the computation sequences that caused the execution histories.

Semantic dependence demonstrated by a pair of *halting* computations is, of course, finitely demonstrated. For ex-

---

[6] The formal definition of semantic dependence, given in the Appendix, contains conditions to ensure that a semantic dependence is not caused by the value of the function assigned to a vertex being undefined for some input. This is done to avoid trivial semantic dependences. When we informally refer to (the semantics of) one program statement affecting the execution behavior of another statement, this restriction is implied.

ample, the semantic dependence of vertex v_5 upon vertex v_2 in the def/use graph of Fig. 1 is finitely demonstrated, because the *Min* and *Max* functions are defined for all pairs of integers. The semantic dependence of vertex v_6 upon vertex v_5 in the def/use graph of Fig. 2 is not finitely demonstrated, because the only way v_5 can affect the execution behavior of v_6 is by determining whether execution of the cycle $v_3 v_4 v_5 v_3$ terminates. Note that even *nonterminating* computations can finitely demonstrate semantic dependence, via their finite initial segments. For example, despite the fact that it makes the program fail to terminate, changing the statement $N := N - 1$ in the program of Fig. 2 to $N := N - 2$ finitely demonstrates that vertex v_5 of the programs' def/use graph is semantically dependent on itself, because the change alters the argument to the second execution of statement 5 for the input $N = 5$.

V. Relating Semantic and Syntactic Dependence

In software testing, debugging, and maintenance, one is often interested in the following question:

> When can a change in the semantics of a program statement affect the execution behavior of another statement?

This question is, however, undecidable in general. Dependence analysis, like data flow analysis, avoids problems of undecidability by trading precision for (efficient) decidability. During dependence analysis, programs are represented by def/use graphs, which contain limited semantic information but are easily analyzed. Dependence analysis allows semantic questions to be answered "approximately," because a program's dependences partially determine its semantic properties. To evaluate the usefulness of dependence analysis in "approximately" answering the question above, we frame the question in terms of def/use graphs, by asking "When is one statement semantically dependent on another?". This leads to our main results.

(The proofs of Theorems 2 and 4 below are sketched in the Appendix. The proofs of Theorems 3 and 5 are given informally with the theorems. Formal versions of all these proofs are found in [21].)

Theorem 2: Let $G = (G, \Sigma, D, U)$ be a def/use graph, and let $u, v \in V(G)$. If u is semantically dependent on v then u is weakly syntactically dependent on v.

It was shown in Section IV that vertex v_6 in the def/use graph of Fig. 2 is semantically dependent on vertex v_5. This is reflected by the fact that v_6 is weakly syntactically dependent on v_5, as shown in Section III-C. However, v_6 is not strongly syntactically dependent on v_5.

Theorem 3: Strong syntactic dependence is not a necessary condition for semantic dependence.

The next theorem shows that strong syntactic dependence does have semantic significance. The theorem in

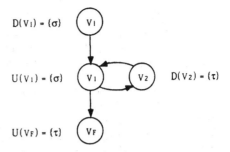

Fig. 3. Direct data flow dependence without semantic dependence.

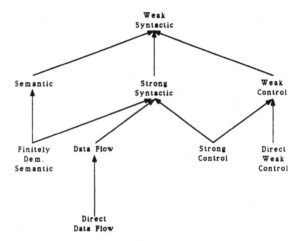

Fig. 4. Relationships of dependence types.

fact justifies some informally-posed applications of dependence analysis (see Section VI).

Theorem 4: Let $G = (G, \Sigma, D, U)$ be a def/use graph, and let $u, v \in V(G)$. If u is semantically dependent on v and this semantic dependence is finitely demonstrated then u is strongly syntactically dependent on v.

It was shown in Section IV that vertex v_5 in the def/use graph of Fig. 1 is semantically dependent on vertex v_2 and that this semantic dependence is finitely demonstrated. This is reflected by the fact that v_5 is strongly syntactically dependent on v_2 (v_5 is directly data flow dependent on v_3, which is strongly control dependent on v_2).

Theorem 5: Neither direct data flow dependence nor data flow dependence is a sufficient condition for semantic dependence.

In the def/use graph of Fig. 3, vertex v_F is directly data flow dependent on vertex v_2. However, v_F is not semantically dependent on v_2. This is because no computation of any program with this def/use graph visits both v_2 and v_F, since the "loop control variable" σ is not redefined in the cycle $v_1 v_2 v_1$.

Corollary 1: Neither weak nor strong syntactic dependence is a sufficient condition for semantic dependence.

Fig. 4 shows the dependence relations considered in this paper, ordered by set inclusion. There is an arrow from a relation R_1 to a relation R_2 if $R_1 \subseteq R_2$.

VI. Implications of the Results

The results of Section V support the following general conclusions about the use of dependence analysis to obtain information about relationships between program statements:

1) The absence of weak syntactic dependence between two statements precludes all relationships between them that imply semantic dependence.

2) The absence of strong syntactic dependence between two statements does not necessarily preclude all relationships between them that imply (nonfinitely-demonstrated) semantic dependence.

3) The absence of strong syntactic dependence between two statements precludes all relationships between them that imply finitely demonstrated semantic dependence.

4) The presence of direct data flow dependence, data flow dependence, or weak or strong syntactic dependence between two statements does not necessarily indicate any relationship between the statements that implies semantic dependence.

Conclusion 1 follows from Theorem 2; any relationship between two statements that implies semantic dependence also implies weak syntactic dependence. Conclusion 2 follows from Theorem 3 and Theorem 4; nonfinitely-demonstrated semantic dependence does not imply strong syntactic dependence. Conclusion 3 follows from Theorem 4; any interstatement relationship that implies finitely demonstrated semantic dependence also implies strong syntactic dependence. Finally, conclusion 4 follows from Theorem 5 and Corollary 1.

Note that conclusion 1 implies that the weak syntactic dependence relation for a program is an "upper bound" for (contains) any relation on the program's statements that implies semantic dependence. Similarly, conclusion 3 implies that the strong syntactic dependence relation for a program bounds any relation on the program's statements that implies finitely demonstrated semantic dependence. Since the syntactic dependences in a program can be computed efficiently, these bounds can be determined easily and used to narrow the search for statements having certain important relationships. For example, if an operator fault at a statement s affects the execution behavior of a statement s', this demonstrates that s' is semantically dependent on s; therefore, only those statements that are weakly syntactically dependent on s could be affected by an operator fault at s. Consequently, weak syntactic dependences can be used to help locate statements that can be affected by an operator fault at a given statement. Of course, whenever a relation R on the statements of a program implies finitely demonstrated semantic dependence, the strong syntactic dependence relation for the program is a "tighter" bound on R than the weak syntactic dependence relation is.

In the sequel, we use the results of Section V to evaluate the semantic basis for several proposed uses of dependences in testing, debugging, and maintenance and to suggest new uses. The results suggest that some proposed uses are mistaken, but provide partial justification, in terms of facilitating search, for other uses.

A. Dependence-Coverage Criteria

In software testing, a *dependence-coverage criterion* is a test-data selection rule based on "covering" or "exercising" certain program dependences. Several coverage criteria have been defined that call for exercising the data flow dependences in a program [10], [16], [19], [22]; these are called "data flow coverage criteria." They require the execution of program walks[7] that demonstrate certain data flow dependences. One rationale for the data flow coverage criteria is that they facilitate the detection of incorrect variable definitions [16], [22], which may be caused by mistaken use of operators and/or variable names. Another is that they facilitate the detection of faults that cause missing and spurious data flow dependences [16]. These two rationales are related, since an incorrect variable definition can cause missing or spurious data flow dependences. In Section VI-A-1 below we use the results of Section V to evaluate the use of dependence coverage criteria for the detection of those incorrect variable definitions that arise from operator faults. In Section VI-A-2, we use the results of Section V to evaluate the use of dependence coverage criteria for the detection of faults that cause missing and spurious dependences.

1) Detection of Operator Faults: The data flow coverage criteria address operator faults by exercising data flow dependences upon potentially faulty variable definitions. This may cause erroneous values produced by an operator fault to propagate, via the sequence of assignments represented by a data flow dependence, and produce an observable failure. The data flow coverage criteria differ with regard to the number and type of data flow dependences exercised and with regard to the number of walks executed that demonstrate a given dependence. For example:

• Rapps and Weyuker's All-Defs criterion [22] exercises one direct data flow dependence, if possible, upon each variable definition in a program.

• Rapps and Weyuker's All-Uses and All-DU-Paths criteria [22] exercise all direct data flow dependences in a program.

• Laski and Korel's Strategy II [16] exercises all direct data flow dependences, but exercises them in combination.

• For a fixed k, Ntafos's Required k-Tuples criterion [19] exercises all chains of k direct data flow dependences; that is, all sequences of $k + 1$ vertices such that each vertex in the sequence except the last is directly data flow dependent on the next.

---

[7]That is, sequences of statements corresponding to walks in a program's control flow graph.

278

It is plausible that the propagation of erroneous values via data flow dependences alone is sufficiently common to make data flow coverage criteria worthwhile, even though, by conclusion 4, that fact that a statement s is data flow dependent on a faulty statement s' does not imply that an erroneous value propagates from s' to s. However, when an operator fault causes a conditional statement to make an incorrect branch, *control dependence* can be critical to the ability of the fault to affect the execution behavior of a particular statement. For example, changing the branch predicate $X > Y$ in the program of Fig. 1 to $X < Y$ changes the number of times statement 3 is executed for the inputs $X = 5$, $Y = 2$ because statement 3 is strongly control dependent on statement 2. Hence, no coverage criterion based only on exercising data flow dependences can, in general, exercise all the syntactic dependences associated with erroneous information flow produced by operator faults. Correspondingly, it is easily seen that data flow dependence is not a necessary condition for even finitely demonstrated semantic dependence.

Some of the data flow coverage criteria mentioned above, such as the All-Uses and Required k-Tuples criteria, incorporate limited forms of control dependence coverage. However, even these criteria do not exercise all syntactic dependences associated with the erroneous information flow produced by operator faults, because the type of syntactic dependences they exercise are still restricted. For any sequence of the letters "C" and "D", it is simple to construct an example of finitely demonstrated semantic dependence for which the corresponding strong syntactic dependence is realized by only one chain of direct data flow dependences and direct strong control dependences, whose ith dependence is a direct strong control dependence (direct data flow dependence) if the ith letter of the sequence is "C" (is "D"). This means that, in general, almost arbitrarily complex chains of data flow and control dependences may have to be exercised to reveal operator faults.

As noted at the beginning of Section VI, it follows from conclusions 1 and 3 that syntactic dependences provide a nontrivial bound on the set of statements that can be affected by an operator fault at a given statement. One might think that to remedy the aforementioned weakness of the data flow coverage criteria it is only necessary to extend them to exercise *all* syntactic dependences upon a potentially faulty definition, instead of just data flow dependences. However, the number of tests required to adequately exercise all syntactic dependences can be impractically large, for the following reasons:

• The number of syntactic dependences in a program can be quadratic in the number of statements.

• A given syntactic dependence may be demonstrated by many program walks (even infinitely many), only one of which is associated with erroneous information flow.

• Erroneous information flow via a particular syntactic dependence may depend not only on which walk is executed, but also on the particular input used.

At the very least, the bounds on erroneous information flow that are implied by a program's syntactic dependences *can* be used to filter out test data, selected without regard to the dependences, that cannot possibly reveal certain faults. More ambitiously, it may be possible to *base* test data selection on the determination of syntactic dependences, by analyzing individual syntactic dependences to determine which dependences, which walks demonstrating them, and which inputs executing these walks are most likely to be associated with erroneous information flow. Implementing this approach might require the development of techniques for more precise semantic analysis of programs and for acquiring reliable statistical information about programmer error-making behavior.

2) Detection of Dependence Faults: Dependence analysis has something to say about other kinds of faults besides operator faults. A *dependence fault* is a fault causing different dependences to exist in an incorrect version of a program than in the correct program. A dependence fault may cause either "missing" or "spurious" dependences or both. A dependence is *missing* if it occurs in the correct program but not in the faulty one; it is *spurious* if the reverse is true. For example, if the wrong variable name, say X, is used on the left-hand side of an assignment statement, this makes every use of X reached by this definition of X spuriously data flow dependent on it. This fault may also cause data flow dependences upon definitions killed by the erroneous definition of X to be missing from the faulty program, although missing and spurious dependences do not always accompany each other. Dependence faults may also involve control dependence, as when a statement is erroneously placed in the body of a conditional branch statement, causing a spurious control dependence. In a sense, dependence faults are the complement of operator faults. Operator faults change only the semantics of a single statement; they do not change a program's def/use graph. Under certain assumptions, it can be shown that any fault that does change a program's def/use graph changes the program's syntactic dependences as well, and is therefore a dependence fault.

The data flow coverage criteria address dependence faults by exercising potentially spurious data flow dependences. To evaluate the soundness of this approach, it is necessary to relate the semantic and syntactic effects of dependence faults. The results of Section V do this for certain types of dependence faults. If a fault causes the function computed by a statement s to be erroneously relevant to the execution behavior of a statement s', it follows from Theorems 2 and 4 that s' is syntactically dependent on s, since s' is semantically dependent on s. If this syntactic dependence exists only by virtue of the fault, then it is spurious. A fault may also cause the function computed by a statement to be erroneously *irrelevant* to the execution behavior of another statement, with the result that a syntactic dependence between the statements is missing by virtue of the fault. By conclusions 1 and 3, if a statement s is not syntactically dependent on a statement s', then the semantics of s' *is* irrelevant to the execution behavior of s. Thus, the presence or absence of syntactic dependences may be evidence of erroneous semantic relationships.

Exercising syntactic dependences, as the data flow coverage criteria do, may reveal when the function computed by one statement is erroneously relevant on the execution behavior of another statement, by exercising a spurious syntactic dependence associated with this fault and thereby eliciting the fault's effects. Of course, it is not sure to. Exercising syntactic dependences may also reveal when the function computed by a statement is erroneously irrelevant to the execution behavior of another statement, particularly if, as is often the case, missing syntactic dependences caused by this fault are accompanied by spurious ones. However, because the data flow coverage criteria exercise only restricted types of syntactic dependences, the results of Section V imply that these criteria do not necessarily exercise all missing and spurious syntactic dependences. In the absence of additional information, the only way to remedy this is to exercise every syntactic dependence in a program. For the reasons given in Section VI-A-1, we believe that this approach is untenable. Nevertheless, determination of syntactic dependences might be used to *guide* more discriminating methods for detecting dependence faults, in ways similar to those proposed in Section VI-A-1 for the detection of operator faults.

B. Anomaly Detection

A *program anomaly* is a syntactic pattern that is often evidence of a programming error, irrespective of a program's specification [9]—for example, a variable being used before it has been defined. Korel [15] proposes using program dependences for the detection of "useless" statements, a type of anomaly detection. *Useless statements* are ones that cannot influence the output of a program and can be removed without changing the function the program computes. Korel claims that a statement is useless if there is no output statement strongly syntactically dependent upon it.

Korel did not prove this informal claim. Nevertheless, conclusion 3 supports a version of it: if no output statement in a program is strongly syntactically dependent on s, then the semantics of s is irrelevant to the *values of variables* output by the program. This is because if a change to the semantics of s affected the value of a variable output at statement s', then this would *finitely demonstrate* that s' was semantically dependent on s. A change to the semantics of a statement can affect the output of a program in ways that imply nonfinitely-demonstrated semantic dependence, however. By conclusion 2, nonfinitely-demonstrated semantic dependence might not be accompanied by strong syntactic dependence. In the factorial program of Fig. 2, changing the branch condition of the *while*-loop to N = N causes the loop to execute forever; consequently, statement 6 is not executed. Thus vertex v_6 of the program's def/use graph is semantically dependent on vertex v_3. However, this semantic dependence is not finitely demonstrated, and v_6 is not strongly syntactically dependent on v_3. Hence, the fact that an output statement is not strongly syntactically dependent on a statement s does not imply that the semantics of s is irrelevant to the behavior of the output statement. However, if no output statement in a program is *weakly* syntactically dependent on s then, by conclusion 1, the semantics of s *is* irrelevant to the program's output.

C. Debugging and Maintenance

In both software debugging and maintenance, it is often important to know when the semantics of one statement can affect the execution behavior of another statement. In debugging, one attempts to determine what statement(s) caused an observed failure. In maintenance, one wishes to know whether a modification to a program will have unanticipated effects on the program's behavior; to determine this, it is helpful to know what statements are affected by the modified ones and what statements affect the modified ones. There are no general procedures for determining absolute answers to these questions, but dependence analysis can be used to answer them approximately.

In his work on program slicing, Weiser proposes that program dependences be used to determine the set of statements in a program—called a "slice" of the program—that are potentially relevant to the behavior of given statements [26]–[28]. Weiser demonstrates how program slices can be used to locate faults when debugging. He claims that if an incorrect state is observed at a statement s, then only those statements that s is strongly syntactically dependent upon could have caused the incorrect state. He argues that by (automatically) determining those statements and then examining them the debugging process can be facilitated.

While most investigators who proposed uses for program dependences made no attempt to justify these uses rigorously, Weiser [26] did recognize the need to do this for the use of dependences in his program slicing technique, and he attempted to provide such justification via both mathematical proofs and a psychological study. To this end, Weiser implicitly defined a type of semantic dependence and examined its relationship to syntactic dependence. Unfortunately, the mathematical part of Weiser's work is flawed. In his dissertation [26], Weiser states a theorem similar to Theorem 2.[8] In his attempted proof of this theorem, Weiser actually assumes, without proof, that strong syntactic dependence is a necessary condition for semantic dependence. Besides being very close to what Weiser is trying to prove, this assumption is false. Weiser does not address the issue of formal justification for slicing in his subsequent writings.

If a program failure observed at one statement is caused by an operator fault at another statement, it follows from conclusion 1 that the search for the fault can be facilitated

---

[8]The theorem is stated in terms of Weiser's problematic "color dominance" characterization of control dependence, which he abandoned in his later writings on slicing, in preference to strong control dependence.

by determining weak syntactic dependences, since the statement where the failure was observed is weakly syntactically dependent upon the faculty statement. If the failure implies finitely demonstrated semantic dependence, it follows from conclusion 3 that strong syntactic dependence can be used to help locate the fault. However, if the failure implies a semantic dependence that is not finitely demonstrated, then strong syntactic dependence cannot necessarily be used to locate the fault. This is illustrated by the example in Section VI-B. Hence, for locating operator faults, Weiser's use of strong syntactic dependence in slicing is justified only when the faults cause failures that finitely demonstrate semantic dependence. In his thesis [26], Weiser does not restrict the type of semantic dependence he attempts to localize with slicing to be finitely demonstrated. In [28], however, Weiser defines slicing for terminating programs only. In general, of course, faulty programs may fail to terminate, so this restriction limits the applicability of slicing.

The implications of conclusions 1–4 for maintenance are similar to those for debugging. If a modification involves only the semantics of a single statement, then, by conclusions 1 and 3, only those statements that are syntactically dependent on the statement to be modified could be affected by the modification. Similarly, only those statements that a modified statement is syntactically dependent on could be relevant to the behavior of the modified statement.

VII. OTHER RELATED WORK

In this section we briefly survey related work, not considered above, on the use of program dependences in testing, debugging, and maintenance.

Bergeretti and Carré [3] present a variant of dependence analysis, called "information flow analysis," that applies to structured programs. They suggest several uses for it, including testing and debugging. They define, by structural induction on the syntax of a programming language, three information flow relations that are similar to strong syntactic dependence.

Recently, several papers have investigated the semantic basis for proposed uses of program dependences [4], [13], [14], [23], [25]. Some of these papers address the use of dependences in software debugging and maintenance. Horwitz *et al.* [13] present a theorem that characterizes when two programs with the same dependences compute the same function. Reps and Yang [23] use a version of this result to prove two theorems about program slicing. One of these states that a slice of a program computes the same function as the program itself on inputs for which the computations of both the program and its slice terminate. The second theorem states that if a program is decomposed into slices, the program halts on any input for which all of the slices halt. The latter two theorems are used by Horwitz *et al.* [14] to justify an algorithm for integrating versions of a program.

This paper differs in three respects from the other recent work on the semantic basis for the use of dependences.

First, the other work does not address the concept of semantic dependence. Second, while the results in those papers are proved for a simple, structured programming language, we adopt a graph-theoretic framework for our results, similar to that in [26], that makes them applicable to programs of any procedural programming language and to unstructured programs as well as structured ones. Third, this paper considers the semantic significance of both weak and strong control dependence, while the above papers consider only strong control dependence.

VIII. CONCLUSION

In summary, we have presented several results clarifying the significance of program dependences for the execution behavior of programs. We have shown that two generalizations of both control and data flow dependence, called weak and strong syntactic dependence, are necessary conditions for certain interstatement relationships involving the effects of program faults and modifications. This implies that weak and strong syntactic dependences, which can be computed efficiently, may be used to guide such activities as test data selection and program debugging. On the other hand, we have also shown that neither data flow nor syntactic dependence is a sufficient condition for the interstatement relationships in question. This result discourages the use of such dependences, in the absence of additional information, as evidence for the presence of these relationships. Finally, we have shown that strong syntactic dependence is not a necessary condition for some interstatement relationships involving program nontermination, and this suggests that some proposed uses of strong syntactic dependence in debugging and anomaly detection are unjustified.

There are several possible lines of further investigation related to the use of program dependences in testing, debugging, and maintenance. For example, our results could be usefully extended to provide information about the effects of larger classes of faults and program modifications. Another possible line of investigation is the development of testing methods that exploit the fact that syntactic dependence bounds the statements that are affected by certain type of faults. For example, Morell [18], Richardson and Thompson [24], and Demillo *et al.* [6] propose test data selection methods that might be adapted to do this, since their methods are based on determining conditions for erroneous program states to occur and then propagate to a program's output. A third possible line of investigation is the development of more sophisticated semantic analysis techniques to complement dependence analysis.

APPENDIX
SKETCH OF THE PROOFS OF THEOREMS 2 AND 4

The proofs of Theorems 2 and 4 are lengthy, so we only sketch them here; complete proofs are found in [21].

To describe the proofs of Theorems 2 and 4, it is necessary to present the complete definition of semantic dependence. This definition uses some notation that we now informally define. An interpretation I of a def/use graph $G = (G, \Sigma, D, U)$ is triple $(\mathfrak{D}, F, N)$. $\mathfrak{D}$ is the set of objects which serve as the inputs, outputs, and intermediate results of a computation, and is called the *domain* of I. F is function that associates with every vertex $v \in V(G)$ a partial recursive function $F(v)$ that maps an assignment of values for the variables in $U(v)$ to an assignment of values for the variables in $D(v)$. F represents the ability of a program statement to alter the value of variables. N is a function that associates with every decision vertex $d \in V_{dec}(G)$ a function $N(d)$ mapping an assignment of values for the variables in $U(d)$ to a successor of d. N represents the ability of a branch condition of a conditional branch statement to determine the order of statement execution. The pair $P = (G, I)$ is called a *program*. The computation sequence induced by executing P on an input $d \in \mathfrak{D}^\Sigma$ is denoted $\mathbb{C}_P(d) = \{(v_i, val_i)\}$.[9] The execution history of $v \in V(G)$ induced by $\mathbb{C}_P(d)$ is denoted $\mathcal{H}_P(v, d)$, and its ith element, if it exists, is denoted $\mathcal{H}_P(v, d)(i)$.

We are now ready to present the formal definition of semantic dependence.

Definition 12: Let $G = (G, \Sigma, D, U)$ be a def/use graph, and let $u, v \in V(G)$. Vertex u is *semantically dependent* on vertex v iff there exist interpretations $I_1 = (\mathfrak{D}, F_1, N_1)$ and $I_2 = (\mathfrak{D}, F_2, N_2)$ of G and an input $d \in \mathfrak{D}^\Sigma$ such that, letting $P_1 = (G, I_1)$ and $P_2 = (G, I_2)$, both of the following conditions are satisfied:

1) For all $w \in V(G) - \{v\}$, $F_1(w) = F_2(w)$ and if $w \in V_{dec}(G)$ then $N_1(w) = N_2(w)$.

2) Either of the following conditions is satisfied:
   a) There is some $i \geq 1$ such that $\mathcal{H}_{P_1}(u, d)(i)$ and $\mathcal{H}_{P_2}(u, d)(i)$ are both defined but are unequal.
   b) $\mathcal{H}_{P_1}(u, d)$ is longer than $\mathcal{H}_{P_2}(u, d)$, and either $\mathbb{C}_{P_2}(d) = \{(v_i, val_i)\}$ is infinite or it visits some vertex v_i from which u is unreachable.

I_1, I_2, and d are said to *demonstrate* that u is semantically dependent on v. If condition 1 holds and either condition 2(a) holds or both of the following conditions are true:

1) $\mathcal{H}_{P_1}(u, d)$ is longer than $\mathcal{H}_{P_2}(u, d)$,

2) u is unreachable from some vertex of $\mathbb{C}_{P_2}(d)$,

then I_1, I_2, and d are said to *finitely demonstrate* that u is semantically dependent on v.

The last part of condition 2(b) may be intuitive. It requires that if a semantic dependence is demonstrated by the fact that one execution history is longer than another, then the computation sequence corresponding to the shorter history must be infinite or must contain a vertex from which the dependent vertex is unreachable. This requirement prevents a semantic dependence from being demonstrated solely as the result of the divergence of a function assigned to a vertex. Such divergence can cause an execution history to be shorter than it would be if the divergence did not occur, by terminating a computation. The reason this possibility is disallowed is that if it were not, then each vertex would be semantically dependent on

every other vertex from which it is reachable via an acyclic initial walk (path), trivializing the semantic dependence relation. If the shorter of two execution histories demonstrating a semantic dependence corresponds to either an infinite computation or to a computation containing a vertex from which the dependent vertex is unreachable, then divergence at a vertex either does not occur or is irrelevant to the demonstration of the dependence, respectively.

The proofs of Theorems 2 and 4 have the following basic form. First, a graph-theoretic structure is defined which represents the potential flow of data to a vertex v along an initial walk Wv in a def/use graph G. This structure is called the "context" of v with respect to Wv. It is then shown that in any execution of a program with def/use graph G, the arguments to an execution of v [that is, the values of the variables in $U(v)$] are completely determined by its context. Next, necessary conditions for semantic dependence are given in terms of walks and contexts. These are obtained by analyzing the pair of possibly infinite "walks" executed by a pair of interpretations and an input that demonstrate semantic dependence. Finally, these conditions are used to prove Theorems 2 and 4. We now describe each of these steps in more detail.

The *context* $CON(v, Wv)$ of a vertex v with respect to an initial walk Wv in a def/use graph $G = (G, \Sigma, D, U)$ is a directed tree (technically an "in-tree" [12]) that represents the cumulative flow of data to v along W. $CON(v, Wv)$ contains a distinguished vertex of outdegree zero, called its *sink*. Each vertex of $CON(v, Wv)$ is labeled with a vertex of G and each arc of $CON(v, Wv)$ is labeled with a variable of Σ. $CON(v, Wv)$ is defined inductively as follows. If W is empty then $CON(v, Wv)$ consists of a single vertex labeled "v". Otherwise, $CON(v, Wv)$ consists of

1) A sink s labeled "v".
2) For each variable $\sigma \in U(v)$ such that $W = XuY$ with $\sigma \in D(u) - D(Y)$, a copy of $CON(u, Xu)$ and an arc from its sink to s labeled "σ".

To see the significance of a context $CON(v, Wv)$, notice that if G represents a "real" program P then $CON(v, Wv)$ is analogous to the set of symbolic values held by the variables of $U(v)$ after the instruction sequence $I(W)$ of P corresponding to W is *symbolically executed* [5] (equivalently, executed under a Herbrand interpretation [11], [17]). These symbolic values define the actual values of the variables in $U(v)$, as functions of the inputs to P, when $I(W)$ is executed normally; hence, the symbolic values determine the actual ones. In the same way, the interpretation of the vertex labels of the context $CON(v, Wv)$ determines the values of the variables in $U(v)$ when Wv is executed for a given input and (abstract) interpretation of G. This is demonstrated formally by induction on the length of W.

To state necessary conditions for semantic dependence in terms of walks and contexts, it is necessary to introduce three auxiliary concepts: "hyperwalks," "consistency," and "reciprocal consistency." Since program computa-

---

[9] The symbol $\mathfrak{D}^\Sigma$ denotes the set of functions from Σ into $\mathfrak{D}$.

tions may fail to terminate, it is necessary to consider infinite "walks" in def/use graphs; a *hyperwalk* in a def/use graph G is sequence of vertices that is either an ordinary walk or an infinite one. A hyperwalk W is *consistent* if there are no two occurrences of a decision vertex d in W that have the same context but are followed by different successors of d. This notion is analogous to the notion of path consistency in program schema theory [11]. Because the context $CON(d, Xd)$ determines the values of the variables in $U(d)$ when Xd is executed, and hence determines the branch taken at d, an executable hyperwalk must be consistent.[10] Reciprocal consistency is similar to consistency, but is a necessary condition for a pair of hyperwalks to be executed by a pair of interpretations I_1 and I_2 that differ at only one vertex—such as a pair of interpretations that demonstrate semantic dependence. A pair of hyperwalks W and X is *reciprocally v-consistent* if

$$W = W_1 u u' W_2 \quad \text{and} \quad X = X_1 u u'' X_2 \quad \text{and} \quad u' \neq u''$$

implies that either $CON(u, W_1 u) \neq CON(u, X_1 u)$ or that $CON(u, W_1 u)$ contains a vertex labeled "v". Intuitively, if W and X are executed by I_1 and I_2, respectively, the only way that $CON(u, W_1 u) = CON(u, X_1 u)$ can hold is if v is the vertex whose interpretation differs between I_1 and I_2 and data flows from v to u via $CON(u, W_1 u)$ and $CON(u, X_1 u)$.

Having defined contexts, hyperwalks, consistency, and reciprocal consistency, and having established their relevance to program execution, it is possible to establish necessary conditions for semantic dependence in terms of walks and contexts.

Theorem 6: Let $G = (G, \Sigma, D, U)$ be a def/use graph and $u, v \in V(G)$. Then u is semantically dependent on v iff there exist initial hyperwalks W and X in G such that each of the following is true:

1) W and X are algorithmically listable; and

2) W and X are consistent and reciprocally v-consistent; and

3) At least one of the following conditions holds:
   a) $W = W_1 u W_2$ and $X = X_1 u X_2$, where u occurs the same number of times in $W_1 u$ as in $X_1 u$, and where either $CON(u, W_1 u) \neq CON(u, X_1 u)$ or $CON(u, W_1 u)$ contains a vertex other than its sink that is labeled "v".
   b) W contains more occurrences of u than X does, and either X is infinite or X contains a vertex from which u is unreachable.

It is interesting to note that these conditions are also *sufficient* for semantic dependence [21], although this fact is not used in proving the results stated in Section V. Condition 1 of Theorem 6, which means that there are some (possibly nonterminating) algorithms for listing W and X, is required for proving the sufficiency of the conditions

but not for proving the results of Section V; hence, we do not discuss it further.

To prove that the conditions of Theorem 6 are necessary for semantic dependence, one lets the hyperwalks W and X of the theorem be the walks executed by interpretations I_1 and I_2 of G, respectively, that, in conjunction with some input d, demonstrate that u is semantically dependent on v. Since these walks are executed by I_1, I_2, and d, they must be consistent and reciprocally v-consistent, for the reasons given above; hence W and X satisfy condition 2 of Theorem 6. Note that condition 3 of Theorem 6 mirrors condition 2 of the definition of semantic dependence; however, the former condition is syntactic, whereas the latter is semantic. Let $P_1 = (G, I_1)$ and $P_2 = (G, I_2)$.

Suppose that condition 2(a) of the definition of semantic dependence is satisfied:

There is some $i \geq 1$ such that $\mathcal{H}_{P_1}(u, d)(i)$ and $\mathcal{H}_{P_2}(u, d)(i)$ are defined and unequal.

Let $W = W_1 u W_2$ and $X = X_1 u X_2$, where u occurs exactly i times in $W_1 u$ and $X_1 u$. Suppose v is not a vertex label in $CON(u, W_1 u)$. Intuitively, then, data does not flow along W_1 from v to the last occurrence of u in $W_1 u$. Since v is the only vertex whose interpretation changes between I_1 and I_2, and since the interpretation of the vertex labels of $CON(u, W_1 u)$ and $CON(u, X_1 u)$ determines the values of the variables in $U(u)$ when $W_1 u$ and $X_1 u$, respectively, are executed for a particular input, $CON(u, W_1 u) \neq CON(u, X_1 u)$. Otherwise, we would have $\mathcal{H}_{P_1}(u, d)(i) = \mathcal{H}_{P_2}(u, d)(i)$. If v is a vertex label in $CON(u, W_1 u)$, then it is possible that $CON(u, W_1 u) = CON(u, X_1 u)$, since different data could flow from v to u via this context under I_1 than under I_2. Thus, if condition 2(a) of the definition of semantic dependence is satisfied then condition 3(a) of Theorem 6 is also satisfied.

On the other hand, suppose that condition 2(b) of the definition of semantic dependence is satisfied:

$\mathcal{H}_{P_1}(u, d)$ is longer than $\mathcal{H}_{P_2}(u, d)$, and either $\mathcal{C}_{P_2}(d)$ is infinite or it visits a vertex from which u is unreachable.

Then clearly condition 3(b) of Theorem 6 is satisfied.

Having established Theorem 6, we show that various subconditions of condition 3 of the theorem, taken together with condition 2, imply various types of syntactic dependence. We assume henceforth that condition 2 is satisfied by W and X.

It is easy to see that if condition 3(a) of Theorem 6 is satisfied by W and X because $CON(u, W_1 u)$ contains a vertex other than its sink that is labeled "v", then u is data flow dependent on v. This is because the head of an arc of $CON(u, W_1 u)$ is directly data flow dependent on its tail, as is clear from the definition of a context. The other subcondition of 3(a), $CON(u, W_1 u) \neq CON(u, X_1 u)$, implies that u is strongly syntactically dependent on v, but this is more difficult to see. The proof of this fact is a pivotal element in establishing the results of Section V, since a generalization of condition 3(a) arises in considering condition 3(b).

Let us refer to the subcondition $CON(u, W_1 u) \neq CON(u, X_1 u)$ of condition 3(a) in Theorem 6 as subcondition 3(a)'. The first step in showing that 3(a)' implies that u is strongly syntactically dependent on v is to show that 3(a)' implies that some vertex-label of $CON(u, W_1 u)$ or $CON(u, X_1 u)$ is strongly control dependent on a decision vertex d having kth occurrences in $W_1 u$ and $X_1 u$ that are followed by different successors. Intuitively, d makes branches that cause $CON(u, W_1 u)$ and $CON(u, X_1 u)$ to differ. Since u is data flow dependent on the vertex labels of its contexts, u is strongly syntactically dependent on d. The existence of d is established by Lemma 1 below. Since W and X are reciprocally v-consistent, it follows either that d is data flow dependent on v or that the initial walks $W_{1.1} d$ and $X_{1.1} d$ of the lemma, which are shorter than $W_1 u$ and $X_1 u$, themselves satisfy the hypothesis of the lemma. Since strong syntactic dependence is a transitive relation, it is evident that an inductive proof that u is strongly syntactically dependent on v can be framed using the lemma. The formalization of this proof is relatively straightforward; hence we focus on the lemma and its proof.

Lemma 1: Let $G = (G, \Sigma, D, U)$ be a def/use graph with $u \in V(G)$, and let $W_1 u$ and $X_1 u$ be initial walks in G containing the same number of occurrences of u. If $CON(u, W_1 u) \neq CON(u, X_1 u)$, then there is a vertex $d \in V(G)$ such that a vertex-label of $CON(u, W_1 u)$ or $CON(u, X_1 u)$ is strongly control dependent on d and such that $W_1 u = W_{1.1} dd' W_{1.2}$ and $X_1 u = X_{1.1} dd'' X_{1.2}$, where $d' \neq d''$ and d occurs equally often in $W_{1.1} d$ and $X_{1.1} d$.

This lemma is proved by assuming that no such vertex d exists, and then showing that this implies that $W_1 u$ and $X_1 u$ have a special structure which precludes u having different contexts with respect to them, which would of course be a contradiction. More precisely, we show, by induction on the length of the longer of $W_1 u$ and $X_1 u$, that if there is no such vertex d then there are walks $R_0, R_1, \cdots, R_n, S_1, S_2, \cdots, S_n$, and $T_1, T_2, \cdots, T_n$ satisfying each of the following conditions:

1) $W_1 u = R_0 S_1 R_1 S_2 R_2 \cdots S_n R_n$.

2) $X_1 u = R_0 T_1 R_1 T_2 R_2 \cdots T_n R_n$.

3) For $i = 1, 2, \cdots, n$, R_i begins with $ifd(r_{i-1})$, where r_{i-1} is the last vertex of R_{i-1}, and $ifd(r_{i-1})$ does not occur in S_i or T_i.

4) For $i = 1, 2, \cdots, n$, the first vertex of $S_i R_i$ is different from the first vertex of $T_i R_i$.

It follows that for $i = 1, 2, \cdots, n$, S_i and T_i consist of vertices that are strongly control dependent on r_{i-1}. It is not difficult to show, using induction and the transitivity of strong control dependence, that if a vertex label of $CON(u, W_1 u)$ or $CON(u, X_1 u)$ occurred in S_i or T_i, then we could let d in the statement of Lemma 1 be some r_j, where $j < i$, to obtain a contradiction. Intuitively, this means that the only part of $W_1 u$ that is relevant to the

structure of $CON(u, W_1 u)$, namely the subsequence $R_0, R_1, \cdots, R_n$, is identical to the only part of $X_1 u$ that is relevant to the structure of $CON(u, X_1 u)$. This implies that the two contexts are identical—which we show formally by induction on the length of $W_1 u$, exploiting the inductive definition of a context. Since this contradicts the hypothesis of the lemma, we conclude the lemma is true. This concludes our sketch of the proof that condition 3(a) of Theorem 6 implies that u is strongly syntactically dependent on v.

Suppose that condition 3(b) of Theorem 6 is satisfied by W and X. This condition is the disjunction of two subconditions, which we will denote 3(b)' and 3(b)". Subcondition 3(b)' is

W contains more occurrences of u than X does, and X is infinite

while subcondition 3(b)" is

W contains more occurrences of u than X does, and X contains a vertex from which u is unreachable.

We show that 3(b)' implies, in conjunction with condition 2 of Theorem 6, that u is weakly syntactically dependent on v (it may or may not be strongly syntactically dependent on v) and that 3(b)" implies that u is strongly syntactically dependent on v. We now sketch these proofs, beginning with that of the second result.

Suppose that subcondition 3(b)" is satisfied. To deal with this case, we prove Lemma 2 below. Note that if we identify the vertex u of 3(b)" with the vertex w of the lemma and let the walks Yw and Zx of the lemma be appropriate prefixes of W and X, respectively, then the lemma applies. The reciprocal v-consistency of W and X implies that either the vertex d of the lemma is data flow dependent on v, which implies that u is strongly syntactically dependent on v, or the walks $Y_1 d$ and $Z_1 d$ of the lemma satisfy the hypothesis of Lemma 1. Since $Y_1 d$ and $Z_1 d$ are shorter than Yw and Zx, respectively, this allows us to frame an inductive proof that u is strongly syntactically dependent on v, similar to that discussed with regard to subcondition 3(a)' of Theorem 6.

Lemma 2: Let G be a control flow graph, $w, x \in V(G)$, and Yw and Zx walks in G. If 1) w is unreachable from x, 2) Yw and Zx begin with the same vertex, and 3) w has more occurrences in Yw than in Zx, then there is a vertex d such that a) w is strongly control dependent on d, b) $Yw = Y_1 dd' Y_2$, and c) $Zx = Z_1 dd'' Z_2$, where $d' \neq d''$ and d has the number of occurrences in $Y_1 d$ as in $Z_1 d$.

The proof of this lemma implicitly demonstrates that if no such vertex d exists, then Yw and Zw have a special structure similar to that discussed above in regard to the proof of Lemma 1, although the proof of Lemma 2 proceeds directly instead of by contradiction. It is shown that if R is the longest common prefix of Yw and Zx then $Yw = RY'w$ and $Zx = RZ'x$, where the first vertex of $Y'w$ is different from that of $Z'x$. If w is strongly control dependent on the last vertex r of R then we may let $d = r$.

284

Suppose that w is not strongly control dependent on r. It is shown that in the case $ifd(r)$, the immediate forward dominator of r, occurs in both $Y'w$ and $Z'x$. Thus, $Y'w = Y_1 ifd(r) Y_2$ and $Z'x = Z_1 ifd(r) Z_2$, where $ifd(r)$ does not occur in Y_1 or Z_1. Each vertex in Y_1 and Z_1 is strongly control dependent on r, so w cannot occur in either walk. This implies that there are more occurrences of w in $ifd(r) Y_2$ than in $ifd(r) Z_2$. Since these walks satisfy the hypothesis of Lemma 2 and are shorter than Yw and Zx, respectively, we may frame an inductive proof of the lemma. By assuming the truth of the lemma for $ifd(r) Y_2$ and $ifd(r) Z_2$, we conclude that $ifd(r) Y_2 = S_1 dd' S_2$ and $ifd(r) Z_2 = T_1 dd'' T_2$, where $d \neq d''$ and d has the same number of occurrences in $S_1 d$ as in $T_1 d$. The vertex d must also have the same number of occurrences $RY_1 S_1 d$ as in $RZ_1 T_1 d$—for otherwise d occurs in Y_1 or Z_1 and so is strongly control dependent on r, which, by the transitivity of strong control dependence, implies that w is strongly control dependent on r.

To demonstrate the implications of subcondition 3(b)' of Theorem 6 it is necessary to introduce a new type of control dependence, called "exit dependence." The exit dependence relation represents the potential ability of a loop exit condition to determine whether a statement outside the loop is executed, by determining whether the loop terminates.

Definition 13: Let G be a control flow graph, and let $u, v \in V(G)$. Vertex u is *exit dependent* on vertex v iff there is a cycle C and a walk vWu in G such that v occurs in C and such that Wu is vertex-disjoint from C.

For example, in the def/use graph of Fig. 2, vertex v_7 is exit dependent on vertex v_3, as can be seen by letting $u = v_7$, $v = v_3$, $C = v_3 v_4 v_5 v_3$, and $vWu = v_3 v_6 v_7$.

In [21], it is shown that the weak control dependence relation of a control flow graph G is the transitive closure of the union of the exit dependence and strong control dependence relations of G. That is, the existence of a chain of exit dependences and strong control dependences from u to v indicates u is weakly control dependent on v, and conversely if u is weakly control dependent on v then such a chain exists. We very briefly describe the basis for this result. A preliminary step in establishing the result is showing that the strong control dependence relation is the transitive closure of the "direct strong control dependence" relation.

Definition 14: Let G be a control flow graph, and let $u, v \in V(G)$. Vertex u is *directly strongly control dependent* on vertex v iff v has successors v' and v'' such that u forward dominates v' but u does not forward dominate v''.

The similarity between this definition and that of direct weak control dependence is obvious, as is the similarly between the definition of weak control dependence and the characterization of strong control dependence in terms of direct strong control dependence. The difference between direct weak and direct strong control dependence, and therefore between weak and strong control dependence, is that u can be directly weakly control dependent

on v because there are infinite walks not containing u that begin with one successor of v but no such walks that begin with the other successor. It can be shown that any such infinite walk contains a cycle that demonstrates that u is exit dependent on either v or some vertex strongly control dependent on v.

Suppose now that subcondition 3(b)' of Theorem 6 is satisfied by W and X, along with condition 2 of that theorem. The following lemma, which is proved by an argument similar to those used to establish Lemmas 1 and 2, shows that subcondition 3(b)' reduces to condition 3(a) of Theorem 6.

Lemma 3: Let G be a control flow graph with $w \in V(G)$, and let Yw and Z be hyperwalks in G such that Yw and Z begin with the same vertex, w has more occurrences in Yw than in Z, Z is infinite, and w is reachable from every vertex in Z. Then there is a vertex $d \in V(G)$ such that each of the following is true:

1) Either w is strongly control dependent on d, w is exit dependent on d, or there is a vertex $x \in V(G)$ such that x is strongly control dependent on d and such that w is exit dependent on x.

2) $Yw = Y_1 dd' Y_2$ and $Z = Z_1 dd'' Z_2$, where $d' \neq d''$ and d has the same number of occurrences in $Y_1 d$ as in $Z_1 d$.

Because the weak syntactic dependence relation for G is the transitive closure of the union of the exit dependence and strong control dependence relations for G, the vertex w of the lemma is weakly control dependent on the vertex d whose existence the lemma asserts. Suppose that w is identified with the vertex u of subcondition 3(b)', and that the lemma is applied to $Z = X$ and a prefix of Yw of W that contains more occurrences of u than X does. Then either the vertex d whose existence the lemma asserts is data flow dependent on v and therefore u is weakly syntactically dependent on v, or the walks $Y_1 d$ and $Z_1 d$ satisfy the hypothesis of Lemma 1. Thus, using the fact that strong syntactic dependence is transitive and implies weak syntactic dependence, we can frame an inductive proof that u is weakly syntactically dependent on v.

REFERENCES

[1] A. V. Aho, J. E. Hopcroft, and J. D. Ullman, *The Design and Analysis of Computer Algorithms.* Reading, MA: Addison-Wesley, 1974.

[2] A. V. Aho, R. Sethi, and J. D. Ullman, *Compilers: Principles, Techniques, and Tools.* Reading, MA: Addison-Wesley, 1986.

[3] J. F. Bergeretti and B. A. Carré, "Information-flow and data-flow analysis of while-programs," *ACM Trans. Program. Lang. Syst.*, vol. 7, no. 1, pp. 37–61, Jan. 1985.

[4] R. Cartwright and M. Felleisen, "The semantics of program dependence," in *Proc. SIGPLAN '89 Conf. Programming Language Design and Implementation*, ACM, New York, 1989, pp. 13–27.

[5] L. A. Clarke and D. J. Richardson, "Symbolic evaluation methods—Implementations and applications," in *Computer Program Testing*, B. Chandrasekaran and S. Radicchi, Eds. Amsterdam, The Netherlands: North-Holland, 1981, pp. 65–102.

[6] R. A. DeMillo, D. S. Guindi, K. N. King, W. M. McCracken, and A. J. Offutt, "An extended overview of the Mothra software testing environment," in *Proc. Second Workshop Software Testing, Verification and Analysis*, Banff, Alberta, July 1988, pp. 142–151.

[7] D. E. Denning and P. J. Denning, "Certification of programs for secure information flow," *Commun. ACM*, vol. 20, no. 7, pp. 504–513, July 1977.

[8] J. Ferrante, K. J. Ottenstein, and J. D. Warren, "The program dependence graph and its use in optimization," *ACM Trans. Program. Lang. Syst.*, vol. 9, no. 5, pp. 319–349, July 1987.

[9] L. D. Fosdick and L. J. Osterweil, "Data flow analysis in software reliability," *ACM Comput. Surveys*, vol. 8, no. 3, pp. 306–330, Sept. 1976.

[10] P. G. Frankl, "The use of data flow information for the selection and evaluation of software test data," Doctoral dissertation, New York Univ., New York, 1987.

[11] S. A. Greibach, *Theory of Program Structures: Schemes, Semantics, Verification.* Berlin: Springer-Verlag, 1975.

[12] F. Harary, *Graph Theory.* Reading, MA: Addison-Wesley, 1969.

[13] S. Horwitz, J. Prins, and T. Reps, "On the adequacy of program dependence graphs for representing programs," in *Proc. Fifteenth ACM Symp. Principles of Programming Languages*, ACM, New York, 1988, pp. 146–157.

[14] ——, "Integrating non-interfering versions of programs," in *Proc. Fifteenth ACM Symp. Principles of Programming Languages*, ACM, New York, 1988, pp. 133–145.

[15] B. Korel, "The program dependence graph in static program testing," *Inform. Processing Lett.*, vol. 24, pp. 103–108, Jan. 1987.

[16] J. W. Laski and B. Korel, "A data flow oriented program testing strategy," *IEEE Trans. Software Eng.*, vol. SE-9, no. 3, pp. 347–354, May 1983.

[17] Z. Manna, *Mathematical Theory of Computation.* New York: McGraw-Hill, 1974.

[18] L. J. Morell, "A theory of error-based testing," Doctoral dissertation, Univ. Maryland, College Park, 1984.

[25] R. P. Selke, "A rewriting semantics for program dependence graphs," in *Conf. Rec. 16th ACM Symp. Principles of Programming Languages*, ACM, New York, 1989, pp. 12–24.

[26] M. Weiser, "Program slices: Formal, psychological, and practical investigations of an automatic program abstraction method," Doctoral dissertation, Univ. Michigan, Ann Arbor, 1979.

[27] ——, "Programmers use slices when debugging," *Commun. ACM*, vol. 25, no. 7, pp. 446–452, July 1982.

[28] ——, "Program slicing," *IEEE Trans. Software Eng.*, vol. SE-10, no. 4, pp. 352–356, July 1984.

[19] S. C. Ntafos, "On required element testing," *IEEE Trans. Software Eng.*, vol. SE-10, no. 6, pp. 795–803, Nov. 1984.

[20] D. A. Padua and M. J. Wolfe, "Advanced compiler optimizations for supercomputers," *Commun. ACM*, vol. 29, no. 12, pp. 1184–1201, Dec. 1986.

[21] A. Podgurski, "The significance of program dependences for software testing, debugging, and maintenance," Doctoral dissertation, Dep. Comput. Inform. Sci., Univ. Massachusetts, Amherst, 1989.

[22] S. Rapps and E. J. Weyuker, "Selecting software test data using data flow information," *IEEE Trans. Software Eng.*, vol. SE-11, no. 4, pp. 367–375, Apr. 1985.

[23] T. Reps and W. Yang, "The semantics of program slicing," Univ. of Wisconsin-Madison, Tech. Rep., 1989.

[24] D. J. Richardson and M. C. Thompson, "The RELAY model of error detection and its application," in *Proc. Second Workshop Software Testing, Verification, and Analysis*, IEEE Computer Society, Los Angeles, CA, 1988.

A Graph Model for Software Evolution

LUQI

Abstract—This paper presents a graph model of software evolution. We seek to formalize the objects and activities involved in software evolution in sufficient detail to enable automatic assistance for maintaining the consistency and integrity of an evolving software system. This includes automated support for propagating the consequences of a change to a software system.

Index Terms—Configuration control, consistency, management, maintenance, software evolution.

I. INTRODUCTION

EVEN though the evolution of software systems accounts for the bulk of their cost, there is currently little automated support for evolution, especially when compared to other aspects of software development. This state of affairs is partially due to lack of tractable formal models for the process of software evolution. We propose a graph model of software evolution to help address this problem, and show how our model can help in maintaining the consistency of a changing system. We are particularly concerned with large and complex systems, which often have long lifetimes and undergo gradual but substantial modifications because they are too expensive to discard and replace. Computer assistance is essential for effective and reliable evolution of such systems because their representations and evolution histories are too complex for unaided human understanding. Computer-aided evolution is particularly important in rapid prototyping, where exploratory design and prototype demonstrations guide the development of the requirements via an iterative process that can involve drastic conceptual reformulations and extensive changes to system behavior [9].

Software evolution involves change requests, software systems, and evolution steps as well as customers, managers, and software engineers. Customers include the people and organizations who use software systems and have funded their development and evolution. Change requests come from customers, and the corresponding changes are controlled by the managers of the software system. Change requests that are approved by the management trigger evolution steps which produce versions of the system incorporating the requested changes. The evolution steps are scheduled by the management, and are carried out by the software engineers.

Both software systems and evolution steps typically have hierarchical structures. Software systems are viewed and manipulated as structured collections of software components of many different types, such as requirements, specifications, design descriptions, source code modules, test cases, manuals, etc. Similarly, evolution steps are viewed and scheduled as structured collections of related substeps, such as job assignments for organizations and individuals, and changes to subsystems and individual software objects. A software component or a step is *composite* if it can be viewed as a collection of related parts, and is *atomic* otherwise. The customers are usually directly concerned only with the top levels of these structures, which correspond to delivered systems and responses to change requests, respectively. Top-level components and steps can be either atomic or composite. For large systems, top-level components and steps are usually composite, with several levels of decomposition between the top level and the atomic parts.

As systems change, they go through many different versions. An *object* is a software component that is subject to change. Objects can be either composite or atomic, and can represent both systems and individual modules. A *version* is an immutable snapshot of an object. Versions have unique identifiers. New versions can be created, but versions cannot be modified after they are created. Objects can be changed only by creating new versions. Because previous versions are not destroyed when a new version is created, the state of an object consists of a partially ordered set of versions, rather than a single version.

This paper explores the general class of objects subject to version control. We view each type of software object—such as a specification or a program—as a subclass of the general class "versioned-object." Each subclass provides additional operations and properties relevant to each kind of software object. Our discussion is independent of the additional operations and properties provided by the more specific subclasses.

A distinguishing characteristic of versioned-objects is that they are persistent. Thus versioned-objects are more closely related to the objects in object-oriented databases than they are to the objects in object-oriented programming languages. In the rest of this paper we refer to versioned-objects simply as objects.

Large systems change gradually, in relatively small steps. The direct effect of each step in the evolution of a system is a change in one or more of the component objects comprising a system. These changes affect the functionality and the performance of the system as well as its

Manuscript received December 15, 1989; revised April 9, 1990. Recommended by M. Zelkowitz. This work was supported in part by the National Science Foundation under Grant CCR-8710737.

The author is with the Department of Computer Science, Naval Postgraduate School, Monterey, CA 93943.

IEEE Log Number 9036535.

Reprinted from *IEEE Trans. Software Eng.*, Vol. 16, No. 8, Aug. 1990, pp. 917–927.

representation, and must respect many dependencies between the components to avoid damaging the system. Considering the complexity of current software systems and the scope and frequency of the changes they typically undergo, complete and effective control over the set of configurations is imperative for successful system evolution. Two of the main objectives of version management are ensuring that consistency constraints are met and coordinating concurrent updates to subcomponents of a system.

Evolution steps can be represented as dependency relations between versions. There are often very many evolution steps in the lifetime of a system, and some of these steps may fork off new branches to create families of alternative versions of the system, which may differ in functionality of performance, and may interface to different operating environments, peripherals, or external systems. The complexity of this structure and the dependence of future changes on past design decisions makes it important to record the evolution history of a system.

We assume that each object has one or more alternative *variations*. A variation of an object is a totally ordered sequence of versions of the object which represents the evolution history of an independent line of development. Each version of an object belongs to exactly one variation. Each variation has a unique identifier. All variations of an object share some common properties which characterize the identity of the object. A new variation for an object is created when one of its lines of development branches. Different variations of an object have different properties of interest to the designers, such as those listed above. Variations can be organized using *generalization per category* [8], which provides a structure useful for supporting browsing tools and mapping values for sets of categorical properties meaningful to the users into internal unique identifiers, thus supporting retrieval and specification of variations based on information familiar to the users.

We seek to formalize the evolution history to provide computer aid for maintaining the consistency of the configurations in the product repository. After summarizing some relevant previous work in Section II and presenting the details of our formalized graph model in Section III, we describe the possibilities for computer aid in Section IV and present some conclusions in Section V.

II. SUMMARY OF PREVIOUS WORK

We briefly review some recent work on configuration management, emphasizing the aspects most closely related to this paper. Our work adapts and extends some of the concepts and structures introduced in earlier models [3], [4]. This section concludes with a summary of the relevant aspects of these models. The rest of the paper refines and extends these concepts to reflect specifics of software evolution.

A. Related Work on Configuration Management

The goals of configuration management include recording the development history of evolving systems, maintaining the integrity of such systems, and aiding the management of the systems in guiding and controlling their evolution. Until relatively recently, configuration management was carried out via a combination of manual and administrative procedures. Early attempts at providing automated support for these functions were aimed at identifying and efficiently storing many versions of the same document, and at keeping versions of mechanically derived software objects up to date.

The problem of maintaining the integrity of an evolving configuration has been addressed more recently via module interconnection languages [12]. The purpose of a module interconnection language is to record the interdependencies between the components of a system. The approach reported in [12] includes specifications of functional properties of modules, in addition to the structural and syntactic properties captured by earlier approaches. This language provides a textual form for recording which versions are compatible with which other versions in a related family of software systems. A major contribution of this work is the recognition that specifications can be ordered by an upward compatibility relationship, and that one component can be substituted for another even in cases where the specifications of the components differ, provided that the specification of the new component is an upwards compatible extension of the specification for the original component. This idea is orthogonal to our contribution, and can be beneficially combined with the formulation presented in this paper. The Inscape environment [13] provides several refined versions of upward compatibility, as well as strict compatibility and implementation compatibility. Implementation compatibility is a weaker restriction than upward compatibility which allows one specification to be substituted for another in particular contexts. The concept of obligations in the Inscape environment also supports automatically determining whether an induced step needs to actually make any changes, and locating the aspects of a component that must be changed by an induced step.

Our work is concerned with clarifying the concepts associated with configurations to enable automated tool support for exploring design alternatives in the context of prototyping, for providing concurrency control in situations where many designers are simultaneously working on different aspects of the same system, and for aiding management in controlling and directing the evolution of complex systems at a conceptually manageable level of detail. Rather than introducing a special language for recording dependencies, we rely on existing specification languages to represent semantic constraints, and include specification objects in the configuration. This simplifies the dependencies between components, resulting in a graph structure that can be represented and maintained via established database technology, and can be treated uniformly for all types of software objects. Our work explicitly provides frozen versions, which are necessary to provide stability in a project setting, and applies to all kinds of software objects. The work reported in [12] is limited to just specifications and programs.

Other work has addressed the problem of maintaining mechanically-derivable software objects [6]. The main contribution of this work is to do opportunistic evaluation of derived components based on forward chaining and a set of rules and strategies that represent a model of the user's intentions and the systems capabilities. These rules can also be applied via backward chaining, which provides a mechanism for the system to deduce what tools must be applied to which components to achieve a state requested by the user. The problem of maintaining rederivable components is not addressed in this paper, and the solutions to these problems can be profitably integrated with our approach. The work reported in [6] does not directly address frozen versions and the details of managing configurations. Our view of dependencies between source objects can readily be encoded in rules of the style reported in [6], and our model can be implemented using the system described there. Transactions are considered in [7], which proposes some programming language constructs for realizing nested atomic transactions that can take long periods of time without blocking other concurrent activities. This work does not characterize the integrity properties of the software configuration that should be maintained, and does not link the commit protocols of the transactions to management controls. We provide a graph model that captures these integrity properties, and extend the transaction commit protocol to provide management controls on a high level that can be mechanically extended to the detailed evolution steps that realize a high level change.

The work described above [6], [7], [12], [13] appears to be based on the implicit assumption that only the current version of the object is useful. Our work focuses on maintaining the entire history of each object, not just the most current version. This is most important for groups of evolving systems that share evolving reusable components. Histories are considered in the Cosmos system [14], which provides a distributed database for supporting software development environments. This work is compatible with ours, and provides a means for realizing our graph model in a practical setting. Their consistent domains and domain relative addressing provide solutions for the problems of providing concurrency control that allows a high degree of concurrency in a distributed environment without risk of deadlock. Our work sheds some additional light on the properties of consistent domains, and indicates how the boundaries of a consistent domain might be established by automatic means: a consistent domain consists of the results of an evolution step and all of its induced steps. Nested steps give rise to nested consistent domains.

B. Concepts from the Model of Software Manufacture

The model of software manufacture [3] was developed to aid in managing versions of mechanically derived objects, with the goals of minimizing the number of objects that must be rederived in response to a change, and of automatically estimating the computing costs associated with installing a proposed change. Our main concern is with the source objects which are produced under the direct control of the software engineers. Several of the concepts of [3] can be readily adapted for formalizing evolution histories in addition to providing support for creating and managing mechanically derived objects.

The model of software manufacture formalizes the concept of a *configuration*. Configurations are intended to capture all of the information that can distinguish between two different versions of a system. The concept of a configuration is important in software evolution because each top-level evolution step produces a new configuration of the evolving system. A configuration is represented as a triple $[G, E, L]$, where $G = [C, S, I, O]$ is a bipartite directed acyclic graph, $E \subseteq C$ is a set of exported components, and L is a labeling function giving unique identifiers for both components and manufacturing steps. The nodes in the graph represent software components (C nodes) and manufacturing steps (S nodes), and the two kinds of nodes alternate on every path in the graph. The arcs in the graph represent input relations between components and manufacturing steps ($I \subseteq C \times S$), and output relations between manufacturing steps and components ($O \subseteq S \times C$).

Exported components correspond to the deliverable parts of a system. Each configuration contains all of the components that can affect the production of the deliverable parts of a specific version of a system, and no other components. The model of software manufacture has a broad view of components, which can include software tools such as compilers and flow analyzers, and tool inputs such as command line options as well as traditional software objects such as test data files and source code modules.

The unique identifiers assigned by the labeling function ensure that each component is the result of a unique manufacturing step. This can be expressed formally as follows.

$$\text{ALL}(m1\ m2:S,\ c:C::$$

$$[m1, c] \in O\,\&\,[m2, c] \in O \Rightarrow m1 = m2)\quad (1)$$

Different invocations of the computations representing a manufacturing step are considered to be distinct, have different unique id's, and produce two different sets of output components, which also have distinct id's. Thus two components are considered to be distinct if they have different derivation histories, if even if the values of the components happen to be the same. The model of software manufacture is constructed in this way to avoid the assumption that all manufacturing steps must be repeatable, so that derivations can involve computations which have persistent states or may be affected by transient hardware faults. The unique identifiers for components and manufacturing steps also allow the graphs corresponding to several different configurations to be combined via graph unions without loss of information. Since the labeling functions are required to give globally unique identifiers with respect to the set of all possible components and steps rather than with respect to just the components and steps in a single configuration, there is no possibility of losing the distinction between parts of different configurations.

The software components and manufacturing steps in the model of software manufacture correspond to our component versions and evolution steps. However, the model of software manufacture focuses on steps that can be completely automated, such as compilation, and on components that can be automatically generated, such as object code. A typical manufacturing step is illustrated in Fig. 1. Since we are concerned mainly with coordinating the activities of a team of people responsible for the evolution of a software system, rather than on the coordination of a set of programs, our model includes only source objects as component versions and activities involving human interaction as evolution steps. A typical evolution step is illustrated in Fig. 2.

The model of software manufacture provides formal definitions of some concepts useful for describing software evolution. The set of *primitive components* P consists of the components that are not produced by any step, and can be defined formally as follows.

$$P = \left\{ c : C \mid ALL(s : S :: [s, c] \notin O) \right\} \quad (2)$$

In the context of the model of software manufacture, primitive components are the source objects: those which cannot be mechanically generated. In the context of software evolution, the primitive components form the initial configuration of the system, as delivered by the developers. Modified versions of these original source objects are considered to be derived rather than primitive in our model of software evolution.

The dependency relation $D+$ is defined to be the transitive closure of the relation

$$D = (I \cup O) \quad (3)$$

induced by the arcs in the graph. Since the relation D is acyclic, $D+$ is a strict partial ordering. The dependency relation represents the dependencies among the components and the steps in terms of the derivation structure. For example, component $c1$ depends on component $c2$ if $[c2, c1] \in D+$ and step $m1$ depends on step $m2$ if $[m2, m1] \in D+$. This dependency relation plays a central role in both the model of software manufacture and in our model of software evolution. For example, it can be used to define the set of steps affected by a change in a component c as follows.

$$\text{affected-steps}(c : C) = \left\{ s : S \mid [c, s] \in D+ \right\} \quad (4)$$

This set is used to determine which derived components must be recomputed when the component c is changed [3]. In Section IV we develop a refinement of this concept suitable for identifying induced evolution steps.

The model of software manufacture must be extended to represent the issues relevant to software evolution because it does not include any representations for future plans, does not admit parts of derivations that do not lead

Fig. 1. A typical manufacturing step.

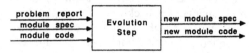

Fig. 2. A typical evolution step.

to delivered products, and does not include any representation of the hierarchical structures involved in software evolution. The relations between components in the model of software manufacture are limited to just the dependencies induced by the derivation history. In particular the model of software manufacture has no representation of whether or not two components are different versions of the same object, or whether one component is a part of another component.

C. Concepts from the Graph Transform Model

The motivation for the graph transform model [4] is similar to that for the model of software manufacture, and several of the concepts of that model are useful in our context. We classify software objects into two categories: *rederivable* and *nonrederivable*. Rederivable objects can be automatically reconstructed by applying a software tool to a set of software objects, without the need for human intervention. All other objects are nonrederivable. An example of a nonrederivable object is a representation of the user input guiding a computer-aided software design tool. The software objects in the graph transform model can have attributes, which can specify computational procedures that can be applied to the components to perform specific transformations.

There are two important relations between nonrederivable and rederivable objects: *uses* and *derives*. These relations have a direction and have natural representations as directed graphs, as illustrated in Fig. 3.

The relation "derives" is defined between general objects and rederivable objects. The relation represents possible transformations of one or more software objects into other objects (e.g., compilation of source code into object code). The "derives" transformations are associated with the use of software tools in the process of programming and are usually invisible to the management and the customers. In the applications of the graph transform model the set of transformations is usually fixed. Individual transformations from the set can be applied automatically using information about the type of the software object and the attributes associated with the objects. The "derives" relation is used for automatically managing derivable objects, which can be either stored or computed on demand depending on the relative importance of response time and use of storage space. This is an important function in a computer aided evolution environment, which

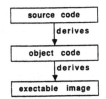

Fig. 3. The derives relation.

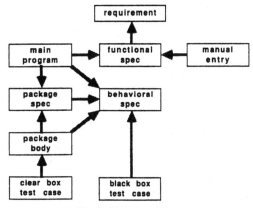

Fig. 4. The uses relation.

we propose to integrate with our approach via the "derives" relationship. The primary focus of our work, however, is the problem of managing the non-re-derivable components of an evolving system.

The "uses" relation is defined between non-re-derivable objects, and represents situations where the semantics or implementation of one software object depends on another software object. An example of this kind of relation is the dependency between Ada packages represented by Ada "with" statements. The "uses" relations between code modules are part of the module decomposition of a software system. These relations may be either defined directly in the components themselves via compiler directives or programming language constructs (e.g., "#include" in C, "with" in Ada, "COPY" in some Cobol dialects) or may be contained in externally specified attributes representing additional information used by the software tools (e.g., library specifications in linking commands). In both cases the relation is defined explicitly, and is not changed often in the evolution process compared to the properties of the individual components. The "uses" relation for implementation modules can be derived automatically from the source code and the external attributes for most programming languages.

In addition to recording dependencies between source code modules, the "uses" relation can include dependencies involving other types of software objects. For example, a clear box test case for a module "uses" the source code of the module, the source code of a module "uses" the behavioral specification for the module as well as the behavioral specifications and the concrete interfaces of the other modules it invokes, the behavioral specification of a module "uses" definitions of properties of the environment from the requirements model, a specification for a user function "uses" the requirements satisfied by the user function, and lower-level requirements "use" the higher-level goals they achieve. Similar relations expressing dependencies not directly related to the source code are that a user manual entry for a user function "uses" the specifications for the user function, and that a black box test case for a code module "uses" the behavioral specifications for the module. These relations are illustrated in Fig. 4. The relationship "*a* uses *b*" is denoted by an arrow directed from *a* to *b*. It is worth noting that in the event a composite module is decomposed into submodules, the implementation of the composite module uses the its own specification and the specifications of the submodules, *but not the implementations of the submodules*. This limits the impact of evolution steps

and provides in incentive for using formal specifications in software evolution. The uses relation can serve as the basis for automatically identifying inputs of proposed evolution steps and the identifying induced steps triggered by a proposed step, as indicated below.

III. MODEL OF SOFTWARE EVOLUTION

The main objective of our model of software evolution is to provide a framework that integrates software evolution activities with configuration control. The model is not concerned with the mechanics and the details of the tasks carried out by the software engineers and evolution programmers. The model is a refinement of some recent work [11] based on a set of organizational paradigms consistent with the ANSI/IEEE standard on Software Configuration Management [1], which are summarized as follows:

1) The management of the software evolution organization exercises a formal type of change control, so that the system configuration changes only as a result of an evolution action authorized by the management.

2) A software configuration management system is used as a tool to coordinate evolution activities for a system.

3) All of the verified software objects are contained in a controlled software library (the configuration repository) and all changes to components of the configuration repository must be authorized by the management.

4) The actual programming work is done using the programmer's workspace, which is outside the configuration repository. When a programmer is assigned to perform an evolution activity, appropriate software objects are copied from configuration repository to the programmer's workspace, where the programmer has free access to them. Final results of the activity are transferred from the programmer's workspace to the configuration repository when the work has been tested, verified and accepted.

5) The deliverable products of the configuration (e.g., user manuals and executable software objects) are derived from the system's configuration repository and installed at the "production" site, which is outside the configuration repository. These software products are the "exports" of the configuration.

6) Since product derivation may be required at any point of time, the system's configuration must be consistent at all times, i.e., the derivation of deliverable objects may not be compromised at any time because of consistency problems in existing software objects.

Such organizational paradigms are common to most software development and evolution organizations that deal with medium and large sized software systems.

A. Definition of the Model

The model of software evolution is composed of two basic elements: system components and evolution steps. We refer to these as components and steps.

Components are versions of nonrederivable software objects: they are immutable, and correspond to the components in the model of software manufacture with the exception that the components must have concrete existence, since they cannot be automatically reconstructed on demand.

The evolution steps correspond to manufacturing steps of the model of software manufacture with the following differences.

1) A top-level evolution step is a representation of an organizational activity concerned with initiation, analysis and implementation of one request for a change in the system.

2) An evolution step may be either atomic or composite.

3) An atomic evolution step produces at most one new version of a system component.

4) The inputs and outputs of a composite step correspond to the inputs and outputs of its substeps.

5) The model of software evolution allows empty steps that do not produce any output components.

6) The model allows steps that do not lead to production of exported components. Such steps represent design alternatives that were explored but not incorporated into any configuration in the repository.

7) Automatic transformations are not considered to be evolution steps and are not represented in the model.

8) The model covers multiple systems which can share components, alternative variations for a single system, and a series of configurations representing the evolution history of each alternative variation of a system.

9) A scope is associated with each evolution step which identifies the set of systems and variations to be affected by the step.

The evolution history is an acyclic bipartite graph G with a global labeling function L, as defined in Section II-B. We interpret C nodes as system components and S nodes as evolution steps. The output edges O relate an evolution step to the components it produces. The input edges I relate a step to the set of system components which must be examined to produce output components that are consistent with the rest of the system. Cycles are not allowed in the graph G, so that sets of software objects with circular dependencies must be packaged as single atomic components in the repository. For example, a set of mu-

tually recursive subprograms must be packaged as an atomic component, as must the data declaration and the operations comprising an abstract data type.

Every configuration in the repository consists of an initial subgraph of G, a set of exported components E, and the global labeling function L. The evolution history graph represents a snapshot of the evolution history at some point in time. New versions of this graph may be created only by consistent extension, i.e., all evolution history graphs representing past states must be initial subgraphs of the current evolution history graph, and must be subject to the same global labeling function.

We formalize some of the above principles and definitions. The set of input components and the set of output components of an evolution step are defined in terms of the arcs in the evolution history graph.

$$\text{input}(s:S) = \big\{c:C \,|\, [c, s] \in I\big\},$$
$$\text{output}(s:S) = \big\{c:C \,|\, [s, c] \in O\big\} \quad (5)$$

The "part-of" relation for steps represents the relationship between a substep of a composite step and the composite step. This relation defines a tree-structured decomposition for each top-level evolution step. Atomic steps are defined as follows.

$$\text{atomic}(s:S) = \neg\,\text{EXISTS}(s':S :: s' \text{ part-of } s) \quad (6)$$

We also need to introduce a relationship that captures indirect dependencies between components. One component *affects* another if both components are identical or if the first component is involved in the derivation of the second component, expressed formally as follows.

$$\text{ALL}(c1\ c2:C :: c1 \text{ affects } c2 \Leftrightarrow c2 \text{ uses* } c1) \quad (7)$$

The relation "uses*" is the reflexive transitive closure of the "uses" relation introduced in Section II-C. The "affects" relation can be derived from the structure of the non-primary inputs of the evolution steps for all components except for the primitive components in the initial configuration. The "uses" relations among the primitive components must be specified when the initial configuration is defined.

The restriction on inputs and outputs of steps can now be stated as follows.

$$\text{ALL}\big(s:S :: \text{atomic}(s) \Rightarrow \big|\text{output}(s)\big| \leq 1\big) \quad (8)$$

Atomic steps produce at most one output.

$$\text{ALL}(s1\ s2:S, c:C ::$$
$$s1 \text{ part-of } s2 \ \& \ c \in \text{output}(s1) \Rightarrow c \in \text{output}(s2))$$
$$(9)$$

The output of a composite step includes all of the outputs of its substeps.

The inputs to both composite and atomic steps are restricted by their parent steps. The inputs to a composite step could be defined to consist of all the inputs of its substeps, but it is more useful to aggregate inputs using a kind of generalization based on the dependencies between components. This simplifies descriptions of composite steps, and supports planning via estimates of the expected sets of inputs to the top-level steps before implementation begins. We achieve this via the following restriction.

$$\text{ALL}\bigl(s1\ s2:S,\ c1:C\ ::$$

$$s1\ \text{part-of}\ s2\ \&\ c1 \in \text{inputs}(s1)\ \Rightarrow$$

$$\text{EXISTS}\bigl(c2:C\ ::\ \bigl(c2 \in \text{input}(s2)\ \&\ c2\ \text{affects}\ c1\bigr)\ \text{or}$$

$$\bigl(c2 \in \text{output}(s1)\ \&\ c2\ \text{uses}\ c1\bigr)\bigr)\bigr)$$

Every input to a substep must either be affected by some input to the parent step, or must affect some output of the substep. For example, if a high-level step changes the specification of a user function, then the substeps can take as input the specifications and code of the modules implementing the user function, since all of those components directly or indirectly "use" the specification of the user function. These indirect dependencies let the inputs to top-level steps be small sets of high-level components which are meaningful to managers, such as the set of requirements affected by the top-level step. If the substep corresponds to a major change that introduces subcomponents that were not used by the previous version, thus introducing some new dependencies, then the specifications of those additional subcomponents will also be inputs to the substep. This is an example of a situation where all of the inputs to the substeps cannot be anticipated in advance. This type of step need not introduce potentials for deadlocks, however, because there is no need to acquire new locks after a transition has started: either the additional subcomponents can be reused without any modifications, or they can be modified by branching off a new variation of the object in question, without affecting any of the other contexts where the object is used.

B. States of Evolution Steps

To model the dynamics of the evolution process, we associate states with evolution steps. We define the following five states of a evolution step.

1) Proposed: In this state a proposed evolution step is analyzed to determine costs, benefits, and potential impact on the system. This includes identifying the software objects in the step's input set. In this state implementation of the change has not yet been approved.

2) Approved: In this state the implementation of the change has been approved, but has not yet been scheduled, and references to generic input objects are not yet bound to particular versions.

3) Scheduled: In this state the implementation has been scheduled, the people responsible for doing the work have been assigned, all inputs of the step have been bound to particular versions, and the work may be in progress. When the step is in this state unique identifiers have been assigned for its output components, but the corresponding components are not yet part of the configuration repository.

4) Completed: In this state the outputs of the step have been verified, integrated, and approved for release. When

a top-level step reaches this state, all output versions associated with the step and all of its direct and indirect substeps are incorporated in the configuration repository. This the final state for all successfully completed steps.

5) Abandoned: In this state the step has been canceled before it is completed. The outputs of the step do not appear as components in the evolution history graph or in the configuration repository. All partial results of the step and the reasons why the step was abandoned are stored as attributes of the step for future reference. The "abandoned" state is the final state for all evolution steps that were not approved by the Software Configuration Control Board or were canceled by the management in the "approved" or "scheduled" states.

Each state corresponds to several phases of the evolution process as they are defined in [10], and corresponding substates can be defined for each of the above states in a detailed implementation of the model.

Transitions of an evolution step from one state to another correspond to explicit decisions made by the management of the evolution organization. By controlling the states of the evolution steps, the management exercises direct control over both the software evolution process and the system configuration. The possible transitions are illustrated in Fig. 5. Evolution steps in the "scheduled" state can be "rolled back" into the "approved" state. Such an action corresponds to a long term delay in a step, and releases the bindings of generic input objects to specific versions. Since this may result in the loss of some or all of the work invested in the step, due to changes in the input objects that may occur before the step returns to the "scheduled" state, decisions to take such transitions should be made with insight and great care. This disadvantage can be reduced by tools for automatically applying a given change to another version of the object. However, automatically combining the results of several steps is the subject of current research [2], [5], and completely automated tools for performing this task reliably have not yet become available for practical use.

C. Constraints on State Transitions

Evolution steps have a tree structure described by the "part-of" relation. In order to ensure consistency in evolution histories containing both composite and atomic steps, we impose the following constraints on some state transitions of composite steps and their substeps:

1) When a step changes from the "proposed" to the "approved" state all of its substeps make the same transition automatically.

2) A step changes automatically from the "approved" state to the "scheduled" state if one of its substeps makes this transition.

3) When a step changes from the "scheduled" to the "approved" state all of its substeps make the same transition automatically.

4) A composite step changes automatically from the "scheduled" state to the "completed" state when all of its substeps have done so.

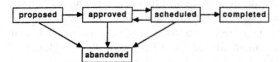

Fig. 5. State transitions for evolution steps.

(a) History of the affected object variation c(v) before the step:
[c(v, 1), ... , c(v, n)]

(b) History of the affected object variation c(v) after the step:
[c(v, 1), ... , c(v, n), c(v, n+1)]

Fig. 6. The effect of an atomic step.

5) A composite step changes automatically to the "abandoned" state when all of its substeps have done so.

6) When a step changes to the "abandoned" state all of its substeps make the same transition automatically.

7) When a new substep is created, it enters the same state as its parent superstep and inherits all version bindings associated with the parent step.

These rules help to ensure that inconsistent configurations are not entered into the repository and that the version bindings for a step are consistent with the version bindings of its substeps. They also reduce clerical effort by allowing management decisions to be explicitly recorded only for the largest applicable composite steps, with mechanical propagation down to the detailed substeps as appropriate.

D. Input Classification for Atomic Evolution Steps

The purpose of an atomic evolution step is to incorporate a single change in a single component of the system. The result of the change is the single output of the atomic step. In order to capture dependencies between different software objects, we distinguish between primary inputs and nonprimary inputs of an atomic step. An input to an atomic step is *primary* if and only if it is a version of the same variation of the same object as the output of the step. Recall that alternative variations of an object represent parallel lines of development for the object which correspond to alternative design choices. The most common case, in which there is exactly one primary input, is illustrated in Fig. 6. We use the notation $c(a, b)$ to denote version b of variation a of object c. The primary input of the step is $c(v, n)$, which is the most recent version of the affected object variation $c(v)$ before the step, and the next to most recent version after the step. The version $c(v, n + 1)$ represents the output from the step.

An atomic step without any primary inputs can arise in several situations. For example, an atomic step may create a new software object as part of a major change which affects the decomposition of the system. An atomic step can also create a new variation of an existing object in cases where the evolution of the object must split into two independent branches. Such a situation can arise in cases where a software object is shared between different systems, and an evolution step acting on one of these systems $S1$ has created a new version of an object which is not suitable for another system $S2$. This new version is therefore not incorporated in any configuration of $S2$. When a later step acting on $S2$ affects the same object, this change must be based on a version of the object that is not the most current one, thus creating a parallel branch in the development of the object, corresponding to a new alternative variation for the object. This is illustrated in Fig.

7. Primary inputs are shown as heavy arrows and nonprimary inputs are shown as thin arrows. Variations are represented as paths with heavy arrows. The versions $c(1, 1..n)$ are shared by systems $S1$ and $S2$, and all belong to variation 1 of the object c. Step $s1$ implements an enhancement to system $S1$ and produces a version $c(1, n + 1)$ which is compatible with system $S1$ but not with system $S2$. Steps $s2$ and $s3$ introduce later chnages in the object c for implementing enhancements to system $S2$. Step $s2$ creates the new variation with index 2, and cannot have a primary input because there are no versions belonging to variation 2 until after step $s2$ is completed. The later step $s3$ has a primary input $c(2, 1)$ which belongs to the same variation as the output version $c(2, 2)$.

We assume that an atomic step has at most one primary input, since it makes sense to include two different versions of an object as inputs to the same step only if those versions have different purposes, and in such a case the two versions should belong to two different alternative variations of the object. An atomic step which acts on several different variations of the affected object represents a change that combines the features of all the variations of a software object. Such a change can either be treated as an enhancement to one of the input variations, in which case there is one primary input corresponding to the existing variation associated with the output, or it can be treated as the creation of a completely new variation of the object, in which case there are no primary inputs.

We can formalize the concept of a primary input by introducing the attributes *object-id* and *variation-id*, both of which apply to versions, and yield unique identifiers for the object and variation associated with the version. Two versions belong to the same variation if they are versions of the same variation of the same object.

$$\text{ALL}(c1 \; c2 : C :: c1 \text{ same-variation } c2 \Leftrightarrow$$
$$\text{object-id}(c1) = \text{object-id}(c2) \; \&$$
$$\text{variation-id}(c1) = \text{variation-id}(c2)) \tag{11}$$

The property *primary-input* can then be defined as follows.

$$\text{ALL}(s : S, \; c1 : C :: c1 \text{ primary-input } s \Leftrightarrow$$
$$c1 \in \text{input}(s) \; \&$$
$$\text{EXISTS}(c2 : C :: c2 \in \text{output}(s) \; \&$$
$$c1 \text{ same-variation } c2)) \tag{12}$$

Some of the nonprimary inputs of an evolution step can be derived from the "uses" relation, since a step can depend on all of the components used by its primary input.

294

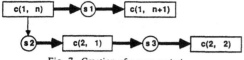

Fig. 7. Creation of a new variation.

This can be expressed formally as follows.

$$\text{ALL}(c1\ c2:C, s:S ::$$

$$c1 \text{ uses } c2 \ \& \ c1 \text{ primary-input } s \Rightarrow c2 \in \text{input}(s))$$
(13)

The set of nonprimary inputs to a step should ideally contain all of the component versions used by the *output* of the step. The above rule approximates this set by the set of component versions used by the primary input of the step, and is intended to define a mechanically derived initial approximation to the set of nonprimary inputs. This initial approximation may need some manual adjustment, since design changes associated with the evolution step can introduce dependencies that did not exist in the previous version, and can remove some dependencies that did exist.

E. Specifying Inputs to Evolution Steps

Inputs to an evolution step can be specified by a reference to either a generic object or a specific version. Generic object references are usually the most common. Informally a generic object reference denotes the "current" version of the object.

Formally a generic object reference consists of an identifier for an object and an identifier for a variation of that object. Each variation of an object consists of a sequence of versions ordered by the dependency relation $D+$, or equivalently by the completion times of the versions. Generic object references for any step are bound to specific versions based on the scheduling of its top-level super-step, at the time the top-level step makes the transition from the "approved" state to the "scheduled" state. The top-level super-step top(s) is defined by the following properties:

$$s \text{ part-of* } \text{top}(s) \ \& \ \neg \text{ EXISTS}(s':S::\text{top}(s) \text{ part-of } s')$$
(14)

where "part-of*" is the reflexive transitive closure of the irreflexive "part-of" relation. The top-level superstep is unique because a step cannot be "part-of" two different supersteps.

The inputs to a step can be specified by generic object references only while the step is in a "proposed" or "approved" state, and must be resolved to specific versions before the step can enter the "scheduled" or "completed" states. The version bindings of a composite step are inherited by its substeps to ensure consistency. Configurations in the repository are completely bound, in the sense that they do not contain any generic object references.

Specific object references are usually used to define in-puts to steps in cases where the current version of an object has features that are not desirable for the proposed new configuration, and some earlier version of the object is acceptable. Specific object references often coincide with the creation of new variations, as discussed in Section III-D.

IV. Evolution Consistency

An important practical problem in the evolution of a large system is ensuring the consistency of each new configuration. While the certification of semantic consistency involves several computationally undecidable problems in the general case, some related consistency criteria based on structural considerations can be maintained automatically with practical amounts of computation. Such support should extend the abilities of an organization responsible for the evolution of a software system to maintain control over the system. We propose to base such support on the concept of an *induced evolution step*.

A. Induced Evolution Steps

A change in a component of a software system can require changes in other components to maintain the consistency of the system. We refer to those other changes as *induced evolution steps*. In this section we define some relationships that enable induced evolution steps to be identified mechanically. These relationships are based on structural considerations, and provide a conservative estimate of the impact of a change. A human designer must either examine the induced steps to determine if they need to produce new versions, or must define uniform policies similar to the "difference predicates" of [3] for filtering out some of the common cases where an induced step can be safely implemented by the identity transformation. Tools for automatically recognizing instances of upwards compatibility relationships [12] would also be useful for this purpose. The purpose of induced evolution steps is to alert the software engineers and the management to the impact of proposed changes and to prevent problems due to incomplete propagation of the consequences of a change. A change in one module can trigger a change in another, which can trigger further changes in a chain of indirect effects. The extent of such chains can be difficult to predict without computer assistance, especially for complex systems.

We call a step that originates such a chain an *inducing step*. The set of induced steps triggered by an inducing step updates the current versions of all components which are affected by the inducing step and are within the scope of the current top-level evolution step. There is need for concern about the scope because there may be multiple systems in the evolution history, which are distinct but may share components. We do not wish to create induced steps which implement unauthorized changes to systems that are not involved in the current top-level evolution step. The purpose of the induced steps is to produce versions of their primary inputs which are consistent with the output version of the inducing step.

A component is current if there is no later version of the same variation of the same object.

$$ALL(c1:C :: current(c1) \Leftrightarrow$$
$$\neg \ EXISTS(c2:C :: c1 \ D + c2 \ \&$$
$$c1 \ same\text{-}variation \ c2)) \tag{15}$$

The scope of a top-level step consists of the components affected by its inputs.

$$scope(s:S) = \Big\{c1:C \ \big| \ EXISTS(c2:C ::$$
$$c2 \in input(top(s)) \ \& \ c2 \ affects \ c1)\Big\} \tag{16}$$

This formulation assumes that the inputs to the top-level steps are the highest-level objects that are affected by the step, such as the system requirements affected by the change.

The set of induced steps can now be characterized as follows.

$$induced\text{-}steps(s1) =$$
$$\Big\{s2:S \ \big| \ EXISTS(c1 \ c2:C :: c1 \ primary\text{-}input \ s1$$
$$\& \ c2 \ primary\text{-}input \ s2 \ \& \ c1 \ affects \ c2$$
$$\& \ current(c2) \ \& \ c2 \in scope(s1))\Big\} \tag{17}$$

Since the inputs of a top-level step are bound to specific versions at the time the step is scheduled, the set of induced steps cannot be influenced by any changes due to parts of any other top-level steps that may be executed concurrently. The predicate "current" is evaluated in the state defined by the version bindings of the top-level step.

An example of induced steps in a small system implemented in Ada is shown in Fig. 8. The initial configuration of the system shown in the figure consists of the three components in the top row. The step $s1$ changes the main program without affecting the package specification, and does not trigger any induced steps. The step $s2$ changes the package body without affecting the package specification, and does not cause any induced steps because there are no other components that use the package body. The step $s3$ does change the package specification, and triggers induces steps $s3.1$ and $s3.2$, which must update the main program and the package body to conform to the new package specification. These induced steps can be derived from the "uses" relationships according to definitions (15)–(17). For all but the initial versions of the components, the "uses" relationships can be derived from the evolution history graph by reversing the directions of the nonprimary input relationships.

In realistic situations there can be longer chains of induced steps, corresponding to paths in the "uses" relation similar to those illustrated in Fig. 4. An example of indirectly induced steps is shown in Fig. 9. Step $s1$ triggers the induced step $s1.1$, which in turn triggers the indirectly induced step $s1.1.1$.

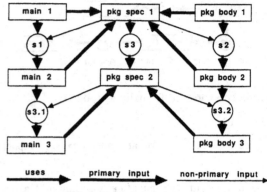

Fig. 8. Induced evolution steps.

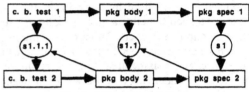

Fig. 9. Indirectly induced steps.

B. Induced State Transitions

To maintain the consistency of the configuration, an inducing step and all of the induced steps must be carried out as an atomic operation. This means that all of the steps in such a set must make their transitions from the "approved" to the "scheduled" states and from the "scheduled" to the "completed" states without other intervening transitions. This can be accomplished by the following rules.

1) An inducing step can enter the "completed" state only if all its induced steps are completed.

2) An induced step enters the "scheduled" state automatically when its inducing step does so.

3) Any "roll back" transition of an inducing step from the "scheduled" state to the "approved" state causes the same transition to be performed on all its induced steps.

4) An induced step can be "rolled back" only by "rolling back" all of its inducing steps.

5) Abandoning an inducing step causes all of its induced steps to be abandoned.

6) An induced step can be abandoned only by abandoning its inducing step.

The first rule ensures that the effects of an inducing step are entered into the repository together with the effects of all the directly and indirectly induced steps. The second rule ensures that the version bindings of the induced steps are consistent with those of the inducing steps. The remaining rules deal with propagating the effects of rollbacks and canceled steps.

V. Conclusion

A formal model of the process of software evolution is needed to serve as a basis for smarter software tools. This paper describes an initial version of such a model and indicates how the model can be used to help maintain the consistency of an evolving system and to help organize and coordinate the activities involved in the evolution of large systems. The model can support aspects of software evolution that are not described in detail in this paper. Some areas for future applications of the model include tools for estimating the cost of proposed changes, and scheduling approved evolution steps. We have found that ideas similar to those underlying techniques for automatically managing versions of automatically rederivable software objects can be applied to nonrederivable source objects, if dependencies between objects are recorded and maintained. We have refined previous approaches to opportunistic construction of derived objects by introducing a link to management approval via the scope of an evolutionary step, as defined in equation (16). This prevents unauthorized and unintended changes to systems caused by propagation of changes to components shared by several systems.

Our model can also serve as the basis for organizing the repository of configurations. Our work has suggested that the configuration repository should contain representations of the steps as well as of the resulting software products. The minimal set of attributes associated with a step are the sets of inputs and outputs. This information is useful for reconstructing the "uses" relation, which is needed in determining the set of induced steps triggered by a proposed evolution step. Other attributes that might be useful include records of time and effort spent on the step, and records of the justifications for the decisions made and the alternatives that were considered and rejected.

Work is needed to address the additional problem of providing computer-aided explanations of the evolution history to support the decisions of the software engineers. This problem is a natural extension of the questions addressed in this paper. Decision support of this type is needed because the groups of people responsible for building a system and those responsible for evolving it are often disjoint, and tend to serve in their positions for short periods of time relative to the lifetime of the system. Thus the evolution history should serve as a "corporate memory," and be capable of supporting current decisions by supplying relevant information about decisions made in the past about the design of the system and past evaluations of alternative designs that were not adopted. Effective representations and analysis procedures for providing adequate decision support for the engineers responsible for system evolution are important areas for future research. We believe such representations can be developed as compatible extensions of the model described in this paper.

REFERENCES

[1] *IEEE Guide to Software Configuration Management*, American National Standards Inst./IEEE, New York, Standard 1042-1987, 1988.
[2] V. Berzins, "On merging software extensions," *Acta Inform.*, vol. 23, no. 6, pp. 607–619, Nov. 1986.
[3] E. Borison, "A model of software manufacture," in *Advanced Programming Environments*, R. Conradi, T. Didriksen, and D. Wanvik, Eds. New York: Springer-Verlag, 1986, pp. 197–220.
[4] D. Heimbigner and S. Krane, "A graph transform model for configuration management environments," in *Proc. ACM Software Eng. Notes/SIGPLAN Notices Software Engineering Symp. Practical-Software Development Environments*, 1988, pp. 216–225.
[5] S. Horowitz, J. Prins, and T. Reps, "Integrating non-interfering versions of programs," *Trans. Program. Lang. Syst.*, vol. 11, no. 3, pp. 345–387, July 1989.
[6] G. Kaiser, P. Feiler, and S. Popovich, "Intelligent assistance for software development and maintenance," *IEEE Software*, pp. 40–49, May 1988.
[7] G. Kaiser, "Modeling configurations as transactions," in *Proc. 2nd Int. Workshop Software Configuration Management*, IEEE, Princeton, NJ, Oct. 1989, pp. 129–132.
[8] M. Ketabchi and V. Berzins, "Generalization per category: Theory and Application," in *Proc. Int. Conf. Information Systems*, 1986; also Tech. Rep. 85-29, Dep. Comput. Sci., Univ. Minnesota.
[9] Luqi, "Software evolution via rapid prototyping," *Computer*, vol. 22, no. 5, pp. 13–25, May 1989.
[10] R. Martin and W. Osborne, *Guidance on Software Maintenance*, Nat. Bureau Standards, U.S. Dep. Commerce, Dec. 1983.
[11] I. Mostov, Luqi, and K. Hefner, "A graph model of software maintenance," Dep. Comput. Sci., Naval Postgraduate School, Tech. Rep. NP552-90-014, Aug. 1989.
[12] K. Narayanaswamy and W. Scacchi, "Maintaining configurations of evolving software systems," *IEEE Trans. Software Eng.*, vol. SE-13, no. 3, pp. 324–334, Mar. 1987.
[13] D. Perry, "The Inscape Environment," in *Proc. 11th Int. Conf. Software Engineering*, IEEE, 1989, pp. 2–12.
[14] J. Walpole, G. Blair, J. Malik, and J. Nichol, "A unifying model for consistent distributed software development environments," *Software Eng. Notes (Proc. ACM Software Engineering Symp. Practical Software Development Environments)*, vol. 13, no. 5, pp. 183–190, Nov. 1988.

Chapter 7
Impact-Determination Techniques

Purpose

Impact-determination techniques use formal dependency models to determine what is affected by a change or proposed change. These techniques, often hidden from end users, play a key role.

The papers in this chapter describe several impact-determination techniques, some used in today's impact-analysis tools: transitive closure, heuristic search, and techniques based on logical inference, analogical reasoning, data-flow analysis, and program slicing.

The techniques are generic in that developers can apply them to various kinds of objects and dependencies. The techniques themselves use formal descriptions of a domain. They tend to have little domain-specific knowledge built into their impact-determination algorithms.

Unless you are building an impact-analysis tool or conducting a study of impact-determination techniques, remembering all the formal details of the techniques is not critical. More important is the understanding of the techniques' purposes because they center on fundamental parts of impact analysis. To that end, it is a good idea to be familiar with the material in chapter 6 because an understanding of impact representations will help you in comprehending impact-determination techniques.

The Papers

Richard Turver and Malcolm Munro begin the chapter with "An Early Impact Analysis Technique for Software Maintenance," in which they describe a method that combines a thematic and stochastic approach to identify the ripple effects of software changes. Developers use *ripple-propagation graphs* and program-slice criteria to identify impacts. (The next paper gives additional information about program slicing.) The stochastic approach is based on work by Frederick Haney [Haney 1972] and is used to reduce the number of ripples in the RPG when identifying impacts. The thematic approach, which Turver and Munro developed, takes the document structure (volumes, chapters, sections, subsections, and segments) as indicators of where to find software ripple effects. This paper is a handy start to

the chapter because it pulls together impact determination that involves both source code and software documents.

In the next paper, "Using Program Slicing in Software Maintenance," Keith Gallagher and James Lyle describe how developers can use program slicing to determine program impacts. Program slicing [Weiser 1984] lets developers abstract only the program statements of interest, for example, those whose execution could possibly affect a variable's value. In this way, it aids in decreasing the scope of a programmer's search for a software bug. The approach is interesting because Gallagher and Lyle show how slicing can be used to eliminate certain kinds of regression tests. Several current tools use program slicing for determining or abstracting programs, so understanding this technique will help you appreciate its power in existing tools.

Transitive closure is a fundamental algorithm for calculating the impact of a change and greatly influences the speed and scalability of performance for common impact-analysis tools. In the next paper, "Efficient Algorithms for the Instantiated Transitive Closure Queries," Ghassap Qadah, Lawrence Henschen, and Jung Kim describe and analyze algorithms for performing a special class of transitive-closure calculation quickly. This paper is based on earlier work, such as "An Efficient Parallel Algorithm for the Transitive Closure Graph," by Pierre Fraisse [Fraisse 1986], which describes an algorithm that depends on having vector hardware and parallel algorithms. Fraisse shows how to calculate transitive closure in $O(n^2 \log n)$ time, where n is the number of nodes in the impact model – a model that specifies the objects and their relationship and how a change in one object can affect other objects. This improves on the original transitive-closure algorithm developed by Stephen Warshall [Warshall 1962], which runs in $O(n^3)$ time, a much slower time.

In the final paper, "Approximate Reasoning about the Semantic Effects of Program Changes," Mark Moriconi and Timothy Winkler describe a logic for determining impacts on the basis of information flow. Information flow is defined simply as A affects B if a change in the value of A could affect the value of B when the program containing them is executed. The logic that Moriconi and Winkler introduce has the advantage of being determinable: developers can handle new program constructs by adding new rules. They can also save and reuse proofs (how inferences are derived) as artifacts in themselves.

References

[Fraisse 1986]   P. Fraisse, "An Efficient Parallel Algorithm for the Transitive Closure Graph," *J. Systems and Software*, May 1986, pp. 165-168.

[Haney 1972]   F. M. Haney, "Module Connection Analysis," *Proc. AFIPS Joint Computer Conf.*, IEEE CS Press, Los Alamitos, Calif., Vol. 41, No. 5, 1972, pp. 173-179.

[Warshall 1962] S. Warshall, "A Theorem on Boolean Matrices," *J. ACM*, Vol. 9, No. 1, 1962, pp. 11-12.

[Weiser 1984]   M. Weiser, "Program Slicing," *IEEE Trans. Software Eng.*, July 1984, pp. 352-357.

An Early Impact Analysis Technique for Software Maintenance

RICHARD J. TURVER AND MALCOLM MUNRO

Centre for Software Maintenance, School of Engineering and Computer Science, University of Durham, Science Laboratories, South Road, Durham.

SUMMARY

The accurate estimation of the resources required to implement a change in software is a difficult task. A method for doing this should include the analysis of the impact of the change on the existing system. A number of techniques for analysing the impact of a change on the source code have been described in the literature. While these techniques provide a good example of how to apply ripple effect analysis to source code, a weakness in these approaches is that they can be difficult to apply in the risk assessment phase of a project. This is because the source code is often not very well understood at this phase, and change proposals are written at a much higher level of abstraction than the code. It is therefore often the case that in practice subjective impact analysis methods are used for risk assessment and project investment appraisal. The underestimated resources for dealing with the ripple effects of a change can result in project schedules becoming so tight that only the minimal quality is achieved. This paper surveys existing ripple analysis techniques and then presents a new technique for the early detection of ripple effects based on a simple graph-theoretic model of documentation and the themes within the documentation.

The objective is to investigate the basis of a technique for analysing and measuring the impact of a change on the entire system that includes not only the source code but the specification and design documentation of a system, and an early phase in the maintenance process.

KEY WORDS Documentation Impact analysis Ripple effect Software maintenance

1. INTRODUCTION

In developing software a number of competing quality factors such as reliability, portability, efficiency, understandability, reusability and maintainability have to be taken into account. The increasing cost of developing software has meant that the life of existing systems has been extended, thus putting a greater emphasis on software maintenance. Over the total life of software the software maintenance effort has been estimated to be frequently more than 50% of the life cycle costs (Lientz and Swanson, 1980). This maintenance cost shows no sign of declining (Nosek and Prashant, 1990).

One of the reasons for the high cost of maintenance is the way in which proposals for change are processed. If change proposals are serviced in the order in which they are made then this may involve extra cost because some changes may overlap with the others, resulting in duplication of work and increased complexity. Costs can be reduced by scheduling change proposals and batching similar proposals together. In order to achieve this, detailed analysis of the system is required to determine the effect of each change on other programs and documentation. A simple model of the software maintenance process from the release planning perspective is (Arthur, 1988):

(1) rank change proposals into a priority order;
(2) select highest priority changes that can be made with available resources;
(3) secure agreement on the content and timing of system releases;
(4) obtain approval to implement the changes;
(5) schedule work into groups to maximize productivity;
(6) prepare release information.

The objectives of release planning are to establish a schedule of system releases and to determine the contents of each release. It is important to rank the changes in some priority order so that, for example, those changes which most improve the profitability of the business may be given a higher priority. The ranking of changes is an important activity which has an impact on the profitability of a system. However, in practice subjective ranking methods are the norm (Foster, 1989). The software maintenance process can be optimized by the use of release-engineering techniques. Examples of such optimizations are a reduction in both project costs and introduced defects by scheduling and batching of releases, based on change impact or ripple effect information. The software maintenance process can only be optimized if precise and unambiguous information is available about the potential ripple effects of a change on an existing system. Measurement techniques can be used in release planning in order to assign numbers to attributes of change proposals in such a way as to describe them according to clearly defined rules. This assignment of numbers to change proposal attributes allows comparisons to be made between the change proposals. The earlier the information is produced in a project the greater will be the size of the process optimization.

This paper investigates ripple effect analysis on source code and documentation of an existing software system. The motivation behind this work is to improve the maintainability of software systems, optimize the release planning activity and thus reduce the maintenance costs. Reduction in costs can be achieved by reducing the time between a proposed change, its implementation and its delivery, whilst at the same maintaining quality.

2. PROCESSING CHANGE PROPOSALS

A software system should not be considered only in terms of its source code. It consists of many other related items such as specification and design documentation. Often a change has system wide ramifications which are not obvious. When considering a change to the source code of a system it is important to assess the impact of that change, not only on the source code but on the other elements of the system. If this process is not carried out then the different elements of the system will become out of step and will lead to a system that is much more difficult to maintain. For example the design documentation may not match the implementation in the source code, thus making the system more difficult to understand.

In carrying out software maintenance it is important to have a model of the process for dealing with change proposals and scheduling releases. Most maintenance models are request-driven showing how a proposal is dealt with and how it flows through the model

(Liu, 1976; Swanson, 1976; Sharpley, 1977; Yau *et al.*, 1978; Parikh, 1982; Martin and McClure, 1983; Patkau, 1983; Osborne, 1987).

A simple idealised model of the change proposal evaluation process can be:

(1) inspect the change proposal;
(2) assess how desirable the change is to the business process;
(3) assess whether the change is a legal requirement;
(4) produce a business feasibility study;
(5) translate the business feasibility study into system terminology;
(6) produce a technical proposal feasibility study;
(7) obtain user agreement on the translated technical proposal feasibility study;
(8) trace the impact on other system components;
(9) assess the risk of introducing defects along with the change and the cost of removing these defects based on past experience;
(10) assess the financial impact on the organization if the subsystem being maintained fails at any time when the system goes live;
(11) compare results produced from the preceding two steps and determine the risk involved in financial terms;
(12) develop an initial resource estimate based on the manpower cost of processing this change proposal;
(13) subtract the initial resource estimate from the expected cost benefit;
(14) assess whether the maintenance investment opportunity should be accepted or not;
(15) report to the user the scope of the change, resources required and the expected return on investment which will accrue to the organization as a result of making the change and any risk involved.

The return on investment can be calculated by subtracting the cost of processing the change proposal from the expected cost benefit. It is therefore imperative to derive an accurate assessment of the change impact from the code and documentation affected and to also produce this estimate early in the maintenance process. If the impact of a change is not detected early then the project schedule may become so tight that only minimal quality will be possible. An important decision point has been identified within the software maintenance process detailed above at which impact analysis is needed for objective comparison and for project resource estimation. Existing techniques for analysing the ripple effect of a change concentrate on the impact on the source code. If the problems described above are to be overcome then this analysis must be extended to include changes to documentation.

3. IMPACT ANALYSIS

The ripple effect of a change to the source code of a software system is defined as the consequential effects on other parts of the system resulting from that change. These effects can be classified into a number of categories such as logical effects, performance effects, or understanding effects. For example a logical ripple effect may be caused by a change in the definition of a data item, which may then cause inconsistencies in the definition and use of other data items.

Impact analysis is the assessment of the effect of a change, to the source code of a module, on the other modules of the system. It determines the scope of a change and provides a measure of its complexity. This type of analysis allows the maintenance managers and programmers to assess the consequences of a particular change to the source code. It can be used as a measure of the cost of a change. The more the change causes other changes to be made ('ripples') then, in general, the higher the cost. Carrying out this analysis before a change is made allows an assessment of the cost of the change and allows management to make a tradeoff between alternative changes.

However, the usual use of impact analysis is to determine the ripple effect of a change after it has been made. None of the existing impact analysis systems (Yau *et al.*, 1978; Haney, 1972; Wild *et al.*, 1991) use analysis to control the maintenance process (Pfleeger and Shawn, 1990). This suggests that the level of information provided by these systems is not sufficiently extensive to allow resource estimation and reasoning about the proposed change.

The most basic ripple effect analysis can be performed using a text editor. However, data flow analysis tools, program slicers and program database tools can provide more detailed information. It is even better to use dedicated tools and techniques for ripple effect analysis. Examples of such ripple effect analysis tools and techniques are described below.

A technique developed by Yau, Collofello, and MacGregor (Yau *et al.*, 1978) analyses the ripple effect from the functional and performance point of view. One aspect of this technique involves identification of the program areas which require additional maintenance activity to ensure their consistency with the initial change. The analysis of performance ripple effect requires the identification of modules whose performance may change as a consequence of software modification. Quantitative estimates for effort involved in making a change are not discussed in this paper.

An approach to impact analysis based on the extended use of traceability to the tracking of requirements to make predictions about the effects of changes on requirements were made using ALCIA (RADC, 1986). The granularity of the unit of analysis is document information content.

A ripple effect analysis technique based on both semantic and syntactic information is presented by Collofello and Vennergrund (1987). In this approach attempts are made to reason about the impact of a change. Semantic descriptions are linked to syntactic dependencies. If a procedure is changed and the semantic condition linked to it is affected, then all other components which depend on that condition are possibly impacted.

Pfleeger and Bohner (1990) recognize impact analysis as a primary activity in software maintenance and present a framework for software metrics which could be used as a basis for measuring stability of the whole system including documentation. The framework is based on a graph, called the traceability graph, which shows the interconnections among source code, test cases, design documents and requirements. This framework provides a good example of the inclusion of software work products as part of the system, although it is anticipated that the level of detail on a diagram is insufficient to make detailed stability measurements. The theoretical basis for extracting impact measures within the meaning of measurement theory has also not been addressed in this work.

A decision view of documentation is presented by Wild, Maly and Liu (Wild *et al.*, 1991). The view structures the document base according to the decisions made during the problem solving process and provides a new way of viewing the software document base. The decision dependency graph links requirements to the documentation which can be used to assess the impact of a proposed change. This paradigm helps identify the parts of the documentation affected by a change. However, the assessment of effort is left to human judgement.

A large amount of information is produced by some techniques such as logical ripple effect techniques (Yau *et al.*, 1978). This information can often be the worst-case impact. The source-code-based techniques are difficult to apply at the production engineering phase because the level of abstraction of the system knowledge at this phase is too high-level. Semantic ripple effect techniques are useful to reason about changes, although the power of the information used to reason is only as useful as the information entered. These semantic conditions can also be linked to source code. However, large systems will make the presentation of all the information a practical problem unless sophisticated windowing systems are used. Impact analysis based on identifying a decision closure provides a useful approach for maintaining documentation. The location of these decisions must be recorded in the development phase. To summarize, the early detection of ripple propagation is difficult during the production engineering phase of software maintenance using the existing techniques unless the semantic information or decision structure is already known.

The main criticisms that can be levelled against existing impact analysis systems is that they do not provide sufficient detail for obtaining accurate estimates of the effect of a change. This is because most of the emphasis is on the impact on the source code. Another weakness is that existing techniques are difficult to apply at the risk assessment phase of a project because not all of the information is known at that time. Once a maintenance project has been committed, then it is of little use for maintenance team to proceed to the detailed design phase or to the analysis of detailed technical design documentation only to find that the change is considerably more involved than intuitive judgement led them to believe.

The software maintenance projects have a poor reputation for coping with the ripple effect. The impact analysis phase of risk assessment is either conducted subjectively or by simply making contingency plans and as a result, projects often fail to meet deadlines and cost targets. As maintenance projects become larger and more structurally complicated and as software systems evolve, so the need for impact analysis techniques will be increased particularly when projects have large capital expenditure. The problems associated with existing impact analysis techniques will therefore become more important and will merit further investigation as software systems increase in size and complexity.

4. STABILITY ANALYSIS

Stability analysis differs from impact analysis in that it considers the sum of the potential ripple effects rather than a particular ripple effect caused by a change. Stability is considered as one of the major attributes of maintainability because the understanding and modification of a program, and the calculation of possible ripple effects constitutes a major proportion of the software maintenance effort. Program stability has been defined by Yau and Collofello (1980) as: 'the resistance of a program to the amplification of changes in the program'. A number of stability measures have been proposed, all concentrating on the stability of the program source code by directly scanning the source code or by predicting program source code stability from higher-level design documentation. None of the existing techniques address the stabilization of documentation itself. This is surprising as documentation such as data flow diagrams, test, and algebraic specifications must also be maintained with the source code. Documentation such as this is also prone to a rippling effect during maintenance.

Haney (1972) describes a technique which models the stabilization of a large system as a function of internal structure. This technique includes a matrix formula for modelling the rippling effect of changes in a system. The matrix records the probability that a change in one module will necessitate a change in any other module in the system. For example a release information sheet can be used to revise the probabilities of module ripple propagation by recording the changes made to modules and to the other modules affected. It is intuitive that the more this technique is used the more predictive value the model will have. The matrix formula based on these probabilities can be used for explaining why the process of changing a system is more involved than intuition leads maintainers to believe. The technique can be used to estimate the number of changes required as a result of changing one particular module. No data is presented to show that the estimated total changes is related to cost or actual changes required. A weakness in this technique is the assumption that all modifications to a module have the same ripple effect and could make the estimation of change resources inaccurate.

A program stability measure was also developed by Song (1977). A technique is presented to quantify the quality of a program in terms of its information structure which is based on the sharing of information between components of a program. The technique is based on a connectivity matrix and random Markovian processes and also makes a similar assumption to the technique described by Haney, in which all modules share the same information content and also sharing of information between modules is equal. This technique is more complicated than that of Haney and has also not been validated.

A measure of the logical stability of software systems consisting of modules was proposed by Yau and Collofello (1980). The logical stability of a module is a measure of the resistance to the impact of such a modification on other modules in the program in terms of logical considerations. In this work logical stability measures are developed for a program and the modules of which the program is composed. There are two parts of logical ripple effect considered by Yau and Collofello in their stability measure. One part concerns intra-module change propagation and the other concerns inter-module change propagation. The metric is based partly on a complexity metric, and partly on probabilities that a modification to a module will affect a particular variable. This stability measure is useful; however, a weakness is that it is very time-consuming to apply the technique to large programs since all the source code must be statically analysed.

Yau and Chang (1984) developed a new stability analysis technique which is similar to the technique described above but easier to apply to large programs. It is not a code-based technique and it is intended to be applied to the design phase of software project. The technique is more efficient because the source code is not statically analysed. The complete information regarding variable definition and usage is not a requirement of this technique. Instead dependencies between global variables and modules are extracted from design documents. This approach uses whatever design information is available.

Yau and Collofello (1985) also developed design stability measures that are intended to be used for assessing the quality of program designs based on design documentation in the design phase of software development. They are based on the counting of assumptions made about module interfaces and shared global data structures. This information is taken from program design documentation.

It is evident that the existing techniques for stability analysis can only be applied to source code and source code detailed documentation. It would be useful to know just how interconnected is the higher level technical documentation, since it is the higher level documentation which is assimilated by maintenance staff first in the processing of a change proposal.

5. DOCUMENTATION STABILITY

The previous sections have described how maintenance process costs can be reduced by batching and scheduling projects in an optimum order. This optimization can be achieved by analysing the impact of a proposed change on an existing system and servicing change proposals which have least impact and have the largest cost benefit to the organization. The weaknesses of existing techniques for impact and stability analysis are:

- the measurement of documentation is not included in the analysis;
- it is difficult to use the existing techniques at an early phase in the maintenance process.

Existing ripple effect techniques extended to include the analysis of documentation would facilitate more accurate estimates for maintenance work and earlier estimates of the potential ripple effect of a change. The remainder of this paper investigates a technique for analysing the impact of a change on the entire system. It includes not only the source code but the specification and design documentation.

As a system evolves the source code changes but the documentation usually either remains the same or lags behind. Even when an effort is made to update to documentation subtle points are often overlooked in the rush to produce a new release. The accumulation of errors and omissions in documentation produces documentation that cannot be relied upon thus making the system harder to understand and thus maintain. Only by systematic analysis of the resistance to the potential ripple effect of document entities on other document entities can specification and design documentation be effectively maintained. The factors which affect the stability of documentation are the ways in which:

- the source code modules are connected;
- the source code modules are connected to the documentation;
- the documentation is connected together;
- the information is shared between source code modules;
- the information is shared between documentation.

The structure, form and organization of documentation is defined by the way in which its document entities are put together and by the mutual relations between the documents. The mutual relations represent document coupling.

The stability analysis techniques described above do not have a natural extension into documentation because of the difficulty in analysing the structure and content of documents and the lack of a suitable formal model of documentation from which a theoretical basis for analysis can be developed. The sheer diversity of the constructs and facilities which form documentation poses a challenge to formal models of the structure of documentation.

It is possible, however, to analyse documents provided that the following observations about documentation are taken into consideration:

- documentation has some sort of topology which can be subjected to analysis;
- documentation consists of one or more documents;
- documentation can be hierarchical in structure;
- documents can contain hierarchically structured sections;
- documents are logically connected through the mutual information they share;
- documents can contain text and/or graphics;
- sections at the bottom level can be decomposed into segments;
- the irreducible segments can represent the smallest primitive component of a document;
- documents can contain inter- and intra-document dependencies;
- some documents may be missing or incomplete;
- some sections of documents may be missing or incomplete;
- document segments may contain subjects or topics which will be called themes.

From these observations the hierarchical structure of documentation can be modelled for subsequent analysis. The structure of documentation can be modelled by considering its hierarchical structure and by observing a pattern of co-occurrences of themes in document segments. This will provide a model of the thematic structure of documentation. The provision of such a model of the interconnection of documentation will enable quantitative statements to be made about the content. Such statements are necessary in order to facilitate:

- the description of the structure of the content of documentation precisely and concisely;
- the precise description of the ripple effect of a change on documentation.

Using this structure of documentation to facilitate impact analysis makes this approach different from other work in the field. The uniqueness can be summarized as:

- the technique is based on the notion of the structure of documentation;
- the ripple effects are analysed by determining the themes of documentation entities;
- the ripple effect technique can be applied in the investment appraisal phase and production engineering phase of software maintenance for batching and scheduling projects, rather than in the implementation phase of software maintenance;
- the technique consolidates the existing ideas of calculating the logical worst-case impact (Yau *et al.*, 1978) with the idea of calculating the stochastic or most likely impact based on past experience (Haney, 1972) into a hybrid ripple effect analysis technique which can be applied to higher levels of abstraction than module connection information and source code;
- consideration of the problem from first principles has led to the development of a new kind of interconnection graph called a ripple propagation graph which forms the theoretical basis of this approach.

The following section investigates the utility of combining hierarchical documentation structure with a categorical and thematic structure for the purpose of analysing the impact of a change on one or more document sections. The analysis of the thematic impact on documentation will indicate the source code impacted by a change and also the risk of introducing defects at a much earlier phase in the maintenance process than existing techniques allow.

6. EARLY DETECTION OF RIPPLE PROPAGATION

The observations about documentation described above were very general in nature. In order to devise and describe algorithms for impact analysis these general observations have to be transformed into a logical model of documentation. This logical model will have to reflect the specific hierarchy of documentation; such a model is:

(1) Documentation Libraries
(2) Volume Entities
(3) Chapter Entities
(4) Section Entities
(5) Subsections Entities
(6) Segment Entities

In this model the relationship between each level of the hierarchy is that of 'consists-of'. So that, for example, Chapter Entities consists-of one or more Section Entities. This 'consists-of' relationship can represent the hierarchy of any documentation. Any entity in the hierarchy above the segment entity is called composite entity.

The desirable approach for impact analysis is to make the technique rigorous and applicable to any development or maintenance method and the abstractions the method manipulates. Any measurements made should be measurements of mathematical objects and not measurements of features of a particular documentation method.

6.1 Ripple propagation graphs

The documentation hierarchical structure described above can be modelled with an acyclic directed graph which can be labelled. A graph consists of a set of elements called vertices, and a set of edges connecting the vertices. An acyclic graph does not contain a sequence of vertices which connect back to the start vertex. A directed graph has edges with an arrow on the edge indicating the direction of a flow or dependency between two vertices. When information is associated with the vertices and edges of a graph the graph, is called a labelled graph.

In the model, the graph vertices represent documentation entities and the graph edges represent a relation of the vertices. The relation is consists-of which represents documentation decomposition. The graph model consist of layers of hierarchical interconnection graphs (HIGs). For example vertex V_2 is a root vertex of the graph $\{(V_2,C_1), (V_2,C_2)\}$ (see Figure 1).

Further information can be added to the Segment Entities such as theme or themes in that segment. This can be defined with additional vertices called theme vertices. The relationship between a Segment Entity and a theme vertex is that of has-theme. Dependenc-

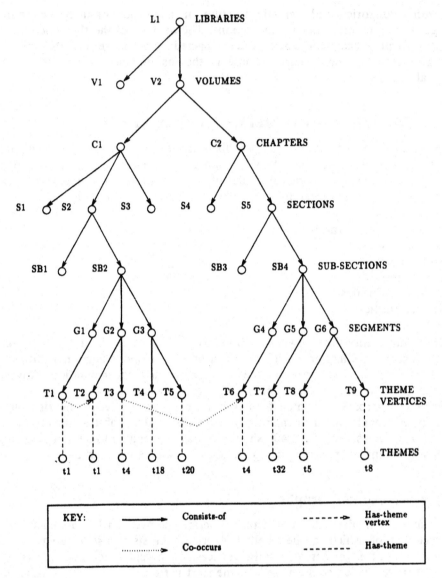

LIBRARIES

VOLUMES

CHAPTERS

SECTIONS

SUB-SECTIONS

SEGMENTS

THEME
VERTICES

THEMES

| KEY: | Consists-of | Has-theme vertex |
| | Co-occurs | Has-theme |

Figure 1. Ripple propagation graph

ies between theme vertices represent co-occurrences of these themes and form the thematic structure of documentation. The relationship between co-occurrences of themes is that of *co-occurs*.

A thematic interconnection graph (TIG) represents the connection between two segment entities for example $\{(G_1, G_2), (G_2, G_4)\}$ (see Figure 1). It is the TIG which records the potential ripple propagation in a documentation system.

Collectively the acyclic graph combining the hierarchical and thematic structure is called the ripple propagation graph (RPG) as it records how potential ripple effects can be propagated through the connectivity in a documentation hierarchy if one document entity is perturbed with a change. The RPG is a selection of documentation features which would otherwise not be visible because of the size and complexity of documentation. Formally the RPG is a tuple which consists of two sets:

$$\text{RPG} = (\textit{Documentation Entities, Relations})$$

(1) a set of *Documentation Entities* that are the components of interconnection, i.e., a set of graph vertices $\{n_1, ..., n_\xi\}$
(2) a set of *Relations* that define the interconnection that exists among documentation entities, i.e. a set of ordered pairs representing the graph edges $\{(n_i, n_j) | n_i, n_j \in$ *Documentation Entities*$\}$, called an edge set.

This can be further formalized:

(1) *Documentation Entities* =
   Composite Components $\cup$ *Segment Components* $\cup$ *Thematic Components* $\cup$ *Themes*
(2) *Relations* =
   Consists-of Relations $\cup$ *Has-theme Vertex Relations* $\cup$ *Has-theme Relations* $\cup$ *Co-occurs Relations*
   (a) *Consists-of Relation* =
      $\{(i,j) \mid i \in$ *Composite Components*, $j \in$ *Composite Components* $\cup$ *Segment Components*$\}$
   (b) *Has-theme Vertex Relation* =
      $\{(G,T) \mid G \in$ *Segment Components*, $T \in$ *Thematic Components*$\}$
   (c) *Has-theme Relation* =
      $\{(T,t) \mid T \in$ *Thematic Components*, $t \in$ *Themes*$\}$
   (d) *Co-occurs Relation* =
      $\{(t_1, t_2) \mid t_1, t_2 \in$ *Thematic Components*$\}$

The graph structure records different types of documentation such as data flow diagrams, algebraic specification, and other formally structured textual documentation. The RPGs provide an appropriate theoretical basis for empirical and observational studies and will also enable the development of new structural hypothesis about all material which serves to describe the semantics of software.

6.2. RPG Crystallization

The objective of RPG crystallization is to determine the constituent entities of the documentation. The technique partitions the document into entities, which are then further subdivided into other entities. This represents the *consists-of* dependency. For each document entity factored a new HIG is derived. This process is repeated until all the irreducible segment entities are identified. A ripple propagation graph can be crystallized from a documentation system or subsystem using the following steps:

(1) Create the hierarchical graph structure of the documentation.
(2) Define a set of application themes (data objects in the documentation).

311

(3) Analyse each Segment Entity for themes and for each theme found, create a theme vertex and attach it to the segment vertex. This records the thematic dependencies.

(4) Connect together each co-occurrences of themes.

The resulting frequencies of theme occurrences can be observed to determine how interconnected the documentation is in terms of the themes. Structured documentation and documentation with formally defined syntax and semantics are suitable for theoretical analysis and measurement. The mapping from the documentation domain to the ripple propagation graph co-domain 'θ: *Documentation* $\rightarrow$ RPG' must be bijective (symmetric) to facilitate objective analysis.

6.3. Set representation of the RPG

A notation is required which describes the possible connections between documentation entities and which can be analysed to deduce the possible consequence of modifying a particular documentation entity. Set notation is a suitable notation to represent the RPGs. A standard set representation of graphs can be used for describing the hierarchical structure from Library Entities down to Theme Vertices. Additional information is required in order to represent the co-occurrence relation between the theme vertices. This can be achieved by associating each theme vertex with a set of segments which refer to it. For example the RPG of Figure 1 can be described in the following way:

Composite Components $= \{L_1,V_1,V_2,C_1,C_2,S_1,S_2,S_3,S_4,S_5,SB_1,SB_2,SB_3,SB_4\}$

Segment Components $= \{G_1,G_2,G_3,G_4,G_5,G_6\}$

Thematic Components $= \{T_1,T_2,T_3,T_4,T_5,Y_6,T_7,T_8,T_9\}$

Themes $= \{t_1,t_4,t_5,t_8,t_{18},t_{20},t_{32}\}$
Hierarchical Interconnection Graph:

   Consists-of Relations $=$
     $\{(L_1,V_1),(L_1,V_2),(V_2,C_1),(V_2,C_2),(C_1,S_1),(C_1,S_2),(C_1,S_3),(C_2,S_4),(C_2,S_5),$
     $(S_2,SB_1),(S_2,SB_2),(S_5,SB_3),(S_5,SB_4),(SB_2,G_1),(SB_2,G_2),(SB_2,G_3),$
     $(SB_4,G_4),(SB_4,G_5),(SB_4,G_6)\}$

Thematic Interconnection Graph:

   Has-theme Vertex Relations $=$
   $\{(G_1,T_1),(G_2,T_2),(G_2,T_3),(G_3,T_4),(G_3,T_5),(G_4,T_6),(G_5,T_7),(G_6,T_8),(G_6,T_9)\}$

   Has-theme Relations $=$

   $\{(T_1,t_1),(T_2,t_1),(T_3,t_4),(T_4,t_{18}),(T_5,t_{20}),(T_6,t_4),(T_7,t_{32}),(T_8,t_5),(T_9,t_8)\}$

   Co-occurs Relations $= \{(T_1,T_2),(T_3,T_6)\}$

312

6.4. Documentation ripple effect analysis

A logical ripple effect algorithum can be used to determine the transitive closure of a proposed change, thus determining all the parts of a document affected by a change. Each of the themes mentioned in a change proposal P are identified and recorded in a change set S, where

$$S = \{t \mid t \in \text{Themes and } t \text{ mentioned in } P\}$$

The impact of a change is derived using a ripple effect algorithm over the RPG. A change set which contains all the elicited themes from the change proposal are analysed in terms of their co-occurrences in the RPG to determine the worst possible ripple effect. The ripple effect algorithm described below is based on a graph slicing operation and is similar to the program slice introduced by Weiser (1984). The RPG slicing operation uses set intersection operations as a means of creating a new set from two existing sets, one of these sets being the sets contained within the RPG. For example an elementary slicing criterion of a documentation system RPG is a tuple (g, T), where g denotes a specific segment in RPG and T is a subset of themes in RPG. An elementary slicing criterion determines a projection function from a documentation segment trajectory in which only the value of themes in T are preserved. This RPG slicing operation provides a restriction transformation which provides a mapping from one set to another and removes any vertices in the RPG not satisfying a particular slicing criterion.

6.4.1. Documentation ripple effect analysis algorithm

The applications of algorithms over the RPGs can provide the maintainer with views of an application system. The graph slicing operation is denoted as:

Thematic Slice(RPG(*Documentation Entities, Relations*),*S*)

where S is the slicing criterion that restrict the vertices and edges which appear in the resulting graph. The graph slicing operation for a conducting documentation ripple effect analysis can be specified with the following sets which represent the applications of RPG slicing to remove RPG vertices and edges not impacted by the change. The algorithm for this slicing operation can be specified as follows:

Thematic Slice : RPG $\times$ $S \rightarrow$ RPG (V)

Thematic Slice (RPG, S) is defined as:

(1) Determine the *Thematic Components Impacted:*
    (a) *Thematic Components Impacted =*
        $\{T_i \mid (T_i, T_n) \in$ *Has-theme Relation* and $t_n \in S\}$
    (b) Extract all *Thematic Components Impacted* by S
(2) Determine the *Segment Components Impacted:*
    (a) *Segment Components Impacted =*

$\{G_i \mid (G_i, T_n) \in$ *Has-theme Vertex Relation* and
$T_n \in$ *Thematic Components Impacted*$\}$

(b) Extract all *Segment Components Impacted* by *Thematic Components Impacted*

(3) Determine the *Composite Components Impacted*:
- (a) (i) *Composite Components Impacted* =
  $\{A_i \mid (A_i, G_n) \in$ *Consists-of Relation* and $G_n \in$ *Segment Components*$\}$
  - (ii) Extract the *Composite Components Impacted*;
- (b) (i) *Composite Components Impacted'* =
  $\{A_i \mid (A_i, A_j) \in$ *Consists-of Relation* and $A_j \in$ *Composite Components Impacted*$\}$
  - (ii) Extract other *Composite Components Impacted*;
- (c) Repeat step (3b) for each hierarchical level in the RPG until the newly calculated set of *Composite Components Impacted* does not change

(4) Determine all *Documentation Entitites Impacted*:
- (a) *Documentation Entities Impacted* =
  Composite Components Impacted $\cup$ *Segment Components Impacted*
- (b) Determine the total *Documentation Entities Impacted*;

(5) Determine the size of the ripple effect in terms of segments affected:
- (a) *Ripple Magnitude* = | *Segment Components Impacted* |
- (b) Determine the magnitude of the ripple effect

6.4.2. Example

For example, given the RPG in (Figure 1) and given the set of themes S extracted from a change proposal describing changes to C_1, where $S = \{t_1, t_4, t_{20}\}$ the following sets can be derived by applying the above algorithm over the RPG.

(1) *Thematic Components Impacted* = $\{T_1, T_2, T_3, T_5, T_6\}$
(2) *Segment Components Impacted* = $\{G_1, G_2, G_3, G_4\}$
(3) *Composite Components Impacted* = five iterations of slicing operation 3:
- (a) *Composite Components Impacted'* = $\{SB_2, SB_4\}$
- (b) *Composite Components Impacted'* = $\{SB_2, SB_4, S_2, S_5\}$
- (c) *Composite Components Impacted'* = $\{SB_2, SB_4, S_2, S_5, C_1, C_2\}$
- (d) *Composite Components Impacted'* = $\{SB_2, SB_4 S_2, S_5, C_1, C_2, V_2\}$
- (e) *Composite Components Impacted'* = $\{SB_2, SB_4, S_2, S_5, C_1, C_2, V_2, L_1\}$

(4) *Documentation Entities Impacted* = $\{L_1, V_2, C_1, C_2, S_2, S_5, SB_2, SB_4, G_1, G_2, G_3, G_4\}$
(5) *Ripple Magnitude* = four segments affected

In this example although the change proposal S is directed towards the application documented in C_1, owing to the thematic interconnectivity recorded in the RPG, the ripple effect propagated to C_2 is detected.

In order to produce a graph-theoretic model RPG of the impact of the change proposal the sliced RPG can be reconstructed using the sets above. To summarize the algorithm above, the RPG' is created by slicing a subgraph from a given RPG according to the documentation entities impacted by the change, i.e., set S. After applying this slicing algorithm over the RPG, the set of impacted segments are identified as the *Segment*

314

Components Impacted and the total cost of dealing with the ripple effect of the impact can be estimated. The cost of maintaining individual segments will be dependent on the specification and design documentation methods used. These costs can be determined experimentally. For example a segment in an algebraic specification will have a maintenance cost different from a segment in a data flow diagram method.

6.4.3. Probability connection matrix for documentation

Since the ripple effect algorithm above is based on existing ideas for ripple effect analysis on source code and module connection information (Yau and Collofello, 1980) and therefore detects all documentation containing themes that are present in a change proposal, it is possible that not all document entities will require maintaining.

The above algorithm detects the worst-case manifestation of the potential ripple effect. However, a situation could occur where a business feasibility study makes a strong case for a maintenance project but the impact of the technical proposal on the existing system indicates a net loss. This would mean that the project would not be carried out, although it is possible that the actual magnitude impact of the change may not be as bad as the ripple effect analysis indicates. To overcome this weakness the thematic ripple effect technique is extended to include some of the stochastic characteristics of the stability analysis techniques described in Song (1977) and Haney (1972). It seems logical to adjust the ripple effect interpretation with a stochastic element to produce the probable maximum ripple effect. This will allow the maintenance manager to make a logical inference about the probable maximum ripple effect of the project based on recorded past experience and thus help the maintenance manager focus on the important impacted documentation and source code. By combining change probability with the HIGs and TIGs a new kind of interconnection graph is contributed which concentrates on ripple propagation. This is why the name ripple propagation graph has been suggested.

A probability connection matrix for documentation can be updated for each project. It can be assued that documentation consists of n segments and that there are n^2 pairwise relationships of the form:

P_{ij} = Probability that a change in segment entity i propagates the requirement for a change in document segment entity j

The matrix is an $n*n$ structure with the documentation segment entities labelled on each side of the matrix G_1 to G_n. Each cell in the matrix represents the probability of a ripple effect between segment entities. Associated with each segment entity are segment attributes and are the following:

(1) Technology interfaces affected by a change to the segment.
(2) System interfaces affected by a change to the segment.
(3) Other application systems affected by change to the segment.
(4) Maximum source code defects introduced by changes to the segment.
(5) Maximum documentation code defects introduced by changes to the segment.
(6) Test files affected.
(7) Average number of lines of code affected by changes to the segment.
(8) Average cost of changing the segment and associated source code.

315

At the release phase of a project the release information is stored in the probability connection matrix. This information will be used to enhance the thematic ripple effect information particularly for risk assessment. Currently it is very difficult to obtain this type of information at an early phase in a maintenance project such as risk assessment.

The interconnection matrix can be used in the following way. For each pair of segment entities (G_1, G_2) impacted in the RPG:

(1) Consult the matrix to find the probability of the ripple effect actually occurring between G_1 and G_2.
(2) If the ripple effect is highly probable, then the attributes associated with G_2 can then be investigated.
(3) The attributes associated with G_2 provide information on the impact of G_2 on the system, the impact on other systems, the impact on the source code, and the likely defects which may be introduced when changing this particular segment.

The information in the probable impacted segment attributes should be accumulated over the life of the system and be used to help a maintenance manager to answer the following types of questions concerning project priorities:

(1) What are the technology interfaces affected by the change?
(2) What are the system interfaces affected by the change?
(3) What are the other application systems affected by a proposed change?
(4) What is the magnitude of the affected areas of documentation and source code?
(5) How much source code will need to be understood to make the change?
(6) What is the risk of introducing defects if these areas are maintained?
(7) How much program testing will be required?
(8) What is the probable cost of dealing with the affected areas of documentation and source code?

The thematic slicing algorithm determines the segment of documentation which might be impacted by a proposed software change. By interpreting the probability connection matrix which contains document segment change history information, the above questions can be answered. The answers to the above questions will provide the maintenance manager with an understanding of the potential spreading of ripple effects and their consequences. This will enable a quick validation of the maintenance manager's own intuitive understanding of the effect of a proposed change. If an application subsystem interface is affected by the change proposal but the subsystem does not seem intuitively affected then this module can be investigated at an early phase in the maintenance process.

The linking of syntactic constructs in the source code with the thematic structure will also improve the precision of the ripple effect information produced at this early phase.

7. CONCLUSIONS

This paper investigates a technique for the early detection of ripple propagation when making a change to software as part of the software maintenance process. Identifying change proposals which affect documentation and source code components which are potential high-risk ripple propagators, can allow a maintenance manager to optimize the allocation of budget and effort.

Existing impact and stability analysis measurement techniques have been reviewed and evaluated. While existing techniques provide a good example of how to conduct ripple effect and stability analysis, a weakness in these approaches is that only the source code is considered when analysing contending change proposals. The main thesis of this work rejects the idea of analysing the impact of a software change on a system by only considering the application source modules and excluding documentation. Source-code-based ripple effect techniques imply that the source code is well understood when the techniques are applied. This is not the case at the investment appraisal phase of the project as only some preliminary high-level design work will have been conducted at this phase. Therefore, if impact analysis techniques are to be used at this early phase, they must address the part of the software which is at a similar level of abstraction to that of the feasibility study or change proposal, that is the documentation.

A new ripple effect technique based on a graph-theoretic approach to the modelling of documentation has been presented. Using this approach facilitates a more objective analysis of the impact of a change on the intrinsic structure of documentation at the risk assessment phase. To analyse these graphs a ripple effect algorithm has been produced based on existing techniques for ripple effect analysis and the thematic structure of documentation. This algorithm is also combined with historical data to provide an assessment of a more probable impact of a change in addition to the worst case impact of a change.

The limitation of the present approach is that the ripple propagation graph crystallization process may not produce graphs which are 100% reproducible. This is because the allocation of a segment document entity to a theme category depends on the segment theme interpretation of the human and therefore is currently subjective. An efficient segment document characterization and classification scheme is important in order to obtain a bijective mapping between the real world documentation and the theoretical graph model. Document entity content description graphs called thematic property models are being investigated for such a characterization and classification scheme.

Using thematic ripple effect analysis an ordered preference relationship can be developed for contending change proposals. It is argued that it is possible to get some indication of the impact of a change to documentation and source code at an early phase in the maintenance process using thematic structure algorithms, but this must be revised with existing techniques later in the maintenance project. With this hybrid ripple effect analysis approach applied earlier in maintenance projects, the value added to project scheduling should be increased.

References

Arthur, J. (1988) *Software Evolution*, John Wiley, New York, pp. 74–75.

Collofello, J. S. and Vennergrund, D. A. (1987) 'Ripple effect based on semantic information', *Proceedings AFIPS Joint Computer Conference*, Vol. 56, pp. 675–682.

Foster, J. R. (1989) 'Priority control in software maintenance', *Proceedings of the 7th International Conference Software Engineering for Telecommunications Switching Systems*, Bournemouth, UK, pp. 163–167.

Haney, F. M. (1972) 'Module connection analysis', *Proceedings AFIPS Joint Computer Conference*, Vol. 41(5), pp. 173–179.

Lientz, B. P. and Burton Swanson, E. (1980) *Software Maintenance Management*, Addison-Wesley, Reading, MA.

Liu, C. (1976) 'A look at software maintenance', *Datamation*, **22**(11), 51–55.

Martin, J. and McClure, C. (1983) *Software Maintenance — The Problem and its Solution*, Prentice Hall, Englewood Cliffs, NJ.

Nosek, J. T. and Prashant, P. (1990) 'Software maintenance management: change in the last decade', *Journal of Software Maintenance Research and Practice*, **2**(3), 157–174.

Osborne, W. M. (1987) 'Building and sustaining software maintainability', *Proceedings, Conference Software Maintenance*, 1987, IEEE Computer Society Press, Washington, DC, pp. 13–23.

Parikh, G. (1982) *Some Tips, Techniques, and Guidelines for Program and System Maintenance*, Winthrop Publishers, Cambridge, MA, pp. 65–70.

Patkau, B. H. (1983) 'A foundation for software maintenance', Ph.D. Thesis, Department of Computer Science, University of Toronto.

Pfleeger, S. L. and Bohner, S. A. (1990) 'A framework for software maintenance metrics', *Proceedings, Conference Software Maintenance*, 1989, IEEE Computer Society Press, Washington, DC, pp. 320–327.

Pfleeger, S. L. and Shawn, A. B. (1990) 'A framework for software maintenance metrics' *Proceedings, Conference Software Maintenance*, 1989, IEEE Computer Society Press, Washington, DC, pp. 320–321.

RADC (1986) 'Automated life cycle impact analysis system', Technical Report, RADC-TR-86-197, Rome Air Development Center, Air Force Systems Command, Griffiths Air Force Base, Rome, New York.

Robillard, P. N. and Boloix, G. (1989). 'The interconnectivity metrics: a new metric showing how a program is organised', *Journal of Systems and Software*, **10**, 29–38.

Sharpley, W. K. (1977) 'Software maintenance planning for embedded computer systems', *Proceedings, IEEE COMPSAC 77*, pp. 520–526.

Song, N. L. (1977) 'A program stability measure', *Proceedings. 1977 Annual ACM Conference*, pp. 163–173.

Swanson, E. B. (1976). 'The dimensions of maintenance', *Proceedings of 2nd IEEE International Conference on Software Engineering*, pp. 492–497.

Weiser, M. D. (1984) 'Program slicing', *IEEE Transactions on Software Engineering*, **SE-10**(4), 352–357.

Wild, C., Maly, K. and Liu, L. (1991) 'Decision-based software development', *Software Maintenance: Research and Practice*, **3**(99), 17–43.

Yau, S. S. and Chang, S. C. (1984). 'Estimating logical stability in software maintenance', *IEEE Computer Society Computer Software and Applications Conference*, pp. 109–119.

Yau, S. S. and Collofello, J. S. (1980). 'Some stability measures for software maintenance', *IEEE Transactions on Software Engineering*, **6**(6), 545–552.

Yau, S. S. and Collofello, J. S. (1985) 'Design stability measures for software maintenance', *IEEE Transactions on Software Engineering*, **SE-11**(9), 849–856.

Yau, S. S., Collofello J. S. and MacGregor, T. (1978) 'Ripple effect analysis of software maintenance', *Proceedings IEEE COMPSAC*, pp. 60–65.

Using Program Slicing in Software Maintenance

Keith Brian Gallagher and James R. Lyle, *Member, IEEE*

Abstract—Program slicing, introduced by Weiser, is known to help programmers in understanding foreign code and in debugging. We apply program slicing to the maintenance problem by extending the notion of a program slice (that originally required both a variable and line number) to a *decomposition slice*, one that captures all computation on a given variable; i.e., is independent of line numbers. Using the lattice of single variable decomposition slices ordered by set inclusion, we demonstrate how to form a slice-based decomposition for programs. We are then able to delineate the effects of a proposed change by isolating those effects in a single component of the decomposition. This gives maintainers a straightforward technique for determining those statements and variables which may be modified in a component and those which may not. Using the decomposition, we provide a set of principles to prohibit changes which will interfere with unmodified components. These semantically consistent changes can then be merged back into the original program in linear time. Moreover, the maintainer can test the changes in the component with the assurance that there are no linkages into other components. Thus decomposition slicing induces a new software maintenance process model which eliminates the need for regression testing.

Index Terms—Software maintenance, program slicing, decompostion slicing, software process models, software testing, software tools, impact analysis.

I. INTRODUCTION

IN "Kill that Code!" [32], G. Weinberg alludes to his private list of the world's most expensive program errors. The top three disasters were caused by a change to exactly one line of code: "Each one involved the change of a *single digit* in a previously correct program." The argument goes that since the change was to only one line, the usual mechanisms for change control could be circumvented. And, of course, the results were catastrophic. Weinberg offers a partial explanation: "Unexpected linkages," i.e., the value of the modified variable was used in some other place in the program. The top three of this list of ignominy are attributed to linkage. More recently, Schneidewind [30] notes that one of the reasons that maintenance is difficult is that it is hard to determine when a code change will affect some other piece of code. We present herein a method for maintainers to use that addresses this issue.

While some may view software maintenance as a less intellectually demanding activity than development, the central premise of this work is that software maintenance is *more* demanding. The added difficulty is due in large part to the semantic constraints that are placed on the maintainer. These

Manuscript received March 17, 1989; revised April 5, 1991. Recommended by R. A. DeMille.

K. B. Gallagher is with the Computer Science Department, Loyola College in Maryland, 4501 N. Charles Street, Baltimore, MD 21210.

J. R. Lyle is with the University of Maryland, Baltimore Campus, 5401 Wilkens Avenue, Baltimore, MD 21228.

IEEE Log Number 9101139.

constraints can be loosely characterized as the attempt to avoid unexpected linkages. Some [4], [14] have addressed this problem by attempting to eliminate these semantic constraints and then providing the maintainer with a tool which will pinpoint potential inconsistencies after changes have been implemented. This makes maintenance appear to be more like development, since the programmer does not need to worry about linkages: Once the change is made, the tool is invoked and the inconsistencies (if any) are located. One would expect that the tool would proceed to resolve these inconsistencies, but it has been shown that this problem is NP-hard [14]. Thus the maintainer can be presented with a problem which is more difficult to resolve than the original change.

We take the opposite view: Present the maintainer with a semantically constrained problem and let him construct the solution which implements the change within these constraints. The semantic context with which we propose to constrain the maintainer is one that will *prohibit* linkages into the portions of the code that the maintainer does not want to change. This approach uncovers potential problems earlier than the aforementioned methods, and, we believe, is worth any inconvenience that may be encountered due to the imposition of the constraints.

Our program slicing-based techniques give an assessment of the impact of proposed modifications, ease the problems associated with revalidation, and reduce the resources required for maintenance activities. They work on unstructured programs, so they are usable on older systems. They may be used for white-box, spare-parts, and backbone maintenance without regard to whether the maintenance is corrective, adaptive, perfective, or preventive.

II. BACKGROUND

Program slicing, introduced by Weiser [33], [36], is a technique for restricting the behavior of a program to some specified subset of interest. A slice $S(v, n)$ (of program P) on variable v, or set of variables, at statement n yields the portions of the program that contributed to the value of v just before statement n is executed. $S(v, n)$ is called a *slicing criteria*. Slices can be computed automatically on source programs by analyzing data flow and control flow. A program slice has the added advantage of being an executable program. Slicing is done implicitly by programmers while debugging [33], [35]; slices can be combined to isolate sections of code likely to contain program faults and significantly reduce debugging times [23]–[25].

There has been a flurry of recent activities where slicing plays a significant role. Horwitz *et al.* [15], [16], [28] use slices in integrating programs. Their results are built on the seminal work of Ottenstein and Ottenstein [7], [27], combining slicing with the robust representation afforded by program dependence graphs. Korel and Laski [20]–[22] use slices combined with execution traces for program debugging and testing. Choi *et al.* [6] use slices and traces in debugging parallel programs. Reps and Wang [29] have investigated termination conditions for program slices. Hausler [13] has developed a denotational approach to program slicing. Gallagher [8] has improved Lyle's [23] algorithm for slicing in the presence of GOTO's and developed techniques for capturing arbitrarily placed output statements. We will not discuss slicing techniques in this paper and instead refer the interested reader to these works.

Since we want to avoid getting bogged down in the details of a particular language, we will identify a program with its flowgraph. Each node in the graph will correspond to a single-source language statement. Henceforth the term statement will mean a node in the flowgraph. Using a common representation scheme makes the presentation clear, although it is clear that any tool based on these techniques will need to account for the nuances of the particular language. In this paper we also ignore problems introduced by having dead code in the source program, and declare that the programs under consideration will not have any dead code. See [8] for slicing-based techniques to eliminate dead code.

Figs. 2–6 illustrate slicing on the program of Fig. 1, a bare bones version of the Unix utility **wc**, word count, taken from [19]. The program counts the number of characters, words, and lines in a text file. It has been slightly modified to illustrate more clearly the slicing principles. The slices of Figs. 2–4 are complete programs which compute a restriction of the specification. The slice on **nw** (Fig. 2) will output the number of words in a file; the slice on **nc** (Fig. 3) will count the number of characters in the input text file; and the slice on **nl** (Fig. 4) will count the number of lines in the file.

III. USING SLICES FOR DECOMPOSITION

This section presents a method for using slices to obtain a decomposition of the program. Our objective is to use slicing to decompose a program "directly" into two (or more) components. A program slice will be one of the components. The construction is a two step process. The first step is to build, for one variable, a *decomposition slice*, which is the union of certain slices taken at certain line numbers on the given variable. Then the other component of the decomposition, called the *complement*, will also be obtained from the original program. The complement is constructed in such a way that when certain statements of the decomposition slice are removed from the original program, the program that remains is the slice that corresponds to the *complement* (in a sense to be defined) of the given criteria with respect to the variables defined in the program. Thus the complement is also a program slice.

The decomposition slice is used to guide the removal of statements in a systematic fashion to construct the complement. It is insufficient to merely remove the slice statements from the original program. Since we require that a slice be executable, there will be certain crucial statements that are necessary in both the slice and its complement. For example,

```
1    #define YES 1
2    #define NO 0
3    main()
4    {
5        int c, nl, nw, nc, inword ;
6        inword = NO ;
7        nl = 0;
8        nw = 0;
9        nc = 0;
10       c = getchar();
11       while ( c != EOF ) {
12           nc = nc + 1;
13           if ( c == '\n')
14               nl = nl + 1;
15           if ( c == ' ' || c == '\n' || c == '\t')
16               inword = NO;
17           else if (inword == NO) {
18               inword = YES ;
19               nw = nw + 1;
20           }
21           c = getchar();
22       }
23       printf("%d \n",nl);
24       printf("%d \n",nw);
25       printf("%d \n",nc);
26   }
```

Fig. 1. Program to be sliced.

```
1    #define YES 1
2    #define NO 0
3    main()
4    {
5        int c, nw, inword ;
6        inword = NO ;
8        nw = 0;
10       c = getchar();
11       while ( c != EOF ) {
15           if ( c == ' ' || c == '\n' || c == '\t')
16               inword = NO;
17           else if (inword == NO) {
18               inword = YES ;
19               nw = nw + 1;
20           }
21           c = getchar();
22       }
24       printf("%d \n",nw);
26   }
```

Fig. 2. Slice on nw: word counter.

```
3    main()
4    {
5        int c, nc ;
9        nc = 0;
10       c = getchar();
11       while ( c != EOF ) {
12           nc = nc + 1;
21           c = getchar();
22       }
25       printf("%d \n",nc);
26   }
```

Fig. 3. Slice on nc: character counter.

if we start with the slice of Fig. 2 and remove *all* its statements from the original program, the resulting object will not even compile!

```
3    main()
4    {
5        int c, nl, ;
7        nl = 0;
10       c = getchar();
11       while ( c != EOF ) {
13           if ( c == '\n')
14               nl = nl + 1;
21           c = getchar();
22       }
23       printf("%d \n",nl);
26   }
```

Fig. 4.   Slice on **nl**: line counter.

```
1    #define YES 1
2    #define NO 0
3    main()
4    {
5        int c, inword ;
6        inword = NO ;
10       c = getchar();
11       while ( c != EOF ) {
15           if ( c == ' ' || c == '\n' || c == '\t')
16               inword = NO;
17           else if (inword == NO) {
18               inword = YES ;
20           }
21           c = getchar();
22       }
26   }
```

Fig. 5.   Slice on **inword**.

```
3    main()
4    {
5        int c ;
10       c = getchar();
11       while ( c != EOF ) {
21           c = getchar();
22       }
26   }
```

Fig. 6.   Slice on **c**.

We use this decomposition to break the program into manageable pieces and automatically assist the maintainer in guaranteeing that there are no ripple effects induced by modifications in a component. We use the complement to provide a semantic context for modifications in the decomposition slice; the complement must remain fixed after any change.

The decomposition ideas presented in this section are independent of a particular slicing method. Once a slice is obtained by any slicing algorithm, a program decomposition may be computed. Clearly, the quality of the decomposition will be affected by the quality of the slice, in the sense that more refined slices give a finer granularity and also deliver more semantic information to the maintainer.

A program slice is dependent on a variable and a statement number. A *decomposition slice* does not depend on statement numbers. The motivation for this concept is easily explained using the example of Fig. 7. The slice $S(t,4)$ is statements 1, 2, 3, 4, while the slice $S(t,6)$ is statements 1, 2, 5, 6. Slicing at statement *last* (in this case 6) of a program is insufficient to get all computations involving the slice variable

```
1    input a
2    input b
3    t = a + b
4    print t
5    t = a - b
6    print t
```

Fig. 7.   Requires a decomposition slice.

t. A decomposition slice captures all relevant computations involving a given variable.

To construct a decomposition slice, we borrow the concept of *critical instructions* from an algorithm for dead code elimination as presented in Kennedy [18]. A brief reprise follows. The usual method for dead code elimination is to first locate all instructions that are useful in some sense. These are declared to be the critical instructions. Typically, dead code elimination algorithms start by marking output instructions to be critical. Then the *use-definition* [18] chains are traced to mark the instructions which impact the output statements. Any code that is left unmarked is useless to the given computation.

Definition 1:   Let $Output(P,v)$ be the set of statements in program P that output variable v, let *last* be the last statement of P, and let $N = Output(P,v) \cup \{last\}$. The statements in $\bigcup_{n \in N} S(v)$ form the decomposition slice on v, denoted $S(v)$.

The decomposition slice is the union of a collection of slices, which is still a program slice [36]. We include statement *last* so that a variable which is not output may still be used as a decomposition criteria; this will also capture any defining computation on the decomposition variable after the last statement that displays its value. To successfully take a slice at statement last, we invoke one of the crucial differences between the slicing definitions of Reps [29], with those of Weiser [36], Lyle [23], and this work. A Reps slice must be taken at a point p with respect to a variable which is defined or referenced at p. Weiser's slices can be taken at an arbitrary variable at an arbitrary line number. This difference prohibits Reps's slicing techniques from being applicable in the current context, since we want to slice on every variable in the program at the last statement.

We now begin to examine the relationship between decomposition slices. Once we have this in place, we can use the decomposition slices to perform the actual decompositions. To determine the relationships, we take the decomposition slice for each variable in the program and form a lattice of these decomposition slices, ordered by set inclusion. It is easier to gain a clear understanding of the relationship between decomposition slices if we regard them *without* output statements. This may seem unusual in light of the above definition, since we used output statements in obtaining relevant computations. We view output statements as windows into the current state of computation, which do not contribute to the realization of the state. This coincides with the informal definition of a slice: the statements which yield the portions of the program that contributed to the value of v just before statement n is executed. Assuming that output statements do not contribute to the value of a variable precludes from our discussion output statements (and therefore programs) in which the output values are reused, as is the case with random access files or output to files which are later reopened for input. Moreover, we are describing a decomposition technique which is not dependent on any particular slicing technique; we have no way of knowing whether or not the slicing technique includes output statements or not. We say a slice is *output-restricted* if all its output statements are removed.

Definition 2: Output restricted decomposition slices $S(v)$ and $S(w)$ are *independent* if $S(v) \cap S(w) = \emptyset$.

It would be a peculiar program that had independent decomposition slices; they would share neither control flow or data flow. In effect, there would be two programs with nonintersecting computations on disjoint domains that were merged together. The lattice would have two components. In Ott's slice metric terminology [26], independence corresponds to low (coincidental or temporal) cohesion.

Output-restricted decomposition slices that are not independent are said to be *(weakly) dependent*. Subsequently, when we speak of independence and dependence *of slices,* it will always be in the context of output-restricted decomposition slices.

Definition 3: Let $S(v)$ and $S(w)$ be output-restricted decomposition slices, $w \neq v$, and let $S(v) \subset S(w)$. $S(v)$ is said to be *strongly dependent* on $S(w)$.

Thus output-restricted decomposition slices strongly dependent on independent slices are independent. The definitions of independence and dependence presented herein are themselves dependent on the notion of a slice. The analogous definitions are used by Bergeretti and Carré [3] to *define* slices. In Ott's metric terminology [26], strong dependence corresponds to high (sequential or functional) cohesion.

Strong dependence of decomposition slices is a binary relation; in most cases, however, we will not always need an explicit reference to the containing slice. Henceforth we will write "$S(v)$ is strongly dependent" as a shorthand for "$S(v)$ is strongly dependent on some other slice $S(w)$" when the context permits it.

Definition 4: An output-restricted slice $S(v)$ that is *not* strongly dependent on any other slice is said to be *maximal.*

Maximal decomposition slices are at the "ends" of the lattice. This definition gives the motivation for output restriction; we do not want to be concerned with the possible effects of output statements on the maximality of slices or decomposition slices. This can be observed by considering the decomposition slices on **nw** and **inword**, of Figs. 2 and 5. If we regarded output statements in defining maximal, we could force the slice on **inword** to be maximal by the addition of a *print* statement referencing **inword** along with the others at the end of the program. Such a statement would not be collected into the slice on **nw**. Since this added statement is not in any other slice, the slice on **inword** would be maximal and it should not be.

Fig. 8 gives the lattice we desire. $S(nc)$, $S(nl)$, and $S(nw)$ are the maximal decomposition slices. $S(inword)$ is strongly dependent on $S(nw)$; $S(c)$ is strongly dependent on all the other decomposition slices. The decomposition slices on $S(nw), S(nc)$, and $S(nl)$ (Figs. 2-4) are weakly dependent and maximal when the output statements are removed. There

$$S(nc) \quad S(nl) \quad S(nw)$$
$$\uparrow$$
$$S(inword)$$
$$\searrow \quad \uparrow \quad \nearrow$$
$$S(c)$$

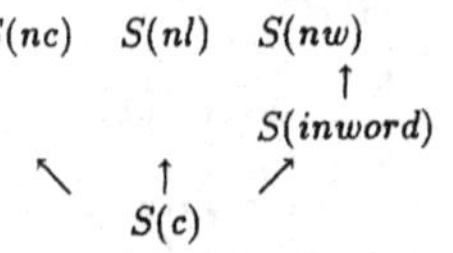

Fig. 8. Lattice of decomposition slices.

are no independent decomposition slices in the example. Recall that independent decomposition slices cannot share any control flow: the surrounding control statements would make them dependent.

We now begin to classify the individual statements in decomposition slices.

Definition 5: Let $S(v)$ and $S(w)$ be output-restricted decomposition slices of program P. Statements in $S(v) \cap S(w)$ are called *slice dependent statements.*

Slice independent statements are statements which are not slice dependent. We will refer to slice dependent statements and slice independent statements as *dependent statements* and *independent statements.* Dependent statements are those contained in decomposition slices which are interior points of the lattice; independent statements are those in a maximal decomposition slice which are not in the union of the decomposition slices which are properly contained in the maximal slice. The terms arise from the fact that two or more slices *depend* on the computation performed by dependent statements. Independent statements do not contribute to the computation of any other slice. When modifying a program, dependent statements cannot be changed or the effect will ripple out of the focus of interest.

For example, statement 12 of the slice on **nc** (Fig. 3) is a slice independent statement with respect to any other decomposition slice. Statements 13 and 14 of the slice on **nl** (Fig. 4) are also slice independent statements with respect to any other decomposition slice. The decomposition slice on **c** (Fig. 6) is strongly dependent on all the other slices; thus all its statements are slice dependent statements with respect to any other decomposition slice. Statements 6 and 15–20 of the slice on **nw** (Fig. 2) are slice independent statements with respect to decomposition slices $S(nc), S(nl)$, and $S(c)$: only statement 19 is slice independent when compared with $S(inword)$. Statements $6, 15–18$, and 20 of the decomposition slice on **inword** (Fig. 5) are slice independent statements with respect to decomposition slices $S(nc), S(nl)$, and $S(c)$; no statements are slice independent when compared with $S(nw)$.

We have a relationship between maximal slices and independent statements. This proposition permits us to apply the terms "(slice) independent statement" and "(slice) dependent statement" in a sensible way to a particular statement in a given maximal decomposition slice without reference to the binary relation between decomposition slices which is required in definition 5.

Proposition 1: Let 1) Varset(P) be the set of variables in program P; 2) $S(v)$ be an output-restricted decomposition slice of P; 3) Let $M = \{m \in \text{Varset}(P) | S(m) \text{ is maximal}\}$; 4) Let $U = M - \{v\}$. The statements in $S(v) - \bigcup_{u \in U} S(u)$ are independent.

Proof: Let $U = \{u_1, \ldots, u_m\}$. $S(v) - \bigcup_{u \in U} S(u) = S(v) - S(u_1) \ldots - S(u_m)$. ◊

There is a relationship between the maximal slices and program. (Recall that dead code has been excluded from our discussions.)

Proposition 2: Let $M = \{m \in \text{Varset}(P) | S(m)$ is maximal$\}$. Then $\bigcup_{m \in M} S(m) = P$.

Proof: Since $S(m) \in P$, $\bigcup_{m \in M} S(m) \subset P$. If $P \not\subseteq \bigcup_{m \in M} S(m)$, then the statements in P that are not in $\bigcup_{m \in M} S(m)$ are dead code. ◊

Maximal slices capture the computation performed by the program. Maximal slices and their respective independent statements also are related.

Proposition 3: An output-restricted decomposition slice is maximal if it has at least one independent statement.

Proof: Suppose $S(v)$ is maximal. By definition, $S(v)$ has at least one statement that no other slice has. This statement is an independent statement.

Now suppose that $S(v)$ has an independent statement s. Then s is not in any other slice, and the slice that contains s is maximal. ◊

Conversely, a slice with no independent statements is strongly dependent.

We also have another characterization of strongly dependent slices.

Proposition 4: Let 1) $\text{Varset}(P)$ be the set of variables in program P; 2) $S(v)$ be an output-restricted decomposition slice of P; 3) Let $D = \{w \in \text{Varset}(P) | S(v)$ is strongly dependent on $S(w)\}$; 4) Let $M = \{m \in \text{Varset}(P) | S(m)$ is maximal$\}$; 5) Let $U = M - \{v\}$. An output-restricted decomposition slice $S(v)$ is strongly dependent (on some $S(d)$) if $\bigcup_{u \in U} S(u) = P$.

Proof: Suppose $S(v)$ is strongly dependent. We need to show that D has a maximal slice. Partially order D by set inclusion. Let d be one of the maximal elements of D. The element d is maximal; if it is not, then it is properly contained in another slice d_1, which is in D and contains $S(v)$. Then $d \in M, d \neq v$, and $S(v)$ makes no contribution to the union.

Suppose $\bigcup_{u \in U} S(u) = P$. Since $U \subseteq M, S(v)$ makes no contribution to the union. By proposition 3, $S(v)$ is strongly dependent. ◊

We are now in a position to state the decomposition principles. Given a maximal output-restricted decomposition slice $S(v)$ of program P, delete the independent and output statements of S and P. We will denote this program $\sum(v)$ and call it the *complement of decomposition slice* $S(v)$ (with respect to P). Henceforth, when we speak of complements, it will always be in the context of decomposition slices. The decomposition slice is the subset of the program that computes a subset of the specification; the complement computes the rest of the specification.

Figs. 9–11 give the complements of the slices on **nw, nc,** and **nl** of Figs. 2–4. Using proposition 4, we obtain that the complement of both the slice on **inword** and the slice on **c** is the entire program.

This yields the approximation of a direct sum decomposition of a program which preserves the computational integrity

```
3     main()
4     {
5         int c, nl, nw, nc, inword ;
7         nl = 0;
9         nc = 0;
10        c = getchar();
11        while ( c != EOF ) {
12            nc = nc + 1;
13            if ( c == '\n')
14                nl = nl + 1;
21            c = getchar();
22        }
23        printf("%d \n",nl);
25        printf("%d \n",nc);
26    }
```

Fig. 9. $\sum(nw)$. Complement of slice on **nw**: computes line count and character count.

```
1     #define YES 1
2     #define NO 0
3     main()
4     {
5         int c, nl, nw, nc, inword ;
6         inword = NO ;
7         nl = 0;
8         nw = 0;
9         nc = 0;
10        c = getchar();
11        while ( c != EOF ) {
12            nc = nc + 1;
13            if ( c == '\n')
14                nl = nl + 1;
15            if ( c == ' ' || c == '\n' || c == '\t')
16                inword = NO;
17            else if (inword == NO) {
18                inword = YES ;
19                nw = nw + 1;
20            }
21            c = getchar();
22        }
23        printf("%d \n",nl);
24        printf("%d \n",nw);
26    }
```

Fig. 10. $\sum(nc)$. Complement of slice on **nc**: computes word count and line count.

of the constituent parts. This also indicates that the only useful decompositions are done with maximal decomposition slices. A complement $\sum$ of a maximal slice can be further decomposed, so the decomposition may be continued until all slices with independent statements (i.e., the maximal ones) are obtained.

In practice, a maintainer may find a strongly dependent slice as a starting point for a proposed change. Our method will permit such changes. Such a change may be viewed as properly *extending* the domain of the partial function that the program computes, while preserving the partial function on its original domain.

IV. APPLICATION TO MODIFICATION AND TESTING

Statement independence can be used to build a set of guidelines for software modification. To do this, we need to make one more set of definitions regarding variables which appear in independent and dependent statements. With these

```
1    #define YES 1
2    #define NO 0
3    main()
4    {
5        int c, nl, nw, nc, inword ;
6        inword = NO ;
8        nw = 0;
9        nc = 0;
10       c = getchar();
11       while ( c != EOF ) {
12           nc = nc + 1;
15           if ( c == ' ' || c == '\n' || c == '\t')
16               inword = NO;
17           else if (inword == NO) {
18               inword = YES ;
19               nw = nw + 1;
20           }
21           c = getchar();
22       }
24       printf("%d \n",nw);
25       printf("%d \n",nc);
26   }
```

Fig. 11. $\sum (nl)$. Complement of slice on **nl**: computes character count and word count.

```
1    main()
2    {
3        int a, b, c, d, e, f;
4        c = 4;
5        b = c;
6        a = b + c;
7        d = a + c;
8        f = d + b;
9        e = d + 8;
10       b = 30 + f;
11       a = b + c;
12   }
```

Fig. 12.   Dependent variable sample program.

```
1    main()
2    {
3        int a, b, c, d, e, f;
4        c = 4;
5        b = c;
6        a = b + c;
7        d = a + c;
8        f = d + b;
10       b = 30 + f;
11       a = b + c;
12   }
```

Fig. 13.   Slice on **a**.

```
1    main()
2    {
3        int a, b, c, d, e, f;
4        c = 4;
5        b = c;
6        a = b + c;
7        d = a + c;
9        e = d + 8;
12   }
```

Fig. 14.   Slice on **e**.

```
1    main()
2    {
3        int a, b, c, d, e, f;
4        c = 4;
5        b = c;
6        a = b + c;
7        d = a + c;
8        f = d + b;
10       b = 30 + f;
12   }
```

Fig. 15.   Slice on **b**.

definitions we give a set of rules which maintainers must obey in order to make modifications without ripple effects and unexpected linkages. When these rules are obeyed, we have an algorithm to merge the modified slice back into the complement and effect a change. The driving motivation for the following development is: "What restrictions must be placed on modifications in a decomposition slice so that the *complement* remains intact?"

Definition 6: A *variable* that is the target of a dependent assignment statement is called a *dependent variable*. Alternatively and equivalently, if *all* assignments to a variable are in independent statements, then the variable is called an *independent variable*.

An assignment statement can be an independent statement while its target is not an independent variable. In the program of Fig. 12, the two maximal decomposition slices are $S(a)$ and $S(e)$ (Figs. 13 and 14). Slice $S(b)$ (Fig. 15) is strongly dependent on $S(a)$, and $S(f)$ (Fig. 16) is strongly dependent on $S(b)$ and $S(a)$. $S(d)$ and $S(c)$ (not shown) are strongly dependent on both maximal slices. In $S(a)$, statements 8, 10, and 11 are independent, by the proposition. But *variables* **a** and **b** are targets of assignment statements 6 and 5, respectively. So, in the decomposition slice $S(a)$, only variable **f** is an independent variable.

A similar argument applies for independent control flow statements which reference dependent variables. A dependent variable in an independent statement corresponds to the situation where the *variable* in question is required for the compilation of the complement, but the *statement* in question does not contribute to complement. If a variable is referenced in a dependent statement, it is necessary to the complement and cannot be independent.

If a decomposing on a single variable yields a strongly dependent slice, we are able to construct a slice where the original slice *variable* is an independent variable.

Proposition 5: Let 1) Varset(P) be the set of variables in program P; 2) $S(v)$ be a strongly dependent output restricted decomposition slice of P; 3) Let $D = \{w \in \text{Varset}(P)|S(v)$ is strongly dependent on $S(w)\}$; 4) Let $M = \{m \in \text{Varset}(P)|S(m)$ is maximal$\}$; 5) Let $U = D \cap M$; 6) Let $T = \bigcup_{u \in U} S(u)$. The variable v is an independent variable in T.

In other words, when $S(v)$ is a strongly dependent slice and T is the union of all the maximal slices upon which $S(v)$ is strongly dependent, then v is an independent variable in T.

Proof: We show that the complement of T, $P-T$ has no references to v: if variable v is in the complement of T, then there is a maximal slice in the complement upon which

```
1  main()
2  {
3     int a, b, c, d, e, f;
4     c = 4;
5     b = c;
6     a = b + c;
7     d = a + c;
8     f = d + b;
12 }
```

Fig. 16. Slice on f.

$S(v)$ is strongly dependent. This contradicts the hypotheses, so the complement if T has no references to v and the variable v is independent in T. ◇

This can be interpreted as the variable version of Proposition 1, which refers to statements.

This has not addressed the problem that is presented when the decomposition slice on variable is maximal, but the variable itself remains dependent. This is the situation that occurred in the example at the beginning of the chapter; the slice on variable a (Fig. 13) is maximal, but the variable is dependent. The solution is straightforward: we construct the slice that is the union of all slices in which the variable is dependent.

Proposition 6: Let 1) Varset(P) be the set of variables in program P; 2) $S(v)$ be an output-restricted decomposition slice of P; 3) Let $E = \{w \in \text{Varset}(P) | v$ is a dependent variable in $S(w)\}$; 4) Let $T = \bigcup_{e \in E} S(e)$.

We have two cases: 1) $E = \varnothing$ (and thus T is empty also), in which case v is an independent variable; 2) $E \neq \varnothing$, so T is not empty and the variable v is an independent variable in T.

Proof:
Case 1: $E = \varnothing$
$S(v)$ contains all references to v. In particular, $S(v)$ contains all assignments to v. So v is an independent variable in $S(v)$.
End Case 1

Case 2: $E \neq \varnothing$
T contains references to v. In particular, T contains all assignments to v. So v is an independent variable in T. *End Case 2* ◇

This proposition is about *variables*.

A. Modifying Decomposition Slices

We are now in a position to answer the question posed at the beginning of this section. We present the restrictions as a collection of rules with justifications.

Modifications take three forms: additions, deletions, and changes. A change may be viewed as a deletion followed by an addition. We will use this second approach and determine only those statements in a decomposition slice that can be deleted, and the forms of statements that can be added. Again, we must rely on the fact that the union of decomposition slices is a slice, since the complementary criteria will usually involve more than one maximal variable. We also assume that the maintainer has kept the modified program compilable and has obtained the decomposition slice of the portion of the software that needs to be changed. (Locating the code may be a highly

nontrivial activity; for the sake of the current discussion, we assume its completion.)

Since independent statements do not affect data flow or control flow in the complement, we have:

Rule 1: Independent statements may be deleted from a decomposition slice.

Reason: Independent statements do not affect the computations of the complement. Deleting an independent statement from a slice will have no impact on the complement. ◇

This result applies to control flow statements and assignment statements. The statement may be deleted, even if it is an assignment statement which targets a dependent variable or a control statement which references a dependent variable. The point to keep in mind is that if the statement is independent, it does *not* affect the complement. If an independent statement is deleted, there will certainly be an effect in the slice. But the purpose of this methodology is to keep the complement intact.

There are a number of situations to consider when statements are to be added. We progress from simple to complex. Also note that for additions, new variables may be introduced *as long as the variable name does not clash with any name in the complement.* In this instance the new variable is independent in the decomposition slice. In the following, *independent variable* means an independent variable or a new variable.

Rule 2: Assignment statements that target independent variables may be added anywhere in a decomposition slice.

Reason: Independent variables are unknown to the complement. Thus changes to them cannot affect the computations of the complement. ◇

This type of change is permissible even if the changed value flows into a dependent variable. In Fig. 13, changes are permitted to the assignment statement at line 8, which targets **f**. A change here would propagate into the values of dependent variables **a** and **b** at lines 10 and 11. The maintainer would then be responsible for the changes which would occur to these variables. If lines 10 and 11 were dependent (i.e., contained in another decomposition slice), line 8 would also be contained in this slice and variable **f** would be dependent.

Adding control flow statements requires a little more care. This is required because control statements have two parts: the logical expression, which determines the flow of control, and the *actions* taken for each value of the expression. (We assume no side effects in the evaluation of logical expressions.) We discuss only the addition of **if-then-else** and **while** statements, since all other language constructs can be realized by them [5].

Rule 3: Logical expressions (and output statements) may be added anywhere in a decomposition slice.

Reason: We can inspect the state of the computation anywhere. Evaluation of logical expressions (or the inclusion of an output statement) will not even affect the computation of the slice. Thus the complement remains intact. ◇

We must guarantee that the statements which are controlled by newly added control flow do not interfere with the complement.

Rule 4: New control statements that surround (i.e., control) any dependent statement will cause the complement to change.

Reason: Suppose that newly added code controls a dependent statement.

Let C be the criteria which yield the complement. When using this criteria on the modified program, the newly added control code will be included in this complementary slice. This is due to the fact that the dependent statements are in both the slice and the complement. Thus any control statements which control dependent statements will also be in the slice and the complement. ◊

By making such a change we have violated the principle that the complement remain fixed. Thus new control statements may not surround any dependent statement.

This short list is necessary and sufficient to keep the slice complement intact. This also has an impact on testing the change that will be discussed later.

Changes may be required to computations involving a dependent variable v in the extracted slice. the maintainer can choose one of the following two approaches:

1) Use the techniques of the previous section to extend the slice so that v is independent in the slice.
2) Add a new local variable (to the slice), copy the value to the new variable, and manipulate the new name only. Of course, the new name must not clash with any name in the complement. This technique may also be used if the slice has no independent statements; i.e., it is strongly dependent.

B. Merging the Modifications into the Complement

Merging the modified slice back into the complement is straightforward. A key to understanding the merge operation comes from the observation that through the technique, the maintainer is editing the *entire program*. The method gives a view of the program with the unneeded statements deleted and with the dependent statements restricted from modification. The slice gives a smaller piece of code for the maintainer to focus on, while the rules of the previous subsection provide the means by which the deleted and restricted parts cannot be changed accidentally.

We now present the merge algorithm.

1) Order the statements in the original program. (In the following examples we have one statement per line, so that the ordering is merely the line numbering.) A program slice and its complement can now be identified with the subsequence of statement numbers from the original program. We call the sequence numbering from the slice the *slice sequence,* and the numbering of the complement, the *complement sequence.* We now view the editing process as the addition and deletion of the associated sequence numbers.
2) For deleted statements, delete the sequence number from the slice sequence. Observe that since only independent statements are deleted, this number is not in the complement sequence.
3) For statements inserted into the slice, a new sequence number needs to be generated. Let P be the sequence number of the statement preceding the statement to be inserted. Let M be the least value in the slice sequence

greater than P. Let $F = \min(\text{int}(P + 1), M)$. Insert the new statement at sequence number $(F + P)/2$. (Although this works in principle, in practice, more care needs to be taken in the generation of the insertion sequence numbers to avoid floating point errors after 10 inserts.)
4) The merged program is obtained by merging the modified slice sequence values (i.e., statements) into the complement sequence.

Thus the unchanged dependent statements are used to guide the reconstruction of the modified program. The placement of the changed statements within a given control flow is arbitrary. Again, this becomes clearer when the editing process is viewed as a modification to the entire program. The following example will help clarify this.

C. Testing the Change

Since the maintainer must restrict all changes to independent or newly created variables, testing is reduced to testing the modified slice. Thus the need for regression testing in the complement is eliminated. There are two alternative approaches to verifying that only the change needs testing. The first is to slice on the original criteria, plus any new variables, minus any eliminated variables, and compare its complement with the complement of the original: they should match exactly. The second approach is to preserve the criteria which produced the original complement. Slicing out on this must produce the modified slice exactly.

An axiomatic consideration illumines this idea. The slice and its complement perform a subset of the computation; where the computations meet are the dependencies. Modifying the code in the independent part of the slice leaves the independent part of the complement as an invariant of the slice (and vice versa).

If the required change is "merely" a module replacement, the preceding techniques are still applicable. The slice will provide a harness for the replaced module. A complete independent program supporting the module is obtained. One of the principal benefits of slicing is highlighted in this context: any side effects of the module to be replaced will also be in the slice. Thus the full impact of change is brought to the attention of the modifier.

As an example, we make some changes to $S(nw)$, the slice on **nw**, the word counter of Fig. 2. The changed slice is shown in Fig. 17. The original program determined a word to be any string of "nonwhite" symbols terminated by a "white" symbol (space, tab, or newline). The modification changes this to the requirement to be alphabetical characters terminated by white space. (The example is illustrating a change, not advocating it.) Note the changes. We have deleted the independent "variables" YES and NO; added a new, totally independent variable **ch**; and revamped the independent statements. The addition of the C macros **isspace** and **isalpha** is safe, since the results are only referenced. We test this program independently of the complement. Fig. 18 shows the reconstructed, modified program. Taking the decomposition slice on **nw** generates the program of Fig. 17. Its complement is already given in Fig. 9.

```
3     main()
4     {
*           int ch;
5           int c, nw ;
*           ch = 0;
8           nw = 0;
10          c = getchar();
11          while ( c != EOF ) {
*                 if (isspace(c) && isalpha(ch))
*                       nw = nw + 1;
*                 ch = c ;
21                c = getchar();
22          }
24          printf("%d \n",nw);
26    }
```

Fig. 17. Modified slice on **nw**, the word counter.

```
3     main()
4     {
*           int ch;
5           int c, nl, nw, nc ;
*           ch = 0;
7           nl = 0;
8           nw = 0;
9           nc = 0;
10          c = getchar();
11          while ( c != EOF ) {
*                 if (isspace(c) && isalpha(ch))
*                       nw = nw + 1;
*                 ch = c ;
12                nc = nc + 1;
13                if ( c == '\n')
14                      nl = nl + 1;
21                c = getchar();
22          }
23          printf("%d \n",nl);
24          printf("%d \n",nw);
25          printf("%d \n",nc);
26    }
```

Fig. 18. Modified program.

the starred (∗) statements indicate where the new statements would be placed using the line-number-generation technique above.

V. A New Software Maintenance Process Model

The usual Software Maintenance Process Model is depicted in Fig. 19. A request for change arrives. It may be adaptive, perfective, corrective, or preventive. In making the change, we wish to minimize defects, effort, and cost, while maximizing customer satisfaction [12]. The software is changed, subject to pending priorities. The change is composed of two parts: Understanding the code, which may require documentation, code reading, and execution. Then the program is modified. The maintainer must first design the change (which may be subject to peer review), then alter the code itself, while trying to minimize side effects. The change is then validated. The altered code itself is verified to assure conformance with the specification. Then the new code is integrated with the existing system to insure conformance with the system specifications. This task involves regression testing.

The new model is depicted in Fig. 20. The software is changed, subject to pending priorities. The change is com-

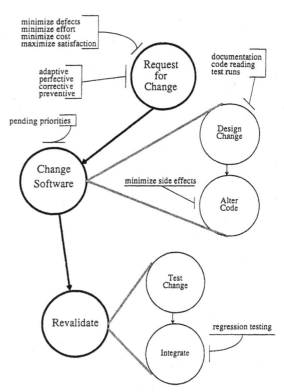

Fig. 19. A software maintenance process model.

posed of two parts: Understanding the code will now require documentation, code reading, execution, and the use of decomposition slices. The decomposition slices may be read and executed (a decided advantage of having executable program slices). The code is then modified, subject to the strictures outlined. Using those guidelines, no side effects or unintended linkages can be induced in the code, even by accident. This lifts a substantial burden from the maintainer.

The change is tested in the decomposition slice. Since the change cannot ripple out into other modules, regression testing is unnecessary. The maintainer need only verify that the change is correct. After applying the merge algorithm, the change (of the code) is complete.

VI. Future Directions

The underlying method and the tool based on it [9] need to be empirically evaluated. This is underway using the Goal-Question-Metric paradigm of Basili et al. [2]. Naturally, we are also addressing questions of scale, to determine if existing software systems decompose sufficiently via these techniques, in order to effect a technology transfer. We are also evaluating decomposition slices as candidates for components in a reuse library.

Although they seem to do well in practice, the slicing algorithms have relatively bad worst-case running times of $O(n\ e\ \log(e))$, where n is the number of variables and e is the number of edges in the flowgraph. To obtain all the slices, this running time becomes $O(n^2 e\ \log(e))$. These worst-case times would seem to make an interactive slicer

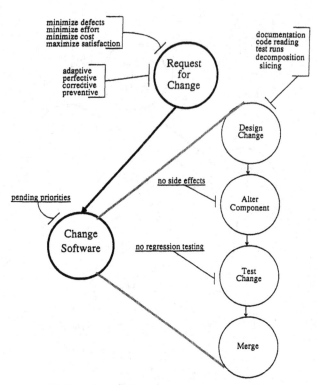

Fig. 20. A new software maintenance process model.

for large (i.e., real) programs impractical. This difficulty can be assuaged by making the data-flow analysis one component of the deliverable products which are handed off from the development team to the maintenance team. An interactive tool could then be built using these products. Then as changes are made by the maintainers, the data flow data can be updated, using the incremental techniques of Keables [17].

Interprocedural slices can be attacked using the techniques in Weiser [36] and Barth [1]. The interprocedural slicing algorithms of Horwitz *et al.* [16] cannot be used, since they require that the slice be taken at a point where the slice variable id **def**ed or **ref**ed; we require that all slices be taken at the last statement of the program. For separate compilation, a worst-case assumption must be made about the external variables if the source is not available. If the source is available, one proceeds as with procedures.

Berzins [4] has attacked the problem of software merges for *extensions* of programs. To quote him:

"An extension extends the domain of the partial function without altering any of the initially defined values, while a modification redefines values that were defined initially."

We have addressed the modification problem by first *restricting* the domain of the partial function to the slice complement, modifying the function on the values defined by the independent variables in the slice, then merging these two disjoint domains.

Horwitz *et al.* [15] have addressed the modification problem. They start with a *base* program and two modifications it, *A* and *B*:

"Whenever the changes made to *base* to create *A* and *B* do not 'interfere' (in a sense defined in the paper), the algorithm produces a program *M* that integrates *A* and *B*. The algorithm is predicated on the assumption that differences in the *behavior* of the variant programs from that of *base*, rather than the differences in *text*, are significant and must be preserved in *M*."

Horwitz *et al.* do not restrict the changes that can be made to *base*; thus their algorithm produces an approximation to the undecidable problem of determining whether or not the behaviors interfere. We have side-stepped this unsolvable problem by constraining the modifications that are made. Our technique is more akin to the limits placed on software maintainers. Changes must be done in a context: independence and dependence provides the context. It is interesting to note, however, that their work uses program slicing to determine potential interferences in the merge.

They do note that program *variants*, as they name them, are easily embedded in the change control system, such as RCS [31]. Moreover, the direct sum nature of the components can be exploited to build related families of software. That is, components can be "summed" as long as their dependent code sections match exactly, and there is no intersection of the independent domains. We also follow this approach for component construction.

Weiser [34] discusses some slice-based metrics. *Overlap* is a measure of how many statements in a slice are found only in that slice, measured as a mean ratio of nonunique-to-unique statements in each slice. *Parallelism* is the number of slices that has few statements in common, computed as the number of slices that have pairwise overlap below a certain threshold. *Tightness* is the number of statements in every slice, expressed as a ratio over program length. Programs with high overlap and parallelism but with low tightness would decompose nicely: the lattice would not get too deep or too tangled.

We have shown how a data flow technique, program slicing, can be used to form a decomposition for software systems. The decomposition yields a method for maintainers to use. The maintainer is able to modify existing code cleanly, in the sense that the changes can be assured to be completely contained in the modules under consideration and that no unseen linkages with the modified code is infecting other modules.

REFERENCES

[1] J. M. Barth, "A practical interprocedural dataflow analysis algorithm," *Comm. Assoc. Computing Machinery*, vol. 21, no. 9, pp. 724–726, Sept. 1978.
[2] V. Basili, R. Selby, and D. Hutchens, "Experimentation in software engineering," *IEEE Trans. Software Eng.*, vol. 12, pp. 352–357, July 1984.
[3] J.-F. Bergeretti and B. Carré, "Information-flow and data-flow analysis of **while**-programs," *ACM Trans. Programming Languages and Systems*, vol. 7, no. 1, pp. 37–61, Jan. 1985.
[4] V. Berzins, "On merging software extensions," *Acta Informatica*, vol. 23, pp. 607–619, 1985.
[5] C. Bohm and G. Jacopini, "Flow diagrams and languages with only two formation rules," *CACM*, vol. 9, no. 5, pp. 366–371, May 1966.
[6] J.-D. Choi, B. Miller, and P. Netzer, "Techniques for debugging parallel programs with flowback analysis," Univ. Wisconsin–Madison, Tech. Rep. 786, Aug. 1988.
[7] J. Ferrante, K. Ottenstein, and J. Warren, "The program dependence graph and its use in optimization," *ACM Trans. Programming Languages*

328

and Systems, vol. 9, no. 3, pp. 319–349, July 1987.

[8] K. B. Gallagher, "Using program slicing in software maintenance," Ph.D. thesis, Univ. Maryland, Baltimore, Dec. 1989.

[9] K. B. Gallagher, "Surgeon's assistant limits side effects," IEEE Software, vol. 7, p. 64, May 1990.

[10] K. B. Gallagher and J. R. Lyle, "Using program decomposition to guide modifications," in Proc. Conf. Software Maintenance—1988, Oct. 1988, pp. 265–268.

[11] K. B. Gallagher and J. R. Lyle, "A program decomposition scheme with applications to software modification and testing," in Proc. 22nd Int. Conf. System Sciences (Hawaii), Jan. 1989, vol. II, pp. 479–485.

[12] R. Grady, "Measuring and managing software maintenance," IEEE Software, vol. 4, Sept. 1987.

[13] P. Hausler, "Denotational program slicing," in Proc. 22nd Hawaii Int. Conf. System Sciences, Jan. 1989, vol. II (Software Track), pp. 486–494.

[14] S. Horwitz, J. Prins, and T. Reps, "Integrating non-interfering versions of programs," in Proc. SIGPLAN'88 Symp. Principles of Programming Languages, Jan. 1988.

[15] S. Horwitz, J. Prins, and T. Reps, "Integrating non-interfering versions of programs," ACM Trans. Programming Languages and Systems, vol. 11, no. 3, pp. 345–387, July 1989.

[16] S. Horwitz, T. Reps, and D. Binkley, "Interprocedural slicing using dependence graphs," ACM Trans. Programming Languages and Systems, vol. 12, no. 1, pp. 35–46, Jan. 1990.

[17] J. Keables, K. Robertson, and A. von Mayrhauser, "Data flow analysis and its application to software maintenance," in Proc. Conf. Software Maintenance—1988, Oct. 1988, pp. 335–347.

[18] K. Kennedy, "A survey of data flow analysis techniques," in Program Flow Analysis: Theory and Applications, S. S. Muchnick and N. D. Jones, Eds. Englewood Cliffs, NJ: Prentice-Hall, 1981.

[19] B. Kernighan and D. Ritchie, The C Programming Language. Englewood Cliffs, NJ: Prentice-Hall, 1978.

[20] B. Korel and J. Laski, "Dynamic program slicing," Inform. Process. Lett., vol. 29, no. 3, pp. 155–163, Oct. 1988.

[21] B. Korel and J. Laski, "STAD—a system for testing and debugging: User perspective," in Proc. 2nd Workshop on Software Testing, Verification and Analysis (Banff, Alberta, Can.), July 1988, pp. 13–20.

[22] J. Laski, "Data flow testing in STAD" Systems and Software, to be published.

[23] J. R. Lyle, "Evaluating variations of program slicing for debugging," Ph.D. thesis, Univ. of Maryland, College Park, Dec. 1984.

[24] J. R. Lyle and M. D. Weiser, "Experiments in slicing-based debugging aids," in Empirical Studies of Programmers, E. Soloway and S. Iyengar, Eds. Norwood, NJ: Ablex, 1986.

[25] J. R. Lyle and M. D. Weiser, "Automatic program bug location by program slicing," in Proc. 2nd Int. Conf. Computers and Applications (Peking, China), June 1987, pp. 877–882.

[26] L. Ott and J. Thuss, "The relationship between slices and module cohesion," in Proc. 11th Int. Conf. Software Eng., May 1989, pp. 198–204.

[27] K. Ottenstein and L. Ottenstein, "The program dependence graph in software development environments," ACM SIGPLAN Notices, vol. 19, no. 5, pp. 177–184, May 1984; see also, Proc. ACM SIG-SOFT/SIGPLAN Software Eng. Symp. Practical Software Development Environments.

[28] T. Reps and S. Horwitz, "Semantics-based program integration," in Proc. 2nd European Symp. Programming (ESOP '88) (Nancy, France), Mar. 1988, pp. 133–145.

[29] T. Reps and W. Yang, "The semantics of program slicing," Univ. Wisconsin–Madison, Tech. Rep. 777, June 1988.

[30] N. Schneidewind, "The state of software maintenance," IEEE Trans. Software Eng., vol. SE-13, pp. 303–310, Mar. 1987.

[31] W. Tichy, "RCS: A system for version control," Software—Practice and Experience, vol. 15, no. 7, pp. 637–654, July 1985.

[32] G. Weinberg, "Kill that code!," Infosystems, pp. 48–49, Aug. 1983.

[33] M. Weiser, "Program slicing: Formal, psychological and practical investigations of an automatic program abstraction method," Ph.D. thesis, Univ. Michigan, Ann Arbor, 1979.

[34] M. Weiser, "Program slicing," in Proc. 5th Int. Conf. Software Eng., May 1981, pp. 439–449.

[35] M. Weiser, "Programmers use slicing when debugging," CACM, vol. 25, no. 7, pp. 446–452, July 1982.

[36] M. Weiser, "Program slicing," IEEE Trans. Software Eng., vol. SE-10, pp. 352–357, July 1984.

Efficient Algorithms for the Instantiated Transitive Closure Queries

Ghassan Z. Qadah, *Member, IEEE*, Lawrence J. Henschen, and Jung J. Kim

Abstract—This paper studies and compares the performance of several algorithms suitable for processing an important class of recursive queries, the so-called *instantiated* transitive closure (TC) queries. These algorithms are the two well known algorithms *wavefront* and *δ-wavefront* and a newly proposed generic algorithm called *super-TC*. During the evaluation of a TC query, the first two algorithms may read a given disk page more than once, whereas super-TC reads the disk page at most once. This paper also presents a comprehensive performance evaluation of these three algorithms using rigorous analytical and simulation models. Such a study reveals that the relative performance of the algorithms is a strong function of the parameters which characterize the processed TC query and the relation referenced by that query. Furthermore, it points out the superiority of one of the *super-TC* variants over all of the other presented algorithms.

Index Terms— Algorithms, performance evaluation, recursive rules, relational database, transitive closure queries.

I. INTRODUCTION

THE development of efficient algorithms to process the transitive closure (TC) type of logic rules and queries has attracted recently a large amount of research efforts [1], [4], [6], [11], [12], [13], [18]. This is due to a number of reasons. Firstly, the importance of recursion in general, in improving the expressive power and intelligence of database systems. Secondly, the fact that in most application domains the transitive closure rules and queries are the most frequently found type of recursion. Thirdly, the fact that many complex recursive query types can be translated into expressions which involve transitive closure queries [2]. Developing efficient algorithms for processing the transitive closure queries is, therefore, an important step towards the development of future intelligent database systems.

A rule is *linearly recursive* if the rule's head predicate appears only once in its body.[1] A linear recursive rule is a *transitive closure (TC) rule* if its body contains only a one-sided join with the recursive predicate. For example, the following rule is a TC rule:

$$R(X,Y) :- A(X,Z), R(Z,Y) \qquad (1)$$

where $A(X,Z)$ is an extensional (base) predicate. Within the context of deductive databases [10], $A(X,Z)$ is defined, as shown in Fig. 1(a), by a two-attribute normalized database relation with very many tuples of data (another common view for the base relation is the one shown in Fig. 1(b), where the base relation is represented as a directed (possibly cyclic) graph. The nodes in

Manuscript received January 24, 1990; revised November 1, 1990. Recommended by F. B. Bastani. This work was supported by the National Science Foundation under Grant DCR-860-8311. The contribution of Jung J. Kim is the development of the computer programs used to simulate the different algorithms presented in this paper.

The authors are with the Department of Electrical Engineering and Computer Science, Northwestern University, Evanston, IL 60208.

IEEE Log Number 9041667.

[1] This paper uses PROLOG notation to express logic rules and queries.

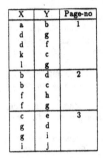 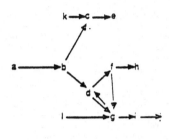

X	Y	Page-no
a	b	1
d	g	
d	f	
k	c	
l	g	
b	d	2
b	c	
f	h	
f	g	
c	e	3
g	d	
g	i	
i	j	

Fig. 1. The binary relation A. (a) In table form. (b) In graph form.

such a graph are the set of distinct values in the two columns of the base relations. For every tuple (x,y) of the base relation, there exists, in the corresponding digraph, a directed edge from node x to node y.

To generate solutions from the recursive rule (1), another nonrecursive rule, the **exit** rule, which defines the predicate $R(X,Y)$ must exist. For example the following rule is an exit rule for R:

$$R(X,Y) :- A(X,Y). \qquad (2)$$

A TC query is a headless rule whose predicate is defined by a transitive closure rule and an associated exit rule. For example,

$$:-R(X,Y) \qquad (3)$$

is a TC query. In general, a two-place unit query, such as (3), may have different forms depending on whether the query variables are instantiated or not. When X and Y are both instantiated $(:-R(c_1,c_2)$, where both c_1 and c_2 are constants), the query is referred to as *fully instantiated*. When neither X nor Y is instantiated $(:-R(X,Y))$, the query is *uninstantiated*, and when one of the variables X or Y (but not both) is instantiated $(:-R(c,Y)$ or $:- R(X,c))$, the query is *(partially) instantiated*. A generalization of the last query form is the one in which one of the query's variables is instantiated to a set of constants. Different solution sets are generated as a result of processing the different forms of a query. The fully instantiated query generates only one solution, *true* or *false*. The uninstantiated query generates the set of tuples $\{(x_i,y_j)|\ x_i$ and y_j are constants and $R(x_i,y_i)$ is *"true"*$\}$. Depending on the nature of the solution set generated by a partially instantiated query, such a query can be one of two types, $type_1$ and $type_2$. The $type_1$ query generates values for only the uninstantiated variable. The $type_2$ query, on the other hand, generates the set of tuples with values for both the instantiated and the uninstantiated variables of the query. For example, let $\{c_1,c_2\cdots,c_n\}$ be the set of constants to which the variable X, in $:-R(X,Y)$, is instantiated, then the sets $\{y_j|R(c_i,y_j)$ is true and $i \in \{1,2\cdots,n\}\}$, and $\{(c_i,y_j)|R(c_i,y_j)$ is true and $i \in$

$\{1, 2, \cdots, n\}\}$ are generated by $type_1$ $(: -R^1(\{c_1, c_2 \cdots, c_n\}, Y)$ and $type_2$ $(: -R^2(\{c_1, c_2 \cdots, c_n\}, Y)$ *partially instantiated* queries, respectively.

The generation of solutions for a general query, such as (3), can be done using a compilation-based evaluation scheme [7], [17]. Using such a scheme, the set of rules which define the processed query is transformed into an equivalent set of relational algebra expressions, each containing extensional relations only. The union of the solutions generated by evaluating these expressions on the extensional database constitutes the set of solutions which satisfy the given query. Applying the compilation scheme to query (3) and the set of rules (1) and (2) generates the following infinite set of expressions:

$$A$$
$$AoA$$
$$AoAoA$$
$$.$$
$$.$$
$$.$$
$$AoAoA \cdots oA \qquad (4)$$

The operator o in (4) is the composition operator defined as follows:

$$AoA = \pi_{1,4}\{A \bowtie_{1.2=2.1} A\} \qquad (5)$$

where π and $\bowtie$ are the relational algebra operators projection and join, respectively. "1.2" and "2.1" in (5) refer to the second and first attributes of the base relation A, respectively. Viewing the binary relation A as a directed graph, as shown in Fig. 1(b), then the union of the set of expressions, (4) forms the transitive closure of such a graph, A^+ (for the definition of A^+ refer to [8]). The evaluation of A^+ generates the set of solutions which satisfies $: -R(X, Y)$. Using the same compilation technique, one can derive similar formulas for the other forms of the transitive closure query. For example, the compilation of $: -R^1(c, Y)$ and $: -R^2(c, Y)$ generates the expressions $[\pi_2(\sigma_{X=c}(A^+))]$ and $[\sigma_{X=c}(A^+)]$, respectively, where σ is the relational algebra operator selection. $: -R(c_1, c_2)$, on the other hand, generates the expression $[\sigma_{X=c_1 \& Y=c_2}(A^+)]$("$: -R(c_1, c_2)$" is true if a nonempty relation results from the evaluation of the latter expression).

The scheme presented above suggests a general approach to generate solutions for a TC query, that is, computing the full transitive closure of the referenced relation A, and storing the result in the database. When a particular query form is received, the proper selection and projection operators (if needed) are applied to the stored relation to generate the required solutions. Because of its generality, simplicity and elegance, such an approach has been seriously considered and many efficient algorithms to compute the full transitive closure of a database relation have been developed and studied [1], [13], [18]. However, for application domains dominated by retrieval and update queries of the instantiated (partial or full) type, such a scheme is inefficient for a number of reasons. First, the storage cost for the transitive closure is high. Second, the time required to compute the full transitive closure of a relation is also high even with the efficient algorithms developed specifically for such a purpose [1]. Third, propagating the updates made to relation A to its transitive closure is time-consuming and may require the recomputation of the relation's transitive closure. Fourth, the processing of the instantiated queries can be mapped into graph problems that use algorithms tailored to

the specific query form and require much less processing time and space than that required by the full computation of the transitive closure. For example, by pushing the selection and projection operators inside the transitive closure computation in the compiled formula of $: -R^1(c, Y)$, i.e., $[\pi_2(\sigma_{X=c}(A^+))]$, the computation is transformed into one which finds all of the nodes in the digraph of relation A which can be reached from node c. An algorithm to perform the reachability problem is much faster and requires less storage than the one performing the full transitive closure operation. Furthermore, the updates made to relation A is no longer problematic since this algorithm always uses the up-to-date version of A (and not its transitive closure) to find solutions.

The argument presented above suggests that designing algorithms customized to the individual query forms is the right path to follow. In [11], an efficient algorithm to evaluate the second type of the partially instantiated TC queries on general (cyclic and acyclic) graphs have been presented. In [5], [6], two algorithms, *wavefront* and *δ-wavefront*, suitable for processing the first type of the partially instantiated TC queries have been proposed. This paper revisits these two algorithms and presents a comprehensive study for their performance using a newly developed set of analytical models. Such a study reveals, among other findings, that *δ-wavefront* is superior to *wavefront* with variable speed advantages reaching orders of magnitude depending on the characteristics of the processed query and the base relation referenced by that query. Furthermore, this paper presents a newly developed generic algorithm, the *super-TC*, together with a number of its variants suitable also for processing the first type of the partially instantiated TC queries. An important characteristic of this algorithm (and every one of its variants) is its linear page-IO complexity with respect to the number of pages storing the base relation (i.e., this algorithms may read a given disk page, storing tuples from the base relation, into main-memory *at most once*). This is in contrast to the nonlinear page IO behavior of *wavefront* and *δ-wavefront* algorithms (i.e., these algorithms may read a given disk page into main-memory more than once). Using rigorous simulation models, this paper compares the performance of the different *super-TC* variants and identifies the best-performing one over a wide range of the performance domain. It then compares the winning variant to the *δ-wavefront* algorithm and shows the superiority of the best-performing *super-TC* variant over the *δ-wavefront* algorithm with speed advantages reaching an order of magnitude.

Section II introduces and defines the basic parameters and assumptions necessary to model the different algorithms presented in this paper. Section III presents and compares the performance of *wavefront* and *δ-wavefront*. Section IV presents the generic *super-TC* algorithm and its different variants. Moreover in this section, the performance of these variants are evaluated and compared and the best performing one is identified. A performance comparison between the best performing *super-TC* variant and *δ-wavefront* is presented in Section V. Finally, Section VI presents some concluding remarks.

II. Modeling Framework

Several analytical and simulation models are developed to study and compare the performance of the different algorithms presented in this paper. In constructing these models, three sets of basic (input) parameters have been used, namely, *relation-related*, *query-related*, and *hardware-related*. These sets together

TABLE I
THE BASIC PARAMETERS CHARACTERIZING THE PERFORMANCE MODELS

Parameters	Definition	Typical_values
Nt	The number of tuples in the base relation A	50 000
W_{tuple}	The length of a tuple in A	32 bytes
$W_{attribute}$	The length of an attribute value	16 bytes
Nd	The size of the domain underlying A's X and Y attributes	variable
Nr	The tuple–domain ratio ($= Nt/Nd$) also called *OutDegree*	0.1–10
Qr	The query constant ratio = (Number of query constants/Number of tuples in relation A)	0.001–0.05
MRA	The ratio (Number of pages allocated in main-memory for relation A/Number of pages in relation A)	variable
MRR	The ratio (Number of pages allocated in main-memory for the closure(dead_closure)/Number of pages in relation A)	variable
p_{size}	Page size in bytes	1024 bytes
$T_{compare}$	Time to compare two attribute values in main-memory	3 μs
T_{move}	Time to move a tuple in main-memory	20 μs
T_{hash}	Time to compute a hash function	9 μs
T_{io}	Time to perform a random I/O	15 ms

with their meanings and the values which they assume throughout our performance studies are presented in Table I. *relation-related* parameters (the top section of Table I) characterize the base relation A (cardinality, tuple length, attribute length, etc.), whereas *hardware-related* parameters (the bottom section of Table I) characterize the hardware resources available for processing the algorithms (main-memory size, page size, time to perform a random I/O, etc.).

The *query-related* set of parameters (the middle section of Table I) characterizes the processed TC query and contains only one parameter Qr. This parameter denotes the ratio "number of constants to which the X argument of the query is instantiated/the cardinality of the base relation." Qr has a significant effect on the studied algorithms because, given a base relation, an algorithm may need to access only a small portion of the relation when given a few initial constants while it may have to process close to the entire relation when given a large set of constants.

To facilitate the development of the different performance models presented in this paper, several fundamental assumptions have been made, namely:

1) The base relation A is binary with attributes X and Y. Its cardinality, as shown in Table I, is Nt. The values in the attributes X and Y are randomly drawn *with replacement* from the same underlying domain. This domain is assumed to be finite with a size Nd and the probability to draw its values is uniform. By fixing the value of Nt and changing the value of $Nt/Nd(= Nr)$, one can generate directed (possibly cyclic) graphs with fixed number of arcs (i.e., base relations of the same cardinality) and variable out-degree nodes.

2) Relation A is stored in pages using a hash-based scheme. A hash function uses the X_attribute value of a given tuple from A to compute the address of the page in which that tuple is stored. The pages storing relation A are assumed to be distributed between the system's main-memory and secondary storage disk.

3) The generated solutions for a processed query is stored using a scheme similar to the one used by the base relation.

4) The different query constants ($Qr * Nt$ of them) are randomly drawn, *without replacement* and using a uniform distribution, from the domain underlying the two attributes of the base relation.

```
Procedure wavefront (input: query_constants, A(base relation); output: closure)
begin
/*
    wave and closure are unary relations with an X_attribute.
    A is a binary relation with X_attribute and Y_attribute.
*/
    wave = {query_constants};
    closure = Φ;
    While (closure does change) Do
        wave = π_Y {wave(X) ⋈_{1.1=2.1} A(X,Y)};    ← ***
        closure = wave ∪ closure;
    endwhile
end.
```

Fig. 2. The *wavefront* algorithm.

III. THE *wavefront* AND δ-*wavefront* ALGORITHMS AND THE EVALUATION OF THEIR PERFORMANCE

This section presents the two algorithms *wavefront* and δ-*wavefront* and a comprehensive study of their performance.

A. The wavefront Algorithm

wavefront is a breadth-first search algorithm. It starts out from some initial nodes in the base graph (the ones corresponding to the constants in the processed query) and iterates to find all of the nodes reachable from these initial ones (the values associated with these nodes constitute the solutions to the processed query). The algorithm, as shown in Fig. 2, employs two temporary relations, *wave* and *closure*. While, the former relation stores those nodes found during one iteration, the latter one accumulates the nodes found during the different iterations of the algorithm. At the beginning of an iteration, say the kth one, *wave*, which contains the set of nodes collected during the $(k - 1)$th iteration, is (semi-)joined with A (refer to the statement in Fig. 2 flagged by "***"). The result relation is projected on its second attribute to yield the set of nodes that are 1 arc away from those nodes in *wave* (or, in other words, k arcs away from the initial nodes). The newly generated nodes which form the new *wave* are "unioned" with *closure* to yield a new *closure*. The iteration process continues until *closure* does not change from one iteration to another. At that point, the nodes in *closure* are the solutions to the processed query.

Fig. 3 presents the processing of relation A of Fig. 1 using *wavefront* to generate all of the solutions to the query " :-$R^1(\{k, l\}, Y)$". The generation of these solutions requires

iteration	old-wave	new-wave	closure	pages_referenced
1	k, l	c, g	c, g	1
2	c, g	e, i, d	c, g, e, i, d	3
3	e, i, d	j, f, g	c, g, e, i, d, j, f	3, 1
4	j, f, g	h, g, i, d	c, g, e, i, d, j, f, h	2, 3
5	h, g, i, d	d, i, j, f, g	c, g, e, i, d, j, f, h	3, 1

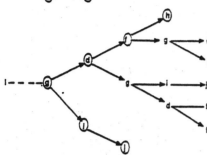

Fig. 3.   The processing of $R^1(\{k, l\}, Y)$? using *wavefront*.

```
Procedure δ-wavefront (input: query_constants, A(base relation); output: closure)
begin
/*
     wave and closure are unary relations with an X_attribute.
     A is a binary relation with an X_attribute and a Y_attribute.
*/
     wave = {query_constants};
     closure = Φ;
     While (wave ≠ Φ) Do
        wave = π_Y {wave(X) ⋈_{1.1=2.1} A(X,Y)};    ← + + +
        wave = wave − closure;                       ← • • •
        closure = wave ∪ closure;
     endwhile
end.
```

Fig. 4.   The *δ-wavefront* algorithm.

iteration	old-wave	new-wave	closure	pages_referenced
1	k, l	c, g	c, g	1
2	c, g	e, i, d	c, g, e, i, d	3
3	e, i, d	j, f, g	c, g, e, i, d, j, f	3, 1
4	j, f	h	c, g, e, i, d, j, f, h	2
5	h	Φ	c, g, e, i, d, j, f, h	none

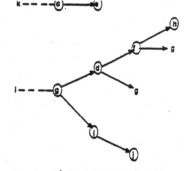

Fig. 5.   The processing of $:-R^1(\{k, l\}, Y)$ using *δ-wavefront*.

five iterations, and Fig. 3 displays, in tabular form, the content of the two relations *wave* and *closure* as well as the pages of relation A referenced during each one of these iterations.

The *wavefront*, presented above, is simple and maintains a relational interface to the database. However, its performance suffers from a serious drawback, namely, it involves some amount of redundant processing when dealing with nonlist or nontree graphs. This drawback is attributed to the fact that the *wavefront* algorithm is *memoryless*, i.e., during an iteration it may process (visit), as shown in Fig. 3, some nodes in the base graph even though these nodes might have been encountered and processed during some earlier iteration. This type of processing is redundant since it does not add any new nodes (solutions) to the ones already found during earlier iterations. A case in point is the processing of node *g* during the fourth iteration in Fig. 3. Such a processing is redundant since node *g* has been encountered during the first iteration and processed during the second iteration of the algorithm. It is easy to see that the redundant processing of *g* during the fourth iteration does not bring any new node to *closure*.

B. The δ-wavefront Algorithm

Fig. 4 presents *δ-wavefront*. It is essentially *wavefront* modified to eliminate the redundant processing of nodes encountered at different levels of execution. Such an elimination is achieved by processing during any iteration only those nodes in *wave* that have not been encountered during any previous iteration (encountered nodes are stored in *closure*). The statement flagged by "* * *" in Fig. 4 accomplishes just that. It filters out from *wave* those nodes already stored in *closure* by computing the set difference "wave-closure".

Fig. 5 presents the processing of relation A of Fig. 1 using *δ-wavefront* to generate all of the solutions to $:-R^1(\{k, l\}, Y)$. In the third and fourth iterations of this figure, one can see the basic mechanism used by *δ-wavefront* to get rid of the redundant processing experienced by *wavefront*. *wave*, generated during the third iteration (nodes *j*, *f*, and *g*), is reduced by deleting those nodes already encountered and processed during earlier iterations (node *g*, processed during the second iteration) before it is joined with relation A during the fourth iteration.

Comparing Figs. 3 and 5 reveals several interesting points. First, both of the algorithms *wavefront* and *δ-wavefront* perform

the same number of iterations for a given query; however, the number of nodes processed by *δ-wavefront* per iteration is usually smaller than that processed by *wavefront*. As a result of the smaller *wave* in *δ-wavefront*, the total number of pages of relation A referenced (processed) throughout the execution may be smaller than that of *wavefront*, resulting in a faster execution time. Second, while *wavefront* might traverse an edge in the graph representing relation A (processing a tuple in the relation) more than once, e.g., edges $\{(g, d), (g, i), (i, j),$ etc.$\}$ in Fig. 3, *δ-wavefront*, on the other hand, traverses (processes) a given edge at most once (refer to Fig. 5). Therefore, it is easy to conclude that the worst case execution time of *δ-wavefront* is linear[2] with respect to the number of tuples in relation A, whereas such a measure is not linear for *wavefront*. The linear behavior of *δ-wavefront* measured in edges processed should not be confused with its nonlinear I/O behavior, i.e., it might read into main-memory a disk page more than once (searching for different tuples of the base relation) due to the limitation on memory size. For example, consider the processing presented in Fig. 5 being carried out by a computer having a main-memory with a storage capacity of one page. The column "pages_referenced" of that figure shows that page 1 of the processed relation will be read twice into the main-memory, once during the first iteration and again during the third iteration, because this page has to be swapped out during the second iteration to make room for page 3.

---

[2] In general, the average execution time of *δ-wavefront* is sublinear with respect to the number of edges in the graph since only a subset of the graphs edges will be traversed for a given instantiated transitive closure query.

Parameter	Definition
$rlength$	The recursion length. The number of iterations performed by $wavefront/\delta\text{-}wavefront$ during the processing of a TC query.
R_i	Number of elements in $closure$ after the ith iteration.
$RG\Delta R_i$	Number of elements in the ith $replicate\text{-}gross\text{-}wave$ ($rgwave_i$). $rgwave_i$ refers to the collection of nodes obtained from joining $wave_{i-1}$ with the base relation A and removing the first column from the result relation.
$G\Delta R_i$	Number of elements in the ith $gross\ wave(gwave_i)$. $gwave_i$ refers to the set of nodes obtains from $rgwave_i$ after removing the duplicate nodes.
ΔR_i	Number of elements in the ith $wave$ ($wave_i$). $wave_i$ refers to the set of nodes obtained from $gwave_i$ after removing the nodes already stored in the current $closure$.
$OutDegree$	The expected number of edges emanating from a node in the graph representation of the base relation A $(= \frac{Nt}{Nd})$.
Ndv_Y	The number of distinct values in the $Y\_attribute$ of relation A.
N_A	Number of pages storing relation A $(= Nt * W_{\text{tuple}} / P_{\text{size}})$.
P_A	The number of main-memory pages allocated to store relation $A(= MRA * N_A)$.
P_R	The number of main-memory pages allocated to store $closure$ $(= MRR * N_A)$

A generic algorithm, the *super-TC*, designed to have a linear IO behavior will be presented in Section IV.

C. Comparing the Performance of the wavefront and δ-wavefront Algorithms

In this section, the performance of *wavefront* and *δ-wavefront* is quantitatively compared using the measure total-execution-time (*TTime*). In a single processor environment, *TTime* of a given algorithm is defined as the time required to execute the algorithm assuming there exists no overlap between the activities of the CPU and I/O subsystems.

Analytical modeling techniques have been used to compute the measures *TTime(wavefront)* and *TTime(δ-wavefront)*. The sets of formulas which relate these measures to the basic parameters of Table I are presented next. In the course of deriving these formulas, the notation presented in Table II has been used. Moreover, we have assumed that *wave* is *main-memory resident*, whereas *closure* is *disk-resident* with some main-memory pages (specified by the parameter P_R of Table II) allocated for it. *closure* is stored on disk using a hash-based technique similar to the one used to store the base relation A (see assumption 3 of Section II).

1) Derivation of Formulas for TTime(δ-wavefront): *TTime(δ-wavefront)*, the total time required for the execution of *δ-wavefront*, can be computed as follows:

$$TTime(\delta\text{-}wavefront) =$$
$$\sum_{i=1}^{rlength} join\text{-}project\text{-}time_i(\delta\text{-}wavefront)$$
$$+ union\text{-}diff\text{-}time_i(\delta\text{-}wavefront) \qquad (6)$$

where the *join-project-time_i(δ-wavefront)* is the time required to join (refer to the statement of Fig. 4 flagged by "+++") the $(i-1)$th (nonreplicate and nonredundant) *wave*, i.e., $wave_{i-1}$, with relation A during the ith iteration of *δ-wavefront*, project the result relation on its second attribute and remove the replicate nodes to generate the ith *gross-wave(gwave_i)*. *union-diff-time_i(δ-wavefront)*, on the other hand, is the time required to remove from $gwave_i$ the redundant nodes (the nodes of $gwave$ already stored in *closure*) to generate the ith *wave(wave_i)* and append it to *closure* (refer to the statement of Fig. 4 flagged by "***" and the statement directly following it). *join-project-time_i(δ-wavefront)* can be computed using the following formula:

$$join\text{-}project\text{-}time_i(\delta\text{-}wavefront) = \qquad (7)$$

$T_{hash} * \Delta R_{i-1} +$ /* for every value in $wave_{i-1}$, locate the page of relation A with matching tuples */

$T_{io} * \Delta R_{i-1} * (1 - MRA) +$ /* bring the page into main-memory (if not already there) */

$T_{compare} * \Delta R_{i-1} * \frac{P_{size}}{W_{tuple}} +$ /* search through the page for matching tuples */

$T_{hash} * RG\Delta R_i +$ /* hash the values of the $Y\_attribute$ of the matching tuples to $gwave_i$ */

$T_{compare} * RG\Delta R_i +$ /* search to check for duplicates */

$T_{move} * G\Delta R_i$ /* store distinct values in $gwave_i$ */

In deriving the above formula, we have assumed that some pages from relation A, specified by the parameter $P_A (= MRA * N_A)$, are stored in main-memory prior to the start of the algorithm's execution. Furthermore, $gwave_i$ is assumed to be stored in a hash table that resides completely in main memory.

union-diff-time_i(δ-wavefront) of (6) can be computed as follows:

$$union\text{-}diff\text{-}time_i(\delta\text{-}wavefront) = \qquad (8)$$

$T_{hash} * G\Delta R_i +$ /* for every value (node) in $gwave_i$, locate the page of *closure* with matching nodes */

$T_{io} * G\Delta R_i * \frac{max((avgClosure_i - P_R), 0)}{avgClosure} +$ /* bring the *closure* page into main-memory (if it is not already there) */

$T_{compare} * G\Delta R_i * \frac{P_{size}}{W_{attribute}} +$ /* search through the page to check if the node already exist in *closure* */

$2 * T_{move} * \Delta R_i$ /* store the node in the *closure* and $wave_i$ (if it is not already in *closure*) */

where $avgClosure_i$ in the above formula, is the average size, in pages, of *closure* during the ith iteration. It can be computed using the following approximate formula:

$$avgClosure_i = \left(R_{i-1} + \frac{\Delta R_i}{2}\right) * \frac{W_{attribute}}{P_{size}}. \qquad (9)$$

The values of the various i-subscripted quantities (for $i \geq 1$) in (7)–(9) are computed by iterating the following set of equations, beginning with $R_0 = 0$, $G\Delta R_0 = \Delta R_0 = Nt * Q_r$ and $i = 1$.

$$RG\Delta R_i = \Delta R_{i-1} * OutDegree \qquad (10)$$

$$G\Delta R_i = Ndv_Y * \left(1 - e^{-\frac{RG\Delta R_i}{Ndv_Y}}\right) \tag{11}$$

$$\Delta R_i = G\Delta R_i * \left(1 - \frac{R_{i-1}}{Ndv_Y}\right) \tag{12}$$

$$R_i = R_{i-1} + \Delta R_i \tag{13}$$

where ndv_Y, the number of distinct values in the $Y\_attribute$ of relation A, can be computed using the following formula:

$$Ndv_Y = Nd * \left(1 - e^{-\frac{Nt}{Nd}}\right). \tag{14}$$

In deriving (10)–(14), we have used the average probabilistic modeling technique, presented in [14], [16], which takes advantage of the fact that the values in the X and Y attributes of the base relation A are uniformly distributed over the underlying domain. Furthermore, the derivation of (11) and (14) have used the classical ball-box occupancy model [9], i.e., given n boxes and m balls, the expected number of boxes occupied after throwing the n balls into the m boxes, assuming it is equally probable that a ball lands into any one of the boxes, is "$n * \left(1 - e^{-\frac{m}{n}}\right)$". In (14), m and n correspond to the number of tuples in the base relation and the number of distinct values in the underlying domain, respectively, whereas in (11) they correspond to the number of elements in $rgwave_i$ and the number of distinct values in the $Y\_attribute$ of the base relation.

The derivation of (12), on the other hand, makes use of the following argument: let B be the set of distinct values in the $Y\_attribute$ of the base relation. Since, $closure_{i-1}$ is a subset of B, the probability that a value from $gwave_i$ does not find a duplicate in $closure$ is the same as the probability that such a value maps into the portion of B not occupied by the elements of $closure_{i-1}$, i.e., $\frac{Ndv_Y - R_{i-1}}{Ndv_Y} = 1 - \frac{R_{i-1}}{Ndv_Y}$.

The computation of the parameter $rlength$ of (6) is presented in Section III-C-3.

2) Derivations of Formulas for TTime(wavefront): TTime(wave-front), the total time required for the execution of *wavefront*, can be expressed as follows

$$TTime(wavefront) =$$
$$\sum_{i=1}^{rlength} join\text{-}project\text{-}time_i(wavefront)$$
$$+ union\text{-}time_i(wavefront) \tag{15}$$

where the *join-project-time(wavefront)* is the time required to join $gwave_{i-1}$ with relation A during the ith iteration of *wavefront* and then to project the result to remove the replicate nodes and generate $gwave_i$. *union-time(wavefront)*, on the other hand, is the time required to union $gwave_i$ with $closure_{i-1}$ to generate $closure_i$. *join-project-time_i(wavefront)* can be computed using formula (7) provided it undergoes the following modification: the parameter ΔR_{i-1} in formula (7) must be replaced by $G\Delta R_{i-1}$ to reflect the fact that at the beginning of each iteration, *wavefront* joins the *current gwave* with relation A and not the *wave* itself as is done in *δ-wavefront*.

In an analogous way, a slightly modified version of (8) can be used to compute *union-time_i(wavefront)*. The factor "$2 * T_{move} * \Delta R_i$" in formula (8) must be replaced by "$T_{move} * \Delta R_i$" to reflect the need to only store the surviving nodes of the current

gwave in *closure* since a nonreplicate and nonredundant *wave* does not need to be created.

To compute the quantities R_i, ΔR_i, $G\Delta R_i$, and $RG\Delta R_i$ when $i \geq 1$, the set of recurrence equations (10)–(13) can be used provided that the parameter ΔR_{i-1} in (10) is changed to $G\Delta R_{i-1}$. Such a change is needed because *wavefront* generates the *next gwave* using the *current gwave* and not the *current wave* as in the case of *δ-wavefront.*. The parameter *rlength* of (11) is the same as the one in (6). The computation of this parameter is presented next.

3) The Computation of rlength: The derivation of a closed form formula which directly computes *rlength* from the models' input parameters has proved to be a formidable task. Instead, we have used the recurrence set of equations (10)–(13) to perform such a computation. By counting the iterations (the value of i) through which these equations must be computed until the value of ΔR_i drops below the value of "1" (i.e., *wave* becomes empty), an *approximate* value for *rlength* can be obtained.

Fig. 6 displays *rlength*, computed as stated above, versus $Nr(Outdegree$ of the base graph) for $Nt = 50\ 000$ tuples. The different curves in that figure correspond to the query constant ratios (Qr), 0.001, 0.01, and 0.05. A quick look at Fig. 6 reveals the following interesting points:

- *rlength* is a strong function of *OutDegree*, a fact neglected in current literature [6], [18] (Some researchers assume acyclic graphs, and treat *rlength* and *OutDegree* as two independent variables [18]. However, even in an acyclic graph case, the two should be a function of each other assuming random generation of a relation with a fixed Nt.). When *OutDegree* is small ($\ll 1$), the graph has numerous, isolated small segments; hence paths tend to terminate quickly. When *OutDegree* is around 1, a path, once started, has the best probability of extending. In other words, the graph has sizable segments, and they do not exhibit too many cycles yet. When *OutDegree* grows larger ($\gg 1$), segments in the graph start to merge together rapidly and cycles develop heavily; hence, paths again tend to terminate quickly, but this time due to cycles.

- *rlength* is also affected by Qr (another fact mistreated in current literature [6]). When *OutDegree* < 1, higher Qr leads to slightly longer *rlength* because the more starting points there are, the better the chance that some of the paths will "survive" longer. For *OutDegree* > 1, however, higher Qr leads to shorter *rlength*. This is because more starting points translate into higher probability of merging among their paths, thus cutting one another short.

To check for the accuracy of our method in computing *rlength*, we have used simulation. For each $Nr(OutDegree)$ value, we have generated 10 random relations (graphs) each of which has 50 000 tuples. In turn, each one of these relations is, then, fed into a simulator for *δ-wavefront*. By running this simulator for a specific Qr, we were able to obtain the corresponding value of *rlength*. The 10 values obtained in this fashion for *rlength* are then averaged to get a representative value for *rlength*. This process was repeated for each combination of Qr and *OutDegree*.

Fig. 7 plots two graphs representing the values of *rlength* obtained through simulation and calculation for $Nt = 50\ 000$ tuples for $Qr = 0.01$. This figure reveals that the calculated *rlength* is a very good overall approximation to the simulated one with the maximum error occurring around *OutDegree* = 1. The plots for the simulated and calculated *rlength* for other values of Qr (these plots are not included here) have revealed similar behavior. They have also revealed that the calculated

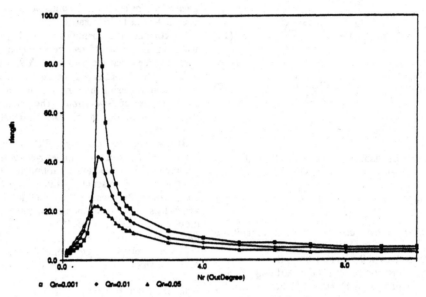

Fig. 6. The calculated recursion length (*rlength*).

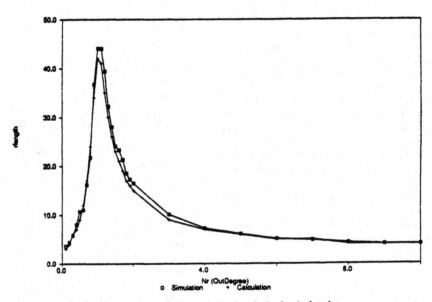

Fig. 7. Comparing the calculated and simulated *rlength*.

rlength tends to slightly overestimate the simulated one when Qr is relatively small and underestimate *rlength* when Qr is relatively large with the best estimation taking place somewhere in between.

4) The Performance Comparison Results: Using the formulas presented in the previous sections, we have computed the measure *TTime* for *wavefront* and *δ-wavefront*. The results of these computations are presented in Figs. 8–10. Specifically, Fig. 8 plots *TTime(wavefront)* versus the ratio $Nr(OutDegree)$ for $Nt = 50\,000$ tuples, $MRA = 0.1$, $MRR = 0.15$, and $Qr = 0.001$, 0.01, and 0.05. This figure points out the strong dependence of the total execution time of the studied algorithm on the characteristics of the base relation (the value of the parameter *OutDegree*) and (to a less degree) on the characteristics of the processed TC query (the value of the parameter Qr). Furthermore, Fig. 8 points

out an anomaly in the behavior of *wavefront*. That is, for those relations with $OutDegree \geq 1$, an increase in the number of query constants will actually result in a decrease in the total execution time instead of an increase. Such a finding is very important and shows that splitting the query constants among a number of processors each of which is running *wavefront* (on its own copy of the base relation) will not reduce the query execution time, but rather increase it (in comparison to a processor having a main-memory size equal to the sum of all main-memories in the parallel system), i.e., *wavefront* is unsuitable for this type of distributed processing.

The effect of changing the main-memory size allocated to the base relation on *TTime (wavefront)* has been studied. In general, the shape of *TTime(wavefront)* versus Nr has been found to remain the same as MRA is changed, however, its

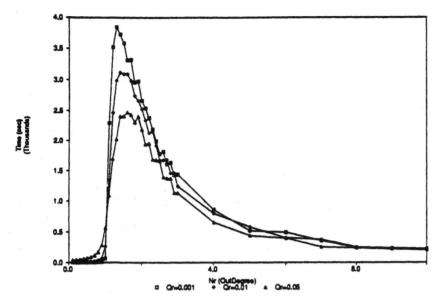

Fig. 8. The total execution time of *wavefront*.

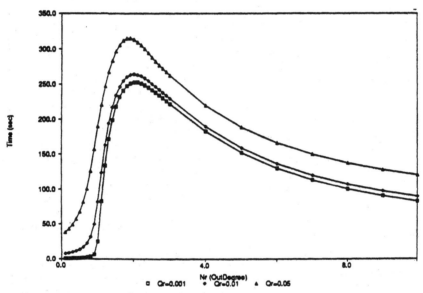

Fig. 9. The total execution time of *δ-wavefront*.

magnitude is found to be very sensitive to changes in *MRA*, i.e., a slight change in the values of MRA substantially changes the magnitude of the measure *TTime(wavefront)*. The effect of changing the main-memory size allocated to the *closure* on *TTime(wavefront)* has also been studied. We have found that an increase in the value of *MRR* beyond 0.15 does not bring any reduction in the value of *TTime(wavefront)* (this leads us to conclude that *MRR* = 0.15 is enough to keep the *closure* main-memory resident), whereas decreasing *MRR* below 0.15 increases the magnitude of *TTime(wavefront)*, however, such an increase is not dramatic.

The observations, presented above, lead us to conclude that *TTime(wavefront)* is much more sensitive to changes in *MRA* than to changes in *MRR*. This implies that if an extra amount of main-memory is available to the *wavefront*, it is always a wise decision to allocate a larger portion of this memory to the base relation.

Fig. 9 plots *TTime(δ-wavefront)* versus *Nr(OutDegree)* for *Qr* = 0.001, 0.01, and 0.05, *MRA* = 0.1 and *MRR* = 0.15. It is interesting to see that the general behavior of *TTime (δ-wavefront)* is similar to that of *TTime(wavefront)* except that the anomalous behavior experienced by *wavefront* does not extend to *δ-wavefront*, which suggests its suitability for parallel processing environments. Furthermore, the magnitude of *TTime(δ-wavefront)* is substantially smaller than that of *wavefront* (for the same parameter settings) and *TTime(δ-wavefront)* is more sensitive to changes in *MRR* than *TTime(wavefront)*.

To compare the speed of *δ-wavefront* to that of *wavefront*, we have used the measure speed-ratio (SR), defined as "*TTime(wavefront)/TTime(δ-wavefront)*." Fig. 10 plots SR

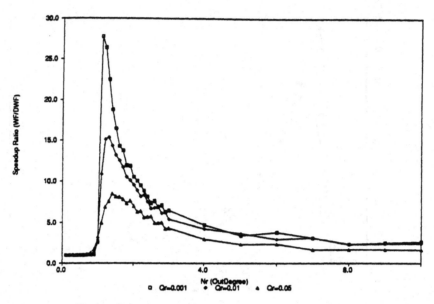

Fig. 10. Comparing the performance of *wavefront* and *δ-wavefront*.

versus *OutDegree* for *MRA* = 0.1 and *MRR* = 0.15. A quick examination of this figure reveals the following interesting points.

- Over the entire range of the performance input parameters, SR is ≥ 1, i.e., *δ-wavefront* is as fast or faster than *wavefront*, with large SR's being possible.
- SR is a strong function of the parameter *OutDegree* (base relation) hitting a maximum when *OutDegree* is about 1 (base relations with relatively few but very long chains of nodes) and decreasing rapidly as *OutDegree* gets smaller than 1. SR also decreases in value, but at a slower rate, as *OutDegree* gets larger than 1.
- When *OutDegree* < 1, SR is somewhat independent of the parameter *Qr*. However, when *OutDegree* ≥ 1, SR is a strong function of the parameter *Qr*, decreasing in value as *Qr* gets larger.

It is interesting to note here that the comparison of Fig. 10 to other figures which plot SR for different combinations of *MRA* and *MRR* values (these figures are not included here to keep the size of this paper down) has shown that SR is insensitive to changes in the values of *MRA* and *MRR* remains almost constant at the values presented in Fig. 10.

IV. THE GENERIC *super-TC* ALGORITHM AND ITS VARIANTS

This section presents the generic *super-TC* algorithm and its different variants. It also presents a comparative performance study of these variants to identify the best performing one(s).

A. The Generic super-TC Algorithm

super-TC is a generic transitive closure algorithm designed to overcome the nonlinear I/O problem encountered in *δ-wavefront* (and *wavefront*). That is, it is designed to read any given page from the base relation at most once. Such a desirable property is achieved as follows: when *super-TC* chooses a node, say node *a* of Fig. 1, to search for its children, the page(s) which stores the edges that link the given node to its children (tuples with *X_*attribute value equal to *a*) is read into the processor's main-memory. *super-TC* separates the tuples of the read page(s), page 1 in our example, into three groups. The first group contains those

tuples which will be used by *a* to find its children (tuple (*a, b*) of page 1). The second group contains those tuples which will never be referenced during the future processing of nodes (tuples (*k, c*) and (*l, g*)) and the third group contains those tuples which have the possibility of being referenced during the future processing of nodes (tuples (*d, g*) and (*d, f*)). Once the tuples in the first group have been used to find the processed node's children, they will never be used again by any future node (since these tuples will not lead to any new nodes that are not already in *closure*) and can be discarded. The tuples of the second group can also be discarded, since these tuples will never be referenced by any future node. However, the tuples of the third group need to be saved for a possible future reference and cannot be discarded. *super-TC* saves these tuples in main memory and can, therefore, safely eliminate the need for reading the processed page(s) once again. Any future reference to such a page(s) will be directed to those tuples of the page already stored in the processor's main-memory.

When a page(s) is read into memory in response to a node, finding the tuples of the first group is very easy: just match the given node with those tuples in the page(s). However, finding the tuples of the second and third groups is more complicated and requires some knowledge about all of the tuples in the processed relation. To find the tuples which belong to these groups, *super_TC* takes advantage of the following observation: a node in the graph (and therefore the edges that directly descend from that node) will never be referenced if both of the following conditions are satisfied (refer to Fig. 1).

1) The node has no incoming arcs. That is, there exists no tuple in the processed relation whose *Y_*attribute value is equal to the node.
2) The node does not match a query constant.

The two conditions presented above provide us with an easy procedure for testing the possibility of a future reference to a given tuple. Take the *X_*attribute value of the tuple and compare it to the set of query constant and the set of values in the *Y_*attribute of the processed relation. If a match does not occur, then the tuple belongs to the second group and can be discarded. If, on the other hand, a match exists, then, the tuple belongs to the third group

Procedure super_TC (input: *query_constants*, *A(base relation)*; output: *dead_closure*)
begin
/*
   wave and closure are unary relations with an X_attribute.
   A is a binary relation with an X_attribute and a Y_attribute.
   A fast access path is defined on the X_attribute of A.
   A bit_vector BV_Y encodes the values of the Y_attribute.
   A mark bit is associated with every node to be inserted in the alive_closure.
*/
   update BV_Y with *query_constants*;
   mem_save = Φ;
   dead_closure = Φ;
   alive_closure = {*query_constants* with mark bits set to 1};
   While (alive_closure $\neq$ Φ) Do
      choose a driver from alive_closure, call it d; ⟵ +++
      delete d from the alive_closure;
      if mark(d) = 0, then insert d into the dead_closure;
      read (from disk) the pages, of A , with tuples which match d (if not
         already in mem_save), store those tuples with X_attribute value
         in BV_Y into mem_save;
      find those tuples in mem_save which match d, call the resulting relation M;
      project M over its second(Y)_attribute; call the resulting set of nodes W;
      set mark(W) = 0;
      delete the set of tuples M from mem_save;
      alive_closure = alive_closure $\bigcup$ [W − dead_closure]; ⟵ ***
      mark(alive_closure) = mark(alive_closure) AND mark(W);
   endwhile
end.

Fig. 11.   The *super-TC* algorithm.

alive_closure	dead_closure	mem_save	page_read
$\underline{k}^+, l^+$	Φ	$(d, g), (d, f), (l, g).$ $(k, c)^*$	1
$\underline{c}, l^+$	c	$(d, g), (d, f), (l, g),$ $(g, d), (g, i), (i, j).$ $(c, e)^*$	3
$\underline{e}, l^+$	c, e	$(d, g), (d, f), (l, g),$ $(g, d), (g, i), (i, j).$	none
$\underline{l}^+$	c, e	$(d, g), (d, f), (g, d),$ $(g, i), (i, j).$ $(l, g)^*$	−
$\underline{g}$	c, e, g	$(d, g), (d, f), (i, j).$ $(g, d)^*, (g, i)^*$	−
$\underline{d}, i$	c, e, g, d	$(i, j).$ $(d, g)^*, (d, f)^*$	−
$\underline{f}, i$	c, e, g, d, f	$(i, j), (b, d), (b, c)$ $(f, h)^*, (f, g)^*.$	2
$\underline{h}, i$	c, e, g, d, f, h	$(i, j), (b, d), (b, c).$	none
$\underline{i}$	c, e, g, d, f, h, i	$(b, d), (b, c).$ $(i, j)^*$	−
$\underline{j}$	c, e, g, d, f, h, i, j	$(b, d), (b, c).$	−
Φ	$\underbrace{c, e, g, d, f, h, i, j}_{closure}$	$(b, d), (b, c).$	−

Fig. 12.   The processing of $:-R^1(\{k, l\}, Y)$ using *super-TC*.

and must be saved. It is interesting to note here that a technique somewhat similar to the one presented above has been used by Lu [12] to reduce the size of the base relation while evaluating its full transitive closure. However, to the best of our knowledge this technique has never been used before in processing the instantiated type of the transitive closure operation.

Fig. 11 presents *super-TC*. It assumes that an access path is defined on the X_attribute of the base relation A which permits the quick identification of the page(s) relevant to a given node. Furthermore, *super-TC* uses a main-memory resident bit_vector BV_Y, similar to the ones used in [3], [14], [16] to improve the processing speed of the join operation, to encode the Y_attribute values found in A. Such a structure provides *super-TC* with a quick way of finding out whether a given value does exist in the Y_attribute without incurring a high main-memory storage cost. The process of encoding a set of values uses a suitable hash function HF to transform these values into addresses to the bit_vector and sets the corresponding bits to 1's. To check for the presence of a given value within the encoded set, such a value is transformed using HF into an address to the bit_vector. The corresponding bit is then tested, and the value may exist if the corresponding bit in the bit_vector is *set*. Due to the collision phenomenon associated with hash schemes, some false alarms will be generated, i.e., a value might hash to a *set* bit in BV_Y even though it is not one of the values in the Y_attribute of the base relation, nor one of the query constants. In *super-TC* false alarms do not introduce any error but may degrade system performance. Using an appropriate size for BV_Y, such a degradation can be brought to a negligible minimum [3].

super-TC, as shown in Fig. 11, starts the execution of a given query by encoding the query constants and updating BV_Y accordingly.[3] It also uses two unary relations, *dead_closure* and *alive_closure*, and one binary relation *mem_save*. At any point during execution, *dead_closure* stores those nodes in the graph already found (visited) and processed (children already found). Initially *dead_closure* is set to empty. *alive_closure*, on the other hand, stores those nodes already found (visited) but not yet

---

[3] Thus, BV_Y will encode not only the values in the Y_attribute of relation A, but also the query constants. Therefore, BV_Y can be used for checking the possible future references to a tuple.

processed (children not yet found). This relation is initialized to the set of query constants. *mem_save*, on the other hand, stores those tuples from the pages already read into memory which have the potential to be referenced (used) in the future. *super-TC* proceeds by choosing a node d from *alive_closure* for processing. d is then deleted from *alive_closure* and inserted into *dead_closure* (if it is not a query constant). The processing of d continues by fetching, from the secondary store, those pages from relation A with tuples having d in their X_attribute into main-memory (if they are not already there). As these pages are read in, they are first filtered through BV_Y to remove those tuples that will never be referenced during the processing of any future node. The remaining tuples are then stored into *mem_save*, which, in turn, is interrogated for the set of tuples M that match d. M is then deleted from *mem_save*, projected over the Y_attribute to yield the set of nodes W that are the children of d. W is then compared with the nodes in *dead_closure* (refer to the statement in Fig. 11 flagged by "***") to eliminate from W those nodes already stored there. The set of surviving nodes are then "unioned" with the ones in *alive_closure* for future processing. The processing of nodes continues until *alive_closure* is empty, at that point *dead_closure* will contain all of the solutions to the processed query.

As an example, Fig. 12 presents the processing of relation A of Fig. 1 using *super-TC* to generate solutions to $:-R^1(\{k, l\}, Y)$. The nodes in *alive_closure* flagged with "+" are initial query constants, and once processed, they will not be included in *dead_closure*. The unflagged nodes, on the other hand, are generated during the execution of the algorithm and, therefore, once processed, are included in *dead_closure*. During the processing of a node (an underlined node in *alive_closure*), the tuples which match that node in *mem_save* are flagged by "*". Once these tuples are used to find the children of the processed node, they are deleted from *mem_save*. On the other hand, the unflagged tuples in *mem_save* are those accumulated from the pages already read into main memory and have the potential of being referenced during the processing of the remaining unprocessed nodes.

It is interesting to note (as indicated by the statement flagged by "+++" in Fig. 11) the absence of a specific rule by which *super-TC* selects the next node from the *alive_closure* for processing (hence, it is called generic). Next we use this generic algorithm to generate some of its variants and compare their performance to select the best performing one(s).

339

B. The Different super-TC Variants and the Evaluation of Their Performance

Different variants to the generic *super-TC* can be generated by providing it with alternate rules for selecting the next node out of *alive_closure* for processing. In general, several selection rules exist. Among those considered are the following.

1) Random: The variant adopting this selection rule implements its *alive_closure* as an unordered set, i.e., the next node to be processed is selected from such a set at random. The *super-TC* variant adopting this selection rule carries out its graph search in a random fashion and hence referred to as *rsuper-TC*.

2) First-in First-Out (FIFO): The variant adopting this selection rule implements its *alive_closure* as a queue, i.e., the newly generated nodes are added to the rear of the queue, whereas a new node is selected for processing from the front of the queue. The *super-TC* variant adopting this selection rule carries out its graph search in a breadth-first fashion and hence referred to as *bfsuper-TC*.

3) Last-in First-out (LIFO): The *alive_closure* is implemented as a stack, i.e., a newly generated node or the next node selected for processing is added to or taken from the top of this stack. The *super-TC* variant adopting this selection rule carries out its graph search in a depth-first fashion and hence referred to as *dfsuper-TC*.

4) Good-first: The variant adopting this selection rule implements its *alive_closure* as two unordered sets, *in-memory* and *out-memory*. At any point during execution, *in-memory* stores those modes of *alive_closure* whose base relation pages have already been read into main memory (the useful tuples in these pages are stored in *mem-save*), whereas *out-memory* stores those nodes of *alive_closure* whose pages are still residing on disk. This variant selects its next node for processing in random from those ones in *in-memory*. Only when *in-memory* is empty, the next node will be selected at random from those stored in *out-memory*. The *super-TC* algorithm which adopts this selection rule is referred to as *gfsuper-TC*.

5) Best-first: The *alive_closure* in the variant adopting this rule is implemented exactly as the one in *gfsuper-TC*. Furthermore, its processing of nodes proceeds as in *gfsuper-TC* as long as *in-memory* is not empty. However, when *in-memory* is empty, the next page to be fetched from disk is the one referenced by the maximum number of nodes in *out-memory*. The chosen page is then brought into *mem-save*, the nodes referencing this page are transferred to *in-memory*, and the processing of nodes continues by randomly selecting one node out of *in-memory*. The *super-TC* variant which adopts this selection rule is referred to as *bestsuper-TC*. It is important to note here that the implementation of this selection rule is much more expensive than the previous ones since *bestsuper-TC* needs to maintain a fetch-list which contains the addresses of those disk pages referenced by the nodes in *out-memory*. Moreover, the fetch-list must be ordered according to the number of nodes in *out-memory* which reference each one of the pages on this list. The list needs to be updated each time a new node is added to *out-memory*.

It is interesting to notice that the execution time for the different *super-TC* variants are almost the same (assuming the availability of unlimited amount of main-memory) since all of these variants require the same amount of disk IO (the largest component in the execution time of these algorithms). However, the maximum sizes of *mem-save* required by these variants are different, and therefore, we are interested in the *super-TC* variant which generates the smallest *mem-save*.

To compute the maximum sizes of *mem-save* required by the different *super-TC* variants, we have used simulation. Our simulator generates a random base relation according to a given specification, i.e., fixed Nt and *OutDegree*, and stores the corresponding tuples, after clustering them according to their X_attribute values, in disk pages, i.e., all of the tuples in the relation with the same X_attribute values (the relational version of a successor list) are stored in the same (or consecutive) disk page(s). It, then, generates a query (also according to a given Qr), runs this query on the generated relation using each one of the *super-TC* variants and records the maximum size of the corresponding *mem-save*. This process is repeated 10 times for each Nt, *OutDegree*, and Qr combination and the resulting values generated for each variant are averaged to obtain a representative estimate for the size of the corresponding *mem-save*.

Fig. 13 plots the maximum size of *mem-save* (as a % of the base relation size) versus *OutDegree* for the different *super-TC* variants and for $Qr = 0.001$. This figure shows that the maximum size of *mem-save* for all of the variants is a strong function of the parameter *OutDegree*. When *OutDegree* < 1, the size of *mem-save* is almost the same for all of the variants. However, for *OutDegree* $\geq$ 1, the size of *mem-save* for *gfsuper-TC* and *bestsuper-TC* is almost the same and is much smaller than those required by the other *super-TC* variants. Since the cost of implementing the selection rule in *gfsuper-TC*, in terms of main-memory storage and CPU time, is much less than that of implementing the rule in *bestsuper-TC*, we conclude that *gfsuper-TC* is the best performing variant for *super-TC*. This conclusion has been found to hold for the other values of Qr as well.

Fig. 14 plots the maximum size of *mem-save* required by the best performing *super-TC* variant, namely, *gfsuper-TC* versus *OutDegree* for $Qr = 0.001$, 0.005, 0.01, and 0.05. This plot reveals that the *worst-case size* for *mem-save* is around 50% of the base relation and drops slightly as Qr is increased in value. It is interesting to notice that such a worst-case situation occurs in a narrow band around *OutDegree* = 1 (i.e., for relations with tuples forming a small number of long chains, not very frequent in real life), dropping exponentially as *OutDegree* get away from that value.

It is important to note here that the above results obtained for *mem-save* are based on the assumption that the tuples of the base relation are clustered in disk pages according to their X_attribute values, i.e., the tuples which share the same X_attribute value are stored in the same disk page. In general, a number of other storage schemes exists, among them: random, depth-first, and breadth-first. The random scheme stores the tuples into pages without establishing any clustering order, i.e., the tuples which share the same X_attribute values might reside in several different disk pages. The depth-first (breadth-first) scheme stores those tuples which lie along a depth-first (breadth-first) search path in the base relation graph into the same (or in consecutive) disk page(s).

When the random storage scheme is used, the *mem-save* sized generated by the *super-TC* variants tends to be somewhat higher than those presented in Fig. 13, since each one of the processed nodes will now bring into main-memory a larger number of pages, thus requiring a larger *mem-save* to store the useful tuples contained in these pages.

When one of the depth-first or breadth-first schemes is used, the *mem-save* sizes generated by some of the *super-TC* variants will be substantially smaller than the ones presented in Fig. 13. For example, when the tuples of the base relation are stored in a depth-first fashion, the maximum sizes of *mem-save* generated by *dfsuper-TC* will be very small, whereas when these tuples are stored in a breadth-first fashion, the sizes of *mem-save* generated

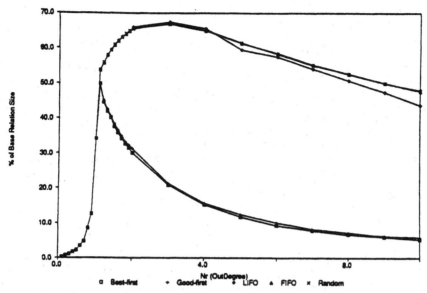

Fig. 13. Comparing the maximum size of *mem-save* in the different variants of *super-TC*.

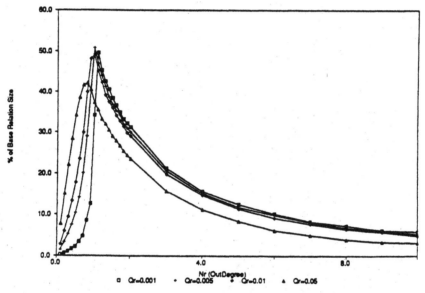

Fig. 14. Comparing the maximum size of *mem-save* in *gfsuper-TC* for different values of *Qr*.

by *bfsuper-TC* will be very small. In both of these cases, however, the size of *mem-save* generated by *gfsuper-TC* (and *bestsuper-TC*) will be as small as the ones generated by *dfsuper-TC* (when depth-first clustering is used) or *bfsuper-TC* (when breadth-first clustering is used). This is due to the fact that *gfsuper-TC* can automatically configure itself as a depth-first or breadth-first search algorithm taking advantage of the way the relation is clustered on disk to further reduce its *mem-save* requirements. This is a great advantage for *gfsuper-TC*.

V. COMPARING THE PERFORMANCE OF THE *δ-wavefront* AND *gfsuper-TC* ALGORITHMS

The performance comparison between the *δ-wavefront* and *gfsuper-TC* algorithms has been carried out using the measure

Speed-ratio defined as the ratio "IOP(*δ-wavefront*)/IOP(*gfsuper-TC*). For a given algorithm *X*, IOP (IO page) is defined as the total number of page I/O from the base relation performed by *X*. In computing IOP (*gfsuper-TC*), we have assumed that the bit-vector BV_Y is already constructed and stored on disk prior to the evaluation of the TC query. The IOP (*gfsuper-TC*), therefore, includes the cost of only reading the bit-vector pages into main-memory. The fact that the bit-vector will have to be constructed only once and then used in processing many TC operations (as well as other relational operations such as the join operation [16], [14]) justifies such an assumption.

To compute IOP for the studied algorithms, we have used simulation. Our simulator consists of two parts, the database generator and the algorithm simulator. The database generator takes the values of the relation-related parameters of Table I as

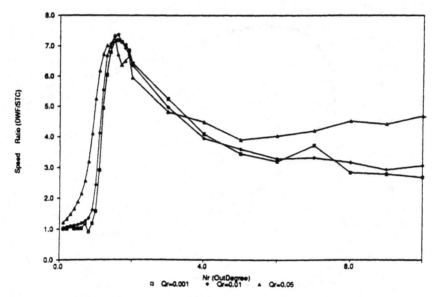

Fig. 15. The speed of *gfsuper-TC* relative to that of *δ-wavefront*.

input and generates the tuples of the binary base relation A as output. The two attributes of the generated relation are defined on a common domain of size Nd (the domain of positive integers from 0 up to and including the value $Nd - 1$). The values in the generated tuples are randomly drawn (with replacement) from this common domain using a random number generator with a range equal to the size of the domain.

The program simulator, on the other hand, takes the tuples of the generated base relation, the hardware-related parameters, and some of the relation-related parameters as input and simulates the studied algorithms. It starts such a simulation by splitting the input tuples, based on their X_attribute, into pages using a simple hash function. The simulator then generates the proper number of initial query constants, specified by $Qr * Nt$, by randomly drawing them (without replacement) from the domain which underlies the attributes of the base relation. The simulator then runs the *gfsuper-TC* algorithm to find the corresponding value of the performance measure IOP and the maximum amount of main-memory storage (*mem-save* size + bit-vector size) required to support the algorithm during this run. The simulator then allocates the same amount of main-memory to the *δ-wavefront* algorithm and executes it using the same relation and the same query constants as before to obtain a value of IOP for the *δ-wavefront* algorithm. To obtain a more accurate value of the performance measure for each one of the evaluated algorithms, the above process is repeated 10 times and the final value of IOP is the average of the performance values obtained during these repetitions.

Fig. 15 plots the measure *Speed-ratio* versus *OutDegree* for $Qr = 0.001$, 0.01, and 0.05. This figure indicates that although the *Speed-ratio* is a strong function of the parameters *OutDegree* and Qr, nevertheless, it is always greater than 1 and reaches the value of 7, a substantial speed improvement of *gfsuper-TC* over *δ-wavefront* given the fact that both of these algorithms are running with the same amount of main-memory storage. The speed advantage displayed by *fgsuper-TC* over *δ-wavefront* is attributed to the fact that the former algorithm manages its assigned portion of main-memory more intelligently than the *δ-wavefront* algorithm does. While the *super-TC* variant keeps

in main-memory only those tuples that are relevant to the future processing of the nodes, the *δ-wavefront* keeps in main-memory the relevant and the unrelevant tuples, thus effectively reducing the amount of useful main-memory available to process such an algorithm. For a fixed amount of allocated main-memory, the *super-TC* algorithm will, therefore, perform a much less amount of page IO than that performed by the *δ-wavefront* algorithm, thus, the good performance of the former algorithm over the latter one.

It is important to note here that despite the ample of evidence, presented in this paper, indicating that the size of mem-save for the super-TC algorithm will, in most practical cases, be relatively small in comparison with the size of the base relation, nevertheless there will always be the case when the size of *mem-save* would be incorrectly estimated resulting in memory overflow. The *super-TC* algorithm can handle such a situation by simply requesting some extra space from the memory manager or by paging *mem-save* and swapping some of these pages to the disk. Our initial investigation of the latter remedy shows that a *super-TC* equipped with a modified version of the good-first selection rule (in this version, *in-memory* is redefined to store those unprocessed nodes which reference the tuples residing in the main-memory portion of *mem-save*. When *in-memory* is empty a new page (form disk *mem-save* or disk base relation; a choice which depends on the referencing nature of the current unprocessed nodes in *out-memory*) will be brought into main memory) is still superior to the *δ-wavefront* algorithm. The reason for such a behavior is the fact that the total size of *mem-save* is, in most practical cases, much smaller than that of the base relation which implies that the *super-TC* algorithm will perform a smaller amount of page swapping than the *δ-wavefront* algorithm would do, thus the superiority of the *super-TC* over the *δ-wavefront*.

VI. Conclusions

This paper studies and compares the performance of several algorithms suitable for processing the first type of the *partially instantiated* transitive closure queries. These algorithms are *wavefront, δ-wavefront,* and generic *super-TC,* and a number of its variants, namely, *rsuper-TC, bfsuper-TC, dfsuper-TC, gfsuper-TC*, and *bestsuper-TC*. While *wavefront* and δ-*wavefront* may read a given base relation page more than once, *super-TC* and its variants read each page at most once.

A comprehensive performance evaluation of the algorithms using rigorous analytical and simulation models has also been presented. The results of our study suggest that the relative performance of the algorithms is a strong function of the parameters which characterize the processed query and the base relation referenced by that query. Furthermore, it points out the superiority of one variant of the *super-TC* algorithm, *gfsuper-TC*, over the rest of the variants and over δ-*wavefront* (for the same amount of main-memory storage, *gfsuper-TC* achieves up to seven times the speed of δ-*wavefront*) which in turn is superior to the *wavefront* algorithm (up to one or more orders of magnitude of speed advantage). The speed improvement achieved by the *super-TC* algorithm is attributed to the fact that the *super-TC* manages its assigned portion of main-memory more intelligently than the δ-*wavefront* algorithm does. While the *super-TC* keeps in main-memory only those tuples that are relevant to the future processing of the nodes, the δ-*wavefront* keeps in main-memory the relevant and the unrelevant tuples, thus effectively reducing the amount of useful main-memory available to process such an algorithm. For a fixed amount of allocated main-memory, the *super-TC* algorithm will, therefore, perform a much less amount of page IO than that performed by the δ-*wavefront* algorithm, thus, the good performance of the former algorithm over the latter one.

REFERENCES

[1] R. Agrawal and H. V. Jagadish, "Direct algorithms for the transitive closure of database relations," in *Proc. 13th Int. Conf. VLDB*, Sept. 1987, pp. 255–266.
[2] R. Agrawal, "Alpha: An extension of relational algebra to express a class of recursive queries," *IEEE Trans. Software Eng.*, vol. 14, no. 7, July 1988.
[3] E. Babb, "Implementing a relational database by means of specialized hardware," *ACM TODS*, vol. 4, no. 6, pp. 414–429, June 1979.
[4] F. Bancilhon and R. Ramakrishnan, "An amateur's introduction to recursive query processing strategies," in *Proc. 1986 ACM-SIGMOD Conf.*, 1986.
[5] J. Han and L. Henschen, "Compiling and processing transitive closure queries in relational database systems," Dept. EECS, Northwestern Univ., Tech. Rep. 86-06-DMB-02.
[6] J. Han, G. Qadah, and C. Chaou, "The processing of the transitive closure queries," in *Proc. 1988 Int. Conf. Extending Database Technology*, Venice, Italy, pp. 49–75.
[7] L. Henschen and S. Naqvi, "On compiling queries in recursive first-order databases," *J. ACM*, pp. 47–86, Jan. 1984.
[8] E. Horowitz and S. Sahni, *Fundamentals of Data Structures in Pascal*, 2nd ed. Rockville, MD: Computer Science Press, 1987.
[9] W. Feller, *An Introduction to Probability Theory and its Application*, vol. 1. New York: Wiley, 1967.
[10] H., Gallaire, J. Minker, and J. Nicolas, "Logic and databases: A deductive approach," *Comput. Surveys*, vol. 16, no. 2, pp. 153–185, June 1984.
[11] Y. E. Ioannidis and R. Ramakrishnan, "Efficient transitive closure algorithms," in *Proc. 14th VLDB Conf.*, 1988, pp. 382–394.
[12] H. Lu, "New strategies for computing the transitive closure of a database relation," in *Proc. 13th VLDB Conf.*, 1987.
[13] H. Lu, K. Mikkilineni, and J. P. Richardson, "Design and evaluation of algorithms to compute the transitive closure of a database relation," in *Proc. 3rd Int. Conf. Data Engineering*, 1987, pp. 112–119.
[14] G. Z. Qadah, "Filter-based join algorithms on uniprocessor and distributed-memory multiprocessor database machines," in *Proc. Int. Conf. Extending Database Technology*, 1988, pp. 388–413.
[15] ——, "An inference model and a tree-structured multiprocessor for large data-intensive logic bases," in *Proc. Fifth Int. Workshop Database Machines*, Oct. 1987, pp. 503–516.
[16] G. Z. Qadah and K. B. Irani, "The join operation on a shared-memory multiprocessor database machine," *IEEE Trans. Software Eng.*, vol. 14, no. 11, pp. 1688–1683, Nov. 1988.
[17] R. Reiter, "Deductive question-answering on relational databases," in *Logic and Databases*, H. Gallaire and J. Minker, Eds. New York: Plenum, 1978.
[18] P. Valduiez and H. Boral, "Evaluation of recursive queries using join indices," in *Proc. 1st Expert Database Systems Conf.*, Apr. 1986, pp. 197–208.

Approximate Reasoning About the Semantic Effects of Program Changes

MARK MORICONI, MEMBER, IEEE, AND TIMOTHY C. WINKLER

Abstract—The incremental cost of a change to a program often is disproportionately high because of inadequate means of determining the semantic effects of the change. A practical logical technique is presented for finding the semantic effects of changes through a direct analysis of the program. The programming language features considered include parameterized modules, procedures, and global variables.

The logic described in this paper is *approximate* in that weak (conservative) results sometimes are inferred. The basis for an approximation is a structural interpretation of the information-flow relationships among program objects. The approximate inference system is concise, abstract, extensible, and decidable, giving it significant advantages over the main alternative formalizations. Our implementation of the logic records the justification for each flow dependency to explain in detail how indirect effects occur.

Index Terms—Analysis of changes, approximate reasoning, formal methods, information flow, program analysis.

I. INTRODUCTION

FOR large systems, the overall cost of even a small change can be extremely high. This is true even for well-structured systems, which minimize but do not eliminate the interconnections among system objects that lead to unexpected effects. A significant reduction in cost could be achieved if there were a way to determine the indirect effects of changes automatically.

Conventional formal methods are not effective in the analysis of changes. The question of whether a change to a program effects a certain system object boils down to determining whether a formula in the specification language is a theorem. This reduction would take place in a Hoare logic involving pre-and postconditions, as well as in a logic based on the equivalence of functions. Unfortunately, the expressive behavioral specification languages are undecidable and some are incomplete. They also have insufficient mechanical theorem proving support. Consequently, any approach based on a behavioral specification language would tend to be impractical for everyday use.

To obtain a practical solution, we make a sharp distinction between the kind of property to be analyzed and the kind of method used to analyze it. In particular, we reason about the semantic effects of changes through a structural analysis of a program. We believe that the right structural abstraction for capturing the "effects" relation between system objects is that of "information flow." Intuitively, information flows from an object x to an object y if, when the program is executed, a change in the value associated with x can change the value associated with y. This is a qualitative question in that we are interested only in whether *any* information flows from one object to another, not the amount of information that flows. For system objects x and y, a change to x is said to affect y provided the pair $< x,y >$ is in the closure of the information-flow relation with respect to a set of special axioms. The axioms do not include the usual transitivity rule. If there is flow from x to y and from y to z, there is not necessarily flow from x to z.

We define a logic for approximating the direct and indirect information flows in a large program. Each construct in a programming language is described declaratively by a rule of inference. Each rule is syntax-directed in that its application is driven by the abstract syntax of the programming language. The programming features covered include parameterized modules, procedures, global variables, functions without side effects, recursion, and various statements, such as assignment, while loop, and conditional. The entire logical system is concise and comprehensible.

Our formalization has three important characteristics that increase its practical utility. First, our logic is decidable, obviating the problems associated with semantic approaches. Decidability is achieved in part because we do not require formal, detailed specifications. Since programs are often constructed without any specification, this decision has the additional benefit of making our method more widely applicable. Second, new constructs can be handled simply by adding more rules. Third, the implementation of our logic facilitates the interpretation of computed results. In particular, proofs are saved in a comprehensible form that makes explicit the justifications for each pair in a closure. Justifications are particularly useful in examining an approximation that is believed to be too inexact.

Because our logic is approximate and conservative, it has the logical property that it is complete but not sound. Let $\mathfrak{I}$ denote the set of true information flows in a given program and let $\mathfrak{a}$ denote our approximate inference system. In addition, let $x \Rightarrow y$ indicate that there is information flow from object x to object y, where an object is a module, procedure, function, or variable. Then, we have

$$\text{if } \vDash_{\mathfrak{I}} x \Rightarrow y \text{ then } \vdash_{\mathfrak{a}} x \Rightarrow y$$

Manuscript received October 15, 1989; revised May 1, 1990. Recommended by N. G. Leveson. This work was supported by the Office of Naval Research under Contract N00014-86-C-0775 and by Meidensha Corporation.

The authors are with the Computer Science Laboratory, SRI International, 333 Ravenswood Avenue, Menlo Park, CA 94025.

IEEE Log Number 9037078.

but the converse is false. Of course, the converse is desirable in classical logic, but, for our application, completeness is the crucial property. An overestimate (completeness and unsoundness) will not cause us to overlook an object affected by a change, but it may point to objects that are not relevant.

Another nice property of our axiomatization $\mathcal{C}$ is that failure to derive a flow means that the flow definitely does not occur. That is,

$$\text{if } \vdash_{\mathcal{C}} x \Rightarrow y \text{ then } \models_{\mathcal{G}} x \Rightarrow y$$

which is just the contrapositive of the completeness property above.

The remainder of the paper is organized as follows. The next section compares our work to related work involving the semantic and structural analysis of programs. Section III presents the abstract syntax for the language discussed in the body of the paper. Section IV gives a mathematical definition of information flow, illustrates its intransitivity, and defines rules for computing transitive flows across statements, including procedure calls. Section V introduces a logical method for referring to values of variables at specific program points. Section VI shows how to state questions about changes and presents computer-generated analyses that answer positive and negative questions. The questions involve various program objects, including variables, procedures, and modules. Section VII shows that changes are analyzed in polynomial time. Section VIII discusses modules and sketches how to handle a subtle example. Section IX concludes with a brief summary of our results.

An earlier paper [1] presented similar results in a different logical framework. The main improvement in this paper is that the inference rules can be applied directly to a program, making it trivial to compute detailed justification for the indirect effects of a change. The earlier paper gave a logic for analyzing an abstract model of a program, but did not specify a mechanical procedure for deriving (from a program) the basic relations in a model. The technique in this paper is considerably more efficient.

II. RELATED WORK

A. Semantic Approaches

In 1972 Floyd [2] described an imagined interaction between a computer programmer and a formal program verification system that he believed might be feasible within the next decade. One of the main ideas in the scenario was for the computer to carry the burden of maintaining the consistency of specifications, programs, and lemmas following incremental changes. In 1978 Moriconi [3] developed and implemented a technique for this purpose based on a Hoare-style axiomatization of the programming language semantics. Most verification systems, past and present, are based at least implicitly on Hoare logic [4].

A proof of a program in Hoare logic is a sequence of steps, where each step is an instance of a Hoare axiom, a Hoare sentence derived from a previous step by a rule of inference, or a theorem in the underlying logic. Maintain-

ing consistency in the presence of change boils down to determining theoremhood in the underlying theory (which is no easier than determining functional correctness). The underlying logic is determined by the specification language. The existing languages that we are familiar with are undecidable and, moreover, there typically is insufficient theorem proving power to handle the formulas that arise in practice. The undecidable specification languages include Anna [5], [6], EHDM [7], Gypsy [8], Larch [9], [10], OBJ [11], [12], VDM [13], and Z [14].

Perry [15], [16] recently suggested a similar approach based on Hoare logic for extending configuration management systems. He attempts to simplify matters by using the subset relation instead of logical implication to relate assertions. This transliteration works if the specifications are properly encoded in set theory. But the encoding offers no apparent gain, since the formulas to be proved are no simpler than before. Truth maintenance systems (e.g., [17], [18]) provide a different way of thinking about the problem, but we are still left with the intractable problem of testing for theoremhood.

B. Structural Approaches

Qualitative information flow has been studied extensively in the field of computer security by Denning [19] and others.[1] A program's security can be certified at compile-time through a conservative interpretation of the information-flow relation. A variety of formalisms have been used for this purpose, including attribute grammars [21] and logical rules [22]. Representative security analysis tools are those of McHugh and Good [23] and Rushby [24].

Our research has a very different orientation than work in computer security. Our focus is on flows local to an operation and, most importantly, on nonlocal flows between operations. Work in security has focused almost exclusively on local flows. If every local flow in a system is secure, it is valid to conclude that the entire system is secure. Kemmerer [25] gives a technique for detecting covert channels from an abstract model of a system; the technique involves an information-flow closure with respect to the special model. The connection between his model and the program is left unspecified and the technique does not apply directly to programs.

Bergeretti and Carré [26] use the concept of information flow in program development to detect certain kinds of errors and anomalies. Their work is more limited than ours in that it is oriented toward intraprocedural flows, although they do present preliminary ideas for procedures without recursion, without globals, and with very conservative assumptions about parameters. They adopt a relational approach for computing all possible facts, many of which may not be relevant to the specific change. Their relational approach does not address the problem of providing flow justifications. Our logical approach supports the derivation of specific results justified explicitly by for-

[1]Classical information theory, developed by Shannon [20] and others, is concerned with the *amount* of information generated by a particular event. We are interested in the simpler question of whether *any* information is generated by an event.

mal proofs. We describe how to use the results of an analysis to reason about large-grain program objects, not just variables.

The information flow relation can be interpreted within a classical program flow-analysis framework. Only a crude interpretation can be provided using coarse-grain relations, such as the "calls" relation between procedures or the "uses" relation between modules. It appears that def/use chains could be put together across procedure boundaries to yield an interpretation equivalent to the one given in this paper. (A def/use chain represents the set of uses u of a variable x from a point p such that there is a path from p to u that does not redefine x). Intraprocedural def/use chains have been used by Podgurski and Clarke [27] in defining a general notion of variable dependence that seems to be equivalent to intraprocedural information flow.

Our logical approach has a number of advantages over a graph-based flow-anlysis framework that stem from differences in objectives. This paper focuses on the abstract information-flow relation, the specification and prototyping of an analysis technique, and on the explication of analysis results. In contrast, program flow analysis has been studied primarily for use in optimizing compilers or other settings in which low-level relations and efficiency are of primary importance. In fact, our inference system can be viewed as a specification for a def/use implementation of the closure. Our logic can directly provide flow justifications, which would require a significant extension to a flow analysis implementation.

Recent work by Horwitz, Reps, and Binkley [28] is somewhat related. They describe a complex but efficient flow-analysis algorithm for computing program slices, a concept originally introduced by Weiser [29]. A slice is the set of all statements and predicates of a program that affect a variable at a given point. The computation of a slice inherently has a backward orientation, whereas tracking the effects of changes has a forward orientation. However, the assertions computed by our rules can be used to determine slices.

III. Abstract Syntax

We begin by focusing on programs that consist of a collection of (global) variables, functions, and procedures. Procedures can refer to global variables; functions always behave as pure mathematical functions. Parameters of procedures have a value-result semantics (copy-in/copy-out). Three kinds of statements are treated: assignment, a looping construct, and a conditional.

Our logic does not depend on the concrete syntax of a particular programming language. Instead, it refers to an *abstract syntax* containing the features just described. The abstract syntax is defined in functional notation, specifically a many-sorted logic with subsorts. For example, the subsort declaration $Var \subseteq Expr$ means that every variable is an expression. Operators are defined in a mixfix syntax in which an underbar is a placeholder indicating where arguments should appear. This notation is borrowed from OBJ [12].

```
sorts
    Const Expr ExprList Name Param
    ParamKind ParamList PrimOp
    Program Stmt Unit Var
subsorts
    Var, Const ⊆ Expr
    PrimOp ⊆ Name
    Unit ⊆ Program
operators
    ExprList = List[Expr]

    _(_) : Name ExprList → Expr

    _ := _ : Var Expr → Stmt
    _(_) : Name ExprList → Stmt
    if _ then _ else _ fi : Expr Stmt Stmt → Stmt
    while _ do _ od : Expr Stmt → Stmt
    null : → Stmt
    _;_ : Stmt Stmt → Stmt

    value,value-result,result : → ParamKind
    _ _ : ParamKind Var → Param
    ParamList = List[Param]

    var_ : Var → Unit
    procedure _(_)_ : Name ParamList Stmt → Unit
    function _(_)_ : Name ParamList Stmt → Unit
    _ _ : Unit Program → Program
```

Fig. 1. Abstract syntax (without modules).

The abstract syntax for programs (without modules) is contained in Fig. 1. To simplify the discussion, we assume that procedures, functions, and globals have unique names. In addition, locals of different procedures are distinct.

The discussion does not include structured objects and expressions with side effects, although we believe that our logic could be adapted to analyze them. Pointers and call-by-reference parameters can be added, but not as easily. Types are omitted from the abstract syntax because they are not used in the analysis.

IV. Definition of Information Flow for Statements

A. Notation

We consistently use certain variables to range over particular classes of objects. The metavariable c ranges over constants of sort *Const*. Letters u, v, x, y, and z are metavariables ranging over variables and constants in the language. We let *primop* range over the primitive operators of the language (i.e., those that are not user defined), e, t_i ($i > 0$), and b (for boolean) range over expression instances, and S and S_i range over statement instances. The letters f and p range over the names of functions and procedures, whose parameters are of kind k_i. Finally, the letter $\mathcal{C}$ denotes a context in which a particular analysis takes place. These naming conventions are summarized in Fig. 2.

The predicates in Fig. 3 will be used in defining information flow for the constructs in the abstract syntax. Two predicates are needed for statements, one for asserting flows across the statement and another for asserting which variables are modified directly or indirectly by the statement. Information can flow into an expression, so a predicate is needed to describe such flows. Interprocedural flow assertions model the variable bindings that result from a procedure call. The relation $\Rightarrow_f$ denotes a flow from an actual to a formal and $\Rightarrow_b$ denotes a formal to actual

346

Notation	Sort
c	Const
u, v, x, y, z	Var or Const
$primop$	PrimOp
e, t_i, b	Expr
S, S_i	Stmt
f, p	Name
k_i	ParamKind
C	Context

Fig. 2. Summary of naming conventions.

Notation	Interpretation (with respect to context C)
$C \triangleright [S] x \Rightarrow y$	the value of x before execution of S affects the value of y after execution of S
$C \triangleright [S] \bmod x$	execution of statement S may modify the value of variable x
$C \triangleright x \Rightarrow \text{val}(e)$	the value of x affects the value of expression e
$C \triangleright [S] x \Rightarrow_f y$	intersubprogram forward flow from formal x to actual y for call S
$C \triangleright [S] x \Rightarrow_b y$	interprocedural backward flow from actual x to formal y for call S
$C \triangleright \text{global}(x)$	x is a global variable
$C \triangleright \text{value}(p, i)$	the ith formal parameter of procedure p is a value parameter
$C \triangleright \text{result}(p, i)$	the ith formal parameter of procedure p is a result parameter
$C \triangleright \text{param}(p, i, x)$	the ith formal parameter of procedure p is x
$C \triangleright \text{func}(p, S)$	p is a function with body S
$C \triangleright \text{proc}(p, S)$	p is a procedure with body S

Fig. 3. Summary of predicates used in inference rules.

flow. The relations apply to implicit parameters, i.e., globals.

The context C is used in assertions to denote collected assumptions about the entities in a program. A context is a pair in which the first element is the set of global variables and the second is a mapping from procedure or function names to their descriptions. Specifically,

$$\text{Context} = \text{Globals} \times$$
$$(\text{Name} \rightarrow \text{Kind} \times \text{ParamList} \times \text{Stmt})$$

where the sort *Globals* is a set of variables and *Kind* indicates whether the name is that of a procedure or function. The mapping also specifies the parameter list and body of the named entity.

Inference rules are used to axiomatize the basic information-flow predicates in Fig. 3. Inference rules describe how assertions can be derived. An inference rule of the form

$$\frac{P_1 \cdots P_n}{C}$$

states that conclusion C can be inferred from the premises P_i. Typically, each P_i and C is an instance of a predicate in Fig. 3. If a rule has no premises, we write it without the horizontal bar. The rules are syntax-directed; at least one axiom or rule is given for each construct in the abstract syntax. The context referred to in an assertion must be derived from a program using the rules given in the Appendix. We have implemented a program analyzer in Common Lisp that directly applies the rules given below to compute assertions.

The style of our inference rules is inspired by Plotkin's "structural operational semantics" [30]. This style of formalism is intended to produce concise, comprehensible definitions that are independent of internal representation details. The formalism has been used as a common framework for specifying, among other things, type checking,

type inference, translation, and interpretation [31], and it is becoming a popular notation for language-directed specifications.

B. Mathematical Definition of Information Flow Predicates

The meaning of information flow can be illustrated with a few simple examples. Execution of the assignment statement **x := y** causes a flow from **y** to **x**. Execution of the conditional

if x = 0 then y := 0 else y := 1

causes a flow from **x** to **y**. A procedure call initiates a set of flows that reflect the actual/formal parameter bindings.

Before defining information flow, we introduce some sorts and functions. Let the sort *Val* denote the values of variables. The sort *Env* consists of mappings from variable names to values. The operations *val* and *set* retrieve and set the value, respectively, of a variable in an environment. The function *eval* evaluates an expression in a given environment and context; expressions have no side-effects. Function *exec* executes a statement in a given environment and context, and produces a new environment. Nonterminating execution produces the value "undefined." The signature for the operations is given below.

sorts Val Env
operators
    val : Var Env → Val
    set : Var Val Env → Env
    eval : Expr Env Context → Val
    exec : Stmt Env Context → Env

We now make the following definitions:

$$C \triangleright [S]x \Rightarrow y \text{ iff } (\exists env: \text{Env})(\exists v: \text{Val})$$
$$\left[\text{val}(y, \text{exec}(S, env, C)) \right.$$
$$\left. \neq \text{val}(y, \text{exec}(S, \text{set}(x, v, env), C)) \right]$$

$$C \triangleright x \Rightarrow \text{val}(e) \text{ iff } (\exists env: \text{Env})(\exists v: \text{Val})$$
$$\left[\text{eval}(e, env, C) \right.$$
$$\left. \neq \text{eval}(t, \text{set}(x, v, env), C) \right]$$

$$C \triangleright [S] \bmod x \text{ iff } (\exists env: \text{Env})\left[\text{val}(x, env) \right.$$
$$\left. \neq \text{val}(x, \text{exec}(S, env, C)) \right].$$

These are the exact mathematical definitions of the first three predicates in Fig. 3.

The first definition says that there is flow from x to y provided the value of y after execution of S differs when only the value of x is changed in the initial environment *env*. The second definition says that there is a flow from x to expression e if the value of e differs when only the value of x is changed. The third definition says that S modifies x provided the value of x after execution of S can be different from its value before.

Our inference rules approximate the mathematical definitions. We do not include the rules for defining the *mod* relation. They are straightforward and give a relatively exact interprocedural version of the "modifies" relation commonly used for program optimization [32].

The fact that the information flow relation is not transitive in the usual sense is illustrated by the example below.

Example 1 (Intransitivity of information flow): Consider the following program fragment:

procedure addinc (value-result sum, value-result i);
    add (sum, i); inc (i)

procedure add (value-result a, value-result b);
    a := a+b

procedure inc (value-result z);
    add (z, 1)

Suppose that we want to know whether a change to the value of variable **sum** can affect the value of variable **z**. The call to **add** in **addinc** gives a flow from **sum** to **a** and the call from **inc** to **add** gives a backward flow from **a** to **z**. Hence, a flow from **sum** to **z** is in the transitive closure. But there is no execution sequence for which the value of **sum** affects **z**. The problem, of course, is that transitive flows are determined in part by the flow of control. For procedures, the interplay between control and information flow can be complex. □

C. Approximate Logic for Statements

Any constant or variable that appears in an expression affects the value of the expression.

expr-var

$$\mathcal{C} \triangleright x \Rightarrow val(x) \qquad x: Var$$

expr-const

$$\mathcal{C} \triangleright c \Rightarrow val(c)$$

-expr

$$\frac{\mathcal{C} \triangleright x \Rightarrow val(t_i)}{\mathcal{C} \triangleright x \Rightarrow val(primop(t_1, \cdots, t_n))} \qquad i = 1, \cdots, n.$$

The first rule says that any change in the value of x affects the value of x. The second says that a constant affects its value. Strictly speaking, a constant cannot change, so

___

if-cond

$$\frac{\mathcal{C} \triangleright x \Rightarrow val(b) \quad (\mathcal{C} \triangleright [S_1] \bmod y \vee \mathcal{C} \triangleright [S_2] \bmod y)}{\mathcal{C} \triangleright [\text{if } b \text{ then } S_1 \text{ else } S_2 \text{ fi}]x \Rightarrow y}$$

___

there can be no information flow from a constant to something else. We include this rule because the programmer may edit a constant in a program, in which case we may want to see what depends on the constant. The third rule

says that a change that affects any component of an expression affects the value of the expression. The sort *PrimOp* denotes built-in functions; user-defined functions are handled differently.

Anything that affects the value of the right-hand side of an assignment affects the value of the variable on the left-hand side.

:=

$$\frac{\mathcal{C} \triangleright x \Rightarrow val(e)}{\mathcal{C} \triangleright [y := e]x \Rightarrow y}$$

It also is necessary to specify invariants over assignments. In particular, if an assignment does not modify some variable (i.e., the variable does not appear on the left-hand side), then the value of the variable before the assignment is said to affect its value afterwards.

not-mod

$$\frac{\neg (\mathcal{C} \triangleright [S] \bmod x)}{\mathcal{C} \triangleright [S]x \Rightarrow x}$$

In practice, S can be restricted to be an assignment, the null statement, or a procedure call. Note that constants are always invariant across statements.

Statement composition is handled by the following rule:

seq

$$\frac{\mathcal{C} \triangleright [S_1]x \Rightarrow y \quad \mathcal{C} \triangleright [S_2]y \Rightarrow z}{\mathcal{C} \triangleright [S_1; S_2]x \Rightarrow z}.$$

Two flows are composed when the intermediate variable is the same and the two statements appear in sequence. In the absence of the not-mod rule, the composition rule could not be applied when one statement in a sequence does not modify a variable modified by another statement in the sequence.

Conditional statements are broken into two cases. The first deals with the flows on the two branches of the if-then-else. The second deals with the flow from the condition through the branches.

if

$$\frac{\mathcal{C} \triangleright [S_i]x \Rightarrow y}{\mathcal{C} \triangleright [\text{if } b \text{ then } S_1 \text{ else } S_2 \text{ fi}]x \Rightarrow y} \qquad i = 1 \text{ or } i = 2$$

The first rule says that the flows created by the statements in the branches are created by the conditional statement as a whole. The first premise of the second rule says that a variable x can affect the choice of the branch. The second premise says that variable y is affected by one of the branches. In this situation, x indirectly affects y. This rule does not take into account the fact that y could have the same value on both branches.

The while rules deal with three possibilities.

while-null

$$\mathcal{C} \triangleright [\text{while } b \text{ do } S \text{ od}]x \Rightarrow x$$

while

$$\frac{\mathcal{C} \triangleright [\text{while } b \text{ do } S \text{ od}]x \Rightarrow y \quad \mathcal{C} \triangleright [S]y \Rightarrow z}{\mathcal{C} \triangleright [\text{while } b \text{ do } S \text{ od}]x \Rightarrow z}$$

while-cond

$$\frac{\mathcal{C} \triangleright [\text{while } b \text{ do } S \text{ od}]x \Rightarrow y \quad \mathcal{C} \triangleright y \Rightarrow \text{val}(b) \quad \mathcal{C} \triangleright [S] \text{ mod } z}{\mathcal{C} \triangleright [\text{while } b \text{ do } S \text{ od}]x \Rightarrow z}$$

The first rule handles the situation in which the body S of the while loop is never executed. This means that the effect of the statement is exactly the same as the null statement. The second rule is recursive. If a flow from x to y is created by the while statement and a flow from y to z is created by the body S of the while statement, then the two flows can be composed. The third rule also is recursive, indicating that a transitive flow occurs when y affects

---

func (expression)

$$\frac{\mathcal{C} \triangleright \text{func}(f, S) \quad \mathcal{C} \triangleright [f(t_1, \cdots, t_n)]u \Rightarrow_f x \quad \mathcal{C} \triangleright [S]x \Rightarrow \text{value}}{\mathcal{C} \triangleright u \Rightarrow \text{val}(f(t_1, \cdots, t_n))}$$

---

condition C. The condition governs whether S is executed and therefore affects any variable modified by S.

We next deal with parameter passing in functions and procedures. Before stating the function and procedure rules, we first introduce rules for parameter passing. The first two rules deal with the transmission of values from a call site and the last two deal with return values. Globals and constants are implicit parameters at every call site. They are transmitted by the rule

$$\frac{\mathcal{C} \triangleright \text{global}(x) \vee x\text{: Const}}{\mathcal{C} \triangleright [p(t_1, \cdots, t_n)]x \Rightarrow_f x}$$

which asserts that the value of a global or constant at the call site is the same as the value when the called procedure is entered. The rule

asserts that a flow from a variable u into an actual parameter t_i is transmitted to the corresponding formal value parameter x_i. Globals are returned to themselves, analogously to the forward transmission of globals.

$$\frac{\mathcal{C} \triangleright \text{global}(x)}{\mathcal{C} \triangleright [p(t_1, \cdots, t_n)]x \Rightarrow_b x}$$

Result parameters of procedures are transmitted back to the actual parameter.

$$\frac{\mathcal{C} \triangleright \text{result}(p, i) \quad \mathcal{C} \triangleright \text{param}(p, i, x) \quad t_i\text{: Var}}{\mathcal{C} \triangleright [p(t_1, \cdots, t_n)]x \Rightarrow_b t_i}$$
$$i = 1, \cdots, n$$

The first two premises assert that x is the ith parameter of procedure p and x is also a result parameter. The third premise requires that t_i be a variable; from the conclusion, t_i must be an actual parameter in the call to p. Under these conditions, we can conclude that the call to p results in a backward flow from formal x to actual t_i.

We can now define the information-flow semantics of function and procedure calls. The rule for function calls is

The first premise checks that f is a function and S is its body. The second premise asserts that the call to f causes a forward flow from u to x; by the parameter passing rules, u and x are the same constant, the same global, or describe a flow from an actual to a formal. The last premise asserts that there is flow from x to the special program variable called *value*, which is used to indicate the return value of a function. The conclusion says that the value of u affects the value of the call.

The procedure call rule is complicated by the possibility of multiple backward flows. The idea behind the rule is that a forward flow into a procedure can be passed through the procedure through transitive local flows and then back to the caller via a backward flow.

$$\frac{\mathcal{C} \triangleright \text{value}(p, i) \quad \mathcal{C} \triangleright \text{param}(p, i, x) \quad \mathcal{C} \triangleright u \Rightarrow \text{val}(t_i)}{\mathcal{C} \triangleright [p(t_1, \cdots, t_n)]u \Rightarrow_f x} \quad i = 1, \cdots, n$$

proc (statement)

$$\frac{\mathbb{C} \rhd \text{proc}(p, S) \quad \mathbb{C} \rhd [p(t_1, \cdots, t_n)]u \Rightarrow_f x \quad \mathbb{C} \rhd [S]x \Rightarrow y \quad \mathbb{C} \rhd [p(t_1, \cdots, t_n)]y \Rightarrow_b v}{\mathbb{C} \rhd [p(t_1, \cdots, t_n)]u \Rightarrow v}$$

The first premise asserts that p is a procedure and S is its body. The second premise asserts that the call to p results in a forward flow from u to x. The third says that there is a local flow from x to y. The last requires a backward return flow from y to v. From these four conditions, we can infer that the call to p has the net effect of causing a flow from u to v.

V. VARIABLES AT PROGRAM POINTS

The assertions in Fig. 3 involve variables that denote values before and after a given program statement. They do not allow us to make assertions that relate variables at two arbitrary points in a program. In addition, we cannot ask whether a change to a local variable of a given procedure can affect the value of a local of another procedure, since the locals are in different scopes. To provide this capability, we provide a mechanism for introducing names, which have global scope, for the values of variables at specific points in a program. The new names are called *label variables* of sort *LabelVar* (a subsort of *Var*). For the purposes of this paper, a variable ending in "0" is a label variable, otherwise it is an ordinary variable. One way to introduce label variables involves modifying the program; another requires no modification but involves new inference rules. Both approaches are presented below.

For a given variable and point, we may be interested in tracing flows forward, backward, or both. To trace forward from a point between two statements, we insert the assignment $x := \exp(x, x0)$ where x is the variable of interest and $x0$ is a new unique label variable. Primitive operator **exp** has the property that its value depends on x and $x0$. This follows from a direct application of the expression rule (**expr**). To trace backward, we insert $x0 := \exp(x, x0)$ and both are needed to trace both directions. An example is given in the next section.

Although this approach is simple, it is unattractive in that we must modify the program. This is particularly serious if we are interested in a large number of program points. Fortunately, modification of a program is not necessary, as we can introduce label variables during the inference process. For this purpose, we introduce the following rules.

$$\frac{\mathbb{C} \rhd [S]x \Rightarrow y}{\mathbb{C} \rhd [S]l \Rightarrow y}$$

$$\frac{\mathbb{C} \rhd [S]x \Rightarrow y}{\mathbb{C} \rhd [S]x \Rightarrow l}$$

$$\mathbb{C} \rhd l \Rightarrow \text{val}(e)$$

where l is a label variable. It is necessary to record the association among label variable, the renamed ordinary variable, and the statement or expression in order to properly interpret results of an analysis. For example, in the first rule, l represents the value of x before execution of statement S. Renamings must be complete and uniform for this approach to be equivalent to the previous one that introduced assignments.

Label variables have two important properties. The first is that they are treated as globals by the parameter passing rules, allowing them to be moved from scope to scope. Second, there is always a flow from a label variable to itself across all statements. That is,

$$\mathbb{C} \rhd [S]l \Rightarrow l.$$

This is guaranteed in the first approach by the choice of assignments and in the second because no assignments to l can exist. This fact is used to propagate labeled flows through statement sequences.

VI. DEDUCING THE EFFECTS OF PROGRAM CHANGES

We want to ask questions about changes to a number of different kinds of objects: variables (including globals), procedures, functions, and parameterless modules. Questions involving large-grain objects are reduced to questions involving only our assertions about statements, possibly involving label variables. For example, a change to variable v affects module M provided v flows into a variable associated with M. In general, the questions of interest have the following pattern: does a change to object X affect the behavior of object Y?

A query can be any first-order formula with finite quantification. This means that we can quantify over the objects in a program, such as its modules or procedures. An analysis of the program (using the inference rules of the previous sections) produces all of the ground (variable-free) facts about the program. These facts are positive and facts not in this set are assumed to be false. First-order queries are defined recursively in terms of the ground facts. For a specific program, sorts are interpreted with respect to the objects in the current program. For example, x: *Var* indicates that x ranges over the finite set of variables in the current program, not the countably infinite set of variables that could occur in a program. Formulas in this section will make use of four new relations, which are summarized in Fig. 4.

We will find it convenient to have notation for asserting that execution of a procedure or function creates a certain flow. For a name P, we have

$$\mathbb{C} \rhd [P]x \Rightarrow y \text{ iff } (\exists S)[\mathbb{C} \rhd \text{sub}(P, S)$$
$$\wedge \; \mathbb{C} \rhd [S]x \Rightarrow y]$$

Notation	Interpretation (with respect to context C)
$C \triangleright \text{orig}(l, x)$	x is the variable associated with label variable l
$C \triangleright \text{varof}(x, p)$	x is a variable referenced in procedure or function p
$C \triangleright \text{sub}(p, S)$	p is a procedure or function with body S
$C \triangleright \text{subof}(p, M)$	procedure or function p is in module M

Fig. 4. Summary of predicates used in questions.

This says that there is a flow from x to y for P if and only if P is a procedure or function subprogram in context C and there is a flow from x to y in its body S.

Example 2 (Absence of an interprocedural flow):
Consider again the following program.

procedure addinc (value-result sum, value-result i);
   add (sum, i); inc (i)

procedure add (value-result a, value-result b);
   a := a+b

procedure inc (value-result z);
   add (z, 1)

Our implementation of the inference rules produces the following assertions for the body of **addinc**.

```
0: [add (sum, i); inc (i)]i = > sum
1: [add (sum, i); inc (i)]sum = > sum
2: [add (sum, i); inc (i)]i = > i
3: [add (sum, i); inc (i)]1 = > i
4: [add (sum, i); inc (i)]1 = > 1
```

Suppose that we are interested in whether the value of sum on entry to addinc affects the value of **i** on exit. Formally, we want to know whether $C \triangleright [addinc]sum \Rightarrow i$ and it is easy to see that it is false. Note that there is no need for label variables in this example, since the basic assertion deals with before and after values for **addinc**. Because approximations are conservative, we know that there really is no flow from **sum to i**. □

Example 3 (Presence of an interprecedural flow):
Suppose that we are interested in whether the value of **i**

before the call to **inc** affects the value of **a** on entry to **add**. To answer this question, we introduce label variables **i0** and **a0**.

var i0, a0;

procedure addinc (value-result sum, value-result i);
   add (sum,); i := exp (i, i0); inc (i)

procedure add (value-result a, value-result b);
   a0 := exp (a, a0); a := a+b

procedure inc (value-result z); ´
   add (z, i)

The new assignment in **addinc** associates **i0** with the value of **i** before the call to **inc**. The one in **add** associates the value of **a** upon entry with **a0**. The assignments have a different form because **i0** is to be propagated forwards and **a0** backwards.

We want to find a procedure P in our program such that $C \triangleright [P]i0 \Rightarrow a0$. Of the ground facts generated by the computer, here are the ones for **addinc**.

```
 0: [. . .]i0 = > i0
 1: [. . .]i0 = > a0
 2: [. . .]i0 = > i
 3: [. . .]i = > a0
 4: [. . .]i = > i
 5: [. . .]a0 = > a0
 6: [. . .]sum = > a0
 7: [. . .]sum = > sum
 8: [. . .]i = > sum
 9: [. . .]1 = > i
10: [. . .]1 = > 1
```

Ellipses denote the body of **addinc**.

We can see that the second assertion validates the desired flow, i.e., it proves $C \triangleright [addinc]i0 \Rightarrow a0$. Since this is a positive assertion, there is no guarantee that the flow actually occurs. Below is a formal machine-generated proof that validates this assertion.

Proof of [add (sum, i); i := exp (i, i0); inc (i)]i0 = > a0

(1)	[add (sum, i)]i0 = > i0	- not-mod i0
	Also proc[add (sum, i)]i0 = > f i0 [a0 := exp (a, a0); a := a+b]i0 = > i0 = > b i0	
(2)	i0 = > [i0]	- expr-var
(3)	i0 = > [exp (i, i0)]	- expr[2] (2)
(4)	[i := exp (i, i0)]i0 = > i	- := (3)
(5)	[add (sum, i); i := exp (i, i0)]i0 = > i	- seq (1) (4)
(6)	[inc (i)]i = > f z	- = > f[1]
(7)	[add (z, 1)]z = > f a	- = > f[1]
(8)	a = > [a]	- expr-var
(9)	a = > [exp (a, a0)]	- expr[1] (8)
(10)	[a0 := exp (a, a0)]a = > a0	- := (9)
(11)	[a := a+b]a0 = > a0	- not-mod a0
(12)	[a0 := exp (a, a0); a := a+b]a = > a0	- seq (10) (11)
(13)	[add (z, 1)]z = > a0	- proc[1->] (7) z = > f a (12) a0 = > b a0

(14) [inc (i)]i = > a0
(15) [add (sum, i); i := exp (i, i0); inc (i)]i0 = > a0

- proc[1->] (6) i = > f z (13) a0 = > b a0
- seq (5) (14)

The justifications are keyed to the labels on the rules. The proof shows how the flow from **i0** to **a0** actually occurs, including the relevant control path. Steps (1)–(5) establish that **i0**, starting at the new assignment in **addinc**, flows into the value of **i** immediately before the call to **inc**. Steps (8)–(12) verify that there is a flow from the value of **a** on entry to **add** to the point associated with **a0**. Steps (7) and (13) are assertions about the body of **inc**, verifying an interprocedural flow from formal **z** of **inc** to **a0**. Steps (6) and (14) verify that the call to **inc** creates a flow from **i** to **a0**. The last step composes the assertions at (5) and (14) creating the desired flow for the body of **addinc**. □

We now consider more general questions. In the formulas below, free variables in formulas can be instantiated to form a specific question. For simplicity, we assume that label variables have been introduced for every variable at every program point. (In practice, the number of label variables can be reduced based on the particular question.)

Example 4 (Effect on a variable): Suppose that we are interested in whether a change to a variable x affects a variable y. The formula

$$(\exists P: \text{Name})(\exists u, v: \text{LabelVar})[\mathcal{C} \rhd \text{orig}(u, x)$$
$$\wedge \mathcal{C} \rhd \text{orig}(v, y) \wedge \mathcal{C} \rhd [P]u \Rightarrow v],$$

where x and y are free, says that a change to a variable x can affect the value of a variable y if a change to a label variable u associated with x can affect a label variable v associated with y when some procedure P is executed.

Our earlier question about whether *sum* affects *i* can be stated as an instance of this formula. Substituting *sum* for x and *i* for y, we obtain

$$(\exists P: \text{Name})(\exists u, v: \text{LabelVar})[\mathcal{C} \rhd \text{orig}(u, sum)$$
$$\wedge \mathcal{C} \rhd \text{orig}(v, i) \wedge \mathcal{C} \rhd [P]u \Rightarrow v].$$

We did not use label variables before, but this formulation is equivalent. □

Example 5 (Effect on a procedure): To ask whether a change to a variable x affects an arbitrary procedure P, we use the defining formula

$$(\exists R: \text{Name})(\exists u, v: \text{LabelVar})(\exists y: \text{Var})$$
$$[\mathcal{C} \rhd \text{orig}(u, x) \wedge \mathcal{C} \rhd \text{orig}(v, y)$$
$$\wedge \mathcal{C} \rhd \text{varof}(y, P) \wedge \mathcal{C} \rhd [R]u \Rightarrow v],$$

where x and P are free. Observe that R can be any procedure, including P. It will be different from P when the procedure that owns x is not called, directly, or indirectly, by P.

If instead we are interested in whether the value of x at a certain point affects a procedure P, we would use the formula

$$(\exists R: \text{Name})(\exists v: \text{LabelVar})(\exists y: \text{Var})$$
$$[\mathcal{C} \rhd \text{orig}(v, y) \wedge \mathcal{C} \rhd \text{varof}(y, P)$$
$$\wedge \mathcal{C} \rhd [R]u \Rightarrow v]$$

where u is free and to be instantiated with the label variable for x at the point of interest. □

Example 6 (Effect on a module): A change to a variable x can affect module M if the change affects a procedure contained in M. That is, we must prove an instance of

$$(\exists P, R: \text{Proc})(\exists u, v: \text{LabelVar})(\exists y: \text{Var})$$
$$[\mathcal{C} \rhd \text{orig}(u, x) \wedge \mathcal{C} \rhd \text{orig}(v, y)$$
$$\wedge \mathcal{C} \rhd \text{varof}(y, P) \wedge \mathcal{C} \rhd \text{subof}(P, M)$$
$$\wedge \mathcal{C} \rhd [R]u \Rightarrow v],$$

where x and M are free. □.

VII. COMPLEXITY

The time complexity of our inference algorithm is linear in the size of the program and polynomial with respect to the total number of variables and constants. For a large program, the size of the program usually should dominate.

In abstract syntax trees, different copies of the same syntactic structure are treated as distinct. The parameters used in the following analysis are given below.

c Number of constants in program.
g Number of global variables in program.
l Largest number of locals in a procedure.
v Number of vars ($g + l$).
s Program size (number of nodes in tree).

Label variables are counted as globals.

The basic evaluation strategy involves an initial pass to compute invariant or static parameter passing relations, the *mod* relation, and the initial assertions, followed by the application of a worklist-based inference algorithm. Most of the rules for the parameter passing relations can be applied in an initial pass of the program, since they are invariant over the inference process. The cost of this is small in comparison to total cost, so the details are omitted.

The inference process is carried out by a worklist algorithm. The elements of the worklist are assertions of the form $\mathcal{C} \rhd [S]x \Rightarrow y$, $\mathcal{C} \rhd x \Rightarrow \text{val}(e)$, or $\mathcal{C} \rhd [p(t_1, \cdots, t_n)]u \Rightarrow_f x$. The worklist is initialized by a first scan of the program that applies the direct rules requiring no antecedent conditions (such as **expr-var**, **expr-const**, :=, and **not-mod**). The worklist of new assertions is processed until it is empty. When an assertion is removed from the worklist, all possible derived assertions are created and the new ones are added to the worklist.

The total cost of applying the inference rules is bounded at a given node by the cost of systematically applying the rules for all possible subsidiary assertions. The bound on the total number of assertions for any program element is $(c + v)v + c$. The worklist algorithm propagates new assertions in a complex pattern, but the total cost paid is just the sum of the incremental costs of exploring the possible new consequences of each subsidiary assertion at each node. For example, in the **seq** rule, if a new assertion $\mathcal{C} \rhd [S_1]x \Rightarrow y$ is considered, we need to find all assertions $\mathcal{C} \rhd [S_2]y \Rightarrow z$ that might be used with this assertion in the rule. There can be at most v such assertions and so the incremental cost is v. There are $(c + v)v + c$ possible assertions so the total cost is roughly $(c + v)v^2$ (ignoring some special cases associated with constants). The analysis is the same for an assertion coming in on the right, since the cost is always the total number of possible antecedents of the rule.

The **while** rule is costly since the incremental cost of an assertion is the cost of doing a simple transitive closure process. (This probably could be improved with a more sophisticated algorithm.) The cost of applying inference rules at a **while** node is $(c + v)v^3 + cv^2 + c$.

The total cost of information flow analysis is the sum of the costs of all the program elements:

$$O\big(s(c + v)v^3\big).$$

If there are no while loops or no recursive procedures, the cost would be

$$O\big(s(c + v)v^2\big).$$

We have assumed that the cost of adjoining a variable to a set of variables is constant. In practice, the cost may depend on implementation details. The actual cost may be $c + v$, which would be an additional factor in the above cost formulas.

VIII. EXTENSIONS

A. Parameterized Modules

A module consists of variables, functions, and procedures. A parameter to a module can be a variable, function, or procedure. Functions and procedures that are passed as values cannot reference global variables.

The basic idea for the analysis of modules is to use assumptions about the parameters of a module to derive conditional results (summary information) that depend on those assumptions. For a particular instantiation of the parameterized module, we can discharge assumptions to get specific unconditional results. When doing analysis under assumptions A, the existing rules are used along with some special rules that involve conditions in A. If an assertion P is a result of this analysis, then the conditional summary is $A \supset P$. We take this approach for simplicity; it would be better to associate assumptions with individual assertions.

In the analysis of variable parameters, we must know which formals correspond to the same actuals. The assertion $x \equiv y$ says that formals x and y are instantiated with

the same actual variable. The assumptions for variables are a conjunction of assertions of this form.

The special rules say that equivalent variable parameters can be interchanged in assertions. One such rule is

$$\frac{\mathcal{C} \rhd [S]u \Rightarrow x}{\mathcal{C} \rhd [S]u \Rightarrow y} \quad \text{if } x \equiv y.$$

The assumptions for procedures are of the form

$$[p(x_1, \cdots, x_n)]x_i \Rightarrow x_j$$
$$[p(x_1, \cdots, x_n)]c \Rightarrow x_j$$

where the x_i are considered to be specific variables and c is any constant. The first assertion says that a call to procedure p creates a flow from the ith parameter to the jth parameter. The second assertion describes a flow from a constant. An example of a special rule for procedures is

$$\frac{\mathcal{C} \rhd u \Rightarrow \mathrm{val}(t_i) \quad t_j : \mathrm{Var}}{\mathcal{C} \rhd [p(t_1, \cdots, t_n)]u \Rightarrow t_j}$$
$$\text{if } \mathcal{C} \rhd [p(x_1, \cdots, x_n)]x_i \Rightarrow x_j.$$

The rules for functions are similar.

There can be a problem with combinatorial explosion since arbitrary subsets of the conditions on the parameters may appear as conditions in the results of analysis of the parameterized object. In practice, it may be preferable to wait until the actual parameters are given before attempting an analysis.

B. A Difficult Example

Weiser's paper on slicing [28] presents an example which shows the limitations of the method presented in that paper. The fundamental problem in the example appears not to have been addressed in the literature. The same problem can occur when reasoning about information flows.

Here is Weiser's example:

```
A := constant
WHILE P(k) DO
   IF Q(C) THEN BEGIN
      B := A
      X := 1
   ELSE BEGIN
      C := B
      Y := 2
      END
   K := K + 1
   END
Z := X + Y
WRITE(Z)
```

Our analysis technique would indicate incorrectly that there is a flow from **constant** to **Z**. However, any execution path where the value of **A** has affected the value of **C**, in which case the value of **A** might indirectly affect the value of **X** or **Y** (and hence **Z**), both **X** and **Y** have already been assigned constant values that are not changed by either branch of the conditional. Therefore, no conditional flow from **A** to **Z** can occur.

To correctly analyze this program, it is necessary to keep track of the information flows that occur *together* along the same path and to require, for conditional flows, that there be a different modification of the dependent variable in the two branches.

Let

$$\mathcal{C} \triangleright [S]x \rightarrow y$$

have definition

$$\mathcal{C} \triangleright [S]x \rightarrow y \text{ iff } \forall c: \text{Env}\big[\text{val}(x, c)$$
$$= \text{val}(y, \text{exec}(S, c, \mathcal{C}))\big]$$

which asserts that execution of S has the logical effect of the assignment "$y := x$". We treat $x \rightarrow y$ as a separate syntactic entity that can occur in more complex expressions.

The special connectives $\wedge$ and $\vee_U$ (where U is, in general, a set of variables) have similar properties to the familiar logical connectives, such as commutative and associative laws (the details are tricky for $\vee_U$). The general form of a statement assertion is

$$\mathcal{C} \triangleright [S]A$$

where A is formed using $x \rightarrow y$ assertions and the $\wedge$ and $\vee_U$ connectives. During analysis, a single assertion of this form is derived for each statement. An analysis successively refines the assertion until a fixpoint is reached.

An expression of the form $A \vee_U B$ corresponds to a logical expression of the form $(C(U) \wedge A) \vee (\neg C(U) \wedge B)$, where $C(U)$ is the predicate of a conditional expression.

The flow assertion $x \rightarrow y$ indicates an explicit nonconditional flow. Given an assertion $\mathcal{C} \triangleright [S]A$, there is a conditional dependence on a variable x if $\vee_U$ occurs in A and $x \in U$. The variables modified (i.e., occurring on the right of a $\rightarrow$) in the arguments to the occurrence of $\vee_U$ are conditionally dependent on x.

The following rules are used to analyze the program.

$$\frac{\mathcal{C} \triangleright [S]A \quad \mathcal{C} \triangleright [S]B}{\mathcal{C} \triangleright [S]A \wedge B}$$

$$\frac{\neg \mathcal{C} \triangleright [S] \bmod x}{\mathcal{C} \triangleright [S]x \rightarrow x}$$

$$\mathcal{C} \triangleright [y := x]x \rightarrow y$$

$$\frac{v \neq y}{\mathcal{C} \triangleright [y := x]v \rightarrow v}$$

$$\frac{\mathcal{C} \triangleright [S_1]A \quad \mathcal{C} \triangleright [S_2]B}{\mathcal{C} \triangleright [S_1; S_2](A; B)}$$

$$\frac{\mathcal{C} \triangleright U \Rightarrow \text{val}(b) \quad \mathcal{C} \triangleright [S_1]A \quad \mathcal{C} \triangleright [S_2]B}{\mathcal{C} \triangleright [\text{if } b \text{ then } S_1 \text{ else } S_2 \text{ fi}](A \vee_U B)}$$

In the last rule, U may be a set of variables. The last occurrence of "$;$" in the preceding rule is a new operator satisfying the distributive laws

$$(A \vee_U B); C = (A; C) \vee_U (B; C)$$

$$C; (A \vee_U B) = (C; A) \vee_{(C;U)} (C; B)$$

where $C; U$ is the inverse image of the set of variables in U under the basic flow mappings in C. (It can be arranged that C is a conjunction of these by always applying the first distributive law first). If A and B are conjunctions of basic $\rightarrow$ assertions, then $A; B$ is a conjunction of basic $\rightarrow$ assertions consisting of the assertions obtained by chaining assertions from A with assertions from B. That is, if $x \rightarrow y$ is in A and $y \rightarrow z$ is in B, then $A; B$ includes $x \rightarrow z$.

A critical property of $\vee_U$ is the following idempotence law

$$A \vee_U A = A.$$

This captures the idea that if there is no difference in the two branches or cases of a conditional, then there is really no conditionality.

A simple example of the problem in Weiser's program is illustrated by the following program fragment.

if q (c) then b := a; x := 1 else c := b; y := 2 fi;
if q (c) then b := a; x := 1 else c := b; y := 2 fi;
if q (c) then b := a; x := 1 else c := b; y := 2 fi;

We are interested in whether there is a conditional flow from **a** to **x** or **y**. If we analyze this program fragment, we derive several assertions, including

$$\mathcal{C} \triangleright [b := a; x := 1](a \rightarrow a \wedge a \rightarrow b \wedge c \rightarrow c \wedge 1$$
$$\rightarrow x \wedge y \rightarrow y)$$

$$\mathcal{C} \triangleright [c := b; y := 2](a \rightarrow a \wedge b \rightarrow b \wedge b \rightarrow c \wedge x$$
$$\rightarrow x \wedge 2 \rightarrow y)$$

$$\mathcal{C} \triangleright [\text{if } q(c) \text{ then } b := a; x := 1 \text{ else } c := b; y := 2 \text{ fi}]$$
$$(a \rightarrow a \wedge a \rightarrow b \wedge c \rightarrow c \wedge 1 \rightarrow x \wedge y \rightarrow y)$$
$$\vee_{\{c\}}(a \rightarrow a \wedge b \rightarrow b \wedge b \rightarrow c \wedge x \rightarrow x \wedge 2 \rightarrow y)$$

These assertions precisely describe the effects of parts of the program fragment.

Analysis of one if statement gives

$$(a \rightarrow a \wedge a \rightarrow b \wedge c \rightarrow c \wedge 1 \rightarrow x \wedge y \rightarrow y)$$
$$\vee_{\{c\}}(a \rightarrow a \wedge b \rightarrow b \wedge b \rightarrow c \wedge x \rightarrow x \wedge 2 \rightarrow y)$$

Let A denote this expression. Then, the result of the analysis of the complete program fragment is $A; A; A$. Let C be the assertion $(a \rightarrow a \wedge a \rightarrow b \wedge a \rightarrow c \wedge 1 \rightarrow x \wedge 2 \rightarrow y)$. The key point in simplifying $A; A; A$ is that the only context in which the variable a occurs in a $\vee_U$ is $C \vee_{\{a\}} C$, which simplifies to C, eliminating the conditional dependence on a.

This completes the sketch of an extension to our logic

for handling in Weiser's example. It is not at all clear how this can be done in a graph-based flow analysis framework. Graph-based methods treat individual dependencies in isolation and do no extend naturally to situations in which combinations of flows must be considered.

IX. Conclusion

Reasoning about changes is necessary in practical software development primarily due to continual changes in requirements and the support environment. We have developed and implemented a logical technique for determining the semantic effects of program changes based on an analysis of the abstract syntax of a generic programming language containing many of the features used in building large systems. The key idea behind the logic is that of approximate reasoning about changes based on a conservative interpretation of the semantic information-flow relation. Our logical formalization has several advantages over competing formalizations and is comparable in efficiency to the best alternative formalization in a program flow-analysis framework. We hope that automatic formal reasoning about the direct and indirect effects of changes will become a standard component of everyday programming environments.

Appendix
Definition of the Context Function

The context $\mathbb{C}$ used in the assertions is derived from the abstract syntax tree of the program by the function CreateContext defined below. In the presentation, the lowercase name of a sort stands for an element of the sort.

Context = Globals × Descriptions
Globals = Set[Var]
Descriptions = (Name → Description)
Description = Kind × ParamList × Stmt
sort Kind
operators
  proc, func: → Kind

CreateContext: Program → Context
AddToContext: Def Context → Context

CreateContext(*def program*) =
  AddToContext(*def*, CreateContext(*program*))
CreateContext(*def*) = AddToContext(*def*,
  $<\{ \}, \text{empty}>$)

AddToContext(var x, $<globals, descriptions>$) =
  $<globals \cup \{x\}, descriptions>$
AddToContext(procedure *name*(*parmlist*)
    varlist; *stmt*,
  $<globals, descriptions>$) =
  $<globals, (name \mapsto <\text{proc}, paramlist, stmt>,$
  $descriptions)>$
AddToContext(function *name*(*paramlist*)
    varlist; *stmt*,
  $<globals, descriptions>$) =
  $<globals, (name \mapsto <\text{func}, paramlist,$
  $stmt>, descriptions)>$

Note that Descriptions are treated as having the following operations:

empty: → Descriptions
-,-: Descriptions Descriptions → Descriptions
- $\mapsto$ -: Name Description → Descriptions

The function GetDescription looks up information for a procedure or function in a context:

operators
GetDescription: Descriptions → Descr

GetDescription(*name*, empty) = error
GetDescription(*name*, (*name* $\mapsto$ *descr*, *descriptions*)) = *descr*
Get Description(*name*, (*aname* $\mapsto$ *descr*, *descriptions*)) = GetDescription(*name*, *descriptions*) if *name* ≠ *aname*

definition $\mathbb{C} \triangleright \text{global}(x)$

$$\frac{x \in globals}{<globals, descriptions> \triangleright \text{global}(x)}$$

definition $\mathbb{C} \triangleright \text{value}(p, i)$

$$\frac{<kind, (k_1x_1, \cdots, k_nx_n), stmt> = \text{GetDescription}(p, descriptions) \quad (k_i = \text{value}) \vee (k_i = \text{value-result})}{<globals, descriptions> \triangleright \text{value}(p, i)}$$

definition $\mathbb{C} \triangleright \text{result}(p, i)$

$$\frac{<kind, (k_1x_1, \cdots, k_nx_n), stmt> = \text{GetDescription}(p, descriptions) \quad (k_i = \text{result}) \vee (k_i = \text{value-result})}{<globals, descriptions> \triangleright \text{result}(p, i)}$$

definition $\mathbb{C} \triangleright \text{param}(p, i, x)$

$$\frac{<kind, (k_1x_1, \cdots, k_nx_n), stmt> = \text{GetDescription}(p, descriptions) \quad x = x_i}{<globals, descriptions> \triangleright \text{param}(p, i, x)}$$

defintion $\mathbb{C} \triangleright \mathrm{func}(p, S)$

$$\frac{< \mathrm{func},\ paramlist,\ S > \ =\ \mathrm{GetDescription}(p,\ descriptions)}{< globals,\ descriptions > \ \triangleright\ \mathrm{func}(p, S)}$$

defintion $\mathbb{C} \triangleright \mathrm{proc}(p, S)$

$$\frac{< \mathrm{proc},\ paramlist,\ S > \ =\ \mathrm{GetDescription}(p,\ descriptions)}{< globals,\ descriptions > \ \triangleright\ \mathrm{proc}(p, S)}$$

REFERENCES

[1] M. Moriconi, "A practical approach to semantic configuration management," in *Proc. ACM SIGSOFT Conf. Software Testing, Analysis, and Verification*, Key West, FL, Dec. 1989, pp. 103–113.

[2] R. W. Floyd, "Toward interactive design of correct programs," in *Proc. IFIP Congress 71*, 1972, pp. 7–10.

[3] M. Moriconi, "A designer/verifier's assistant," *IEEE Trans. Software Eng.*, vol. SE-5, pp. 387–401, July 1979; reprinted in *Artificial Intelligence and Software Engineering*, C. Rich and R. Waters, Eds. Los Altos, CA: Morgan Kaufmann, 1986; also reprinted in *Tutorial on Software Maintenance*, G. Parikh and N. Zvegintzov, Eds. IEEE Computer Society Press, 1983.

[4] C. A. R. Hoare, "An axiomatic basis for computer programming," *Commun. ACM*, vol. 12, no. 10, pp. 576–583, 1969.

[5] D. C. Luckham and F. W. von Henke, "An overview of Anna, a specification language for Ada," *IEEE Software*, vol. 2, no. 2, pp. 9–23, Mar. 1985.

[6] D. C. Luckham, F. W. von Henke, B. Krieg-Brückner, and O. Owe, *ANNA, A Language for Annotating Ada Programs* (Lecture Notes in Computer Science, Vol. 260). New York: Springer-Verlag, 1987.

[7] *The EHDM Specification Language*, Comput. Sci. Lab., SRI International, May 1989.

[8] D. I. Good, R. L. Akers, and L. M. Smith, "Report on Gypsy 2.05," Computational Logic Inc., Austin, TX, Tech. Rep. CLI-1, 1986.

[9] J. V. Guttag, J. J. Horning, and J. M. Wing, "The Larch family of specification languages," *IEEE Software*, vol. 2, no. 5, pp. 24–36, Sept. 1985.

[10] J. V. Guttag, J. J. Horning, and J. M. Wing, "Larch in five easy pieces," Digital Systems Research Center, Palo Alto, CA, Tech. Rep. 5, July 1985.

[11] K. Futatsugi, J. Goguen, J.-P. Jouannaud, and J. Meseguer, "Principles of OBJ2," in *Proc. Twelfth Symp. Principles of Programming Languages*, ACM, 1985, pp. 52–66.

[12] J. Goguen and T. Winkler, "Introducing OBJ3," Comput. Sci. Lab., SRI International Tech. Rep. SRI-CSL-88-9, Aug. 1988.

[13] D. Bjorner and C. B. Jones, *Formal Specification and Software Development (Series in Computer Science)*. Englewood Cliffs, NJ: Prentice-Hall International, 1982.

[14] I. Hayes, Ed., *Specification Case Studies (Series in Computer Science)*. Englewood Cliffs, NJ: Prentice-Hall International, 1987.

[15] D. E. Perry, "Software interconnection models," in *Proc. 9th Int. Conf. Software Engineering*, Monterey, CA, Mar. 1987, pp. 61–69.

[16] ——, "Version control in the Inscape environment," in *Proc. 9th Int. Conf. Software Engineering*, Monterey, CA, Mar. 1987, pp. 142–149.

[17] J. de Kleer, "An assumption-based TMS," *Artificial Intell.*, vol. 28, pp. 127–162, 1986.

[18] J. Doyle, "A truth maintenance system," *Artificial Intell.*, vol. 12, pp. 231–272, 1979.

[19] D. E. Denning, "A lattice model of secure information flow," *Commun. ACM*, vol. 19, no. 5, pp. 236–242, 1976.

[20] C. E. Shannon, "A mathematical theory of communication," *Bell Syst. Tech. J.*, vol. 27, pp. 379–423 (July), pp. 623–656 (Oct.), 1948.

[21] D. E. Denning and P. J. Denning, "Certification of programs for secure information flow," *Commun. ACM*, vol. 20, no. 7, pp. 504–513, 1977.

[22] G. R. Andrews and R. P. Reitman, "An axiomatic approach to information flow in parallel programs," *ACM Trans. Program. Lang. Syst.*, vol. 2, no. 1, pp. 56–76, Jan. 1980.

[23] J. McHugh and D. I. Good, "An information flow tool for Gypsy," in *Proc. 1985 Symp. Security and Privacy*, IEEE Comput. Soc., Oakland, CA, Apr. 1985, pp. 46–48.

[24] J. M. Rushby, "The security model of enhanced HDM," in *Proc. 7th DoD/NBS Computer Security Initiative Conf.*, Gaithersburg, MD, Sept. 1984, pp. 120–136.

[25] R. A. Kemmerer, "Shared resource matrix methodology: An approach to identifying storage and timing channels," *ACM Trans. Comput. Syst.*, vol. 1, no. 3, pp. 256–277, Aug. 1983.

[26] J.-F. Bergeretti and B. A. Carré, "Information-flow and data-flow analysis of while-programs," *ACM Trans. Program. Lang. Syst.*, vol. 7, no. 1, pp. 37–61, Jan. 1985.

[27] A. Podgurski and L. A. Clarke, "The implications of program dependencies of software testing, debugging, and maintenance," in *Proc. ACM SIGSOFT Conf. Software Testing, Analysis, and Verification*, Key West, FL, Dec. 1989, pp. 168–178.

[28] S. Horwitz, T. Reps, and D. Binkley, "Interprocedural slicing using dependence graphs," in *Proc. ACM SIGPLAN 88 Conf. Programming Language Design and Implementation*, Atlanta, GA, June 1988, pp. 35–46.

[29] M. Weiser, "Program slicing," *IEEE Trans. Software Eng.*, vol. SE-10, pp. 352–357, July 1984.

[30] G. D. Plotkin, "A structural approach to operational semantics," Dep. Comput. Sci., Aarhus Univ., Aarhus, Denmark, Rep. DAIMI FN-19, Sept. 1981.

[31] D. Clément, J. Despeyroux, T. Despeyroux, L. Hascoet, and G. Kahn, "Natural semantics on the computer," in *Proc. France–Japan Artificial Intelligence and Computer Science Symp.*, Oct. 1986, pp. 49–89.

[32] K. D. Cooper and K. Kennedy, "Efficient computation of flow insensitive interprocedural summary information," in *Proc. ACM SIGPLAN Symp. Compiler Construction*, June 1984, pp. 247–258.

Chapter 8

Final Remarks

Why this Tutorial Now?

Understanding the impacts of software change has been a challenge since software systems were first developed. With the increasing size and complexity of these systems, the need has become more dramatic. With the new century less than four years away, many legacy software systems will need to examine the way that they handle dates. Software change impact analysis is a key technology to address this prevalent situation.

Software technology continues to advance quickly. Tools and techniques applied to large software systems development and maintenance are enabling software systems to be built and changed more readily. At the heart of these advancements is the use of repositories to manage and support software evolution. Also assisting in the advancement of software technology are new ways of organizing software process and products to take advantage of information technology.

While many software organizations have been successful in putting software artifacts into repositories and even getting them out when needed, there has been little done to analyze the contents of the repository for purposes of supporting software change. Like many learning endeavors, one must go through the learning stages at a lower level to understand the benefits of the next level. More concretely, now that we have learned how to store software life-cycle objects in a repository, we are ready to learn how to use the structure and contents of the repository for other benefits. The benefit that this tutorial targets is the ability to identify potential impacts of software changes from relationships between software life-cycle objects stored in a repository.

Material in this tutorial results from research into software change impact analysis technology conducted over several years. Even in the time that it took to compile this material, there have been significant advancements in the field. With increasing awareness of benefits from software repositories and dependency analysis technology, software technologists are incorporating software change impact analysis tools in their software engineering environments. Requirements engineering tools are providing traceability capabilities that allow users to identify related requirements and software artifacts. Software source code analysis tools are providing the ability to combine control flow and data flow analysis and create views or "slices" of programs for examination during modifications.

Impact analysis using traceability relationships at the artifact or document level concentrates on relationships between SLOs of different kinds across the lifecycle. In contrast, impact analysis using dependency analysis focuses on relationships between SLOs of the same kind within a particular phase or activity of the lifecycle. While these may seem distinctive and quite separate, actually they are congruent and complementary. When applied together, they provide an effective capability for determining the effects of a software change.

Summary of Material Covered

For this tutorial, we selected papers that provide up-to-date information on software change impact analysis. We included work from software source code dependency analysis and software traceability analysis. We proposed how results from both of these areas can be integrated to more effectively support impact analysis in software engineering repositories. We outlined why impact representation and determination techniques are at the heart of both source dependency analysis and traceability analysis.

The introductory paper entitled, "An Introduction to Software Change Impact Analysis," pulled together the themes of software dependency analysis and traceability. It provided usable definitions for impact analysis related terms and presented an overview of the technology that parallels the structure of the tutorial.

After the introductory paper, Chapter 1 examined the nature of software change impact analysis by outlining critical issues in changing software. This chapter introduced the reader to impact analysis in the software change process, established a framework for comparing various types of impact analysis, and examined impact analysis from the perspective of how it is employed in a real-world situation — the upcoming "date change" problems for the twenty-first century. This chapter gave insight into the nature of software change and the importance of detecting and predicting changes to software in advance of its implementation.

Chapter 2 familiarizes the reader with some of the ways software impacts are addressed in practice. That is, it shows how software change impacts are addressed in today's software organizations. Although impact analysis is an important area in software development and maintenance, it persists in being hard to do in practice. To be effective, it requires an understanding of software changes, their relationships between software life-cycle objects, a discipline to account for the changes, and automated support. Papers in Chapter 3 focused on where current technology is applied to managing software artifacts and their respective change.

Chapter 3 presented automated support for impact analysis by introducing some example prototype systems that support impact analysis. Automated support is essential for effective impact analysis since there is considerable work in manually identifying change impacts in the plethora of software artifacts produced during development and maintenance. By examining examples of impact analysis tools and environments, Chapter 3 provided the reader with some background on automated support for different types of impact analysis and alerted the reader to some key tool technologies that can be applied to impact analysis.

Chapter 4 examined dependency modeling and representation techniques to give the reader an appreciation for techniques and formalisms employed in representing software program dependencies. The chapter described how software dependency analysis provides an effective way to identify software change impacts. It emphasized that programming languages provide a reasonable structure to capture data definition and use information as well as logic and control flow information. With this information, a programmer can make reasonable decisions on what statements, modules, and data elements might be effected in the event of a software change. Chapter 4 outlined some of the key issues in analyzing software source code dependencies from the data, control, and component perspectives.

Chapter 5 examined traceability analysis. Much of the material for this chapter was presented from the perspective of software development environments and documentation systems. This chapter covered traceability technology used to determine the effects of software changes. Advances in software development environments and repository technology have enabled software engineers to trace impacts of software changes using traceability relationships. Traceability relationships are often represented in a graph structure which is amenable to navigation with a hypertext system. Chapter 5 discussed issues about determining impacts from relationships between software artifacts of differing types.

Chapter 6 presented a perspective on how software change impacts can be represented for analysis. This chapter along with Chapter 7 provided the most detailed and technical information in this tutorial. While impacts can be represented in many ways ranging from simple marks on program statements to sophisticated truth maintenance rules, effective analysis requires an understanding of software changes, their relationships between software life-cycle objects, a discipline to account for the changes, and automated support to be effective. Chapter 6 discusses impact representation methods that support many of the requirements espoused in this tutorial.

The papers in Chapter 7 discussed several techniques frequently encountered in impact analysis tools today. Impact determination techniques help use formal models of dependencies to derive impacts of a change. These techniques included transitive closure, heuristic search techniques, techniques based on logical inference, analogical reasoning, data flow analysis, and program slicing. Chapter 8 provided insight into several key impact determination techniques that assist in detecting impacts of a change.

After these closing remarks, the tutorial is concluded with a comprehensive annotated bibliography. This bibliography contains several good references to impact analysis related material, each with a few sentences to describe its significance with respect to this tutorial. We encourage readers to examine these and obtain some of these interesting readings.

What Does the Future Hold?

One of our main reasons for assembling this tutorial on software change impact analysis was to integrate ideas and concepts from two areas of software engineering: dependency analysis and traceability analysis. The future of software change impact analysis will involve efforts to leverage these two technology areas, and such efforts will benefit from having an integrated impact-analysis perspective.

The focus of dependency analysis is on the detailed dependencies and control, data, and component information that developers can detect from source code. However, because this analysis is applied *only* to source code, its scope is narrow in light of all the other software artifacts in a project.

Traceability analysis focuses on the relationships among software life-cycle objects, such as requirements, design, and code. SLOs are software work products representing documents of one kind or another containing varied levels of software information. In most traceability tools, the granularity of SLOs is represented at the document level — too high to accurately assess the impact of a software change. If the SLO relationships are too coarse, they must be decomposed to understand complex relationships. On the other hand, if they are too granular, it is difficult to reconstruct them into recognizable, easily understood software work products. This is the dilemma repository developers face.

Both dependency analysis and traceability analysis are available in some form in commercial tools like the Rational Development Environment. But such tools are rare. It is our hope that the limitations of today's impact-analysis technology will be overcome by the great need for this technology and the great promise of new methods that integrate techniques to make impact analysis more effective.

Each area has disadvantages that are overcome by the other. Traceability analysis overcomes dependency analysis' lack of support for SLOs other than code. Dependency analysis overcomes traceability analysis' lack of detailed representations.

With challenges like the date-change problem expressed in "Millenium Now: Solutions for Century Data Change Impact" (in Chapter 3), it is clear that software change impact analysis is a valuable technology that needs to evolve. While improvements will occur with the marriage between dependency analysis and traceability analysis, the opportunities for better analysis are just opening up. A vision for the future includes using software change impact analysis to

- determine more accurate effort and cost estimates for software changes;

- provide guidance for making changes through navigation links on concept relationships embedded in the SLO repository;

- examine software-change design choices to determine the design solution with the least impact, thus guiding software-design evolution; and

- ultimately influence the way software is changed by providing better visibility into the change possibilities and better decisions about software changes.

Annotated Bibliography

There is much more information on software change impact analysis than we had space to include. The following articles, research papers, technical reports, and books are excellent additional reading. We encourage you to explore this many-sided topic through these sources. The asterisks beside an item indicate that the paper is in this book.

For updates, a fruitful source for research papers on impact analysis is the annual *Proceedings of the Conference on Software Maintenance* (IEEE Computer Society Press).

[Adams 1989]   **Adams, E. W., M. Honda, and T. C. Miller, "Object Management in a CASE Environment," *Proc. Int'l Conf. Software Eng.*, IEEE CS Press, Los Alamitos, Calif., 1989, pp. 154-163.**

Describes the philosophy and approach of Sun Microsystems' Network Software Environment. The authors outline the object-management solution to traditional configuration and change-management situations as well as those to do with distributed, parallel development. They also discuss component dependencies as well as inheritance and type extensions. Their repository approach to managing software life-cycle objects makes it easier to conduct an impact analysis.

[Anezin 1993]   **Anezin, D. L., "Process and Methods for Requirements Tracing," Ph.D. dissertation, George Mason Univ., Nov. 1993; available from Univ. Microfilms Int'l Dissertation Services, Ann Arbor, Mich.**

The author describes a process and its associated methods to support forward and backward requirements tracing. The approach is novel in that it uses automation to construct requirement classifications and clustering techniques for analyzing and tracing requirements. Patterns are detected to relate and connect requirements, thus expediting the process of populating and updating requirements-traceability records. This work is based on much of the requirements research conducted at George Mason University.

*[Arango 1993]   **Arango, G., E. Schoen, and R. Pettengill, "A Process for Consolidating and Reusing Design Knowledge," *Proc. Int'l Conf. Software Eng.*, IEEE CS Press, Los Alamitos, Calif., 1993, pp. 231-241.**

The authors examine traceability from the perspectives of evolution and reuse. They present a validated process for constructing workspaces to support product-family design, and evolution. Although the paper does not address traceability directly, it does show how developers can use traceability information to evolve software systems.

*[Arnold 1993]   **Arnold, R. S., and S. A. Bohner, "Impact Analysis — Towards A Framework for Comparison," *Proc. Conf. Software Maintenance*, IEEE CS Press, Los Alamitos, Calif., 1993, pp. 292-301.**

The authors propose a definition of impact analysis that clearly delineates the basis for comparing impact-analysis capabilities. They present a framework model of impact analysis and discuss underlying ideas according to this definition. The paper classifies several impact-analysis approaches according to this definition.

*[Arnold 1995]   Arnold R. S., "Millennium Now: Solutions for Century Data Change Impact," *Application Development Trends,* Jan. 1995, pp. 60-66.

The author describes the nature of the impact-analysis problem through the date-change problem that is likely to plague software organizations at the turn of the century. He suggests steps to take in planning for the transition as well as the tools and techniques necessary to accomplish the effort. Taking a software-assets approach, the author suggests that early assessment is the key to addressing the impacts to an organization's software portfolio.

[Basili 1981]   Basili, V., and D. Weiss, "Evaluation of a Software Requirements Document by Analysis of Change Data," *Proc. Int'l Conf. Software Eng.,* IEEE CS Press, Los Alamitos, Calif., 1981, pp. 314-323.

The authors describe reasons for changing requirements and the relationships among them. This information makes it easier to see potential traceability relationships among requirements and design artifacts. The authors discuss data-collection methods and the results of applying the methods to the requirements of the U.S. Navy's A-7 flight software. They also examine the feasibility of using data-collection methods to analyze the maintainability of a requirements document.

[Belady 1976]   Belady, L., and M. M. Lehman, "A Model of Large Program Development," *IBM Systems J.,* Vol. 15, No.3, 1976, pp. 225-252.

The article outlines program development and evolution characteristics and relationships. It presents an analysis of OS/360 data to explore the programming process. The authors propose "laws" of program-evolution dynamics and outline five parameters in a change model of the programming process.

[Berzins 1995]   Berzins, V., *Software Merging and Slicing,* IEEE CS Press, Los Alamitos, Calif., 1995.

This book is a collection of papers that discuss merging or consolidating program versions, and slicing, for "slicing away" parts of a program that are irrelevant to a change. The papers provide good technical background on these topics. The book as a whole is a useful companion volume to *Software Change Impact Analysis.*

[Bigelow 1988]   Bigelow, J., "Hypertext and CASE," *IEEE Software,* Mar. 1988, pp. 23-29.

The article outlines an approach to using hypertext/hypermedia to connect software documentation. The underlying hypertext abstract machine is a powerful mechanism for representing the relationships among life-cycle objects. The author gives examples of how this mechanism works with changes, expressed as configuration-management deltas (change increments), in source code.

[Bohner 1989b]   Bohner, S. A., "Hypermedia for Information Analysis," *Proc. Annual Intelligence Community Artificial Intelligence/Advanced Computing Symp.,* 1989.

This paper describes the use of the graph-theoretic approach to analyzing impacts in software life-cycle objects. The author outlines the connectivity of informational objects and how they can be navigated using hypermedia technology. Because the symposium supports the intelligence community (even though it is conducted in a public forum), an example of actual use would be classified information. Thus, the author uses the traceability of software work products and dependencies among work products in the example.

[Bohner 1991a] **Bohner, S. A., "Impact Analysis Using Hypermedia,"** *Proc. Annual Intelligence Community Artificial Intelligence/Advanced Computing Symp.*, Mar. 1991.

This paper extends the work presented in the paper from the 1989 proceedings (see above). The graph-theoretic approach is described again, but in the more definitive terms of analyzing software life-cycle objects, such as source code (data and function) and software documents (requirements, design, code, and test).

[Bohner 1991b] **Bohner, S. A., "Impact Analysis to Support Re-engineering,"** *Proc. Annual Naval Surface Warfare Center's Systems Reengineering Workshop*, U.S. Naval Surface Warfare Center, 1991.

The author introduces an approach that uses software change impact analysis to support software reengineering. The focus is on improving software-maintenance characteristics by improving the visibility into software traceability and dependency relationships. The author recognizes that successful software reengineering often requires the accurate capture of software life-cycle objects. This, in turn, requires considerable insight into the relationships among those objects. The author addresses these problems by describing a traceability approach to discovering the objects.

*[Bohner 1991c] **Bohner, S. A., "Software Change Impact Analysis for Design Evolution,"** *Proc. Int'l Conf. Software Maintenance and Reengineering*, USPDI, 1991.

The author introduces a process model for software maintenance that stresses impact analysis. Using directed graphs, the author describes traditional process and product metrics as well as new impact-analysis metrics that address the traceability of software work products and the dependencies among them. Developers can use these metrics to understand and control changes to the system design. As changes are requested, developers can measure them, assess their impacts, and make enlightened design decisions.

[Bohner 1995] **Bohner, S. A., "A Graph Traceability Approach for Software Change Impact Analysis,"** Ph.D. dissertation, George Mason Univ., Aug. 1995; available from Univ. Microfilms Int'l Dissertation Services, Ann Arbor, Mich.

This research concentrates on improving software change impact identification by developing and demonstrating an effective impact-analysis method that incorporates source-code dependency and requirements-traceability information. The method employs software-project database (repository) technology to broaden detection of impacts from source code to other important software artifacts, such as requirements and design. The author shows the feasibility of implementing the graph-traceability representation method using automation.

[Cimitile 1992] **Cimitile, A., F. Lanubile, and G. Visaggio, "Traceability Based on Design Decisions,"** *Proc. Conf. Software Maintenance*, IEEE CS Press, Los Alamitos, Calif., 1992, pp. 309-317.

The authors present a view of software structure as conceptual models that connect source code with design decisions and map them onto the target model. The view is in the context of a conversion from Pascal to Ada. The conceptual models — essential design and language-oriented design — are represented in a graph model, which is used in the authors' Traceability Support System, also described.

[Collofello 1987] **Collofello, J. S., and J. J. Buck, "Software Quality Assurance for Maintenance,"** *IEEE Software*, Sept. 1987, pp. 46-51.

The authors describe the ripple effect, an important aspect of software change. The ripple effect is "the effect caused by making a small change to a system which [affects] many other parts of a system." The authors outline a project study in which a large software system (telephone switching system) is undergoing maintenance. Although the focus of the investigation is on software-change defects and testing, there is useful information on ripple-effect analysis. Reviews are expanded to address the inadvertent side-effects of software changes.

*[Collofello 1988]   Collofello, J., and M. Orn, "A Practical Software Maintenance Environment," *Proc. Conf. Software Maintenance*, IEEE CS Press, Los Alamitos, Calif., 1988, pp. 45-51.

The authors report on a project to develop a software-maintenance environment. The project, begun at Arizona State University in 1983, focuses on a number of maintenance tasks, including understanding software, changing software, tracing ripple effects, releasing changed software, documenting acquired knowledge, and planning/scheduling maintenance tasks. In their coverage of ripple-effect analysis, the authors' description of relationships is particularly significant for impact analysis.

[Conklin 1987]   Conklin, J., "Hypertext: An Introduction and Survey," *Computer*, Sept. 1987, pp. 17-41.

The author surveys the state of the art in 1987 with respect to hypertext/hypermedia systems and applications. The article gives a good perspective on hypermedia technology and reasonable expectations for its application. There is also a summary of existing hypertext systems and their respective capabilities. The benefits of hypertext in other applications suggest that it would be useful in categorizing traceability relationships – which, in turn, could greatly aid the navigation of impact-analysis results.

*[Cross 1987]   Cross, G. M., "Requirements and Traceability Management," Software for Guidance and Control, Sept. 1991, pp. 41-45.

The author discusses the contribution of requirements traceability to all phases of system development in the context of applying the Requirements and Traceability Management tool. He outlines traceability-tool requirements, requirements capture and stripping, requirements engineering, analysis and design, testing, and impact analysis. The important part of this paper from the perspective of impact analysis is the recognition by the requirements-tool industry that impact analysis is a necessary part of a software environment.

[Dhar 1988]   Dhar, V., and M. Jarke, "Dependency Directed Reasoning and Learning in Systems Maintenance Support," *IEEE Trans. Software Eng.*, Feb. 1988, pp. 211-227.

This paper is for those interested in the theory behind system-change relationships. The authors describe the Remap formalism (Representation and Maintenance of Process Knowledge), which links design-decision dependencies with domain-specific design rules. They identify four classes of process knowledge that support design-specific knowledge about design dependencies (for example, a specific design decision to format unformatted data), general knowledge about design rules (for example, unformatted data requires formatting), knowledge about the essence of conditions for certain design decisions, and knowledge about analogical properties among design situations.

[Dorfman 1981]   Dorfman, M., and R. F. Flynn, "ARTS — An Automated Requirements Traceability System," *Proc. AIAA Computers in Aerospace Conf.*, 1981, pp. 418-428; also in *J. Systems and Software*, Apr. 1984, pp. 63-74.

The authors describe the storage and retrieval of large quantities of requirements that have been constructed in a tree using the Automated Requirements Traceability System. ARTS maintains pointers between requirements and the requirements from which they were derived and reports on requirements coverage.

[Doyle 1979]   **Doyle, J., "A Truth Maintenance System," *Artificial Intelligence*, May 1979, pp. 231-272.**

The author describes the inferencing necessary to detect dependencies in a rule base. Although he explores ideas in the belief systems area of artificial intelligence, the article provides ideas that parallel application in impact analysis. Rather than focusing on a matrix or graph of dependencies, developers use a set of rules for dependency-directed backtracking to change a set of assumptions. Truth-maintenance techniques show promise for reducing the search space of impact analysis for large systems.

[Farrow 1976]   **Farrow, R., K. Kennedy, and L. Zucconi, "Graph Grammars and Global Program Data Flow Analysis," *Proc. IEEE Symp. Foundations of Computer Science*, IEEE Press, New York, 1976, pp. 42-56.**

This is an early paper on the mathematical foundations of structured-programming constructs and their representation in the Grammar for Semi-Structured Flow Graphs. The authors introduce GSSFG as an improvement on Bohm-Jacopini graph grammars and reducing many limitations of the B-J graphs. The authors examine graph-reduction techniques that apply to data-flow and control-flow analysis. Although this paper is compiler-oriented, you can get good insight into the graph representations useful for flow analysis.

[Feldman 1979]   **Feldman, S. I., "Make: A Program for Maintaining Computer Programs," *Software Practice and Experience*, Wiley-Interscience, New York, Apr. 1979, pp. 255-265.**

This early paper outlines the dependencies among programs and their compilers, linkers, loaders, and the like. The author describes how to derive program-build dependencies from dependency graphs and graph grammars as well as how to use this derivation in managing program updates.

[Ferrante 1987]   **Ferrante, J., K. J. Ottenstein, and J. D. Warren, "The Program Dependence Graph and Its Use in Optimization," *ACM Trans. Programming Languages and Systems*, July 1987, pp. 319-349.**

The authors describe the Program Dependence Graph representation, which makes data-flow and control-flow dependencies apparent with respect to program operations. The PDG supports incremental optimization and lets developers apply transformations to the affected dependencies. The authors also present an incremental approach to modifying the data dependencies that result from branch deletion or loop unrolling.

*[Forte 1990]   **Forte, G., "Configuration Management Survey," *CASE Outlook*, Summer 1990, pp. 24-51.**

The article is an in-depth survey of leading configuration-management products as of 1990, but the concepts and ideas are still valid. The author reviews the range of capabilities and features available in configuration-management tools and relates these capabilities to the basic requirements for improved software development and maintenance. He also comments on how they address important issues like impact analysis and traceability. An insightful companion sidebar by Alex Lobba targets key configuration-management issues in software development and maintenance.

[Fraisse 1986]   Fraisse, P., "An Efficient Parallel Algorithm for the Transitive Closure Graph," *J. Systems and Software*, May 1986, pp. 165-168.

The author examines an efficient algorithm $O(n^2 \log n)$ for determining the transitive closure of a graph using a parallel-vector approach. This algorithm applies to the transformation of a connectivity graph (of all relationships of a given software life-cycle object) into a reachability graph (determining objects that may be affected by a change to an object).

*[Gallagher 1991]   Gallagher, K. B., and J. R. Lyle, "Using Program Slicing in Software Maintenance," *IEEE Trans. Software Eng.*, Aug. 1991, pp. 751-761.

This comprehensive paper extends the notion of a program slice to a decomposition slice. It encompasses all the computation on a given variable (what remains is the complement of the program slice). The decomposition slice represents an impact analysis with respect to a given variable of interest. The authors also address the software-maintenance process with respect to software change and regression testing.

*[Garg 1989]   Garg, P., and W. Scacchi, "A Hypertext System to Manage Software Life-Cycle Documents," *IEEE Software*, May 1990, pp. 90-98.

The authors describe the Document Integration Facility part of the Software Factory and an experiment in the use of hypertext mechanisms to manage software artifacts. DIF addresses traceability through the use of hypertext links and navigation mechanisms. The authors present it as an alternative to project-database approaches and discuss its usefulness in development and maintenance environments.

*[Gotel 1994]   Gotel, O. C., and A. C. Finkelstein, "An Analysis of the Requirements Traceability Problem," *Proc. Int'l Conf. Requirements Eng.*, IEEE CS Press, Los Alamitos, Calif., Apr. 1994, pp. 94-101.

In this in-depth exploration of the requirements-traceability problem, the authors formally define requirements traceability and present a framework for examining tool support. They divide the requirements-traceability problem into dilemmas before requirements specification and after, emphasizing that most work is done after requirements specification.

[Gulla 1992]   Bjorn, G., "Improved Maintenance Support by Multi-Version Visualization," *Proc. Conf. Software Maintenance*, IEEE CS Press, Los Alamitos, Calif., 1992, pp. 376-383.

The author discusses the increasing use of software repositories and the need to use visualization techniques to identify requisite software components in the software-change process. He describes visualization techniques in terms of difference, affected, entropy, probability, structure variance, and backbone structure views. These views assist in program comprehension and in impact analysis.

[Hamilton 1979]   Hamilton, M., and S. Zeldin, "Requirements Definition Within Acquisition and Its Relationship to Post-Deployment Software Support," Tech. Report TR-22, Higher Order Software, 1979.

The authors define 36 interrelated factors that affect system requirements and describe each in terms of how it affects respective product attributes. They describe in detail the interrelationships of requirements, specifications, and the implementations of a set of cooperating processes. They also outline the types of information in a requirements specification from the acquisition perspective.

366

[Haney 1972]   Haney, F. M., "Module Connection Analysis," *Proc. AFIPS Joint Computer Conf.*, Vol. 41, No. 5, IEEE CS Press, Los Alamitos, Calif., 1972, pp. 173-179.

This early paper describes the stability (in terms of ripple effects) of large programs as a function of internal structure. The technique presented records dependencies in a matrix for the analysis of ripple effects (leading to a stability measure). This predictive model of program stability suggests that identified modules have a probability of change with respect to a given change to the system.

[Harrington 1993]   Harrington, G. A., and K. M. Rondeau, "An Investigation of Requirements Traceability to Support Systems Development," master's thesis, Naval Postgraduate School; available from Defense Technical Information Center, Springfield, Va., AD-A273 167, 1993.

The authors look at what information should be captured for a requirements-traceability scheme. They describe linkages among system requirements and various software-development activities and investigate how developers can implement DoD-Std-2167A, a mandate for requirements traceability in software development.

*[Harrold 1993]   Harrold, M. J., and B. Malloy, "A Unified Interprocedural Program Representation for a Maintenance Environment," *IEEE Trans. Software Eng.*, June 1993, pp. 584-593; also in *Proc. Conf. Software Maintenance*, IEEE CS Press, Los Alamitos, Calif., 1991, pp. 138-147.

The authors present a graph technique for representing interprocedural program dependencies, in which Unified Interprocedural Graphs are used to represent interactions among code procedures. UIGs are designed to save storage space and access times in their representations.

[Hartmann 1990]   Hartmann, J., and D. Robson, "Techniques for Selective Revalidation," *IEEE Software*, Jan. 1990, pp. 31-36.

The authors extend an integer-programming approach to identifying sections of source code that may have to be retested in a maintenance change. They also examine languages other than Fortran. The approach uses integer-programming techniques to ascertain the minimum set of paths that should retested with respect to changes in source-code statements. The retest problem they present mirrors the problem presented in identifying the ripple effects of changes in software artifacts in a repository.

[Henry 1981]   Henry, S., and D. Kafura, "Software Structure Metrics Based on Information Flow," *IEEE Trans. Software Eng.*, Sept. 1981, pp. 510-518.

The authors define and validate a set of metrics appropriate for evaluating software systems. They define metrics for procedure complexity, module complexity, and coupling and correlate these complexity measures with the occurrence of software changes to the Unix operating system. They also examine the ideas of information flow (fan-in and fan-out) with respect to the decisions that must be made in designing software and the associated changes that may occur.

*[Horowitz 1986]   Horowitz, E., and R. Williamson, "SODOS: A Software Document Support Environment — Its Definition," *IEEE Trans. Software Eng.*, Aug. 1986, pp. 849-859.

The authors explore the mechanisms necessary to support an automated software-documentation system. Using Smalltalk-80, a relational database-management system, and a graph model of software documentation, they construct a prototype system to manage software documents. The graph model and support for traceability are of particular interest because they are needed to provide a basis for impact analysis at the software-work-product level.

*[Horwitz 1990]   Horwitz, S., T. Reps, and D. Binkley, "Interprocedural Slicing Using Dependence Graphs," *ACM Trans. Programming Languages and Systems*, Jan. 1990, pp. 35-46.

This paper is an in-depth treatment of program slicing and the components of dependence graphs that enable slices to be taken across several procedures. The authors introduce the notion of a system dependence graph to account for multiple procedures in a program.

*[Kaiser 1989]   Kaiser, G. E., P. H. Feiler, and S. S. Popovich, "Intelligent Support for Software Development and Maintenance," *IEEE Software*, May 1988, pp. 40-49.

The authors report on the Professor Marvel project, which supports two aspects of an intelligent assistant. First, it provides visibility into the system structure and relationships in the software product to make developers aware of the consequences of tasks being performed. Second, it participates in development activities through "opportunistic" processing — it detects jobs that it can do and does them, so developers are relieved of some of the burden. The model of relationships is interesting from the impact-analysis perspective, since it offers semantics on the links among software objects.

*[Keables 1988]   Keables, J., K. Robertson, and A. von Mayrhauser, "Data Flow Analysis and Its Application to Software Maintenance," *Proc. Conf. Software Maintenance*, IEEE CS Press, Los Alamitos, Calif., 1988, pp. 335-347.

The authors explore the use of data-flow analysis to support software-maintenance activities. They examine insertion, deletion, and modification of nodes (data statements) in a program with respect to definition/use graphs and describe a tool kit developed for data-flow analysis.

[Kennedy 1981]   Kennedy, K., "A Survey of Data Flow Analysis Techniques," in *Program Flow Analysis: Theory and Applications*, S. S. Muchnick and N. D. Jones, eds., Prentice-Hall, Englewood Cliffs, N.J., 1981.

This comprehensive look at data-flow analysis techniques touches on graph analysis techniques, optimization, and language considerations. Tje author describes the Grammar for Semi-Structured Flow Graphs as well as interprocedural analysis techniques.

[Kuhn 1988]   Kuhn, D. R., "Static Analysis Tools for Software Security Certification," *Proc. Nat'l Computer Security Conf.*, 1988, pp. 290-298.

The author examines the tools necessary to assist specialists in software-security certification in detecting security risks that may be caused by modifications. He describes the use of Unix tools to achieve some level of confidence that important control-flow and data-flow constraints are not subverted when software is changed.

*[Kung 1994]   Kung, D., et al., "Change Impact Identification in Object Oriented Software," *Proc. Conf. Software Maintenance*, IEEE CS Press, Los Alamitos, Calif., 1994, pp. 202-211.

The authors present an object-oriented model of change-impact identification as it pertains to software maintenance. They discuss the types of code changes in an object-oriented class library and suggest various automated approaches to identifying different kinds of code changes and their respective impacts. They also describe an object-oriented software-maintenance environment that implements the resulting impact-analysis techniques. The paper offers an object-oriented perspective to analyzing software-change impacts by examining encapsulation, aggregation, inheritance, polymorphism, and dynamic binding.

[Lehman 1980]   Lehman, M. M., "Programs, Life Cycles, and Laws of Software Evolution," *Proc. IEEE*, IEEE Press, New York, 1980, pp. 1060-1076.

The author classifies programs according to program-development and program-evolution characteristics and relationships, proposes "laws": of program evolution formulated by quantified studies, and outlines five parameters in an example of program-release planning. You can get good insight into the causes of software change and where an impact analysis should concentrate.

[Leintz 1980]   Leintz, B. P., and E. B. Swanson, *Software Maintenance Management*, Addison-Wesley, Reading, Mass., 1980.

The authors survey software maintenance in management information systems, providing an early definition of currently accepted maintenance types (corrective, perfective, and adaptive). On the basis of their experience in the maintenance of large information systems, they advocate the need for software understanding. The book is a good reference for maintenance-management strategies. From the impact-analysis perspective, it shows that different types of changes need different analyses. Additionally, because it focuses on management, the book clarifies the visibility aspects of impact analysis.

*[Loyall 1993]   Loyall, J. P., and S. A. Mathisen, "Using Dependence Analysis to Support Software Maintenance," *Proc. Conf. Software Maintenance*, IEEE CS Press, Los Alamitos, Calif., 1993, pp. 282-291.

The authors give a language-independent definition of interprocedural dependency analysis and describe its implementation in a prototype tool that supports software maintenance. They also formally define data, control, and syntactic dependence and explore the definitions.

*[Luqi 1990]   Luqi, "A Graph Model for Software Evolution," *IEEE Trans. Software Eng.*, Aug. 1990, pp. 917-927.

In a formal examination of software evolution, the author seeks to formalize objects and activities involved in software evolution in sufficient detail to enable automation. A key contribution is the basis for automated software-change propagation. This model of software evolution serves as a good foundation for program-change semantics.

*[Madhavji 1991]   Madhavji, N. H., "The Prism Model of Changes," *Proc. Int'l Conf. Software Eng.*, IEEE CS Press, Los Alamitos, Calif., 1991, pp. 166-177.

The paper gives a broad perspective on change with respect to people, policies, laws, resources, processes, and results. Although it addresses automated systems, the necessary expansion to other environmental factors underlines the complexity of change. The author distinguishes changes to the items from changes to the environment that houses them. He describes the Prism Dependency Structure facility. The Dependency Structure supports classifying, recording, and analyzing change-related data from a qualitative perspective by describing items and their interdependencies as well as identifying the possible effects of changes.

*[Moreton 1990]   Moreton, R., "A Process Model for Software Maintenance," *J. Information Technology*, June 1990, pp. 100-104.

The author underlines the need for an effective software-maintenance process in light of the increasing size and complexity of software systems. He believes a key part of the software-maintenance process is impact analysis, in which the effects of a change request are elaborated for estimates. There is also a discussion on formalizing the software-maintenance process, and the author relates this to a survey of 24 commercial organizations belonging to the Butler Cox Productivity Enhancement Programme.

*[Moriconi 1990]   **Moriconi, M., and T. C. Winkler, "Approximate Reasoning about the Semantic Effects of Program Changes," *IEEE Trans. Software Eng.*, Sept. 1990, pp. 980-992.**

The authors present logical techniques for finding and reasoning about the semantic effects of program changes. Their approach to analyzing programs is based on the use of parameterized modules, procedures, and global variables. The approximate reasoning is a model of the information-flow relationships among program objects. The key idea is that approximate reasoning about changes is based on a conservative (logical) interpretation of semantic information flow. That is, approximate reasoning about the direct and indirect effects of changes can be determined algorithmically and can thus be automated.

*[Moser 1990]   **Moser, L. E., "Data Dependency Graphs for Ada Programs," *IEEE Trans. Software Eng.*, May 1990, pp. 498-509.**

The author describes a compositional method for constructing data dependency graphs for Ada programs. The method combines composition-rule techniques with data dependency graphs to construct larger aggregate units. The method examines composition rules for iteration, recursion, exception handling, and tasking. The dependency graphs appear to be useful for determining impacts, although the author does not directly address this application.

[Nejmeh 1988]   **Nejmeh, B. A., and T. E. Dickey, "Traceability Technology at the Software Productivity Consortium," Software Productivity Consortium, Tech. Report SPC-1.0-881130-40-00-N, Herndon, Va., Nov. 1988.**

This expanded version of the condensed paper that appeared with coauthor Steve Wartik in the *Proceedings of the 1989 International Federation for Information Processing* outlines the Software Productivity Consortium's approach to building a traceability tool. Although the authors describe only plans to develop a requirements-traceability tool, the demonstration prototype did show some interesting technologies that might support traceability in a project-library database. The approach focuses on documentation requirements in DoD-Std-2167A.

[Ottenstein 1984]   **Ottenstein, K. J., and L. M. Ottenstein, "The Program Dependence Graph in a Software Development Environment," *ACM SIGPLAN Notices*, May 1984, pp. 177-184.**

The authors describe the Program Dependence Graph, which represents program data-flow and control-flow information in a dependency graph. This representation is useful for program slicing and for incremental data-flow analysis. The authors examine PDGs in light of their utility in a software-development environment that supports language-sensitive editors and debugging tools. They also address the idea of PDGs to support software-complexity metrics.

[Penedo 1985]   **Penedo, M. H., and E. D. Stuckle, "PMDB — A Project Master Database for Software Engineering Environments," *Proc. Int'l Conf. Software Eng.*, IEEE CS Press, Los Alamitos, Calif., 1985, pp. 150-157.**

The authors present TRW's approach to addressing project databases. In their treatment of traceability issues, they acknowledge that software objects and their associated relationships play an important role in the utility of a software-development environment. The components and relationships are loosely based on DoD-Std-2167 , since TRW is an aerospace company supporting the U.S. Department of Defense. The representation focuses on management's need to account for tasks in software development.

[Perry 1989]   **Perry, D. E., "The Inscape Environment," *Proc. Int'l Conf. Software Eng.*, IEEE CS Press, Los Alamitos, Calif., 1989, pp. 2-12.**

The author introduces Inscape, a software-development environment to support large-system development. He presents software-component dependencies in terms of knowledge about the system-construction process. Inscape addresses change propagation at the module and interface levels as well as at the policy level.

[Pfleeger 1991]   **Pfleeger, S. L., *Software Engineering: The Production of Quality Software*, 2nd ed., Macmillan, New York, 1991.**

The author gives a good overview of software-engineering practices. The new edition presents perspectives on recent advances in reuse, CASE technology, and software maintenance. Chapter 10 has a discussion on software change impact analysis, including a definition, that outlines a vision for impact analysis based on a graph-representation approach.

[Pierce 1978]   **Pierce, R. A., "A Requirements Tracing Tool," *ACM Software Eng. Notes*, Nov. 1978, pp. 67-71.**

The author describes a simple requirements-tracing tool used to maintain cross references among sets of requirements. The tool also addresses relationships among requirements and design software life-cycle objects.

[Pirnia 1981]   **Pirnia, S., "Requirements Definition Approach for an Automated Requirements Traceability Tool," *Proc. IEEE Nat'l Aerospace and Electronics Conf.*, 1981, pp. 389-394.**

The author briefly describes a requirements-tracing tool used to maintain relationships among sets of requirements. The author also examines the types of analyses performed to determine the tool's relationship database and presents a requirements-definition process for the functional requirements of a program to automate requirements traceability.

*[Podgurski 1990]   **Podgurski, A., and L. A. Clarke, "A Formal Model of Program Dependencies and Its Implications for Software Testing, Debugging, and Maintenance," *IEEE Trans. Software Eng.*, Sept. 1990, pp. 965-979.**

The authors present a formal, general model of program-level dependencies, describing two ideas of control-flow and data-flow dependency information: weak and strong syntactic dependencies. They then relate these ideas to semantic dependence models — the ability of a program statement to affect the execution of other statements.

[Powers 1993]   **Powers, T. P., and C. D. Stubbs, "An Investigation of Requirements Traceability to Support Systems Development," master's thesis, Naval Postgraduate School; available from Defense Technical Information Center, Springfield, Va., AD-A273 405, Sept. 1993.**

The authors describe current practices with the use of traceability technology, reporting on a survey of 35 systems-development organizations. They also present a detailed case study of traceability in a U.S. Department of Defense organization.

[Purdom 1970]   **Purdom, P. Jr., "A Transitive Closure Algorithm," *BIT*, Vol. 10, 1970, pp. 76-99.**

The author describes an algorithm for determining the transitive closure of a graph that applies to the transformation of a connectivity graph (of all relationships of a given software life-cycle object) into a reachability graph (determining the objects that may be affected by a change to that object).

*[Qadah 1991]   **Qadah, G. Z., L. J. Henschen, and J. J. Kim, "Efficient Algorithms for the Instantiated Transitive Closure Queries," *IEEE Trans. Software Eng.*, Mar. 1991, pp. 296-309.**

The authors do not directly address traceability or impact analysis but they explore an important notion about traceability relationships: all software life-cycle objects have relationships that are recursive. The algorithms efficiently address transitive-closure relationships in the process of turning a connectivity graph into a reachability graph. This reduces the time to analyze impacts in large software systems.

[Queille 1994]   **Queille, J., et al., "The Impact Analysis Task in Software Maintenance: A Model and a Case Study," *Proc. Conf. Software Maintenance*, IEEE CS Press, Los Alamitos, Calif., 1994, pp. 234-242.**

The authors present a general model of impact analysis as it pertains to software maintenance. Impacts are represented as declarative propagation rules (in a Prolog fashion) to describe the way software objects affect each other. Although the authors assert the need for a precise way to describe the semantics of a software change, they do not give details. They describe the application of a prototype impact-analysis tool in a small case study (changes to a 2,100-line program) to demonstrate the potential for this type of analysis on C code. They also construct a Ripple Propagation Graph (see [Turver 1993]) by reading documents (manually) and identifying themes.

[RADC 1986]   **"Automated Life Cycle Impact Analysis System," Tech. Report RADC-TR-86-197, Rome Laboratories, U.S. Air Force Systems Command, Griffiss Air Force Base, Rome, N.Y., Dec. 1986.**

This is the first known report to address software impact analysis broadly from a traceability perspective. The report outlines a research project that examines a methodology for analyzing and assessing change impacts in the DoD-Std-2167 environment. The report describes the Alicia prototype system (Automated Life Cycle Impact Analysis) along with potential algorithms for assessing impacts. The paper also examines what is needed to support cost/schedule, performance, and quality impacts.

[Rang 1985]   **Rang, E. R., and K. H. Thelen, "A Requirements to Test Tracking System," *Proc. Nat'l ACM Conf.*, ACM Press, New York, 1985, pp. 387-391; also as "Summary of Requirements to Test Tracking System (RTTS)," Tech. Report 48SRC51, Honeywell Systems and Research Division, 1984.**

The Requirements to Test Tracking System was developed by Honeywell to track documents for software projects using the U.S. Navy's Mil-Std-1679 software-documentation standard. The RTTS is a special-purpose tool to support a data model reflecting the Navy's software process. As the name indicates, RTTS concentrates on supporting testing activities with traceability information.

*[Simon 1994]   **Simon, A., "The Integrated CASE Manifesto," *American Programmer*, July 1994, pp. 3-7.**

The author outlines integrated computer-assisted software-engineering technology for the future. Integration, the "I" in ICASE, is described in terms of data, control, presentation, process, and platform. The author lists the 10 "must haves" of ICASE, of which the first two are: bidirectional traceability across tools and life-cycle steps and bidirectional impact analysis. These must haves make a reasonable case for putting impact analysis at the core of future CASE tools and their repositories.

[Sommerville 1986]   Sommerville, I., et al., "SOFTLIB — A Documentation Management System," *Software Practice and Experience*, Feb. 1986, pp. 131-143.

The authors describe SoftLib, a software system designed to support the development and management of software documents. SoftLib uses a sophisticated change-management scheme to ensure that documents remain complete and consistent during change activities throughout development. Although this is a coarse-grained approach to traceability, it represents a useful application of document dependencies.

[Taha 1988]   Taha, A., and S. Thebaut, "Program Change Analysis Using Incremental Data Flow Techniques," Tech. Report SERC-TR-26-F, Software Eng. Research Center, Univ. of Florida, Gainesville, Fla., Jan. 1988.

The authors outline incremental data-flow techniques to support software-change analysis and allocate resources for testing. They describe data-flow analysis as a tool for identifying changes in definition-use paths to better estimate the testing effort and to improve the efficiency of testing modified programs.

*[Turver 1994]   Turver, R. J., and M. Munro, "An Early Impact Analysis Technique for Software Maintenance," *J. Software Maintenance: Research and Practice*, Vol. 6, 1994, pp. 35-52.

The authors outline a thematic/stochastic approach for identifying the ripple effects of software changes using Ripple Propagation Graphs and a slice criterion to identify impacts. The stochastic part of the approach uses a method created by Frederick Haney (see [Haney 1972]) to reduce the number of ripples in the RPG in identifying impacts. The thematic part of the approach is an original contribution that takes the document structure (volumes, chapters, sections, subsections, and segments) as indicators of where to find software ripple effects.

[Weiser 1984]   Weiser, M., "Program Slicing," *IEEE Trans. Software Eng.*, July 1984, pp. 352-357.

This often-referenced work on program slicing introduces the salient aspects of this technique. The author describes major definitions concerning slices, finding slices, and interprocedural slicing. He concludes that the power of slicing is derived from four features: slices can be generated automatically, slices are smaller than original programs, slices execute independently, and each slice reproduces a projection of the original program's behavior. He also concedes that slices can be expensive to find and are not guaranteed to be useful and that the independence of slices may cause additional complexities.

[Wilde 1987]   Wilde, N., and B. A. Nejmeh, "Dependency Analysis: An Aid for Software Maintenance," Tech. Report SERC-TR-23-F, Software Eng. Research Center, Univ. of Florida, Gainesville, Fla., Jan. 1987.

The authors examine dependency analysis in terms of data-flow, definition, calling, and functional dependencies. They outline how to classify program dependencies in these terms and give good examples of each type as the analysis is broken down. They also discuss the advantages of dependency graphs.

[Wilde 1989]   Wilde, N., R. Huitt, and S. Huitt, "Dependency Analysis Tools: Reusable Components for Software Maintenance," Tech. Report SERC-TR-26-F, Software Eng. Research Center, Univ. of Florida, Gainesville/Purdue Univ., West Lafayette, Ind., 1989; also in *Proc. Conf. Software Maintenance*, IEEE CS Press, Los Alamitos, Calif., 1989, pp. 126-131.

The report is an extension of the work described in [Wilde 1987]. The authors present techniques for tracing program dependencies and visualizing programs. They discuss the context in which dependency-analysis tools can be used and some perspectives on commercial tools to support software analysis.

[Wilde 1990]   Wilde, N., "Understanding Program Dependencies," (Software Eng. Inst. curriculum module), Tech. Report SEI-CMU-26, Software Eng. Inst., Carnegie Mellon Univ., Pittsburgh, Pa., 1990.

In a good overview of program dependency analysis for understanding source code, the author presents typical program elements that can be analyzed in the framework of program understanding. He examines a classification of program dependencies consisting of data-item, data-type, subprogram, source-file, and source-location relationships as a nonexhaustive list of major dependencies. He also discusses techniques for tracing program dependencies and visualizing programs.

*[Wilde 1992]   Wilde, N., and R. Huitt, "Maintenance Support for Object-Oriented Programs," *IEEE Trans. Software Eng.*, Dec. 1992, pp. 1038-1044.

This paper builds on the work described in [Wilde 1987 and 1989] but focuses on issues in object-oriented programs, such as inheritance. The authors discuss tool support for the dependency analysis of object-oriented programs and for software analysis in general.

[Yau 1978]   Yau, S. S., J. S. Collofello, and T. MacGregor, "Ripple Effect Analysis of Software Maintenance," *Proc. Compsac*, IEEE CS Press, Los Alamitos, Calif., 1978, pp. 60-65.

The authors introduce the concept of ripple-effect analysis (a source-code beginning to software change impact analysis). The paper is short but packed with information about the importance of examining software-change ripple effects. The authors provide a first definition for ripple-effect analysis and discuss how to identify and use ripple effects.

[Yau 1985]   Yau, S. S., and J. S. Collofello, "Design Stability Measures for Software Maintenance," *IEEE Trans. Software Eng.*, Sept. 1985, pp. 849-856.

The authors examine the software-maintenance process and outline the importance of accounting for ripple effects. They present a high-level software-maintenance process model that supports the concept of design stability and propose an algorithm for computing design stability. This metric is based on modules invoking module M, modules invoked by M, parameters passed in and out of M, and global data defined and used by M.

[Yau 1987]   Yau, S. S., and J. J. Tsai, "Knowledge Representation of Software Component Interconnection information for Large-Scale Software Modifications," *IEEE Trans. Software Eng.*, Mar. 1987, pp. 545-552.

The authors describe an approach based on the use of a first-order logic representation of software-interconnection knowledge. They apply directed graphs to model the structure and behavior of large software systems. The resulting graphs, component-interconnection graphs, make it easier to automate reasoning about software modifications. Using this representation, developers can make informed decisions about the validity of a software change.

Author Biographies

Shawn A. Bohner

Shawn A. Bohner is a lead scientist at Mitretek Systems, Inc. (formerly The MITRE Corp.), where he leads efforts in software-systems modernization, process improvement, and business-process reengineering. Before joining Mitretek, he was a senior member of the technical staff in the Software Engineering Laboratory at GTE Laboratory's Technology Center, where he organized and led a corporate initiative for software-maintenance technologies that served business units with research in software-maintenance process, methods, and tools; reengineering technology; and CASE/CASM tools. Dr. Bohner has also held positions at the Software Productivity Consortium and Ford Aerospace Corp. and has served in the United States Air Force.

Dr. Bohner's research interests include software change impact analysis, software maintenance, systems reengineering, process modeling and analysis, software-engineering environments, and knowledge-based systems. He has authored and coauthored more than 20 refereed technical papers and is active in both the ACM and IEEE. He is the past chair of the ACM Professional Development Committee in Washington, DC, and a vice-chair for the IEEE Technical Council on Software Engineering. He has also served on various conference program committees (most recently the International Conference on Software Maintenance, National Business Process Reengineering Conference, Reverse Engineering Forum, and Working Conference on Reverse Engineering), and various software-standards committees.

Dr. Bohner received a PhD in information technology and engineering from George Mason University. His dissertation entitled, "A Graph Traceability Approach for Software Change Impact Analysis," developed methods and tools for analyzing software change impacts. He also received an MS in computer science from Johns Hopkins University and a BS in computer science from the University of Maryland.

Dr. Bohner may be reached at Mitretek Systems; 7525 Colshire Dr., McLean, VA 22102; (703) 610-1606; fax: (703) 610-1603; bohner@mitretek.org.

Robert S. Arnold

Robert S. Arnold is president of Software Evolution Technology, Inc., a firm providing solutions in planning, methodology, tools, and services for companies dealing with software maintenance, reengineering, impact analysis, and the Year 2000 Problem. He is a member of the editorial board for the *Journal of Software Maintenance* and editor of *Year 2000 News*, an Internet newsletter devoted to the Year 2000 Problem. He is also the author of *Software Reengineering* (IEEE CS Press, 1993), and *Tutorial on Software Restructuring* (IEEE CS Press, 1986). He has published numerous articles on software maintenance and software evolution in both the research literature and trade press. In 1993, he received the IEEE Computer Society's Certificate of Appreciation for his technical contribution to software maintenance and reengineering activities. He was program chair of the Conference on Software Maintenance in 1985 and 1987, its general chair in 1988, and chair of its Steering Committee from 1991 to 1993.

Dr. Arnold has also been a reengineering project manager at the Software Productivity Consortium and has worked at The MITRE Corp. and the IBM San Jose Research Laboratory. He received a PhD in computer science from the University of Maryland in empirical measurement of software maintenance quality. He received an MS in computer science from Carnegie Mellon University and a BA with highest distinction from Northwestern University.

Dr. Arnold may be reached at Software Evolution Technology, Inc., 12613 Rock Ridge Rd., Herndon, VA 22070; (703) 450-6791; fax: (703) 450-6791, ext. 11; rarnold@sevtec.com.

6/11/96